Syed J. Hussain
Seattle Silicon
November 26 1987

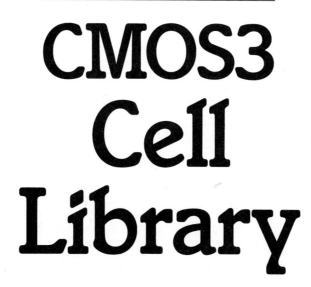

CMOS3 Cell Library

Edited by

Dennis V. Heinbuch

ADDISON-WESLEY PUBLISHING COMPANY

Reading, Massachusetts   Menlo Park, California   New York
Don Mills, Ontario   Wokingham, England   Amsterdam   Bonn   Sydney
Singapore   Tokyo   Madrid   Bogotá   Santiago   San Juan

This book is in the **Addison-Wesley VLSI Systems Series**
Lynn Conway and Charles Seitz, **Consulting Editors**

Computer Aids for VLSI Design	Steven M. Rubin, 1987
VLSI Signal Processing: A Bit-Serial Approach	Peter Denyer and David Renshaw, 1985
The Design and Analysis of VLSI Circuits	Lance A. Glasser and Daniel W. Dobberpuhl, 1985
Principles of CMOS VLSI Design: A Systems Perspective	Neil Weste and Kamran Eshraghian, 1985
The VLSI Designer's Library	John Newkirk and Robert Mathews, 1983

Library of Congress Cataloging-in-Publication Data

Heinbuch, Dennis V.
  CMOS3 cell library.

  Includes index.
    1. Integrated circuits—Very large scale integration—
Design and construction.   I. Title.
TK7874.B35   1987   621.381'73   86-21355
ISBN 0-201-11257-4

The cell data pages in Chapters 11 and 12 and others in Chapters 2 and 3 were reproduced from computer-generated camera ready copies supplied by the NSA.

Preface

The CMOS3 cell library has been designed in a mainstream multisourceable 3-micron CMOS technology for implementation of United States Government systems requiring this capability. A very extensive effort was made to identify original technology ground rules and to develop and verify industrial sources for this technology. A parametric test vehicle, CHARGER, was developed by the government. This vehicle has been processed by potential industrial sources and evaluated by the government. Today this technology is widely accepted as a baseline CMOS technology throughout the semiconductor industry.

The development of the CMOS3 library was undertaken to meet a wide range of military applications. In this cell book the performance of the cell family is documented over a user voltage range of 3 to 7 volts and the military temperature range of $-55°C$ to $125°C$. A conservative set of electrical parameters have been used to develop a wide range of processing tolerances to allow for the processing variations among many 3-micron semiconductor fabrication facilities. The data in this book can, therefore, be taken as aggressively or as conservatively as each individual designer or design requires.

Acknowledgment

The CMOS3 Cell Library was developed by the Integrated Circuit Engineering Office of the National Security Agency, Fort Meade, Maryland in conjunction with several major industrial semiconductor manufacturers.

National Security Agency
Fort Meade, Maryland

Dennis V. Heinbuch
Manager
Integrated Circuit Engineering

Foreword

This book represents the culmination of nine years' work. It gives me a great feeling of personal satisfaction to be invited by Addison-Wesley to write this Foreword, not because of any deep technical contribution that I made to this work, but because I had the pleasure of leading the group of people who initiated the work at the National Security Agency (NSA) in 1978. Subsequent to my departure from that agency, I have maintained an interest in their progress and now celebrate with them in the fulfillment of the vision that motivated us in its beginnings.

Nine years is a long time in a field as rapidly changing as is semiconductor technology. Yet the early motivations have been confirmed in a set of designs that will continue to be valuable into the next decade. Further, the approach used to generate this cell family is worthy of elaboration. It makes an interesting story, in part because it was done inside NSA and reveals some of the technologically exciting things that happen in that agency, but mostly because it shows that a work of durable value can still be accomplished by a small group of motivated people. Unfortunately, I will not be able to give credit to those who contributed to this project. Many have since moved on to other jobs in the government or in industry. But, for those who remain inside NSA, I must respect a wish for anonymity that is characteristic of this group—laboring quietly on technologically exciting things within the confidences of a highly competitive industry. So, rather than give credit to some and not others, I will merely acknowledge their work and that of the industry collaborators who together made this project possible.

For over a decade prior to this project, NSA had established a unique relationship with the semiconductor industry. The sequence of technologies beginning

v

with metal-gate PMOS, then silicon-gate PMOS, metal-gate CMOS, and silicon-gate CMOS/SOS served to create a network of industrial vendors who would collaborate with NSA in an unusual environment of mutual trust. An underlying assumption was that technology was not continuously changing, but that well-defined thresholds existed where the prudent designer could depend on the availability of a process over an extended period of time from several suppliers. The trick was to identify these thresholds. NSA personnel, as noncompetitors, developed sufficient confidence and credibility in the industry to obtain information about the most advanced processes from a group of about 20 companies over this period. In learning what each company planned, often in excruciating detail, common characteristics were distilled and smart decisions could be made on which processes could be expected to support large product lines and hence have long life. A second, more controversial assumption was that a clean specification of design rules could be defined for designers, either at NSA or at its system contractors, that would enable several vendors to fabricate their chips. The motivation for the government was, of course, that an economical source of supply would exist when needed and that any of the vendors would have the opportunity to bid on the basis of their ability to produce in a competitive environment.

Both of these controversial assumptions continue to be hotly debated. In this highly competitive industry, the mystique of rapid technological change and the proprietary "edge" of a unique process runs counter to the objectives of organizations such as NSA. It has been only recently that the introduction of "silicon foundries" to produce a customer's design and the broad development of the Application Specific Integrated Circuit (ASIC) market combined to bring credence to the argument for this broader vendor base. The existence of a well-defined and relatively static interface with the semiconductor manufacturers provides the stability needed to develop a new market, one in which the major value added to the component is in the product-related ideas of the designer. The cell family documented in this book, along with the several CAD systems that support it and the many vendors who run the process are the leading examples of this new trend.

The first indicators were detected in 1978 during an otherwise unsuccessful survey of NSA's industrial friends. The purpose of that survey was to identify a successor to the then widely used metal-gate CMOS. A mainstream process was not found at that time, but it was obvious that silicon-gate CMOS would evolve to become widely used across the industry. It was decided to launch a somewhat more ambitious project. This project would look in detail at things that would contribute to the development of this process and NSA would attempt to get into the technology earlier than ever before by working with a few potential vendors in developing the process. What would be the next threshold? By looking at the capabilities of state-of-the-art semiconductor manufacturing equipment, the constraints imposed by semiconductor physics, the properties that would be needed by circuit and system designers, and the potential markets for low power, high-density circuitry, the team was able to set 3-micron silicon-gate CMOS as their objective. The basic rationale was that it would be within the capabilities of equipment that was expected to be in manufacturing facilities in the early 1980s, it would be tolerant of problems such as latch-up and hot carriers at reasonable supply voltages, it would be competitive with LS/TTL in performance yet would exhibit the same low power properties of CMOS, it would enable chips of roughly 2000 SSI equivalent cells complexity to be implemented with the aid of CAD software, and it was expected to be broadly useful for both defense and commercial applications.

Armed with this information, the team set out to verify their objectives with the industry. Over 20 companies were contacted and most of them were visited. In each case, the potential processes were reviewed in detail to determine reasonable limits of the technology. Back at NSA, where the proprietary aspects of each company's plans could be protected, the information was evaluated and a draft set of design rules and target electrical parameters was prepared. Rather than adopt a composite set of rules as had been done in the past, this draft was more ambitious and attempted to set a common goal for the industry based on the more global view that this team had assembled. This was a bit tricky. They could not, of course, disclose unique processing methods that were proprietary to particular companies. For example, the means employed to control the doping profiles at the edge of the well varied greatly across companies and directly affected several rules relating to spacings relative to the edge of the well mask. The team had to define rules that would accommodate the broadest vendor base, yet would not reveal these unique and proprietary processes. The draft rules were reviewed with each of the contributing companies and a final set of modifications made on the basis of their feedback. Interestingly, most of the companies were motivated to participate, not because of potential future business, but because it provided them with a detailed picture of their progress relative to the industry as a whole. This kind of information at this stage of process development was extremely difficult to obtain otherwise.

Two years had elapsed since the 1978 survey and now the project shifted into high gear with the detailed design of the test vehicle that would be used to develop the process and to verify the performance of the process lines. Named CHARGER, this test chip was more ambitious than any that had been attempted before. It included 10 specific classes of tests encompassing electrical parametrics, process control structures, circuit delay, across-chip and across-wafer variations, input protection, oxide integrity, a sample functional circuit, design rule verification, contact arrays, and miscellaneous structures for measuring alignment, critical dimensions, etc. Altogether, many thousands of individual tests could be made over the surface of a die that was at the limit of the stepper technology then in use. These were documented and provided to the initial vendors who competed for these initial development contracts. Two vendors were awarded contracts in mid-1979 to perform a series of process runs using the CHARGER chip, testing it at their discretion, and finally delivering wafers to NSA for evaluation. One of these vendors successfully delivered samples of the chip on schedule and the other soon afterward. Having verified the test structures and programs, the CHARGER test vehicle was released to other potential vendors and was successfully processed by over 10 vendors in subsequent years. In late 1981 the results were reviewed with the vendors and the design rules and electrical parameters were finalized. These are included in this book.

Meanwhile, work was proceeding at NSA. A second chip was designed to answer a series of questions posed by the circuit designers. This chip, named AUGEUS, was fabricated along with CHARGER by three vendors and provided much of the data needed to ultimately design the cell family. Now work could begin in earnest. NSA, beginning in the 1960s, had developed a comprehensive approach to the design of cell families. Based on their experience in automated chip layout, an additional set of common rules was developed pertaining to both physical chip layout and the expected electrical loading on interconnects. This "higher level" set of rules also is documented in this book and defines the set of standards that must be followed if automatic chip layout is to be used. Further, it defines a set of constraints for cell design that, at NSA, has evolved into a rigorous discipline. Beginning with the circuit schematic, the connectivity is extracted and electrical properties are estimated for initial transient circuit analysis. This is used to approximate transistor sizes needed to achieve the desired performance. Then detailed layout and design rule checks are performed. Finally the geometries defined for the masks are modified in the computer to approximate the changes that will occur in the actual processing of the circuit and the detailed electrical properties of the circuit are extracted from these modified geometries. These electrical properties are then used for exhaustive simulation of the circuit across the limits of worst case process spread, temperature extremes, expected resistive and capacitive loading, and supply voltages. The performance data for each cell in this book is the result of the many hours of computer time needed to do this exhaustive simulation.

The first release of the cell family consisting of 38 cells was completed in September 1982. A third test chip named PRISM was then designed and fabricated to verify the cell family design. In subsequent years the family has been extensively checked and updated to conform with the broadest vendor base. Many additional cells have been added, most recently the MSI level functions were added in 1985. Many of the semiconductor manufacturers who participated in this development effort now use the family in their own designs. Over 100 chip types are known to have been successfully built using the family.

While most of the above activity was taking place in the early 1980s, another related project was underway sponsored by the Defense Advanced Research Agency (DARPA). The objective here was to create the opportunity for breakthroughs in advanced computer architecture by providing timely and inexpensive access to semiconductor manufacturing for the purpose of prototyping new ideas. This work built on the early success of the Mead/Conway text that was rapidly becoming a standard across the educational community. While this work was based on nMOS technology, it was clear when I assumed responsibility for the DARPA VLSI program in 1981 that a conversion to CMOS was vital to the long-term objectives of the overall computer science research program. Consequently, the Jet Propulsion Laboratory (JPL) who had been tasked under the DARPA program with the development of new processes and the University of Southern California Information Sciences Institute (USC/ISI) who were responsible for the MOSIS implementation service were given the additional task of introducing a bulk-silicon CMOS fabrication service to the U.S. research community. NSA provided information on the standard 3-micron design rules and on the CHARGER test vehicle.

A slight problem was encountered at this point. The original NSA work had not planned for the development of a second layer of metal. In fact, most of the industry would not see two layers of metalization in CMOS production until 1986 and then it would be tailored to the 2-micron process. Many would not retrofit existing 3-micron processes to add this new capability. But two layers of metal interconnect were judged to be of such exceptional value to the future generations of VLSI designs expected to come out of the U.S. research community that a departure was needed from the NSA rules. It was decided to accept the risk of developing the appropriate rules for two-layer metal rather than force the entire community to design initially in one set of rules and then change to another when two-layer metal became more widely available. In particular, this decision was based on the expected long lead time to develop and widely install CAD software.

The NSA design rules were released to the research community in August 1982 and USC/ISI set about the task of establishing a vendor base that would provide fast-turnaround fabrication for this community of users. Turnaround time and the desired two layers of metal continued to be a problem until 1984. Subsequent to that time the frequency of the runs has increased from one per month to one every two weeks and turnaround time has been reduced to 8–10 weeks. During the summer of 1985, a course for teachers was held at USC/ISI and representatives from 42 different institutions attended. The number of CMOS designs submitted to MOSIS has since surpassed the number of nMOS designs and is now clearly established as a standard serving U.S. educational institutions under an NSF program and serving the U.S. research community under both NSF and DARPA sponsorship. In July 1984 approval was given to USC/ISI to provide these services to industrial users experimentally on a cost reimbursement basis.

Also in 1984, the idea of using MOSIS as a central point of distribution and configuration control for the NSA cell family was introduced. The objective was to create a single, industrywide source for the cells already in the family and for the designs that would come out of the U.S. research community. The need for configuration control was urgent. As the family became available to industrial companies, much of the task of interfacing the family to the various CAD systems fell on the staff of each company. Not only was duplicate work being performed, but the problem of assuring that the integrity of the family be maintained was becoming impossible. Members of the USC/ISI staff and I met with officers of the major CAD companies during late 1984 and early 1985 to discuss how this might best be accomplished. Normally a cell family owned by a semiconductor vendor is encoded and maintained by that vendor for any specific CAD system. Since data standards for the translation of data from one CAD system to another do not presently encompass all the types of data developed for this cell family, it was clear that some work would have to be done manually. There was the initial problem of who would pay for (or even actually perform) the data preparation and then the problem of who would distribute and assume liability for errors in manually prepared data. Informal agreement was reached with four companies to support the family on their systems and USC/ISI was tasked with the maintenance of a controlled copy of the family under a program that is jointly supported by NSA and DARPA. Mentor Graphics was the first CAD company to publicly announce availability of the cell family on their system in early 1986.

It is useful to now look back at the assumptions made nearly a decade ago at the beginning of this project: first, that thresholds of semiconductor processes exhibiting long durability exist and that this is one such threshold, and second, that a clear interface can be specified between the designer and the fabricator so that each can depend on the other to perform his part of the job independently. The 3-micron cell family described herein is an existence proof, but not without qualification. Clearly the family is well proven, not only on many designs performed by many designers, but also through fabrication by many sources. The conservative method of design and characterization helps to assure that the specified performance will be well within the tolerances that one can expect of modern fabrication facilities. Further, the process is extensively used for a large variety of commercial products and is likely to be available for many years to come. In fact, design at 3 microns has certain advantages for applications that require voltages higher than the specified 5 volts for the logic circuits. Consequently, even though more advanced processes are now available, one should seriously question the need for more complex processes if they are not needed. Secondly, the concept of "silicon foundries" is now well accepted and is an important part of the ASIC portion of the semiconductor industry. The second assumption is proven valid by the marketplace as manufacturers now compete for production of customer-generated designs.

But nothing is without risk. Two-micron CMOS has emerged as the next threshold and in this industry, smaller is frequently interpreted as better, even if it is not needed for density or performance. In particular, many ASIC vendors are now recommending that new designs be done at 2 microns. While many designs do not need the attributes of the more advanced process, the appeal is strong. But this is as it should be. While I fully expect to be able to find sources for this cell library in the next decade, we cannot be too complacent. Technology continues to march forward, not only in ever-reduced geometries, but in many ways as we learn more about the flexibility and power of new semiconductor manufacturing equipment. Thus I hope that this book will be the first of a series, each more useful than the previous to create new products and open new markets.

Paul Losleben
Associate Director
for Program Development
Center for Integrated Systems
Stanford University

Contents

6 **CELL CHARACTERIZATION PLAN** **43**

7 **CELL USER'S GUIDE** **53**

1

Introduction

The CMOS3 standard cell family documented in this library is part of NSA's 3-micron silicon gate CMOS/BULK technology development program. This cell family is intended to meet the requirements of moderate speed, moderate density random logic applications, and is designed to a set of layout rules and electrical parameters that provide maximum sourceability. In addition, CMOS3 is designed for easy exportability and allows in-house designers and contractors to utilize a full range of computer-aided design tools, including various automatic layout programs.

In 1978, NSA representatives visited several semiconductor manufacturers in an effort to identify the future direction of MOS technology development. As a result of this survey, a set of layout rules and electrical parameters for a 3-micron minimum feature size bulk CMOS process was developed. Production sources for processes compatible with these rules were expected to be available in the 1981–1982 time frame.

Contracts were awarded to two vendors in 1979 for the development and demonstration of this technology. CHARGER, an NSA-designed 3-micron CMOS parametric test vehicle, was fabricated by these vendors and tested by NSA to evaluate design rules and electrical parameters.

A second survey was conducted in late 1981 and early 1982 to establish the current vendor base for this technology. As a result of this survey, the original design rules and electrical parameters were modified slightly to make them consistent with the capabilities of the current vendors. These design rules and electrical parameters are contained in Chapter 2.

In the Spring of 1982, CHARGER and AUGEAS, an NSA-designed 3-micron CMOS circuit design test vehicle, were processed by several of the potential vendors and were evaluated by NSA to verify compliance with the NSA rules. These test vehicles will continue to be used for evaluation as additional vendors arise.

The CMOS3 cell family was developed in 1982 and the initial release consisted of 38 cells, including I/O pads. CMOS3 cells were designed with the following goals and guidelines.

- Cells were designed in accordance with the NSA 3-Micron Gate Design Rules and Electrical Parameters (Chapter 2).
- The cell structure is "double-entry" or "multi-port," in which I/O terminals are present on both the top and bottom edges of the cell.
- Cells were designed to meet stringent cell level design constraints. The cell structure, terminal locations, and terminal numbering conventions were defined to be compatible with the automatic layout programs PRF and MP2D (see Chapter 3). Depending on the characteristics of the logic being implemented and the quality of the layout algorithms, these programs permit the placement and routing of 1000 to 1400 CMOS3 cells on a 250 mil square chip.
- The performance of each cell has been characterized over the extremes of electrical parameters and over a wide range of operating conditions including voltage (3V to 7V), temperature (−55°C to 125°C), series load resistance (0 ohms to 10K ohms), and parasitic capacitance (0.5 pF to 6 pF for functional cells; 10 pF to 60 pF for output pads). For more details on cell characterization,

see Chapter 6. These performance characteristics indicate that CMOS3 can meet design goals of a 20 MHz system clock rate through three or four levels of logic with two or three fanouts per output at 5V, 125°C, and under worst case processing conditions.

■ Neither cell performance nor cell density was totally optimized at the expense of the other.

2

Design Rules and Electrical Parameters

This chapter contains the design rules and electrical parameters for the NSA 3-micron CMOS/BULK technology. The CMOS3 cell family has been laid out in accordance with these design rules. The cell performance characteristics presented in this library have been generated using the NSA MOSTRAN circuit simulation program (models 15 and 25) and the electrical parameters defined in this chapter.

2.1 GEOMETRIC LINE KEY

THE FOLLOWING KEY PROVIDES THE SYMBOLS USED TO DESCRIBE THE TOPOLOGICAL LAYOUT RULES.

LAYER	LINE KEY
1. P- WELL	
3. ACTIVE AREA	
4. POLY	
5. P+	
6. N+	
7. CONTACT	
8. METAL 1	
9. PASSIVATION	
13. VIA	
14. METAL 2	

2.1.1   P- WELL   MICRONS

  * A. P-WELL WIDTH   5

    B. P-WELL TO P-WELL SPACING (DIFFERENT POTENTIALS)   15

    C. P-WELL TO P-WELL SPACING (SAME POTENTIAL)   9

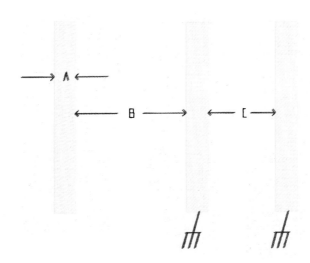

  * REVISED P-WELL WIDTH 1 FEB 1985.

2.1.2   ACTIVE AREA

A. ACTIVE AREA OPENING   4

B. P+ ACTIVE AREA TO P+ ACTIVE AREA SPACING   4

C. N+ ACTIVE AREA TO N+ ACTIVE AREA SPACING   4

D. P+ ACTIVE AREA IN N-SUBSTRATE TO P-WELL   8
    EDGE SPACING

E. N+ ACTIVE AREA IN N-SUBSTRATE TO P-WELL   7
    EDGE SPACING

F. N+ ACTIVE AREA IN P-WELL TO P-WELL   4
    EDGE SPACING

G. N+ ACTIVE AREA TO P+ ACTIVE AREA   4
    SPACING OUTSIDE P-WELL

H. N+ ACTIVE AREA TO P+ ACTIVE AREA   4
    SPACING INSIDE WELL

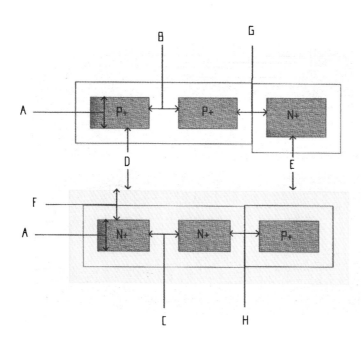

2.1.3   <u>POLY</u>

     A. POLY WIDTH   3

     B. POLY TO POLY SPACING   3

     C. FIELD POLY TO ACTIVE AREA SPACING   2

     D. POLY GATE EXTENSION OVER FIELD   3

     E. GATE POLY TO ACTIVE AREA SPACING   3

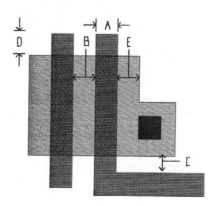

10

2.1.4   <u>P+</u>

A. P+ MASK OVERLAP OF ACTIVE AREA   2

B. P+ MASK OVERLAP OF POLY IN ACTIVE AREA   3.5

C. P+ MASK TO P+ MASK SPACING IN ACTIVE AREA   3

D. P+ MASK TO N+ ACTIVE AREA SPACING   2
    (IF P+ MASK AND N+ MASK ARE COINCIDENT)

E. P+ MASK OVERLAP OF N+ MASK TO ACHIEVE   0
    SHORTING CONTACT

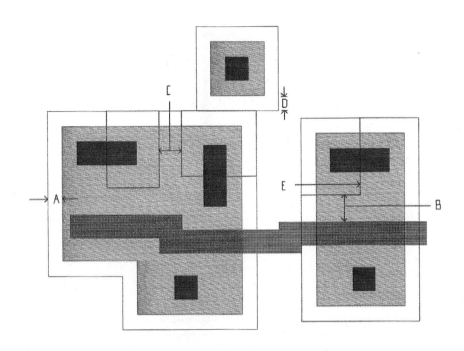

2.1.5   <u>N+</u>

A. N+ MASK OVERLAP OF ACTIVE AREA   2

B. N+ MASK OVERLAP OF POLY IN ACTIVE AREA   3.5

C. N+ MASK TO N+ MASK SPACING IN ACTIVE AREA   3

D. N+ MASK TO P+ ACTIVE AREA SPACING
    (IF N+ MASK AND P+ MASK ARE COINCIDENT)   2

E. N+ MASK OVERLAP OF P+ MASK TO ACHIEVE   0
    SHORTING CONTACT

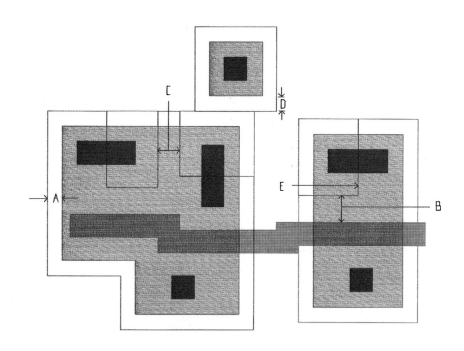

2.1.6   CONTACT

A. CONTACT SIZE   3 X 3

B. MAXIMUM CONTACT SIZE   3 X 8

C. CONTACT TO CONTACT SPACING   3

D. POLY OVERLAP OF CONTACT   2

E. POLY OVERLAP OF CONTACT IN DIRECTION OF METAL   2.5

F. CONTACT TO POLY CHANNEL SPACING   3

G. METAL OVERLAP OF CONTACT   2

H. CONTACT TO ACTIVE AREA SPACING   2

I. CONTACT TO P+ AND N+ MASK SPACING   3

J. N+/P+ SHORTING CONTACT SIZE   3 X 8

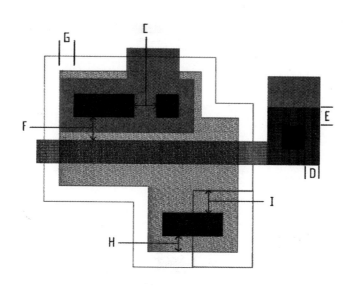

2.1.7   <u>METAL 1</u>

    A. METAL 1 WIDTH (INTERCONNECT)   3

    B. BUS METAL 1 CURRENT DENSITY (MAX)   0.7 MIL AMP/UM

    C. METAL 1 TO METAL 1 SPACING   4

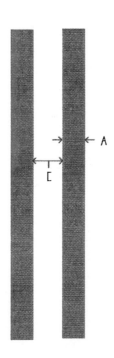

2.1.8   <u>VIA</u>

A. MINIMUM VIA DIMENSION   3X3

B. MINIMUM VIA TO VIA SPACING   3

C. MINIMUM VIA TO CONTACT SPACING   3

D. MINIMUM VIA TO POLY EDGE SPACING   4

E. MINIMUM METAL 1 OVERLAP OF VIA IN ALL DIRECTIONS   2

F. MINIMUM METAL 2 OVERLAP OF VIA IN ALL DIRECTIONS   2

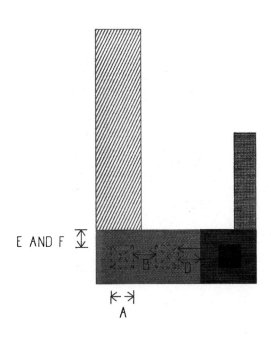

2.1.9 METAL 2

A. METAL 2 WIDTH (INTERCONNECT)   5

B. BUS METAL 2 CURRENT DENSITY (MAX)   0.7 MIL AMP/UM

C. METAL 2 TO METAL 2 SPACING   5

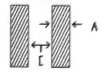

DOUBLE LAYER METAL PADS

D. BONDING PAD METAL 1 AND METAL 2 AREA   100 X 100

E. BONDING PAD SPACING (PAD METAL TO PAD METAL)   100

F. PROBING PAD METAL 1 AND METAL 2 AREA   75 X 75

G. PROBING PAD SPACING (PAD METAL TO PAD METAL)   30

H. BONDING PAD TO PROBING PAD SPACING   30

I. PAD METAL 1 AND PAD METAL 2 TO CIRCUIT METAL 1,   40
   METAL 2, ACTIVE AREA, AND POLY SPACING

J. PAD METAL 1 AND METAL 2 OVERLAP OF P-WELL   3

K. PAD METAL 1 AND METAL 2 OVERLAP OF PASSIVATION   5

L. PAD METAL 1 AND METAL 2 OVERLAP OF VIA   5

M. PAD METAL 1 AND METAL 2 TO SCRIBE   50

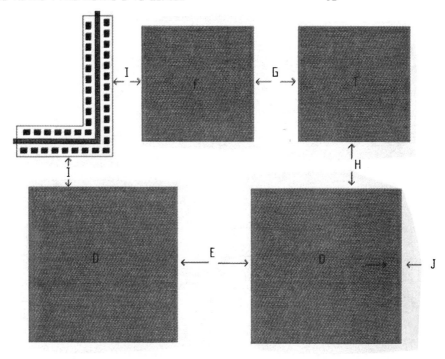

2.1.10   <u>PASSIVATION</u>

    A.   BONDING PAD OPENING   90 X 90

    B.   PROBING PAD OPENING   65 X 65

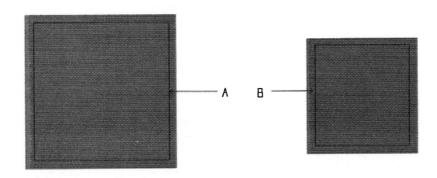

2.2 ELECTRICAL PARAMETERS (25°C)

		MIN	MAX	UNITS
a.	P-channel threshold voltage	−0.5	−1.1	volts
b.	N-channel threshold voltage	0.5	1.1	volts
c.	P-channel process constant $(K'_p = \mu C_{ox}/2)$	6	12	A/V²
d.	N-channel process constant $(K'_n = \mu C_{ox}/2)$	15	30	A/V²
e.	Gate oxide capacitance (600 A)		5.7E4	pF/cm²
f.	Metal over substrate capacitance		5.2E3	pF/cm²
g.	Field poly over substrate capacitance		6.5E3	pF/cm²
h.	Metal over field poly capacitance		1.22E4	pF/cm²
i.	N+/P− junction capacitance		6.0E4	pF/cm²
j.	N−/P+ junction capacitance		4.1E4	pF/cm²
k.	Metal 2 over substrate capacitance		3E3	pF/cm²
l.	Metal 2 over metal capacitance		5E3	pF/cm²
m.	Metal 2 over field poly capacitance		4E3	pF/cm²
n.	Lateral diffusion (per side)		0.4	micron
o.	Operating voltage		7	volts
p.	P+ sheet rho	25	140	ohms/square
q.	N+ sheet rho	10	60	ohms/square
r.	N+ poly sheet rho		30	ohms/square
s.	N− poly sheet rho		35	ohms/square
t.	P− sheet rho		3000	ohms/square

Note: To clarify how the threshold voltage and process constant are measured, the following discussion is presented. Threshold voltage (V_t) and the process constant (K') are obtained from a low drain voltage (V_{ds} greater than or equal to 50 mV) conductivity curve of drain current (I_{ds}) versus gate voltage (V_{qs}). In the linear portion of the curve (i.e., where V_{qs} has not yet started to affect mobility), the equation presented below describes the transfer characteristic of the curve.

$$I_{ds} = 2K' \frac{W_{eff}}{L_{eff}} \cdot [(V_{gs} - V_t) \cdot V_{ds}]*$$

Note that V_t is the extrapolated x-intercept ($I_{ds} = 0$) and K' is determined from the slope of the curve.

---

*Reference — A. S. Grove: *Physics and Technology of Semiconductor Devices.* New York, Wiley and Sons, 1967, p. 324.

3

Cell and I/O Pad Layout

Cells and I/O pads must adhere to strict layout rules and numbering conventions in order to allow for the placement of cells with their side edges abutting, to allow for the proper connection of intercell wiring to the top and bottom cell edges, and to remain compatible with various automatic layout programs.

The reference point of all cell/pad types is the lower left corner of the cell. All functional cells currently have a height of 150 microns and a width that is a multiple of 12 microns. A 12 micron terminal-to-terminal spacing has been maintained for the cell family.

3.1 FUNCTIONAL CELLS

3.1.1 Design Tips

Each cell should contain two shorting contacts (one V_{DD} to N-substrate; one V_{SS} to P– well). For larger cells, no transistor channel should be more than 70 microns from an associated shorting contact.

Long runs of minimum width (4 microns) active area should be avoided due to the relatively high resistance created by the "bird's beak" effect.

Design rule 2.1.3E (Chapter 2), gate poly to active area spacing for source and drain areas should be increased from 3 microns to at least 4 microns for gate widths greater than 8 microns. This spacing should be increased to a minimum of 5 microns for gate widths greater than 25 microns. As in (b) above, this is necessary to lower the resistance in these areas resulting from the "bird's beak" effect.

Design rule 2.1.3B (Chapter 2), poly to poly spacing in active area, should be increased from 3 microns to 4 microns in instances where the poly runs are adjacent for more than 16 microns. This is intended to lower the resistance of this narrow active area.

If a contact is placed under an 8 micron power bus, the area over the contact should not be included as part of the width of the bus. The bus metal should be widened around the contact to insure that an 8 micron uncontacted metal width results.

The channel width of a bent device is calculated by summing the centerlines of each of the straight portions of the device and adding one half of the centerline distance of each corner (see Fig. 3.1). The intent of this guideline is to arrive at a conservative estimate of effective channel width. It may be noticed that some of the devices in cells from Releases 1 and 2 of this library are slightly inconsistent with this guideline because they were designed before this rule was introduced. All subsequent designs will utilize this rule.

3.1.2 Edge Layout Rules

Pages 22–26 describe the layout constraints at the edges of each functional cell for various layers.

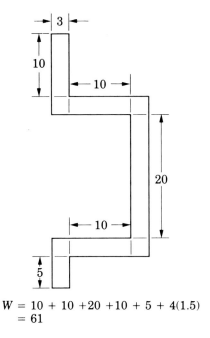

$$W = 10 + 10 + 20 + 10 + 5 + 4(1.5)$$
$$= 61$$

■**Figure 3.1**

3.1.3 Terminals

All terminals fall on incremental spacings of 12 microns. The first possible terminal location is 6 microns in from the left or right cell edge. As a result, all cell sizes are increments of 12 microns.

The first terminal of a cell is denoted as terminal number 2 and is the lower left-most terminal of that cell. Terminal numbers increase from left to right along the bottom edge of the cell. Terminals on the top edge of the cell are numbered as the corresponding bottom terminal "+10" (for instance, 12, 14, 15). Terminal numbers on the top edge are also in ascending order from left to right and, therefore, the terminal functions must be in the same order as the bottom terminals.

Care must be exercised in the layout of areas in the vicinity of terminals so that if a wiring via (cell 8680) is centered on a terminal no design rule violations occur.

3.1.4 Bus Structure

Power buses are included within each cell and bus crosser (cell 8630). Each bus runs horizontally and is a minimum of 8 microns wide not including the areas over the contact cuts. The bottom bus, V_{SS}, is centered on a y-coordinate of 12 microns. The left V_{SS} terminal is 99 and the right terminal is 95. The top bus, V_{DD}, is centered on a y-coordinate of 138 microns. The left V_{DD} terminal is 98 and the right terminal is 96.

P-WELL:

     P-WELL WILL BE COINCIDENT WITH CELL EDGE TO
A HEIGHT OF 50 UM. MINIMUM WIDTH AT THE CELL
EDGE IS 1.5 UM. ABOVE 50 UM THE P-WELL MUST BE
INSIDE CELL EDGE BY 4.5 UM. *

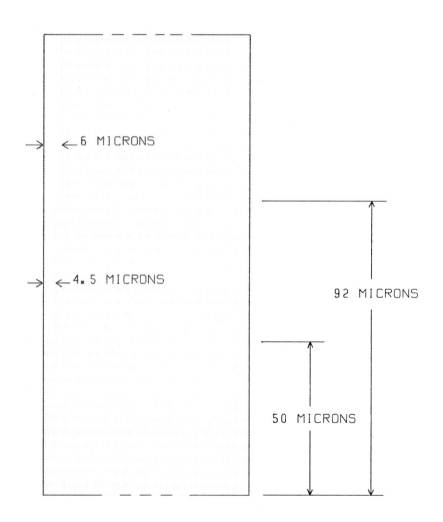

*THIS PARAMETER ALLOWS FOR P+ A.A. IN ADJACENT
CELL TO BE 3.5 UM FROM EDGE.

N+ ACTIVE AREA IN P-WELL:

N+ ACTIVE AREA TO BOTTOM OF CELL   4

N+ ACTIVE AREA TO CELL SIDE
   (4 UM TO 46 UM)   4
   (46 UM TO 88 UM)   8.5
   (88 UM TO 146 UM)   10

N+ ACTIVE AREA TO TOP OF CELL   4

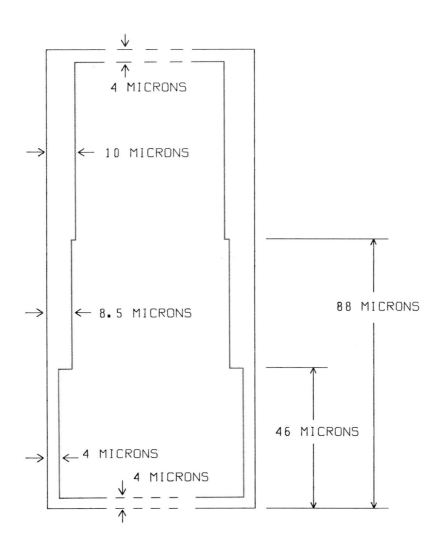

P+ ACTIVE AREA OUTSIDE OF P-WELL:

P+ ACTIVE AREA TO BOTTOM OF CELL   2

P+ ACTIVE AREA TO CELL SIDE
    (2 UM TO 58 UM)   8
    (58 UM TO 100 UM)   3.5
    (100 UM TO 148 UM)   2

P+ ACTIVE AREA TO TOP OF CELL   2

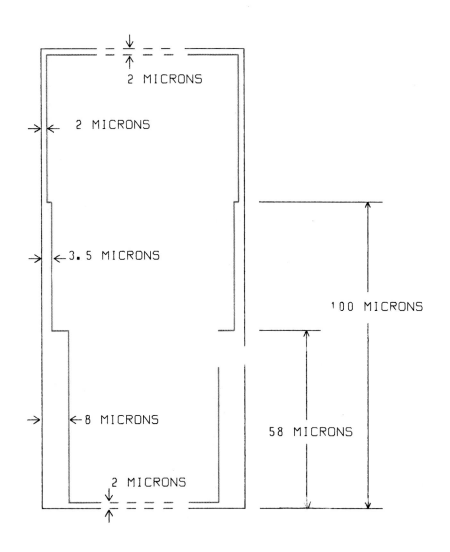

POLY:

POLY TO CELL EDGE (LEFT AND RIGHT SIDES)   1.5

POLY TO CELL EDGE (TOP AND BOTTOM)   0

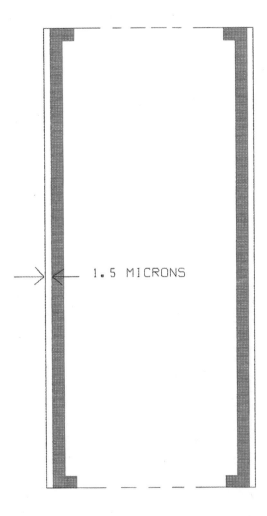

1.5 MICRONS

METAL:

METAL TO CELL EDGE:
    LEFT AND RIGHT SIDES   2
    TOP AND BOTTOM   8

BUS:
    WIDTH   8
    VSS Y-COORDINATE   12
    VDD Y-COORDINATE   138

NO METAL OUTSIDE OF VSS, VDD

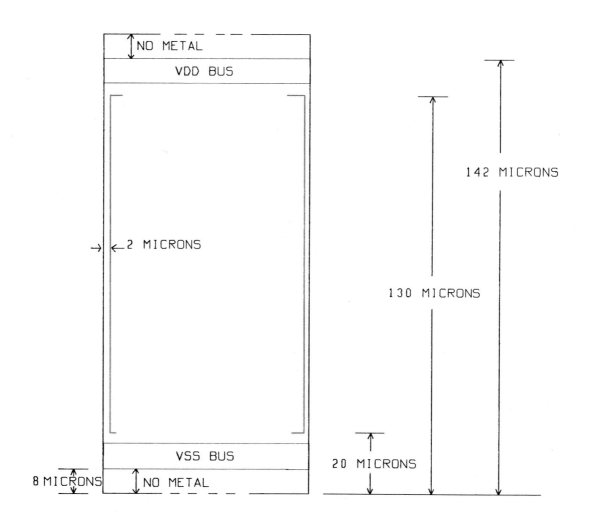

3.2 I/O PADS

3.2.1 Pad Size

Except for special instances, all pads will be 313 microns tall and will be at least 204 microns wide with the width varying in increments of 12 microns. The power pad (9320) is a special exception to these rules.

3.2.2 Terminals

All terminals fall on incremental spacings of 12 microns and are governed by the same rules for structure and numbering as the functional cells (see Section 3.1.3). No terminals are associated with the bonding pad areas, and the power pad (9320) contains no terminals.

3.2.3 Bus Structure

Except for the power pad, each I/O pad function has two implementations resulting from an inverted bus structure. Pad types with an even number in the "tens" place (e.g., 92$\underline{2}$0) have V_{DD} as the bottom bus (closest to the reference point) and V_{SS} as the top bus. Pad types with an odd number in the "tens" place (e.g., 92$\underline{1}$0) have V_{SS} as the bottom bus and V_{DD} as the top bus. This arrangement allows the power buses on the left and right edges of the chip to feed the cell rows inside the chip. See Chapter 10.

The bottom power bus on an I/O pad looks exactly like the bottom bus on a functional cell — it is 8 microns wide, runs horizontally and is centered on a y-coordinate of 12 microns. The top power bus is 50 microns wide and is positioned such that the lower edge of the bus is located at a y-coordinate of 134 microns, thereby lining up with the lower edge of the top power bus in a functional cell.

3.2.4 Output Drive

Output pads in CMOS3 exhibit a 20 ns propagation delay and 50 ns output transition time when driving a 50 pF, 0 ohm load at 5 volts, 125°C, and utilizing worst case processing paramenters.

3.2.5 Input Protection and Guardbanding

Special structures have been included in the I/O pads to protect against electrostatic discharge (ESD) and to reduce the possibility of latch-up.

Spark Gap   A spark gap is utilized on all input circuits to minimize the voltage spike present at the gates of internal circuits and to alleviate some of the current stress on the resistor/diode configuration. One side of the spark gap is connected to the pad signal line prior to the input resistor and the other side is connected to the "top" power bus of the pad. The gap is constructed of offset (staggered) teeth with a point-to-point spacing of 12 microns, and this sawtooth region remains unpassivated. The metal in the signal path must be a minimum of 10 microns from the nearest power bus prior to the input resistor and 7 microns after the resistor to help prevent sparking in the passivated regions and to prevent metal bridging if sparking does occur.

Resistor   The input resistor has a value of approximately 1K ohm and is composed of a P+ diffusion in a P− tub. The P+ diffusion is approximately 12 squares and is connected in parallel with 2 to 4 squres of P− diffusion. The P− diffusion provides a large cross-sectional area to help minimize the current stress on the P+ resistor at large currents. The P− diffusion is connected to the signal line and, therefore, a 15 micron spacing to any other P− material or to the cell edge must be maintained.

Diodes   After the input resistor, the signal line is connected in metal to a P+/N− diode and an N+/P− diode. The diode areas are as large as possible to enhance their current handling capability. The P+/N− diode is surrounded by an N+ ring tied to V_{DD} and the N+/P− diode is surrounded by a P+ ring tied to V_{SS}.

Output Pads   The only precaution against ESD on the output pads is an increase in the metal-to-metal spacing between the output signal line and the adjacent power bus. On the bonding pad side of the "top" power bus, a spacing of 10 microns is maintained between the metal in the output signal line and the bus. On the opposite side of the top metal bus, a spacing of 7 microns is maintained between the metal in the output signal line and that bus.

Guard Banding and Special Configurations   To reduce the potential for latch-up, a P+ active area guard ring surrounds the N-channel transistors and an N+ active area guard ring surrounds the P-channel transistors. The P+ guard ring is at least 4 microns wide. The inside edge of this ring may overlap or abut the P− well, but may not be more than 1 micron outside the P− well. This rule guarantees that the P− well, even when diffused outward by as much as 5 microns from the as-drawn geometries, will still be surrounded by P+ active area (see Fig. 3.2). No such special rules apply to the N+ guard ring.

Substrate currents under the bonding pad may arise due to hole injection into the substrate during rapid transition swings. In order to minimize these effects, a P+/P− "U"-shaped isolation region tied to V_{SS} is provided around the bonding pad area. The P− region must be at least 3 microns wide and is separated from any other P− region by the minimum spacing for this layer. The P+ acts as a lower resistance path on top of the P− and connects the P− to V_{SS}. This P− region must obey all the P− rules which apply to the cell edges for standard cells and must do so for both power bus configurations. When the top bus is V_{DD}, a P− to

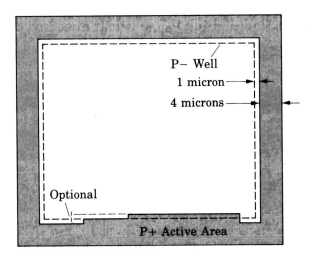

■Figure 3.2

cell edge spacing of 6 microns must be maintained above a y-coordinate of 150 microns. When the top bus is V_{SS}, a P– to cell edge spacing of 15 microns applies between the y-coordinates of 150 microns and 165 microns. Above 165 microns, this spacing returns to 6 microns.

4

SSI Cell Description

The library entry for each cell consists of several pages of data. Header information on each page consists of the following:

- cell family name
- cell type number and name
- cell design date and revision

4.1   PAGE 1

4.1.1   Terminal Information

The terminal name and the terminal number for both the top and bottom edges of the cell are specified along with the capacitance of each input. No capacitance is specified for output terminals because this capacitance is included in the cell characterizations.

The Logic Field refers to the format of the input data to the U.S. Government's LOGICV logic simulation program. Cells are referenced in the ELEMENTS category of LOGICV through the following convention:

(card image format)

	CELL TYPE NUMBER	FIELD #1	FIELD #2	FIELD #3	FIELD #4	FIELD #5	FIELD #6	FIELD #7	TAG
COLUMN:	1	5	15	25	35	45	55	65	75

Fields 1 through 5 are reserved for inputs.
Fields 6 and 7 are reserved for outputs.

Each I/O terminal of a cell is assigned to a unique LOGICV field. For example, the ELEMENTS category entry for the 1130, 3-Input NOR is:

1130A		B	C			OUT		TAG
1	5	15	25	35	45	55	65	75

For cells with more than five inputs and/or more than two outputs, a continuation card may be used. The logic field numbers increase as follows:

CONT	FIELD #8	FIELD #9	FIELD #10	FIELD #11	FIELD #12	FIELD #13	FIELD #14	TAG

As many CONT cards as necessary may be used.

The TAG field specified on these cards is the number (element number, instance number) associated with each unique usage of a cell.

4.1.2 Truth Table

A three state (1, 0, X = don't know) truth table is provided for each cell. For simplicity, an asterisk (*) represents a "don't care" condition. An "IC" denotes a possible illegal condition. For example, a P-channel and an N-channel device may be "on" simultaneously creating a direct path from V_{DD} to V_{SS}. This condition is treated as a "don't know" (X) in logic simulation. A separate page is used when the complete truth table does not fit in the space allotted.

4.1.3 Logic Diagrams and Symbols

The logic symbol is provided with the appropriate terminal names and one of the associated terminal numbers. A logic diagram is provided when more detail is necessary to describe the functionality of the cell.

4.1.4 Worst Case Delay Information

This information is intended to be used for quick cell-to-cell performance comparisons. The delay time and rise/fall time are specified for the following conditions: worst case processing parameters, 5 volts, 125°C, and a typical loading of 1.5K ohm lumped series resistance and 1.5 pF load capacitance with an input transition time of 10 ns.

4.1.5 Logic Equations

The relevant logic equations are provided using the appropriate terminal names.

4.1.6 Notes

Any appropriate application notes for the particular cell are provided here.

4.2 PAGE 2

This page contains the circuit schematic with all I/O terminal numbers identified. Each device is labeled with the device number used in the analysis of the circuit and the device dimensions in microns are contained in brackets (LENGTH/WIDTH). The device numbering convention is as follows:

numbers 20–49 are P-channel devices
numbers 50–89 are N-channel devices

4.3 PAGE 3

Performance characteristics under various conditions are contained on this page in either equation or table form. See Chapter 6, Cell Characterization Plan, and

Chapter 7, Cell User's Guide, for more detail on the derivation and use of these
equations.

4.3.1 Output Characteristic Equations

These equations represent the actual propagation delays and output transition
times. They are calculated by adding the compensating effects of input transition
time and lumped series resistance to the corresponding nominal values, which
are a function of capacitance only (see Section 4.3.2). The propagation delays are
measured between the 50% points of the input and output signals, and the rise
and fall times represent a trapezoidal waveform having a transition time defined
as 0% to 100% of the signal.

4.3.2 Equations

These equations represent propagation delays and output transition times as a
function of output load capacitance only. They are presented for several operating
conditions: worst case electrical parameters at operating temperatures of 25°C,
95°C, and 125°C and best case electrical parameters at a 125°C operating temperature. The input transition time for all four cases is 10 ns.

4.3.3 Voltage Table

A table is included for calculating the effects of supply voltage on propagation
delay and output transition time. Results of the characteristic equation calculations are to be multiplied by the respective entries in the table for the appropriate voltage. A typical output loading of 1.5 pF/1.5K ohm was used.

Because of the nonlinear relationship of delay to RC loading over the voltage
range, caution must be exercised in using this table. Between 4V and 6V, the
accuracy of the table is within 10%. In the ranges of 3V to 4V and 6V to 7V, the
accuracy is within 20%. Heavy output loading (RC greater than or equal to 15 ns)
can result in significant error and, in these cases, detailed simulation should be
used.

4.4 PAGE 4

The curves on this page are linear representations of output delay and transition
time versus capacitive loading for three different values of lumped series resistance: 10K ohms, 1.5K ohms, and 0.2K ohms. The 10K ohm curves represent a
worst case lumped series resistance below which 90% of the nets on a chip should
fall and can be used for rough timing analysis. The 1.5K ohm curves represent a
typical resistive loading; 50% of the nets on a chip should fall below this threshold. The 0.2K ohm curves represent a best case resistive loading that should
cover only 10% or less of the nets on a chip. All the curves presented here are generated at 125°C and 5 volts. For a more detailed description of how to utilize
these curves, refer to the Cell User's Guide (Chapter 7).

4.5 ADDITIONAL PAGES

For cells with multiple outputs, additional pages are necessary for presenting the electrical characteristics of each output. The output represented by each page is specified in the center of the data block.

Additional pages are also necessary to present specialized timing information for the more complicated circuits, such as flip-flops.

4.6 LAST PAGE

The last page for each cell contains a color plot of the cell geometries along with the terminal numbers and device numbers.

5

MSI Cell Data Description

The documentation for the MSI cells is different from that of the SSI cells. With the exception of the 4600s, there are no geometry plots. Timing equations are supplied for worst case processing at 125°C and best case processing at 125°C, only. Box plots are included to show the location of all I/0.

5.1 CELL STRUCTURE

MSI slices are 363 microns tall. Typically, they are composed of two rows of SSI cells flush against the top and bottom of the 363 microns. From top to bottom, the four power busses are V_{DD}, V_{SS}, V_{DD}, V_{SS}. From y-coordinates 0–150 and 213–363, the MSI slices must conform to the SSI edge rules. For the 63 microns of space between the rows of SSI cells, there will generally be horizontal metal wires that come to the sides of the slice. This is how the slices communicate to form an MSI function. The polysilicon terminals on the top and bottom of an MSI slice conform to the SSI rules.

MSI functions are also 363 microns tall. The only difference between MSI functions and MSI slices, structurally speaking, is that between y-coordinates 150–213, material in an MSI function must be inside the cell edge by one half of the spacing rule.

Because of their slice configurations, some MSI functions will have metal wires that seem to hang in space. These lines are outputs and not inputs needing to be tied off. They will not cause problems.

Some of the MSI functions have gaps in the P– well of 12 microns or some multiple thereof. Again, there is no problem. These anomalies are brought to the user's attention to avoid surprises.

5.2 TERMINAL NAMES

The terminal naming conventions of the SSI cells have been discarded. Every terminal has two names. The ETER name is descriptive of the terminal's function and is shared among electrically equivalent terminals. The TERM name indicates the terminal location relative to other terminals. For example, the ETER Q may refer to four terminals with TERM's T2, B2, L5, and R6. T, B, L, and R indicate top, bottom, left, and right. L5 means the fifth terminal from the top on the left side of the cell. B2 means the second terminal from the left on the bottom of the cell.

Each ETER is described by function codes; I, O, F, P, and G, meaning input, output, feed-thru, power, and ground.

5.3 DOUBLE-LEVEL METAL

A second level of metal was not used in the MSI cells. Since the I/0 pads are configured for double-level metal (DLM), even a single metal chip could be run on a

DLM line. On the other hand, a second level of metal could be used at the chip level. Running metal 2 over the MSI functions could provide a significant area savings. Using metal 2 instead of poly eliminates series parasitic resistance outside of the cell.

5.4 n-BIT FUNCTIONS

As was noted earlier, MSI functions of a user-defined bit size can be built using slices. Usually, one beginning and one ending slice is required with some number of middle slices. In order to use such a user-defined function, the user must build the function.

Timing for n-bit functions is provided in the form of equations in n and C_L.

5.5 CHARACTERIZATION

5.5.1 Conditions

The cells were simulated under worst case and best case processing conditions, the parameters for which can be found in the User's Guide, Chapter 7.

All cells were simulated at 125° with V_{DD} at 5 volts.

Input signal levels were at 0 and 5 volts. The input transition times were 30 ns for worst case processing and 15 ns for best case.

Although the circuit simulator could not account for polysilicon resistance, all parasitic capacitors were simulated. The load in a cell output consisted of a series resistor and a shunt capacitor. The resistor was set equal to the output resistance of the cell. The capacitor was varied between 1.5 and 4.0 pF.

5.5.2 Delay Time

Delay time is measured from 50% of the input transition to 50% of the output transition. Data points are taken at 1.5 and 4.0 pF. Delay is assumed to be linear with capacitive load (C_L) and is presented in equation form for worst case and best case processing.

5.5.3 Transition Time

Transition time is measured from 10% to 90% (or vice versa) of V_{DD}. The measured transition time is then multiplied by 1.25 to correct it to 0% and 100% of V_{DD}. Transition time is presented on the documentation pages in a way similar to delay time.

5.5.4 Set-up Time

MSI functions with flip-flops have special timing requirements on the input signals. Set-up time refers to the requirement that one signal must be present and stable for so long before a second signal transition. Generally, data must precede clock by the set-up time. Set-up time for an MSI function is measured in the following manner. First the set-up time for the flip-flop is found under the conditions: V_{DD} at 5 volts, clock transition time and data transition time at 30 ns. Then two different delay times are determined: the time it takes the clock to get from the function terminal to the flip-flop terminal, and a similar delay time for data. Function set-up time = flip-flop set-up time + data delay time − clock delay time.

5.5.5 Hold Time

Hold time generally refers to the requirement that data not change for so long after the negative clock transition. Hold time for the flip-flop is found under conditions: V_{DD} at 7 volts, clock transition time and data transition time at 30 ns. Function hold time = flip-flop hold time − data delay time + clock delay time.

5.6 EXTRAPOLATION

Variations in certain conditions can be accounted for through the use of equations based upon theory and empirical data. Such equations hold for all cells and they save a great deal of computer time and manpower.

The simulation conditions with which this section deals are V_{DD}, temperature, and tau. Tau is an equivalent resistance times an equivalent capacitance for a distributed RC network. Tau can be calculated in any number of ways that can lead to either very conservative or very optimistic results.

Sensitivity factors (SF) are developed for variations of each condition from the norm. For V_{DD}, SF(V_{DD}) is developed for five different cases:

1. $3.0 \langle V_{DD} \rangle 7.0$, typical case, $\mathrm{SF}(V_{DD}) = 4.0/(V_{DD} - 1.0)$
2. $3.0 \langle V_{DD} \langle 5.0$, worse case, $\mathrm{SF}(V_{DD}) = 4.0/(V_{DD} - 1.0)^{1.07}$
3. $5.0 \langle V_{DD} \langle 7.0$, worst case, $\mathrm{SF}(V_{DD}) = 4.0/(V_{DD} - 1.0)^{0.20}$
4. $3.0 \langle V_{DD} \langle 5.0$, best case, $\mathrm{SF}(V_{DD}) = 4.0/(V_{DD} - 1.0)^{0.20}$
5. $5.0 \langle V_{DD} \langle 7.0$, best case, $\mathrm{SF}(V_{DD}) = 4.0/(V_{DD} - 1.0)^{1.07}$

5.6.1 Temperature

For variation in temperature, $\mathrm{SF}(T) = 1.0 + 0.0038 \cdot (T - 125)$, where T is in degrees centigrade.

5.6.2 Series Resistance

For series load resistance due to interconnect:

$$\mathrm{SF}(R_S) = 0.69 \cdot (R_S) \cdot (C_L), \text{ for delay times}$$
$$\mathrm{SF}(R_S) = 2.18 \cdot (R_S) \cdot (C_L), \text{ for transition time}$$
$$\mathrm{SF}(R_S) = 0.0, \text{ for best case for both}$$

5.6.3 All Conditions

In order to calculate a delay time based on all parameters (process, C_L, V_{DD}, T, R_S), first determine the time based only on process and C_L from the pages for the cell of interest. Call this Time(C_L).

$$\text{Time}(C_L,\ V_{DD},\ T,\ R_S),\ =\ \text{SF}(V_{DD})\cdot\text{SF}(T)\cdot\text{Time}(C_L) + \text{SF}(R_S,\ C_L)$$

6

Cell Characterization Plan

This chapter describes the procedures used to characterize the performance of the CMOS3 cells. The data presented in this library is distilled from the output of at least 18 electrical simulations for even the simplest of cells and covers a range of loading, temperature, and processing conditions.

6.1 DEFINITIONS

6.1.1 Electrical Parameters/Device Modeling Parameters

The CMOS3 cells were characterized using the electrical parameters in Section 2.2 and the U.S. Government's MOSTRAN circuit simulation program. Model numbers 15 and 25 from this program were used to simulate the P and N-channel devices, respectively.

A lateral diffusion of 0.25 microns per side was used for the calculation of gate-to-source and gate-to-drain overlap capacitances. 0.25 microns per side was also used in the circuit simulations resulting in an effective channel length of 2.5 microns for a 3-micron (as drawn) device.

Several electrical parameters are temperature dependent. K' ($= \mu C_{ox}/2$) is modified according to the classical relationship of mobility and temperature ($\mu \alpha T^{-3/2}$). The threshold voltage, V_t, varies inversely with temperature by 3mV/°C. In other words, for a temperature, T,

$$V_t(T) = V_t(25°C) + 0.003 \cdot (25 - T)$$

The polysilicon resistivity was also varied according to the temperature/mobility relationship, which is probably a larger variation than is seen in practice. This variation was only accounted for in the calculation of the internal poly resistance between a cell's output device and its output terminal.

Table 6.1 is a summary of the temperature-dependent parameters used in simulating the CMOS3 cells. Simulations using "worst case" parameters represent the "slowest" process. Conversely, simulations using "best case" parameters represent the "fastest" process.

Table 6.2 is a summary of the remaining temperature-independent parameters used in MOSTRAN for these simulations.

6.1.2 Output Loading

The output of each cell drives a load represented by the resistance of the output terminals of the cell connected to an equivalent RC load denoted by $R_S C_L$ (see Fig. 6.1).

C_L represents the total interconnect and fanout (cell input) capacitance. R_S represents the equivalent series resistance of a net and is a value that can be calculated in several ways (see Chapter 7). C_N is present only to allow the MOSTRAN simulator to have a capacitance associated with that node. R_{POLY}

TABLE 6.1 Temperature-Dependent Electrical Parameters

	K' ($\mu A/V^2$)				V_t (VOLTS)				RESISTIVITY (K ohms/square)
	BEST CASE		WORST CASE		BEST CASE		WORST CASE		
	P	N	P	N	P	N	P	N	
−55°C	16.8	42.0	8.4	21.0	−0.71	0.71	−1.31	1.31	0.021
25°C	12.0	30.0	6.0	15.0	−0.50	0.50	−1.10	1.10	0.030
95°C	8.75	21.9	4.37	10.93	−0.29	0.29	−0.89	0.89	0.040
125°C	7.8	19.5	3.9	9.75	−0.20	0.20	−0.80	0.80	0.046

Note: The following abbreviations are often used to specify combinations of parameters:
WNWP—worst N and worst P-channel parameters
WNBP—worst N and best P-channel parameters
BNWP—best N and worst P-channel parameters
BNBP—best N and best P-channel parameters

TABLE 6.2 Temperature Independent Simulation Parameters

	P	N
Lateral diffusion (per side)	0.25 microns	0.25 microns
Surface doping	1×10^{15} cm^{-3}	1×10^{16} cm^{-3}
Bulk doping	1×10^{15} cm^{-3}	1×10^{16} cm^{-3}
Oxide capacity	0.37 pF/mil^2	0.37 pF/mil^2
Mobility constant	9.0	14.0
Mobility exponent	1.1	1.3

is the largest of the internal polysilicon resistances of the cell from the drain of the output device to the associated output terminal. As noted in the previous section, R_{POLY} is temperature-dependent and it is the only resistor in the simulation that is handled in this manner. All capacitances are viewed as voltage independent with the exception of the P+/N− and N+/P− junction capacitances, which are modeled as voltage-variable capacitances.

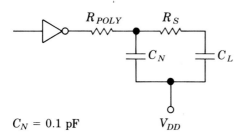

$C_N = 0.1$ pF

■**Figure 6.1**

6.1.3 Transition Time

The rise and fall times (T_R, T_F) in this library represent 0% to 100% of the signal swing. These values are derived from the electrical simulation by measuring the time required for a signal to go from 10% to 90% of its rail values and then by multiplying the result by 1.25.

6.1.4 Output Delay and Transition Time

The output delay of a circuit includes both the throughput delay and the delay of the output transition. The set of input signal conditions for a cell that results in the longest delay for each direction of output transition is the set that is used for characterization.

6.2 OUTPUT CURVES

The curves represent output delay and transition time as a function of capacitive loading for three values of series resistance (0.2K, 1.5K, and 10K ohms). In all cases, the curves are generated at 5 volts, 125°C, using worst case process parameters and an input transition time of 10 ns. Each curve is a straight line approximation based on two points: capacitance values of 1.5 pF and 4.0 pF.

6.3 EQUATIONS

The equations also represent output delay and transition time as a function of capacitive loading. The equations are generated at 5 volts with 0.2K ohm series resistance and an input transition time of 10 ns. Three sets of equations are generated using worst case process parameters: 25°C, 95°C, and 125°C. The fourth set of equations is generated at 125°C using best case process parameters (i.e., the highest values of K' and the lowest threshold voltages). Each equation is a straight line approximation based on two values of C_L: 1.5 pF and 4.0 pF.

6.4 OUTPUT CHARACTERISTIC EQUATIONS

These equations add the compensating effects of input transition time and output series resistance to their respective values, which are a function of load capacitance only (Section 6.3).

The effect of input transition time on propagation delay and output transition time is calculated by maintaining a loading of 0.2K ohm and 1.5 pF on the output and simulating the circuit at 5V, 125°C, and using worst case processing parameters. The coefficient for the term expressing change in transition time is the slope of a two point curve of output delay or transition time versus input transition time. The two input transition time points are 10 ns and 30 ns.

The effect of series resistance on delay and output transition time is represented by a coefficient for the $R_S C_L$ term of the characteristic equation. This coefficient is generated by finding the slope of the output delay and transition times versus resistive loading and dividing by the capacitive value used in generating these curves. Worst case process parameters, V_{DD} = 5V, 125°C, and C_L = 1.5 pF are used for this calculation. Resistance values of 0.2K ohm and 10K ohm were used to generate this curve. The coefficient is then the difference in output delay or transition time divided by 14.7 (= $\Delta R \cdot C_L$ = 9.8·1.5).

For cell types with two outputs in which the characteristics of one output (Output #2) are a function of the loading on the other output (Output #1), another term is added to the characteristic equation for Output #2. The equations and characteristic equations for Output #2 are calculated with a loading of 0.2K ohms and 0.2 pF on Output #1. The additional loading term is a function of the capacitive loading on Output #1. Changes in the resistive loading on Output #1 will not increase the delay to Output #2. To obtain the coefficient for this factor, the loading on Output #2 is fixed at 0.2K ohm and 1.5 pF while the resistive load on Output #1 is held at 0.2K ohm. The delay and transition times for Output #2 are then calculated for capacitive loadings on Output #1 of 1.5 pF and 4.0 pF. The slope of the lines for delay and transition times versus capacitive loading is the coefficient for this term.

6.5   VOLTAGE TABLE

The voltage table reflects the change in output characteristics resulting from changes in V_{DD}. This table was generated from electrical simulations with V_{DD} equal to 3,4,5,6, and 7 volts. A loading of 1.5K ohm, 1.5 pF was used along with worst case process parameters, 125°C, and an input transition time of 10 ns.

The factors in the table represent the output characteristics at a given voltage divided by the output characteristics at 5V. Factors which fall on half volt points (3.5V, 4.5V etc.) are straight line approximations between the two whole voltage values.

6.6   SPECIAL CASES

6.6.1   Transmission Gate (T-Gate) Cells

Each of the T-gate cells is characterized for two conditions: 1) when the T-gate is ON preceding the arrival of a signal from the cell that drives the data input of the T-gate and 2) when the T-gate is OFF (with a signal present at the data input) and then turns ON.

ON T-gate   A 1310 cell (INVERTER) with an ON T-gate between the output and the load cell is characterized in the manner described in Sections 6.2–6.5. The differences between these results and the normal 1310 cell characteristics are the ON T-gate characteristics.

It is expected that the ON T-gate will appear as a lumped resistance under these circumstances. Thus, the characteristics may be expressed as an equation in the same manner as the series resistance compensation factor.

OFF-ON T-gate For this condition, the reference for the output characteristics is the control signal input to the T-gate. Although the control signal is the reference, the cell driving the data input to the T-gate has a major impact on the output characteristics. A 1310 cell is used to drive the data input to the T-gate and the output characteristics for this situation are determined in the manner described in Sections 6.2–6.5.

6.6.2 SET/RESET Register Cells (Latches)

SET/RESET register cells (1410 and 1420) may be viewed as simple multi-output cells. In this regard, they are characterized in the manner described in Section 6.4. Because each of these circuits is symmetrical, only one set of output equations/curves is provided per cell.

6.6.3 Register Cells

Output Characteristics Relative to Input Signals The CLOCK, SET, and RESET signals are treated the same as any other input signal in determining the standard output characteristics.

For register cell timing characterization, the data input must remain stable at least 50 ns before, to 50 ns after, any clock transition to limit the effects of data set-up and hold.

Maximum Clock Rise Time The maximum clock rise time is determined in the following manner:

The flip-flop is simulated under the following conditions:

1. $V_{DD} = 7.0$V
2. Best case process parameters
3. $T = -55°$C
4. Output loading = 0.2K ohm/0.2 pF

The clock rise time is increased until the input data ripples through to the output on a single positive clock transition. This is done for both DATA = 0 and DATA = 1 to determine which is more susceptible to ripple-thru.

A 1310 cell (INVERTER) is then simulated under the following conditions:

1. $V_{DD} = 7.0$V
2. Best case process parameters
3. $T = -55°$C
4. Input fall time = 10 ns
5. Output loading = 0.2K ohm/variable capacitance (C_L)

C_L is varied until the output rise time matches the flip-flop clock rise time that caused ripple-thru (above).

The best case rise time is translated to an equivalent worst case value by simulating the 1310 under the following conditions:

1. V_{DD} = 7.0V
2. Worst case process parameters
3. T = 125°C
4. Input fall time = 10 ns
5. Output loading = 0.2K ohm/C_L from above

The resulting output rise time is the *maximum clock rise time.*

In order to confirm that the ripple-thru does not occur, the flip-flop is then simulated using this rise time and the following conditions:

1. V_{DD} = 7.0V
2. Worst case process parameters
3. T = 125°C
4. Output loading = 0.2K ohm/1.5 pF

Minimum Clock Pulse Width   The flip-flop is simulated under the following conditions:

1. V_{DD} = 3.0V
2. Worst case process parameters
3. T = 125°C
4. Output loading = 0.2K ohm/1.5 pF

A triangular pulse is used for the input clock signal. The R/F times are varied until the flip-flop fails (see Fig. 6.2).

Minimum Reset Pulse Width   The flip-flop is simulated under the following conditions:

1. V_{DD} = 3.0V
2. Worst case process parameters
3. T = 125°C
4. Output loading = 0.2K ohm/1.5 pF

A triangular pulse is used for the input reset signal. The R/F times are varied until the flip-flop fails (see Fig. 6.3).

Minimum Set Pulse Width   The flip-flop is simulated under the following conditions:

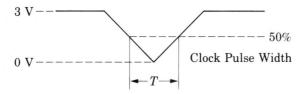

■**Figure 6.2**

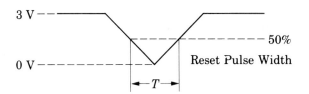

■**Figure 6.3**

     1. V_{DD} = 3.0V
     2.   Worst case process parameters
     3. T = 125°C
     4.   Output loading = 0.2K ohm/1.5 pF

A triangular pulse is used for the input set signal. The R/F times are varied until the flip-flop fails (see Fig. 6.4).

Minimum Data Set-up Time Data set-up time is the length of time that the data input signal to a flip-flop must be stable before the clock signal can make a transition. Data set-up time is measured from the clock transition relative to the input data transition at the 50% points (see Fig. 6.5).

    The minimum data set-up time is established in the following manner:

    a.   First, the set of conditions that results in the slowest set-up time in the master stage of the flip-flop must be determined. This is done by simulating the flip-flop under combinations of the following conditions:
        1.   DATA = 0; DATA = 1
        2. V_{DD} = 3V; V_{DD} = 7V

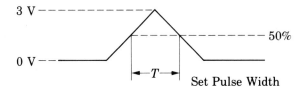

■**Figure 6.4**

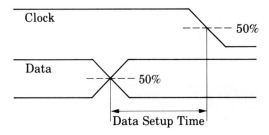

■**Figure 6.5**

3. $T = 125°C$
4. Processing parameters: WNWP; WNBP; BNWP; BNBP
5. Clock transition time = 10 ns
6. Output loading = 0.2K ohm/1.5 pF

b. Next, three "standard" delay times are established that will be used in the determination of the minimum data set-up time. These delay times are found by simulating the flip-flop using the set of conditions established in paragraph (a) above. Clock transition times of 10 ns, 30 ns, and 60 ns are used and the data signal remains stable from 50 ns before to 50 ns after any clock transition.

c. Now, once again using the set of conditions from paragraph (a), six different minimum data set-up times are generated for clock transition times 10 ns, 30 ns, and 60 ns and data transition times of 10 ns and 60 ns.

The minimum data set-up time is derived by moving the input data signal and clock signal closer together until the flip-flop fails or until the output delay increases by more than 10% of the corresponding "standard" delay time (established above).

Because data set-up time is very dependent on the supply voltage, it is useful to establish set-up times for 5V operation in addition to the worst case values just derived. This is done by repeating the procedure described in paragraphs (a) through (c) above, but with a fixed V_{DD} of 5 volts.

The data is presented as curves of data set-up time versus data R/F time for clock R/F times of 10 ns, 30 ns, and 60 ns.

Minimum Hold Time Hold time is the length of time that the data input signal to a flip-flop must be stable after the clock signal has made a transition. It is measured between the 50% points of the clock and data signals (see Fig. 6.6).

The minimum hold time is established in the following way:

a. First, the set of conditions that results in the longest hold time must be determined. This is done by simulating the flip-flop under combinations of the following conditions:
1. DATA = 0; DATA = 1
2. $V_{DD} = 3V$; $V_{DD} = 7V$
3. $T = 125°C$
4. Processing parameters: WNWP; WNBP; BNWP; BNBP

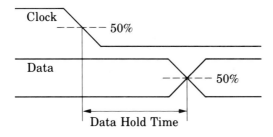

■**Figure 6.6**

      5. Clock transition time = 10 ns

      6. Output loading = 0.2K ohm/0.2 pF

b. Next, three "standard" delay times are established that will be used in the determination of the minimum hold time. These delay times are found by simulating the flip-flop using the set of conditions established in paragraph (a) above. Clock transition times of 10 ns, 30 ns, and 60 ns are used and the data signal remains stable from 50 ns before to 50 ns after any clock transition.

c. Now, once again using the set of conditions from paragraph (a), six different minimum hold times are generated for clock transition times of 10 ns, 30 ns, and 60 ns and data transition times of 10 ns and 60 ns.

The minimum hold time is derived by moving the input data signal and clock signal closer together until the flip-flop fails or until the output delay increases by more than 10% of the corresponding "standard" delay (established above). The minimum allowable hold time is 0 ns (negative values are not permitted).

The data is presented as curves of minimum hold time versus data R/F time for clock R/F times of 10 ns, 30 ns, and 60 ns.

7

Cell
User's Guide

This chapter contains a description of how to apply the information contained in the cell library to perform chip level timing analysis. Highlighted here are some major limitations and some suggestions on how the data pages should be used.

All the data presented here has been generated using the procedures outlined in the cell characterization plan (Chapter 6). This data is presented to allow for reliable timing analysis over a wide range of system requirements.

7.1   DELAY AND TRANSITION TIME VERSUS CAPACITIVE LOADING CURVES

Three different delay versus capacitive loading curves are provided representing three different values for series resistance in a net (0.2K, 1.5K, and 10K ohms). The appropriate curve for the value of series resistance in a particular net can be used to provide the delay and output transition times for the cell of interest. A trapezoidal input having a rise or fall time of 10 ns (0% to 100%) has been used to generate these curves. If the input is different than 10 ns, the delay and output transition times will differ by the relationship presented in the characteristic equations. This relationship should always be considered when using the curves.

The resistance values mentioned here are in addition to the internal cell output resistance. This internal poly resistance was included when the curves were generated. To consider the effect of resistance in the interconnect path, the curve with the same or higher value of resistance must be used. For example, if a path has a load of 2.5K ohms of resistance and 2.0 pF of capacitance, then the 10K ohms resistance curve should be used. Using the higher resistance curve will, of course, result in a more conservative timing analysis.

7.2   CHARACTERISTIC EQUATIONS

The characteristic equations can be used for more accurate timing that includes the effects of the input transition times, series load resistance, and, to some extent, temperature. These equations allow for simple hand calculations, but can be implemented in computer software for large volumes of calculations.

The "Equations" category provides the basic timing equations as a function of capacitive loading at three temperatures (25°C, 95°C, and 125°C) and assuming worst case electrical parameters. Also included is a set of equations at 125°C using best case electrical parameters (BC). The appropriate temperature of 95°C or 125°C and worst case parameters are to be used for worst case system timing analysis at the maximum system temperature specification. The set of equations at 25°C and worst case parameters can be used for timing comparisons when testing the performance of a chip at room temperature; for instance, during chip characterization. The 125°C BC equations are provided for timing signals that have potential race conditions, such as interchip signals in which one chip type is assumed to have been processed under best case conditions and the other is assumed to have been processed under worst case conditions. These equations have been generated using a resistor to model the internal poly resistance of the cell output path. In addition, a 200 ohm resistor is added at each output terminal (see Chapter 6).

The value calculated in each case by the "Equations" is used in the characteristic equations to account for the effects of series resistance and input transition times. The input transition time is considered to be a trapezoidal waveform having a specific rise and fall time (0% to 100% of V_{DD}). The calculations using the equations for transition time produce results for such a waveform. 10 ns is subtracted from the input transition in the characteristic equations, since this is the time used in generating all the other constants of the equations.

The $R_S C_L$ factor in the characteristic equations is the time constant resulting from the series resistance in the net. This factor can be arrived at in several ways. The most conservative way is the lumped RC time constant, which is calculated by summing all the series resistances in the net and the total capacitance of the net and taking the product. This time constant is often much larger than the actual time constant. A more accurate method for calculating the $R_S C_L$ factor used in these equations is to consider each individual resistance multiplied by the capacitance that this resistance "sees" as a time constant for this resistor. The capacitance that a resistor "sees" is the capacitance that is charged or discharged by the current that must flow through that resistor. To calculate the time to drive from a source to a specific input, only those RC time constants that appear in this specific path need to be considered. This method is still fairly conservative, but can produce much smaller RC factors for specific paths. See Section 7.3 for an example.

7.3 LOADING REDUCTION EXAMPLE

Method 1　The quickest method of calculating the C_L and $R_S C_L$ loading for the sample interconnect circuit of Fig. 7.1 is to add all the capacitances to get C_L and add all the resistances to get R_S:

$$C_L = C_A + C_B + C_C$$
$$R_S = R_A + R_B + R_C$$
$$R_S C_L = (C_A + C_B + C_C) \cdot (R_A + R_B + R_C)$$

This method, although simple and straightforward, can lead to a larger $R_S C_L$ factor than is necessary from the output to each input.

Method 2　Another method that is relatively simple takes into account only those RC factors between the output and each individual input. A tau (RC factor) is calculated for each branch of the interconnect by multiplying the resistance of that branch by the total capacitance that resistance "sees." This total

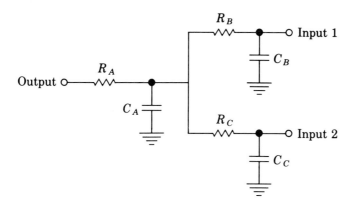

■**Figure 7.1**

capacitance is the capacitance in the net that occurs after that particular resistance. For the sample circuit:

$$\tau_A = R_A \cdot (C_A + C_B + C_C)$$
$$\tau_B = R_B \cdot C_B$$
$$\tau_C = R_C \cdot C_C$$

A tau is then calculated for each input by adding those taus for the branches that appear between the output and each individual input; i.e.,

$$\text{Input } 1 = \tau_A + \tau_B = R_A \cdot (C_A + C_B + C_C) + R_B \cdot C_B$$
$$\text{Input } 2 = \tau_A + \tau_C = R_A \cdot (C_A + C_B + C_C) + R_C \cdot C_C$$

This method is helpful if there is a large resistance in only part of the net. This resistance does not affect the timing calculations to other parts of the net. For instance, if R_B is a large resistance, the effect on the delay to Input 2 is minimal in this calculation as well as in reality.

The C_L is the total capacitance for the net calculated by adding all the individual capacitances.

Method 3 The RC network may be mathematically reduced to a single RC. This method is much more complicated but is probably the most accurate.

7.4 TIMING ANALYSIS EXAMPLE

Figure 7.2 shows an example that will be used to demonstrate the timing analysis possible from the data in the cell library. The taus ($R_S C_L$ factors) shown for the loading of the interconnect network could have been calculated by either methods 1 or 2 described in the preceding section. The cell input capacitances must be added to the interconnect capacitances as shown in Fig. 7.2. This timing analysis will be performed at both 5 and 3 volts at 125°C.

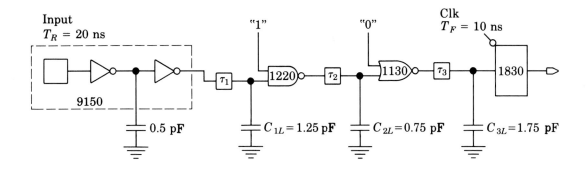

Taus: Capacitances:
$\tau_1 = 1.5$ ns $C_{nI} =$ inputs $C_1 = C_{1L} + C_{1I} = 1.25$ pF+ 0.25 pF= 1.5 pF
$\tau_2 = 1.0$ ns   capacitance $C_2 = C_{2L} + C_{2I} = 0.75$ pF+ 0.25 pF= 1.0 pF
$\tau_3 = 1.0$ ns $C_3 = C_{3L} + C_{3I} = 1.75$ pF+ 0.25 pF= 2.0 pF

■**Figure 7.2**

5 Volt Timing Analysis

Delay and rise time through the 9150 input pad:

Given: $T_R = 20$ ns	(Figure 7.2)
$R_S C_L = 1.5$ ns $= \tau_1$	(Figure 7.2)
$C_L = 1.5$ pF $= C_1$	(Figure 7.2)
$C_{LINV} = 0.5$ pF	(Figure 7.2)

$P_{DC}(0\text{–}1) = (1.81)\cdot(1.5 \text{ pF}) + 5.88 \text{ ns}$ (Page 9150-5)
$\qquad = 8.60 \text{ ns}$

$T_{RC} = (5.78)\cdot(1.5 \text{ pF}) + 3.51 \text{ ns} = 12.18 \text{ ns}$ (Page 9150-5)

$P_D(0\text{–}1) = 8.60 \text{ ns} + 0.12\cdot(20 - 10) + 0.64\cdot(1.5 \text{ ns})$ (Page 9150-5)
$\qquad + 1.84\cdot(0.5 \text{ pF}) = 11.68 \text{ ns}$

$T_R = 12.18 \text{ ns} + 0.03\cdot(20 - 10) + 2.48\cdot(1.5 \text{ ns})$ (Page 9150-5)
$\qquad + 1.10\cdot(0.5 \text{ pF}) = 16.75 \text{ ns}$

Delay and fall time for 1220:

Given: $T_R = 16.75$ ns	(From above)
$R_S C_L = 2.0$ ns $= \tau_2$	(Figure 7.2)
$C_L = 1.0$ pF $= C_2$	(Figure 7.2)

$P_{DC}(1\text{–}0) = (3.01)\cdot(1.0 \text{ pF}) + 3.61 \text{ ns} = 6.62 \text{ ns}$ (Page 1220-3)

$T_{FC} = (10.79)\cdot(1.0 \text{ pF}) + 1.78 \text{ ns} = 12.57 \text{ ns}$ (Page 1220-3)

$P_D(1\text{–}0) = 6.62 \text{ ns} + 0.21\cdot(16.75) - 10) + 0.63\cdot(2.0 \text{ ns})$ (Page 1220-3)
$\qquad = 9.30 \text{ ns}$

$T_F = 12.57 \text{ ns} + 0.15\cdot(16.75 - 10) + 2.60\cdot(2.0 \text{ ns})$ (Page 1220-3)
$\qquad = 18.78 \text{ ns}$

Delay and rise time for 1130:

Given: $T_F = 18.78$ ns   (From above)

          $R_S C_L = 1.0$ ns $= \tau_3$ (Figure 7.2)

          $C_L = 2.0$ pF $= C_3$ (Figure 7.2)

$P_{DC}(0\text{--}1) = 3.8 \cdot (2.0 \text{ pF}) + 5.56 \text{ ns} = 13.16 \text{ ns}$ (Page 1130-3)

$T_{RC} = 11.76 \cdot (2.0 \text{ pF}) + 7.01 \text{ ns} = 30.53 \text{ ns}$ (Page 1130-3)

$P_D(0\text{--}1) = 13.16 \text{ ns} + 0.23 \cdot (18.78 - 10) + 0.62 \cdot (1.0 \text{ ns})$ (Page 1130-3)

        $= 15.80 \text{ ns}$

$T_R = 30.53 \text{ ns} + 0.12 \cdot (18.78 - 10) + 2.27 \cdot (1.0 \text{ ns})$ (Page 1130-3)

        $= 33.85 \text{ ns}$

Set-up time for the 1830:

Given: Data rise time: 33.85 ns   (From above)

          Clock fall time: 10 ns   (Figure 7.2)

Using the 1830 curves for set-up time versus data $T_{R/F}$ (Page 1830-7)

transition times:

Data set-up time = 5.9 ns

Summary of delays for 5 volts, 125°C, and worst case processing parameters

TRANSITION	CELL TYPE	DELAY
0–1	9150	11.68 ns
1–0	1220	9.30 ns
0–1	1130	15.80 ns
Set-up time	1830	5.90 ns
Total Delay:		**42.68 ns**

3 Volt Timing Analysis

This analysis follows the 5 volt timing analysis using the appropriate voltage factors (V.F.) to increase each delay and output transition time.

Delay and rise time through the 9150 input pad:

From the 5V calculations:

$P_D(0\text{--}1) = 11.68 \text{ ns}$

$T_R = 16.75 \text{ ns}$

Applying the appropriate voltage factor:

$P_D(0\text{--}1) = (11.68 \text{ ns}) \cdot (1.69) = 19.74 \text{ ns}$ (Page 9150-5)

$T_R = (16.75 \text{ ns}) \cdot (1.46) = 24.46 \text{ ns}$ (Page 9150-5)

Delay and fall time for 1220:

Given: $T_R = 24.46$ ns   (From above)

$R_S C_L = 2.0$ ns $= \tau_2$ (Figure 7.2)

$C_L = 1.0$ pF $= C_2$ (Figure 7.2)

$P_{DC}(1\text{--}0) = 3.01 \cdot (1.0 \text{ pF}) + 3.61$ ns   (Page 1220-3)

$\quad\quad\quad = 6.62$ ns

$T_{FC} = (10.79) \cdot (1.0 \text{ pF}) + 1.78 \text{ ns} = 12.57$ ns   (Page 1220-3)

$P_D(1\text{--}0) = [6.62 \text{ ns} + 0.21 \cdot (24.46 - 10) + 0.63 \cdot (2.0)] \cdot (\text{V.F.})$

$\quad\quad\quad = (10.92 \text{ ns}) \cdot (1.88) = 20.53$ ns

$T_F = [12.57 \text{ ns} + 0.15 \cdot (24.46 - 10) + 2.60 \cdot (2.0)] \cdot (\text{V.F.})$

$\quad\quad = (19.94 \text{ ns}) \cdot (1.34) = 26.72$ ns

Delay and rise time for 1130:

Given: $T_F = 26.72$ ns   (From above)

$R_S C_L = 1.0$ ns $= \tau_3$ (Figure 7.2)

$C_L = 2.0$ pF $= C_3$ (Figure 7.2)

$P_{DC}(0\text{--}1) = 13.16$ ns (same as for 5 volts)

$T_{RC} = 30.53$ ns (same as for 5 volts)

$P_D(0\text{--}1) = [13.16 \text{ ns} + 0.23 \cdot (26.72 - 10) + 0.62 \cdot (1.0 \text{ ns})] \cdot (\text{V.F.})$

$\quad\quad\quad = (17.63 \text{ ns}) \cdot (1.68) = 29.61$ ns

$T_R = [30.53 \text{ ns} + 0.12 \cdot (26.72 - 10) + 2.27 \cdot (1.0 \text{ ns})] \cdot (\text{V.F.})$

$\quad\quad = (34.81 \text{ ns}) \cdot (1.61) = 56.04$ ns

Set-up time for the 1830:

Given: Data rise time: 56.04 ns   (From above)

Clock fall time: 10 ns   (Figure 7.2)

Using the 1830 curves for set-up time versus data $T_{R/F}$ (Page 1830-7)
transition times:

Data Set-up Time = 13.40 ns

Summary of delays for 3 volts, 125°C, and worst case processing parameters

TRANSITION	CELL TYPE	DELAY
0–1	9150	19.74 ns
1–0	1220	20.53 ns
0–1	1130	29.61 ns
Set-up time	1830	13.40 ns
Total Delay:		**83.28 ns**

8

LOGICV
Appendix

This chapter describes the logical simulation of tri-state functions using LOGICV, a three-state simulator.

The reasoning for the decisions on how the high impedance state would be logically simulated was driven by how an individual die would logically function at wofer probe. With this premise, there may be some discrepancies between how an individual chip in a system will logically function and how the entire system will logically function.

In general, LOGICV will simulate the high impedance state as a logical 1. LOGICV defaults to a "WIRED AND" condition if more than one output is in the same net. This implementation makes the following assumption: When the output of more than one cell with a high impedance stat is "WIRE ANDED" together only one of the cells may be active at one time. The "WIRED AND" function will assign the logical value of the active cell to the net. In general, LOGICV will simulate the high impedance state for pads different than the high impedance state for cells.

8.1   CELLS WITH HIGH IMPEDANCE STATE

8.1.1   1340 Tri-State Buffer

The truth table for an individual 1340 as logically simulated by LOGICV is as follows:

ENABLE	DATA	OUT
0	0	1
0	1	1
0	X	1
1	0	0
1	1	1
1	X	X
X	0	X
X	1	X
X	X	X

Shown in Fig. 8.1 is an example of how two 1340s may be implemented in a chip design and Table 8.1 shows how LOGICV will simulate this example.

8.1.2   1370 Transmission Gate

The truth table for the individual 1370 Transmission Gate as simulated by LOGICV is shown at the top of page 64.

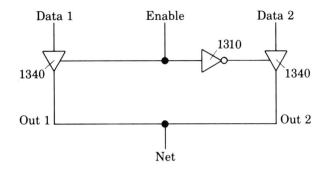

■**Figure 8.1**

Table 8.1

DATA1	DATA2	ENABLE	OUT1	OUT2	NET
0	0	0	1	0	0
0	1	0	1	1	1
0	X	0	1	X	X
1	0	0	1	0	0
1	1	0	1	1	1
1	X	0	1	X	X
X	0	0	1	0	0
X	1	0	1	1	1
X	X	0	1	X	X
0	0	1	0	1	0
0	1	1	0	1	0
0	X	1	0	1	0
1	0	1	1	1	1
1	1	1	1	1	1
1	X	1	1	1	1
X	0	1	X	1	X
X	1	1	X	1	X
X	X	1	X	1	X
0	0	X	X	X	X
0	1	X	X	X	X
0	X	X	X	X	X
1	0	X	X	X	X
1	1	X	X	X	X
1	X	X	X	X	X
X	0	X	X	X	X
X	1	X	X	X	X
X	X	X	X	X	X

CONTROL	DATA	OUT
0	0	1
0	1	1
0	X	1
1	0	0
1	1	1
1	X	X
X	0	X
X	1	X
X	X	X

Also shown, Fig. 8.2, is an example of how two 1370s may be implemented in a chip design and Table 8.2 shows how LOGICV will simulate this example.

8.1.3   1430 Pull-Up

In order to use this cell, LOGICV requires the following line to be placed in the EXTERNALS category:

$VDD 0 1

By taking advantage of the "WIRE AND" option in LOGICV the output of the 1430 is subordinate to the input to any Pad. For example, the following situation may occur (see Fig. 8.3).

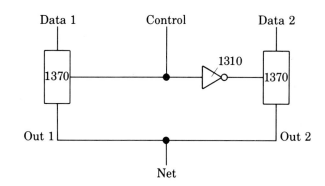

■**Figure 8.2**

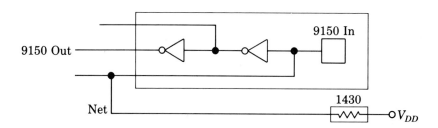

■**Figure 8.3**

Table 8.2

DATA1	DATA2	CONTROL	OUT1	OUT2	NET
0	0	0	1	0	0
0	1	0	1	1	1
0	X	0	1	X	X
1	0	0	1	0	0
1	1	0	1	1	1
1	X	0	1	X	X
X	0	0	1	0	0
X	1	0	1	1	1
X	X	0	1	X	X
0	0	1	0	1	0
0	1	1	0	1	0
0	X	1	0	1	0
1	0	1	1	1	1
1	1	1	1	1	1
1	X	1	1	1	1
X	0	1	X	1	X
X	1	1	X	1	X
X	X	1	X	1	X
0	0	X	X	X	X
0	1	X	X	X	X
0	X	X	X	X	X
1	0	X	X	X	X
1	1	X	X	X	X
1	X	X	X	X	X
X	0	X	X	X	X
X	1	X	X	X	X
X	X	X	X	X	X

LOGICV will simulate the example shown in Fig. 8.3 as follows:

1430 OUT	9150 IN	NET	9150 OUT
1	0	0	0
1	1	1	1
1	X	X	X
1	Hi−Z=1	1	1

Care must be taken if both a 1430 Pull-Up and a 1440 Pull-Down cell are used in the same simulation and an electrical overdrive condition is being simulated for both cell types. This is due to the use of the "WIRE OUTPUT" option by LOGICV, which will not support the correct logical simulation for both cell types in one simulation.

8.1.4 1440 Pull-Down

In order to use this cell, LOGICV requires the following line to be in the EXTER-NALS category:

$VSS 0 0

LOGICV simulates the output of this cell to always be a logical 0 using the "WIRE AND" option in LOGICV (default "WIRE" condition). By using the "WIRE OR" option in LOGICV, a correct logic simulation can be generated for an electrical overdrive condition. LOGICV will simulate the example in Figure 8.4 using the "WIRE OR" option as follows:

1440 OUT	9150 IN	NET	9150 OUT
0	0	0	0
0	1	1	1
0	X	X	X
0	Hi$-$Z$=$0	0	0

Care must be taken if both a 1430 Pull-Up and a 1440 Pull-Down cell are used in the same simulation and an electrical overdrive condition is being simulated for both cell types. This is due to the use of the "WIRE OUTPUT" option by LOGICV, which will not support the correct logical simulation for both cell types in one simulation.

8.1.5   9650 and 9660 N-Channel Buffer

The high impedance state is modeled as an "X". This is due to the fact that when the input signal is a logical 1, the transistor is disabled in the N-channel buffer. When the transistor is disabled, there is no active drive to the pad metal, hence the output is unknown. The truth table then is shown at the top of page 67.

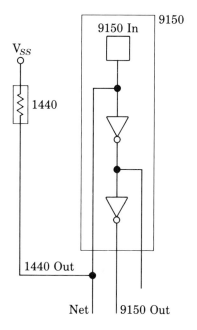

■**Figure 8.4**

INPUT A	PAD
0	0
1	X
X	X

8.1.6 9670 and 9680 Tri-State I/O Pad

These pads are logically modeled by LOGICV to be either an input pad or an output pad. LOGICV will not allow the pads to operate in the high impedance condition. When ENABLE is a logical 0, the Pad operates as an input pad. When ENABLE is a logical 1 the Pad operates as an output pad. When ENABLE is an unknown "X" the output is unknown. The truth table is then:

DATA	ENABLE	PAD	OUT
0	0	0	0
0	0	1	1
0	0	X	X
1	0	0	0
1	0	1	1
1	0	X	X
X	0	0	0
X	0	1	1
X	0	X	X
0	1	0	0
1	1	0	1
X	1	0	X
0	1	1	0
1	1	1	1
X	1	1	X
0	1	X	0
1	1	X	1
X	1	X	X
*	X	*	X

In order for LOGICV to simulate these pads correctly, the signal names must be in these logic fields:

Field	1	Data
	2	Enable
	3	Input Pad Signal
	6	Out
	7	Output Pad Signal

The input pad signal in logic field 3 and the output pad signal in logic field 7 cannot use the same signal name verbatim, even though both signals are the same electrically and refer to the same physical pad.

8.1.7 9710 and 9720 Tri-State Output Pad

The high impedance state is modeled as an "X". This is due to the fact that when the ENABLE signal is a logical 0, the transistors that drive the output pad are disabled. When these transistors are disabled there is no active drive to the pad metal, hence the output is unknown. The truth table is then:

ENABLE	DATA	PAD
0	0	X
0	1	X
0	X	X
1	0	0
1	1	1
1	X	X
X	0	X
X	1	X
X	X	X

9

Stackable Shift Register Cell Implementation

The following is a list of the stackable shift register cells designed for the CMOS3 cell family:

2900 Stackable Shift Register
2910 Two-phase Clock Driver
2920 Serial/Parallel Data Select Mux
2930 Bus Crosser/Interface
2940 Bus Crosser/Interface

These cells are designed to be used in applications in which long, medium-to-slow speed (10 MHz) shift registers are required. The cells are intended to be compatible with commercially available cell routers, but are primarily developed for hand pack placement. All cells are designed such that no design rule violations will occur.

9.1 BASIC CELL DESCRIPTION

9.1.1 2900

This is the basic stackable shift register cell. It is a D flip-flop, without Set or Reset inputs, or QBAR output. A stack can be wired to be either negative or positive triggered by changing the clock driver input signal. Since there are no Sets or Resets, the cell can only be cleared or preset by clocking in a new bit stream. The architecture is such that the D input of a cell mates with the Q output of a previous cell. V_{DD}, V_{SS}, Clock, and Clockbar signals also mate in this fashion. By reflecting the cell vertically and joining the V_{DD} (or V_{SS}) busses, very high density can be achieved.

9.1.2 2910

Every horizontal row of shift register cells must have (at least) one clock driver element. The clock driver provides the signals necessary to switch the register elements. The driver is intended to drive up to 32 2900 cells in a single row without causing ripple-thru of the register elements. The 2910 will normally be placed at the end of each cell row. Since the 2900 has no clock buffering, it is susceptible to ripple-thru, and care must be taken to assure that it does not occur when using the 2910 cell. Ripple-thru susceptibility for the 2900 cells is provided in the cell documentation.

The 2910 used in conjunction with the 2900 generates negative triggered registers; that is, Q outputs change on the negative transition of the clock driver input.

Simulations show that the 2900 cells are particularly susceptible to ripple-thru if the clock skew is significant. Thus, the user of the 2910 and 2900 cells should assure that the loading on both clock phases is identical. 2900 clock inputs are designed to have identical capacitive and resistive loading on both clock phases. The 2910 cell is designed to have balanced rise, fall, and delay times on both clock outputs provided the capacitive loading is identical.

Simulations also show that ripple-thru susceptibility for the 2900 cell is sensitive to clock and clockbar rise/fall times, and to clock skew. The 2910 has sufficient drive for over 32 shift register cells; the rise and fall times on clock and clockbar are more than sufficient to prevent ripple-thru. However, clock skew will vary depending on the operating voltage, temperature, process variations, and rise/fall time at the input of the 2910 clock driver.

The designers should be cognizant that a significant hold time can occur with these cells due to clock driver delay. This delay should be considered by the designer when performing critical timing analysis.

Since the clock lines are routed entirely in metal, distributed loading on these lines was considered in simulations. For the 2910 driving 32 2900 cells, the delay differences between the closest and farthest cells from the clock driver had (according to simulations) less than 1.0 ns. This is considered negligible.

9.1.3 2920

There may be applications where a block of data must be latched and clocked out serially. To perform such a function, a Serial/Parallel Data Select Mux was created. It is functionally identical to the 1350 cell found in the CMOS3 cell library. Shown is an example of a 4-bit Parallel-Load/Serial-Out shift register. The 2920 cell has metal signal lines to pass clock and clockbar signals for the shift register cells, but play no part in the actual operation of the 2920. In most instances, the 2920 cell placement should be along the outer edges of the shift register stack, since external data and control signals must be provided. However, this cell is not necessarily restricted in this manner.

9.1.4 2930

The feed-out cell is an interface to allow the capability of tapping off outputs or providing external input data. It also acts as a bus crosser and a feed-thru for internal data.

9.1.5 2940

This cell is similar to the 2930, except it cannot be used to directly tap off (or in) internal shift register data. It permits access to data that may be imbedded deep in a stack. It should be noted that if the vertical bus crosser signal is not used, "stray matter" may occur in checking the network for correct connectivity. This is okay and expected, but should be verified by the design engineer. If the 2930 cell is substituted, then no stray matter errors will occur, but more capacitance will be present on the output of the 2900 cells.

9.2 SPECIAL NOTES APPLICABLE TO 2900 SERIES CELLS

For terminals at the top or bottom of cells, polysilicon connections must often be added to complete the design. Terminal placement is such that wiring vias cannot be used to make direct connection.

The Clock and Clockbar side terminal locations are not precisely centered on the signal line, but are 0.5 microns below center.

When feeding a common clock input, it is recommended that the clock path through the 2910 cells flow in a direction opposite the direction of data flow through the registers. If data enters at the top of the stack, then clock should enter at the bottom. This will help eliminate any problems associated with the clock driver input resistance causing ripple between cell rows.

Routing 2910 output signals to other than 2900 series cells is not recommended, since this could cause imbalance between clock signals or excessive loading. In addition, the designer could have a problem in the shift registers if each clock driver in an array does not drive identical capacitance in all rows. If there is an imbalance in capacitance between rows, then one row of registers could switch faster than another, causing timing problems.

10

Chip Level Design Rules and Layout

This chapter covers the chip level design rules and guidelines for cell and pad placement, interconnect routing, power distribution, and other considerations.

10.1 CELL AND PAD PLACEMENT

The functional cells and pads are structured to allow placement of any type adjacent to any other functional cell or pad. Cells and pads may be mixed on any edge of the chip if care is exercised in maintaining the proper bus configurations. When pads are placed adjacent to each other, a bonding area to bonding area pitch of at least 204 microns (8 mils) results.

10.2 BUS STRUCTURE

Each functional cell and bus crosser has a horizontal V_{SS} power bus centered on a y-coordinate of 12 microns and a horizontal V_{DD} power bus centered on a y-coordinate of 138 microns. For cells and bus crossers, these power buses are 8 microns wide. These buses can be widened, if desired, by adding metal to the outside of the buses. This metal must extend 8 microns into the cell from the top and bottom edges in order to contact the existing bus and may extend as far as desired beyond the top and bottom edges. Note that an area penalty will result by forcing the first horizontal wiring channels, top and bottom, farther from the cell (see Fig. 10.1).

Each I/O pad also has horizontal V_{SS} and V_{DD} buses. It was noted in Chapter 3 that two type numbers exist for each I/O pad function. Pads with an odd number in the ten's place of the type number (e.g., 92<u>1</u>0) have V_{SS} as the bottom bus and V_{DD} as the top bus. Pads with an even number in the ten's place of the type

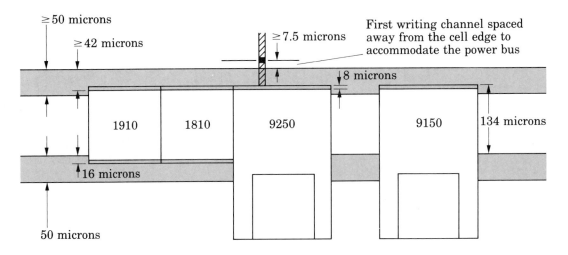

■Figure 10.1

number (e.g., 92$\underline{2}$0) have V_{DD} as the bottom bus and V_{SS} as the top bus. This dual arrangement allows the rows of functional cells to receive power from the innermost power bus of the I/O pads on the left and right edges of the chip (see Fig. 10.2). The top power bus is 50 microns wide and its lower edge is at a y-coordinate of 134 microns, allowing it to line up with the lower edge of the bus in a functional cell. This bus cannot be widened. The bottom power bus is centered on a y-coordinate of 12 microns and is 8 microns wide. The bottom bus of an I/O pad may be widened to any width in the same manner as described above for the functional cells (see Fig. 10.1).

10.3 POWER DISTRIBUTION

Several alternatives are available for chip power distribution. Power buses in the pads on the left and right edges of the chip can be connected to the end of each cell row (see Fig. 10.3a). This arrangement requires that V_{DD} be the innermost bus on one side of the chip and that V_{SS} be the innermost bus on the other side. Implementation of this approach involves the selection of I/O pads with the appropriate bus polarities and the incorporation of power pads into the pad rows.

A second approach may be utilized which will isolate the I/O pad circuitry from the internal logic. This may be desirable if a significant amount of high speed I/O is used or if internal logic is especially sensitive to power fluctuations. This approach involves the use of a power bus structure for the interior of the

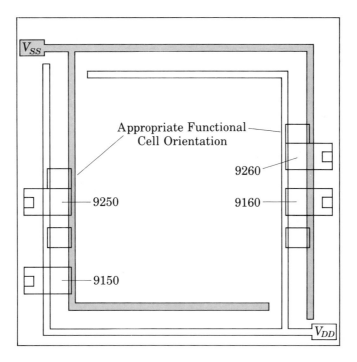

■Figure 10.2

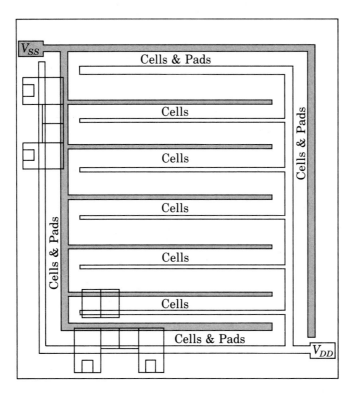

■**Figure 10.3a**

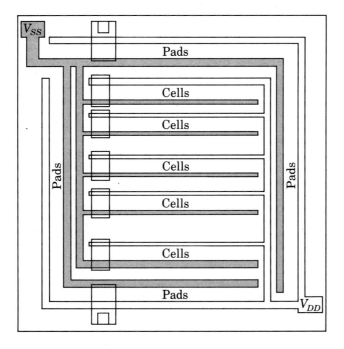

■**Figure 10.3b**

chip that is distinct from the power structure of the I/O pads. These two networks are common only at the power pads (see Fig. 10.3b).

Multiple V_{SS} and V_{DD} pads may also be used.

10.4 CELL INTERCONNECT

The horizontal interconnect wiring, which is almost exclusively metal, has a width of 3 microns and a spacing of 6 microns, yielding a pitch of 9 microns. The vertical interconnect wiring, which is primarily polysilicon, has a width of 8 microns and a spacing of 4 microns, yielding a pitch of 12 microns. Notice that the functional cells have a terminal-to-terminal pitch of 12 microns, also. When metal is used for vertical interconnect, the 3 micron width/6 micron spacing rules mentioned above apply. Metal may be connected to polysilicon by centering a wiring via at the junction of the metal and poly interconnect centerlines (see Fig. 10.4).

The 9 micron metal interconnect pitch requires that two wiring vias not be placed side by side in adjacent metal rows. If this condition is allowed, the wiring pitch becomes 11 microns (see Fig. 10.5).

The first horizontal wiring channel is centered on the top and bottom edge of each cell. This channel must contain only metal unless two adjacent cell I/O terminals (12 microns apart) are to be connected in poly. All cell terminals are 8 micron wide poly; thus, the endpoints of the centerline of the 8 micron wide poly interconnect end at the I/O terminal point and the poly may or may not extend by one half the poly interconnect width past the endpoint. I/O terminals are connected to metal in the first wiring channel by using a wiring via (see Fig. 10.6).

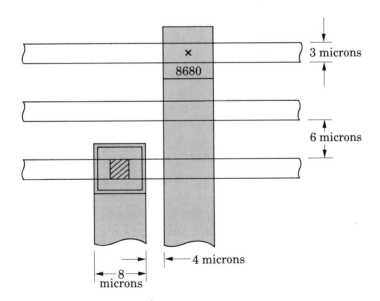

■Figure 10.4

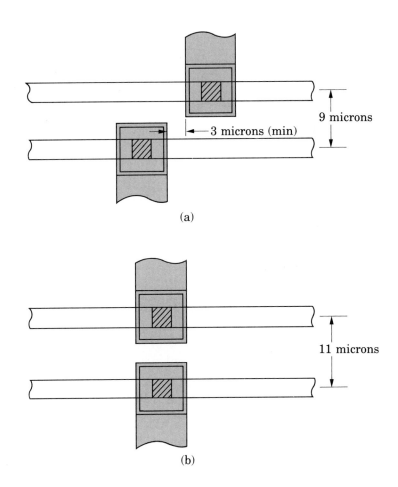

(a)

(b)

■**Figure 10.5**

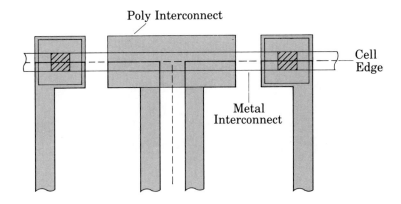

■**Figure 10.6**

10.5 MISCELLANEOUS

The following structures should be included on every chip:

- Level Identifiers and Critical Dimension Bars
8010	P–
8030	Active Area
8040	Poly
8050	P+ Diffusion
8060	N+ Diffusion
8070	Contact
8080	Metal
8090	Passivation
8130	Via
8140	Metal 2
- Test Transistors (when space allows)
8200
8210
- Test Resistors (when space allows)
8220

Part number, date codes, etc. should be digitized at the geometry level and placed on all mask layers.

The recommended scribe region is 4 mils wide and its inside edge should be 2 mils outside the pad metal. The scribe region should appear on levels 3 (Active Area), 7 (Contact), 9 (Passivation), and 13 (Via).

11

SSI Cell
Data Pages

SSI Cell Index

CELL NUMBER	CELL NAME	NUMBER OF PAGES
1100	Dual Inverter	5
1120	2-Input NOR	5
1130	3-Input NOR	5
1140	4-Input NOR	5
1220	2 NAND	5
1230	3 NAND	5
1310	Inverter	5
1320	Non-Inverting Buffer	5
1340	Tri-State Buffer	7
1350	Data Select	6
1370	Transmission Gate	7
1410	NAND Latch	5
1420	NOR Latch	5
1430	Pull-Up	4
1440	Pull-Down	4
1480	D Flip-Flop w/S, R, Q, $\overline{Q}$	14
1510	4X Non-Inverting Buffer	5
1520	4X Inverting Buffer	5
1530	Clocked Latch	10
1540	Hi=Impedance Inverter	5
1550	Hi=Impedance Buffer	5
1560	Delay Cell	5
1570	D Flip-Flop w/Asy R, Q	10
1580	D Flip-Flop w/Asy R, Q, $\overline{Q}$	12
1610	$\overline{AB}$ Decode	5
1620	A or $\overline{B}$	5
1660	2-Input NAND/AND	7
1670	3-Input NAND/AND	7
1680	4-Input NAND/AND	7
1740	4-Input OR	5
1760	2-Input OR/NOR	7
1770	3-Input OR/NOR	7
1810	3, 2 AND/OR MUX	5
1830	D Flip-Flop w/Q, $\overline{Q}$	9
1850	Full Adder	7
1870	2, 2 AND/NOR MUX	5
1910	4, 2 AND/OR MUX	6
1930	2, 3 AND/OR MUX	5
1970	2, 2 AND/OR MUX	5
2310	EXCLUSIVE OR	5
2350	Exclusive NOR	5
2900	Stackable Shift Register	7
2910	Stackable Two Phase Clock Driver	7
2920	Stackable Data Select	5
2930	Stackable Bus Crosser	2
2940	Stackable Bus Crosser	2

SSI Cell Index (continued)

CELL NUMBER	CELL NAME	NUMBER OF PAGES
8010–8140	Level Identifiers	2
8200	N-Channel Test Devices	2
8210	P-Channel Test Devices	2
8220	Test Resistors	2
8630	Bus Crosser	2
8640	Metal2 Bus Crosser	2
8660	RC Load Cell	2
8670	Poly-Metal2 Via	2
8680	Wiring Via	2
8690	Metal1–Metal2 Via	2
9110	VSS-Diode Only Input Pad	5
9120	VSS-Diode Only Input Pad	5
9150	Input Pad	7
9160	Input Pad	7
9250	Output Buffer	5
9260	Output Buffer	5
9320	Power Pad	2
9460	Schmitt Triggered Input Pad	6
9470	Schmitt Triggered Input Pad	6
9530	Level Shifter Input Pad	7
9540	Level Shifter Input Pad	7
9620	Butterfly	2
9650	N-Channel Buffer	5
9660	N-Channel Buffer	5
9670	Tri-State I/0 Pad	9
9680	Tri-State I/0 Pad	9
9710	Tri-State Output Pad	7
9720	Tri-State Output Pad	7

3 MICRON CMOS/BULK CELL FAMILY -CMOS3-	1100 DUAL INVERTER CELL HEIGHT 150 WIDTH 48	DATE: 09/01/83 REVISION: A

TERMINAL INFORMATION

TERMINAL NAME	TERMINAL NUMBER	LOGIC FIELD	CAPACITANCE (PF)
A	3,13	1	.25
B	4,14	2	.25
OUT1	2,12	6	
OUT2	5,15	7	

LOGIC DIAGRAM

A,3 ▷○ OUT1,2

B,4 ▷○ OUT2,5

TRUTH TABLE

A	OUT1	B	OUT2
0	1	0	1
1	0	1	0
X	X	X	X

LOGIC SYMBOLS

A,3

OUT1,2

B,4

OUT2,5

WORST CASE DELAY INFORMATION

P_D = 6.2 NS $T_{R/F}$ = 16.8 NS

R_S = 1.5KΩ, C_L = 1.5PF, V=5V, T=125°C

LOGIC EQUATION(S)

OUT1 = $\overline{A}$

OUT2 = $\overline{B}$

NOTES

1. THE TWO INVERTERS HAVE APPROXIMATELY THE SAME DRIVE, SO ONLY 1 SET OF OUTPUT CURVES WILL BE PRESENTED.

1100-1

84

CIRCUIT SCHEMATIC

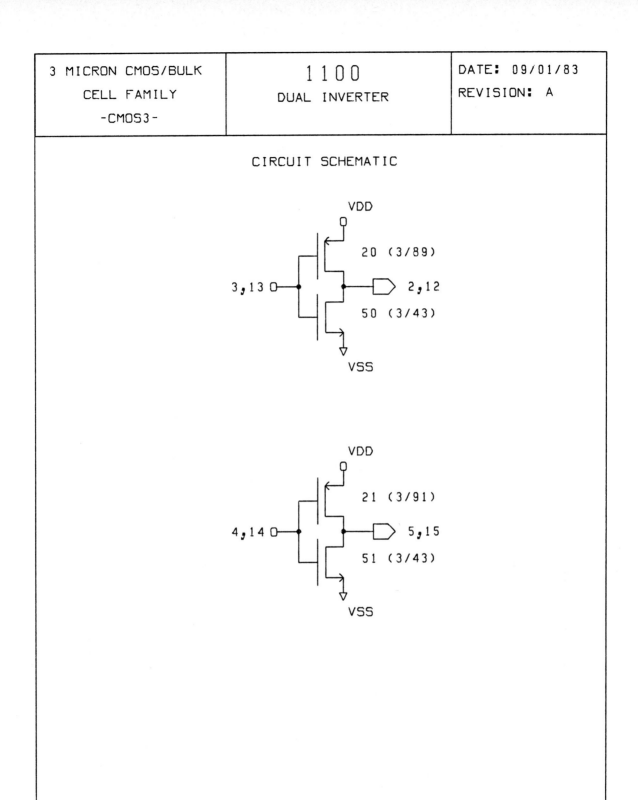

3 MICRON CMOS/BULK CELL FAMILY -CMOS3-	1100 DUAL INVERTER	DATE: 09/01/83 REVISION: A

OUTPUT CHARACTERISTIC EQUATIONS

$$P_D(0-1) = P_{DC}(0-1) + .15 (T_{R/F} - 10) + .62 R_S C_L$$

$$P_D(1-0) = P_{DC}(1-0) + .11 (T_{R/F} - 10) + .62 R_S C_L$$

$$T_R = T_{RC} + .24 (T_{R/F} - 10) + 2.58 R_S C_L$$

$$T_F = T_{FC} + .26 (T_{R/F} - 10) + 2.61 R_S C_L$$

EQUATIONS

25°C

$$P_{DC}(0-1) = 1.4 C_L + 2.2$$

$$P_{DC}(1-0) = 1.28 C_L + 2.6$$

$$T_{RC} = 4.5 C_L + 2.5$$

$$T_{FC} = 3.8 C_L + 2.3$$

95°C

$$P_{DC}(0-1) = 1.56 C_L + 2.5$$

$$P_{DC}(1-0) = 1.72 C_L + 2.4$$

$$T_{RC} = 5.8 C_L + 2.65$$

$$T_{FC} = 4.94 C_L + 2.3$$

125°C

$$P_{DC}(0-1) = 1.92 C_L + 2.4$$

$$P_{DC}(1-0) = 1.6 C_L + 2.8$$

$$T_{RC} = 6.5 C_L + 2.8$$

$$T_{FC} = 5.4 C_L + 2.3$$

125°C BC

$$P_{DC}(0-1) = 1.04 C_L + 1.4$$

$$P_{DC}(1-0) = .94 C_L + 1.6$$

$$T_{RC} = 3.4 C_L + 3.2$$

$$T_{FC} = 2.86 C_L + 3.0$$

VOLTAGE TABLE

VOLTAGE	DEVIATION FACTOR			
	TRANSITION		PROP DELAY	
	TR	TF	1-0	0-1
3.0	1.28	1.26	1.83	1.44
3.5	1.18	1.16	1.56	1.29
4.0	1.09	1.06	1.28	1.15
4.5	1.05	1.03	1.14	1.08
5.0	1.00	1.00	1.00	1.00
5.5	.97	.98	.92	.95
6.0	.95	.97	.83	.91
6.5	.93	.94	.78	.88
7.0	.91	.92	.72	.85

1100-3

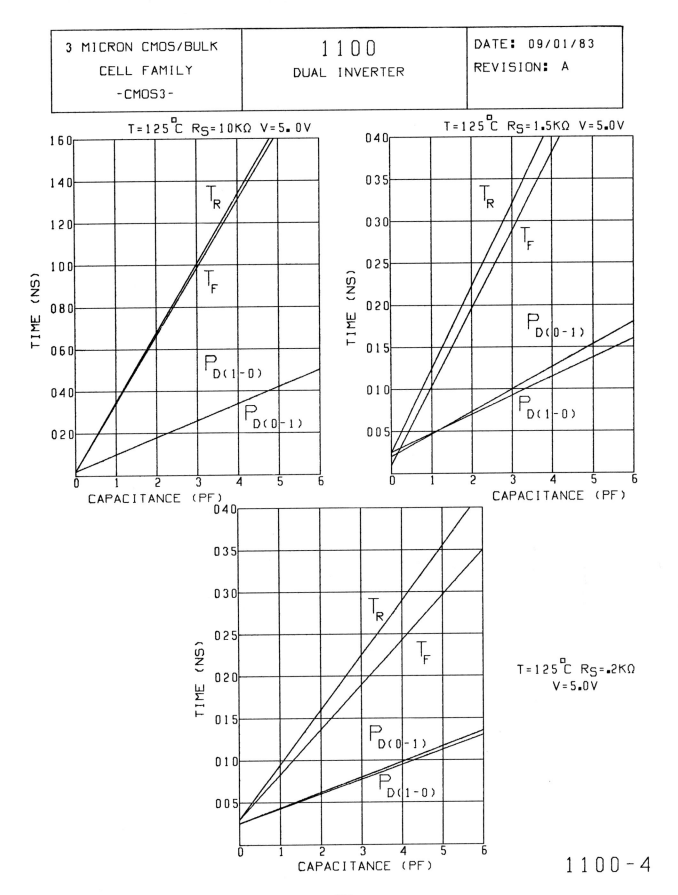

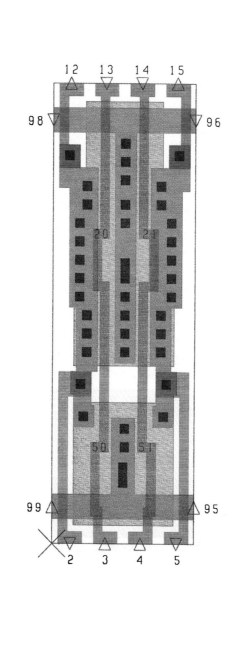

3 MICRON CMOS/BULK CELL FAMILY -CMOS3-	1120 2 INPUT NOR CELL HEIGHT 150 WIDTH 35	DATE: 04/01/85 REVISION: B

TERMINAL INFORMATION

TERMINAL NAME	NUMBER	LOGIC FIELD	CAPACITANCE (PF)
A	2,12	1	.23
B	3,13	2	.23
OUT	4,14	6	

LOGIC DIAGRAM

SAME AS LOGIC SYMBOL

TRUTH TABLE

A	B	OUT
0	0	1
0	X	X
X	0	X
1	*	0
*	1	0
X	X	X

LOGIC SYMBOLS

A,2
B,3 — OUT,4

WORST CASE DELAY INFORMATION

P_D=10.06 NS $T_{R/F}$=25.01 NS

R_S=1.5KΩ, C_L=1.5PF, V=5V, T=125°C

LOGIC EQUATION(S)

OUT = $\overline{A+B}$

NOTES

1120-1

3 MICRON CMOS/BULK CELL FAMILY -CMOS3-	1120 2 INPUT NOR	DATE: 04/01/85 REVISION: B

CIRCUIT SCHEMATIC

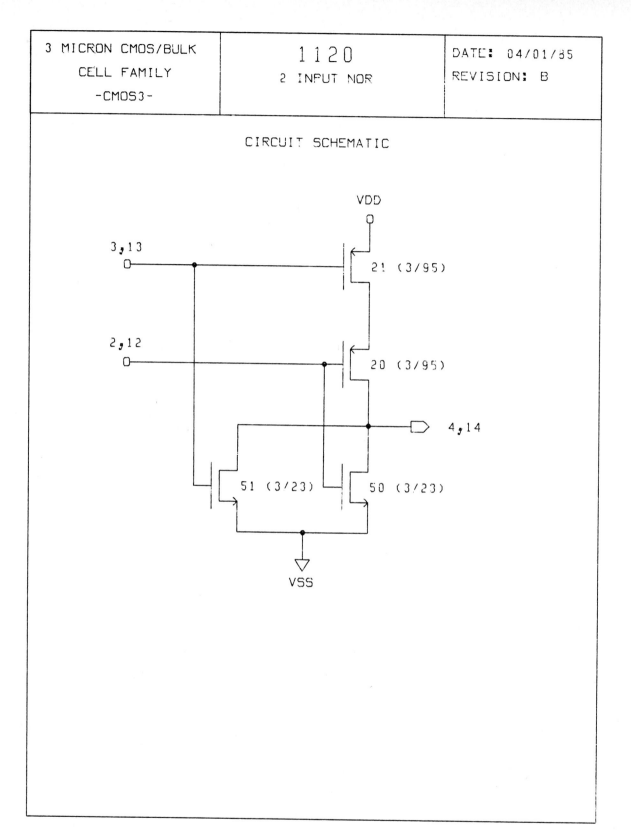

OUTPUT CHARACTERISTIC EQUATIONS

$$P_D(0-1) = P_{DC}(0-1) + 0.20 \ (T_{R/F} - 10) + 0.63R_SC_L$$

$$P_D(1-0) = P_{DC}(1-0) + 0.22 \ (T_{R/F} - 10) + 0.59R_SC_L$$

$$T_R = T_{RC} + 0.17 \ (T_{R/F} - 10) + 2.43R_SC_L$$

$$T_F = T_{FC} + 0.21 \ (T_{R/F} - 10) + 2.41R_SC_L$$

EQUATIONS

25°C

$$P_{DC}(0-1) = 2.33C_L + 3.64$$

$$P_{DC}(1-0) = 2.08C_L + 4.02$$

$$T_{RC} = 7.69C_L + 3.57$$

$$T_{FC} = 6.43C_L + 3.32$$

95°C

$$P_{DC}(0-1) = 3.00C_L + 3.95$$

$$P_{DC}(1-0) = 2.63C_L + 4.37$$

$$T_{RC} = 10.12C_L + 4.20$$

$$T_{FC} = 8.42C_L + 3.30$$

125°C

$$P_{DC}(0-1) = 3.29C_L + 4.08$$

$$P_{DC}(1-0) = 2.85C_L + 4.52$$

$$T_{RC} = 11.17C_L + 4.48$$

$$T_{FC} = 9.27C_L + 4.04$$

125°C BC

$$P_{DC}(0-1) = 1.60C_L + 2.85$$

$$P_{DC}(1-0) = 1.38C_L + 2.97$$

$$T_{RC} = 5.66C_L + 3.12$$

$$T_{FC} = 4.58C_L + 3.70$$

VOLTAGE TABLE

VOLTAGE	DEVIATION FACTOR			
	TRANSITION		PROP DELAY	
	TR	TF	1-0	0-1
3.0	1.45	1.51	1.64	1.54
3.5	1.29	1.33	1.42	1.36
4.0	1.14	1.15	1.20	1.17
4.5	1.07	1.08	1.10	1.09
5.0	1.00	1.00	1.00	1.00
5.5	.96	.96	.95	.95
6.0	.92	.92	.89	.90
6.5	.89	.90	.86	.87
7.0	.87	.87	.82	.84

1120-3

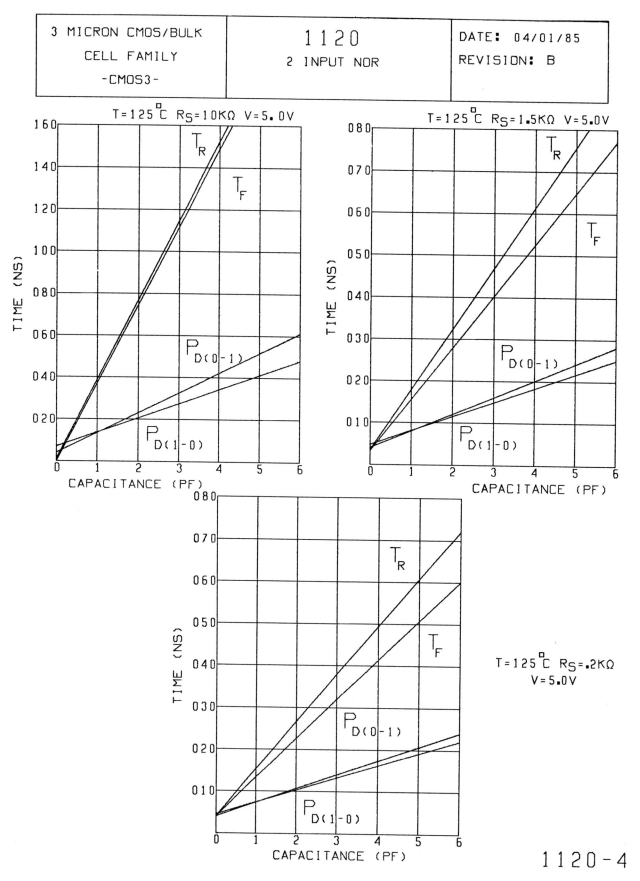

1120-4

92

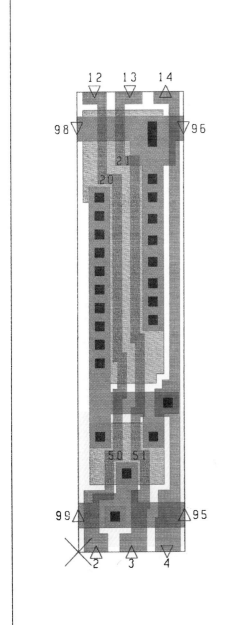

1120-5

3 MICRON CMOS/BULK CELL FAMILY ·CMOS3·	1130 3 INPUT NOR CELL HEIGHT 150 WIDTH 48	DATE: 09/01/83 REVISION: A

TERMINAL INFORMATION

TERMINAL NAME	NUMBER	LOGIC FIELD	CAPACITANCE (PF)
A	2,12	1	.26
B	3,13	2	.26
C	4,14	3	.26
OUT	5,15	6	

LOGIC DIAGRAM

SAME AS LOGIC SYMBOL

TRUTH TABLE

A	B	C	OUT
0	0	0	1
*	*	1	0
*	1	*	0
1	*	*	0
ALL OTHER COMBINATIONS			X

LOGIC SYMBOLS

A,2
B,3
C,4 —OUT,5

WORST CASE DELAY INFORMATION

P_D=12.23 NS $T_{R/F}$=27.89 NS

R_S=1.5KΩ, C_L=1.5PF, V=5V, T=125°C

LOGIC EQUATION(S)

OUT = $\overline{A+B+C}$

NOTES

1130-1

94

CIRCUIT SCHEMATIC

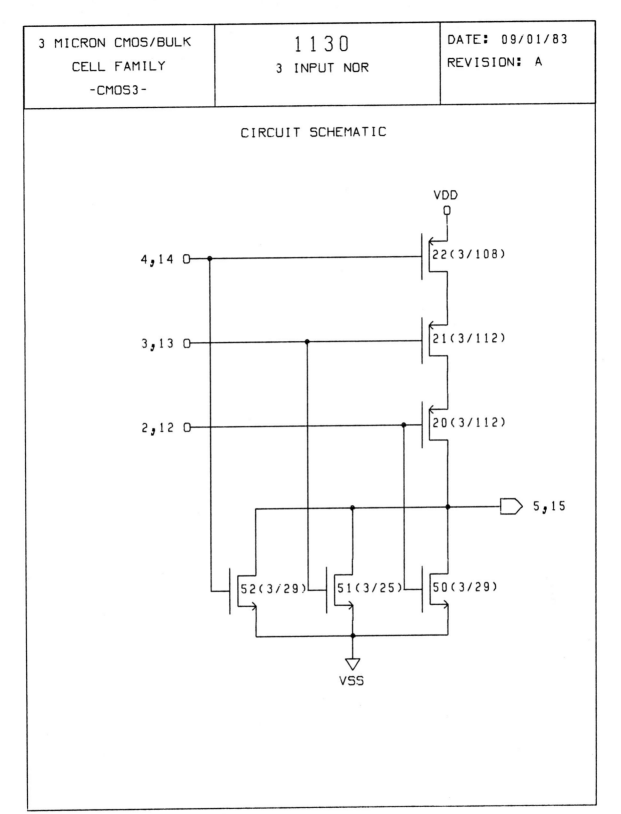

1130-2

95

3 MICRON CMOS/BULK CELL FAMILY -CMOS3-	1130 3 INPUT NOR	DATE: 09/01/83 REVISION: A

OUTPUT CHARACTERISTIC EQUATIONS

$$P_D(0-1) = P_{DC}(0-1) + .23 \ (T_{R/F} - 10) + .62 \ R_S C_L$$

$$P_D(1-0) = P_{DC}(1-0) + .21 \ (T_{R/F} - 10) + .60 \ R_S C_L$$

$$T_R = T_{RC} + .12 \ (T_{R/F} - 10) + 2.27 R_S C_L$$

$$T_F = T_{FC} + .26 \ (T_{R/F} - 10) + 2.33 R_S C_L$$

EQUATIONS

$25\,^{\circ}C$

$$P_{DC}(0-1) = 2.75 C_L + 4.73$$

$$P_{DC}(1-0) = 1.60 C_L + 4.10$$

$$T_{RC} = 8.27 C_L + 5.09$$

$$T_{FC} = 4.33 C_L + 4.24$$

$95\,^{\circ}C$

$$P_{DC}(0-1) = 3.50 C_L + 5.32$$

$$P_{DC}(1-0) = 2.00 C_L + 4.46$$

$$T_{RC} = 10.73 C_L + 6.41$$

$$T_{FC} = 5.59 C_L + 5.10$$

$125\,^{\circ}C$

$$P_{DC}(0-1) = 3.8 \ C_L + 5.56$$

$$P_{DC}(1-0) = 2.14 C_L + 4.62$$

$$T_{RC} = 11.76 C_L + 7.01$$

$$T_{FC} = 6.12 C_L + 5.47$$

$125\,^{\circ}C$ BC

$$P_{DC}(0-1) = 1.64 C_L + 3.81$$

$$P_{DC}(1-0) = 0.98 C_L + 2.86$$

$$T_{RC} = 5.41 C_L + 3.96$$

$$T_{FC} = 2.72 C_L + 4.88$$

VOLTAGE TABLE

VOLTAGE	DEVIATION FACTOR			
	TRANSITION		PROP DELAY	
	TR	TF	1-0	0-1
3.0	1.61	1.57	1.67	1.68
3.5	1.41	1.37	1.44	1.45
4.0	1.20	1.17	1.21	1.22
4.5	1.10	1.09	1.11	1.11
5.0	1.00	1.00	1.00	1.00
5.5	.94	.96	.94	.94
6.0	.89	.91	.88	.88
6.5	.85	.89	.84	.84
7.0	.82	.86	.80	.80

1130-3

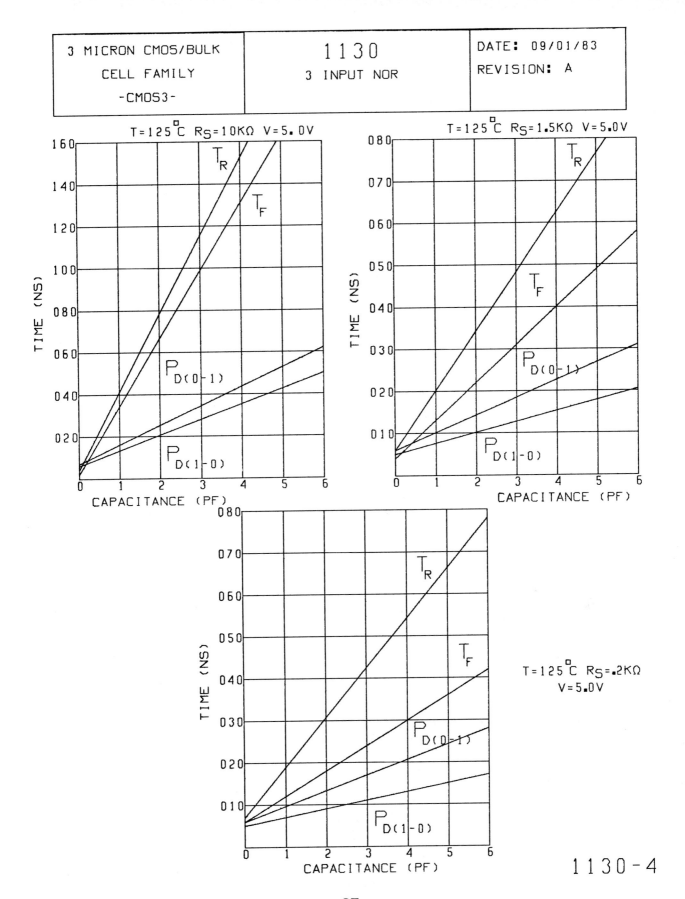

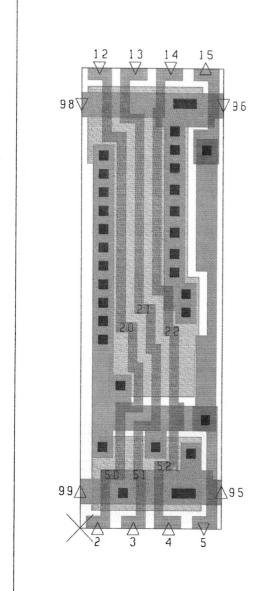

1130-5

98

3 MICRON CMOS/BULK CELL FAMILY -CMOS3-	1140 4-INPUT NOR CELL HEIGHT 150 WIDTH 60	DATE: 04/01/85 REVISION: A

TERMINAL INFORMATION

TERMINAL NAME	TERMINAL NUMBER	LOGIC FIELD	CAPACITANCE (PF)
A	2,12	1	.27
B	3,13	2	.25
C	4,14	3	.25
D	5,15	4	.26
OUT	6,16	6	

LOGIC DIAGRAM

SAME AS LOGIC SYMBOL

TRUTH TABLE

A	B	C	D	OUT
0	0	0	0	1
1	*	*	*	0
*	1	*	*	0
*	*	1	*	0
*	*	*	1	0
ALL OTHER COMBINATIONS				X

LOGIC SYMBOLS

A,2
B,3
C,4 ———— OUT,6
D,5

WORST CASE DELAY INFORMATION

$P_D = 16.99$ NS $\qquad T_{R/F} = 38.40$ NS

$R_S = 1.5K\Omega$, $C_L = 1.5PF$, $V = 5V$, $T = 125°C$

LOGIC EQUATION(S)

$OUT = \overline{A+B+C+D}$

NOTES

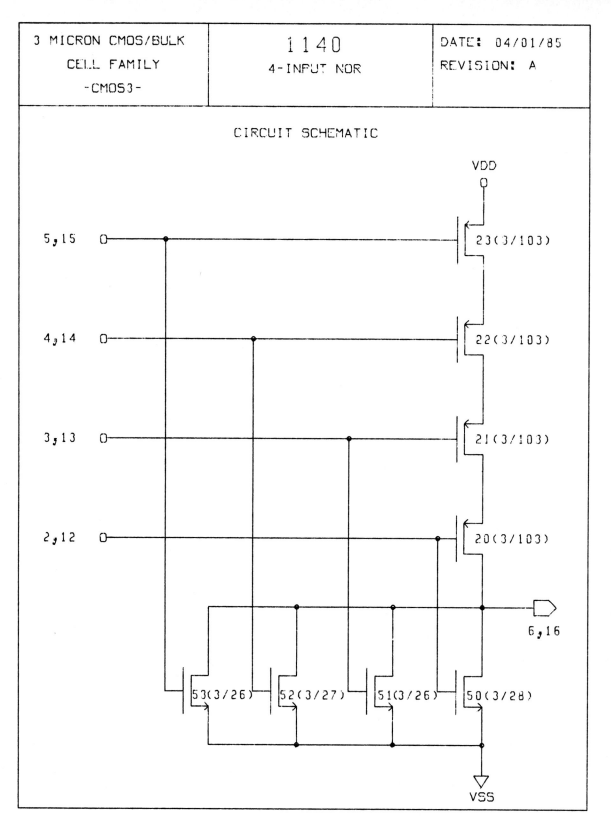

3 MICRON CMOS/BULK CELL FAMILY -CMOS3-	1140 4-INPUT NOR	DATE: 04/01/85 REVISION: A

CIRCUIT SCHEMATIC

VDD

5,15   23(3/103)

4,14   22(3/103)

3,13   21(3/103)

2,12   20(3/103)

6,16

53(3/26)   52(3/27)   51(3/26)   50(3/28)

VSS

REL 3   1140-2

100

3 MICRON CMOS/BULK CELL FAMILY -CMOS3-	1140 4-INPUT NOR	DATE: 04/01/85 REVISION: A

OUTPUT CHARACTERISTIC EQUATIONS

$$P_D(0-1) = P_{DC}(0-1) + .21 (T_{R/F} - 10) + .60 R_S C_L$$

$$P_D(1-0) = P_{DC}(1-0) + .07 (T_{R/F} - 10) + .60 R_S C_L$$

$$T_R = T_{RC} + .20 (T_{R/F} - 10) + 2.12 R_S C_L$$

$$T_F = T_{FC} + .24 (T_{R/F} - 10) + 2.36 R_S C_L$$

EQUATIONS

25°C
$$P_{DC}(0-1) = 3.90 C_L + 6.51$$
$$P_{DC}(1-0) = 1.73 C_L + 3.97$$
$$T_{RC} = 11.58 C_L + 7.48$$
$$T_{FC} = 4.85 C_L + 3.60$$

95°C
$$P_{DC}(0-1) = 4.96 C_L + 7.55$$
$$P_{DC}(1-0) = 2.06 C_L + 4.45$$
$$T_{RC} = 14.95 C_L + 9.85$$
$$T_{FC} = 6.3 C_L + 4.14$$

125°C
$$P_{DC}(0-1) = 5.38 C_L + 7.98$$
$$P_{DC}(1-0) = 2.38 C_L + 4.36$$
$$T_{RC} = 16.36 C_L + 10.83$$
$$T_{FC} = 6.86 C_L + 4.48$$

125°C BC
$$P_{DC}(0-1) = 2.29 C_L + 4.70$$
$$P_{DC}(1-0) = 1.06 C_L + 2.70$$
$$T_{RC} = 7.50 C_L + 5.17$$
$$T_{FC} = 3.06 C_L + 4.17$$

VOLTAGE TABLE

VOLTAGE	DEVIATION FACTOR			
	TRANSITION		PROP DELAY	
	TR	TF	1-0	0-1
3.0	1.67	1.59	1.65	1.76
3.5	1.45	1.39	1.43	1.50
4.0	1.22	1.18	1.21	1.24
4.5	1.11	1.09	1.10	1.12
5.0	1.00	1.00	1.00	1.00
5.5	.94	.96	.94	.93
6.0	.87	.91	.88	.86
6.5	.83	.88	.84	.82
7.0	.79	.85	.80	.77

REL 3   1140-3

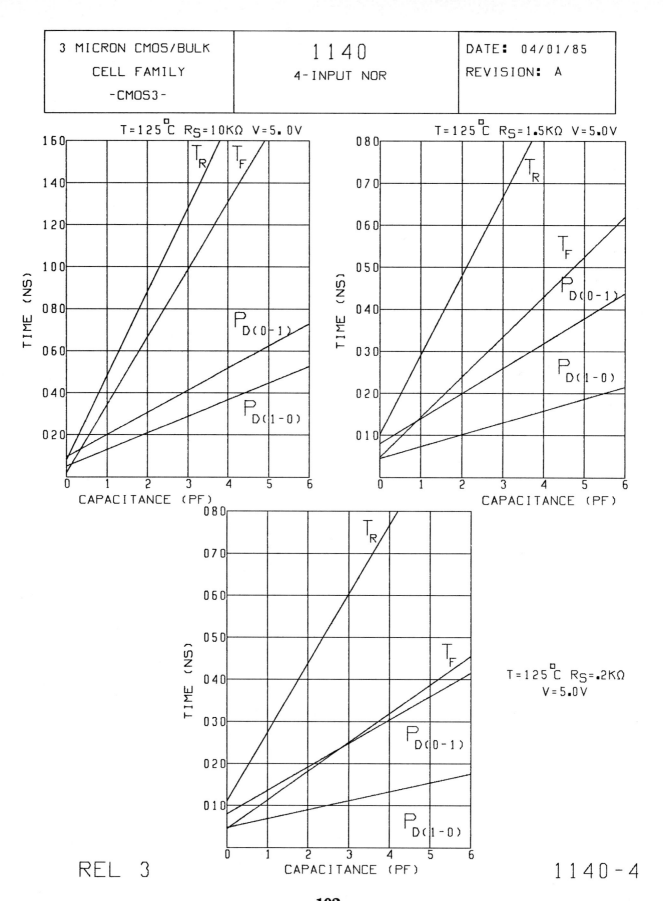

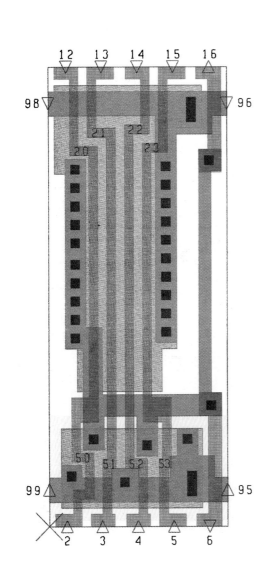

REL 3   1140-5

103

3 MICRON CMOS/BULK CELL FAMILY -CMOS3-	1220 2-NAND CELL HEIGHT 150 WIDTH 35	DATE: 09/01/83 REVISION: A

TERMINAL INFORMATION

TERMINAL NAME	LOGIC NUMBER	CAPACITANCE FIELD	(PF)
A	2,12	1	.24
B	3,13	2	.23
OUT	4,14	6	

LOGIC DIAGRAM

SAME AS LOGIC SYMBOL

TRUTH TABLE

A	B	OUT
0	*	1
*	0	1
1	1	0
1	X	X
X	1	X
X	X	X

LOGIC SYMBOLS

A,2
B,3 —OUT,4

WORST CASE DELAY INFORMATION

$P_D = 9.13$ NS $T_{R/F} = 24.1$ NS

$R_S = 1.5K\Omega$, $C_L = 1.5PF$, $V = 5V$, $T = 125°C$

LOGIC EQUATION(S)

OUT = $\overline{A*B}$

NOTES

1220-1

104

CIRCUIT SCHEMATIC

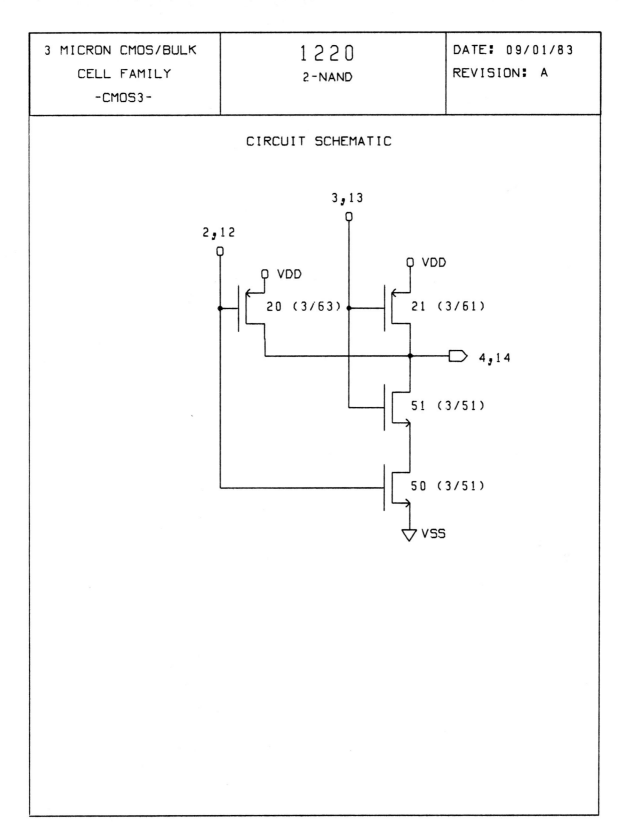

1220-2

3 MICRON CMOS/BULK CELL FAMILY -CMOS3-	1220 2-NAND	DATE: 09/01/83 REVISION: A

OUTPUT CHARACTERISTIC EQUATIONS

$$P_D(0-1) = P_{DC}(0-1) + .15 \ (T_{R/F} - 10) + .63 \ R_S C_L$$

$$P_D(1-0) = P_{DC}(1-0) + .21 \ (T_{R/F} - 10) + .63 \ R_S C_L$$

$$T_R = T_{RC} + .20 \ (T_{R/F} - 10) + 2.53 R_S C_L$$

$$T_F = T_{FC} + .15 \ (T_{R/F} - 10) + 2.50 R_S C_L$$

EQUATIONS

$25^\circ C$	$95^\circ C$	$125^\circ C$
$P_{DC}(0-1) = 2.17 C_L + 2.75$	$P_{DC}(0-1) = 2.83 C_L + 2.95$	$P_{DC}(0-1) = 3.11 C_L + 3.03$
$P_{DC}(1-0) = 2.12 C_L + 3.34$	$P_{DC}(1-0) = 2.74 C_L + 3.52$	$P_{DC}(1-0) = 3.01 C_L + 3.61$
$T_{RC} = 7.73 C_L + 2.27$	$T_{RC} = 10.27 C_L + 2.42$	$T_{RC} = 11.39 C_L + 2.49$
$T_{FC} = 7.34 C_L + 1.79$	$T_{FC} = 9.32 C_L + 1.57$	$T_{FC} = 10.79 C_L + 1.78$

$125^\circ C$ BC

$$P_{DC}(0-1) = 1.70 C_L + 2.07$$

$$P_{DC}(1-0) = 1.53 C_L + 2.63$$

$$T_{RC} = 6.21 C_L + 2.31$$

$$T_{FC} = 6.02 C_L + 1.7$$

VOLTAGE TABLE

VOLTAGE   DEVIATION FACTOR

VOLTAGE	TRANSITION		PROP DELAY	
	TR	TF	1-0	0-1
3.0	1.30	1.34	1.55	1.39
3.5	1.18	1.22	1.58	1.25
4.0	1.09	1.09	1.27	1.13
4.5	1.04	1.05	1.14	1.07
5.0	1.00	1.00	1.00	1.00
5.5	.97	.99	.93	.95
6.0	.95	.98	.85	.92
6.5	.93	.95	.80	.90
7.0	.91	.91	.75	.87

1220-3

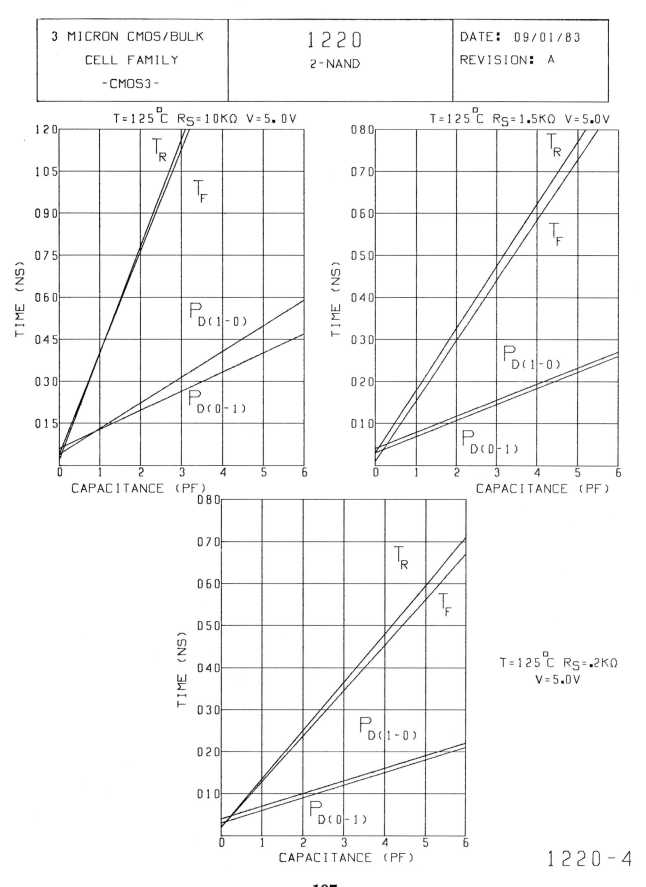

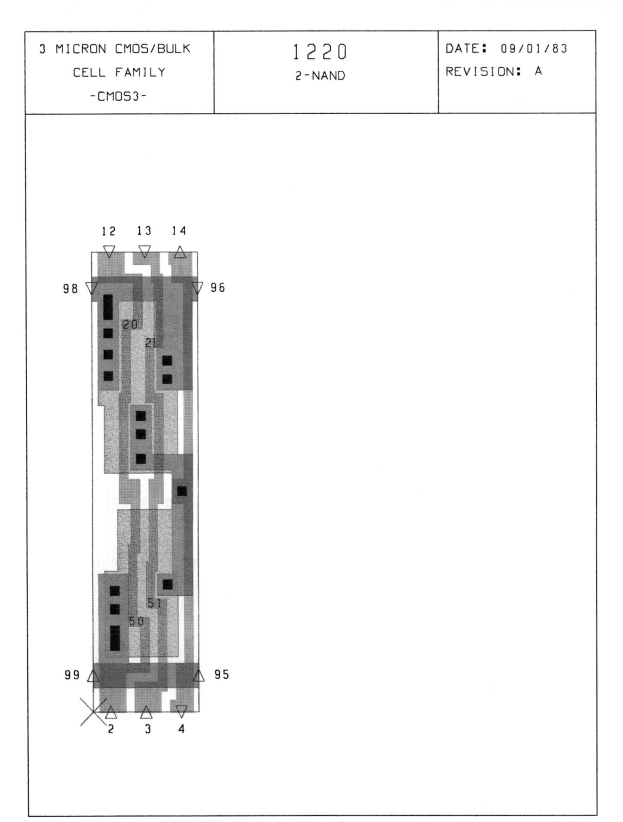

3 MICRON CMOS/BULK	1 2 3 0	DATE: 09/01/83
CELL FAMILY	3 NAND	REVISION: A
-CMOS3-	CELL HEIGHT 150 WIDTH 48	

TERMINAL INFORMATION

TERMINAL NAME	TERMINAL NUMBER	LOGIC FIELD	CAPACITANCE (PF)
A	2,12	1	.23
B	3,13	2	.21
C	4,14	3	.22
OUT	5,15	6	

LOGIC DIAGRAM

SAME AS LOGIC SYMBOL

TRUTH TABLE

A	B	C	OUT
0	*	*	1
*	0	*	1
*	*	0	1
1	1	1	0
ALL OTHER COMBINATIONS			X

LOGIC SYMBOLS

A,2
B,3
C,4
OUT,5

WORST CASE DELAY INFORMATION

P_D=11.13 NS $T_{R/F}$=25.91 NS

R_S=1.5KΩ, C_L=1.5PF, V=5V, T=125°C

LOGIC EQUATION(S)

OUT = $\overline{A \cdot B \cdot C}$

NOTES

1230-1

3 MICRON CMOS/BULK CELL FAMILY -CMOS3-	1230 3 NAND	DATE: 09/01/83 REVISION: A

CIRCUIT SCHEMATIC

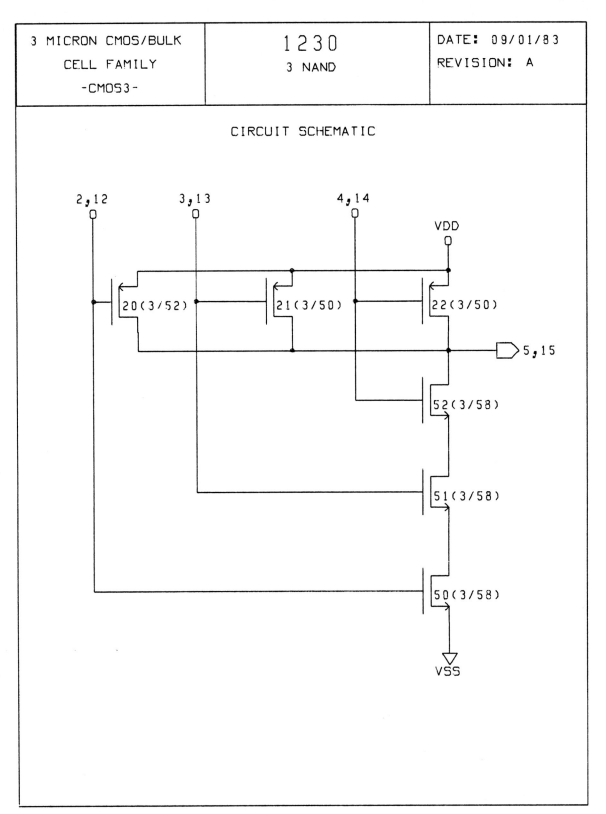

3 MICRON CMOS/BULK CELL FAMILY -CMOS3-	1 2 3 0 3 NAND	DATE: 09/01/83 REVISION: A

OUTPUT CHARACTERISTIC EQUATIONS

$$P_D(0-1) = P_{DC}(0-1) + .13 (T_{R/F} - 10) + .53 R_S C_L$$

$$P_D(1-0) = P_{DC}(1-0) + .24 (T_{R/F} - 10) + .62 R_S C_L$$

$$T_R = T_{RC} + .22 (T_{R/F} - 10) + 2.47 R_S C_L$$

$$T_F = T_{FC} + .13 (T_{R/F} - 10) + 2.49 R_S C_L$$

EQUATIONS

$25^\circ C$

$$P_{DC}(0-1) = 2.33 C_L + 3.71$$

$$P_{DC}(1-0) = 2.49 C_L + 4.41$$

$$T_{RC} = 7.94 C_L + 3.55$$

$$T_{FC} = 3.04 C_L + 2.58$$

$95^\circ C$

$$P_{DC}(0-1) = 3.01 C_L + 4.14$$

$$P_{DC}(1-0) = 3.17 C_L + 4.83$$

$$T_{RC} = 10.51 C_L + 4.15$$

$$T_{FC} = 10.54 C_L + 3.09$$

$125^\circ C$

$$P_{DC}(0-1) = 3.3 C_L + 4.34$$

$$P_{DC}(1-0) = 3.45 C_L + 4.99$$

$$T_{RC} = 11.62 C_L + 4.41$$

$$T_{FC} = 11.6 C_L + 3.28$$

$125^\circ C$ BC

$$P_{DC}(0-1) = 1.70 C_L + 2.34$$

$$P_{DC}(1-0) = 1.70 C_L + 3.50$$

$$T_{RC} = 5.0 C_L + 3.98$$

$$T_{FC} = 5.03 C_L + 2.11$$

VOLTAGE TABLE

VOLTAGE   DEVIATION FACTOR

VOLTAGE	TRANSITION		PROP DELAY	
	TR	TF	1-0	0-1
3.0	1.39	1.54	2.00	1.48
3.5	1.25	1.35	1.65	1.32
4.0	1.12	1.16	1.31	1.16
4.5	1.05	1.08	1.15	1.08
5.0	1.00	1.00	1.00	1.00
5.5	.95	.97	.92	.95
6.0	.93	.93	.84	.91
6.5	.91	.90	.79	.88
7.0	.89	.87	.74	.85

1230-3

111

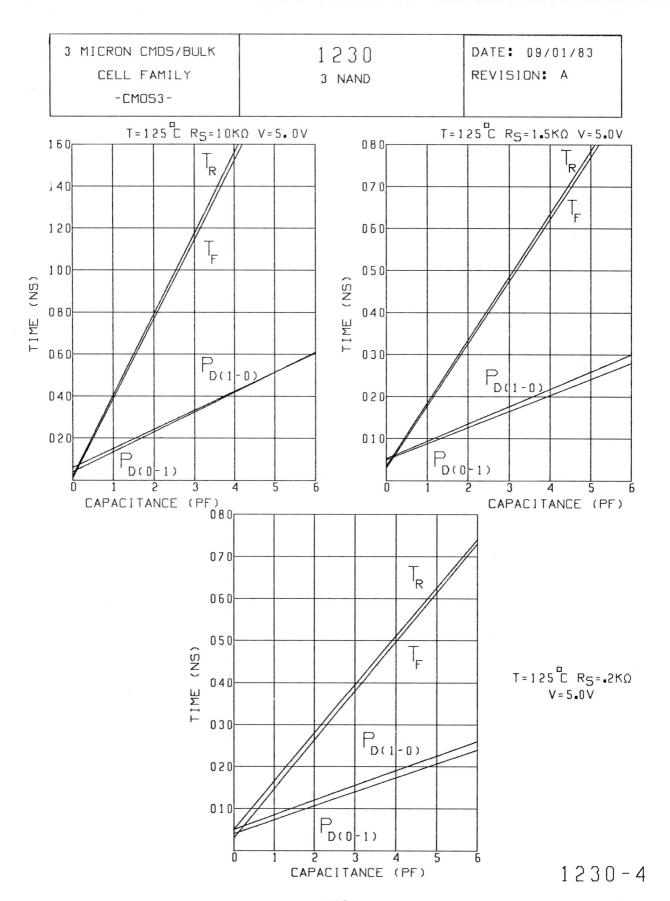

1230-4

112

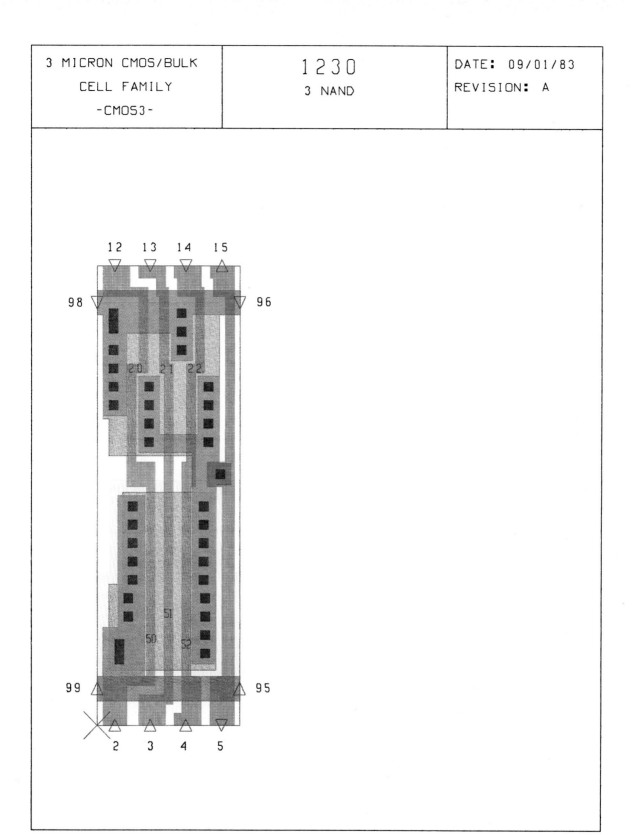

1230-5

113

3 MICRON CMOS/BULK CELL FAMILY -CMOS3-	1310 INVERTER CELL HEIGHT 150 WIDTH 36	DATE: 09/01/83 REVISION: A

TERMINAL INFORMATION

TERMINAL NAME	NUMBER	LOGIC FIELD	CAPACITANCE (PF)
A	3,13	1	.25
OUT	2,12	6	

LOGIC DIAGRAM

SAME AS LOGIC SYMBOL

TRUTH TABLE

A	OUT
1	0
0	1
X	X

LOGIC SYMBOLS

A,3 —▷∘— OUT,2

WORST CASE DELAY INFORMATION

P_D=6.2 NS $T_{R/F}$=16.6 NS

R_S=1.5KΩ, C_L=1.5PF, V=5V, T=125°C

LOGIC EQUATION(S)

OUT = $\overline{A}$

NOTES

1310-1

114

CIRCUIT SCHEMATIC

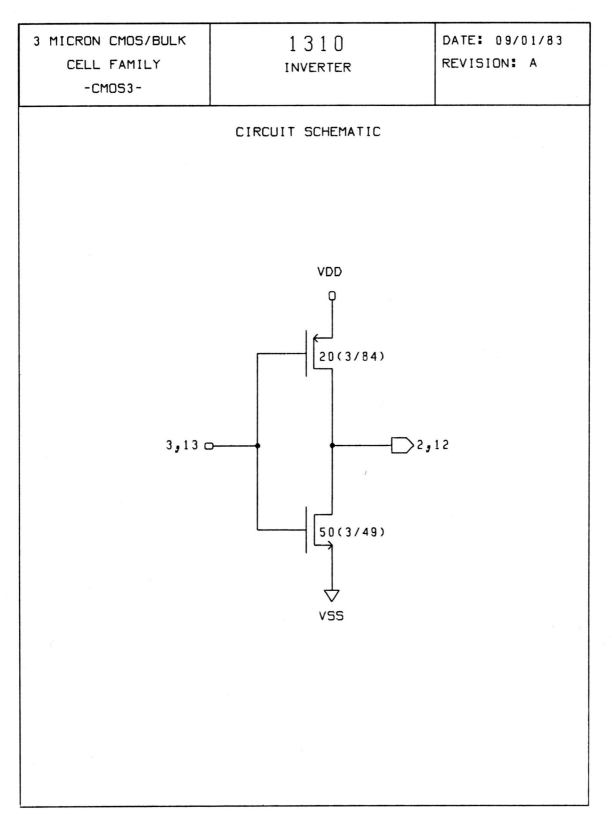

1310-2

3 MICRON CMOS/BULK CELL FAMILY -CMOS3-	1310 INVERTER	DATE: 09/01/83 REVISION: A

OUTPUT CHARACTERISTIC EQUATIONS

$$P_D(0-1) = P_{DC}(0-1) + .12 \ (T_{R/F} - 10) + .60 \ R_S C_L$$

$$P_D(1-0) = P_{DC}(1-0) + .12 \ (T_{R/F} - 10) + .60 \ R_S C_L$$

$$T_R = T_{RC} + .25 \ (T_{R/F} - 10) + 2.5 \ R_S C_L$$

$$T_F = T_{FC} + .35 \ (T_{R/F} - 10) + 2.5 \ R_S C_L$$

EQUATIONS

25°C

$$P_{DC}(0-1) = 1.31 C_L + 2.41$$

$$P_{DC}(1-0) = 1.03 C_L + 2.57$$

$$T_{RC} = 3.97 C_L + 2.98$$

$$T_{FC} = 2.86 C_L + 2.57$$

95°C

$$P_{DC}(0-1) = 1.64 C_L + 2.54$$

$$P_{DC}(1-0) = 1.25 C_L + 2.69$$

$$T_{RC} = 5.19 C_L + 3.2$$

$$T_{FC} = 3.68 C_L + 2.69$$

125°C

$$P_{DC}(0-1) = 1.78 C_L + 2.57$$

$$P_{DC}(1-0) = 1.35 C_L + 2.7$$

$$T_{RC} = 5.70 C_L + 3.32$$

$$T_{FC} = 4.04 C_L + 2.70$$

125°C BC

$$P_{DC}(0-1) = .93 \ C_L + 1.67$$

$$P_{DC}(1-0) = .78 \ C_L + 1.36$$

$$T_{RC} = 2.74 C_L + 3.59$$

$$T_{FC} = 1.98 C_L + 3.41$$

VOLTAGE TABLE

VOLTAGE	TRANSITION		PROP DELAY	
	TR	TF	1-0	0-1
3.0	1.34	1.26	1.82	1.46
3.5	1.23	1.16	1.55	1.30
4.0	1.11	1.06	1.28	1.15
4.5	1.05	1.03	1.14	1.07
5.0	1.00	1.00	1.00	1.00
5.5	.97	1.00	.91	.96
6.0	.94	1.00	.82	.91
6.5	.92	.99	.77	.88
7.0	.90	.92	.71	.85

DEVIATION FACTOR

1310-3

116

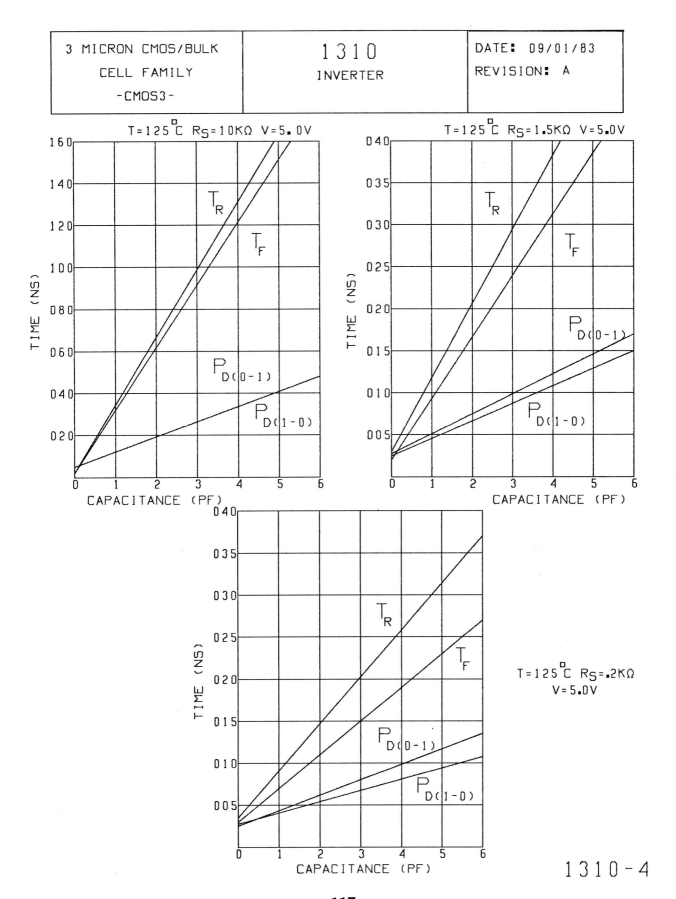

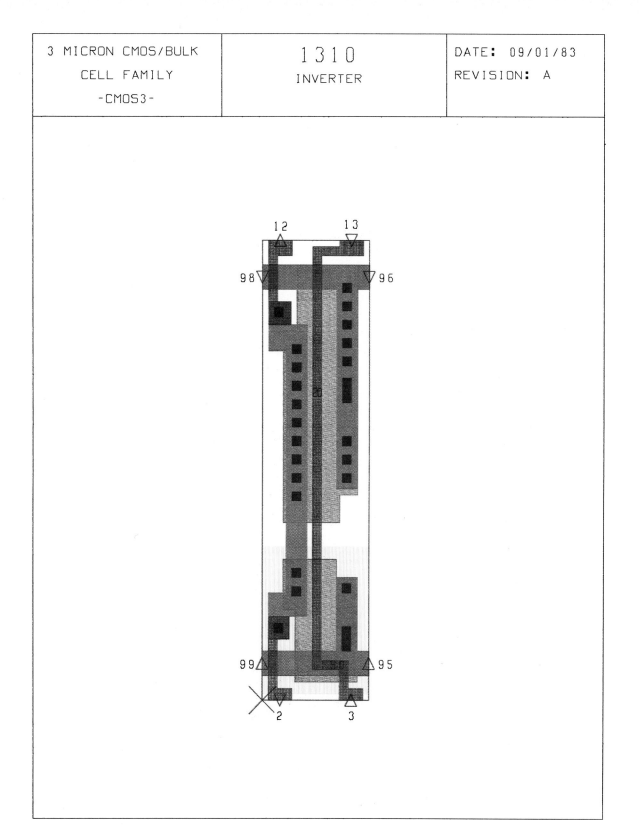

1310-5

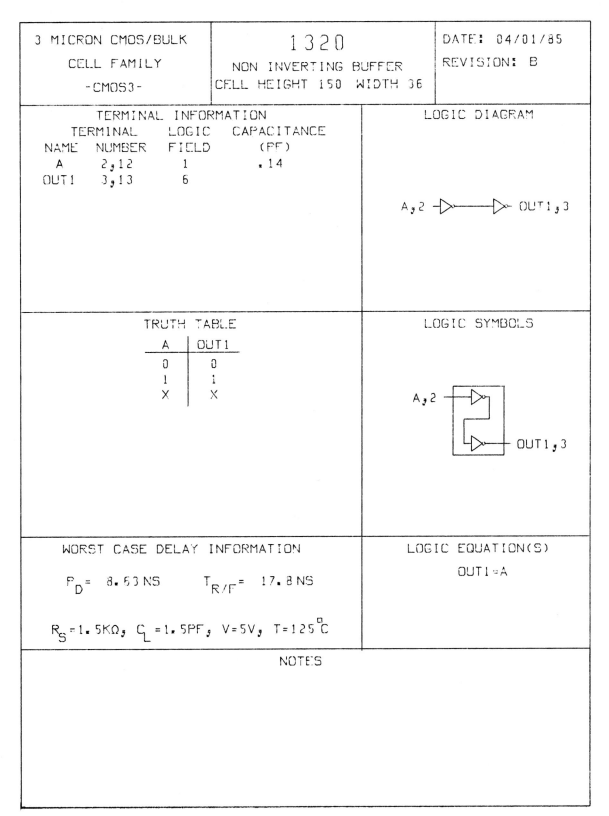

3 MICRON CMOS/BULK	1320	DATE: 04/01/85
CELL FAMILY	NON INVERTING BUFFER	REVISION: B
-CMOS3-	CELL HEIGHT 150 WIDTH 36	

TERMINAL INFORMATION

NAME	TERMINAL NUMBER	LOGIC FIELD	CAPACITANCE (PF)
A	2,12	1	.14
OUT1	3,13	6	

LOGIC DIAGRAM

A,2 outline OUT1,3

TRUTH TABLE

A	OUT1
0	0
1	1
X	X

LOGIC SYMBOLS

A,2   OUT1,3

WORST CASE DELAY INFORMATION

P_D = 8.53 NS $T_{R/F}$ = 17.8 NS

R_S = 1.5 KΩ, C_L = 1.5 PF, V=5V, T=125°C

LOGIC EQUATION(S)

OUT1=A

NOTES

REL 3   1320-1

119

CIRCUIT SCHEMATIC

VDD

VDD

20(3/39)

21(3/66.5)

2,12

3,13

50(3/19.5)

51(3/33.5)

VSS

VSS

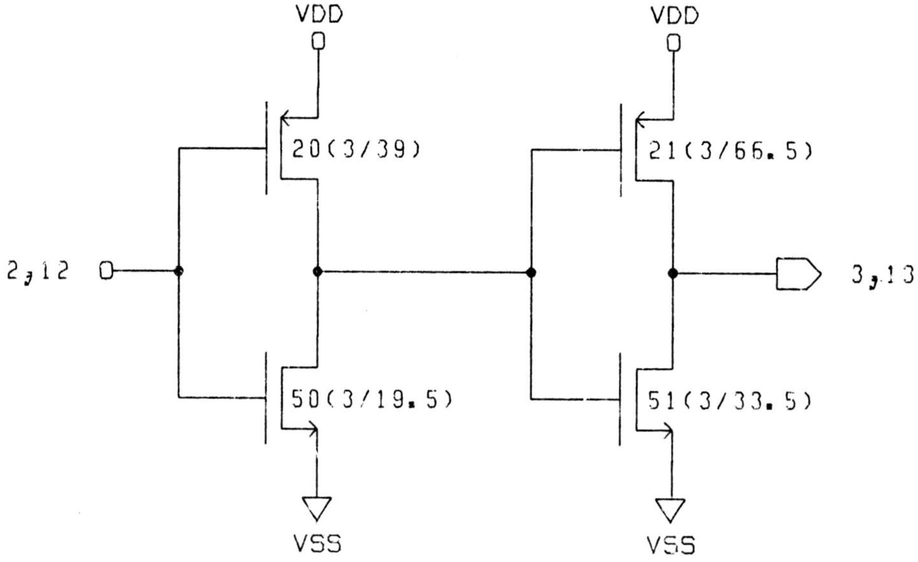

REL 3   1320-2

3 MICRON CMOS/BULK CELL FAMILY -CMOS3-	1320 NON INVERTING BUFFER	DATE: 04/01/85 REVISION: B

OUTPUT CHARACTERISTIC EQUATIONS

$$P_D(0-1) = P_{DC}(0-1) + .09(T_{R/F} - 10) + .64 R_S C_L$$

$$P_D(1-0) = P_{DC}(1-0) + .08(T_{R/F} - 10) + .61 R_S C_L$$

$$T_R = T_{RC} + .02(T_{R/F} - 10) + 2.53 R_S C_L$$

$$T_F = T_{FC} + .03(T_{R/F} - 10) + 2.54 R_S C_L$$

EQUATIONS

$25^\circ C$	$95^\circ C$	$125^\circ C$
$P_{DC}(0-1) = 1.63 C_L + 3.56$	$P_{DC}(0-1) = 2.10 C_L + 4.00$	$P_{DC}(0-1) = 2.29 C_L + 4.17$
$P_{DC}(1-0) = 1.42 C_L + 3.66$	$P_{DC}(1-0) = 1.79 C_L + 4.19$	$P_{DC}(1-0) = 1.94 C_L + 4.40$
$T_{RC} = 5.40 C_L + 1.58$	$T_{RC} = 7.0 C_L + 2.05$	$T_{RC} = 7.68 C_L + 2.23$
$T_{FC} = 4.37 C_L + 1.44$	$T_{FC} = 5.6 C_L + 1.81$	$T_{FC} = 6.12 C_L + 1.97$

$125^\circ C$ BC

$$P_{DC}(0-1) = 1.11 C_L + 2.09$$

$$P_{DC}(1-0) = .93 C_L + 2.25$$

$$T_{RC} = 3.95 C_L + 1.20$$

$$T_{FC} = 3.18 C_L + 1.10$$

VOLTAGE TABLE

VOLTAGE	DEVIATION FACTOR			
	TRANSITION		PROP DELAY	
	TR	TF	1-0	0-1
3.0	1.41	1.45	1.71	1.62
3.5	1.27	1.30	1.47	1.42
4.0	1.13	1.14	1.22	1.21
4.5	1.07	1.07	1.11	1.11
5.0	1.00	1.00	1.00	1.00
5.5	.96	.96	.94	.94
6.0	.92	.92	.87	.88
6.5	.90	.90	.83	.84
7.0	.87	.89	.79	.80

REL 3   1320-3

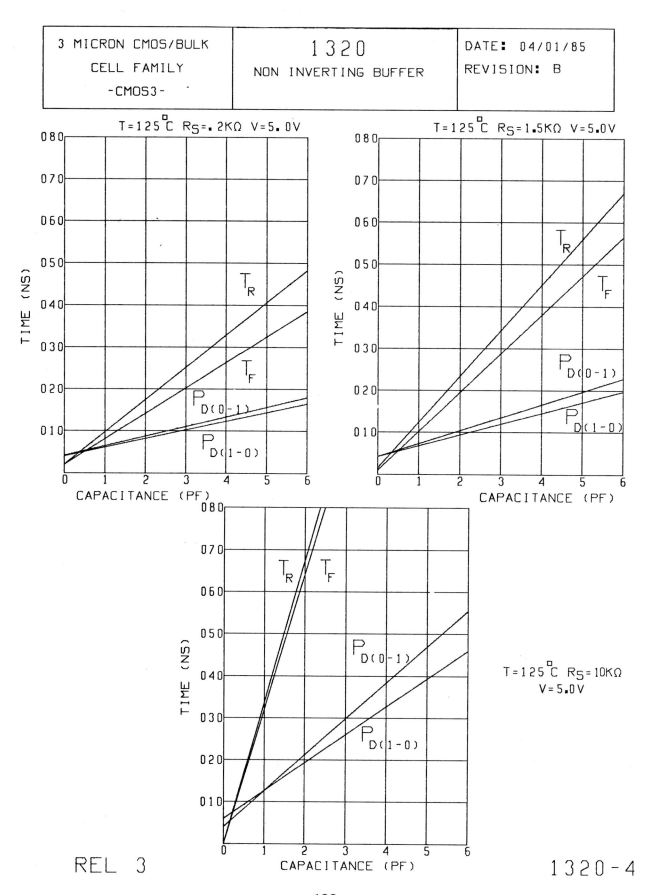

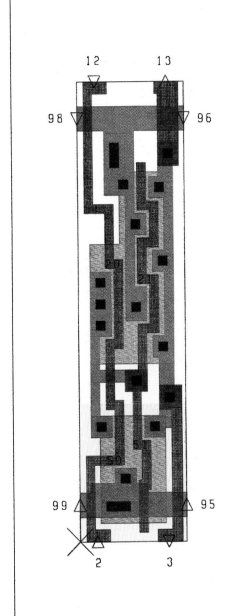

REL 3   1320-5

123

3 MICRON CMOS/BULK CELL FAMILY -CMOS3-	1340 TRI-STATE BUFFER CELL HEIGHT 150 WIDTH 34	DATE: 04/01/84 REVISION: A

TERMINAL INFORMATION

TERMINAL NAME	NUMBER	LOGIC FIELD	CAPACITANCE (PF)
ENABLE	2,12	1	.50
DATA	3,13	2	.27
OUT	4,14	6	

LOGIC DIAGRAM

SAME AS LOGIC SYMBOL

TRUTH TABLE

ENABLE	DATA	OUT
0	*	HI-Z
1	*	DATA
X	*	X

LOGICV SIMULATES THE HI-Z CONDITION AS A 1. SEE LOGICV APPENDIX FOR FURTHER INFORMATION.

LOGIC SYMBOLS

ENABLE,2

DATA,3 —▷— OUT,4

WORST CASE DELAY INFORMATION

ENABLE P_D = 9.03 NS $T_{R/F}$ =17.44 NS

DATA P_D = 9.39 NS $T_{R/F}$ =17.46 NS

R_S =1.5KΩ, C_L =1.5PF, V=5V, T=125°C

LOGIC EQUATION(S)

SEE TRUTH TABLE

NOTES

1. DATA PRESENT WITH ENABLE CHANGING CURVES AND EQUATIONS ARE ON PAGES 3-4
2. ENABLE PRESENT DATA CHANGING CURVES AND EQUATIONS ARE ON PAGES 5-6.

REL 3   1340-1

3 MICRON CMOS/BULK CELL FAMILY -CMOS3-	1340 TRI-STATE BUFFER	DATE: 04/01/84 REVISION: A

CIRCUIT SCHEMATIC

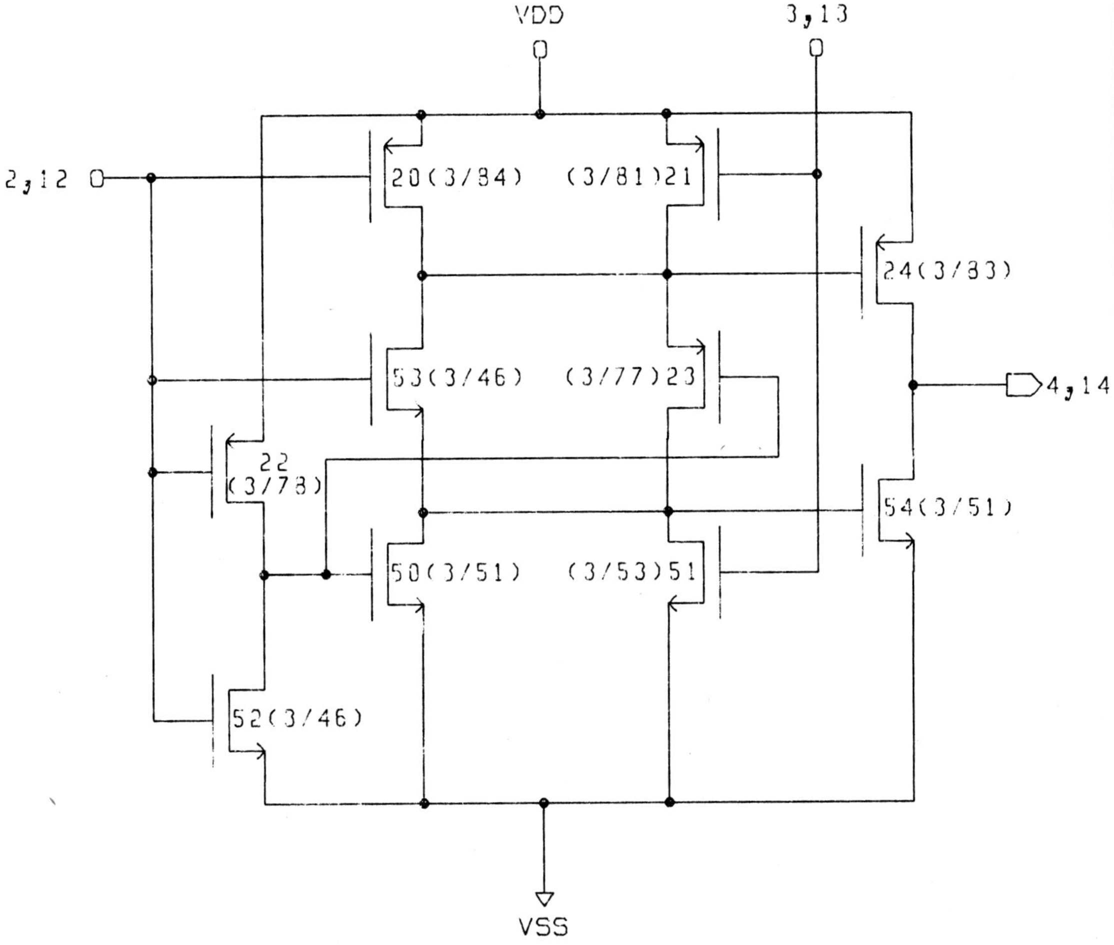

VDD
3,13
2,12
20(3/84)
(3/81)21
24(3/83)
53(3/46)
(3/77)23
4,14
22
(3/78)
54(3/51)
50(3/51)
(3/53)51
52(3/46)
VSS

REL 3 1340-2

3 MICRON CMOS/BULK CELL FAMILY -CMOS3-	1340 TRI-STATE BUFFER ENABLE CHANGING	DATE: 04/01/84 REVISION: A

OUTPUT CHARACTERISTIC EQUATIONS

$$P_D(0-1) = P_{DC}(0-1) + .10 (T_{R/F} - 10) + .65 R_S C_L$$

$$P_D(1-0) = P_{DC}(1-0) + .07 (T_{R/F} - 10) + .63 R_S C_L$$

$$T_R = T_{RC} + .03 (T_{R/F} - 10) + 2.54 R_S C_L$$

$$T_F = T_{FC} + 0.00 (T_{R/F} - 10) + 2.56 R_S C_L$$

EQUATIONS

25°C

$$P_{DC}(0-1) = 1.47 C_L + 3.79$$

$$P_{DC}(1-0) = 1.14 C_L + 4.75$$

$$T_{RC} = 5.06 C_L + 1.69$$

$$T_{FC} = 3.78 C_L + 1.55$$

95°C

$$P_{DC}(0-1) = 1.9 C_L + 4.28$$

$$P_{DC}(1-0) = 1.46 C_L + 5.47$$

$$T_{RC} = 6.58 C_L + 2.22$$

$$T_{FC} = 4.88 C_L + 2.04$$

125°C

$$P_{DC}(0-1) = 2.08 C_L + 4.46$$

$$P_{DC}(1-0) = 1.60 C_L + 5.72$$

$$T_{RC} = 7.24 C_L + 2.43$$

$$T_{FC} = 5.36 C_L + 2.26$$

125°C BC

$$P_{DC}(0-1) = 1.10 C_L + 1.95$$

$$P_{DC}(1-0) = 0.86 C_L + 2.35$$

$$T_{RC} = 3.95 C_L + 1.46$$

$$T_{FC} = 3.17 C_L + 0.79$$

VOLTAGE TABLE

VOLTAGE	DEVIATION FACTOR			
	TRANSITION		PROP DELAY	
	TR	TF	1-0	0-1
3.0	1.35	1.30	1.96	1.66
3.5	1.23	1.18	1.65	1.44
4.0	1.11	1.08	1.33	1.21
4.5	1.05	1.04	1.17	1.11
5.0	1.00	1.00	1.00	1.00
5.5	.97	.97	.93	.94
6.0	.94	.94	.85	.87
6.5	.92	.92	.80	.83
7.0	.90	.90	.76	.79

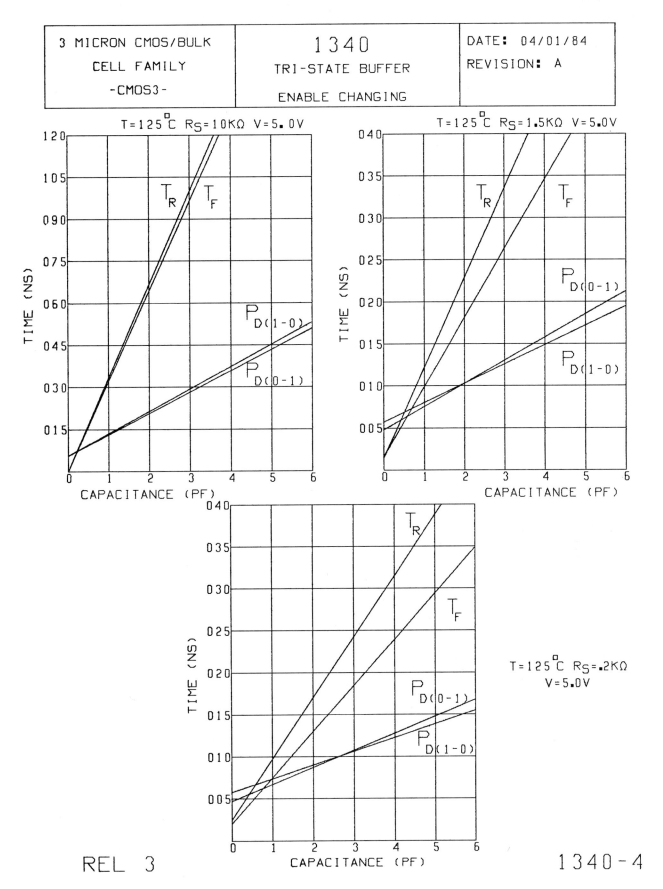

3 MICRON CMOS/BULK CELL FAMILY -CMOS3-	1340 TRI-STATE BUFFER DATA CHANGING	DATE: 04/01/84 REVISION: A

OUTPUT CHARACTERISTIC EQUATIONS

$$P_D(0-1) = P_{DC}(0-1) + .09 \ (T_{R/F} - 10) + .64 \ R_S C_L$$

$$P_D(1-0) = P_{DC}(1-0) + .12 \ (T_{R/F} - 10) + .62 \ R_S C_L$$

$$T_R = T_{RC} + .02 \ (T_{R/F} - 10) + 2.54 R_S C_L$$

$$T_F = T_{FC} + .03 \ (T_{R/F} - 10) + 2.56 R_S C_L$$

EQUATIONS

$25^{\circ}C$	$95^{\circ}C$	$125^{\circ}C$
$P_{DC}(0-1) = 1.46 C_L + 4.68$	$P_{DC}(0-1) = 1.89 C_L + 5.31$	$P_{DC}(0-1) = 2.07 C_L + 5.54$
$P_{DC}(1-0) = 1.15 C_L + 5.42$	$P_{DC}(1-0) = 1.43 C_L + 6.23$	$P_{DC}(1-0) = 1.62 C_L + 6.54$
$T_{RC} = 5.06 C_L + 1.71$	$T_{RC} = 6.53 C_L + 2.23$	$T_{RC} = 7.23 C_L + 2.46$
$T_{FC} = 3.76 C_L + 1.7$	$T_{FC} = 4.86 C_L + 2.18$	$T_{FC} = 5.34 C_L + 2.37$

$125^{\circ}C$ BC

$$P_{DC}(0-1) = 1.09 C_L + 2.45$$

$$P_{DC}(1-0) = 0.88 C_L + 3.31$$

$$T_{RC} = 3.98 C_L + 1.29$$

$$T_{FC} = 3.10 C_L + 1.23$$

VOLTAGE TABLE

VOLTAGE   DEVIATION FACTOR

VOLTAGE	TRANSITION		PROP DELAY	
	TR	TF	1-0	0-1
3.0	1.35	1.35	1.79	1.72
3.5	1.23	1.23	1.52	1.48
4.0	1.11	1.11	1.24	1.23
4.5	1.06	1.06	1.12	1.12
5.0	1.00	1.00	1.00	1.00
5.5	.97	.97	.93	.93
6.0	.94	.94	.86	.86
6.5	.91	.92	.82	.82
7.0	.89	.91	.78	.77

REL 3   1340-5

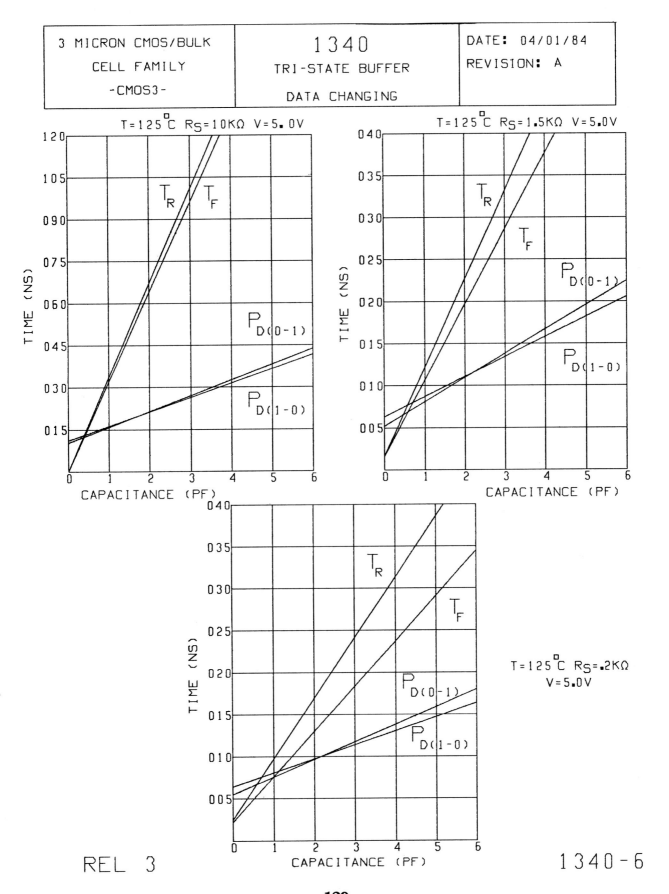

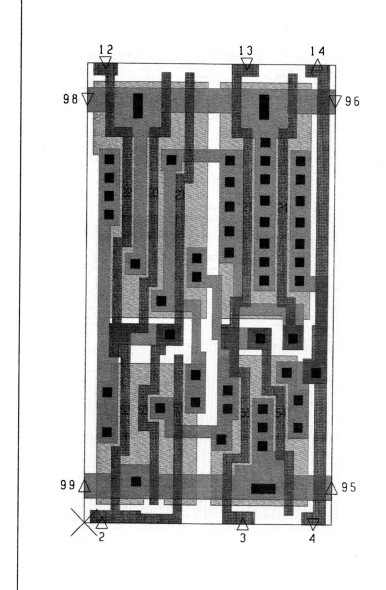

REL 3   1340-7

3 MICRON CMOS/BULK CELL FAMILY -CMOS3-	1350 DATA SELECT CELL HEIGHT 150 WIDTH 84	DATE: 09/07/84 REVISION: B

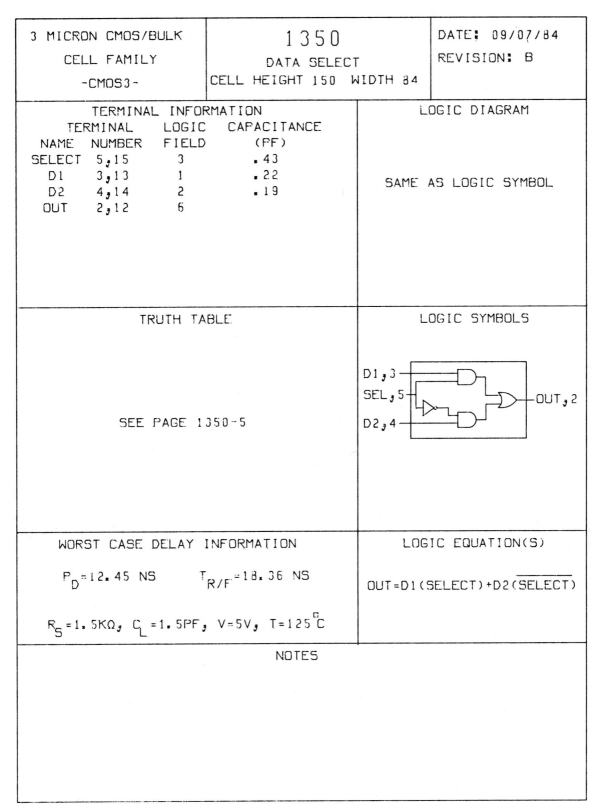

TERMINAL INFORMATION

TERMINAL NAME	NUMBER	LOGIC FIELD	CAPACITANCE (PF)
SELECT	5,15	3	.43
D1	3,13	1	.22
D2	4,14	2	.19
OUT	2,12	6	

LOGIC DIAGRAM

SAME AS LOGIC SYMBOL

TRUTH TABLE

SEE PAGE 1350-5

LOGIC SYMBOLS

D1,3 ─
SEL,5 ─
D2,4 ─   ─ OUT,2

WORST CASE DELAY INFORMATION

P_D=12.45 NS $T_{R/F}$=18.36 NS

R_S=1.5KΩ, C_L=1.5PF, V=5V, T=125°C

LOGIC EQUATION(S)

OUT=D1(SELECT)+D2($\overline{\text{SELECT}}$)

NOTES

REL 3   1350-1

131

CIRCUIT SCHEMATIC

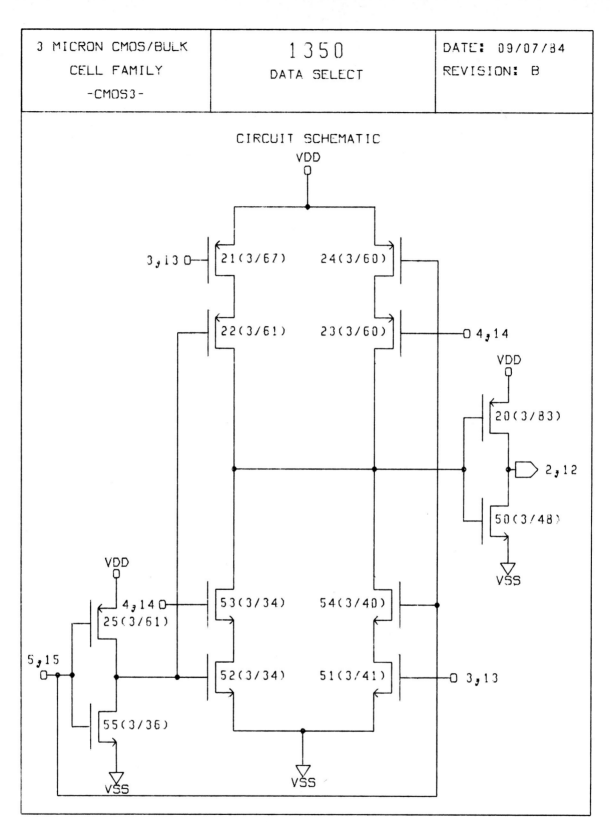

REL 3   1 3 5 0 - 2

3 MICRON CMOS/BULK CELL FAMILY -CMOS3-	1350 DATA SELECT	DATE: 09/07/84 REVISION: B

OUTPUT CHARACTERISTIC EQUATIONS

$$P_D(0-1) = P_{DC}(0-1) + .12 \ (T_{R/F} - 10) + .65 \ R_S C_L$$

$$P_D(1-0) = P_{DC}(1-0) + .12 \ (T_{R/F} - 10) + .53 \ R_S C_L$$

$$T_R = T_{RC} + .01 \ (T_{R/F} - 10) + 2.51 R_S C_L$$

$$T_F = T_{FC} + .01 \ (T_{R/F} - 10) + 2.51 R_S C_L$$

EQUATIONS

$25^\circ C$	$95^\circ C$	$125^\circ C$
$P_{DC}(0-1) = 1.48C_L + 6.29$	$P_{DC}(0-1) = 1.91C_L + 7.29$	$P_{DC}(0-1) = 2.10C_L + 7.68$
$P_{DC}(1-0) = 1.2 \ C_L + 7.06$	$P_{DC}(1-0) = 1.54C_L + 8.39$	$P_{DC}(1-0) = 1.69C_L + 8.91$
$T_{RC} = 5.12C_L + 2.17$	$T_{RC} = 6.66C_L + 2.84$	$T_{RC} = 7.35C_L + 3.09$
$T_{FC} = 3.94C_L + 2.03$	$T_{FC} = 5.09C_L + 2.66$	$T_{FC} = 5.59C_L + 2.95$

$125^\circ C$ BC

$$P_{DC}(0-1) = 1.10C_L + 3.58$$

$$P_{DC}(1-0) = 0.9 \ C_L + 4.44$$

$$T_{RC} = 4.07C_L + 1.41$$

$$T_{FC} = 3.24C_L + 1.41$$

VOLTAGE TABLE

VOLTAGE   DEVIATION FACTOR

VOLTAGE	TRANSITION		PROP DELAY	
	TR	TF	1-0	0-1
3.0	1.37	1.38	1.79	1.76
3.5	1.25	1.25	1.52	1.50
4.0	1.12	1.11	1.25	1.23
4.5	1.06	1.06	1.13	1.12
5.0	1.00	1.00	1.00	1.00
5.5	.97	.97	.93	.93
6.0	.93	.94	.86	.87
6.5	.91	.92	.82	.83
7.0	.89	.90	.77	.78

REL 3   1350-3

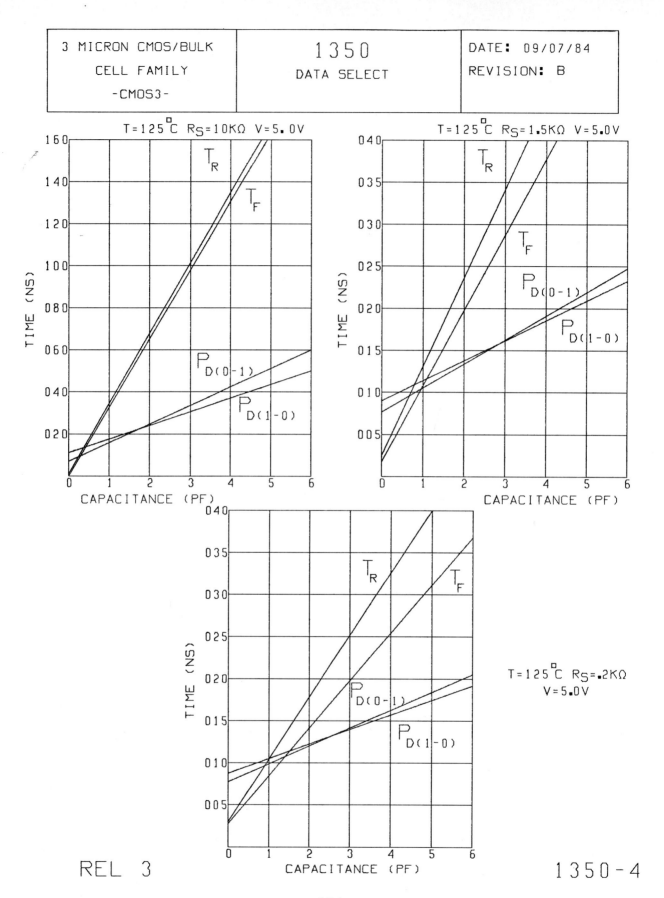

3 MICRON CMOS/BULK	1350	DATE: 09/07/84
CELL FAMILY	DATA SELECT	REVISION: B
-CMOS3-		

REL 3

1350-4

134

SEL	D1	D2	OUT
0	*	*	D2
1	*	*	D1
X	0	0	0
X	0	1	X
X	0	X	X
X	1	0	X
X	1	1	1
X	1	X	X
X	X	*	X

REL 3   1350-5

135

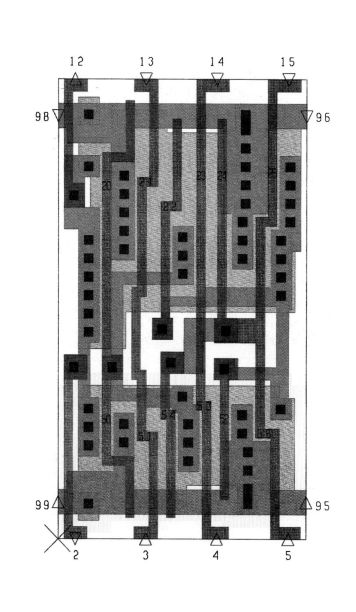

REL 3   1350-6

3 MICRON CMOS/BULK CELL FAMILY -CMOS3-	1370 TRANSMISSION GATE CELL HEIGHT 150 WIDTH 72	DATE: 09/07/84 REVISION: C

TERMINAL INFORMATION

TERMINAL NAME	LOGIC NUMBER	CAPACITANCE FIELD	(PF)
CONTROL	2,12	1	.31
DATA	3,13	2	$1.15+C_L$
OUT	4,14	6	

LOGIC DIAGRAM

CONTROL,2

DATA,3 — OUT,4

TRUTH TABLE

C	D	OUT
1	0	0
1	1	1
1	X	X
0	0	HI-Z
0	1	HI-Z
0	X	HI-Z
X	*	X

LOGICV SIMULATES THE HI-Z CONDITION
AS A 1. SEE LOGICV APPENDIX FOR
FURTHER INFORMATION.

LOGIC SYMBOLS

CONTROL,2

DATA,3 — OUT,4

WORST CASE DELAY INFORMATION

$$P_D = 9.0 \text{ NS} \qquad T_{R/F} = 22.0 \text{ NS}$$

$$R_S = 1.5K\Omega, \ C_L = 1.5PF, \ V=5V, \ T=125^\circ C$$

LOGIC EQUATION(S)

OUT=DATA*CONTROL
(HI-Z AT CONTROL LOW)

NOTES

ALL TIMING ANALYSIS HAS BEEN ACCOMPLISHED BY DRIVING THE
TRANSMISSION GATE WITH AN INVERTER (1310). THE DATA ON THESE PAGES
REPRESENTS THE TIMING THROUGH THE COMBINATION OF INVERTER AND
TRANSIMISSION GATE. TWO SETS OF DATA ARE PRESENTED:THE FIRST IS
FROM THE INPUT OF THE INVERTER WHICH DRIVES THE DATA INPUT TO THE
OUTPUT OF THE T-GATE;THE SECOND IS FROM THE CONTROL TO THE OUTPUT.

1370-1

137

3 MICRON CMOS/BULK CELL FAMILY -CMOS3-	1370 TRANSMISSION GATE	DATE: 09/07/84 REVISION: C

CIRCUIT SCHEMATIC

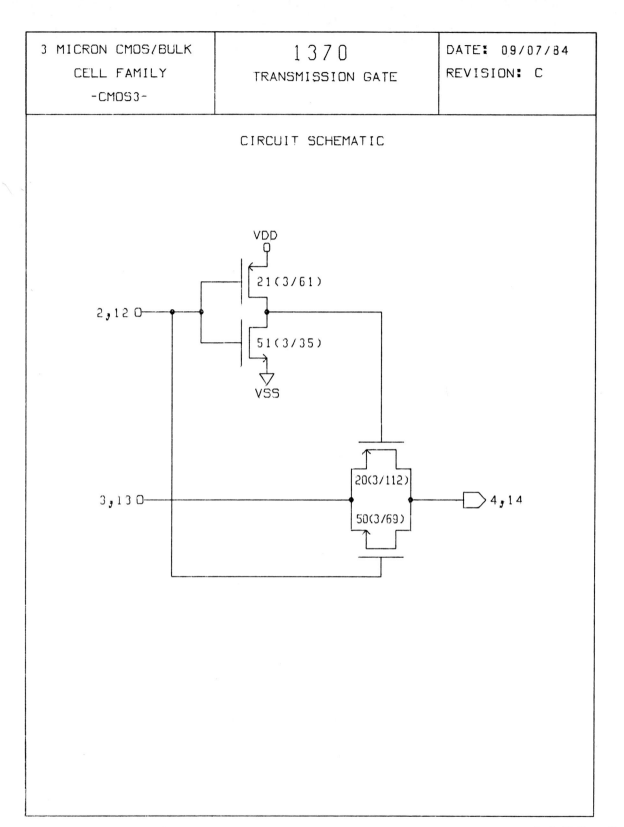

3 MICRON CMOS/BULK CELL FAMILY -CMOS3-	1370 TRANSMISSION GATE DATA	DATE: 09/07/84 REVISION: C

OUTPUT CHARACTERISTIC EQUATIONS

$$P_D(0-1) = P_{DC}(0-1) + .15 \, (T_{R/F} - 10) + .67 \, R_S C_L$$

$$P_D(1-0) = P_{DC}(1-0) + .15 \, (T_{R/F} - 10) + .62 \, R_S C_L$$

$$T_R = T_{RC} + .23 \, (T_{R/F} - 10) + 2.28 R_S C_L$$

$$T_F = T_{FC} + .24 \, (T_{R/F} - 10) + 2.36 R_S C_L$$

EQUATIONS

$25^\circ C$	$95^\circ C$	$125^\circ C$
$P_{DC}(0-1) = 1.63 C_L + 3.89$	$P_{DC}(0-1) = 2.00 C_L + 4.32$	$P_{DC}(0-1) = 2.16 C_L + 4.49$
$P_{DC}(1-0) = 1.25 C_L + 3.82$	$P_{DC}(1-0) = 1.53 C_L + 4.11$	$P_{DC}(1-0) = 1.64 C_L + 4.23$
$T_{RC} = 5.43 C_L + 5.69$	$T_{RC} = 6.94 C_L + 6.92$	$T_{RC} = 7.56 C_L + 7.46$
$T_{FC} = 3.56 C_L + 3.99$	$T_{FC} = 4.49 C_L + 4.64$	$T_{FC} = 4.87 C_L + 4.91$

$125^\circ C$ BC

$$P_{DC}(0-1) = .96 \, C_L + 2.61$$

$$P_{DC}(1-0) = .76 \, C_L + 2.30$$

$$T_{RC} = 3.26 C_L + 5.36$$

$$T_{FC} = 2.03 C_L + 4.23$$

VOLTAGE TABLE

VOLTAGE	DEVIATION FACTOR			
	TRANSITION		PROP DELAY	
	TR	TF	1-0	0-1
3.0	1.59	1.62	1.74	1.68
3.5	1.39	1.41	1.49	1.45
4.0	1.19	1.19	1.23	1.22
4.5	1.10	1.10	1.12	1.11
5.0	1.00	1.00	1.00	1.00
5.5	.94	.95	.93	.93
6.0	.89	.90	.87	.87
6.5	.85	.87	.82	.83
7.0	.82	.84	.78	.79

1370-3

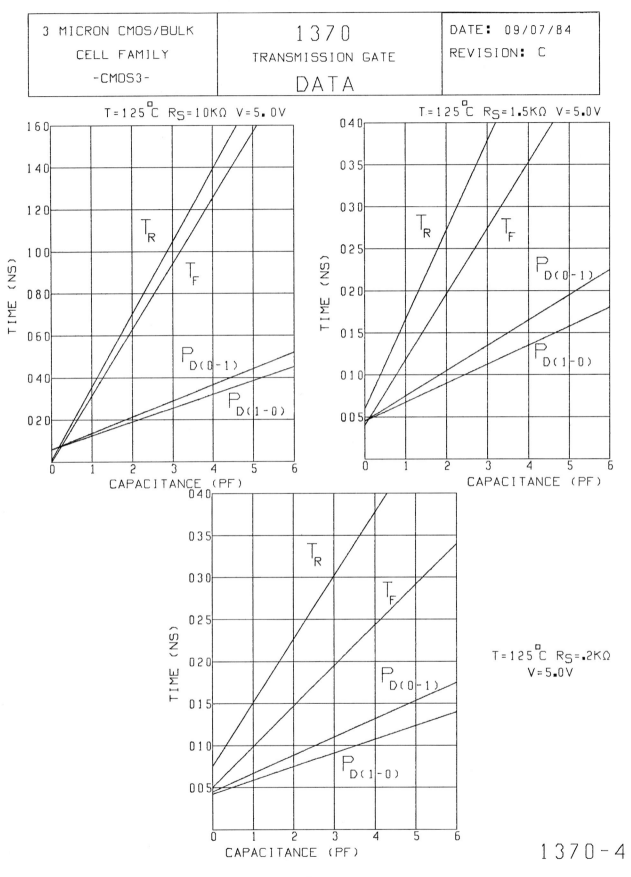

3 MICRON CMOS/BULK CELL FAMILY -CMOS3-	1370 TRANSMISSION GATE CONTROL	DATE: 09/07/84 REVISION: C

OUTPUT CHARACTERISTIC EQUATIONS

$$P_D(0-1) = P_{DC}(0-1) + .07 (T_{R/F} - 10) + .66 R_S C_L$$

$$P_D(1-0) = P_{DC}(1-0) + .06 (T_{R/F} - 10) + .58 R_S C_L$$

$$T_R = T_{RC} + .43 (T_{R/F} - 10) + 2.31 R_S C_L$$

$$T_F = T_{FC} + .28 (T_{R/F} - 10) + 2.39 R_S C_L$$

EQUATIONS

$25^\circ C$	$95^\circ C$	$125^\circ C$
$P_{DC}(0-1) = 1.60 C_L + 2.35$	$P_{DC}(0-1) = 1.95 C_L + 2.4$	$P_{DC}(0-1) = 2.08 C_L + 2.39$
$P_{DC}(1-0) = 1.25 C_L + 2.06$	$P_{DC}(1-0) = 1.53 C_L + 2.02$	$P_{DC}(1-0) = 1.64 C_L + 2.00$
$T_{RC} = 5.34 C_L + 5.13$	$T_{RC} = 6.81 C_L + 6.46$	$T_{RC} = 7.43 C_L + 6.98$
$T_{FC} = 3.51 C_L + 3.60$	$T_{FC} = 4.50 C_L + 4.01$	$T_{FC} = 4.88 C_L + 4.20$

$125^\circ C$ BC

$$P_{DC}(0-1) = .94 C_L + .31$$

$$P_{DC}(1-0) = .84 C_L + .31$$

$$T_{RC} = 3.07 C_L + 5.96$$

$$T_{FC} = 2.02 C_L + 4.18$$

VOLTAGE TABLE

VOLTAGE   DEVIATION FACTOR

VOLTAGE	TRANSITION		PROP DELAY	
	TR	TF	1-0	0-1
3.0	1.54	1.52	2.14	1.71
3.5	1.36	1.32	1.78	1.48
4.0	1.17	1.12	1.41	1.24
4.5	1.09	1.06	1.21	1.12
5.0	1.00	1.00	1.00	1.00
5.5	.95	.96	.81	.92
6.0	.91	.92	.62	.85
6.5	.88	.89	.47	.80
7.0	.85	.86	.32	.75

1370-5

141

3 MICRON CMOS/BULK CELL FAMILY -CMOS3-	1370 TRANSMISSION GATE CONTROL	DATE: 09/07/84 REVISION: C

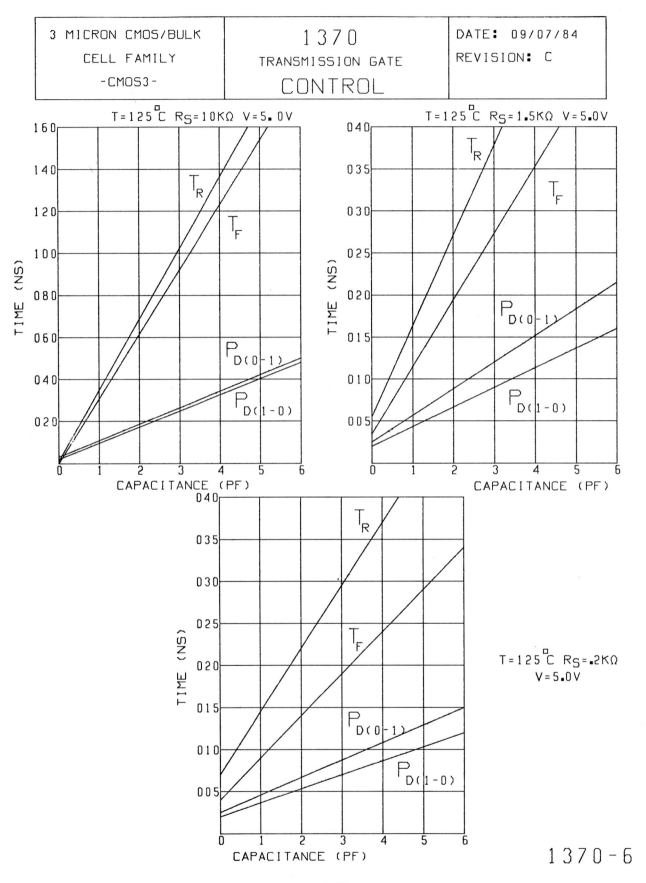

1370-6

142

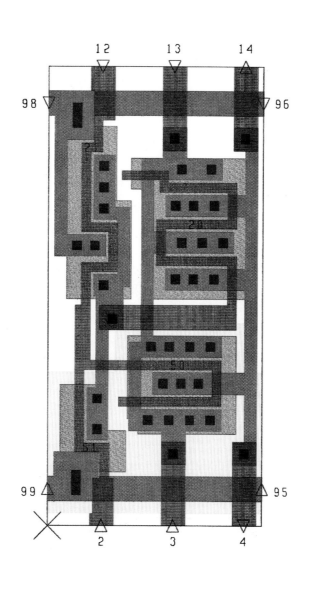

1370-7

3 MICRON CMOS/BULK CELL FAMILY -CMOS3-	1410 NAND LATCH CELL HEIGHT 150 WIDTH 60	DATE: 04/01/84 REVISION: B

TERMINAL INFORMATION

TERMINAL NAME	NUMBER	LOGIC FIELD	CAPACITANCE (PF)
S	4,14	1	.25
R	3,13	2	.25
Q	2,12	6	
$\overline{Q}$	5,15	7	

LOGIC DIAGRAM

TRUTH TABLE

S	R	Q	$\overline{Q}$	
0	0	1	1	
0	1	1	0	
1	0	0	1	
*1	1	Q_{N-1}	$\overline{Q}_{N-1}$	IF $Q_{N-1}=0$ THEN Q=0 AND $\overline{Q}$=1
1	X	X	X	
0	X	1	X	IF $\overline{Q}_{N-1}=0$ THEN Q=1 AND $\overline{Q}$=0
X	1	X	X	
X	0	X	1	
X	X	X	X	

* SEE NOTES

LOGIC SYMBOLS

WORST CASE DELAY INFORMATION

P_D = 11.3 NS $T_{R/F}$ = 19.5 NS

R_S =1.5KΩ, C_L =1.5PF, V=5V, T=125°C

LOGIC EQUATION(S)

$$Q=(Q_{N-1}*S*R)+\overline{S}$$

$$\overline{Q}=(\overline{Q}_{N-1}*S*R)+\overline{R}$$

NOTES

1. DELAY AND TRANSITION TIMES FOR Q AND $\overline{Q}$ ARE APPROXIMATELY THE SAME SO ONLY ONE SET OF EQUATIONS AND CURVES WILL BE GENERATED.

2. C_L^1 FOR THE DELAY AND TRANSISTION EQUATIONS IS THE CAPACITIVE LOADING ON THE OPPOSITE OUTPUT FROM WHERE THE DELAY IS BEING CALCULATED. THE CURVES ARE DRAWN WITH THE OPPOSITE OUTPUT UNLOADED.

*BOTH INPUTS CAN NOT CHANGE FROM 0,0 TO 1,1 SIMULTANEOUSLY, THE OUTPUT GOES TO A DON'T KNOW STATE.

1410-1

CIRCUIT SCHEMATIC

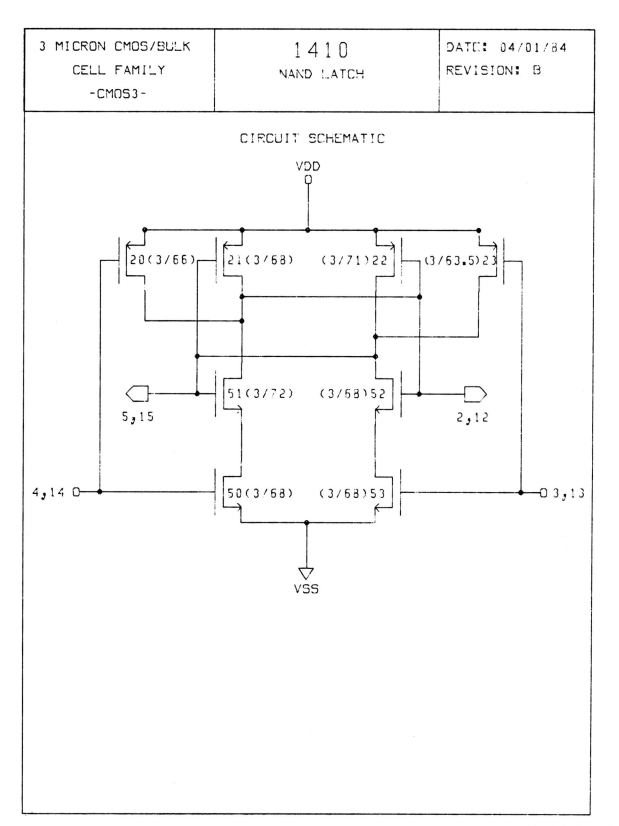

OUTPUT CHARACTERISTIC EQUATIONS

$$P_D(0-1) = P_{DC}(0-1) + .18 \ (T_{R/F} - 10) + .60 \ R_S C_L + 0 \ C_L^1$$

$$P_D(1-0) = P_{DC}(1-0) + .15 \ (T_{R/F} - 10) + .65 \ R_S C_L + 1.56 \ C_L^1$$

$$T_R = T_{RC} + .20 \ (T_{R/F} - 10) + 2.39 R_S C_L + .29 C_L^1$$

$$T_F = T_{FC} + .014(T_{R/F} - 10) + 2.54 R_S C_L + .99 C_L^1$$

EQUATIONS

25°C

$$P_{DC}(0-1) = 1.71 C_L + 3.86$$

$$P_{DC}(1-0) = 1.47 C_L + 5.77$$

$$T_{RC} = 4.38 C_L + 4.73$$

$$T_{FC} = 5.00 C_L + 2.23$$

95°C

$$P_{DC}(0-1) = 2.15 C_L + 4.41$$

$$P_{DC}(1-0) = 1.38 C_L + 6.70$$

$$T_{RC} = 5.75 C_L + 5.52$$

$$T_{FC} = 6.51 C_L + 2.84$$

125°C

$$P_{DC}(0-1) = 2.32 C_L + 4.65$$

$$P_{DC}(1-0) = 2.06 C_L + 7.07$$

$$T_{RC} = 6.35 C_L + 5.83$$

$$T_{FC} = 7.16 C_L + 3.10$$

125°C BC

$$P_{DC}(0-1) = 1.08 C_L + 3.14$$

$$P_{DC}(1-0) = 1.11 C_L + 3.73$$

$$T_{RC} = 3.42 C_L + 4.07$$

$$T_{FC} = 4.14 C_L + 1.27$$

VOLTAGE TABLE

VOLTAGE   DEVIATION FACTOR

VOLTAGE	TRANSITION		PROP DELAY	
	TR	TF	1-0	0-1
3.0	1.44	1.40	1.80	1.48
3.5	1.28	1.26	1.53	1.32
4.0	1.13	1.12	1.26	1.16
4.5	1.06	1.06	1.13	1.08
5.0	1.00	1.00	1.00	1.00
5.5	.97	.97	.92	.95
6.0	.93	.95	.85	.90
6.5	.91	.94	.80	.87
7.0	.89	.93	.76	.84

1410-3

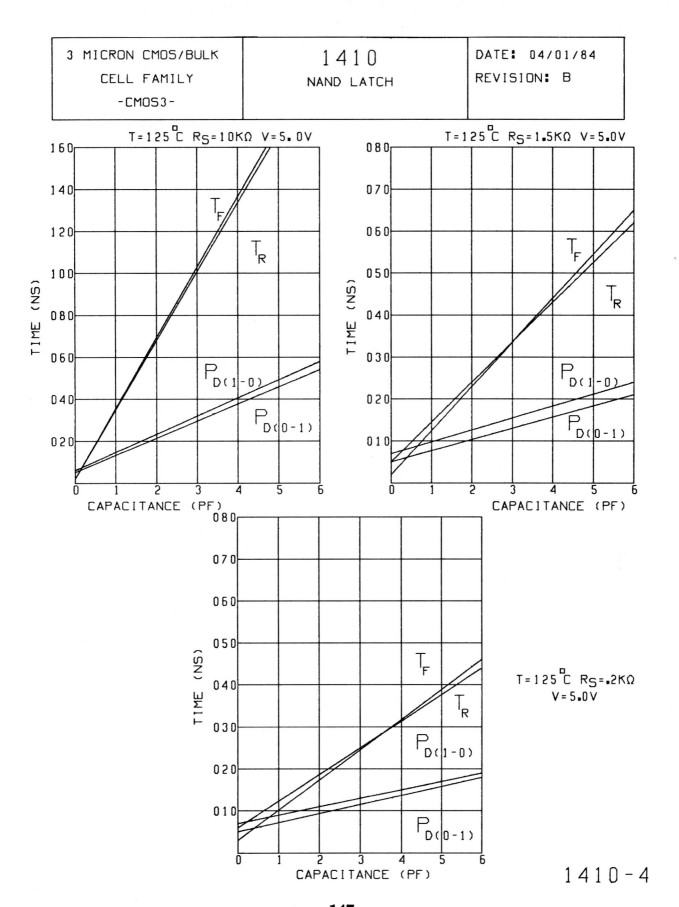

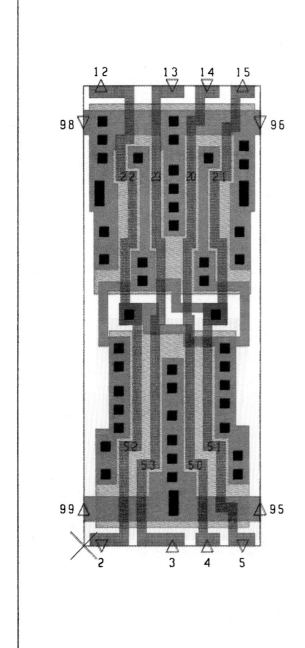

1410-5

TERMINAL INFORMATION

TERMINAL NAME	NUMBER	LOGIC FIELD	CAPACITANCE (PF)
Q	2,12	6	
S	3,13	1	.24
R	4,14	2	.24
$\overline{Q}$	5,15	7	

LOGIC DIAGRAM

S,3 — $\overline{Q}$,5
R,4 — Q,2

TRUTH TABLE

S	R	Q	$\overline{Q}$	
* 0	0	Q_{N-1}	$\overline{Q}_{N-1}$	
1	0	1	0	
0	1	0	1	
1	1	0	0	
X	1	0	X	
X	0	X	X	IF $\overline{Q}_{N-1}=0$ THEN Q=1 AND $\overline{Q}=0$
1	X	X	0	
0	X	X	X	IF $Q_{N-1}=0$ THEN Q=0 AND $\overline{Q}=1$
X	X	X	X	

* SEE NOTES

LOGIC SYMBOLS

S,3 — $\overline{Q}$,5
R,4 — Q,2

WORST CASE DELAY INFORMATION

P_D = 15.3 NS $T_{R/F}$ = 29.3 NS

R_S = 1.5KΩ, C_L = 1.5PF, V=5V, T=125°C

LOGIC EQUATION(S)

$$Q=S\overline{R}+(Q_{N-1}*\overline{S}*\overline{R})$$

$$\overline{Q}=\overline{S}R+(\overline{Q}_{N-1}*\overline{S}*\overline{R})$$

NOTES

1. DELAY AND TRANSISTION TIMES FOR EACH OUTPUT FROM THE INPUT ARE APPROXIMATELY THE SAME. THEREFORE, ONLY ONE SET OF CURVES AND EQUATIONS WILL BE PROVIDED.

2. C_L^1 FOR THE DELAY AND TRANSISTION EQUATIONS IS THE CAPACITIVE LOADING ON THE OPPOSITE OUTPUT FROM WHERE THE DELAY IS BEING CALCULATED. THE CURVES ARE DRAWN WITH THE OPPOSITE OUTPUT UNLOADED.
   *BOTH INPUTS CANNOT CHANGE FROM 1,1 TO 0,0 SIMULTANEOUSLY, THE OUTPUT GOES TO A DON'T KNOW STATE.

1420-1

3 MICRON CMOS/BULK CELL FAMILY -CMOS3-	1420 NOR LATCH	DATE: 04/01/84 REVISION: B

CIRCUIT SCHEMATIC

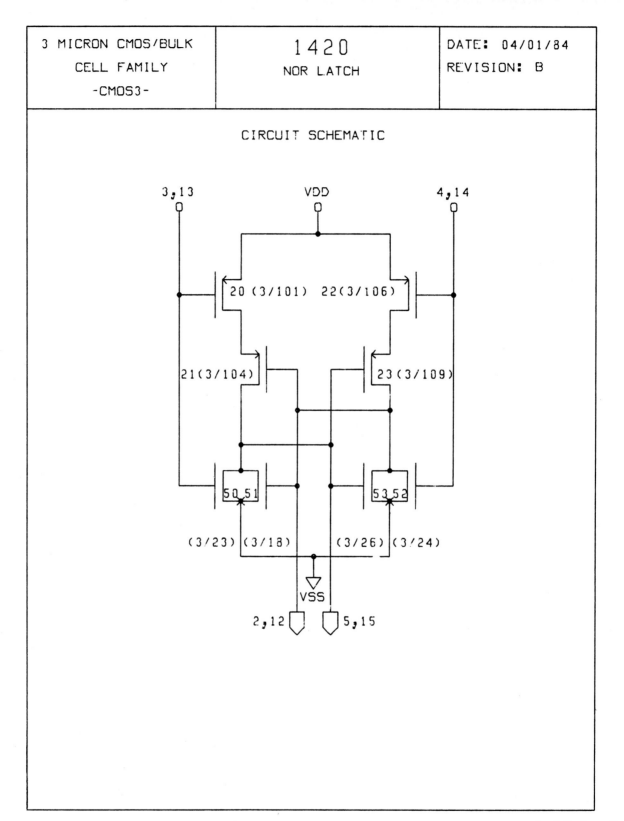

3 MICRON CMOS/BULK CELL FAMILY -CMOS3-	1420 NOR LATCH	DATE: 04/01/84 REVISION: B

OUTPUT CHARACTERISTIC EQUATIONS

$$P_D(0-1) = P_{DC}(0-1) + .19 (T_{R/F}-10) + .66 R_S C_L + 1.35 C_L^1$$

$$P_D(1-0) = P_{DC}(1-0) + .21 (T_{R/F}-10) + .63 R_S C_L + 0 C_L^1$$

$$T_R = T_{RC} + .01 (T_{R/F}-10) + 2.49 R_S C_L + .91 C_L^1$$

$$T_F = T_{FC} + .13 (T_{R/F}-10) + 2.45 R_S C_L + .27 C_L^1$$

EQUATIONS

$25^\circ C$	$95^\circ C$	$125^\circ C$
$P_{DC}(0-1) = 2.48 C_L + 7.01$	$P_{DC}(0-1) = 3.24 C_L + 8.11$	$P_{DC}(0-1) = 3.57 C_L + 8.56$
$P_{DC}(1-0) = 2.29 C_L + 4.66$	$P_{DC}(1-0) = 2.93 C_L + 5.22$	$P_{DC}(1-0) = 3.18 C_L + 5.48$
$T_{RC} = 8.91 C_L + 3.38$	$T_{RC} = 11.76 C_L + 4.42$	$T_{RC} = 13.01 C_L + 4.84$
$T_{FC} = 6.08 C_L + 4.35$	$T_{FC} = 8.06 C_L + 5.05$	$T_{FC} = 8.93 C_L + 5.35$

$125^\circ C$ BC

$$P_{DC}(0-1) = 1.94 C_L + 4.45$$

$$P_{DC}(1-0) = 1.76 C_L + 3.2$$

$$T_{RC} = 7.37 C_L + 2.02$$

$$T_{FC} = 5.22 C_L + 3.44$$

VOLTAGE TABLE

VOLTAGE	DEVIATION FACTOR			
	TRANSITION		PROP DELAY	
	TR	TF	1-0	0-1
3.0	1.39	1.44	1.56	1.64
3.5	1.26	1.27	1.38	1.42
4.0	1.12	1.10	1.18	1.20
4.5	1.06	1.05	1.09	1.10
5.0	1.00	1.00	1.00	1.00
5.5	.96	.97	.95	.94
6.0	.93	.94	.90	.89
6.5	.91	.92	.87	.85
7.0	.88	.90	.83	.81

1420-3

151

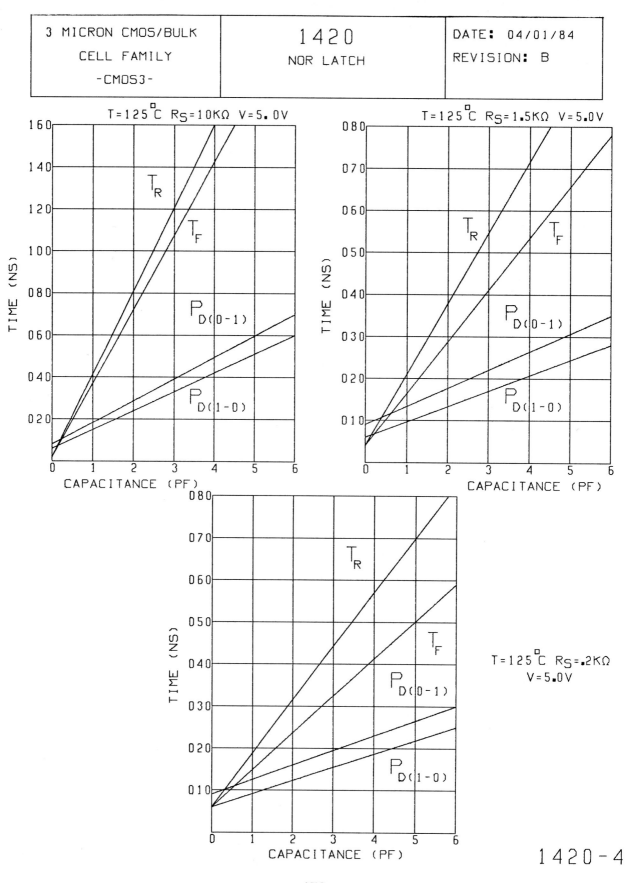

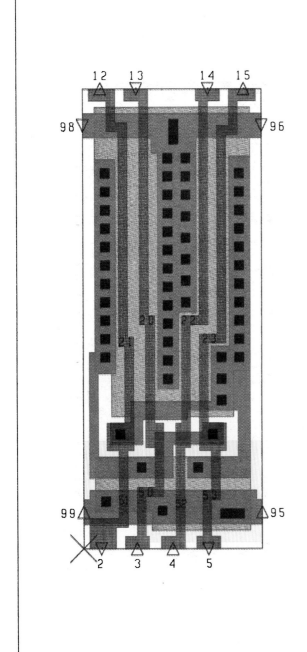

1420-5

153

3 MICRON CMOS/BULK CELL FAMILY -CMOS3-	1430 PULL-UP CELL HEIGHT 150 WIDTH 36	DATE: 04/01/85 REVISION: C

TERMINAL INFORMATION

TERMINAL NAME	NUMBER	LOGIC FIELD	CAPACITANCE (PF)
OUT	2,12	6	

LOGIC DIAGRAM

SAME AS LOGIC SYMBOL.

TRUTH TABLE

N/A

SEE LOGICV APPENDIX FOR SIMULATION INFORMATION.

LOGIC SYMBOLS

VDD

OUT,2

WORST CASE DELAY INFORMATION

P_D = N/A NS $T_{R/F}$ = N/A NS

R_S =1.5KΩ, C_L =1.5PF, V=5V, T=125°C

LOGIC EQUATION(S)

OUT=1

NOTES

THE CURRENT THE 1430 IS ABLE TO SOURCE WHEN AT A SUPPLY VOLTAGE OF 5.0V AND AN OUTPUT VOLTAGE OF 0.0V IS:

TEMPERATURE(*)	CURRENT
125(WNWP)	0.003 MA
25(WNWP)	0.004 MA
95(WNWP)	0.003 MA
125(BNBP)	0.007 MA

ADDITIONAL NOTES ON PAGE 1430-3.

1430-1

CIRCUIT SCHEMATIC

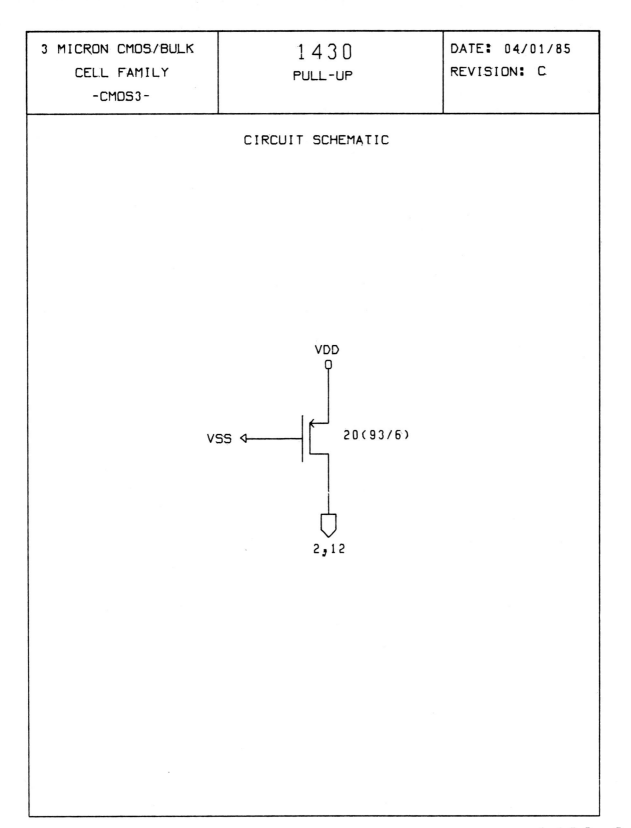

THE 1430 PULL-UP CELL IS INTENDED TO BE USED IN PLACE OF AN ELECTRICAL CONNECTION TO THE POWER BUS IN DEFINING THE CONNECTION FOR AN INPUT TO A CELL OR PAD.   THE CELL WAS NOT INTENDED TO BE USED IN AN ELECTRICAL OVERDRIVE CONDITION EXCEPT FOR WHEN AN INPUT SIGNAL FROM ONTO THE CHIP MAY ELECTRICALLY OVERDRIVE THIS CELL. THIS CONDITION IS SHOWN BELOW:

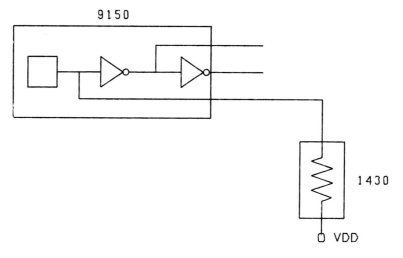

THIS CELL WAS NOT DESIGNED TO OPERATE AT 10 MHZ, AND THE SPEED APPLICATION MUST BE INVESTIGATED FOR EVERY USAGE OF THE CELL.

1430-3

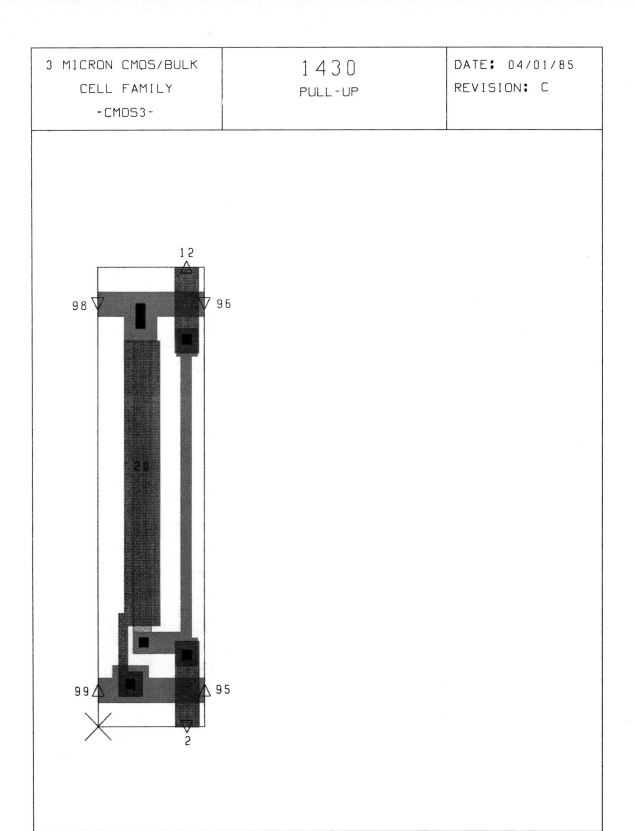

1430-4

157

3 MICRON CMOS/BULK CELL FAMILY -CMOS3-	1440 PULL-DOWN CELL HEIGHT 150 WIDTH 36	DATE: 04/01/84 REVISION: B

TERMINAL INFORMATION

TERMINAL NAME	LOGIC NUMBER	CAPACITANCE FIELD (PF)
OUT	2,12	6

LOGIC DIAGRAM

SAME AS LOGIC SYMBOL.

TRUTH TABLE

N/A

SEE LOGICV APPENDIX FOR SIMULATION INFORMATION.

LOGIC SYMBOLS

OUT,2

VSS

WORST CASE DELAY INFORMATION

P_D= N/A NS $T_{R/F}$= N/A NS

R_S=1.5KΩ, C_L=1.5PF, V=5V, T=125°C

LOGIC EQUATION(S)

OUT=0

NOTES

THE CURRENT THE 1440 IS ABLE TO SINK FOR AN OUTPUT VOLTAGE OF 5.0V IS:

TEMPERATURE(*)	CURRENT	
125(WNWP)	0.007 MA	*FOR N/P CHANNEL
25(WNWP)	0.009 MA	CONDITIONS SEE
95(WNWP)	0.007 MA	TABLE 7.1
125(BNBP)	0.017 MA	

ADDITIONAL NOTES ON PAGE 1440-3.

1440-1

CIRCUIT SCHEMATIC

2,12

VDD O⎯⎯ 50(88/6)

VSS

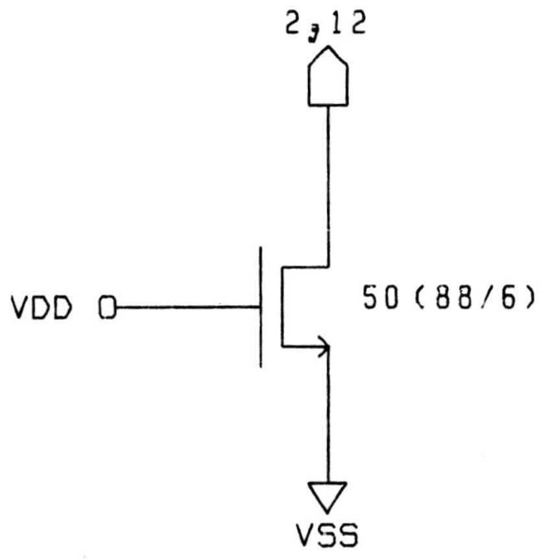

1440-2

THE 1440 PULL-DOWN CELL IS INTENDED TO BE USED IN PLACE OF AN ELECTRICAL CONNECTION TO THE POWER BUS IN DEFINING THE CONNECTION FOR AN INPUT TO A CELL OR PAD. THE CELL WAS NOT INTENDED TO BE USED IN AN ELECTRICAL OVERDRIVE CONDITION EXCEPT WHERE AN INPUT SIGNAL FROM ONTO THE CHIP MAY ELECTRICALLY OVERDRIVE THIS CELL. THIS CONDITION IS SHOWN BELOW:

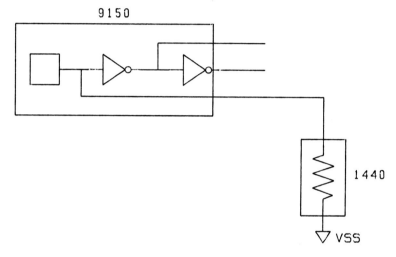

THIS CELL WAS NOT DESIGNED TO OPERATE AT 10 MHZ, AND THE SPEED APPLICATION MUST BE INVESTIGATED FOR EVERY USAGE OF THE CELL.

1440-3

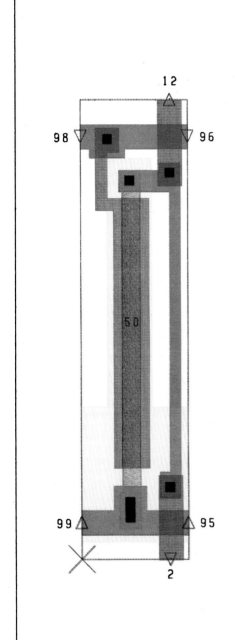

1440-4

161

3 MICRON CMOS/BULK	1480	DATE: 04/01/84
CELL FAMILY	DFF W/R,S,Q,$\overline{Q}$	REVISION: A
-CMOS3-	CELL HEIGHT 150 WIDTH 204	

TERMINAL INFORMATION

TERMINAL NAME	NUMBER	LOGIC FIELD	CAPACITANCE (PF)
CLOCK	2,12	1	.23
DATA	3,13	2	.19
RESET	4,14	3	.33
SET	5,15	4	.45
Q	6,16	6	
$\overline{Q}$	7,17	7	

LOGIC DIAGRAM

TRUTH TABLE

C	D	R	S	Q_N	$\overline{Q}_N$
⟋	*	1	1	Q_{N-1}	$\overline{Q}_{N-1}$
⟋	*	1	1	D_{N-1}	$\overline{D}_{N-1}$
*	*	0	1	0	1
*	*	1	0	1	0
*	*	0	0	1	1

SEE PAGE 1480-13 FOR ADDITIONAL
TRUTH TABLE

LOGIC SYMBOLS

WORST CASE DELAY INFORMATION
FOR RESET TO Q: CLOCK=0.

P_D= 24.75NS $T_{R/F}$= 19.97NS

R_S=1.5KΩ, C_L=1.5PF, V=5V, T=125°C

LOGIC EQUATION(S)

$$Q_N=[Q_{N-1}C+D_{N-1}\overline{C}]*R+\overline{S}$$

$$\overline{Q}_N=[.NOT.Q_N]+\overline{R}$$

NOTES

$\overline{Q}$ IS NOT ALWAYS LOGICAL INVERSE OF Q.
SPECIAL FLIP FLOP TIMING SEE PAGES 1480-11, 12.
SET IS INDEPENDENT OF CLOCK. RESET IS ALSO INDEPENDENT OF CLOCK,
BUT A HAZARD EXISTS IN THE CASE WHERE R=0, S=1, C=1, AND D=1.
IN THIS CASE, THE MASTER SECTION OF THE FLIP-FLOP IS NOT RESET,
AND WILL BE A 1 SINCE D=1 AND C=1. IF C THEN GOES TO 0, THE
MASTER WILL BE RESET. HOWEVER, A SMALL PULSE WILL PROPAGATE
THROUGH THE SLAVE AND BE OUTPUT ON Q (BUT NOT $\overline{Q}$). SIMULATIONS
INDICATE THIS PULSE IS NOT SUFFICIENTLY LARGE TO CLOCK A FLIP-
FLOP. STILL, CARE SHOULD BE TAKEN TO AVOID THIS CONDITION.

REL 3   1480-1

162

CIRCUIT SCHEMATIC

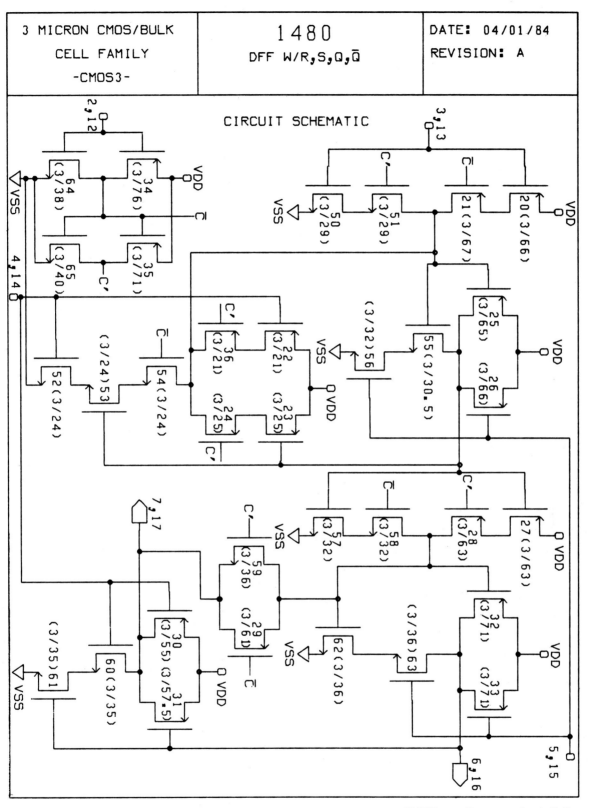

REL 3   1480-2

163

OUTPUT CHARACTERISTIC EQUATIONS

$$P_D(0-1)=P_{DC}(0-1)+.03\ (T_{R/F}-10)+.64\ R_S C_L$$

$$P_D(1-0)=P_{DC}(1-0)+.03\ (T_{R/F}-10)+.58\ R_S C_L$$

$$T_R=T_{RC}+0.0\ (T_{R/F}-10)+2.38 R_S C_L$$

$$T_F=T_{FC}+0.0\ (T_{R/F}-10)+2.19 R_S C_L$$

EQUATIONS

$25°C$

$$P_{DC}(0-1)=1.44C_L+6.15$$
$$P_{DC}(1-0)=2.45C_L+3.29$$
$$T_{RC}=4.42C_L+3.36$$
$$T_{FC}=6.58C_L+4.58$$

$95°C$

$$P_{DC}(0-1)=1.83C_L+7.29$$
$$P_{DC}(1-0)=3.06C_L+9.95$$
$$T_{RC}=5.64C_L+4.46$$
$$T_{FC}=8.32C_L+5.93$$

$125°C$

$$P_{DC}(0-1)=1.99C_L+7.73$$
$$P_{DC}(1-0)=3.30C_L+10.6$$
$$T_{RC}=6.16C_L+4.90$$
$$T_{FC}=9.04C_L+6.49$$

$125°C$ BC

$$P_{DC}(0-1)=0.91C_L+3.62$$
$$P_{DC}(1-0)=1.35C_L+4.71$$
$$T_{RC}=2.99C_L+2.21$$
$$T_{FC}=4.06C_L+2.73$$

VOLTAGE TABLE

VOLTAGE	DEVIATION FACTOR			
	TRANSITION		PROP DELAY	
	TR	TF	1-0	0-1
3.0	1.53	1.79	1.96	1.79
3.5	1.35	1.52	1.63	1.52
4.0	1.17	1.25	1.30	1.25
4.5	1.09	1.13	1.15	1.13
5.0	1.00	1.00	1.00	1.00
5.5	.95	.93	.92	.93
6.0	.90	.86	.83	.85
6.5	.87	.82	.78	.81
7.0	.84	.77	.72	.76

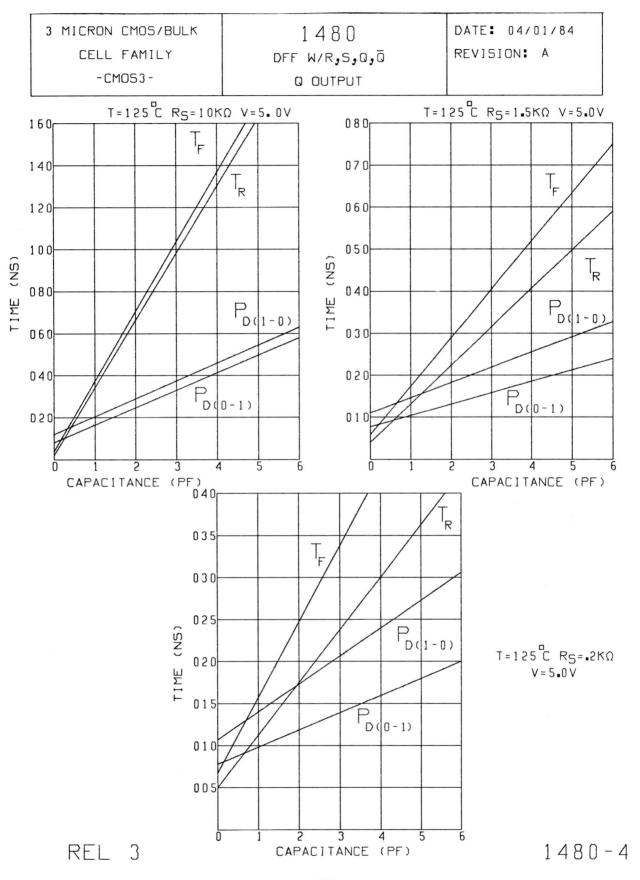

3 MICRON CMOS/BULK CELL FAMILY -CMOS3-	1480 DFF W/R,S,Q,$\overline{Q}$ $\overline{Q}$ OUTPUT	DATE: 04/01/84 REVISION: A

OUTPUT CHARACTERISTIC EQUATIONS

$$P_D(0-1) = P_{DC}(0-1) + .08 \ (T_{R/F} - 10) + .61 \ R_S C_L + 3.90 C_Q$$

$$P_D(1-0) = P_{DC}(1-0) + .08 \ (T_{R/F} - 10) + .57 \ R_S C_L + 2.23 C_Q$$

$$T_R = T_{RC} + 0.0 \ (T_{R/F} - 10) + 2.34 R_S C_L + 2.16 C_Q$$

$$T_F = T_{FC} + 0.0 \ (T_{R/F} - 10) + 2.25 R_S C_L + 0.99 C_Q$$

EQUATIONS

$25\,^\circ C$	$95\,^\circ C$	$125\,^\circ C$
$P_{DC}(0-1) = 1.8 \ C_L + 11.22$	$P_{DC}(0-1) = 2.30 C_L + 13.60$	$P_{DC}(0-1) = 2.50 C_L + 14.52$
$P_{DC}(1-0) = 2.54 C_L + 8.85$	$P_{DC}(1-0) = 3.17 C_L + 10.64$	$P_{DC}(1-0) = 3.42 C_L + 11.33$
$T_{RC} = 5.44 C_L + 3.84$	$T_{RC} = 6.99 C_L + 5.10$	$T_{RC} = 7.64 C_L + 5.61$
$T_{FC} = 6.85 C_L + 3.84$	$T_{FC} = 8.70 C_L + 4.96$	$T_{FC} = 9.46 C_L + 5.42$

$125\,^\circ C$ BC

$$P_{DC}(0-1) = 1.13 C_L + 6.27$$

$$P_{DC}(1-0) = 1.40 C_L + 5.00$$

$$T_{RC} = 3.74 C_L + 2.46$$

$$T_{FC} = 4.34 C_L + 2.27$$

VOLTAGE TABLE

VOLTAGE	DEVIATION FACTOR			
	TRANSITION		PROP DELAY	
	TR	TF	1-0	0-1
3.0	1.55	1.75	1.97	1.92
3.5	1.37	1.50	1.64	1.61
4.0	1.18	1.24	1.31	1.29
4.5	1.09	1.12	1.16	1.15
5.0	1.00	1.00	1.00	1.00
5.5	.95	.94	.92	.92
6.0	.90	.87	.83	.83
6.5	.87	.83	.78	.78
7.0	.83	.78	.72	.73

REL 3   1480-5

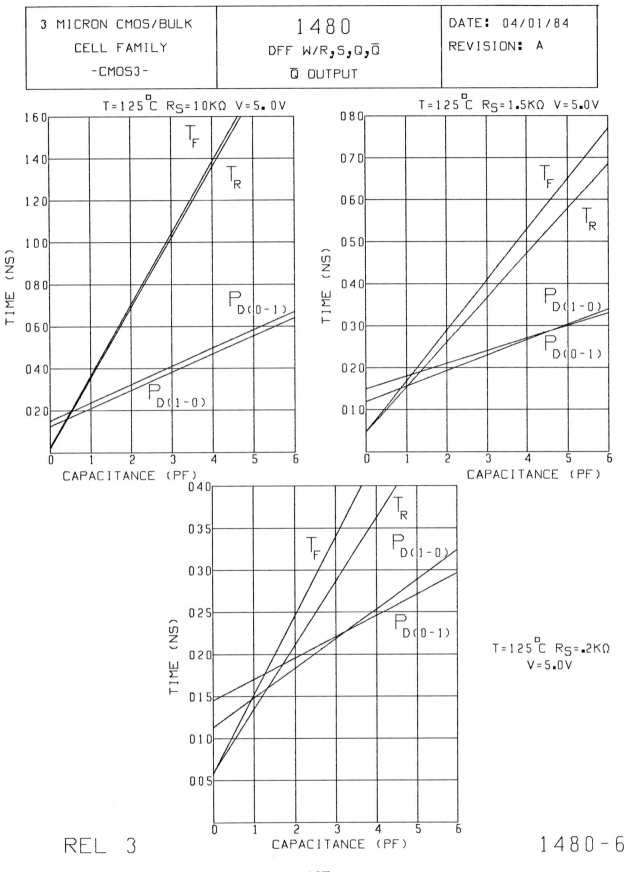

REL 3

1480-6

3 MICRON CMOS/BULK CELL FAMILY -CMOS3-	1480 DFF W/R,S,Q,$\bar{Q}$ SET TO Q,$\bar{Q}$	DATE: 04/01/64 REVISION: A

OUTPUT CHARACTERISTIC EQUATIONS

$$P_D(0-1) = P_{DS}(0-1) + .13(T_{R/F} - 10) + .61 R_S C_L$$

$$P_D(1-0) = P_{DS}(1-0) + .06(T_{R/F} - 10) + .59 R_S C_L + 1.13 C_Q$$

$$T_R = T_{RS} + .28(T_{R/F} - 10) + 2.19 R_S C_L$$

$$T_F = T_{FS} + .02(T_{R/F} - 10) + 2.10 R_S C_L + 0.42 C_Q$$

EQUATIONS

$25^\circ C$	$95^\circ C$	$125^\circ C$
$P_{DS}(0-1) = 1.42 C_L + 3.01$	$P_{DS}(0-1) = 1.80 C_L + 3.16$	$P_{DS}(0-1) = 1.96 C_L + 3.23$
$P_{DS}(1-0) = 2.57 C_L + 5.43$	$P_{DS}(1-0) = 3.20 C_L + 7.60$	$P_{DS}(1-0) = 3.45 C_L + 3.06$
$T_{RS} = 3.70 C_L + 5.30$	$T_{RS} = 4.66 C_L + 6.39$	$T_{RS} = 5.06 C_L + 6.85$
$T_{FS} = 6.78 C_L + 6.39$	$T_{FS} = 3.60 C_L + 8.89$	$T_{FS} = 9.37 C_L + 9.71$

$125^\circ C$ BC
$P_{DS}(0-1) = .96 C_L + 1.76$
$P_{DS}(1-0) = 1.43 C_L + 3.19$
$T_{RS} = 2.01 C_L + 5.34$
$T_{FS} = 4.43 C_L + 4.12$

VOLTAGE TABLE

VOLTAGE   DEVIATION FACTOR

VOLTAGE	TRANSITION		PROP DELAY	
	TR	TF	1-0	0-1
3.0	1.51	1.81	1.90	1.53
3.5	1.34	1.53	1.60	1.36
4.0	1.17	1.25	1.29	1.18
4.5	1.09	1.13	1.15	1.09
5.0	1.00	1.00	1.00	1.00
5.5	.95	.93	.92	.95
6.0	.90	.86	.33	.89
6.5	.87	.32	.78	.85
7.0	.83	.77	.72	.82

REL 3   1480-7

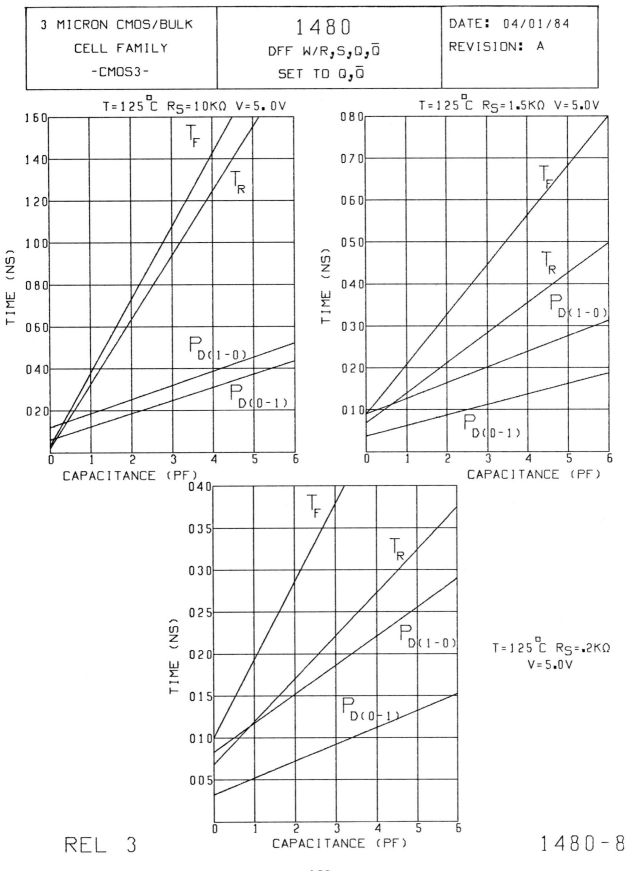

3 MICRON CMOS/BULK	1480	DATE: 04/01/84
CELL FAMILY	DFF W/R,S,Q,$\overline{Q}$	REVISION: A
-CMOS3-	SET TO Q,$\overline{Q}$	

REL 3

1480-8

3 MICRON CMOS/BULK CELL FAMILY -CMOS3-	1480 DFF W/R,S,Q,$\bar{Q}$ RESET TO Q,$\bar{Q}$	DATE: 04/01/84 REVISION: A

OUTPUT CHARACTERISTIC EQUATIONS

$$P_D(0-1)=P_{DR}(0-1)+.17 (T_{R/F}-10)+.61 R_SC_L$$

$$P_D(1-0)=P_{DR}(1-0)+.15 (T_{R/F}-10)+.57 R_SC_L$$

$$T_R=T_{RR}+.26 (T_{R/F}-10)+2.09R_SC_L$$

$$T_F=T_{FR}+0.0 (T_{R/F}-10)+2.19R_SC_L$$

EQUATIONS

25°C
$$P_{DR}(0-1)=1.87C_L+3.70$$
$$P_{DR}(1-0)=2.46C_L+14.89$$
$$T_{RR}=3.98C_L+7.84$$
$$T_{FR}=6.51C_L+4.63$$

95°C
$$P_{DR}(0-1)=2.38C_L+4.08$$
$$P_{DR}(1-0)=3.06C_L+18.37$$
$$T_{RR}=5.09C_L+9.65$$
$$T_{FR}=8.24C_L+5.98$$

125°C
$$P_{DR}(0-1)=2.59C_L+4.26$$
$$P_{DR}(1-0)=3.30C_L+19.79$$
$$T_{RR}=5.57C_L+10.29$$
$$T_{FR}=8.96C_L+6.54$$

125°C BC
$$P_{DR}(0-1)=1.20C_L+2.65$$
$$P_{DR}(1-0)=1.35C_L+9.23$$
$$T_{RR}=2.55C_L+6.32$$
$$T_{FR}=4.03C_L+2.73$$

VOLTAGE TABLE

VOLTAGE	DEVIATION FACTOR			
	TRANSITION		PROP DELAY	
	TR	TF	1-0	0-1
3.0	1.67	1.80	1.98	1.52
3.5	1.44	1.53	1.65	1.35
4.0	1.21	1.25	1.31	1.18
4.5	1.11	1.13	1.16	1.09
5.0	1.00	1.00	1.00	1.00
5.5	.95	.93	.92	.95
6.0	.89	.86	.83	.89
6.5	.85	.82	.78	.86
7.0	.81	.77	.72	.82

REL 3   1480-9

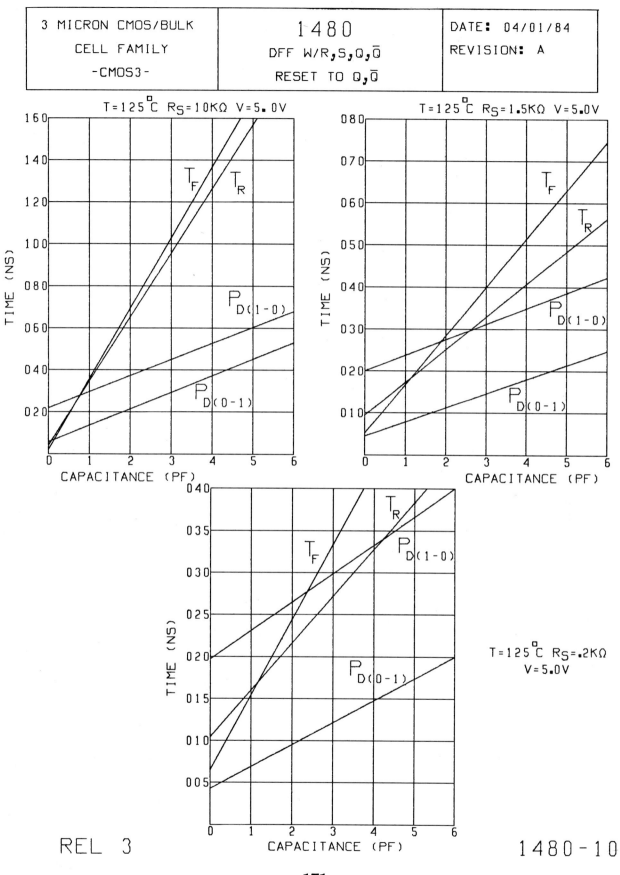

3 MICRON CMOS/BULK CELL FAMILY -CMOS3-	1480 DFF W/R,S,Q,Q̄	DATE: 04/01/84 REVISION: A

SPECIAL FLIP FLOP TIMING

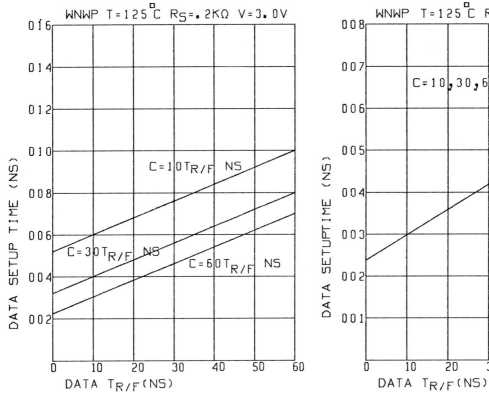

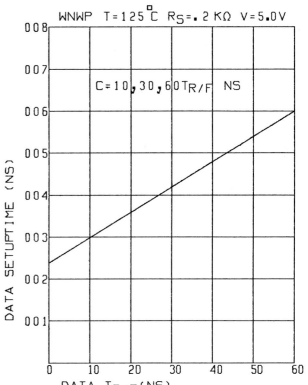

3 MICRON CMOS/BULK CELL FAMILY -CMOS3-	1480 DFF W/R,S,Q,Q̄	DATE: 04/01/84 REVISION: A

SPECIAL FLIP FLOP TIMING

MINIMUM CLOCK PULSE WIDTH = 28NS

MINIMUM RESET PULSE WIDTH = 32NS

MINIMUM SET PULSE WIDTH = 25NS

MAXIMUM CLOCK RISE/FALL TIME = 200NS

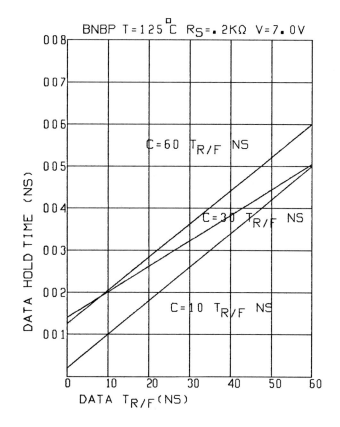

REL 3   1480-12

| 3 MICRON CMOS/BULK CELL FAMILY -CMOS3- | | | 1480 DFF W/R,S,Q,$\overline{Q}$ | | | | DATE: 04/01/84 REVISION: A |

SET	R	C	D	M	Q	$\overline{Q}$	SPECIAL CASES
0	0	*	*	1	1	1	
0	1	*	*	1	1	0	
0	X	*	*	1	1	X	
1	0	0	*	0	0	1	
1	0	1	0	0	0	1	
1	0	1	1	1	0	1	
1	0	1	X	X	0	1	
1	0	X	0	0	0	1	
1	0	X	1	X	0	1	
1	0	X	X	X	0	1	
1	1	0	*	M_{T-1}	M_{T-1}	$\overline{M_{T-1}}$	
1	1	1	0	0	Q_{T-1}	$\overline{Q}_{T-1}$	
1	1	1	1	1	Q_{T-1}	$\overline{Q}_{T-1}$	
1	1	1	X	X	Q_{T-1}	$\overline{Q}_{T-1}$	
1	1	X	0	X	X	X	IF $M_{T-1}=0$ THEN M=0 / IF $M_{T-1}=Q_{T-1}$ THEN $Q=Q_{T-1}$ AND $\overline{Q}=(\overline{Q_{T-1}})$
1	1	X	1	X	X	X	IF $M_{T-1}=1$ THEN M=1 / IF $M_{T-1}=Q_{T-1}$ THEN $Q=Q_{T-1}$ AND $Q=(\overline{Q_{T-1}})$
1	1	X	X	X	X	X	IF $M_{T-1}=Q_{T-1}$ THEN $Q=Q_{T-1}$ AND $\overline{Q}=(\overline{Q_{T-1}})$
1	X	0	*	X	X	X	IF $M_{T-1}=0$ THEN M=0 AND Q=0 AND $\overline{Q}=1$
1	X	1	0	0	X	X	
1	X	1	1	1	X	X	IF $Q_{T-1}=0$ THEN Q=0 AND $\overline{Q}=1$
1	X	1	X	X	X	X	IF $M_{T-1}=0$ THEN M=0
1	X	X	0	X	X	X	IF $M_{T-1}=0$ AND $Q_{T-1}=0$ THEN Q=0 AND $\overline{Q}=1$
1	X	X	1	X	X	X	IF $M_{T-1}=0$ AND $Q_{T-1}=0$ THEN Q=0 AND $\overline{Q}=1$
1	X	X	X	X	X	X	
X	0	0	*	X	X	1	
X	0	1	0	X	X	1	
X	0	1	1	1	X	1	
X	0	1	X	X	X	1	
X	0	X	*	X	X	1	IF $M_{T-1}=1$ THEN M=1 AND Q=1 AND $\overline{Q}=0$
X	1	0	*	X	X	X	
X	1	1	0	X	X	X	IF $Q_{T-1}=1$ THEN Q=1 AND $\overline{Q}=0$
X	1	1	1	1	X	X	
X	1	1	X	X	X	X	IF $M_{T-1}=1$ THEN M=1 / IF $M_{T-1}=1$ AND $Q_{T-1}=1$ THEN Q=1 AND $\overline{Q}=0$
X	1	X	*	X	X	X	IF $M_{T-1}=1$ AND $Q_{T-1}=1$ THEN Q=1 AND $Q=0$
X	1	X	X	X	X	X	
X	X	0	*	X	X	X	
X	X	1	0	X	X	X	
X	X	1	1	1	X	X	
X	X	1	X	X	X	X	
X	X	X	*	X	X	X	

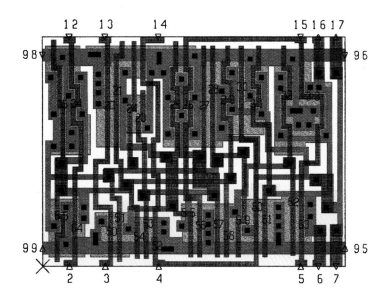

3 MICRON CMOS/BULK CELL FAMILY -CMOS3-	1510 NON INVERTING BUFFER CELL HEIGHT 150 WIDTH 72	DATE: 04/10/86 REVISION:

TERMINAL INFORMATION

NAME	TERMINAL NUMBER	LOGIC FIELD	CAPACITANCE (PF)
IN	3,13	1	.27
OUT	2,12	6	

LOGIC DIAGRAM

IN,3 ▷◦———▷◦ OUT,2

TRUTH TABLE

IN	OUT
0	0
1	1
X	X

LOGIC SYMBOLS

IN,3 ——▷
OUT,2 ——▷

WORST CASE DELAY INFORMATION

P_D = 7.11 NS $T_{R/F}$ = 9.24 NS

R_S = 1.5KΩ, C_L = 1.5PF, V=5V, T=125°C

LOGIC EQUATION(S)

OUT=IN

NOTES

1510-1

176

CIRCUIT SCHEMATIC

VDD
20(3/86)

VDD
21(3/341)

3,13

2,12

50(3/42)

51(3/161)

VSS

VSS

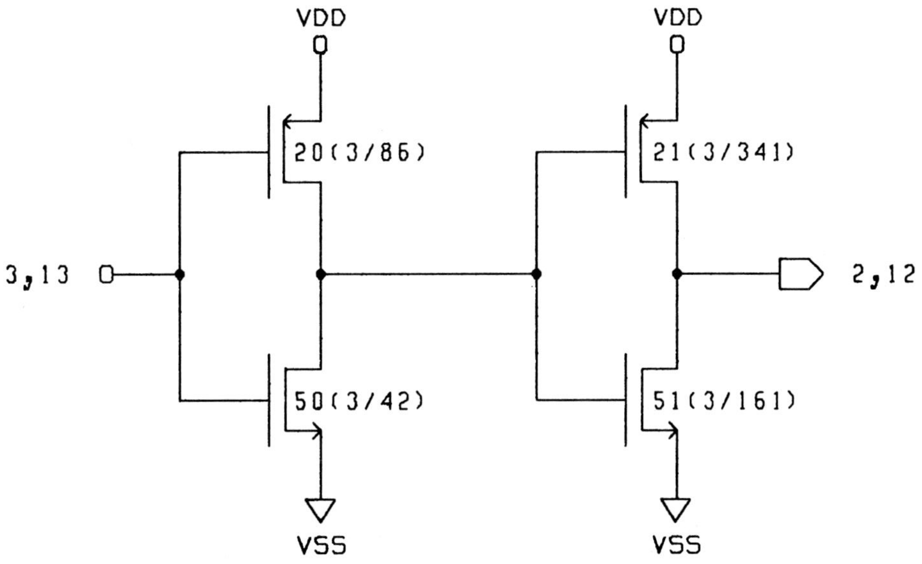

1510-2

3 MICRON CMOS/BULK CELL FAMILY -CMOS3-	1510 NON INVERTING BUFFER	DATE: 04/10/86 REVISION:

OUTPUT CHARACTERISTIC EQUATIONS

$$P_D(0-1) = P_{DC}(0-1) + .12 \ (T_{R/F} - 10) + .67 \ R_S C_L$$

$$P_D(1-0) = P_{DC}(1-0) + .10 \ (T_{R/F} - 10) + .66 \ R_S C_L$$

$$T_R = T_{RC} + .04 \ (T_{R/F} - 10) + 2.63 R_S C_L$$

$$T_F = T_{FC} + .04 \ (T_{R/F} - 10) + 2.63 R_S C_L$$

EQUATIONS

25°C

$$P_{DC}(0-1) = .48 C_L + 4.16$$

$$P_{DC}(1-0) = .46 C_L + 4.25$$

$$T_{RC} = 1.56 C_L + 1.27$$

$$T_{FC} = 1.41 C_L + 1.20$$

95°C

$$P_{DC}(0-1) = .60 C_L + 4.64$$

$$P_{DC}(1-0) = .56 C_L + 4.87$$

$$T_{RC} = 1.93 C_L + 1.63$$

$$T_{FC} = 1.71 C_L + 1.56$$

125°C

$$P_{DC}(0-1) = .65 C_L + 4.80$$

$$P_{DC}(1-0) = .61 C_L + 5.11$$

$$T_{RC} = 2.09 C_L + 1.78$$

$$T_{FC} = 1.84 C_L + 1.71$$

125°C BC

$$P_{DC}(0-1) = .44 C_L + 2.48$$

$$P_{DC}(1-0) = .41 C_L + 2.64$$

$$T_{RC} = 1.50 C_L + 1.29$$

$$T_{FC} = 1.37 C_L + 1.28$$

VOLTAGE TABLE

VOLTAGE   DEVIATION FACTOR

VOLTAGE	TRANSITION		PROP DELAY	
	TR	TF	1-0	0-1
3.0	1.22	1.21	1.60	1.58
3.5	1.14	1.14	1.40	1.38
4.0	1.06	1.06	1.19	1.19
4.5	1.03	1.03	1.09	1.09
5.0	1.00	1.00	1.00	1.00
5.5	.98	.99	.95	.95
6.0	.97	.97	.89	.89
6.5	.96	.96	.85	.85
7.0	.95	.95	.81	.81

1510-3

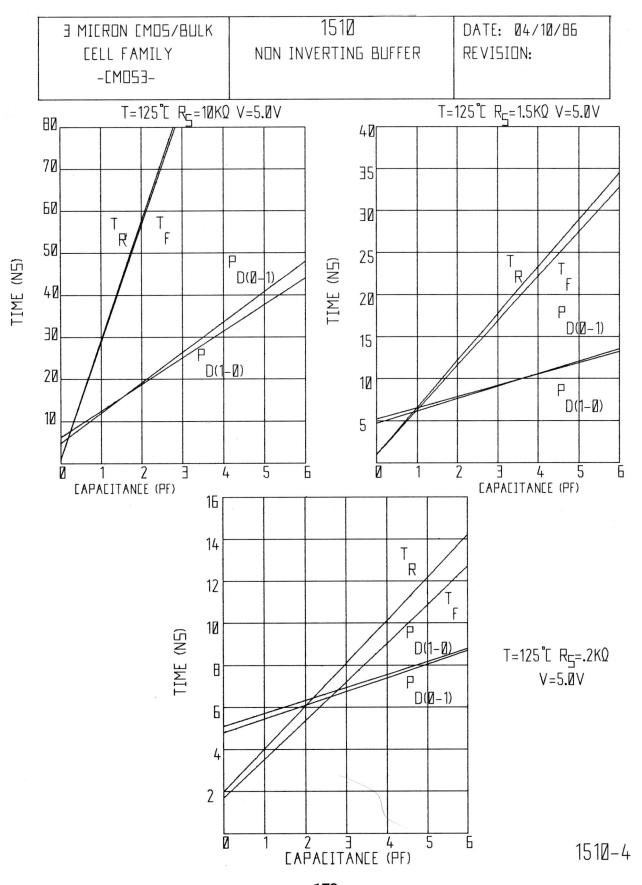

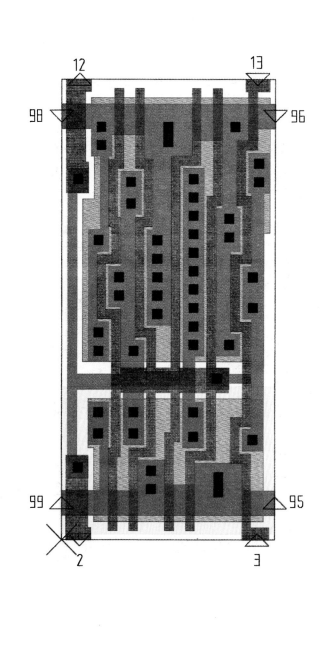

1510-5

180

3 MICRON CMOS/BULK	1520	DATE: 09/01/83
CELL FAMILY	4X INVERTING BUFFER	REVISION:
-CMOS3-	CELL HEIGHT 150 WIDTH 60	

TERMINAL INFORMATION

TERMINAL NAME	LOGIC NUMBER	CAPACITANCE FIELD	(PF)
OUT	2,12	6	
IN	3,13	1	1.03

LOGIC DIAGRAM

SAME AS LOGIC SYMBOL

TRUTH TABLE

IN	OUT
0	1
1	0
X	X

LOGIC SYMBOLS

IN,3 ———▷○——— OUT,2

WORST CASE DELAY INFORMATION

P_D= 3.69 NS $T_{R/F}$= 9.59 NS

R_S=1.5KΩ, C_L=1.5PF, V=5V, T=125°C

LOGIC EQUATION(S)

OUT = $\overline{IN}$

NOTES

REL 3   1520-1

181

CIRCUIT SCHEMATIC

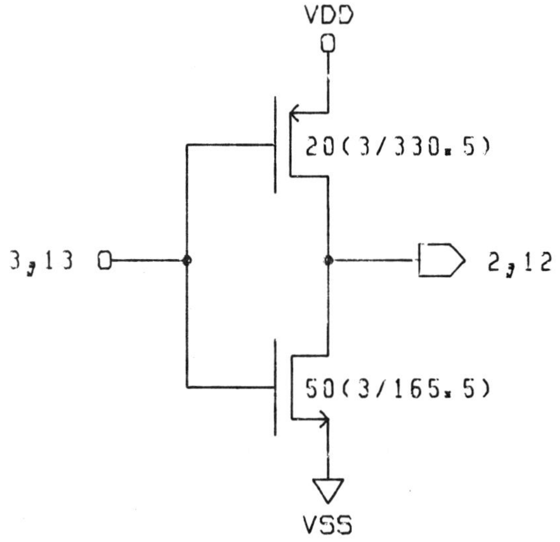

REL 3   1520-2

3 MICRON CMOS/BULK CELL FAMILY -CMOS3-	1520 4X INVERTING BUFFER	DATE: 09/01/83 REVISION:

OUTPUT CHARACTERISTIC EQUATIONS

$$P_D(0-1)=P_{DC}(0-1)+0.05(T_{R/F}-10)+0.65R_SC_L$$

$$P_D(1-0)=P_{DC}(1-0)+0.07(T_{R/F}-10)+0.64R_SC_L$$

$$T_R=T_{RC}+0.23(T_{R/F}-10)+2.55R_SC_L$$

$$T_F=T_{FC}+0.23(T_{R/F}-10)+2.58R_SC_L$$

EQUATIONS

25°C	95°C	125°C
$P_{DC}(0-1)=0.58C_L+1.28$	$P_{DC}(0-1)=0.66C_L+1.43$	$P_{DC}(0-1)=0.70C_L+1.49$
$P_{DC}(1-0)=0.52C_L+1.61$	$P_{DC}(1-0)=0.59C_L+1.76$	$P_{DC}(1-0)=0.62C_L+1.81$
$T_{RC}=1.40C_L+2.54$	$T_{RC}=1.68C_L+3.00$	$T_{RC}=1.92C_L+3.17$
$T_{FC}=1.22C_L+2.19$	$T_{FC}=1.45C_L+2.49$	$T_{FC}=1.54C_L+2.62$

125°C BC

$$P_{DC}(0-1)=0.45C_L+0.80$$

$$P_{DC}(1-0)=0.42C_L+0.86$$

$$T_{RC}=0.97C_L+3.74$$

$$T_{FC}=0.85C_L+3.49$$

VOLTAGE TABLE

VOLTAGE   DEVIATION FACTOR

VOLTAGE	TRANSITION		PROP DELAY	
	TR	TF	1-0	0-1
3.0	1.14	1.12	1.44	1.41
3.5	1.09	1.08	1.30	1.27
4.0	1.04	1.04	1.15	1.14
4.5	1.02	1.02	1.08	1.07
5.0	1.00	1.00	1.00	1.00
5.5	.99	.99	.96	.96
6.0	.98	.98	.91	.93
6.5	.97	.98	.88	.90
7.0	.97	.98	.85	.88

REL 3   1520-3

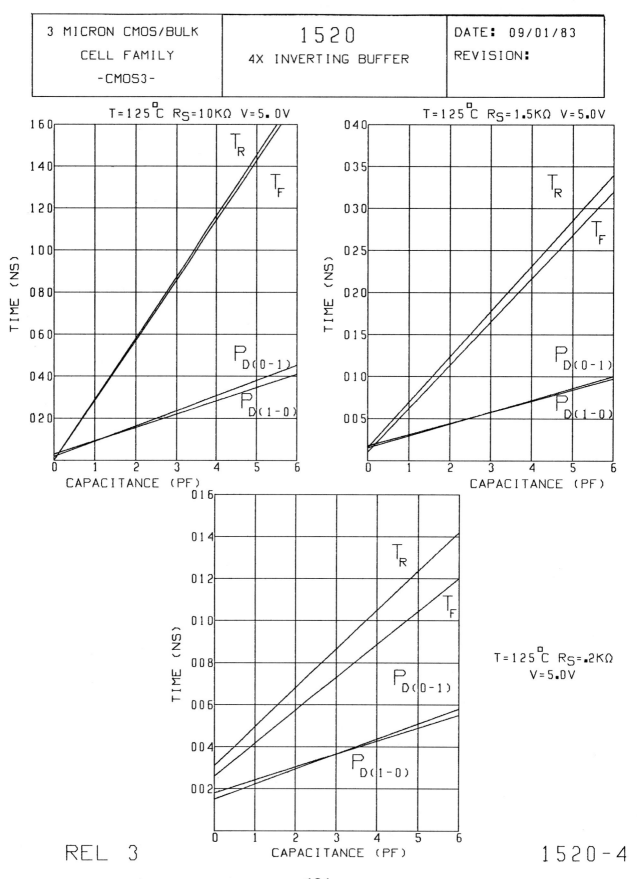

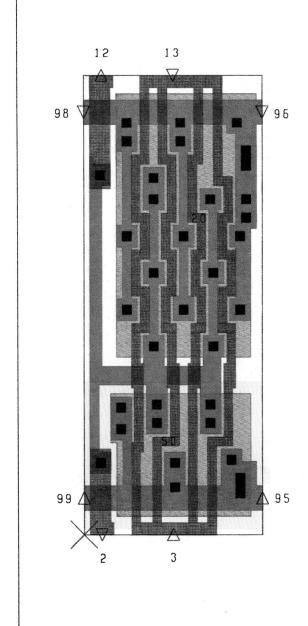

REL 3   1520-5

185

3 MICRON CMOS/BULK CELL FAMILY -CMOS3-	1530 CLOCKED LATCH CELL HEIGHT 150 WIDTH 120	DATE: 04/01/84 REVISION: B

TERMINAL INFORMATION

TERMINAL NAME	NUMBER	LOGIC FIELD	CAPACITANCE (PF)
CLOCK	2,12	1	.26
DATA	3,13	2	.25
$\bar{Q}$	4,14	7	
RESET	5,15	3	.26
Q	6,16	6	

LOGIC DIAGRAM

TRUTH TABLE

C	D	R	Q_N	$\bar{Q}_N$	
⟍	*	1	DATA	DATA	
*	*	0	0	1	
⟍	*	1	Q_{N-1}	$\bar{Q}_{N-1}$	
X	0	1	X	X	IF $Q_{N-1}=0$ THEN Q=0
X	1	1	X	X	IF $Q_{N-1}=1$ THEN Q=1
0	0	X	0	1	
1	*	X	X	X	IF $Q_{N-1}=0$ THEN Q=0
X	0	X	X	X	IF $Q_{N-1}=0$ THEN Q=0

FOR ALL OTHER CONDITIONS Q=X

LOGIC SYMBOLS

WORST CASE DELAY INFORMATION

Q $P_D = 18.71$ NS $T_{R/F} = 16.0$ NS

$\bar{Q}$ $P_D = 19.15$ NS $T_{R/F} = 27.24$ NS

$R_S = 1.5K\Omega$, $C_L = 1.5PF$, V=5V, T=125°C

LOGIC EQUATION(S)

$$Q_N = \overline{(Q_{N-1}C + D\bar{C})R}$$
$$\bar{Q}_N = (Q_{N-1}C + D\bar{C})R$$

NOTES

CIRCUIT SCHEMATIC

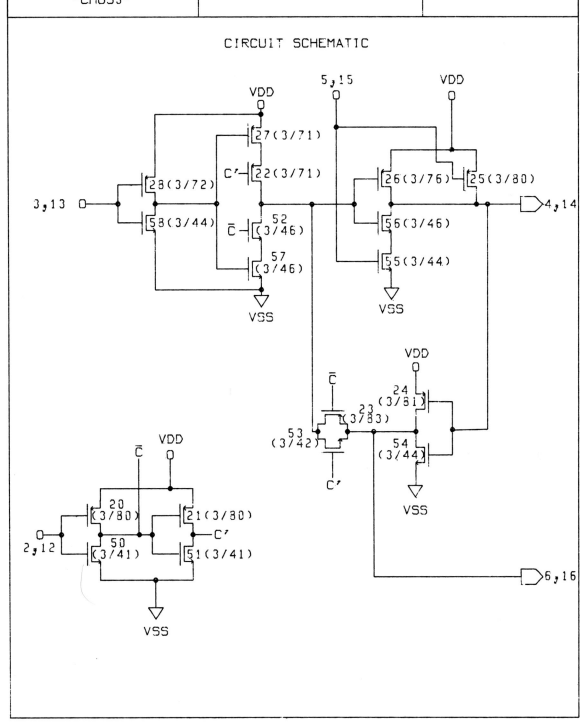

3 MICRON CMOS/BULK CELL FAMILY -CMOS3-	1530 CLOCKED LATCH Q OUTPUT	DATE: 04/01/84 REVISION: B

OUTPUT CHARACTERISTIC EQUATIONS

$$P_D(0-1)=P_{DC}(0-1)+.09\ (T_{R/F}-10)+.62\ R_S C_L+1.24 C_{L_{\bar{Q}}}$$

$$P_D(1-0)=P_{DC}(1-0)+.09\ (T_{R/F}-10)+.62\ R_S C_L+.79 C_{L_{\bar{Q}}}$$

$$T_R=T_{RC}+.00\ (T_{R/F}-10)+2.47 R_S C_L+1.56 C_{L_{\bar{Q}}}$$

$$T_F=T_{FC}+.00\ (T_{R/F}-10)+2.52 R_S C_L+1.18 C_{L_{\bar{Q}}}$$

EQUATIONS

$25^\circ C$	$95^\circ C$	$125^\circ C$
$P_{DC}(0-1)=1.34 C_L+11.51$	$P_{DC}(0-1)=1.72 C_L+13.95$	$P_{DC}(0-1)=1.87 C_L+14.91$
$P_{DC}(1-0)=1.10 C_L+8.48$	$P_{DC}(1-0)=1.40 C_L+10.14$	$P_{DC}(1-0)=1.51 C_L+10.78$
$T_{RC}=4.14 C_L+2.51$	$T_{RC}=5.30 C_L+3.32$	$T_{RC}=5.78 C_L+3.66$
$T_{FC}=3.15 C_L+1.85$	$T_{FC}=3.99 C_L+2.41$	$T_{FC}=4.34 C_L+2.64$

$125^\circ C$ BC

$$P_{DC}(0-1)=.88\ C_L+6.53$$

$$P_{DC}(1-0)=.69\ C_L+4.33$$

$$T_{RC}=2.96 C_L+1.55$$

$$T_{FC}=2.27 C_L+1.09$$

VOLTAGE TABLE

VOLTAGE	DEVIATION FACTOR			
	TRANSITION		PROP DELAY	
	TR	TF	1-0	0-1
3.0	1.47	1.48	1.39	1.91
3.5	1.31	1.32	1.59	1.60
4.0	1.15	1.15	1.28	1.29
4.5	1.08	1.08	1.14	1.15
5.0	1.00	1.00	1.00	1.00
5.5	.96	.96	.92	.92
6.0	.91	.92	.84	.84
6.5	.89	.90	.79	.79
7.0	.86	.87	.74	.73

REL 3   1530-3

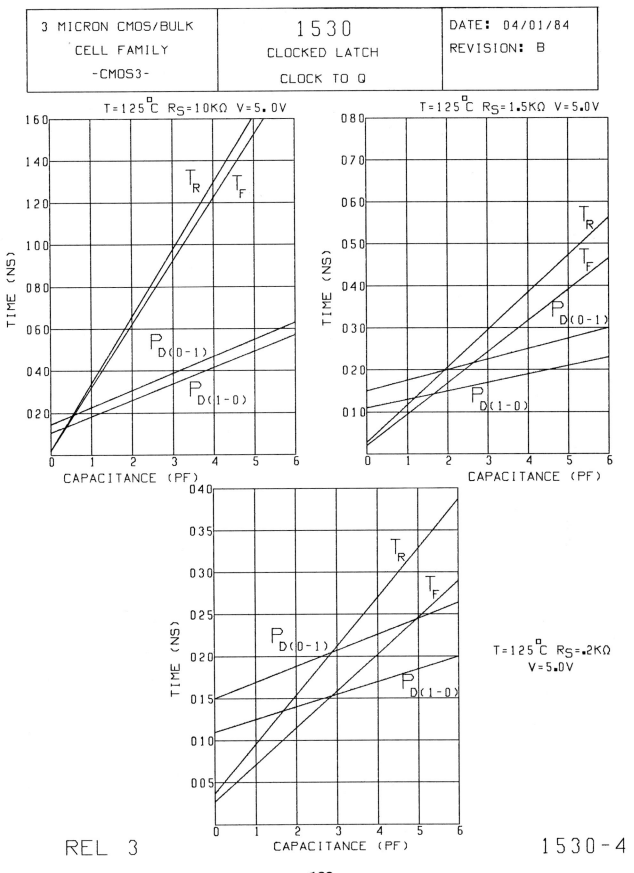

3 MICRON CMOS/BULK CELL FAMILY -CMOS3-	1530 CLOCKED LATCH CLOCK TO Q	DATE: 04/01/84 REVISION: B

REL 3

1530-4

189

3 MICRON CMOS/BULK CELL FAMILY -CMOS3-	1530 CLOCKED LATCH $\bar{Q}$ OUTPUT	DATE: 04/01/84 REVISION: B

OUTPUT CHARACTERISTIC EQUATIONS

$$P_D(0-1) = P_{DC}(0-1) + .09 (T_{R/F} - 10) + .68 R_S C_L$$

$$P_D(1-0) = P_{DC}(1-0) + .09 (T_{R/F} - 10) + .64 R_S C_L$$

$$T_R = T_{RC} + .00 (T_{R/F} - 10) + 2.55 R_S C_L$$

$$T_F = T_{FC} + .00 (T_{R/F} - 10) + 2.46 R_S C_L$$

EQUATIONS

$25^{\circ}C$	$95^{\circ}C$	$125^{\circ}C$
$P_{DC}(0-1) = 2.08C_L + 6.90$	$P_{DC}(0-1) = 2.75C_L + 8.20$	$P_{DC}(0-1) = 3.04C_L + 8.73$
$P_{DC}(1-0) = 2.43C_L + 9.96$	$P_{DC}(1-0) = 3.15C_L + 12.05$	$P_{DC}(1-0) = 3.46C_L + 12.86$
$T_{RC} = 7.64C_L + 2.52$	$T_{RC} = 10.12C_L + 3.28$	$T_{RC} = 11.21C_L + 3.60$
$T_{FC} = 8.27C_L + 3.74$	$T_{FC} = 10.86C_L + 4.80$	$T_{FC} = 12.0C_L + 5.21$

$125^{\circ}C$ BC

$$P_{DC}(0-1) = 1.73C_L + 4.13$$

$$P_{DC}(1-0) = 1.86C_L + 5.74$$

$$T_{RC} = 6.65C_L + 1.43$$

$$T_{FC} = 6.90C_L + 1.98$$

VOLTAGE TABLE

VOLTAGE	TRANSITION		PROP DELAY	
	TR	TF	1-0	0-1
3.0	1.30	1.48	1.82	1.65
3.5	1.20	1.32	1.54	1.43
4.0	1.10	1.15	1.26	1.21
4.5	1.05	1.08	1.13	1.11
5.0	1.00	1.00	1.00	1.00
5.5	.97	.96	.93	.94
6.0	.94	.92	.86	.88
6.5	.93	.90	.82	.85
7.0	.91	.87	.77	.81

REL 3   1530-5

190

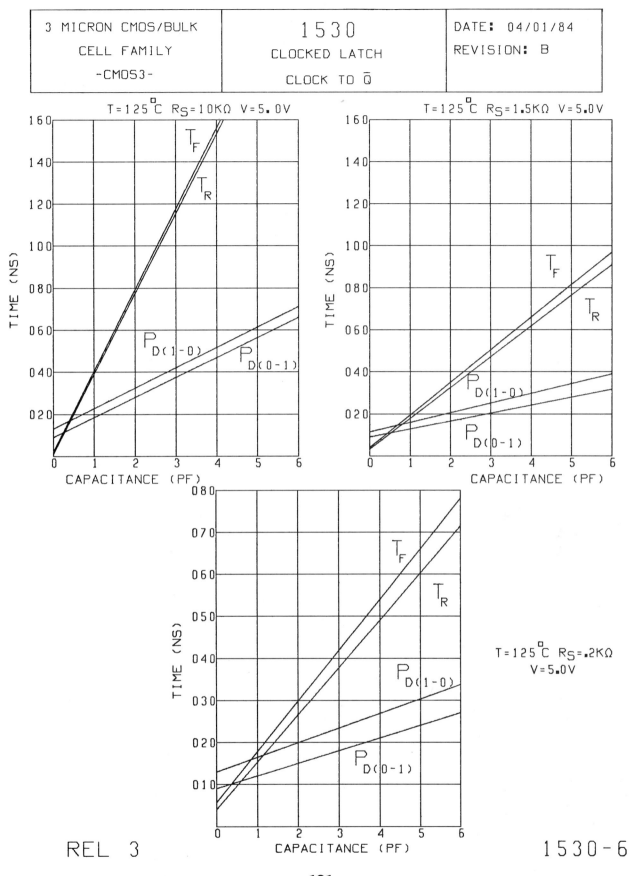

OUTPUT CHARACTERISTIC EQUATIONS

$$P_D(0-1) = P_{DR}(0-1) + .12 (T_{R/F}-10) + .64 R_S C_L$$

$$P_D(1-0) = P_{DR}(1-0) + .10 (T_{R/F}-10) + .64 R_S C_L + .86 C_{L\bar{Q}}$$

$$T_R = T_{RR} + .21 (T_{R/F}-10) + 2.45 R_S C_L$$

$$T_F = T_{FR} + .02 (T_{R/F}-10) + 2.38 R_S C_L + 1.0 C_{L\bar{Q}}$$

EQUATIONS

25°C

$$P_{DR}(0-1) = 2.0 C_L + 3.18$$

$$P_{DR}(1-0) = 1.16 C_L + 5.42$$

$$T_{RR} = 5.96 C_L + 4.73$$

$$T_{FR} = 3.06 C_L + 3.90$$

95°C

$$P_{DR}(0-1) = 2.53 C_L + 3.58$$

$$P_{DR}(1-0) = 1.46 C_L + 6.31$$

$$T_{RR} = 7.93 C_L + 5.50$$

$$T_{FR} = 3.88 C_L + 5.01$$

125°C

$$P_{DR}(0-1) = 2.82 C_L + 3.75$$

$$P_{DR}(1-0) = 1.57 C_L + 6.66$$

$$T_{RR} = 8.82 C_L + 5.79$$

$$T_{FR} = 4.23 C_L + 5.46$$

125°C BC

$$P_{DR}(0-1) = 1.51 C_L + 2.25$$

$$P_{DR}(1-0) = .72 C_L + 3.23$$

$$T_{RR} = 5.22 C_L + 3.89$$

$$T_{FR} = 2.16 C_L + 2.52$$

VOLTAGE TABLE

VOLTAGE	DEVIATION FACTOR			
	TRANSITION		PROP DELAY	
	TR	TF	1-0	0-1
3.0	1.33	1.60	1.71	1.33
3.5	1.22	1.40	1.47	1.26
4.0	1.10	1.19	1.23	1.13
4.5	1.05	1.10	1.12	1.07
5.0	1.00	1.00	1.00	1.00
5.5	.98	.95	.93	.96
6.0	.95	.90	.86	.92
6.5	.94	.87	.82	.89
7.0	.92	.84	.77	.86
	$\bar{Q}$	Q	Q	$\bar{Q}$

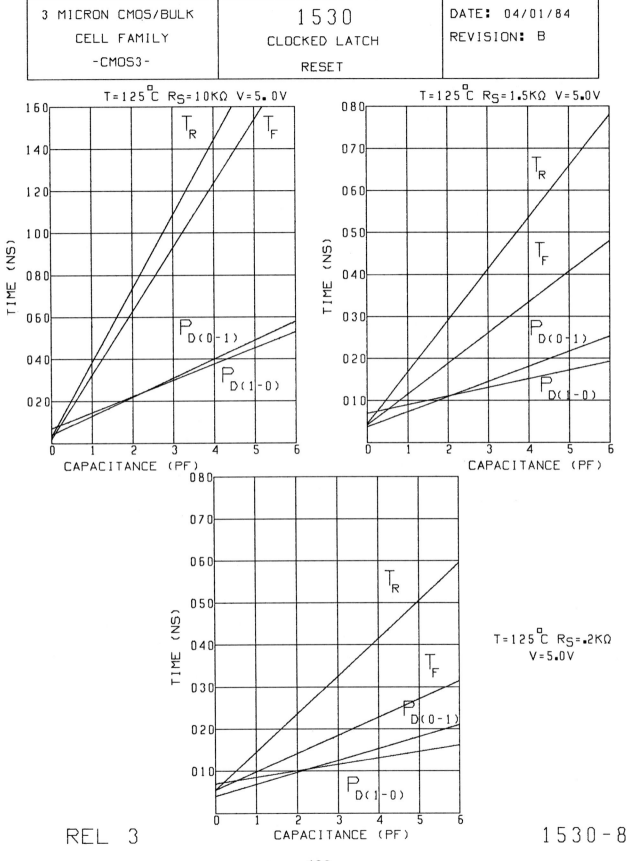

3 MICRON CMOS/BULK CELL FAMILY -CMOS3-	1530 CLOCKED LATCH	DATE: 04/01/84 REVISION: B

SPECIAL FLIP FLOP TIMING

MINIMUM CLOCK PULSE WIDTH = 27NS

MINIMUM RESET PULSE WIDTH = 22NS

HOLD TIME IS 0 NS AT 7V FOR ALL

COMBINATIONS OF: CLOCK $T_{R/F}$ 10NS,30NS,60NS

DATA $T_{R/F}$ 10NS,60NS

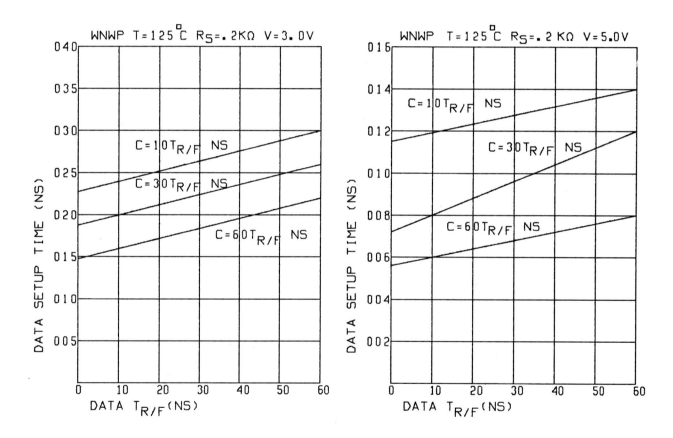

REL 3

1530-9

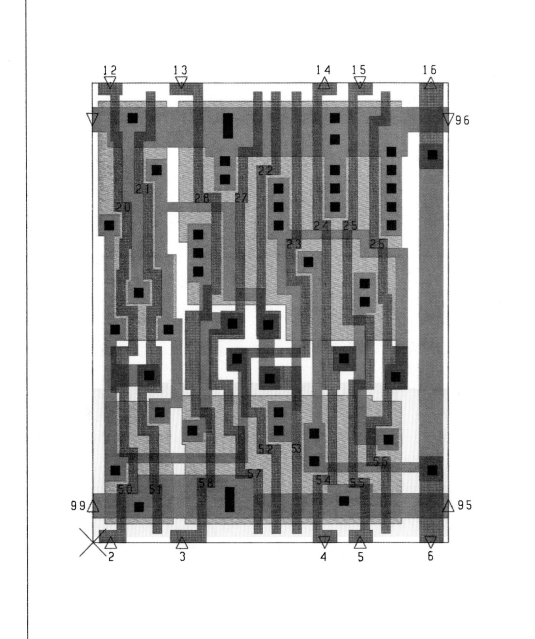

REL 3 1530-10

3 MICRON CMOS/BULK CELL FAMILY -CMOS3-	1540 HI IMPEDANCE INV CELL HEIGHT 150 WIDTH 24	DATE: 04/01/84 REVISION: B

TERMINAL INFORMATION

TERMINAL NAME	TERMINAL NUMBER	LOGIC FIELD	CAPACITANCE (PF)
A	3,13	1	.11
OUT	2,12	6	

LOGIC DIAGRAM

SAME AS LOGIC SYMBOL

TRUTH TABLE

A	OUT
0	1
1	0
X	X

LOGIC SYMBOLS

A,3 ———|>———OUT,2

WORST CASE DELAY INFORMATION

P_D = 56.0 NS $T_{R/F}$ = 162.0 NS

R_S = 1.5KΩ, C_L = 1.5PF, V=5V, T=125°C

LOGIC EQUATION(S)

OUT = $\overline{A}$

NOTES

1. USE FOR LOW SPEED (DELAY) INVERTER.

1540-1

CIRCUIT SCHEMATIC

VDD

20 (4/6)

3,13

2,12

50 (7/5)

VSS

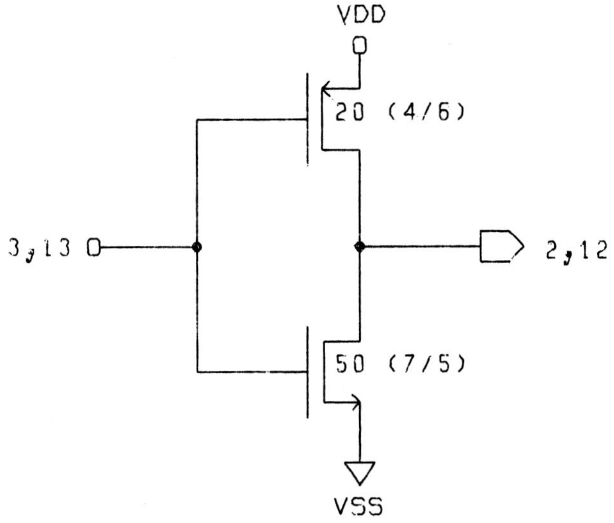

1540-2

3 MICRON CMOS/BULK CELL FAMILY -CMOS3-	1540 HI IMPEDANCE INV	DATE: 04/01/84 REVISION: B

OUTPUT CHARACTERISTIC EQUATIONS

$$P_D(0-1)=P_{DC}(0-1)+.17 \ (T_{R/F}-10)+.36 \ R_S C_L$$

$$P_D(1-0)=P_{DC}(1-0)+.26 \ (T_{R/F}-10)+.28 \ R_S C_L$$

$$T_R=T_{RC}+0 \quad (T_{R/F}-10)+1.84 R_S C_L$$

$$T_F=T_{FC}+.02 \ (T_{R/F}-10)+1.60 R_S C_L$$

EQUATIONS

$25°C$	$95°C$	$125°C$
$P_{DC}(0-1)=22.3C_L+7.07$	$P_{DC}(0-1)=27.0C_L+10.6$	$P_{DC}(0-1)=28.3C_L+13.0$
$P_{DC}(1-0)=23.4C_L+3.19$	$P_{DC}(1-0)=29.3C_L+3.11$	$P_{DC}(1-0)=31.6C_L+3.07$
$T_{RC}=66.2C_L+12.3$	$T_{RC}=86.0C_L+16.1$	$T_{RC}=94.2C_L+17.8$
$T_{FC}=59.8C_L+11.27$	$T_{FC}=76.4C_L+14.4$	$T_{FC}=83.2C_L+15.7$

$125°C$ BC

$$P_{DC}(0-1)=13.3C_L+4.03$$

$$P_{DC}(1-0)=12.6C_L+2.57$$

$$T_{RC}=41.9C_L+7.68$$

$$T_{FC}=35.5C_L+6.75$$

VOLTAGE TABLE

VOLTAGE　　　　DEVIATION FACTOR

VOLTAGE	TRANSITION		PROP DELAY	
	TR	TF	1-0	0-1
3.0	1.68	1.88	2.62	1.73
3.5	1.45	1.58	2.13	1.49
4.0	1.23	1.28	1.65	1.24
4.5	1.11	1.14	1.32	1.12
5.0	1.00	1.00	1.00	1.00
5.5	.93	.92	.91	.93
6.0	.87	.84	.58	.86
6.5	.82	.79	.47	.81
7.0	.78	.73	.35	.76

1540-3

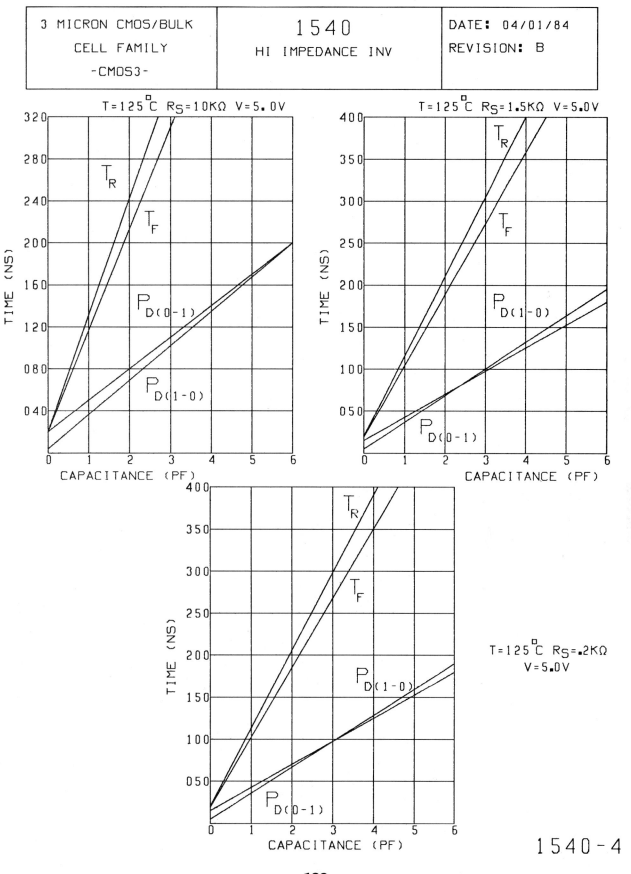

1540-4

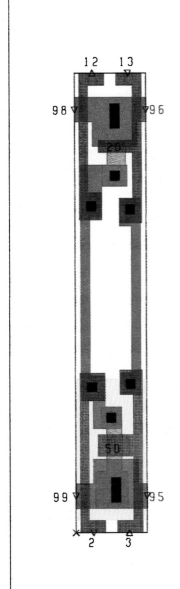

1540-5

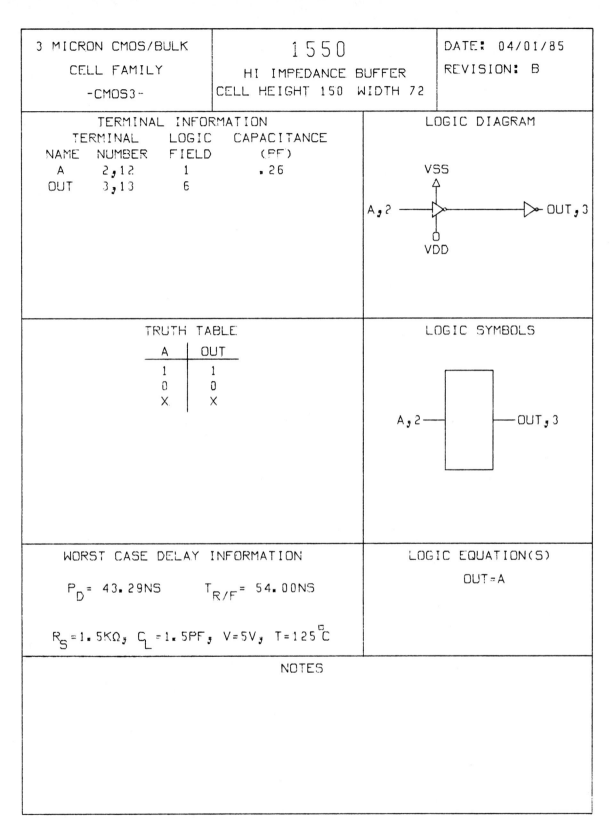

| 3 MICRON CMOS/BULK CELL FAMILY -CMOS3- | 1550 HI IMPEDANCE BUFFER CELL HEIGHT 150 WIDTH 72 | DATE: 04/01/85 REVISION: B |

TERMINAL INFORMATION

TERMINAL NAME	NUMBER	LOGIC FIELD	CAPACITANCE (PF)
A	2,12	1	.26
OUT	3,13	6	

LOGIC DIAGRAM

TRUTH TABLE

A	OUT
1	1
0	0
X	X

LOGIC SYMBOLS

WORST CASE DELAY INFORMATION

P_D = 43.29NS $T_{R/F}$ = 54.00NS

R_S = 1.5KΩ, C_L = 1.5PF, V=5V, T=125°C

LOGIC EQUATION(S)

OUT = A

NOTES

REL 3   1550-1

CIRCUIT SCHEMATIC

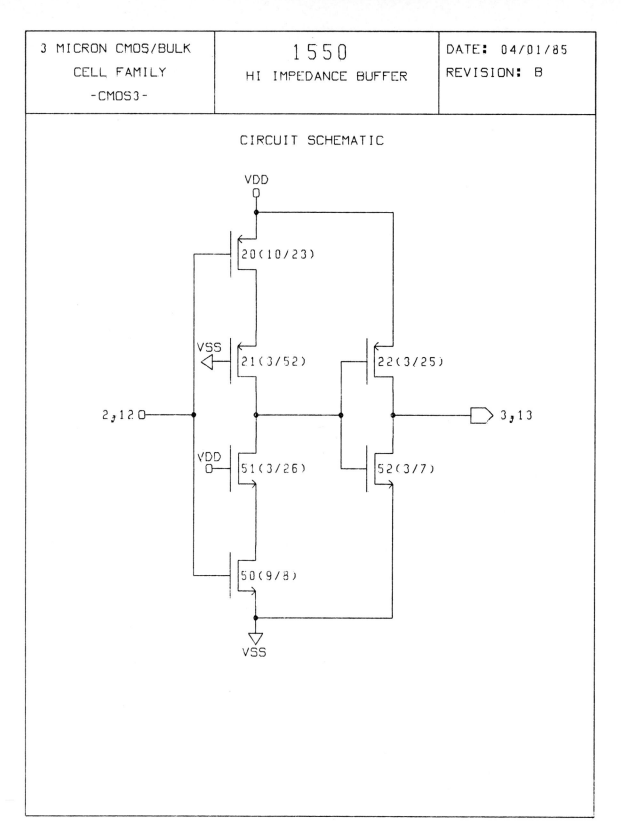

REL 3   1550-2

OUTPUT CHARACTERISTIC EQUATIONS

$$P_D(0-1) = P_{DC}(0-1) + .28 \ (T_{R/F} - 10) + .51 \ R_S C_L$$

$$P_D(1-0) = P_{DC}(1-0) + .17 \ (T_{R/F} - 10) + .41 \ R_S C_L$$

$$T_R = T_{RC} + 0 \quad (T_{R/F} - 10) + 2.09 R_S C_L$$

$$T_F = T_{FC} + 0 \quad (T_{R/F} - 10) + 1.39 R_S C_L$$

EQUATIONS

25°C

$$P_{DC}(0-1) = 4.67 C_L + 13.85$$

$$P_{DC}(1-0) = 6.78 C_L + 21.66$$

$$T_{RC} = 14.17 C_L + 8.98$$

$$T_{FC} = 18.30 C_L + 10.58$$

95°C

$$P_{DC}(0-1) = 6.07 C_L + 22.52$$

$$P_{DC}(1-0) = 8.60 C_L + 27.06$$

$$T_{RC} = 18.57 C_L + 12.14$$

$$T_{FC} = 23.70 C_L + 13.72$$

125°C

$$P_{DC}(0-1) = 6.66 C_L + 23.92$$

$$P_{DC}(1-0) = 9.33 C_L + 29.29$$

$$T_{RC} = 20.46 C_L + 13.49$$

$$T_{FC} = 25.96 C_L + 15.07$$

125°C BC

$$P_{DC}(0-1) = 3.19 C_L + 10.72$$

$$P_{DC}(1-0) = 4.01 C_L + 13.42$$

$$T_{RC} = 10.52 C_L + 6.30$$

$$T_{FC} = 12.39 C_L + 7.01$$

VOLTAGE TABLE

VOLTAGE	DEVIATION FACTOR			
	TRANSITION		PROP DELAY	
	TR	TF	1-0	0-1
3.0	1.53	1.84	1.83	2.09
3.5	1.36	1.54	1.56	1.74
4.0	1.13	1.23	1.28	1.39
4.5	1.09	1.12	1.14	1.20
5.0	1.00	1.00	1.00	1.00
5.5	.95	.94	.92	.87
6.0	.90	.87	.84	.73
6.5	.88	.83	.79	.66
7.0	.85	.79	.73	.58

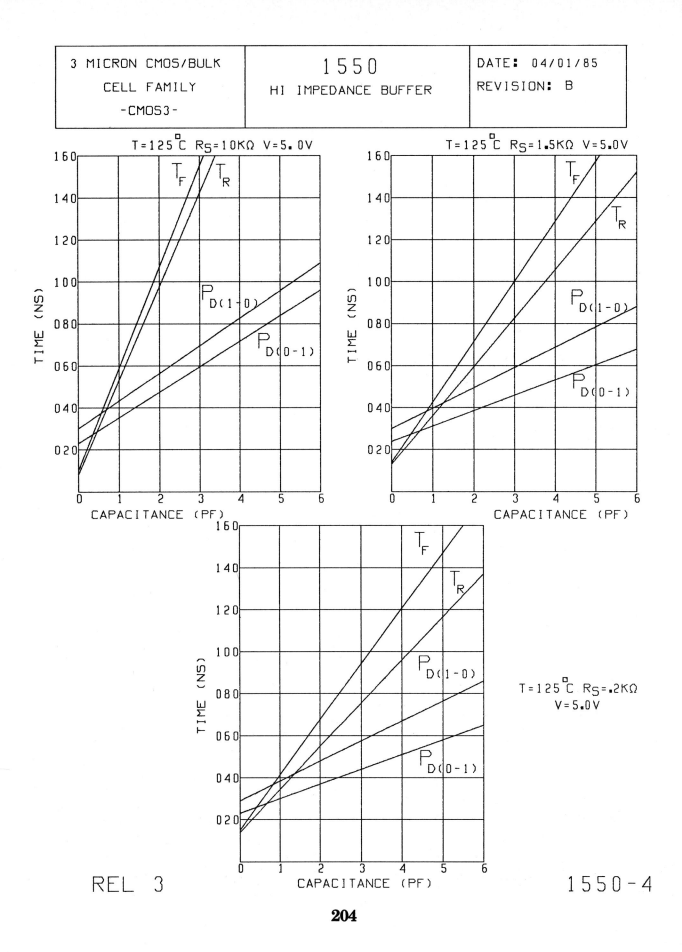

T=125°C R_S=10KΩ V=5.0V

T=125°C R_S=1.5KΩ V=5.0V

T=125°C R_S=.2KΩ
V=5.0V

REL 3

1550-4

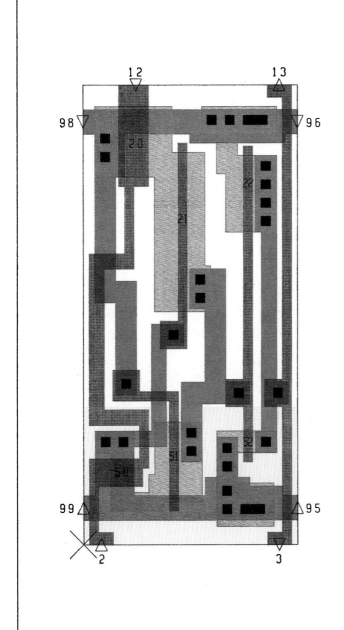

REL 3   1550-5

205

3 MICRON CMOS/BULK CELL FAMILY -CMOS3-	1560 DELAY CELL CELL HEIGHT 150 WIDTH 84	DATE: 04/01/85 REVISION: B

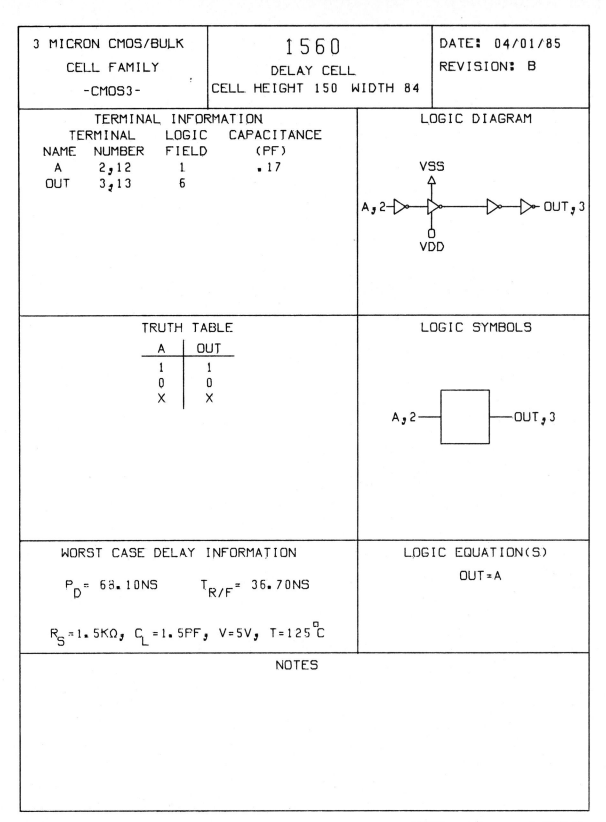

TERMINAL INFORMATION

TERMINAL NAME	NUMBER	LOGIC FIELD	CAPACITANCE (PF)
A	2,12	1	.17
OUT	3,13	6	

LOGIC DIAGRAM

VSS

A,2 — OUT,3

VDD

TRUTH TABLE

A	OUT
1	1
0	0
X	X

LOGIC SYMBOLS

A,2 — OUT,3

WORST CASE DELAY INFORMATION

P_D = 68.10NS $T_{R/F}$ = 36.70NS

R_S = 1.5KΩ, C_L = 1.5PF, V=5V, T=125°C

LOGIC EQUATION(S)

OUT=A

NOTES

REL 3   1560-1

206

CIRCUIT SCHEMATIC

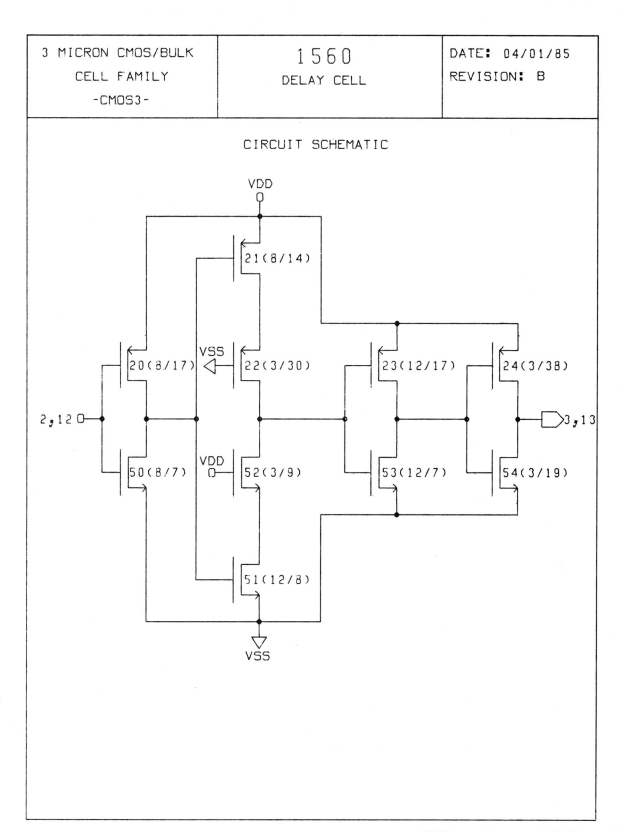

REL 3   1560-2

3 MICRON CMOS/BULK CELL FAMILY -CMOS3-	1560 DELAY CELL	DATE: 04/01/85 REVISION: B

OUTPUT CHARACTERISTIC EQUATIONS

$$P_D(0-1) = P_{DC}(0-1) + .22 (T_{R/F} - 10) + .58 R_S C_L$$

$$P_D(1-0) = P_{DC}(1-0) + .18 (T_{R/F} - 10) + .65 R_S C_L$$

$$T_R = T_{RC} + 0 \quad (T_{R/F} - 10) + 2.22 R_S C_L$$

$$T_F = T_{FC} + 0 \quad (T_{R/F} - 10) + 2.08 R_S C_L$$

EQUATIONS

$25^{\circ}C$

$$P_{DC}(0-1) = 3.38 C_L + 44.81$$

$$P_{DC}(1-0) = 3.16 C_L + 45.49$$

$$T_{RC} = 10.72 C_L + 6.86$$

$$T_{FC} = 9.00 C_L + 7.16$$

$95^{\circ}C$

$$P_{DC}(0-1) = 4.38 C_L + 55.53$$

$$P_{DC}(1-0) = 4.04 C_L + 56.31$$

$$T_{RC} = 14.08 C_L + 9.08$$

$$T_{FC} = 11.74 C_L + 9.50$$

$125^{\circ}C$

$$P_{DC}(0-1) = 4.81 C_L + 59.78$$

$$P_{DC}(1-0) = 4.40 C_L + 60.62$$

$$T_{RC} = 15.54 C_L + 10.03$$

$$T_{FC} = 12.90 C_L + 10.57$$

$125^{\circ}C$ BC

$$P_{DC}(0-1) = 2.38 C_L + 25.69$$

$$P_{DC}(1-0) = 2.14 C_L + 25.43$$

$$T_{RC} = 3.38 C_L + 4.64$$

$$T_{FC} = 6.98 C_L + 5.36$$

VOLTAGE TABLE

VOLTAGE	DEVIATION FACTOR			
	TRANSITION		PROP DELAY	
	TR	TF	1-0	0-1
3.0	1.49	1.55	2.00	1.96
3.5	1.33	1.36	1.66	1.63
4.0	1.16	1.17	1.31	1.30
4.5	1.08	1.09	1.16	1.15
5.0	1.00	1.00	1.00	1.00
5.5	.96	.96	.91	.91
6.0	.91	.91	.82	.82
6.5	.89	.88	.77	.75
7.0	.86	.85	.71	.70

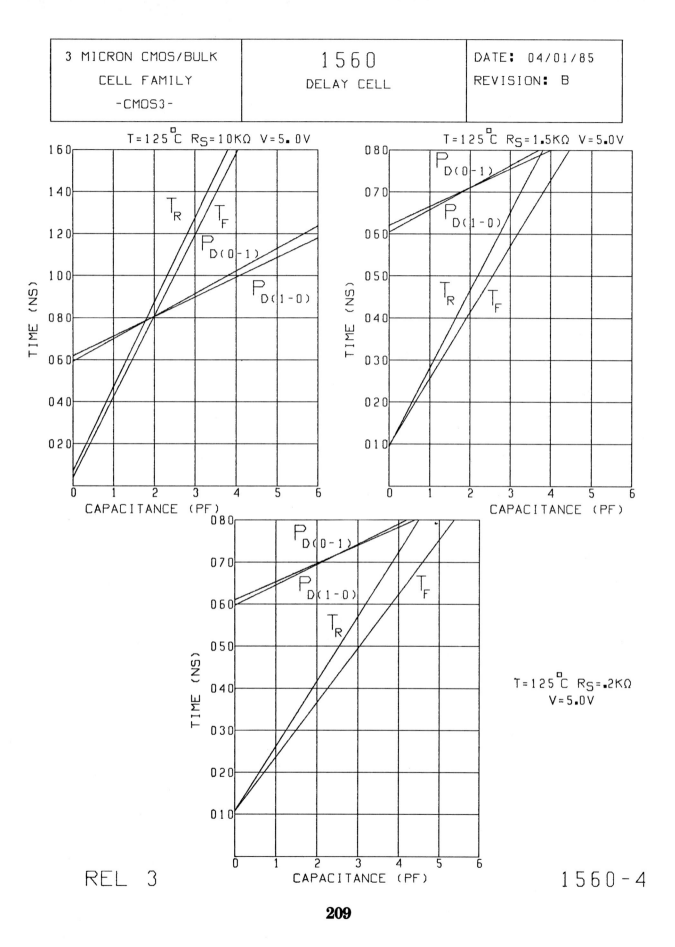

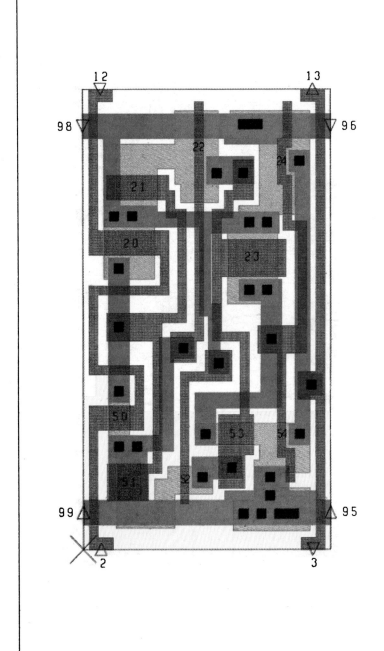

REL 3   1560-5

3 MICRON CMOS/BULK	1570	DATE: 04/01/84
CELL FAMILY	D-FLIP FLOP W/ASY R & Q	REVISION: A
-CMOS3-	CELL HEIGHT 150 WIDTH 144	

TERMINAL INFORMATION

TERMINAL NAME	NUMBER	LOGIC FIELD	CAPACITANCE (PF)
CLOCK	2,12	1	.18
DATA	3,13	2	.21
RESET	4,14	3	.41
Q	5,15	6	

LOGIC DIAGRAM

TRUTH TABLE

C	D	R	Q
⟍	*	1	DATA
⟋	*	1	Q_{N-1}
*	*	0	0
X	*	X	X

SEE PAGE 1570-9 FOR ADDITIONAL

TRUTH TABLE

LOGIC SYMBOLS

WORST CASE DELAY INFORMATION

P_D = 23.46NS $T_{R/F}$ = 16.46NS

R_S =1.5KΩ, C_L =1.5PF, V=5V, T=125°C

LOGIC EQUATION(S)

$$Q_N = (Q_{N-1}C + D_{N-1}\bar{C})R$$

NOTES

SPECIAL FLIP FLOP TIMING SEE PAGES 1570-7 AND 1570-8

REL 3   1570-1

211

CIRCUIT SCHEMATIC

REL 3   1570-2

212

3 MICRON CMOS/BULK	1570	DATE: 04/01/84
CELL FAMILY	D-FLIP FLOP W/ASY R & Q	REVISION: A
-CMOS3-	CLOCK TO Q	

OUTPUT CHARACTERISTIC EQUATIONS

$$P_D(0-1) = P_{DC}(0-1) + 0.11(T_{R/F} - 10) + 0.63R_S C_L$$

$$P_D(1-0) = P_{DC}(1-0) + 0.11(T_{R/F} - 10) + 0.58R_S C_L$$

$$T_R = T_{RC} + 0.00(T_{R/F} - 10) + 2.43R_S C_L$$

$$T_F = T_{FC} + 0.00(T_{R/F} - 10) + 2.30R_S C_L$$

EQUATIONS

$25^\circ C$

$$P_{DC}(0-1) = 1.30C_L + 8.25$$

$$P_{DC}(1-0) = 1.28C_L + 15.22$$

$$T_{RC} = 4.03C_L + 3.03$$

$$T_{FC} = 3.05C_L + 4.41$$

$95^\circ C$

$$P_{DC}(0-1) = 1.67C_L + 9.80$$

$$P_{DC}(1-0) = 1.60C_L + 18.63$$

$$T_{RC} = 5.13C_L + 4.05$$

$$T_{FC} = 3.80C_L + 6.06$$

$125^\circ C$

$$P_{DC}(0-1) = 1.82C_L + 10.40$$

$$P_{DC}(1-0) = 1.73C_L + 19.97$$

$$T_{RC} = 5.66C_L + 4.46$$

$$T_{FC} = 4.10C_L + 6.86$$

$125^\circ C$ BC

$$P_{DC}(0-1) = 0.87C_L + 4.75$$

$$P_{DC}(1-0) = 0.80C_L + 8.78$$

$$T_{RC} = 2.94C_L + 1.94$$

$$T_{FC} = 2.03C_L + 3.61$$

VOLTAGE TABLE

VOLTAGE	DEVIATION FACTOR			
	TRANSITION		PROP DELAY	
	TR	TF	1-0	0-1
3.0	1.49	1.57	1.90	1.83
3.5	1.33	1.37	1.59	1.54
4.0	1.16	1.17	1.23	1.26
4.5	1.08	1.09	1.14	1.13
5.0	1.00	1.00	1.00	1.00
5.5	.96	.96	.92	.92
6.0	.91	.91	.84	.85
6.5	.88	.88	.79	.79
7.0	.85	.85	.73	.74

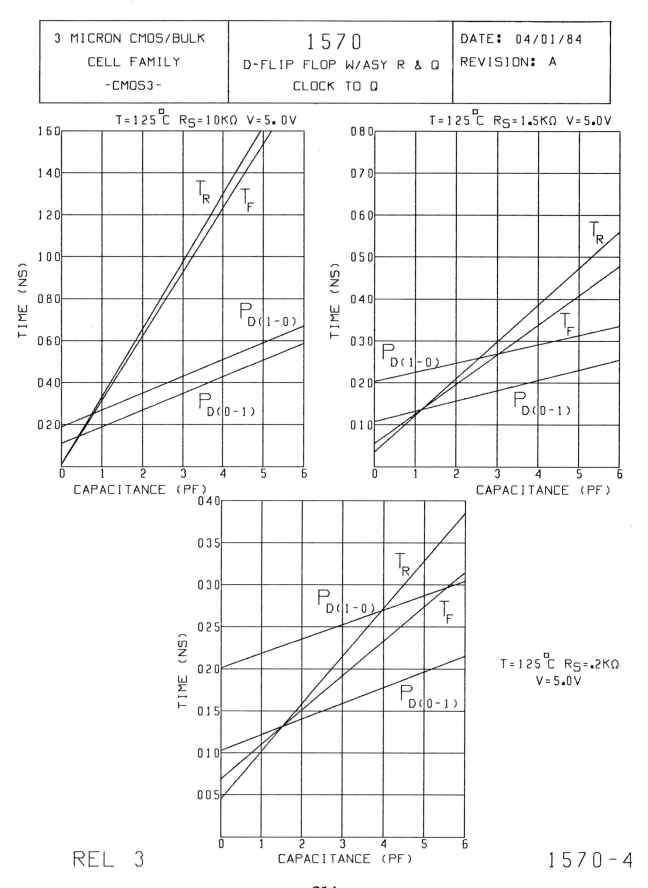

REL 3

1570-4

214

3 MICRON CMOS/BULK CELL FAMILY -CMOS3-	1570 D-FLIP FLOP W/ASY R & Q RESET TO Q	DATE: 04/01/84 REVISION: A

OUTPUT CHARACTERISTIC EQUATIONS

$$P_D(1-0) = P_{DC}(1-0) + 0.18(T_{R/F} - 10) + 0.60R_SC_L$$

$$T_F = T_{FC} + 0.01(T_{R/F} - 10) + 2.41R_SC_L$$

EQUATIONS

$25^\circ C$	$95^\circ C$	$125^\circ C$
$P_{DC}(1-0) = 1.12C_L + 7.62$	$P_{DC}(1-0) = 1.42C_L + 5.98$	$P_{DC}(1-0) = 1.53C_L + 9.52$
$T_{FC} = 2.99C_L + 3.32$	$T_{FC} = 3.73C_L + 4.33$	$T_{FC} = 4.11C_L + 4.73$

$125^\circ C$ BC	VOLTAGE TABLE
$P_{DC}(1-0) = 0.69C_L + 4.96$	
$T_{FC} = 2.13C_L + 1.96$	

VOLTAGE TABLE

VOLTAGE   DEVIATION FACTOR

TRANSITION	PROP DELAY	
	TF	1-0
3.0	1.58	1.79
3.5	1.33	1.52
4.0	1.18	1.25
4.5	1.09	1.12
5.0	1.00	1.00
5.5	.95	.93
6.0	.90	.86
6.5	.87	.81
7.0	.84	.77

REL 3   1570-5

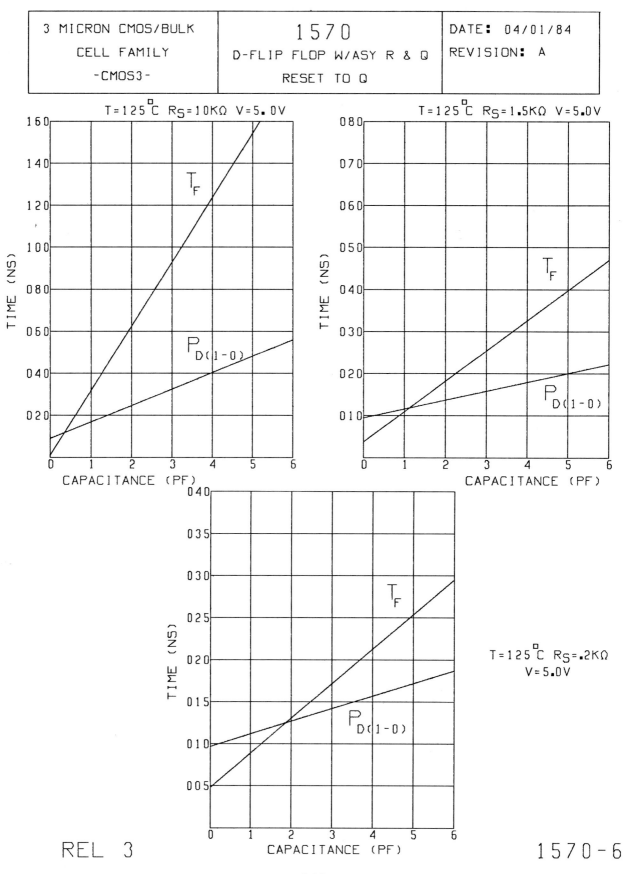

REL 3

1570-6

216

3 MICRON CMOS/BULK CELL FAMILY -CMOS3-	1570 D-FLIP FLOP W/ASY R & Q	DATE: 04/01/84 REVISION: A

SPECIAL FLIP FLOP TIMING

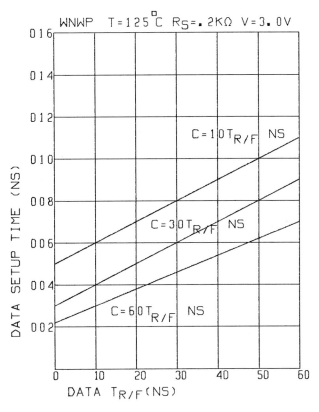

WNWP T=125°C R$_S$=.2KΩ V=3.0V

DATA SETUP TIME (NS)

C=10 T$_{R/F}$ NS

C=30 T$_{R/F}$ NS

C=60 T$_{R/F}$ NS

DATA T$_{R/F}$(NS)

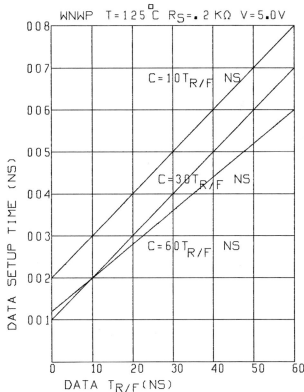

WNWP T=125°C R$_S$=.2KΩ V=5.0V

DATA SETUP TIME (NS)

C=10 T$_{R/F}$ NS

C=30 T$_{R/F}$ NS

C=60 T$_{R/F}$ NS

DATA T$_{R/F}$(NS)

REL 3

1570-7

3 MICRON CMOS/BULK CELL FAMILY -CMOS3-	1570 D-FLIP FLOP W/ASY R & Q	DATE: 04/01/84 REVISION: A

SPECIAL FLIP FLOP TIMING

MINIMUM CLOCK PULSE WIDTH = 29NS

MINIMUM RESET PULSE WIDTH = 17NS

MAXIMUM CLOCK RISE TIME = 200NS

RESET HOLD TIME = 8NS

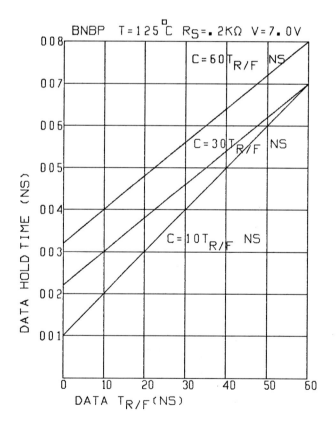

REL 3

1570-8

R	C	D	M	Q	SPECIAL CASES
0	0	*	0	0	
0	1	0	0	0	
0	1	1	1	0	
0	1	X	X	0	
0	X	0	0	0	
0	X	1	X	0	
0	X	X	X	0	
1	0	*	M_{T-1}	M_{T-1}	
1	1	0	0	Q_{T-1}	
1	1	1	1	Q_{T-1}	
1	1	X	X	Q_{T-1}	
1	X	*	X	X	IF $D=M_{T-1}$ THEN $M=M_{T-1}$ / IF $Q_{T-1}=M_{T-1}$ THEN $Q=Q_{T-1}$ / IF $M_{T-1}=0$ THEN M=0 AND Q=0
X	0	*	X	X	
X	1	0	0	X	
X	1	1	1	X	IF $Q_{T-1}=0$ THEN Q=0
X	1	X	X	X	
X	X	*	X	X	IF D=0 AND $M_{T-1}=0$ THEN M=0 / IF $M_{T-1}=0$ AND $Q_{T-1}=0$ THEN Q=0

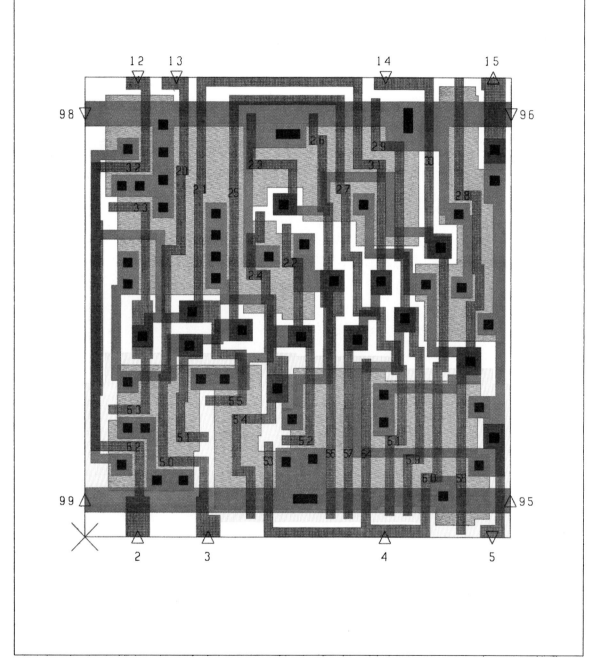

3 MICRON CMOS/BULK CELL FAMILY -CMOS3-	1580 D-FLIP FLOP W/ASY R,Q,Q̄ CELL HEIGHT 150 WIDTH 156	DATE: 04/01/84 REVISION: A

TERMINAL INFORMATION

TERMINAL NAME	TERMINAL NUMBER	LOGIC FIELD	CAPACITANCE (PF)
CLOCK	2,12	1	.22
DATA	3,13	2	.23
RESET	4,14	3	.36
Q	5,15	6	
Q̄	6,16	7	

LOGIC DIAGRAM

TRUTH TABLE

C	D	R	Q	Q̄
⌐_	*	1	DATA	$\overline{DATA}$
_/	*	1	Q_{N-1}	$\bar{Q}_{N-1}$
*	*	0	0	1
X	*	X	X	X

SEE PAGE 1580-11 FOR ADDITIONAL

TRUTH TABLE

LOGIC SYMBOLS

WORST CASE DELAY INFORMATION

Q P_D= 18.15NS $T_{R/F}$= 20.43NS

Q̄ P_D= 19.01NS $T_{R/F}$= 15.93NS

R_S=1.5KΩ, C_L=1.5PF, V=5V, T=125°C

LOGIC EQUATION(S)

$$Q_N = \overline{(Q_{N-1}C + D_{N-1}\bar{C})R}$$

$$\bar{Q}_N = (Q_{N-1}C + D_{N-1}\bar{C})R$$

NOTES

SPECIAL FLIP FLOP TIMING SEE PAGES 1580-9 AND 1580-10

REL 3   1580-1

221

CIRCUIT SCHEMATIC

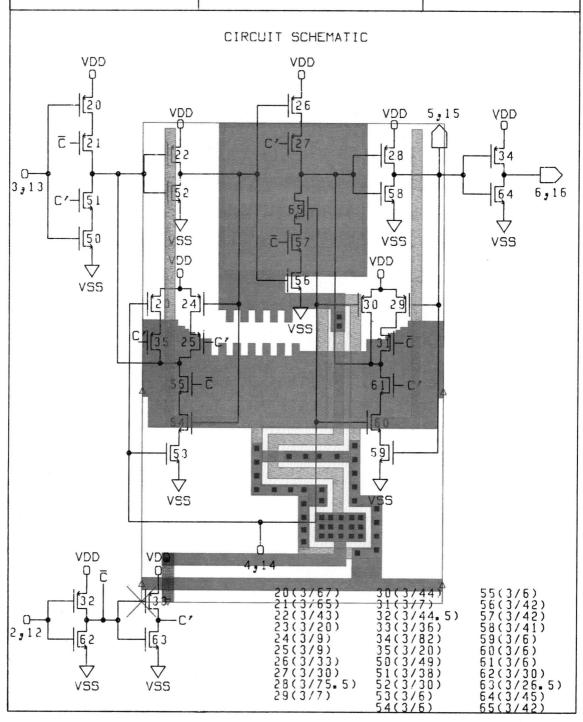

20(3/67)   30(3/44)   55(3/6)
21(3/65)   31(3/7)   56(3/42)
22(3/43)   32(3/44.5) 57(3/42)
23(3/20)   33(3/36)   58(3/41)
24(3/9)   34(3/82)   59(3/6)
25(3/9)   35(3/20)   60(3/6)
26(3/33)   50(3/49)   51(3/6)
27(3/30)   51(3/38)   62(3/30)
28(3/75.5) 52(3/30)   63(3/26.5)
29(3/7)   53(3/6)   64(3/45)
           54(3/6)   65(3/42)

REL 3   1580-2

.3 MICRON CMOS/BULK CELL FAMILY -CMOS3-	1580 D-FLIP FLOP W/ASY R,Q,$\overline{Q}$ RESET TO Q & $\overline{Q}$	DATE: 04/01/84 REVISION: A

OUTPUT CHARACTERISTIC EQUATIONS

$$P_D(0-1)=P_{DC}(0-1)+0.10(T_{R/F}-10)+0.65R_SC_L+0.79C_{L_Q}$$

$$P_D(1-0)=P_{DC}(1-0)+0.11(T_{R/F}-10)+0.65R_SC_L$$

$$T_R=T_{RC}+0.00(T_{R/F}-10)+2.57R_SC_L+0.90C_{L_Q}$$

$$T_F=T_{FC}+0.02(T_{R/F}-10)+2.59R_SC_L$$

EQUATIONS

$25^\circ C$	$95^\circ C$	$125^\circ C$
$P_{DC}(0-1)=1.36C_L+5.53$	$P_{DC}(0-1)=1.74C_L+6.54$	$P_{DC}(0-1)=1.91C_L+6.39$
$P_{DC}(1-0)=1.41C_L+4.70$	$P_{DC}(1-0)=1.62C_L+5.40$	$P_{DC}(1-0)=1.99C_L+5.63$
$T_{RC}=4.56C_L+1.41$	$T_{RC}=5.37C_L+1.83$	$T_{RC}=6.44C_L+2.04$
$T_{FC}=4.89C_L+1.71$	$T_{FC}=6.38C_L+2.11$	$T_{FC}=7.04C_L+2.23$

$125^\circ C$ SC

$$P_{DC}(0-1)=0.95C_L+3.23$$

$$P_{DC}(1-0)=1.10C_L+2.78$$

$$T_{RC}=3.44C_L+0.85$$

$$T_{FC}=4.11C_L+1.12$$

VOLTAGE TABLE

VOLTAGE	DEVIATION FACTOR			
	TRANSITION		PROP DELAY	
	TR	TF	1-0	0-1
3.0	1.33	1.34	1.64	1.72
3.5	1.25	1.22	1.42	1.48
4.0	1.12	1.10	1.20	1.23
4.5	1.05	1.05	1.10	1.12
5.0	1.00	1.00	1.00	1.00
5.5	.97	.97	.94	.94
6.0	.93	.94	.88	.87
6.5	.91	.93	.85	.83
7.0	.88	.91	.81	.78

REL 3   1580-3

223

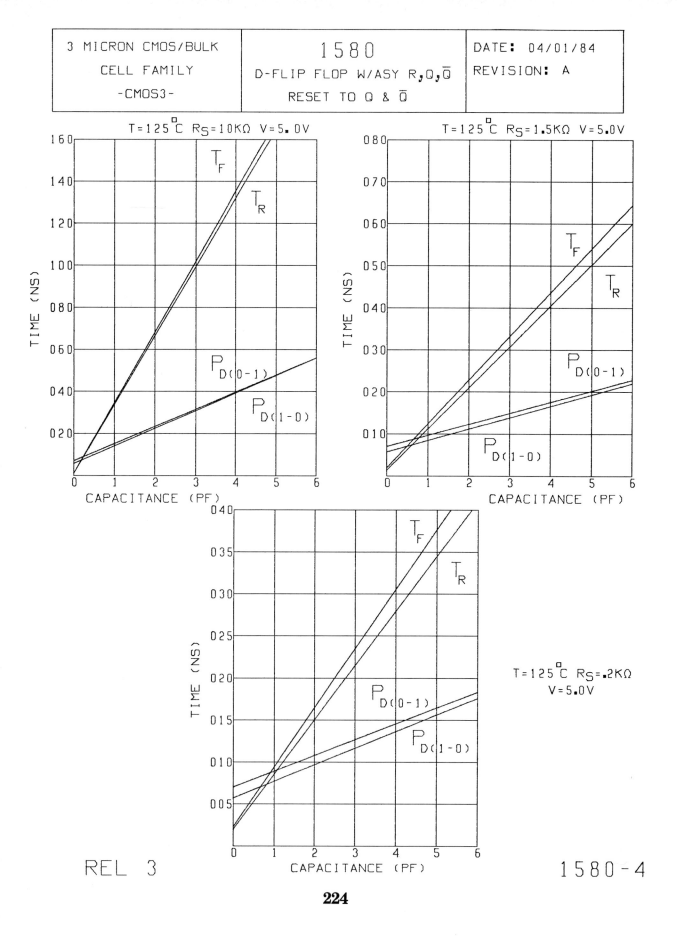

REL 3

1580-4

3 MICRON CMOS/BULK CELL FAMILY -CMOS3-	1580 D-FLIP FLOP W/ASY R,Q,Q̄ CLOCK TO Q	DATE: 04/01/84 REVISION: A

OUTPUT CHARACTERISTIC EQUATIONS

$$P_D(0-1) = P_{DC}(0-1) + 0.10(T_{R/F}-10) + 0.65R_S C_L$$

$$P_D(1-0) = P_{DC}(1-0) + 0.11(T_{R/F}-10) + 0.61R_S C_L$$

$$T_R = T_{RC} + 0.00(T_{R/F}-10) + 2.54R_S C_L$$

$$T_F = T_{FC} + 0.00(T_{R/F}-10) + 2.50R_S C_L$$

EQUATIONS

$25°C$	$95°C$	$125°C$
$P_{DC}(0-1) = 1.71C_L + 6.72$	$P_{DC}(0-1) = 2.22C_L + 7.94$	$P_{DC}(0-1) = 2.44C_L + 8.41$
$P_{DC}(1-0) = 1.51C_L + 10.83$	$P_{DC}(1-0) = 1.94C_L + 13.13$	$P_{DC}(1-0) = 2.13C_L + 14.04$
$T_{RC} = 6.01C_L + 2.20$	$T_{RC} = 7.85C_L + 2.92$	$T_{RC} = 8.66C_L + 3.20$
$T_{FC} = 4.84C_L + 2.63$	$T_{FC} = 6.28C_L + 3.54$	$T_{FC} = 6.89C_L + 3.96$

$125°C$ BC

$$P_{DC}(0-1) = 1.31C_L + 3.79$$

$$P_{DC}(1-0) = 1.14C_L + 6.27$$

$$T_{RC} = 4.90C_L + 1.30$$

$$T_{FC} = 4.02C_L + 1.83$$

VOLTAGE TABLE

VOLTAGE	DEVIATION FACTOR			
	TRANSITION		PROP DELAY	
	TR	TF	1-0	0-1
3.0	1.36	1.41	1.86	1.76
3.5	1.24	1.27	1.57	1.50
4.0	1.12	1.13	1.27	1.24
4.5	1.06	1.07	1.14	1.12
5.0	1.00	1.00	1.00	1.00
5.5	.97	.97	.93	.93
6.0	.93	.93	.85	.86
6.5	.91	.91	.80	.81
7.0	.89	.89	.75	.76

REL 3   1580-5

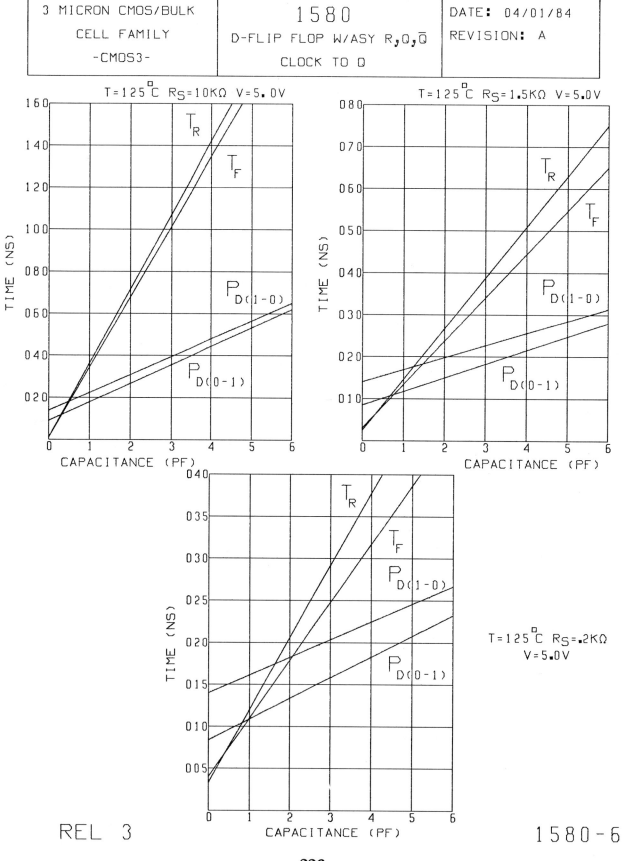

REL 3

1580-6

3 MICRON CMOS/BULK CELL FAMILY -CMOS3-	1580 D-FLIP FLOP W/ASY R,Q,$\bar{Q}$ CLOCK TO $\bar{Q}$	DATE: 04/01/84 REVISION: A

OUTPUT CHARACTERISTIC EQUATIONS

$$P_D(0-1) = P_{DC}(0-1) + 0.11(T_{R/F} - 10) + 0.64R_S C_L + 0.99C_{L_Q}$$

$$P_D(1-0) = P_{DC}(1-0) + 0.10(T_{R/F} - 10) + 0.63R_S C_L + 1.37C_{L_Q}$$

$$T_R = T_{RC} + 0.00(T_{R/F} - 10) + 2.56R_S C_L + 0.88C_{L_Q}$$

$$T_F = T_{FC} + 0.00(T_{R/F} - 10) + 2.58R_S C_L + 1.33C_{L_Q}$$

EQUATIONS

25°C

$$P_{DC}(0-1) = 1.36C_L + 11.62$$

$$P_{DC}(1-0) = 1.11C_L + 7.98$$

$$T_{RC} = 4.54C_L + 1.47$$

$$T_{FC} = 3.49C_L + 1.29$$

95°C

$$P_{DC}(0-1) = 1.75C_L + 14.13$$

$$P_{DC}(1-0) = 1.41C_L + 9.47$$

$$T_{RC} = 5.86C_L + 1.97$$

$$T_{FC} = 4.46C_L + 1.67$$

125°C

$$P_{DC}(0-1) = 1.91C_L + 15.12$$

$$P_{DC}(1-0) = 1.53C_L + 10.04$$

$$T_{RC} = 6.42C_L + 2.19$$

$$T_{FC} = 4.88C_L + 1.84$$

125°C BC

$$P_{DC}(0-1) = 0.95C_L + 6.72$$

$$P_{DC}(1-0) = 0.76C_L + 4.40$$

$$T_{RC} = 3.42C_L + 0.96$$

$$T_{FC} = 2.70C_L + 0.71$$

VOLTAGE TABLE

VOLTAGE	DEVIATION FACTOR			
	TRANSITION		PROP DELAY	
	TR	TF	1-0	0-1
3.0	1.39	1.39	1.90	1.88
3.5	1.26	1.26	1.59	1.58
4.0	1.12	1.12	1.23	1.23
4.5	1.06	1.06	1.14	1.14
5.0	1.00	1.00	1.00	1.00
5.5	.96	.97	.92	.92
6.0	.93	.93	.84	.84
6.5	.91	.91	.73	.79
7.0	.88	.89	.72	.74

REL 3   1580-7

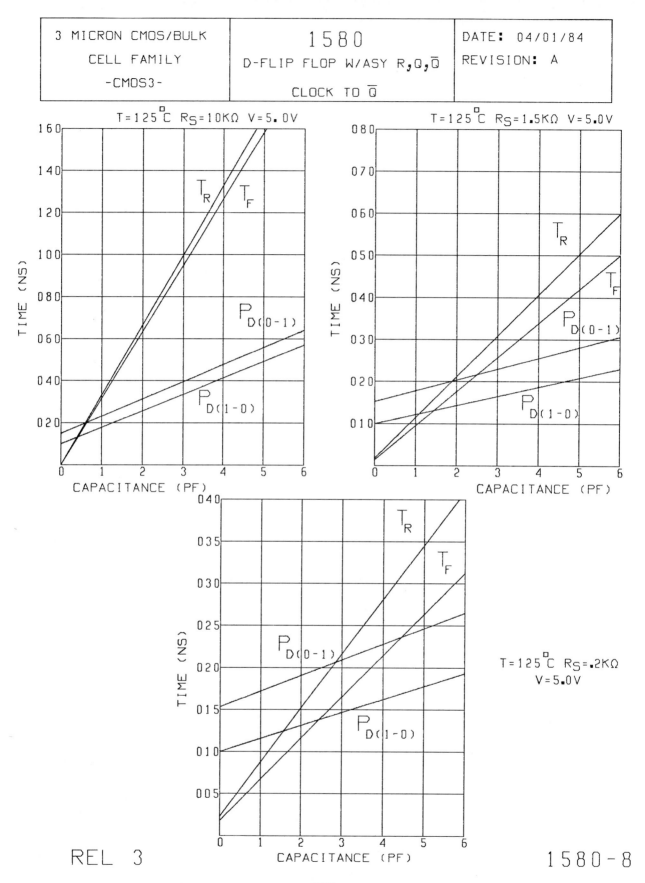

3 MICRON CMOS/BULK CELL FAMILY -CMOS3-	1580 D-FLIP FLOP W/ASY R,Q,Q̄	DATE: 04/01/84 REVISION: A

SPECIAL FLIP FLOP TIMING

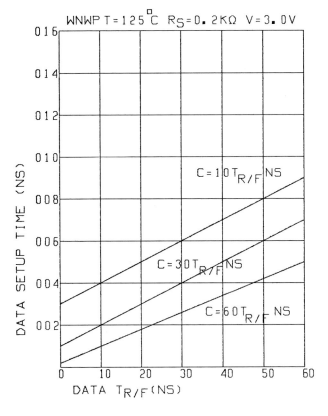

WNWP T=125°C R_S=0.2KΩ V=3.0V

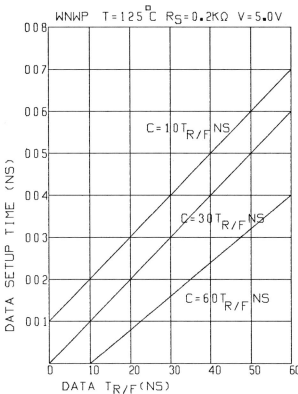

WNWP T=125°C R_S=0.2KΩ V=5.0V

REL 3

1580-9

SPECIAL FLIP FLOP TIMING

MINIMUM CLOCK PULSE WIDTH = 18NS

MINIMUM RESET PULSE WIDTH = 17NS

MAXIMUM CLOCK RISE TIME = 200NS

RESET HOLD TIME = 8NS

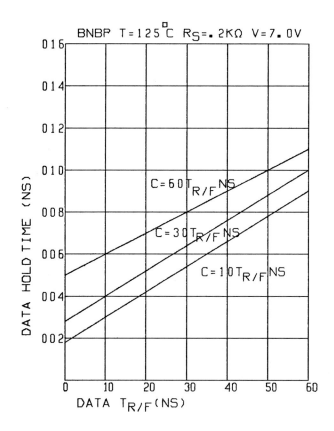

R	C	D	M	Q	Q̄	SPECIAL CASES
0	0	*	0	0	1	
0	1	0	0	0	1	
0	1	1	1	0	1	
0	1	X	X	0	1	
0	X	0	0	0	1	
0	X	1	X	0	1	
0	X	X	X	0	1	
1	0	*	M_{T-1}	M_{T-1}	$\overline{M}_{T-1}$	
1	1	0	0	Q_{T-1}	$\overline{Q}_{T-1}$	
1	1	1	1	Q_{T-1}	$\overline{Q}_{T-1}$	
1	1	X	X	Q_{T-1}	$\overline{Q}_{T-1}$	
1	X	*	X	X	X	IF $D=M_{T-1}$ THEN $M=M_{T-1}$ IF $Q_{T-1}=M_{T-1}$ THEN $Q=Q_{T-1}$ AND $\overline{Q}=\overline{Q}_{T-1}$
X	0	*	X	X	X	IF $M_{T-1}=0$ THEN $M=0$ AND $Q=0$ AND $\overline{Q}=1$
X	1	0	0	X	X	
X	1	1	1	X	X	IF $Q_{T-1}=0$ THEN $Q=0$ AND $\overline{Q}=1$
X	1	X	X	X	X	
X	X	*	X	X	X	IF $D=0$ AND $M_{T-1}=0$ THEN $M=0$ IF $M_{T-1}=0$ AND $Q_{T-1}=0$ THEN $Q=0$ AND $\overline{Q}=1$

REL 3   1580-11

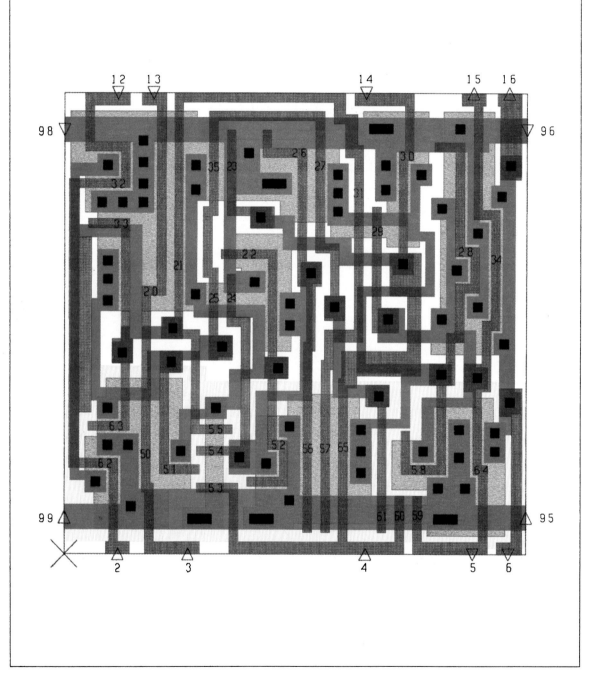

REL 3 1580-12

3 MICRON CMOS/BULK CELL FAMILY -CMOS3-	1610 $\overline{A}B$ DECODER CELL HEIGHT 150 WIDTH 48	DATE: 04/01/84 REVISION: B

TERMINAL INFORMATION

TERMINAL NAME	NUMBER	LOGIC FIELD	CAPACITANCE (PF)
A	3,13	1	.23
B	2,12	2	.21
OUT	4,14	6	

LOGIC DIAGRAM

A,3
B,2 ⊃— OUT,4

TRUTH TABLE

A	B	OUT
*	1	$\overline{A}$
0	*	B
1	0	0
1	X	0
X	0	0
X	X	X

LOGIC SYMBOLS

A,3
B,2 —OUT,4

WORST CASE DELAY INFORMATION

P_D = 12.11 NS $T_{R/F}$ = 27.44 NS

R_S = 1.5KΩ, C_L = 1.5PF, V=5V, T=125°C

LOGIC EQUATION(S)

OUT = $\overline{A}$*B

NOTES

CIRCUIT SCHEMATIC

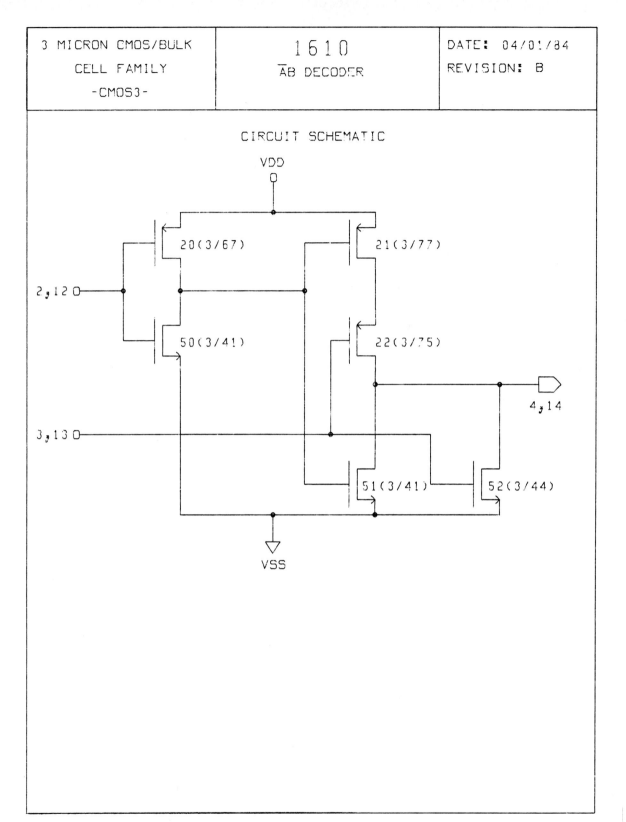

1610-2

234

OUTPUT CHARACTERISTIC EQUATIONS

$$P_D(0-1) = P_{DC}(0-1) + .13 (T_{R/F} - 10) + .62 R_S C_L$$

$$P_D(1-0) = P_{DC}(1-0) + .09 (T_{R/F} - 10) + .63 R_S C_L$$

$$T_R = T_{RC} + .09 (T_{R/F} - 10) + 2.34 R_S C_L$$

$$T_F = T_{FC} + .02 (T_{R/F} - 10) + 2.53 R_S C_L$$

EQUATIONS

25°C

$$P_{DC}(0-1) = 2.74 C_L + 4.55$$

$$P_{DC}(1-0) = 1.24 C_L + 3.73$$

$$T_{RC} = 8.72 C_L + 3.78$$

$$T_{FC} = 4.05 C_L + 1.82$$

95°C

$$P_{DC}(0-1) = 3.51 C_L + 5.14$$

$$P_{DC}(1-0) = 1.56 C_L + 4.36$$

$$T_{RC} = 11.34 C_L + 4.85$$

$$T_{FC} = 5.22 C_L + 2.34$$

125°C

$$P_{DC}(0-1) = 3.82 C_L + 5.39$$

$$P_{DC}(1-0) = 1.69 C_L + 4.61$$

$$T_{RC} = 12.43 C_L + 5.35$$

$$T_{FC} = 5.73 C_L + 2.55$$

125°C BC

$$P_{DC}(0-1) = 1.75 C_L + 3.28$$

$$P_{DC}(1-0) = .89 C_L + 2.43$$

$$T_{RC} = 6.03 C_L + 2.95$$

$$T_{FC} = 3.15 C_L + 1.45$$

VOLTAGE TABLE

VOLTAGE	DEVIATION FACTOR			
	TRANSITION		PROP DELAY	
	TR	TF	1-0	0-1
3.0	1.55	1.39	1.66	1.69
3.5	1.36	1.26	1.44	1.46
4.0	1.17	1.12	1.21	1.22
4.5	1.09	1.06	1.11	1.11
5.0	1.00	1.00	1.00	1.00
5.5	.95	.97	.94	.94
6.0	.90	.93	.88	.88
6.5	.87	.91	.85	.84
7.0	.84	.89	.81	.80

1610-3

235

3 MICRON CMOS/BULK CELL FAMILY -CMOS3-	1 6 1 0 $\overline{A}$B DECODER	DATE: 04/01/84 REVISION: B

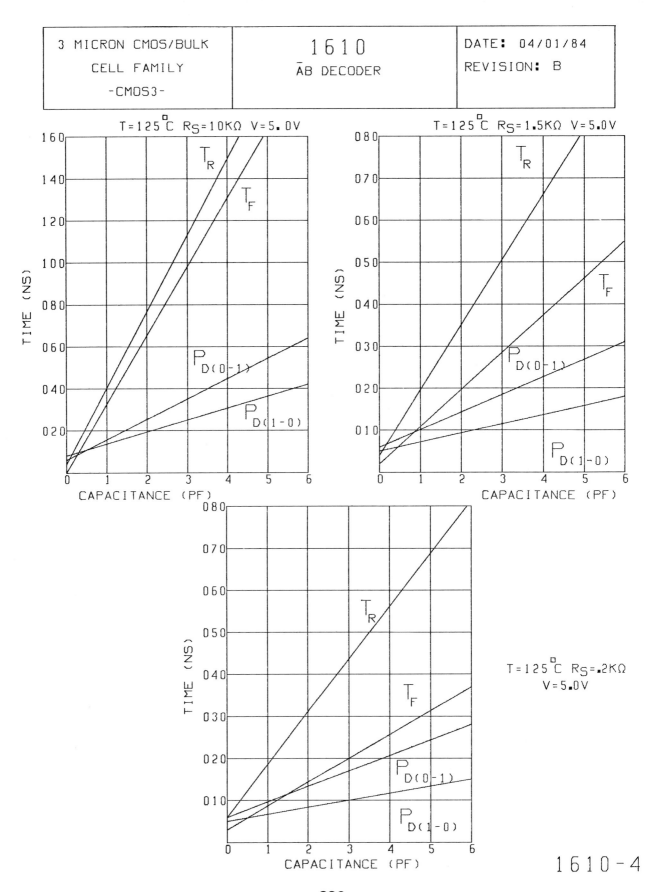

1610-4

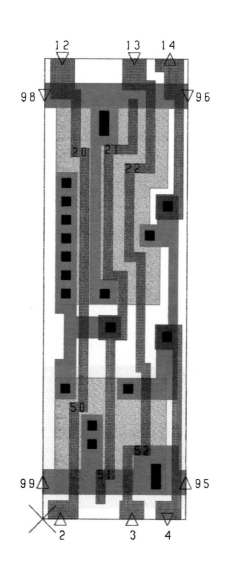

1610-5

237

3 MICRON CMOS/BULK	1 6 2 0	DATE: 09/07/84
CELL FAMILY	A OR $\overline{B}$	REVISION:
-CMOS3-	CELL HEIGHT 150 WIDTH 48	

TERMINAL INFORMATION

TERMINAL NAME	TERMINAL NUMBER	LOGIC FIELD	CAPACITANCE (PF)
A	2,12	1	.22
$\overline{B}$	3,13	2	.23
OUT	4,14	6	

LOGIC DIAGRAM

SAME AS LOGIC SYMBOL.

TRUTH TABLE

A	$\overline{B}$	OUT
0	0	1
0	1	0
1	0	1
1	1	1

LOGIC SYMBOLS

A,2
$\overline{B}$,3
OUT,4

WORST CASE DELAY INFORMATION

P_D= 9.15 NS $T_{R/F}$= 19.73NS

R_S=1.5KΩ, C_L=1.5PF, V=5V, T=125°C

LOGIC EQUATION(S)

OUT=A+$\overline{B}$

NOTES

CIRCUIT SCHEMATIC

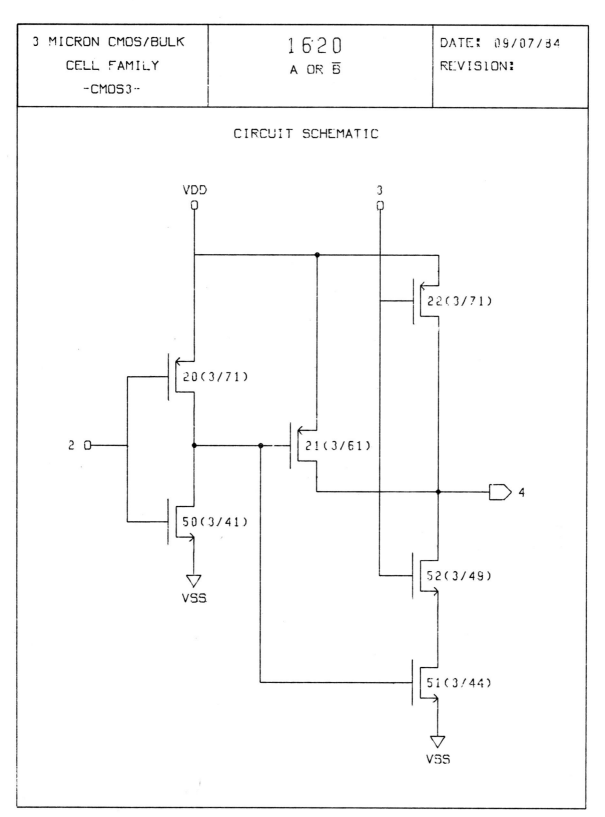

REL 3.3   1620-2

OUTPUT CHARACTERISTIC EQUATIONS

$$P_D(0-1) = P_{DC}(0-1) + .07 \ (T_{R/F} - 10) + .63 \ R_S C_L$$

$$P_D(1-0) = P_{DC}(1-0) + .07 \ (T_{R/F} - 10) + .60 \ R_S C_L$$

$$T_R = T_{RC} + .02 \ (T_{R/F} - 10) + 2.49 R_S C_L$$

$$T_F = T_{FC} + .01 \ (T_{R/F} - 10) + 2.46 R_S C_L$$

EQUATIONS

$25°C$

$$P_{DC}(0-1) = 1.81 C_L + 3.38$$

$$P_{DC}(1-0) = 1.98 C_L + 3.47$$

$$T_{RC} = 6.05 C_L + 1.98$$

$$T_{FC} = 6.02 C_L + 1.95$$

$95°C$

$$P_{DC}(0-1) = 2.32 C_L + 3.89$$

$$P_{DC}(1-0) = 2.49 C_L + 4.04$$

$$T_{RC} = 7.85 C_L + 2.62$$

$$T_{FC} = 7.72 C_L + 2.52$$

$125°C$

$$P_{DC}(0-1) = 2.54 C_L + 4.11$$

$$P_{DC}(1-0) = 2.69 C_L + 4.26$$

$$T_{RC} = 8.62 C_L + 2.92$$

$$T_{FC} = 8.44 C_L + 2.75$$

$125°C$ BC

$$P_{DC}(0-1) = 1.25 C_L + 1.90$$

$$P_{DC}(1-0) = 1.22 C_L + 2.17$$

$$T_{RC} = 4.47 C_L + 1.49$$

$$T_{FC} = 4.27 C_L + 1.28$$

VOLTAGE TABLE

VOLTAGE	DEVIATION FACTOR			
	TRANSITION		PROP DELAY	
	TR	TF	1-0	0-1
3.0	1.42	1.57	1.81	1.63
3.5	1.28	1.37	1.53	1.42
4.0	1.14	1.17	1.25	1.21
4.5	1.07	1.09	1.13	1.11
5.0	1.00	1.00	1.00	1.00
5.5	.96	.96	.93	.94
6.0	.92	.91	.86	.88
6.5	.90	.88	.82	.84
7.0	.88	.85	.78	.80

REL 3.3   1620-3

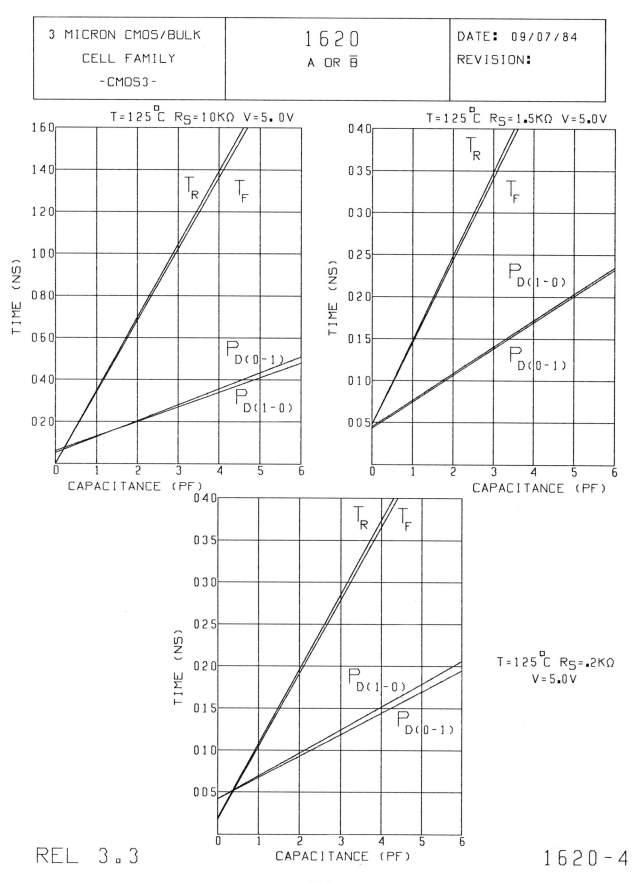

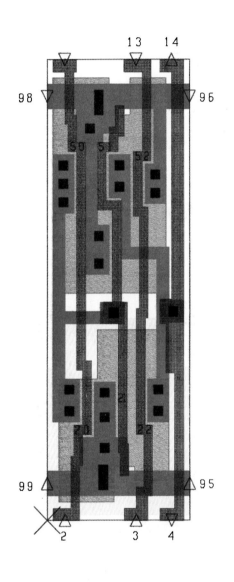

3 MICRON CMOS/BULK CELL FAMILY -CMOS3-	1660 2 NAND/AND CELL HEIGHT 150 WIDTH 48	DATE: 09/07/84 REVISION: B

TERMINAL INFORMATION

TERMINAL NAME	TERMINAL NUMBER	LOGIC FIELD	CAPACITANCE (PF)
A	2,12	1	.25
B	3,13	2	.24
OUT1	4,14	7	
OUT2	5,15	6	

LOGIC DIAGRAM

SAME AS LOGIC SYMBOL.

TRUTH TABLE

A	B	OUT1	OUT2
0	*	1	0
*	0	1	0
1	1	0	1
X	1	X	X
!	X	X	X
X	X	X	X

LOGIC SYMBOLS

A,2
B,3
OUT1,4
OUT2,5

WORST CASE DELAY INFORMATION

OUT1 P_D = 10.04 NS $T_{R/F}$ = 24.28 NS

OUT2 P_D = 11.82 NS $T_{R/F}$ = 23.71 NS

R_S = 1.5KΩ, C_L = 1.5PF, V=5V, T=125°C

LOGIC EQUATION(S)

OUT1 = $\overline{A*B}$

OUT2 = A*B

NOTES

DELAY EQUATIONS OF THE AND OUTPUT TAKE INTO CONSIDERATION THE CAPACITIVE LOADING ON THE NAND OUTPUT. RESISTIVE LOADING ON THE NAND OUTPUT HAS LITTLE EFFECT ON AND DELAY. SEE DESIGN APPLICATION NOTES FOR PROPAGATION DEVIATION OVER VOLTAGE FOR AND DELAY WITH NAND LOADING.

1660-1

3 MICRON CMOS/BULK CELL FAMILY -CMOS3-	1660 2 NAND/AND	DATE: 09/07/84 REVISION: B

CIRCUIT SCHEMATIC

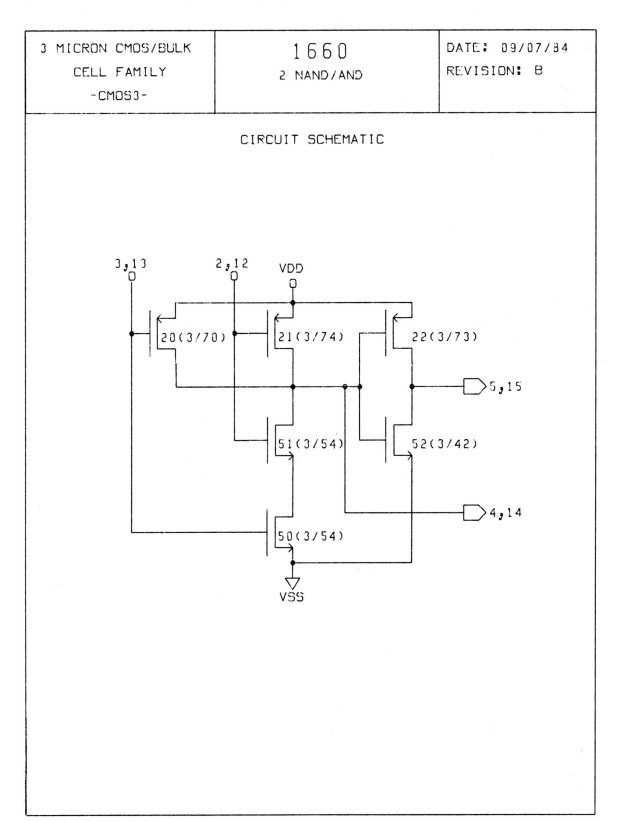

3 MICRON CMOS/BULK CELL FAMILY -CMOS3-	1660 2 NAND/AND NAND	DATE: 09/07/84 REVISION: B

OUTPUT CHARACTERISTIC EQUATIONS

$$P_D(0-1) = P_{DC}(0-1) + .13 (T_{R/F} - 10) + .66 R_S C_L$$

$$P_D(1-0) = P_{DC}(1-0) + .22 (T_{R/F} - 10) + .65 R_S C_L$$

$$T_R = T_{RC} + .19 (T_{R/F} - 10) + 2.52 R_S C_L$$

$$T_F = T_{FC} + .14 (T_{R/F} - 10) + 2.53 R_S C_L$$

EQUATIONS

$25^\circ C$

$$P_{DC}(0-1) = 2.04 C_L + 2.90$$

$$P_{DC}(1-0) = 2.08 C_L + 3.96$$

$$T_{RC} = 7.36 C_L + 3.08$$

$$T_{FC} = 7.32 C_L + 2.76$$

$95^\circ C$

$$P_{DC}(0-1) = 2.66 C_L + 3.16$$

$$P_{DC}(1-0) = 2.70 C_L + 4.23$$

$$T_{RC} = 9.32 C_L + 3.43$$

$$T_{FC} = 9.72 C_L + 3.11$$

$125^\circ C$

$$P_{DC}(0-1) = 2.93 C_L + 3.26$$

$$P_{DC}(1-0) = 2.97 C_L + 4.42$$

$$T_{RC} = 10.91 C_L + 3.54$$

$$T_{FC} = 10.77 C_L + 3.27$$

$125^\circ C$ BC

$$P_{DC}(0-1) = 1.66 C_L + 1.96$$

$$P_{DC}(1-0) = 1.64 C_L + 3.06$$

$$T_{RC} = 6.15 C_L + 3.07$$

$$T_{FC} = 6.11 C_L + 2.28$$

VOLTAGE TABLE

VOLTAGE	DEVIATION FACTOR			
	TRANSITION		PROP DELAY	
	TR	TF	1-0	0-1
3.0	1.26	1.35	1.37	1.37
3.5	1.17	1.23	1.57	1.25
4.0	1.09	1.10	1.27	1.12
4.5	1.04	1.05	1.13	1.06
5.0	1.00	1.00	1.00	1.00
5.5	.98	.99	.92	.94
6.0	.95	.98	.85	.92
6.5	.94	.95	.80	.90
7.0	.92	.91	.76	.87

1660-3

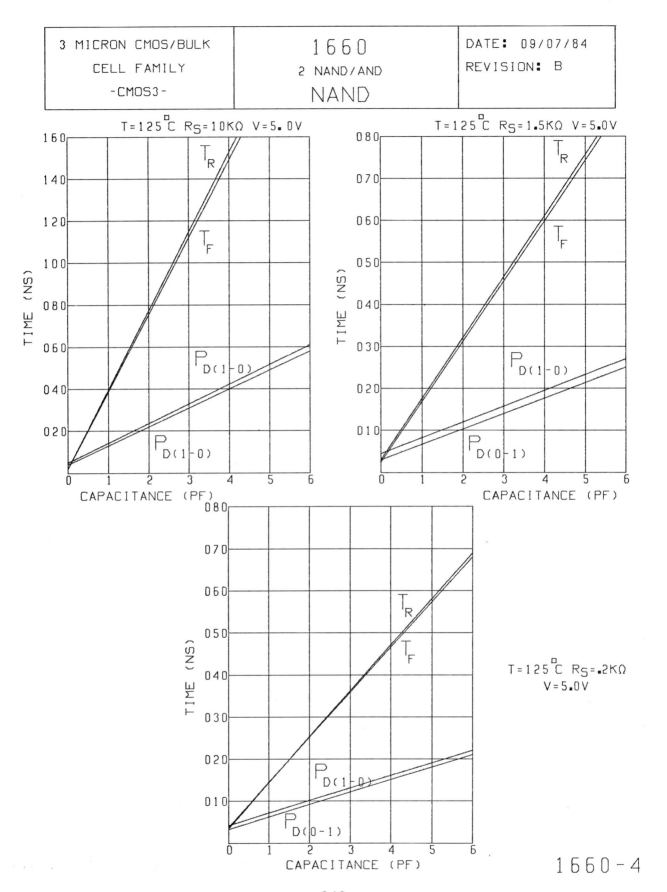

3 MICRON CMOS/BULK CELL FAMILY -CMOS3-	1660 2 NAND/AND AND	DATE: 09/07/84 REVISION: B

OUTPUT CHARACTERISTIC EQUATIONS

$$P_D(0-1) = P_{DC}(0-1) + .19 (T_{R/F} - 10) + .67 R_S C_L + 1.33 C_{LNAND}$$

$$P_D(1-0) = P_{DC}(1-0) + .10 (T_{R/F} - 10) + .65 R_S C_L + 1.73 C_{LNAND}$$

$$T_R = T_{RC} + .01 (T_{R/F} - 10) + 2.61 R_S C_L + .96 C_{LNAND}$$

$$T_F = T_{FC} + .02 (T_{R/F} - 10) + 2.64 R_S C_L + 1.07 C_{LNAND}$$

EQUATIONS

$25^\circ C$	$95^\circ C$	$125^\circ C$
$P_{DC}(0-1) = 2.06 C_L + 5.19$	$P_{DC}(0-1) = 2.71 C_L + 5.87$	$P_{DC}(0-1) = 3.0 C_L + 6.12$
$P_{DC}(1-0) = 1.77 C_L + 4.18$	$P_{DC}(1-0) = 2.32 C_L + 4.30$	$P_{DC}(1-0) = 2.55 C_L + 5.05$
$T_{RC} = 7.67 C_L + 1.54$	$T_{RC} = 10.15 C_L + 2.01$	$T_{RC} = 11.25 C_L + 2.19$
$T_{FC} = 6.60 C_L + 1.22$	$T_{FC} = 8.72 C_L + 1.55$	$T_{FC} = 9.67 C_L + 1.68$

$125^\circ C$ BC

$$P_{DC}(0-1) = 1.71 C_L + 3.68$$

$$P_{DC}(1-0) = 1.52 C_L + 2.47$$

$$T_{RC} = 6.61 C_L + 1.02$$

$$T_{FC} = 5.88 C_L + .88$$

VOLTAGE TABLE

VOLTAGE	DEVIATION FACTOR			
	TRANSITION		PROP DELAY	
	TR	TF	1-0	0-1
3.0	1.26	1.24	1.55	1.57
3.5	1.17	1.15	1.37	1.37
4.0	1.08	1.07	1.18	1.17
4.5	1.04	1.03	1.09	1.09
5.0	1.00	1.00	1.00	1.00
5.5	.98	.98	.95	.95
6.0	.95	.96	.90	.90
6.5	.94	.95	.87	.87
7.0	.92	.94	.83	.84

1660-5

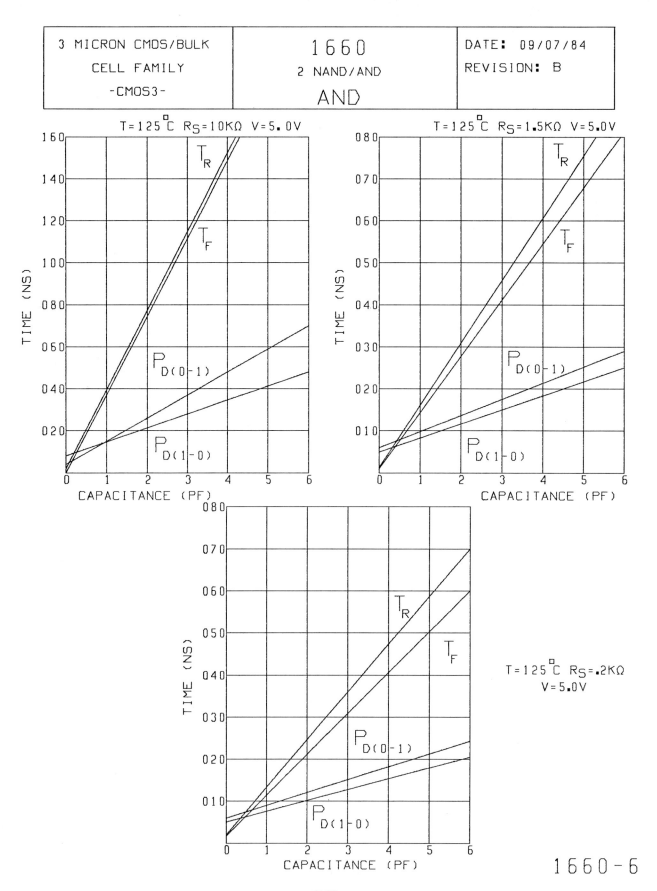

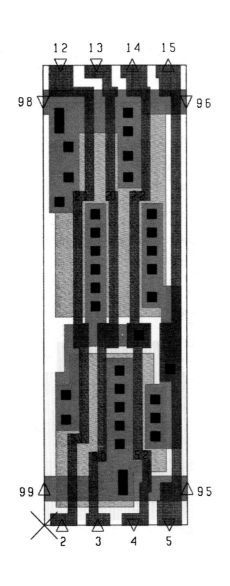

3 MICRON CMOS/BULK	1670	DATE: 04/01/84
CELL FAMILY	3 NAND/AND	REVISION: B
-CMOS3-	CELL HEIGHT 150 WIDTH 60	

TERMINAL INFORMATION

TERMINAL NAME	NUMBER	LOGIC FIELD	CAPACITANCE (PF)
A	2,12	1	.25
B	3,13	2	.23
C	4,14	3	.26
OUT1	5,15	7	
OUT2	6,16	6	

LOGIC DIAGRAM

SAME AS LOGIC SYMBOL.

TRUTH TABLE

A	B	C	OUT1	OUT2
0	*	*	1	0
*	0	*	1	0
*	*	0	1	0
1	1	1	0	1
ALL OTHER COMBINATIONS			X	X

LOGIC SYMBOLS

A,2
B,3
C,4
OUT1,5
OUT2,6

WORST CASE DELAY INFORMATION

NAND P_D =11.6 NS $T_{R/F}$ =29 NS
AND/UNLOADED NAND P_D = 11 NS $T_{R/F}$ =19 NS

R_S =1.5KΩ, C_L =1.5PF, V=5V, T=125°C

LOGIC EQUATION(S)

OUT1=$\overline{A*B*C}$

OUT2=A*B*C

NOTES

THE DELAY EQUATIONS FOR THE AND OUTPUT TAKE INTO CONSIDERATION
THE CAPACITIVE LOADING ON THE NAND OUTPUT. RESISTIVE LOADING
ON THE NAND OUTPUT HAS LITTLE EFFECT ON THE AND DELAY
SEE DESIGN APPLICATION NOTES FOR PROPAGATION DEVIATION OVER
VOLTAGE FOR AND DELAY WITH NAND LOADED.

1670-1

CIRCUIT SCHEMATIC

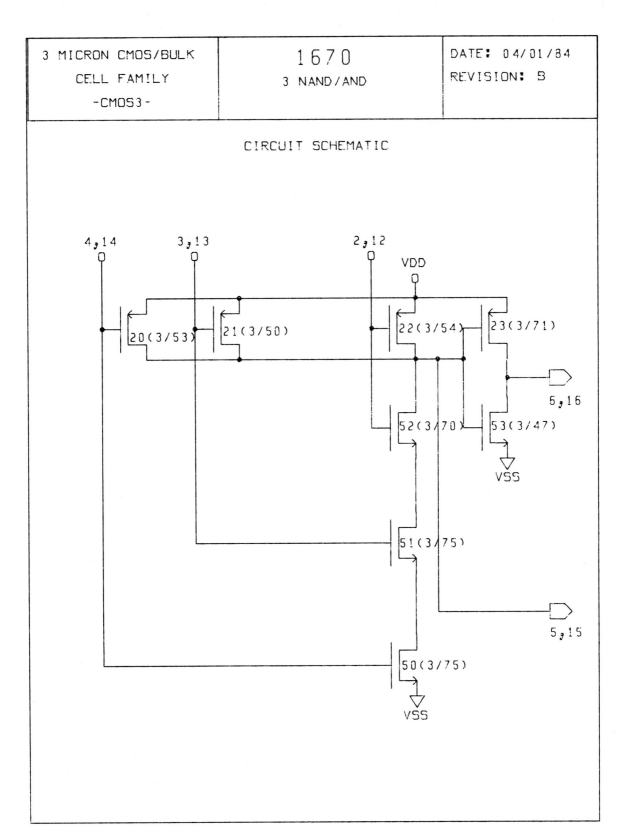

1670-2

251

OUTPUT CHARACTERISTIC EQUATIONS

$$P_D(0-1) = P_{DC}(0-1) + .17(T_{R/F} - 10) + .65 R_S C_L$$

$$P_D(1-0) = P_{DC}(1-0) + .22(T_{R/F} - 10) + .66 R_S C_L$$

$$T_R = T_{RC} + .16(T_{R/F} - 10) + 2.46 R_S C_L$$

$$T_F = T_{FC} + .13(T_{R/F} - 10) + 2.50 R_S C_L$$

EQUATIONS

$25\,^\circ C$

$$P_{DC}(0-1) = 2.54 C_L + 3.82$$

$$P_{DC}(1-0) = 2.26 C_L + 4.76$$

$$T_{RC} = 9.11 C_L + 3.99$$

$$T_{FC} = 3.07 C_L + 3.20$$

$95\,^\circ C$

$$P_{DC}(0-1) = 3.32 C_L + 4.30$$

$$P_{DC}(1-0) = 2.95 C_L + 5.27$$

$$T_{RC} = 12.15 C_L + 4.72$$

$$T_{FC} = 10.70 C_L + 3.82$$

$125\,^\circ C$

$$P_{DC}(0-1) = 3.64 C_L + 4.52$$

$$P_{DC}(1-0) = 3.26 C_L + 5.47$$

$$T_{RC} = 13.48 C_L + 5.03$$

$$T_{FC} = 11.86 C_L + 4.09$$

$125\,^\circ C$ BC

$$P_{DC}(0-1) = 2.0 C_L + 2.86$$

$$P_{DC}(1-0) = 1.80 C_L + 3.53$$

$$T_{RC} = 7.46 C_L + 3.36$$

$$T_{FC} = 6.78 C_L + 2.45$$

VOLTAGE TABLE

VOLTAGE   DEVIATION FACTOR

VOLTAGE	TRANSITION		PROP DELAY	
	TR	TF	1-0	0-1
3.0	1.35	1.40	1.83	1.41
3.5	1.23	1.25	1.57	1.27
4.0	1.11	1.11	1.27	1.13
4.5	1.06	1.06	1.14	1.07
5.0	1.00	1.00	1.00	1.00
5.5	.97	.98	.92	.96
6.0	.94	.96	.84	.92
6.5	.92	.94	.79	.89
7.0	.90	.91	.74	.87

1670-3

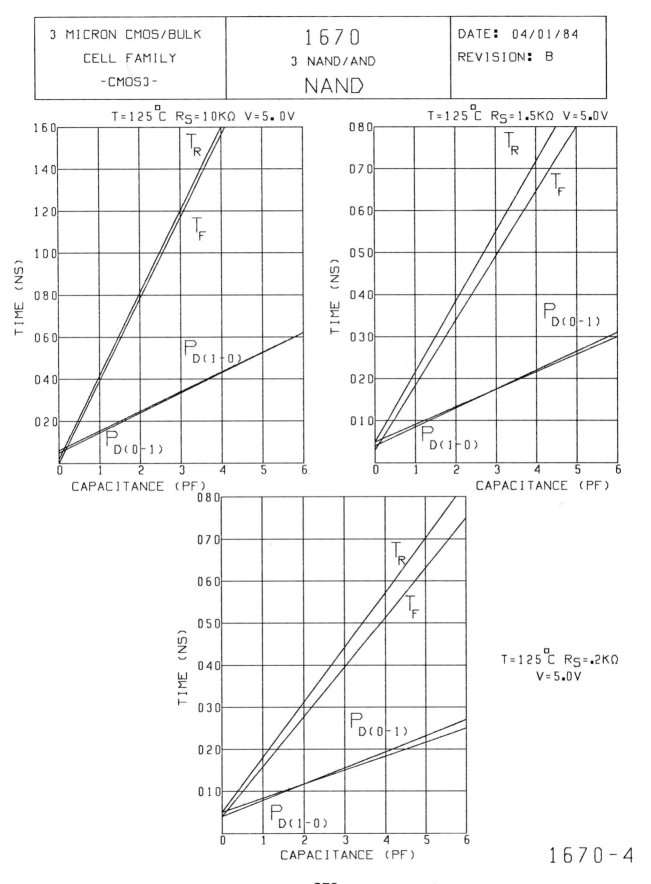

3 MICRON CMOS/BULK CELL FAMILY -CMOS3-	1670 3 NAND/AND AND	DATE: 04/01/84 REVISION: B

OUTPUT CHARACTERISTIC EQUATIONS

$$P_D(0-1) = P_{DC}(0-1) + .20 \ (T_{R/F} - 10) + .66 \ R_S C_L + 1.03 \ C_{LNAND}$$

$$P_D(1-0) = P_{DC}(1-0) + .15 \ (T_{R/F} - 10) + .64 \ R_S C_L + 1.41 \ C_{LNAND}$$

$$T_R = T_{RC} + .01 \ (T_{R/F} - 10) + 2.59 R_S C_L + 1.11 \ C_{LNAND}$$

$$T_F = T_{FC} + .03 \ (T_{R/F} - 10) + 2.63 R_S C_L + 1.37 \ C_{LNAND}$$

EQUATIONS

$25^\circ C$	$95^\circ C$	$125^\circ C$
$P_{DC}(0-1) = 2.0 \ C_L + 6.12$	$P_{DC}(0-1) = 2.62 C_L + 6.98$	$P_{DC}(0-1) = 2.9 \ C_L + 7.3$
$P_{DC}(1-0) = 1.62 C_L + 5.31$	$P_{DC}(1-0) = 2.12 C_L + 6.10$	$P_{DC}(1-0) = 2.34 C_L + 6.42$
$T_{RC} = 7.35 C_L + 1.71$	$T_{RC} = 9.71 C_L + 2.23$	$T_{RC} = 10.76 C_L + 2.43$
$T_{FC} = 5.99 C_L + 1.34$	$T_{FC} = 7.92 C_L + 1.72$	$T_{FC} = 8.78 C_L + 1.86$

$125^\circ C$ BC

$$P_{DC}(0-1) = 1.64 C_L + 4.23$$

$$P_{DC}(1-0) = 1.4 \ C_L + 3.45$$

$$T_{RC} = 6.3 \ C_L + 1.08$$

$$T_{FC} = 5.40 C_L + .95$$

VOLTAGE TABLE

VOLTAGE	DEVIATION FACTOR			
	TRANSITION		PROP DELAY	
	TR	TF	1-0	0-1
3.0	1.29	1.24	1.59	1.68
3.5	1.19	1.16	1.40	1.44
4.0	1.09	1.07	1.18	1.21
4.5	1.05	1.04	1.09	1.11
5.0	1.00	1.00	1.00	1.00
5.5	.97	.98	.95	.95
6.0	.95	.96	.90	.89
6.5	.93	.95	.86	.85
7.0	.92	.94	.83	.82

1670-5

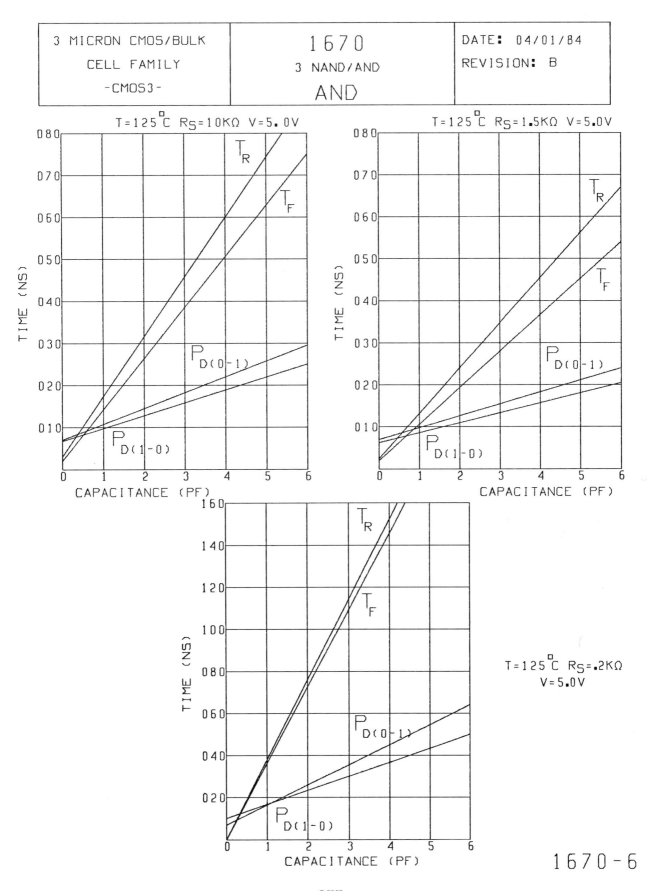

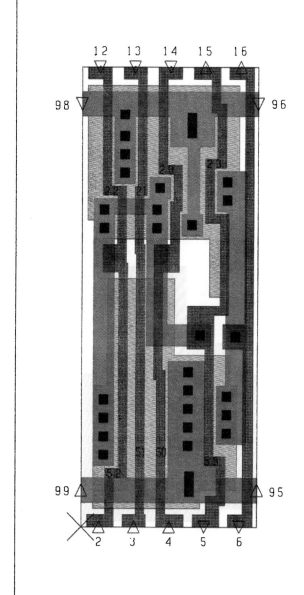

3 MICRON CMOS/BULK CELL FAMILY -CMOS3-	1680 4 NAND/AND CELL HEIGHT 150 WIDTH 72	DATE: 09/01/83 REVISION: A

TERMINAL INFORMATION

TERMINAL NAME	NUMBER	LOGIC FIELD	CAPACITANCE (PF)
A	2,12	1	.25
B	3,13	2	.24
C	4,14	3	.25
D	5,15	4	.26
OUT1	6,16	7	
OUT2	7,17	5	

LOGIC DIAGRAM

SAME AS LOGIC DIAGRAM.

TRUTH TABLE

A	B	C	D	OUT1	OUT2
0	*	*	*	1	0
*	0	*	*	1	0
*	*	0	*	1	0
*	*	*	0	1	0
1	1	1	1	0	1
ALL OTHER COMBINATIONS				X	X

LOGIC SYMBOLS

A,2
B,3
C,4
D,5
OUT1,6
OUT2,7

WORST CASE DELAY INFORMATION

NAND P_D=13.50 NS $T_{R/F}$=33.0 NS

AND P_D=14.07 NS $T_{R/F}$=22.26 NS

R_S=1.5KΩ, C_L=1.5PF, V=5V, T=125°C

LOGIC EQUATION(S)

$$OUT1=\overline{A*B*C*D}$$

$$OUT2=A*B*C*D$$

NOTES

THE DELAY EQUATIONS FOR THE AND OUTPUT TAKE INTO CONSIDERATION THE CAPACITIVE LOADIG ON THE NAND OUTPUT. RESISTIVE LOADING ON THE NAND OUTPUT HAS LITTLE EFFECT ON THE AND DELAY. SEE DESIGN APPLICATION NOTES FOR PROPAGATION DEVIATION OVER VOLTAGE FOR AND DELAY WITH NAND LOADED.

1680-1

3 MICRON CMOS/BULK CELL FAMILY -CMOS3-	1680 4 NAND/AND	DATE: 09/01/83 REVISION: A

CIRCUIT SCHEMATIC

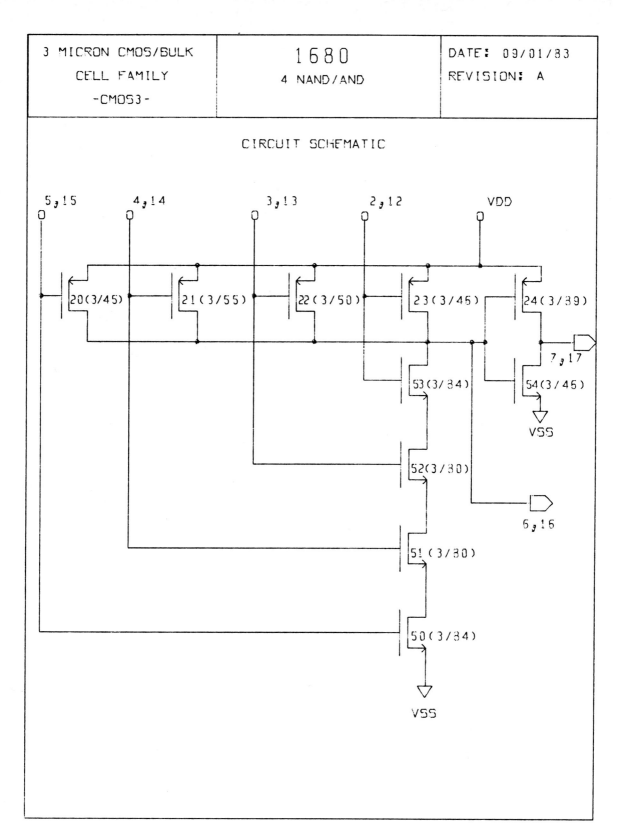

3 MICRON CMOS/BULK CELL FAMILY -CMOS3-	1680 4 NAND/AND NAND	DATE: 09/01/83 REVISION: A

OUTPUT CHARACTERISTIC EQUATIONS

$$P_D(0-1)=P_{DC}(0-1)+.13 \ (T_{R/F}-10)+.64 \ R_S C_L$$

$$P_D(1-0)=P_{DC}(1-0)+.23 \ (T_{R/F}-10)+.65 \ R_S C_L$$

$$T_R=T_{RC}+.16 \ (T_{R/F}-10)+2.41 R_S C_L$$

$$T_F=T_{FC}+.10 \ (T_{R/F}-10)+2.42 R_S C_L$$

EQUATIONS

25°C	95°C	125°C
$P_{DC}(0-1)=2.77C_L+4.25$	$P_{DC}(0-1)=3.59C_L+4.90$	$P_{DC}(0-1)=3.91C_L+5.21$
$P_{DC}(1-0)=2.57C_L+5.79$	$P_{DC}(1-0)=3.32C_L+6.53$	$P_{DC}(1-0)=3.64C_L+6.83$
$T_{RC}=9.74C_L+4.72$	$T_{RC}=12.96C_L+5.67$	$T_{RC}=14.36C_L+6.08$
$T_{FC}=8.78C_L+4.27$	$T_{FC}=11.56C_L+5.38$	$T_{FC}=12.77C_L+5.84$

125°C BC

$$P_{DC}(0-1)=2.11C_L+3.20$$

$$P_{DC}(1-0)=1.92C_L+4.21$$

$$T_{RC}=7.76C_L+3.74$$

$$T_{FC}=7.1 \ C_L+2.91$$

VOLTAGE TABLE

VOLTAGE	DEVIATION FACTOR			
	TRANSITION		PROP DELAY	
	TR	TF	1-0	0-1
3.0	1.41	1.51	1.95	1.45
3.5	1.27	1.33	1.62	1.30
4.0	1.13	1.15	1.29	1.15
4.5	1.07	1.07	1.15	1.07
5.0	1.00	1.00	1.00	1.00
5.5	.96	.97	.92	.96
6.0	.93	.93	.83	.91
6.5	.90	.91	.78	.88
7.0	.88	.88	.73	.86

1680-3

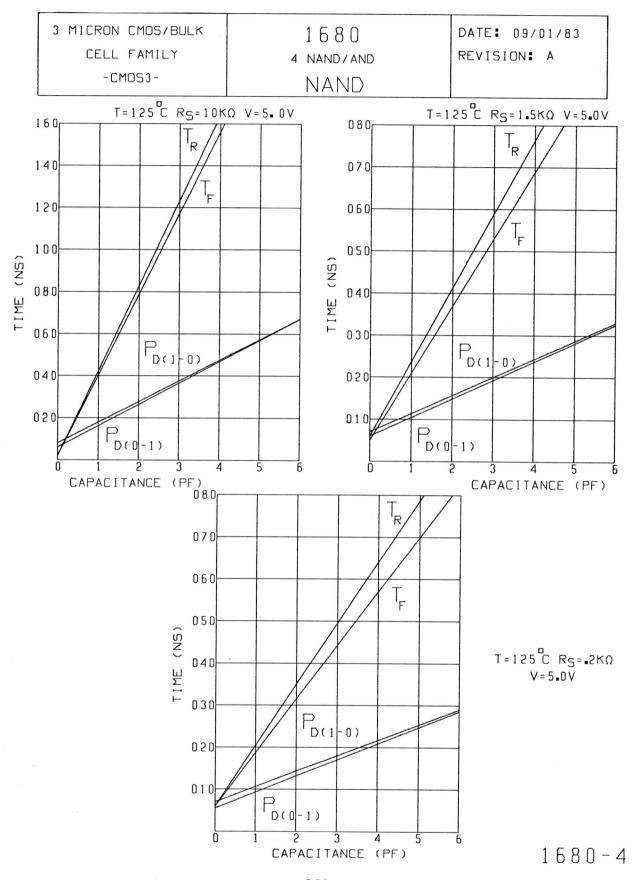

260

1680-4

OUTPUT CHARACTERISTIC EQUATIONS

$$P_D(0-1) = P_{DC}(0-1) + .21 (T_{R/F} - 10) + .66 R_S C_L + 1.5 C_{LNAND}$$

$$P_D(1-0) = P_{DC}(1-0) + .17 (T_{R/F} - 10) + .64 R_S C_L + 2.04 C_{LNAND}$$

$$T_R = T_{RC} + .01 (T_{R/F} - 10) + 2.59 R_S C_L + 1.44 C_{LNAND}$$

$$T_F = T_{FC} + .02 (T_{R/F} - 10) + 2.61 R_S C_L + 1.82 C_{LNAND}$$

EQUATIONS

$25^\circ C$

$$P_{DC}(0-1) = 1.86 C_L + 7.35$$

$$P_{DC}(1-0) = 1.64 C_L + 6.15$$

$$T_{RC} = 5.81 C_L + 1.95$$

$$T_{FC} = 5.97 C_L + 1.59$$

$95^\circ C$

$$P_{DC}(0-1) = 2.45 C_L + 8.42$$

$$P_{DC}(1-0) = 2.14 C_L + 7.14$$

$$T_{RC} = 9.0 C_L + 2.55$$

$$T_{FC} = 7.88 C_L + 2.03$$

$125^\circ C$

$$P_{DC}(0-1) = 2.7 C_L + 8.85$$

$$P_{DC}(1-0) = 2.36 C_L + 7.54$$

$$T_{RC} = 9.96 C_L + 2.80$$

$$T_{FC} = 8.73 C_L + 2.21$$

$125^\circ C$ BC

$$P_{DC}(0-1) = 1.55 C_L + 4.95$$

$$P_{DC}(1-0) = 1.40 C_L + 4.02$$

$$T_{RC} = 5.94 C_L + 1.22$$

$$T_{FC} = 5.36 C_L + 1.06$$

VOLTAGE TABLE

VOLTAGE	DEVIATION FACTOR			
	TRANSITION		PROP DELAY	
	TR	TF	1-0	0-1
3.0	1.29	1.26	1.63	1.78
3.5	1.19	1.17	1.41	1.51
4.0	1.09	1.08	1.19	1.24
4.5	1.05	1.04	1.10	1.12
5.0	1.00	1.00	1.00	1.00
5.5	.97	.98	.94	.94
6.0	.95	.96	.89	.87
6.5	.93	.94	.86	.83
7.0	.92	.93	.82	.80

1680-5

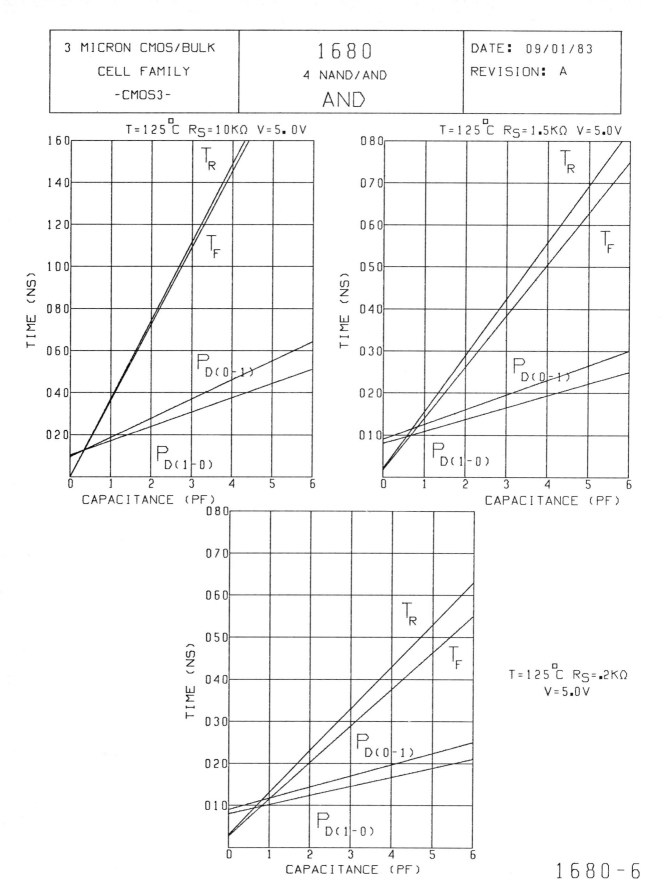

1680-6

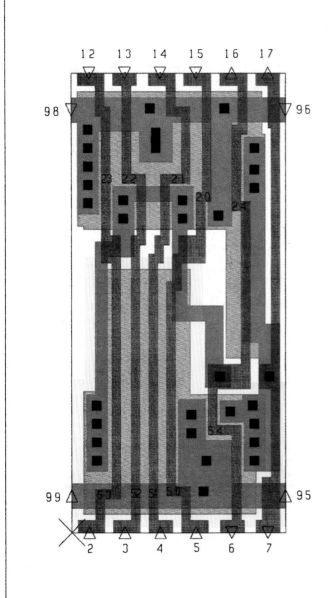

1680-7

263

3 MICRON CMOS/BULK	1740	DATE: 09/01/83
CELL FAMILY	4-INPUT OR	REVISION: A
-CMOS3-	CELL HEIGHT 150 WIDTH 72	

TERMINAL INFORMATION

TERMINAL NAME	NUMBER	LOGIC FIELD	CAPACITANCE (PF)
A	2,12	1	.27
B	3,13	2	.25
C	4,14	3	.25
D	5,15	4	.25
OUT	6,16	5	

LOGIC DIAGRAM

SAME AS LOGIC SYMBOL.

TRUTH TABLE

A	B	C	D	OUT
0	0	0	0	0
*	*	*	1	1
*	*	1	*	1
*	1	*	*	1
1	*	*	*	1
ALL OTHER COMBINATIONS				X

LOGIC SYMBOLS

A,2
B,3
C,4   OUT,6
D,5

WORST CASE DELAY INFORMATION

P_D = 16.0 NS $T_{R/F}$ = 15.5 NS

R_S = 1.5KΩ, C_L = 1.5PF, V=5V, T=125°C

LOGIC EQUATION(S)

OUT=A+B+C+D

NOTES

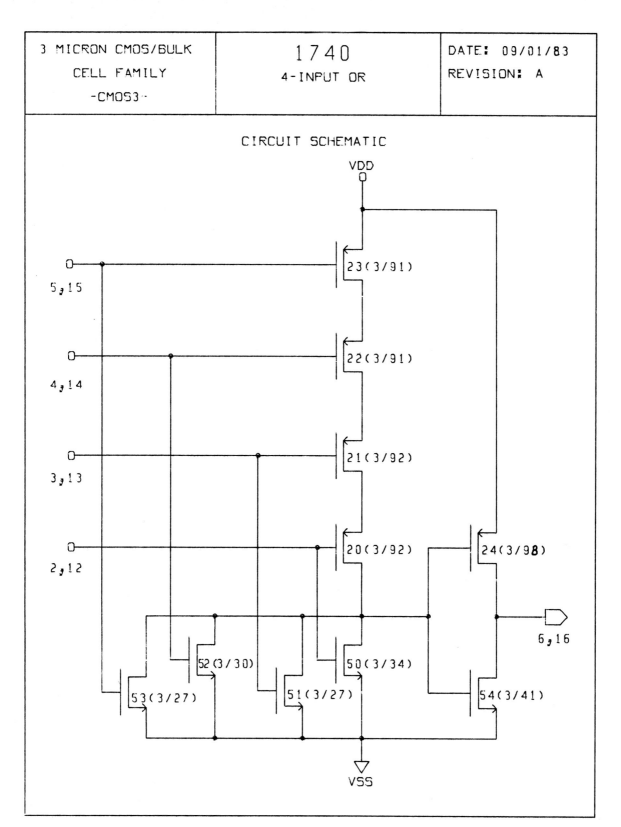

3 MICRON CMOS/BULK CELL FAMILY -CMOS3-	1740 4-INPUT OR	DATE: 09/01/83 REVISION: A

CIRCUIT SCHEMATIC

VDD

5,15

23(3/91)

4,14

22(3/91)

3,13

21(3/92)

2,12

20(3/92)

24(3/98)

6,16

52(3/30)

50(3/34)

53(3/27)

51(3/27)

54(3/41)

VSS

1740-2

3 MICRON CMOS/BULK CELL FAMILY -CMOS3-	1740 4-INPUT OR	DATE: 09/01/83 REVISION: A

OUTPUT CHARACTERISTIC EQUATIONS

$$P_D(0-1) = P_{DC}(0-1) + 0.16(T_{R/F} - 10) + 0.63 R_S C_L$$

$$P_D(1-0) = P_{DC}(1-0) + 0.22(T_{R/F} - 10) + 0.58 R_S C_L$$

$$T_R = T_{RC} + 0.03(T_{R/F} - 10) + 2.53 R_S C_L$$

$$T_F = T_{FC} + 0.02(T_{R/F} - 10) + 2.42 R_S C_L$$

EQUATIONS

$25^\circ C$

$$P_{DC}(0-1) = 1.23 C_L + 5.51$$

$$P_{DC}(1-0) = 1.40 C_L + 9.87$$

$$T_{RC} = 4.07 C_L + 1.83$$

$$T_{FC} = 3.78 C_L + 2.92$$

$95^\circ C$

$$P_{DC}(0-1) = 1.59 C_L + 6.18$$

$$P_{DC}(1-0) = 1.76 C_L + 11.69$$

$$T_{RC} = 5.25 C_L + 2.45$$

$$T_{FC} = 4.82 C_L + 3.82$$

$125^\circ C$

$$P_{DC}(0-1) = 1.74 C_L + 6.45$$

$$P_{DC}(1-0) = 1.92 C_L + 12.42$$

$$T_{RC} = 5.75 C_L + 2.72$$

$$T_{FC} = 5.25 C_L + 4.22$$

$125^\circ C$ BC

$$P_{DC}(0-1) = 0.88 C_L + 3.14$$

$$P_{DC}(1-0) = 0.89 C_L + 6.59$$

$$T_{RC} = 3.04 C_L + 1.84$$

$$T_{FC} = 2.79 C_L + 2.01$$

VOLTAGE TABLE

	DEVIATION FACTOR			
VOLTAGE	TRANSITION		PROP DELAY	
	TR	TF	1-0	0-1
3.0	1.33	1.53	1.88	1.68
3.5	1.25	1.34	1.58	1.45
4.0	1.12	1.16	1.28	1.22
4.5	1.06	1.08	1.14	1.11
5.0	1.00	1.00	1.00	1.00
5.5	.97	.96	.92	.94
6.0	.93	.92	.84	.87
6.5	.91	.89	.79	.83
7.0	.89	.87	.74	.79

1740-3

266

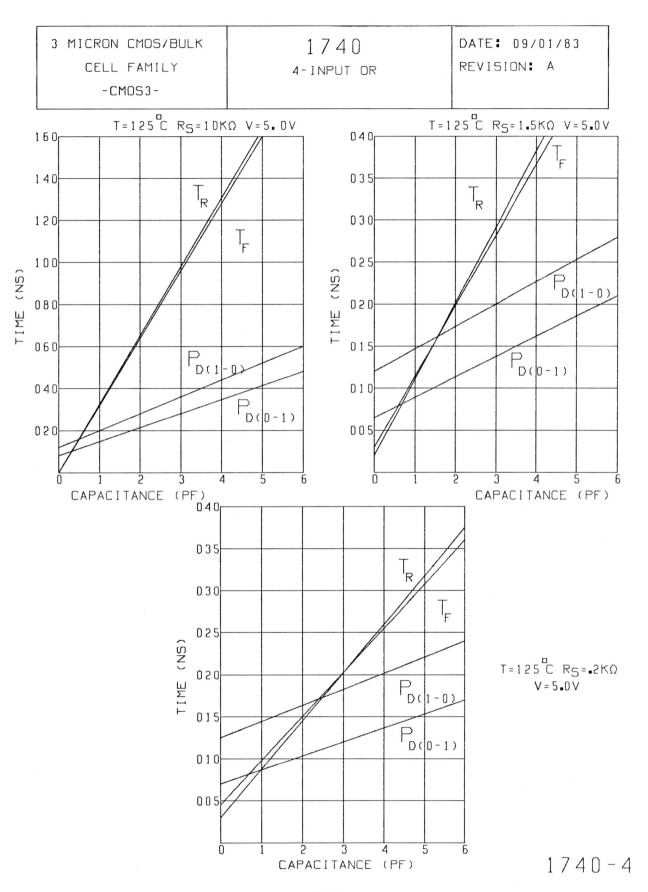

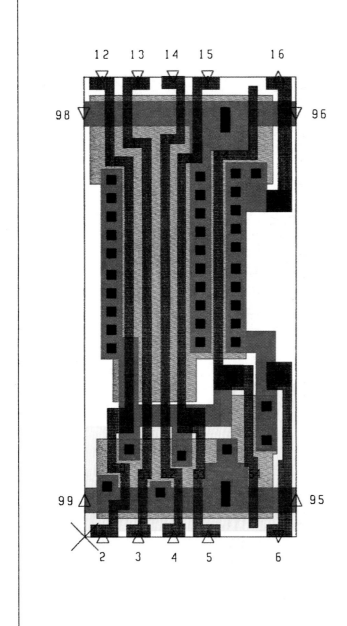

1740-5

OUTPUT CHARACTERISTIC EQUATIONS

$$P_D(0-1)=P_{DC}(0-1)+0.20(T_{R/F}-10)+0.65R_SC_L$$

$$P_D(1-0)=P_{DC}(1-0)+0.22(T_{R/F}-10)+0.62R_SC_L$$

$$T_R=T_{RC}+0.16(T_{R/F}-10)+2.41R_SC_L$$

$$T_F=T_{FC}+0.20(T_{R/F}-10)+2.40R_SC_L$$

EQUATIONS

25°C

$$P_{DC}(0-1)=2.49C_L+4.03$$

$$P_{DC}(1-0)=2.21C_L+4.38$$

$$T_{RC}=8.25C_L+4.50$$

$$T_{FC}=5.94C_L+3.98$$

95°C

$$P_{DC}(0-1)=3.21C_L+4.47$$

$$P_{DC}(1-0)=2.80C_L+4.84$$

$$T_{RC}=10.88C_L+5.41$$

$$T_{FC}=9.11C_L+4.71$$

125°C

$$P_{DC}(0-1)=3.52C_L+4.65$$

$$P_{DC}(1-0)=3.03C_L+5.04$$

$$T_{RC}=12.03C_L+5.77$$

$$T_{FC}=10.04C_L+5.02$$

125°C BC

$$P_{DC}(0-1)=1.74C_L+3.12$$

$$P_{DC}(1-0)=1.51C_L+3.15$$

$$T_{RC}=5.17C_L+3.58$$

$$T_{FC}=5.05C_L+3.95$$

VOLTAGE TABLE

VOLTAGE — DEVIATION FACTOR

VOLTAGE	TRANSITION		PROP DELAY	
	TR	TF	1-0	0-1
3.0	1.46	1.53	1.64	1.55
3.5	1.31	1.34	1.42	1.36
4.0	1.15	1.16	1.20	1.17
4.5	1.07	1.03	1.10	1.09
5.0	1.00	1.00	1.00	1.00
5.5	.95	.96	.95	.95
6.0	.92	.92	.89	.90
6.5	.89	.89	.85	.87
7.0	.86	.87	.82	.84

1760-3

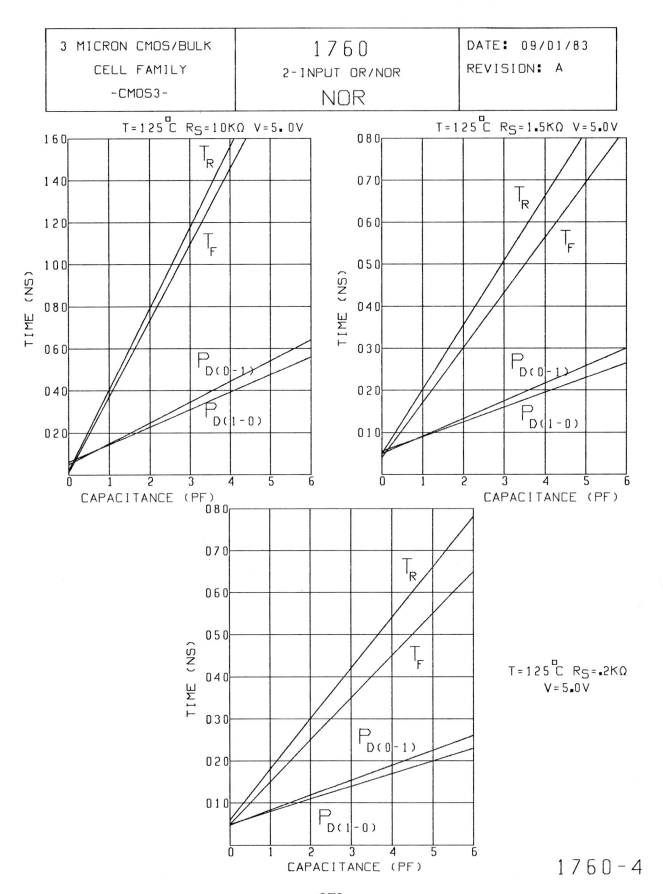

T=125°C R$_S$=10KΩ V=5.0V

T=125°C R$_S$=1.5KΩ V=5.0V

T=125°C R$_S$=.2KΩ
V=5.0V

1760-4

OUTPUT CHARACTERISTIC EQUATIONS

$$P_D(0-1) = P_{DC}(0-1) + 0.19(T_{R/F} - 10) + 0.64R_SC_L + 2.06\ C_{LNOR}$$

$$P_D(1-0) = P_{DC}(1-0) + 0.17(T_{R/F} - 10) + 0.63R_SC_L + 2.89\ C_{LNOR}$$

$$T_R = T_{RC} + 0.02(T_{R/F} - 10) + 2.57R_SC_L + 1.62\ C_{LNOR}$$

$$T_F = T_{FC} + 0.02(T_{R/F} - 10) + 2.57R_SC_L + 2.08\ C_{LNOR}$$

EQUATIONS

$25\,^{\circ}C$	$95\,^{\circ}C$	$125\,^{\circ}C$
$P_{DC}(0-1) = 1.51C_L + 5.90$	$P_{DC}(0-1) = 1.96C_L + 6.69$	$P_{DC}(0-1) = 2.15C_L + 7.00$
$P_{DC}(1-0) = 1.38C_L + 6.07$	$P_{DC}(1-0) = 1.78C_L + 6.99$	$P_{DC}(1-0) = 1.95C_L + 7.35$
$T_{RC} = 5.31C_L + 1.79$	$T_{RC} = 6.94C_L + 2.36$	$T_{RC} = 7.64C_L + 2.52$
$T_{FC} = 4.52C_L + 1.79$	$T_{FC} = 5.99C_L + 2.29$	$T_{FC} = 6.60C_L + 2.49$

$125\,^{\circ}C$ BC

$$P_{DC}(0-1) = 1.15C_L + 3.84$$

$$P_{DC}(1-0) = 1.05C_L + 4.07$$

$$T_{RC} = 4.32C_L + 1.35$$

$$T_{FC} = 3.83C_L + 1.18$$

VOLTAGE TABLE

VOLTAGE   DEVIATION FACTOR

VOLTAGE	TRANSITION		PROP DELAY	
	TR	TF	1-0	0-1
3.0	1.33	1.33	1.80	1.55
3.5	1.22	1.22	1.53	1.43
4.0	1.11	1.10	1.25	1.20
4.5	1.05	1.05	1.13	1.10
5.0	1.00	1.00	1.00	1.00
5.5	.97	.98	.93	.94
6.0	.94	.95	.86	.88
6.5	.92	.94	.81	.85
7.0	.90	.93	.77	.81

1760-5

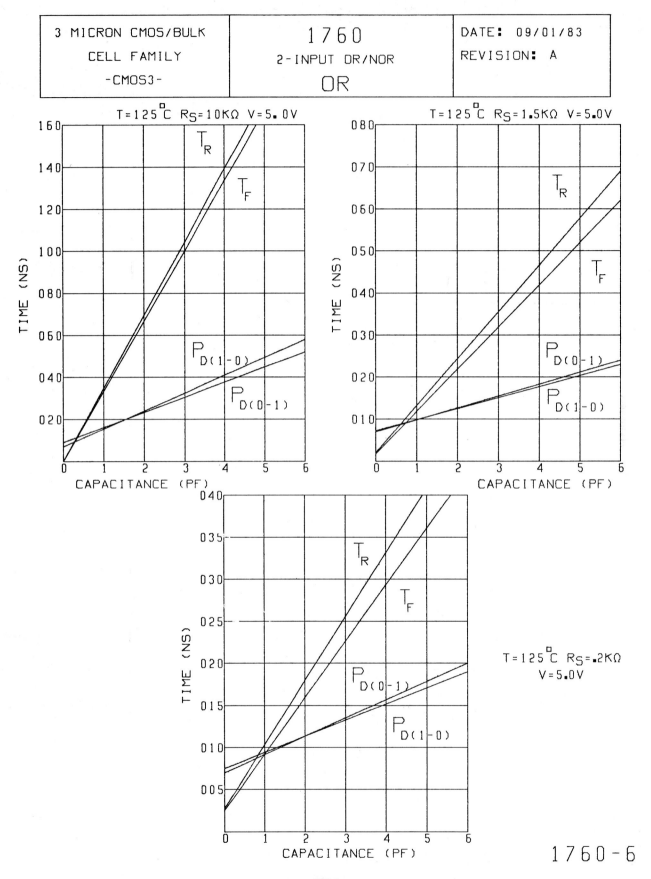

1760-6

274

3 MICRON CMOS/BULK CELL FAMILY -CMOS3-	1760 2-INPUT OR/NOR	DATE: 09/01/83 REVISION: A

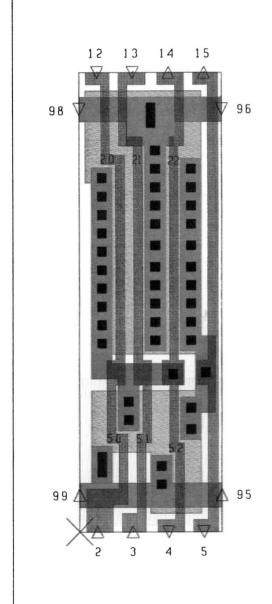

3 MICRON CMOS/BULK CELL FAMILY -CMOS3-	1770 3-INPUT OR/NOR CELL HEIGHT 150 WIDTH 60	DATE: 09/07/84 REVISION: B

TERMINAL INFORMATION

TERMINAL NAME	TERMINAL NUMBER	LOGIC FIELD	CAPACITANCE (PF)
A	2,12	1	.24
B	3,13	2	.24
C	4,14	3	.23
OUT1	6,16	6	
OUT2	5,15	7	

LOGIC DIAGRAM

SAME AS LOGIC SYMBOL.

TRUTH TABLE

A	B	C	OUT1	OUT2
0	0	0	0	1
*	*	1	1	0
*	1	*	1	0
1	*	*	1	0
ALL OTHER COMBINATIONS.			X	X

LOGIC SYMBOLS

A,2
B,3
C,4
OUT2,5
OUT1,6

WORST CASE DELAY INFORMATION

NOR P_D: 15.93 $T_{R/F}$: 38.31
OR/NOR UNLOADED P_D: 14.65 $T_{R/F}$: 15.69

R_S =1.5KΩ, C_L =1.5PF, V=5V, T=125°C

LOGIC EQUATION(S)

$$OUT1 = A + B + C$$

$$OUT2 = \overline{A + B + C}$$

NOTES

THE DELAY EQUATIONS FOR THE OR OUTPUT TAKE INTO CONSIDERATION THE CAPACITANCE LOADING ON THE NOR OUTPUT. RESISITIVE LOADING ON THE NOR OUTPUT HAS LITTLE EFFECT. SEE DESIGN APPLICATION NOTES. SEE USER NOTES FOR PROPAGATION DEVIATIONS OVER VOLTAGE FOR OR DELAY WITH NOR LOADED.

1770-1

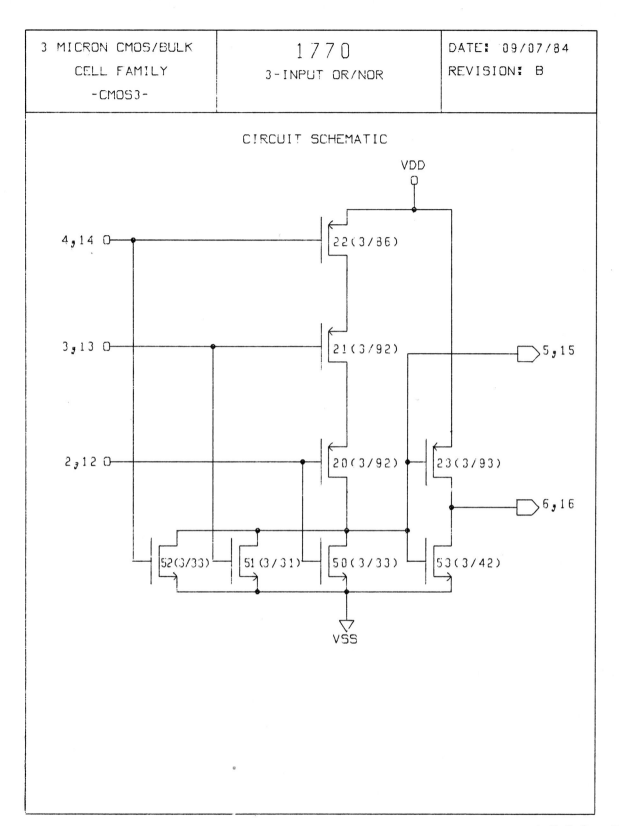

3 MICRON CMOS/BULK CELL FAMILY -CMOS3-	1770 3-INPUT OR/NOR	DATE: 09/07/84 REVISION: B

CIRCUIT SCHEMATIC

VDD

4,14

22(3/86)

3,13

21(3/92)

5,15

2,12

20(3/92) 23(3/93)

6,16

52(3/33) 51(3/31) 50(3/33) 53(3/42)

VSS

1770-2

277

3 MICRON CMOS/BULK CELL FAMILY -CMOS3-	1770 3-INPUT OR/NOR NOR	DATE: 09/07/84 REVISION: B

OUTPUT CHARACTERISTIC EQUATIONS

$$P_D(0-1) = P_{DC}(0-1) + 0.23(T_{R/F} - 10) + 0.65R_SC_L$$

$$P_D(1-0) = P_{DC}(1-0) + 0.18(T_{R/F} - 10) + 0.64R_SC_L$$

$$T_R = T_{RC} + 0.03(T_{R/F} - 10) + 2.21R_SC_L$$

$$T_F = T_{FC} + 0.25(T_{R/F} - 10) + 2.46R_SC_L$$

EQUATIONS

$25°C$

$$P_{DC}(0-1) = 3.57C_L + 6.02$$

$$P_{DC}(1-0) = 1.63C_L + 4.16$$

$$T_{RC} = 11.38C_L + 7.41$$

$$T_{FC} = 5.34C_L + 4.05$$

$95°C$

$$P_{DC}(0-1) = 4.57C_L + 6.98$$

$$P_{DC}(1-0) = 2.01C_L + 4.66$$

$$T_{RC} = 14.86C_L + 9.54$$

$$T_{FC} = 7.09C_L + 4.70$$

$125°C$

$$P_{DC}(0-1) = 4.99C_L + 7.38$$

$$P_{DC}(1-0) = 2.14C_L + 4.9$$

$$T_{RC} = 16.34C_L + 10.42$$

$$T_{FC} = 7.87C_L + 4.95$$

$125°C$ BC

$$P_{DC}(0-1) = 2.32C_L + 4.71$$

$$P_{DC}(1-0) = 1.26C_L + 2.59$$

$$T_{RC} = 3.12C_L + 4.80$$

$$T_{FC} = 4.17C_L + 4.30$$

VOLTAGE TABLE

VOLTAGE	DEVIATION FACTOR			
	TRANSITION		PROP DELAY	
	TR	TF	1-0	0-1
3.0	1.60	1.42	1.55	1.68
3.5	1.41	1.27	1.36	1.45
4.0	1.19	1.13	1.18	1.22
4.5	1.10	1.06	1.09	1.11
5.0	1.00	1.00	1.00	1.00
5.5	.94	.97	.95	.94
6.0	.89	.94	.90	.83
6.5	.85	.92	.86	.84
7.0	.82	.90	.82	.81

1770-3

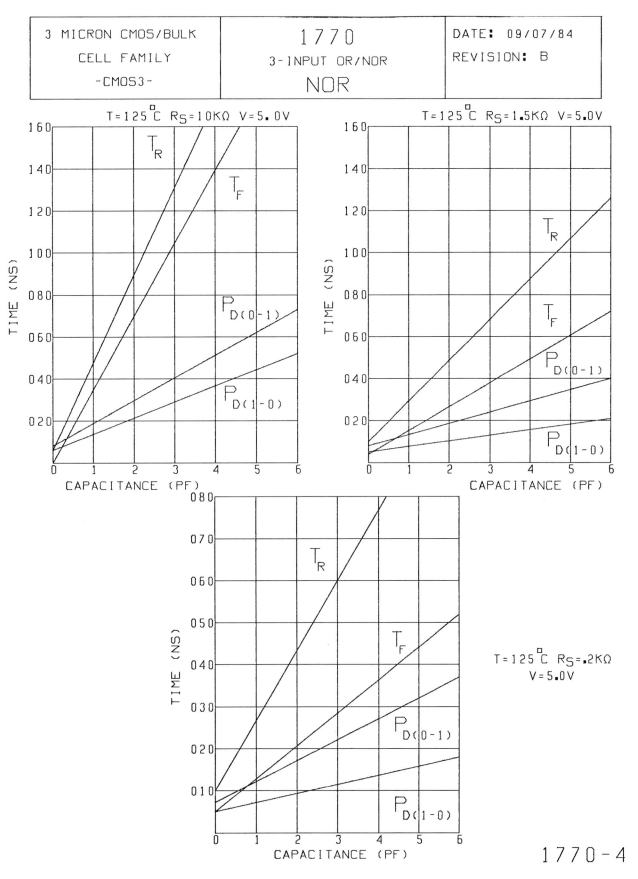

1770-4

OUTPUT CHARACTERISTIC EQUATIONS

$$P_D(0-1) = P_{DC}(0-1) + 0.15(T_{R/F} - 10) + 0.64 R_S C_L + 4.64\ C_{LNOR}$$

$$P_D(1-0) = P_{DC}(1-0) + 0.23(T_{R/F} - 10) + 0.53 R_S C_L + 1.09\ C_{LNOR}$$

$$T_R = T_{RC} + 0.03(T_{R/F} - 10) + 2.6\ R_S C_L + 1.10\ C_{LNOR}$$

$$T_F = T_{FC} + 0.02(T_{R/F} - 10) + 2.5\ R_S C_L + 3.10\ C_{LNOR}$$

EQUATIONS

25°C	95°C	125°C
$P_{DC}(0-1) = 1.27 C_L + 5.33$	$P_{DC}(0-1) = 1.63 C_L + 6.00$	$P_{DC}(0-1) = 1.73 C_L + 6.24$
$P_{DC}(1-0) = 1.35 C_L + 3.87$	$P_{DC}(1-0) = 1.72 C_L + 10.44$	$P_{DC}(1-0) = 1.86 C_L + 11.07$
$T_{RC} = 4.20 C_L + 1.82$	$T_{RC} = 5.42 C_L + 2.41$	$T_{RC} = 5.95 C_L + 2.67$
$T_{FC} = 3.70 C_L + 2.33$	$T_{FC} = 4.94 C_L + 3.37$	$T_{FC} = 5.14 C_L + 4.10$

125°C BC

$$P_{DC}(0-1) = 0.90 C_L + 3.01$$

$$P_{DC}(1-0) = 0.87 C_L + 6.15$$

$$T_{RC} = 3.15 C_L + 1.68$$

$$T_{FC} = 2.76 C_L + 1.93$$

VOLTAGE TABLE

VOLTAGE	TRANSITION		PROP DELAY	
	TR	TF	1-0	0-1
3.0	1.38	1.50	1.38	1.68
3.5	1.25	1.33	1.53	1.45
4.0	1.12	1.15	1.23	1.22
4.5	1.06	1.08	1.14	1.11
5.0	1.00	1.00	1.00	1.00
5.5	.97	.96	.92	.94
6.0	.93	.92	.85	.87
6.5	.91	.90	.80	.83
7.0	.89	.88	.76	.79

DEVIATION FACTOR

1770-5

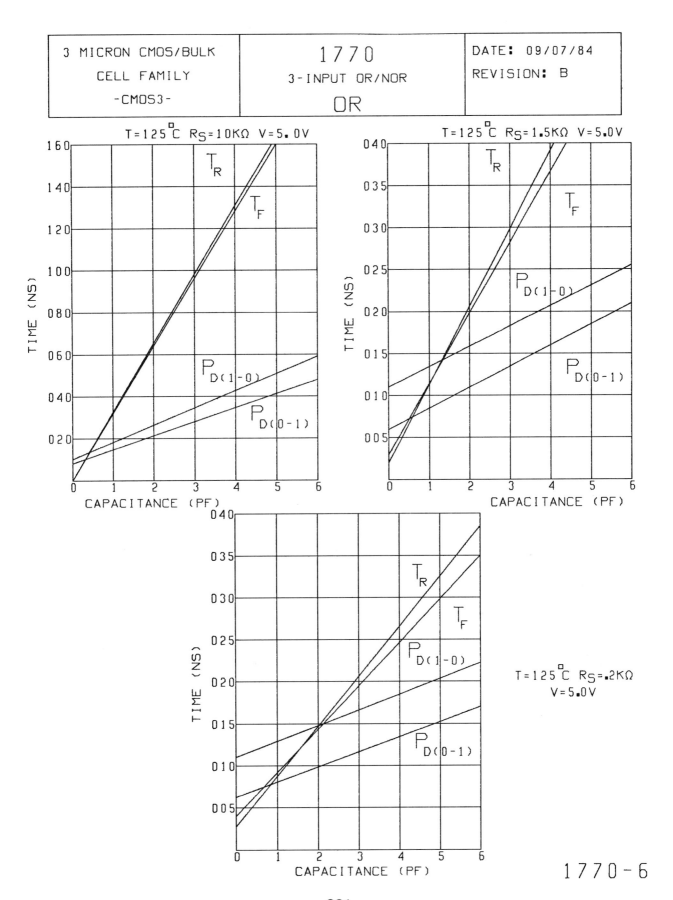

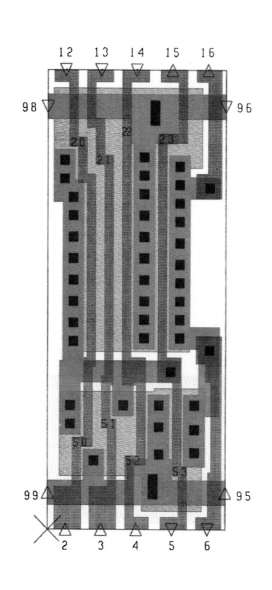

3 MICRON CMOS/BULK CELL FAMILY -CMOS3-	1810 3,2 AND/OR MUX CELL HEIGHT 150 WIDTH 106	DATE: 09/07/84 REVISION: B

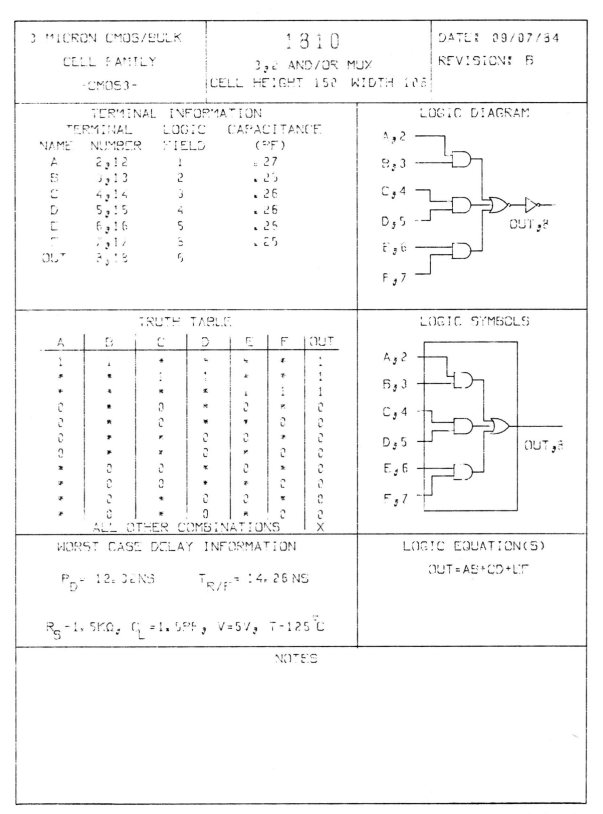

TERMINAL INFORMATION

TERMINAL NAME	NUMBER	LOGIC FIELD	CAPACITANCE (PF)
A	2,12	1	.27
B	3,13	2	.25
C	4,14	3	.26
D	5,15	4	.26
E	6,16	5	.25
F	7,17	6	.25
OUT	8,18	6	

LOGIC DIAGRAM

A,2
B,3
C,4
D,5
E,6
F,7
OUT,8

TRUTH TABLE

A	B	C	D	E	F	OUT
1	1	*	*	*	*	1
*	*	1	1	*	*	1
*	*	*	*	1	1	1
0	*	0	*	0	*	0
0	*	0	*	*	0	0
0	*	*	0	0	*	0
0	*	*	0	*	0	0
*	0	0	0	0	*	0
*	0	0	*	*	0	0
*	0	*	0	0	*	0
*	0	*	0	*	0	0

ALL OTHER COMBINATIONS | X

LOGIC SYMBOLS

A,2
B,3
C,4
D,5
E,6
F,7
OUT,8

WORST CASE DELAY INFORMATION

P_D = 12.02NS $\quad$ $T_{R/F}$ = 14.26 NS

R_S = 1.5KΩ, C_L = 1.5PF, V=5V, T=125°C

LOGIC EQUATION(S)

OUT = AB+CD+EF

NOTES

CIRCUIT SCHEMATIC

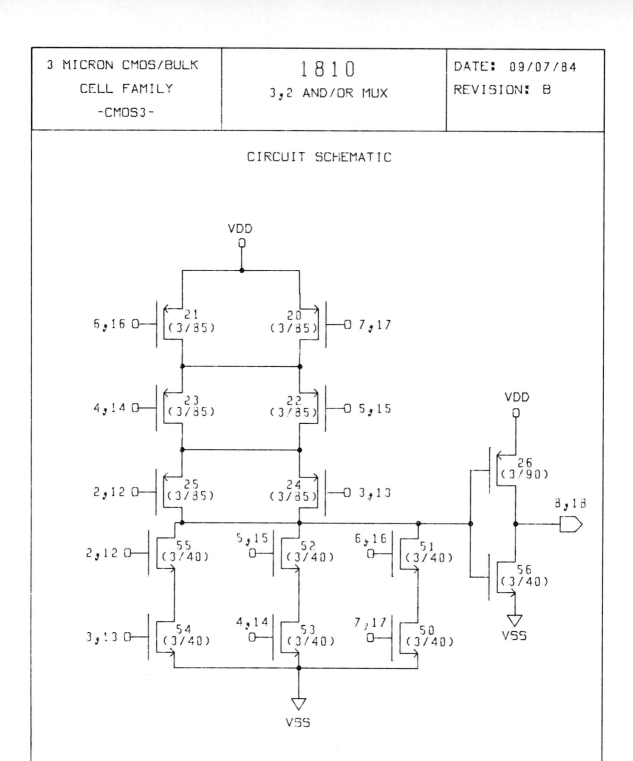

1810-2

284

3 MICRON CMOS/BULK CELL FAMILY -CMOS3-	1810 3,2 AND/OR MUX	DATE: 09/07/84 REVISION: B

OUTPUT CHARACTERISTIC EQUATIONS

$$P_D(0-1) = P_{DC}(0-1) + .11 \ (T_{R/F} - 10) + .59 \ R_S C_L$$

$$P_D(1-0) = P_{DC}(1-0) + .07 \ (T_{R/F} - 10) + .54 \ R_S C_L$$

$$T_R = T_{RC} + .02 \ (T_{R/F} - 10) + 2.41 R_S C_L$$

$$T_F = T_{FC} + .04 \ (T_{R/F} - 10) + 2.39 R_S C_L$$

EQUATIONS

$25^\circ C$	$95^\circ C$	$125^\circ C$
$P_{DC}(0-1) = 1.22 C_L + 7.14$	$P_{DC}(0-1) = 1.55 C_L + 8.44$	$P_{DC}(0-1) = 1.69 C_L + 8.92$
$P_{DC}(1-0) = 1.30 C_L + 6.55$	$P_{DC}(1-0) = 1.64 C_L + 7.88$	$P_{DC}(1-0) = 1.76 C_L + 8.41$
$T_{RC} = 3.23 C_L + 2.60$	$T_{RC} = 4.11 C_L + 3.73$	$T_{RC} = 4.46 C_L + 4.20$
$T_{FC} = 3.00 C_L + 2.58$	$T_{FC} = 3.74 C_L + 3.36$	$T_{FC} = 4.05 C_L + 3.70$

$125^\circ C$ BC

$$P_{DC}(0-1) = .76 \ C_L + 3.95$$

$$P_{DC}(1-0) = .74 \ C_L + 3.80$$

$$T_{RC} = 2.10 C_L + 2.71$$

$$T_{FC} = 1.82 C_L + 2.23$$

VOLTAGE TABLE

VOLTAGE	DEVIATION FACTOR			
	TRANSITION		PROP DELAY	
	TR	TF	1-0	0-1
3.0	1.48	1.61	1.92	1.97
3.5	1.32	1.40	1.60	1.64
4.0	1.16	1.19	1.29	1.31
4.5	1.03	1.10	1.14	1.16
5.0	1.00	1.00	1.00	1.00
5.5	.95	.95	.91	.92
6.0	.91	.90	.83	.83
6.5	.88	.87	.78	.78
7.0	.85	.84	.73	.72

1810-3

285

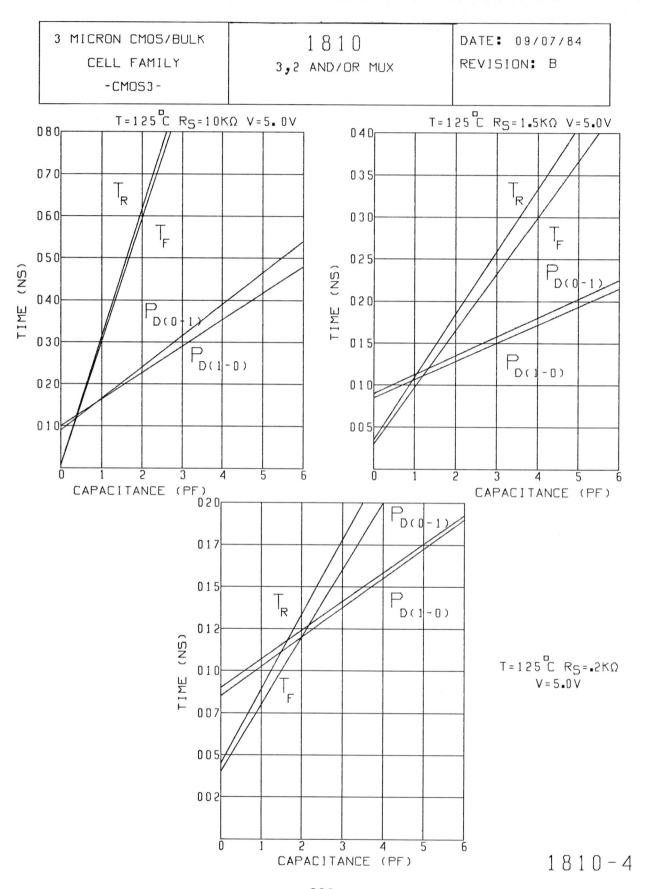

1810-4

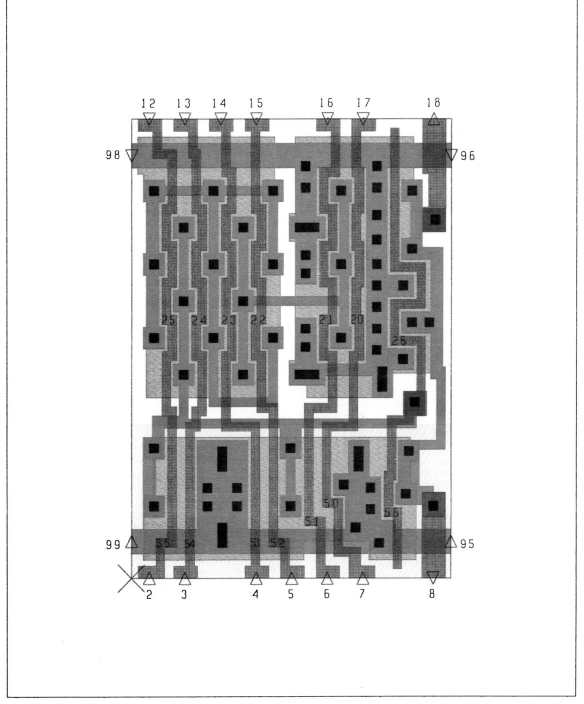

1810-5

287

3 MICRON CMOS/BULK CELL FAMILY -CMOS3-	1830 D-FLIP FLOP W/Q,$\bar{Q}$ CELL HEIGHT 150 WIDTH 132	DATE: 04/01/84 REVISION: A

TERMINAL INFORMATION

TERMINAL NAME	NUMBER	LOGIC FIELD	CAPACITANCE (PF)
DATA	2,12	2	.19
CLOCK	3,13	1	.21
$\bar{Q}$	4,14	7	
Q	5,15	6	

LOGIC DIAGRAM

TRUTH TABLE

C	D	Q	$\bar{Q}$
⌐_	*	DATA	$\overline{DATA}$
_/⌐	*	Q_{N-1}	$\bar{Q}_{N-1}$
X	*	*	*

C=X: IF M_{N-1}=D THEN M=M_{N-1}

IF Q_{N-1}=M_{N-1} THEN Q=Q_{N-1}

LOGIC SYMBOLS

WORST CASE DELAY INFORMATION

$\bar{Q}$ P_D=16.13 NS $T_{R/F}$ =29.36 NS

Q/UNLOADED $\bar{Q}$ P_D=15.79 NS $T_{R/F}$=14.38 NS

R_S=1.5KΩ, C_L=1.5PF, V=5V, T=125°C

LOGIC EQUATION(S)

$$Q_N=Q_{N-1}C+D_{N-1}\bar{C}$$

$$\overline{\bar{Q}_N=Q_{N-1}C+D_{N-1}\bar{C}}$$

NOTES

SPECIAL FLIP FLOP TIMING SEE PAGES 1830-7,8
DELAY EQUATIONS OF THE Q OUTPUT TAKE INTO CONSIDERATION THE
CAPACITIVE LOADING OF THE $\bar{Q}$ OUTPUT. RESISTIVE LOADING ON THE $\bar{Q}$
OUTPUT HAS LITTLE EFFECT ON THE Q DELAY.

REL 3   1830-1

CIRCUIT SCHEMATIC

20(3/60)	50(3/24)
21(3/60)	51(3/24)
22(3/60)	52(3/33)
23(3/19)	53(3/11)
24(3/76)	54(3/31)
25(3/76)	55(3/31)
26(3/99)	56(3/62)
27(3/9)	57(3/11)
28(3/51)	58(3/30)
29(3/49.5)	59(3/31)
30(3/19)	60(3/11)
31(3/9)	61(3/11)

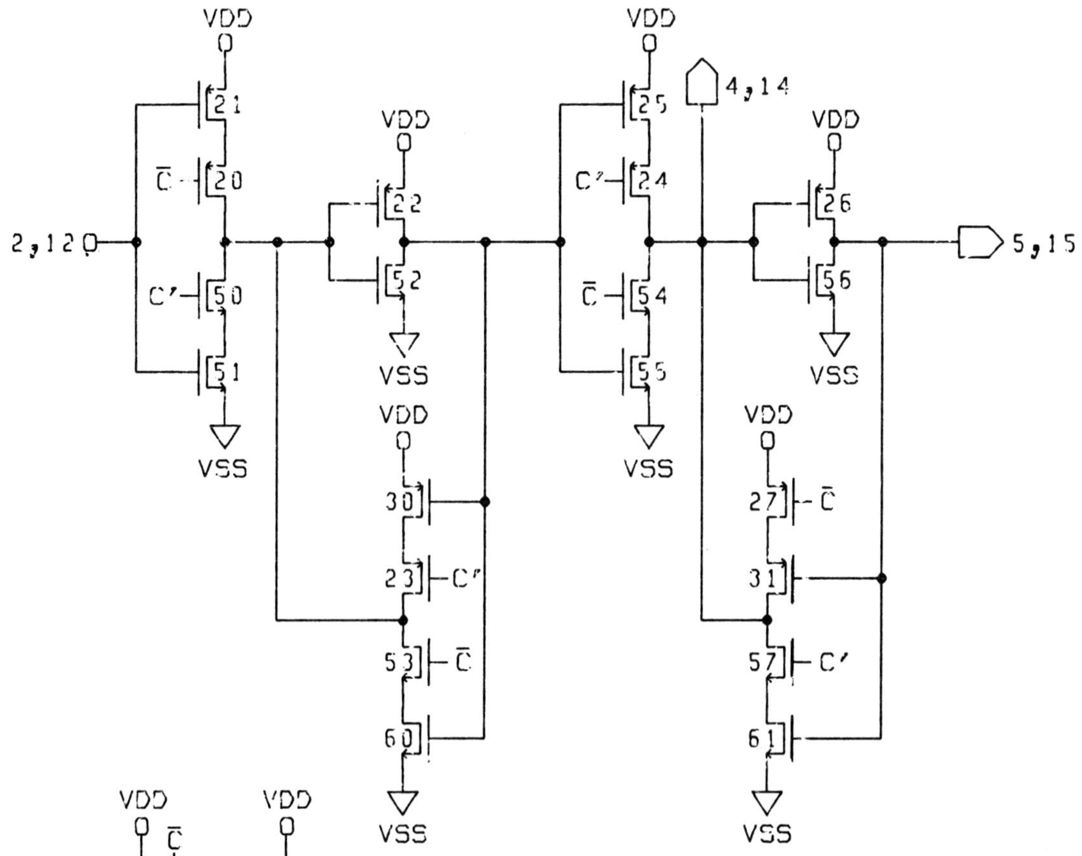

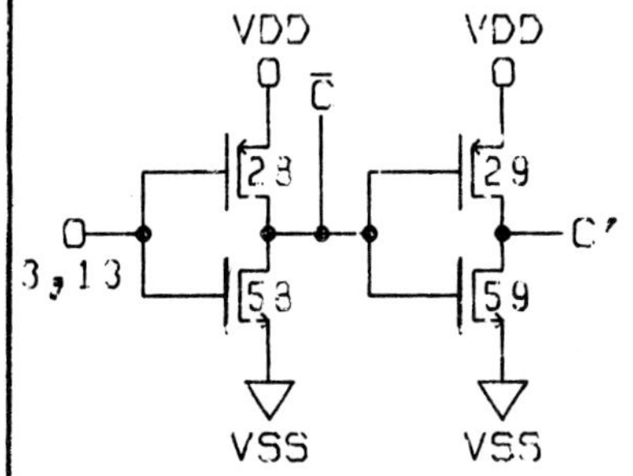

REL 3   1830-2

3 MICRON CMOS/BULK CELL FAMILY -CMOS3-	1830 D-FLIP FLOP W/Q,$\bar{Q}$ CLOCK TO Q	DATE: 04/01/84 REVISION: A

OUTPUT CHARACTERISTIC EQUATIONS

$$P_D(0-1) = P_{DC}(0-1) + .11 \ (T_{R/F} - 10) + .61 \ R_S C_L + 4.44 \ C_{L\bar{Q}}$$

$$P_D(1-0) = P_{DC}(1-0) + .11 \ (T_{R/F} - 10) + .59 \ R_S C_L + 4.00 \ C_{L\bar{Q}}$$

$$T_R = T_{RC} + 0.00 (T_{R/F} - 10) + 2.38 R_S C_L + 2.11 \ C_{L\bar{Q}}$$

$$T_F = T_{FC} + 0.00 (T_{R/F} - 10) + 2.42 R_S C_L + 2.17 \ C_{L\bar{Q}}$$

EQUATIONS

$25^\circ C$	$95^\circ C$	$125^\circ C$
$P_{DC}(0-1) = 1.13 C_L + 9.03$	$P_{DC}(0-1) = 1.43 C_L + 10.71$	$P_{DC}(0-1) = 1.55 C_L + 11.35$
$P_{DC}(1-0) = .91 \ C_L + 10.29$	$P_{DC}(1-0) = 1.14 C_L + 12.33$	$P_{DC}(1-0) = 1.23 C_L + 13.11$
$T_{RC} = 3.00 C_L + 3.41$	$T_{RC} = 3.73 C_L + 4.57$	$T_{RC} = 4.12 C_L + 5.07$
$T_{FC} = 2.04 C_L + 2.73$	$T_{FC} = 2.51 C_L + 3.72$	$T_{FC} = 2.7 \ C_L + 4.13$

$125^\circ C$ BC	VOLTAGE TABLE

$$P_{DC}(0-1) = .69 \ C_L + 5.10$$

$$P_{DC}(1-0) = .54 \ C_L + 5.91$$

$$T_{RC} = 2.00 C_L + 2.42$$

$$T_{FC} = 1.31 C_L + 2.01$$

VOLTAGE	TRANSITION		PROP DELAY	
	TR	TF	1-0	0-1
3.0	1.54	1.54	1.91	1.90
3.5	1.35	1.35	1.50	1.59
4.0	1.17	1.17	1.29	1.23
4.5	1.09	1.09	1.15	1.14
5.0	1.00	1.00	1.00	1.00
5.5	.95	.95	.92	.92
6.0	.90	.91	.84	.84
6.5	.87	.88	.79	.75
7.0	.84	.85	.73	.72

REL 3   1830-3

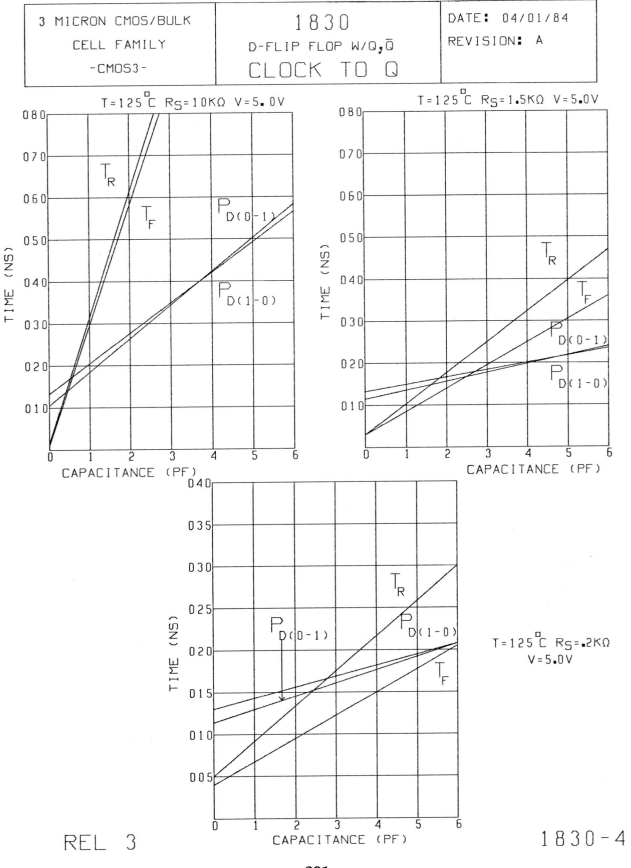

3 MICRON CMOS/BULK CELL FAMILY -CMOS3-	1830 D-FLIP FLOP W/Q,$\bar{Q}$ CLOCK TO $\bar{Q}$	DATE: 04/01/84 REVISION: A

OUTPUT CHARACTERISTIC EQUATIONS

$$P_D(0-1)=P_{DC}(0-1)+.11 (T_{R/F}-10)+.65 R_S C_L$$

$$P_D(1-0)=P_{DC}(1-0)+.12 (T_{R/F}-10)+.59 R_S C_L$$

$$T_R=T_{RC}+0.00(T_{R/F}-10)+2.07R_S C_L$$

$$T_F=T_{FC}+.02 (T_{R/F}-10)+1.93R_S C_L$$

EQUATIONS

25°C	95°C	125°C
$P_{DC}(0-1)=2.60C_L+7.65$	$P_{DC}(0-1)=3.30C_L+9.08$	$P_{DC}(0-1)=3.55C_L+9.63$
$P_{DC}(1-0)=2.86C_L+6.35$	$P_{DC}(1-0)=3.57C_L+7.40$	$P_{DC}(1-0)=3.86C_L+7.50$
$T_{RC}=7.50C_L+7.63$	$T_{RC}=9.64C_L+10.04$	$T_{RC}=10.53C_L+11.02$
$T_{FC}=7.42C_L+7.30$	$T_{FC}=9.39C_L+9.47$	$T_{FC}=10.20C_L+10.37$

125°C BC

$$P_{DC}(0-1)=1.54C_L+4.50$$

$$P_{DC}(1-0)=1.56C_L+3.70$$

$$T_{RC}=4.81C_L+4.78$$

$$T_{FC}=4.42C_L+4.79$$

VOLTAGE TABLE

VOLTAGE	DEVIATION FACTOR			
	TRANSITION		PROP DELAY	
	TR	TF	1-0	0-1
3.0	1.67	1.83	1.91	1.80
3.5	1.45	1.55	1.60	1.53
4.0	1.22	1.26	1.29	1.25
4.5	1.11	1.13	1.15	1.13
5.0	1.00	1.00	1.00	1.00
5.5	.94	.93	.92	.93
6.0	.87	.85	.84	.85
6.5	.83	.80	.78	.81
7.0	.79	.75	.72	.76

REL 3   1830-5

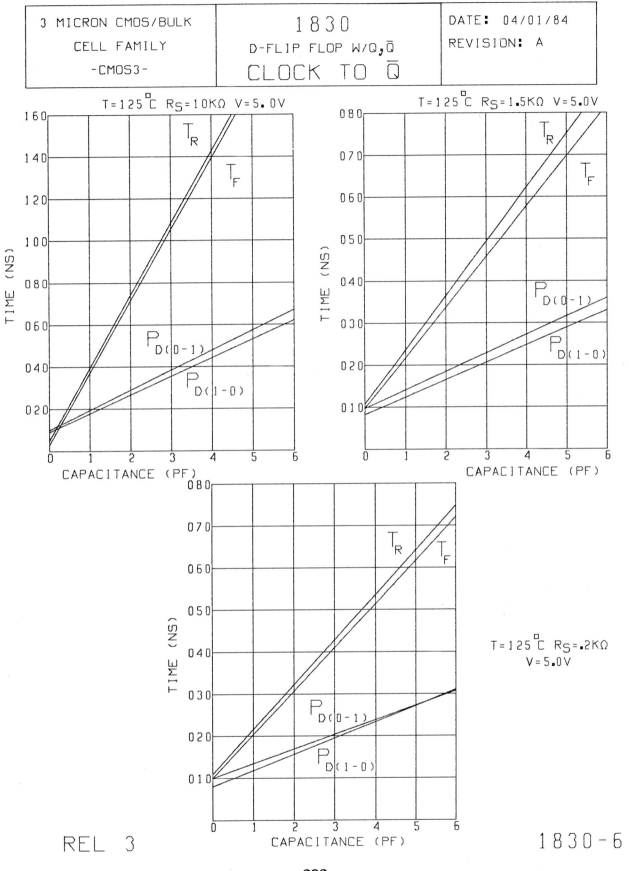

SPECIAL FLIP FLOP TIMING

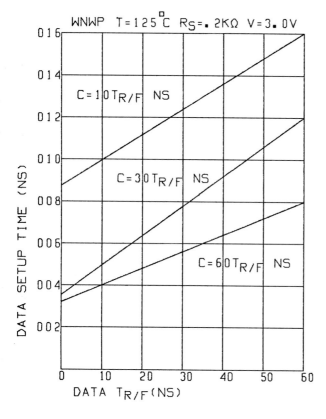

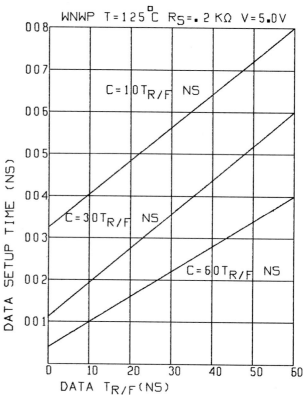

3 MICRON CMOS/BULK CELL FAMILY -CMOS3-	1830 D-FLIP FLOP W/Q,$\overline{Q}$	DATE: 04/01/84 REVISION: A

SPECIAL FLIP FLOP TIMING

MINIMUM CLOCK PULSE WIDTH = 30NS

MAXIMUM CLOCK RISE/FALL TIME = 200NS

DATA HOLD TIME = 2NS   FOR CLOCK $T_{R/F}$ = 30NS

DATA HOLD TIME = 3NS   FOR CLOCK $T_{R/F}$ = 60NS

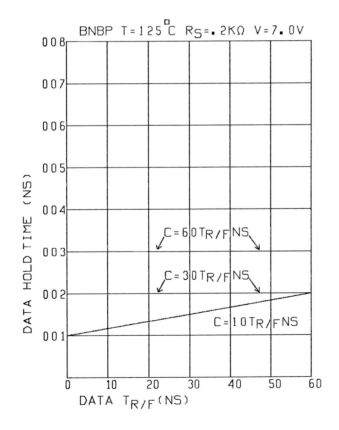

BNBP T=125°C R_S=.2KΩ V=7.0V

REL 3

3 MICRON CMOS/BULK CELL FAMILY -CMOS3-	1830 D FLIP-FLOP W/Q,$\bar{Q}$	DATE: 04/01/84 REVISION: A

REL 3 1830-9

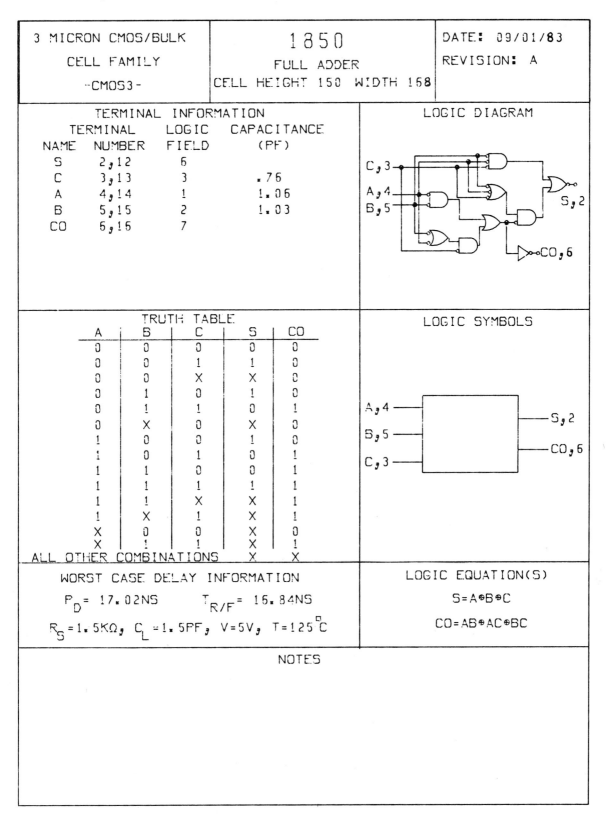

3 MICRON CMOS/BULK CELL FAMILY -CMOS3-	1850 FULL ADDER CELL HEIGHT 150 WIDTH 168	DATE: 09/01/83 REVISION: A

TERMINAL INFORMATION

TERMINAL NAME	NUMBER	LOGIC FIELD	CAPACITANCE (PF)
S	2,12	6	
C	3,13	3	.76
A	4,14	1	1.06
B	5,15	2	1.03
CO	6,16	7	

LOGIC DIAGRAM

TRUTH TABLE

A	B	C	S	CO
0	0	0	0	0
0	0	1	1	0
0	0	X	X	0
0	1	0	1	0
0	1	1	0	1
0	X	0	X	0
1	0	0	1	0
1	0	1	0	1
1	1	0	0	1
1	1	1	1	1
1	1	X	X	1
1	X	1	X	1
X	0	0	X	0
X	1	1	X	1
ALL OTHER COMBINATIONS			X	X

LOGIC SYMBOLS

WORST CASE DELAY INFORMATION

P_D = 17.02NS $T_{R/F}$ = 15.84NS

R_S =1.5KΩ, C_L =1.5PF, V=5V, T=125°C

LOGIC EQUATION(S)

S=A⊕B⊕C

CO=AB⊕AC⊕BC

NOTES

1850-1

CIRCUIT SCHEMATIC

A 4,14
B 5,15
C 3,13

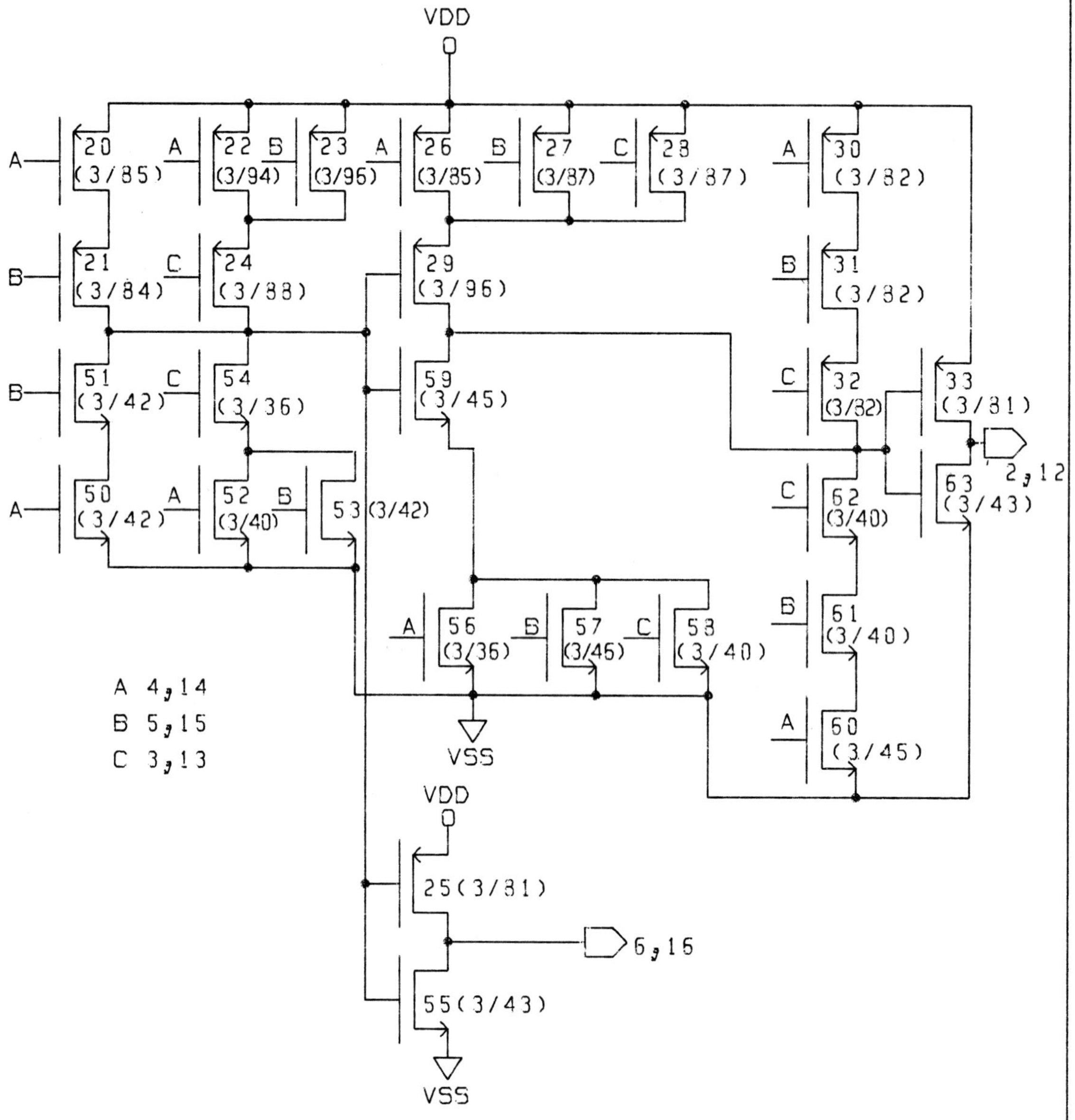

3 MICRON CMOS/BULK CELL FAMILY -CMOS3-	1850 FULL ADDER SUM OUTPUT	DATE: 09/01/83 REVISION: A

OUTPUT CHARACTERISTIC EQUATIONS

$$P_D(0-1) = P_{DC}(0-1) + 0.15(T_{R/F} - 10) + 0.53R_SC_L$$

$$P_D(1-0) = P_{DC}(1-0) + 0.20(T_{R/F} - 10) + 0.59R_SC_L$$

$$T_R = T_{RC} + 0.00(T_{R/F} - 10) + 2.47R_SC_L$$

$$T_F = T_{FC} + 0.00(T_{R/F} - 10) + 2.46R_SC_L$$

EQUATIONS

$25^{\circ}C$	$95^{\circ}C$	$125^{\circ}C$
$P_{DC}(0-1) = 1.38C_L + 10.25$	$P_{DC}(0-1) = 1.76C_L + 12.28$	$P_{DC}(0-1) = 1.92C_L + 13.12$
$P_{DC}(1-0) = 1.22C_L + 10.33$	$P_{DC}(1-0) = 1.54C_L + 12.23$	$P_{DC}(1-0) = 1.67C_L + 13.05$
$T_{RC} = 4.33C_L + 2.55$	$T_{RC} = 5.56C_L + 3.35$	$T_{RC} = 5.09C_L + 3.70$
$T_{FC} = 3.37C_L + 2.59$	$T_{FC} = 4.28C_L + 3.39$	$T_{FC} = 4.56C_L + 3.73$

$125^{\circ}C$ BC

$$P_{DC}(0-1) = 0.92C_L + 6.25$$

$$P_{DC}(1-0) = 0.77C_L + 6.43$$

$$T_{RC} = 3.16C_L + 1.71$$

$$T_{FC} = 2.45C_L + 1.71$$

VOLTAGE TABLE

VOLTAGE	DEVIATION FACTOR			
	TRANSITION		PROP DELAY	
	TR	TF	1-0	0-1
3.0	1.47	1.53	1.89	1.82
3.5	1.31	1.35	1.59	1.54
4.0	1.15	1.16	1.28	1.25
4.5	1.08	1.08	1.14	1.13
5.0	1.00	1.00	1.00	1.00
5.5	.96	.96	.92	.92
6.0	.91	.91	.84	.85
6.5	.89	.89	.79	.80
7.0	.86	.86	.74	.75

1850-3

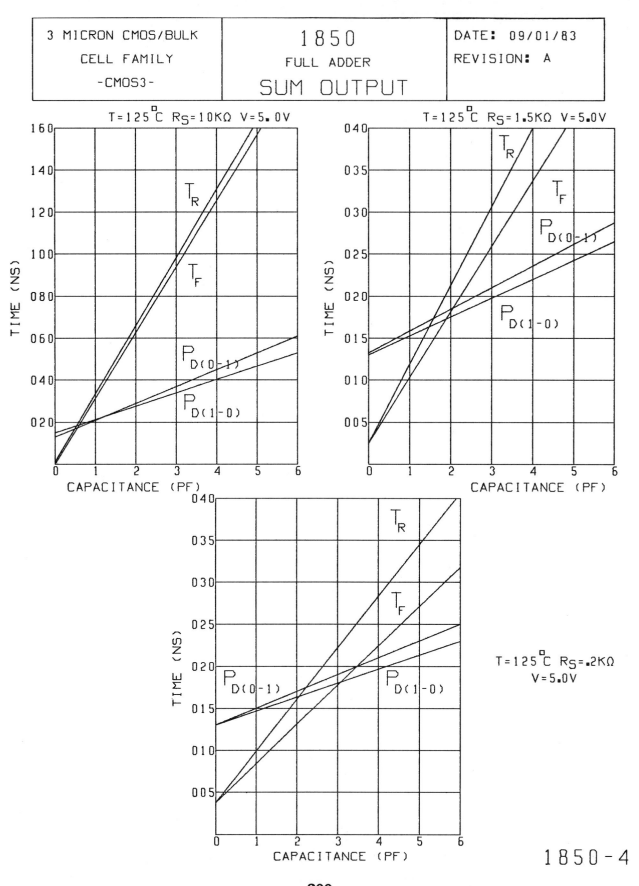

3 MICRON CMOS/BULK	1850	DATE: 09/01/83
CELL FAMILY	FULL ADDER	REVISION: A
-CMOS3-	CARRY OUTPUT	

OUTPUT CHARACTERISTIC EQUATIONS

$$P_D(0-1) = P_{DC}(0-1) + 0.25(T_{R/F} - 10) + 0.52 R_S C_L$$

$$P_D(1-0) = P_{DC}(1-0) + 0.15(T_{R/F} - 10) + 0.59 R_S C_L$$

$$T_R = T_{RC} + 0.01(T_{R/F} - 10) + 2.44 R_S C_L$$

$$T_F = T_{FC} + 0.04(T_{R/F} - 10) + 2.44 R_S C_L$$

EQUATIONS

$25°C$	$95°C$	$125°C$
$P_{DC}(0-1) = 1.42 C_L + 7.67$	$P_{DC}(0-1) = 1.32 C_L + 3.33$	$P_{DC}(0-1) = 1.99 C_L + 9.35$
$P_{DC}(1-0) = 1.26 C_L + 7.91$	$P_{DC}(1-0) = 1.60 C_L + 9.23$	$P_{DC}(1-0) = 1.73 C_L + 9.84$
$T_{RC} = 4.32 C_L + 2.81$	$T_{RC} = 5.55 C_L + 3.75$	$T_{RC} = 6.07 C_L + 4.15$
$T_{FC} = 3.38 C_L + 2.75$	$T_{FC} = 4.23 C_L + 3.62$	$T_{FC} = 4.65 C_L + 4.05$

$125°C$ BC

$$P_{DC}(0-1) = 0.94 C_L + 5.43$$

$$P_{DC}(1-0) = 0.79 C_L + 4.77$$

$$T_{RC} = 3.12 C_L + 1.99$$

$$T_{FC} = 2.31 C_L + 2.68$$

VOLTAGE TABLE

VOLTAGE	DEVIATION FACTOR			
	TRANSITION		PROP DELAY	
	TR	TF	1-0	0-1
3.0	1.48	1.53	1.80	1.80
3.5	1.32	1.35	1.53	1.52
4.0	1.15	1.16	1.26	1.25
4.5	1.08	1.08	1.13	1.12
5.0	1.00	1.00	1.00	1.00
5.5	.96	.96	.93	.93
6.0	.91	.91	.85	.87
6.5	.88	.88	.80	.82
7.0	.86	.86	.75	.78

1850-5

301

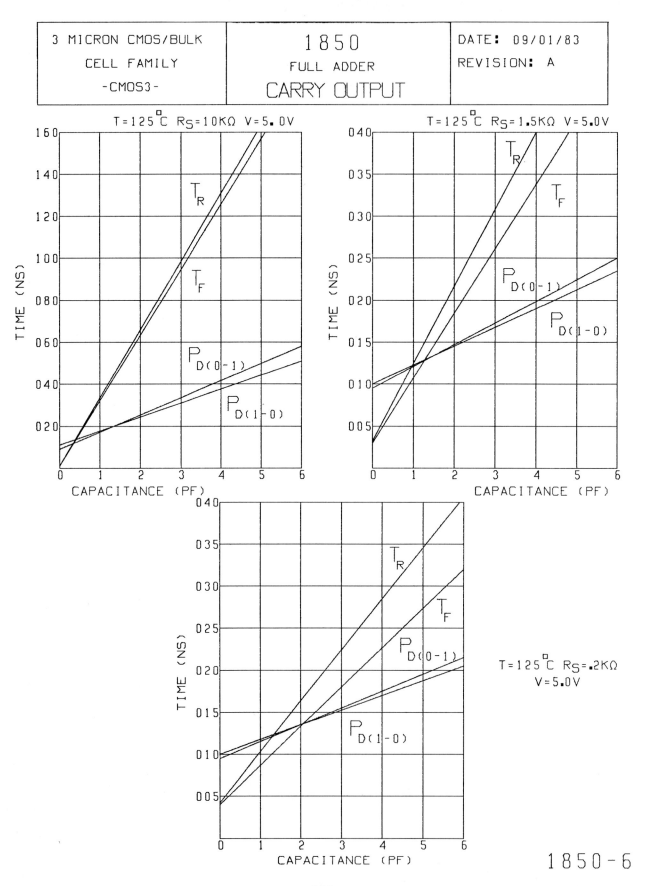

1850-6

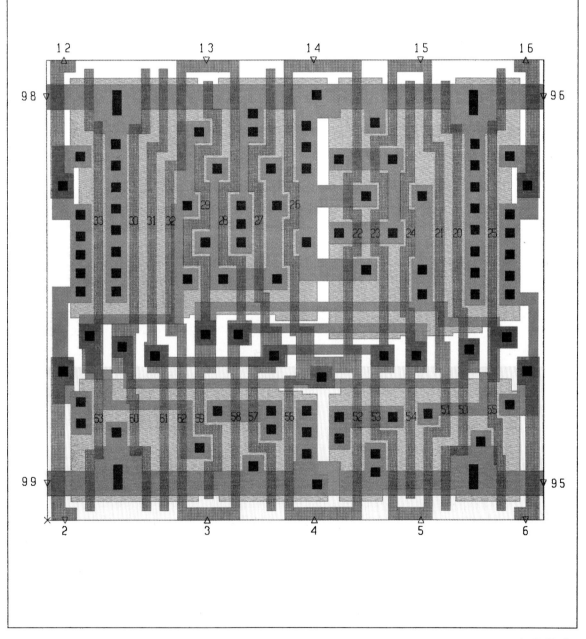

1850-7

3 MICRON CMOS/BULK CELL FAMILY -CMOS3-	1 8 7 0 2,2 AND/NOR MUX CELL HEIGHT 150 WIDTH 72	DATE: 09/01/83 REVISION: A

TERMINAL INFORMATION

TERMINAL NAME	NUMBER	LOGIC FIELD	CAPACITANCE (PF)
A	2,12	1	.27
B	3,13	2	.25
C	4,14	3	.25
D	5,15	4	.25
OUT	6,15	5	

LOGIC DIAGRAM

SAME AS LOGIC SYMBOL

TRUTH TABLE

A	B	C	D	OUT
1	1	*	*	0
*	*	1	1	0
0	*	0	*	1
0	*	*	0	1
*	0	0	*	1
*	0	*	0	1
ALL OTHER COMBINATIONS				X

LOGIC SYMBOLS

A,2
B,3
C,4
D,5

OUT,5

WORST CASE DELAY INFORMATION

P_D = 10.25NS $T_{R/F}$ = 21.38NS

R_S =1.5KΩ, C_L =1.5PF, V=5V, T=125°C

LOGIC EQUATION(S)

OUT=$\overline{AB+CD}$

NOTES

1970 IS A BUFFERED VERSION OF THE 1870.

1870-1

CIRCUIT SCHEMATIC

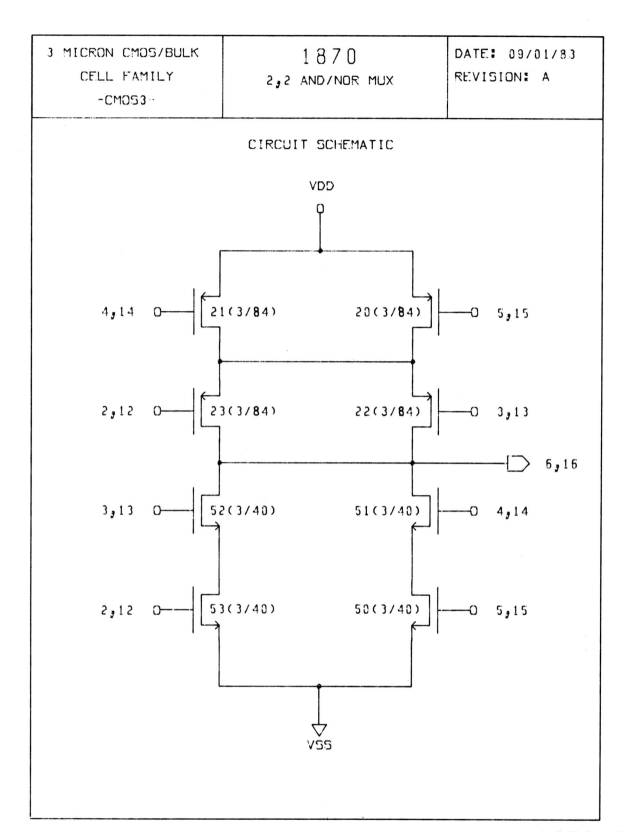

1870-2

3 MICRON CMOS/BULK CELL FAMILY -CMOS3-	1870 2,2 AND/NOR MUX	DATE: 09/01/83 REVISION: A

OUTPUT CHARACTERISTIC EQUATIONS

$$P_D(0-1) = P_{DC}(0-1) + .10 \ (T_{R/F} - 10) + .62 \ R_S C_L$$

$$P_D(1-0) = P_{DC}(1-0) + .11 \ (T_{R/F} - 10) + .57 \ R_S C_L$$

$$T_R = T_{RC} + .24 \ (T_{R/F} - 10) + 2.31 R_S C_L$$

$$T_F = T_{FC} + .17 \ (T_{R/F} - 10) + 2.13 R_S C_L$$

EQUATIONS

$25^\circ C$

$$P_{DC}(0-1) = 1.78 C_L + 2.98$$

$$P_{DC}(1-0) = 2.21 C_L + 4.10$$

$$T_{RC} = 5.05 C_L + 4.45$$

$$T_{FC} = 5.60 C_L + 5.32$$

$95^\circ C$

$$P_{DC}(0-1) = 2.25 C_L + 3.27$$

$$P_{DC}(1-0) = 2.75 C_L + 4.64$$

$$T_{RC} = 6.52 C_L + 5.37$$

$$T_{FC} = 7.11 C_L + 6.78$$

$125^\circ C$

$$P_{DC}(0-1) = 2.45 C_L + 3.39$$

$$P_{DC}(1-0) = 2.97 C_L + 4.84$$

$$T_{RC} = 7.14 C_L + 5.77$$

$$T_{FC} = 7.74 C_L + 7.42$$

$125^\circ C$ BC

$$P_{DC}(0-1) = 1.07 C_L + 1.31$$

$$P_{DC}(1-0) = 1.15 C_L + 2.50$$

$$T_{RC} = 3.03 C_L + 4.90$$

$$T_{FC} = 3.17 C_L + 5.37$$

VOLTAGE TABLE

VOLTAGE	DEVIATION FACTOR			
	TRANSITION		PROP DELAY	
	TR	TF	1-0	0-1
3.0	1.53	1.75	1.95	1.66
3.5	1.35	1.50	1.62	1.44
4.0	1.17	1.24	1.30	1.22
4.5	1.09	1.12	1.15	1.11
5.0	1.00	1.00	1.00	1.00
5.5	.95	.93	.92	.94
6.0	.90	.87	.84	.87
6.5	.87	.83	.79	.83
7.0	.84	.79	.73	.79

1870-3

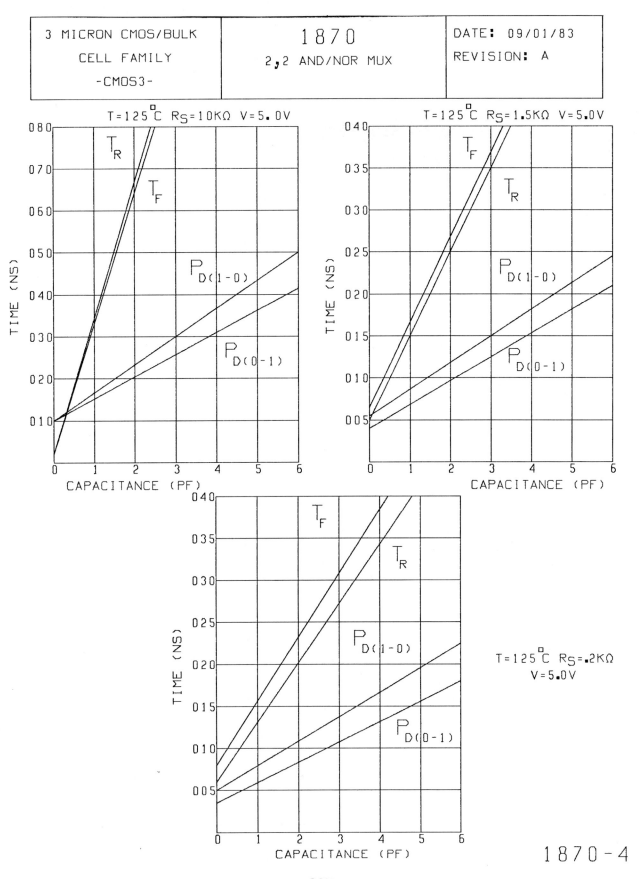

1870-4

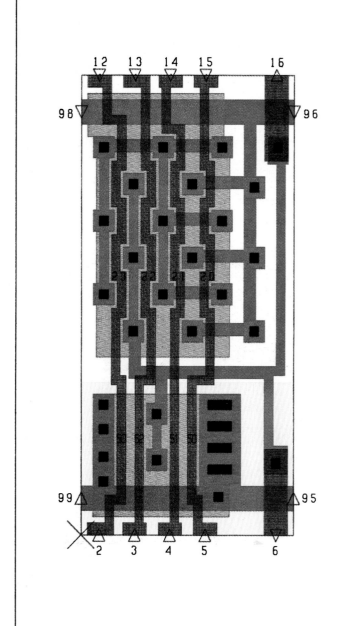

1870-5

3 MICRON CMOS/BULK	1910	DATE: 04/01/85
CELL FAMILY	4,2 AND/OR MUX	REVISION: B
-CMOS3-	CELL HEIGHT 150 WIDTH 144	

TERMINAL INFORMATION

TERMINAL NAME	NUMBER	LOGIC FIELD	CAPACITANCE (PF)
A	2,12	1	.25
B	3,13	2	.25
C	4,14	3	.25
D	5,15	4	.26
E	6,16	5	.27
F	7,17	8	.25
G	8,18	9	.26
H	9,19	10	.25
OUT	10,20	6	

LOGIC DIAGRAM

A,2
B,3
C,4
D,5
E,6
F,7
G,8
H,9

OUT,10

TRUTH TABLE

SEE PAGE 1910-5.

LOGIC SYMBOLS

A,2
B,3
C,4
D,5
E,6
F,7
G,8
H,9

OUT,10

WORST CASE DELAY INFORMATION

$P_D = 15.38NS$ $T_{R/F} = 14.56NS$

$R_S = 1.5K\Omega, \quad C_L = 1.5PF, \quad V = 5V, \quad T = 125^{\circ}C$

LOGIC EQUATION(S)

OUT = AB+CD+EF+GH

NOTES

1910-1

CIRCUIT SCHEMATIC

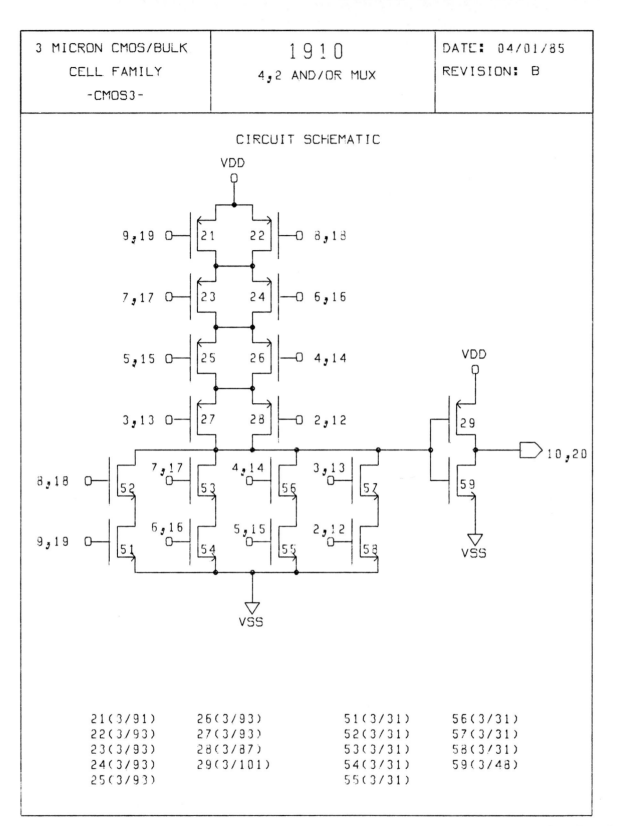

21(3/91)	26(3/93)	51(3/31)	56(3/31)
22(3/93)	27(3/93)	52(3/31)	57(3/31)
23(3/93)	28(3/87)	53(3/31)	58(3/31)
24(3/93)	29(3/101)	54(3/31)	59(3/48)
25(3/93)		55(3/31)	

1910-2

3 MICRON CMOS/BULK CELL FAMILY -CMOS3-	1910 4,2 AND/OR MUX	DATE: 04/01/85 REVISION: B

OUTPUT CHARACTERISTIC EQUATIONS

$$P_D(0-1) = P_{DC}(0-1) + .12 \ (T_{R/F} - 10) + .57 \ R_S C_L$$

$$P_D(1-0) = P_{DC}(1-0) + .04 \ (T_{R/F} - 10) + .54 \ R_S C_L$$

$$T_R = T_{RC} + .00 \ (T_{R/F} - 10) + 2.34 R_S C_L$$

$$T_F = T_{FC} + .04 \ (T_{R/F} - 10) + 2.39 R_S C_L$$

EQUATIONS

25°C

$$P_{DC}(0-1) = 1.20 C_L + 9.43$$

$$P_{DC}(1-0) = 1.21 C_L + 7.07$$

$$T_{RC} = 2.92 C_L + 3.36$$

$$T_{FC} = 2.62 C_L + 2.62$$

95°C

$$P_{DC}(0-1) = 1.52 C_L + 11.32$$

$$P_{DC}(1-0) = 1.51 C_L + 8.61$$

$$T_{RC} = 3.65 C_L + 4.90$$

$$T_{FC} = 3.25 C_L + 3.47$$

125°C

$$P_{DC}(0-1) = 1.66 C_L + 12.08$$

$$P_{DC}(1-0) = 1.63 C_L + 9.24$$

$$T_{RC} = 3.95 C_L + 5.65$$

$$T_{FC} = 3.51 C_L + 3.86$$

125°C BC

$$P_{DC}(0-1) = .76 \ C_L + 5.24$$

$$P_{DC}(1-0) = .69 \ C_L + 3.95$$

$$T_{RC} = 1.86 C_L + 3.52$$

$$T_{FC} = 1.58 C_L + 2.45$$

VOLTAGE TABLE

VOLTAGE	DEVIATION FACTOR			
	TRANSITION		PROP DELAY	
	TR	TF	1-0	0-1
3.0	1.46	1.59	1.91	2.03
3.5	1.31	1.39	1.60	1.68
4.0	1.16	1.18	1.30	1.33
4.5	1.08	1.09	1.15	1.17
5.0	1.00	1.00	1.00	1.00
5.5	.95	.95	.91	.91
6.0	.91	.90	.83	.82
6.5	.88	.87	.77	.76
7.0	.85	.84	.72	.71

1910-3

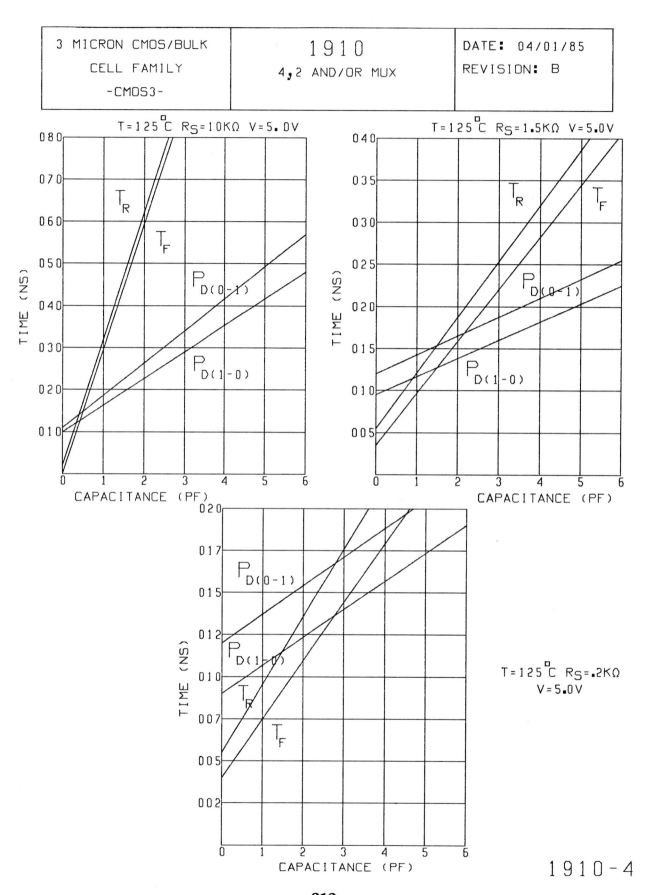

3 MICRON CMOS/BULK CELL FAMILY -CMOS3-	1910 4,2 AND/OR MUX	DATE: 04/01/85 REVISION: B

A	B	C	D	E	F	G	H	OUT
1	1	*	*	*	*	*	*	1
*	*	1	1	*	*	*	*	1
*	*	*	*	1	1	*	*	1
*	*	*	*	*	*	1	1	1
0	*	0	*	0	*	0	*	0
0	*	0	*	0	*	*	0	0
0	*	0	*	*	0	0	*	0
0	*	0	*	*	0	*	0	0
0	*	*	0	0	*	0	*	0
0	*	*	0	0	*	*	0	0
0	*	*	0	*	0	0	*	0
0	*	*	0	*	0	*	0	0
*	0	0	*	0	*	0	*	0
*	0	0	*	0	*	*	0	0
*	0	0	*	*	0	0	*	0
*	0	0	*	*	0	*	0	0
*	0	*	0	0	*	0	*	0
*	0	*	0	0	*	*	0	0
*	0	*	0	*	0	0	*	0
*	0	*	0	*	0	*	0	0
ALL OTHER COMBINATIONS.								X

X=DON'T KNOW
*=DON'T CARE

1910-5

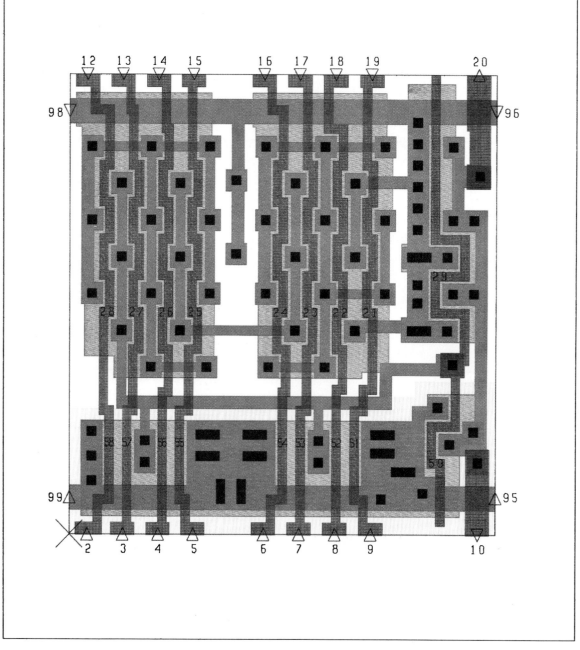

1910-6

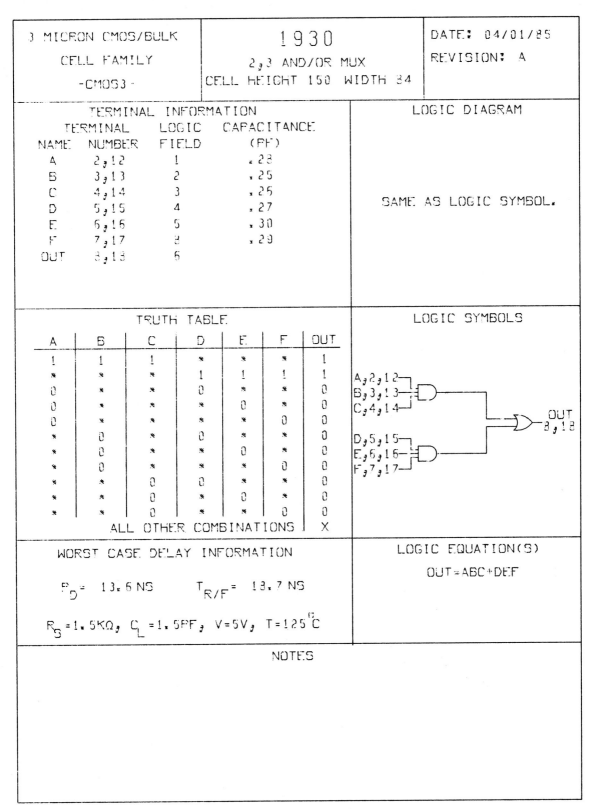

3 MICRON CMOS/BULK	1930	DATE: 04/01/85
CELL FAMILY	2,3 AND/OR MUX	REVISION: A
-CMOS3-	CELL HEIGHT 150 WIDTH 84	

TERMINAL INFORMATION

TERMINAL NAME	TERMINAL NUMBER	LOGIC FIELD	CAPACITANCE (PF)
A	2,12	1	.23
B	3,13	2	.25
C	4,14	3	.25
D	5,15	4	.27
E	6,16	5	.30
F	7,17	8	.29
OUT	8,18	6	

LOGIC DIAGRAM

SAME AS LOGIC SYMBOL.

TRUTH TABLE

A	B	C	D	E	F	OUT
1	1	1	*	*	*	1
*	*	*	1	1	1	1
0	*	*	0	*	*	0
0	*	*	*	0	*	0
0	*	*	*	*	0	0
*	0	*	0	*	*	0
*	0	*	*	0	*	0
*	0	*	*	*	0	0
*	*	0	0	*	*	0
*	*	0	*	0	*	0
*	*	0	*	*	0	0
ALL OTHER COMBINATIONS						X

LOGIC SYMBOLS

WORST CASE DELAY INFORMATION

P_D = 13.6 NS $T_{R/F}$ = 13.7 NS

R_S =1.5KΩ, C_L =1.5PF, V=5V, T=125°C

LOGIC EQUATION(S)

OUT=ABC+DEF

NOTES

CIRCUIT SCHEMATIC

VDD

5,15 21(3/36) 22(3/91.5) 23(3/30)
6,16   7,17

4,14 24(3/83) 25(3/81) 26(3/83) 27(3/64.5)
3,13   2,12

5,15 51(3/44)   4,14 54(3/44)   57(3/33.5)   8,18

6,16 52(3/47)   3,13 55(3/44)

7,17 53(3/49)   2,12 56(3/46)

VSS

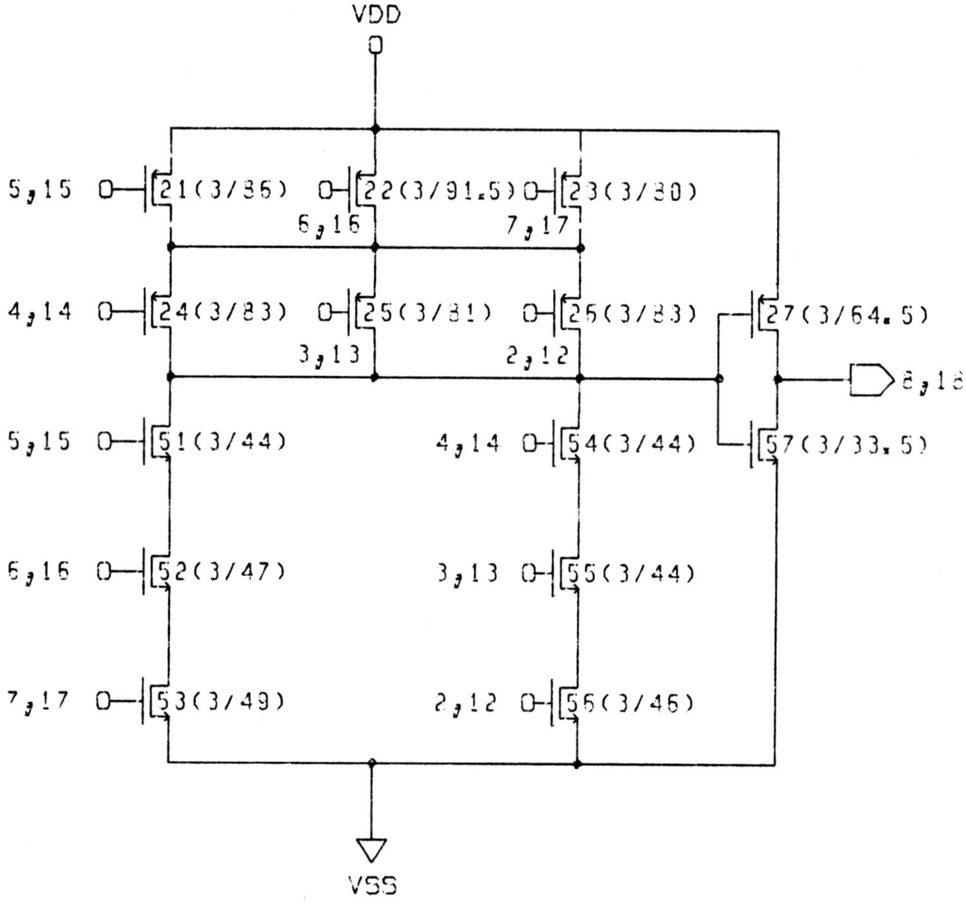

REL 3.3   1930-2

316

3 MICRON CMOS/BULK CELL FAMILY -CMOS3-	1930 2,3 AND/OR MUX	DATE: 04/01/85 REVISION: A

OUTPUT CHARACTERISTIC EQUATIONS

$$P_D(0-1) = P_{DC}(0-1) + .06 (T_{R/F}-10) + .58 R_S C_L$$

$$P_D(1-0) = P_{DC}(1-0) + .10 (T_{R/F}-10) + .56 R_S C_L$$

$$T_R = T_{RC} + .03 (T_{R/F}-10) + 2.38 R_S C_L$$

$$T_F = T_{FC} + .02 (T_{R/F}-10) + 2.43 R_S C_L$$

EQUATIONS

$25^\circ C$

$$P_{DC}(0-1) = 1.70 C_L + 7.12$$

$$P_{DC}(1-0) = 1.46 C_L + 7.15$$

$$T_{RC} = 4.89 C_L + 3.31$$

$$T_{FC} = 3.87 C_L + 2.40$$

$95^\circ C$

$$P_{DC}(0-1) = 2.18 C_L + 8.58$$

$$P_{DC}(1-0) = 1.85 C_L + 8.60$$

$$T_{RC} = 6.26 C_L + 4.45$$

$$T_{FC} = 4.90 C_L + 3.20$$

$125^\circ C$

$$P_{DC}(0-1) = 2.38 C_L + 9.15$$

$$P_{DC}(1-0) = 2.00 C_L + 9.20$$

$$T_{RC} = 6.84 C_L + 4.97$$

$$T_{FC} = 5.72 C_L + 2.97$$

$125^\circ C$ BC

$$P_{DC}(0-1) = 1.08 C_L + 3.94$$

$$P_{DC}(1-0) = .88 C_L + 4.32$$

$$T_{RC} = 3.28 C_L + 2.98$$

$$T_{FC} = 2.54 C_L + 2.20$$

VOLTAGE TABLE

VOLTAGE	DEVIATION FACTOR			
	TRANSITION		PROP DELAY	
	TR	TF	1-0	0-1
3.0	1.54	1.57	1.38	1.98
3.5	1.36	1.38	1.58	1.64
4.0	1.17	1.18	1.28	1.31
4.5	1.09	1.09	1.14	1.15
5.0	1.00	1.00	1.00	1.00
5.5	.95	.95	.92	.91
6.0	.90	.90	.84	.83
6.5	.87	.87	.79	.77
7.0	.84	.84	.74	.72

REL 3.3   1930-3

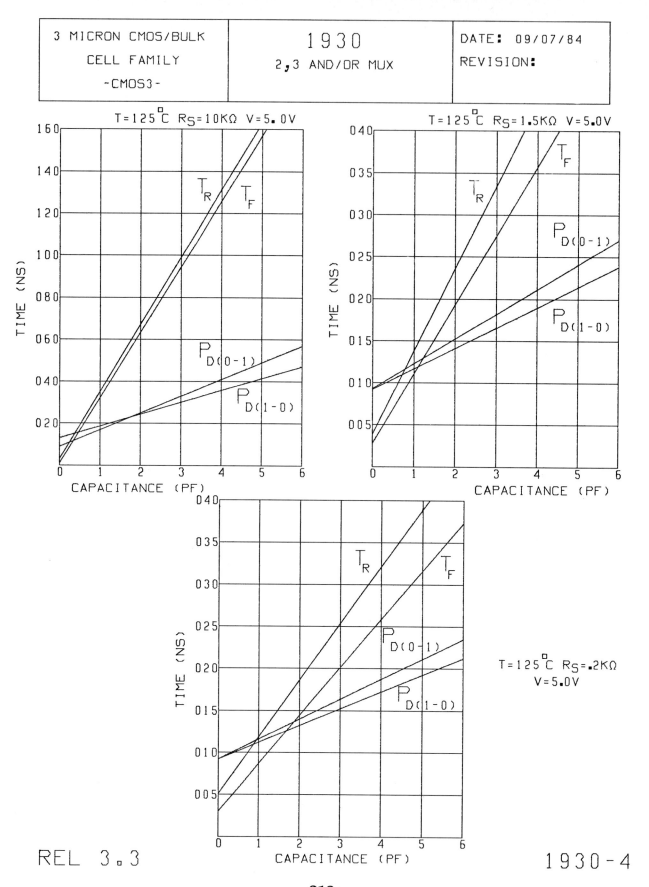

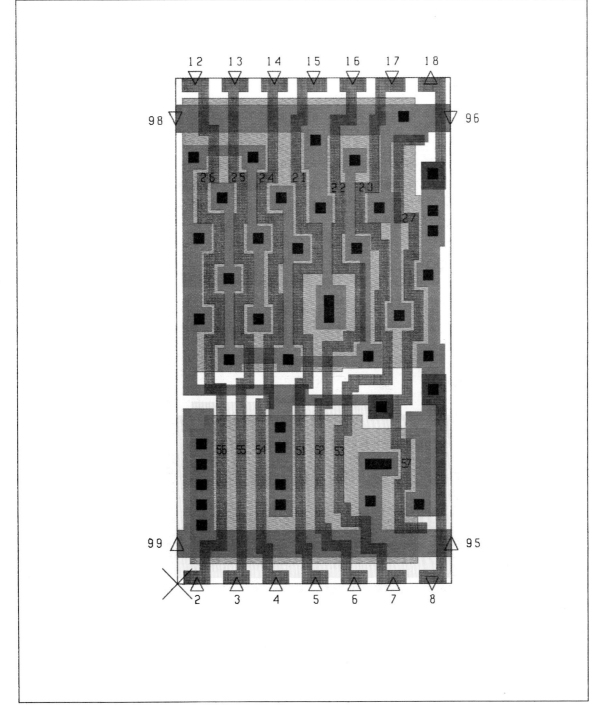

REL 3.3   1930-5

3 MICRON CMOS/BULK CELL FAMILY -CMOS3-	1970 2,2 AND/OR MUX CELL HEIGHT 150 WIDTH 84	DATE: 09/01/83 REVISION: A

TERMINAL INFORMATION

TERMINAL NAME	TERMINAL NUMBER	LOGIC FIELD	CAPACITANCE (PF)
A	2,12	1	.26
B	3,13	2	.24
C	4,14	3	.25
D	5,15	4	.25
OUT	6,16	6	

LOGIC DIAGRAM

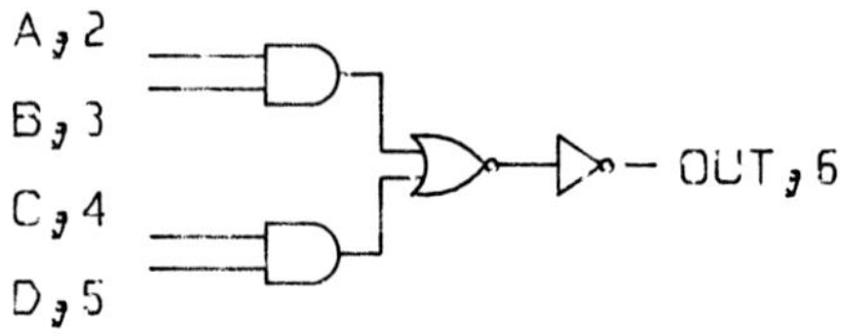

A,2
B,3
C,4
D,5
— OUT,6

TRUTH TABLE

A	B	C	D	OUT
1	1	*	*	1
*	*	1	1	1
0	*	0	*	0
0	*	*	0	0
*	0	0	*	0
*	0	*	0	0
ALL OTHER COMBINATIONS				X

LOGIC SYMBOLS

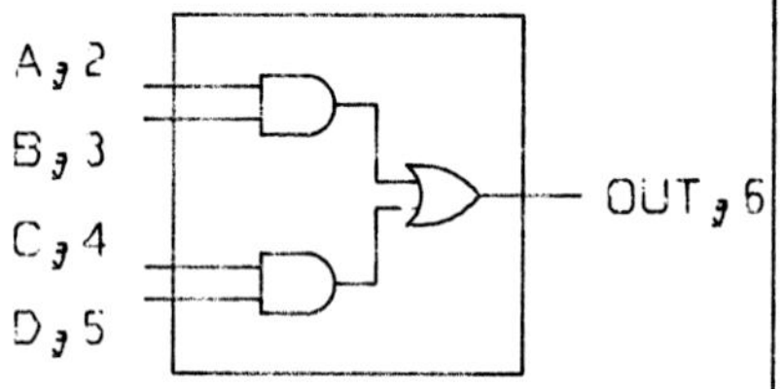

A,2
B,3
C,4
D,5
— OUT,6

WORST CASE DELAY INFORMATION

$$P_D = 10.16NS \qquad T_{R/F} = 13.03NS$$

$$R_S = 1.5K\Omega, \quad C_L = 1.5PF, \quad V=5V, \quad T=125°C$$

LOGIC EQUATION(S)

OUT=AB+CD

NOTES

1970 IS A BUFFERED VERSION OF THE 1870.

1970-1

320

3 MICRON CMOS/BULK CELL FAMILY -CMOS3-	1970 2,2 AND/OR MUX	DATE: 09/01/83 REVISION: A

CIRCUIT SCHEMATIC

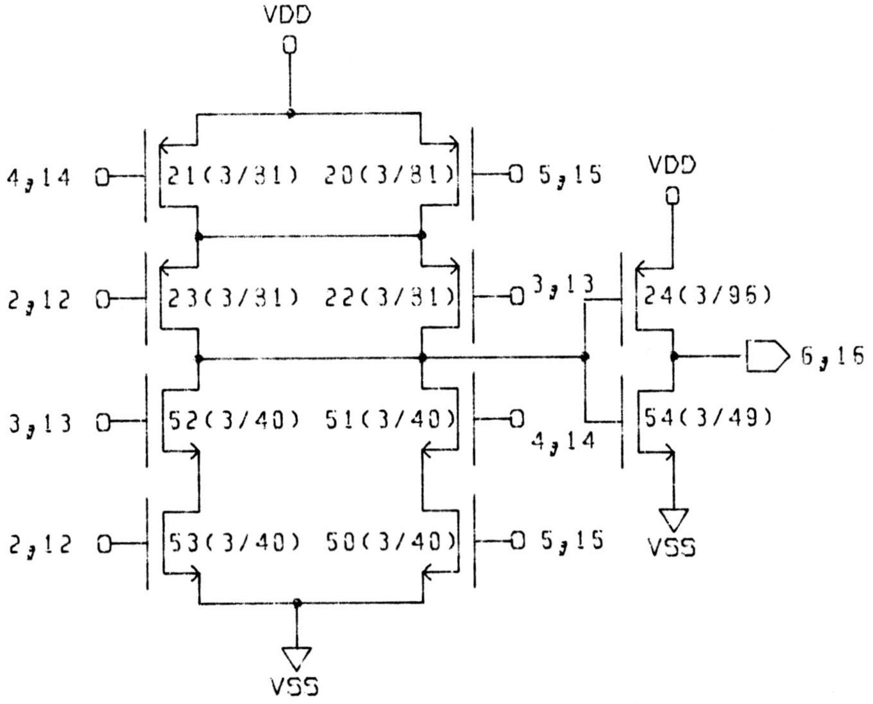

VDD

4,14   21(3/81)   20(3/81)   5,15   VDD

2,12   23(3/31)   22(3/31)   3,13   24(3/95)

6,16

3,13   52(3/40)   51(3/40)   4,14   54(3/49)

2,12   53(3/40)   50(3/40)   5,15   VSS

VSS

3 MICRON CMOS/BULK CELL FAMILY -CMOS3-	1970 2,2 AND/OR MUX	DATE: 09/01/83 REVISION: A

OUTPUT CHARACTERISTIC EQUATIONS

$$P_D(0-1) = P_{DC}(0-1) + .10 \ (T_{R/F} - 10) + .61 \ R_S C_L$$

$$P_D(1-0) = P_{DC}(1-0) + .03 \ (T_{R/F} - 10) + .53 \ R_S C_L$$

$$T_R = T_{RC} + .03 \ (T_{R/F} - 10) + 2.47 R_S C_L$$

$$T_F = T_{FC} + .05 \ (T_{R/F} - 10) + 2.47 R_S C_L$$

EQUATIONS

$25^\circ C$	$95^\circ C$	$125^\circ C$
$P_{DC}(0-1) = 1.10 C_L + 5.64$	$P_{DC}(0-1) = 1.39 C_L + 6.60$	$P_{DC}(0-1) = 1.51 C_L + 6.99$
$P_{DC}(1-0) = 1.01 C_L + 4.75$	$P_{DC}(1-0) = 1.26 C_L + 5.54$	$P_{DC}(1-0) = 1.36 C_L + 5.85$
$T_{RC} = 3.13 C_L + 1.96$	$T_{RC} = 3.94 C_L + 2.73$	$T_{RC} = 4.27 C_L + 3.03$
$T_{FC} = 2.47 C_L + 1.83$	$T_{FC} = 3.03 C_L + 2.35$	$T_{FC} = 3.34 C_L + 2.57$

$125^\circ C$ BC

$$P_{DC}(0-1) = .69 \ C_L + 3.27$$

$$P_{DC}(1-0) = .60 \ C_L + 2.69$$

$$T_{RC} = 2.02 C_L + 2.09$$

$$T_{FC} = 1.54 C_L + 1.80$$

VOLTAGE TABLE

	DEVIATION FACTOR			
VOLTAGE	TRANSITION		PROP DELAY	
	TR	TF	1-0	0-1
3.0	1.45	1.51	1.83	1.90
3.5	1.30	1.33	1.55	1.59
4.0	1.15	1.16	1.26	1.23
4.5	1.07	1.03	1.13	1.14
5.0	1.00	1.00	1.00	1.00
5.5	.95	.95	.92	.92
6.0	.91	.91	.85	.84
6.5	.88	.89	.80	.79
7.0	.86	.87	.75	.74

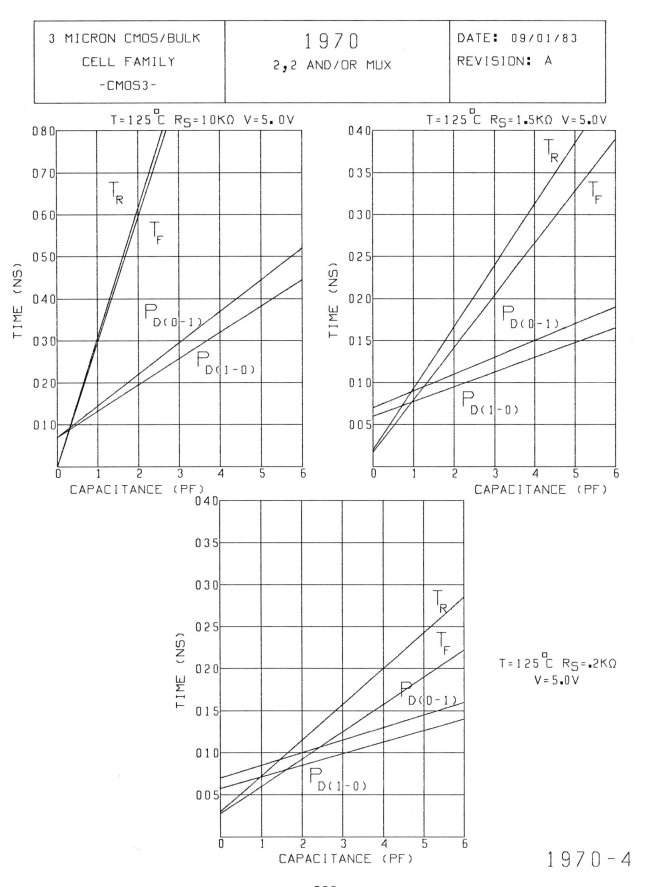

1970-4

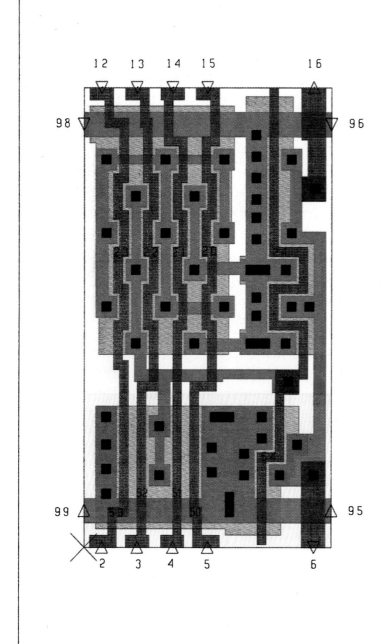

1970-5

324

3 MICRON CMOS/BULK CELL FAMILY -CMOS3-	2310 EXCLUSIVE OR CELL HEIGHT 150 WIDTH 72	DATE: 09/01/83 REVISION: A

TERMINAL INFORMATION

NAME	TERMINAL NUMBER	LOGIC FIELD	CAPACITANCE (PF)
A	2,12	1	.33
B	3,13	2	.28
OUT	4,14	5	

LOGIC DIAGRAM

SAME AS LOGIC SYMBOL.

TRUTH TABLE

A	B	OUT
X	X	X
X	0	X
X	1	X
0	X	X
0	0	0
0	1	1
1	X	X
1	0	1
1	1	0

LOGIC SYMBOLS

A,2
B,3 ——OUT,4

WORST CASE DELAY INFORMATION

$P_D = 11.34NS$ $T_{R/F} = 27.35NS$

$R_S = 1.5K\Omega$, $C_L = 1.5PF$, $V = 5V$, $T = 125^\circ C$

LOGIC EQUATION(S)

$OUT = \overline{A}B + A\overline{B}$

NOTES

2310-1

325

CIRCUIT SCHEMATIC

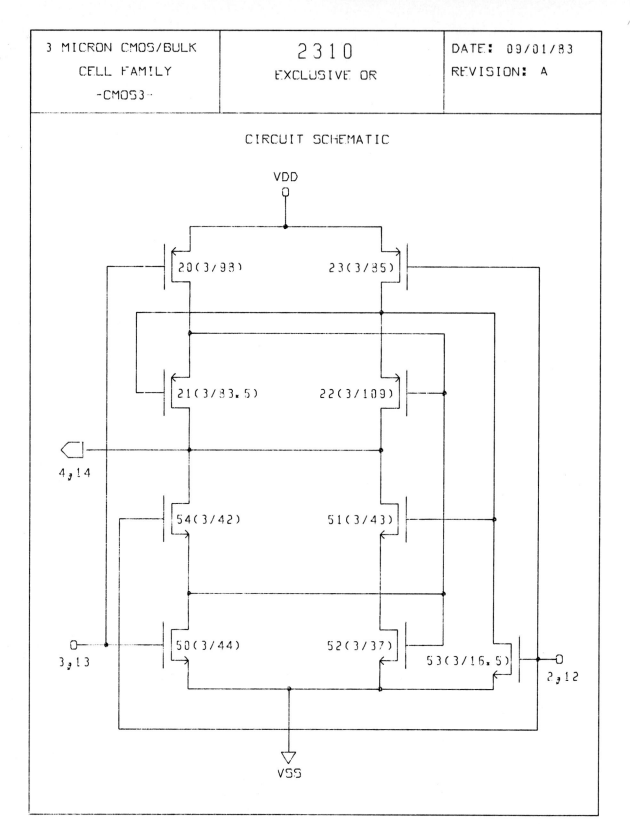

3 MICRON CMOS/BULK CELL FAMILY -CMOS3-	2310 EXCLUSIVE OR	DATE: 09/01/83 REVISION: A

OUTPUT CHARACTERISTIC EQUATIONS

$$P_D(0-1) = P_{DC}(0-1) + .21 (T_{R/F} - 10) + .63 R_S C_L$$

$$P_D(1-0) = P_{DC}(1-0) + .17 (T_{R/F} - 10) + .60 R_S C_L$$

$$T_R = T_{RC} + .11 (T_{R/F} - 10) + 2.39 R_S C_L$$

$$T_F = T_{FC} + .17 (T_{R/F} - 10) + 2.43 R_S C_L$$

EQUATIONS

$25°C$

$$P_{DC}(0-1) = 2.29 C_L + 4.92$$

$$P_{DC}(1-0) = 2.33 C_L + 4.35$$

$$T_{RC} = 3.05 C_L + 4.31$$

$$T_{FC} = 7.55 C_L + 2.47$$

$95°C$

$$P_{DC}(0-1) = 2.94 C_L + 5.44$$

$$P_{DC}(1-0) = 3.00 C_L + 5.15$$

$$T_{RC} = 10.52 C_L + 5.13$$

$$T_{FC} = 9.77 C_L + 3.12$$

$125°C$

$$P_{DC}(0-1) = 3.22 C_L + 5.63$$

$$P_{DC}(1-0) = 3.24 C_L + 5.47$$

$$T_{RC} = 11.53 C_L + 6.67$$

$$T_{FC} = 10.73 C_L + 3.36$$

$125°C$ BC

$$P_{DC}(0-1) = 1.59 C_L + 3.51$$

$$P_{DC}(1-0) = 1.57 C_L + 2.54$$

$$T_{RC} = 5.83 C_L + 4.37$$

$$T_{FC} = 5.64 C_L + 1.4$$

VOLTAGE TABLE

VOLTAGE	DEVIATION FACTOR			
	TRANSITION		PROP DELAY	
	TR	TF	1-0	0-1
3.0	1.54	1.53	1.32	1.62
3.5	1.35	1.33	1.54	1.41
4.0	1.17	1.18	1.25	1.20
4.5	1.09	1.09	1.12	1.10
5.0	1.00	1.00	1.00	1.00
5.5	.95	.95	.93	.94
6.0	.91	.90	.36	.89
6.5	.83	.87	.81	.35
7.0	.85	.85	.77	.82

2310-3

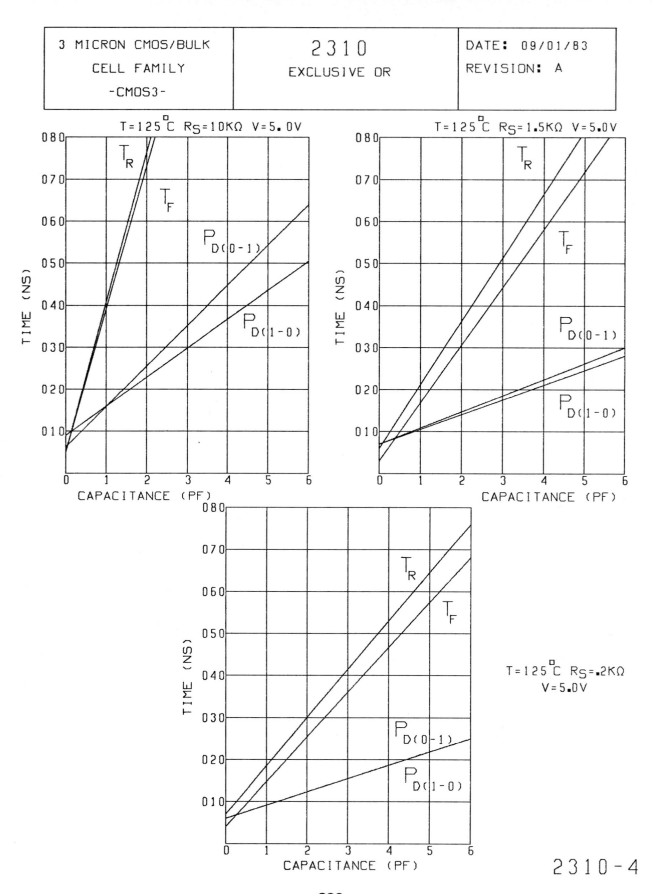

2310-4

3 MICRON CMOS/BULK CELL FAMILY -CMOS3-	2310 EXCLUSIVE OR	DATE: 09/01/83 REVISION: A

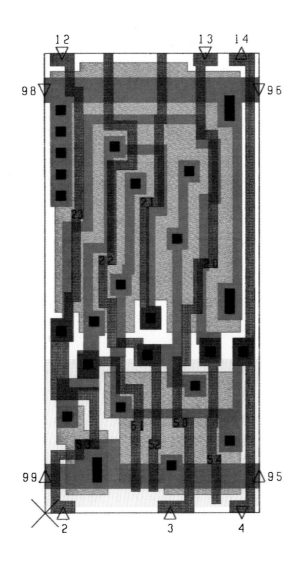

3 MICRON CMOS/BULK CELL FAMILY -CMOS3-	2350 2 INPUT EX-NOR CELL HEIGHT 150 WIDTH 72	DATE: 09/07/84 REVISION:

TERMINAL INFORMATION

TERMINAL NAME	LOGIC NUMBER	CAPACITANCE FIELD	(PF)
A	3,13	1	.42
B	4,14	2	.24
OUT	2,12	6	

LOGIC DIAGRAM

SAME AS LOGIC SYMBOL

TRUTH TABLE

A	B	OUT
0	0	1
0	1	0
1	0	0
1	1	1
0	X	X
1	X	X
X	0	X
X	1	X
X	X	X

LOGIC SYMBOLS

A,3
B,4 — OUT,2

WORST CASE DELAY INFORMATION

$P_D = 12.6NS$ $T_{R/F} = 28.5NS$

$R_S = 1.5K\Omega$, $C_L = 1.5PF$, $V=5V$, $T=125°C$

LOGIC EQUATION(S)

$OUT = \overline{A \oplus B}$

NOTES

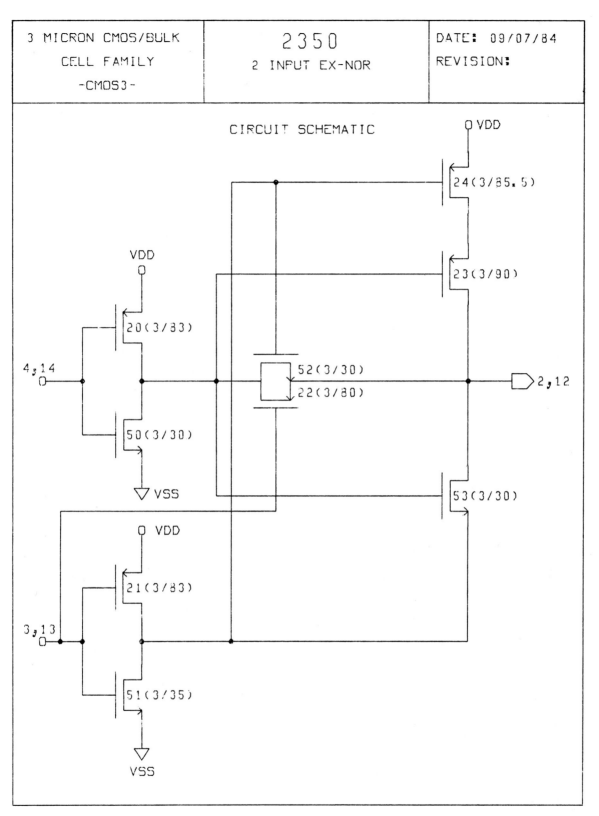

CIRCUIT SCHEMATIC

VDD

24(3/85.5)

23(3/90)

VDD

20(3/33)

4,14

52(3/30)

22(3/80)

2,12

50(3/30)

VSS

53(3/30)

VDD

21(3/83)

3,13

51(3/35)

VSS

REL 3.3   2350-2

331

OUTPUT CHARACTERISTIC EQUATIONS

$$P_D(0-1) = P_{DC}(0-1) + .11 (T_{R/F} - 10) + .65 R_S C_L$$

$$P_D(1-0) = P_{DC}(1-0) + .17 (T_{R/F} - 10) + .59 R_S C_L$$

$$T_R = T_{RC} + .15 (T_{R/F} - 10) + 2.34 R_S C_L$$

$$T_F = T_{FC} + .03 (T_{R/F} - 10) + 2.31 R_S C_L$$

EQUATIONS

25°C	95°C	125°C
$P_{DC}(0-1) = 2.44 C_L + 3.94$	$P_{DC}(0-1) = 3.09 C_L + 4.43$	$P_{DC}(0-1) = 3.34 C_L + 4.71$
$P_{DC}(1-0) = 2.83 C_L + 4.93$	$P_{DC}(1-0) = 3.57 C_L + 5.70$	$P_{DC}(1-0) = 3.86 C_L + 5.98$
$T_{RC} = 8.23 C_L + 5.37$	$T_{RC} = 10.84 C_L + 6.50$	$T_{RC} = 11.93 C_L + 6.93$
$T_{FC} = 8.42 C_L + 3.51$	$T_{FC} = 10.85 C_L + 4.47$	$T_{FC} = 11.86 C_L + 4.83$

125°C BC

$$P_{DC}(0-1) = 1.63 C_L + 2.39$$

$$P_{DC}(1-0) = 1.72 C_L + 3.58$$

$$T_{RC} = 5.85 C_L + 4.46$$

$$T_{FC} = 5.84 C_L + 2.28$$

VOLTAGE TABLE

VOLTAGE | DEVIATION FACTOR

VOLTAGE	TRANSITION		PROP DELAY	
	TR	TF	1-0	0-1
3.0	1.52	1.57	1.82	1.64
3.5	1.35	1.44	1.54	1.43
4.0	1.17	1.21	1.26	1.21
4.5	1.08	1.11	1.13	1.11
5.0	1.00	1.00	1.00	1.00
5.5	.95	.95	.93	.94
6.0	.91	.89	.86	.88
6.5	.88	.85	.82	.84
7.0	.85	.82	.77	.80

REL 3.3   2350-3

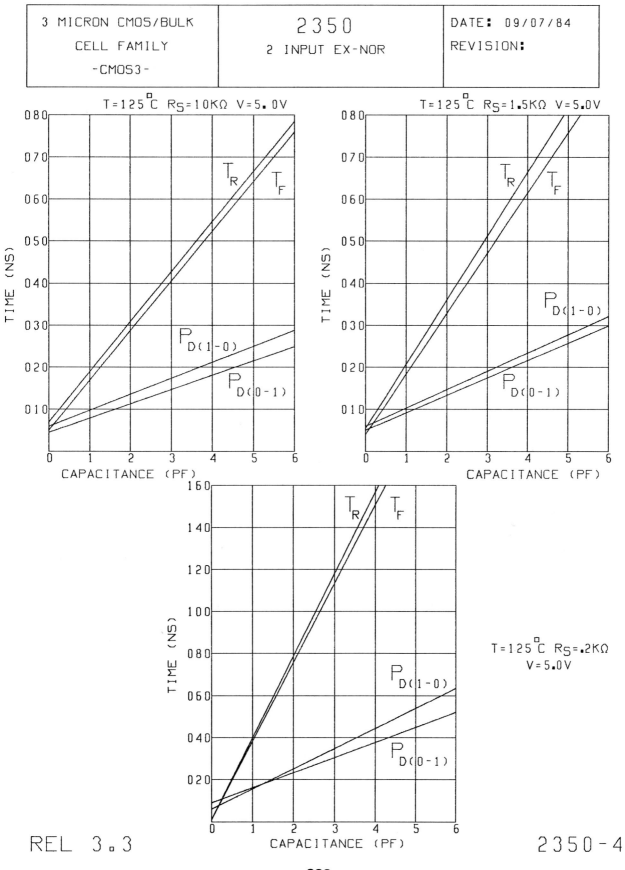

REL 3.3

2350-4

333

3 MICRON CMOS/BULK CELL FAMILY -CMOS3-	2350 2 INPUT EX-NOR	DATE: 09/07/84 REVISION:

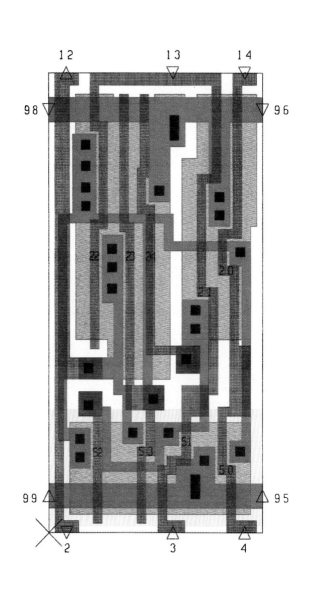

3 MICRON CMOS/BULK	2900	DATE: 09/07/84
CELL FAMILY	STACKABLE SHIFT REGISTER	REVISION:
-CMOS3-	CELL HEIGHT 105 WIDTH 108	

TERMINAL INFORMATION

TERMINAL NAME	NUMBER	LOGIC FIELD	CAPACITANCE (PF)
D	2	3	.132
C	3,13	1	.244
CBAR	4,14	2	.256
Q	5	6	

LOGIC DIAGRAM

TRUTH TABLE

D	C	M_N	Q_N
D	1	D	Q_{N-1}
*	0	M_{N-1}	M_{N-1}
1	X	X	X

IF M=D, M=M_{N-1}
IF S=M, S=S_{N-1}

LOGIC SYMBOLS

C3,13
C̄4,14

WORST CASE DELAY INFORMATION

P_D= 11.26NS $T_{R/F}$= 18.89 NS

W/0NS CLOCK SKEW

R_S=1.5KΩ, C_L=1.5PF, V=5V, T=125°C

LOGIC EQUATION(S)

$$Q=(Q_{N-1}*C)+(D_{N-1}*\bar{C})$$

NOTES

ALL SIMULATIONS FOR THIS CELL ARE PERFORMED WITH A 0.0 NS CLOCK SKEW BETWEEN CLOCK AND CLOCK BAR INPUTS, UNLESS INDICATED OTHERWISE.
   THIS CELL IS NEGATIVE TRIGGERED: DATA TRANSFERS TO Q WHEN CLOCK GOES LOW AND CLOCK BAR GOES HIGH.
   THE 2900-2940 CELLS ARE NON-STANDARD CMOS3 CELLS SPECIFICALLY DESIGNED FOR LONG, HIGH DENSITY SHIFT REGISTER APPLICATIONS. REFER TO THE CMOS3 CELL NOTEBOOK APPENDIX FOR GUIDELINES ON IMPLEMENTING THESE CELLS.

REL 3.3   2900-1

CIRCUIT SCHEMATIC

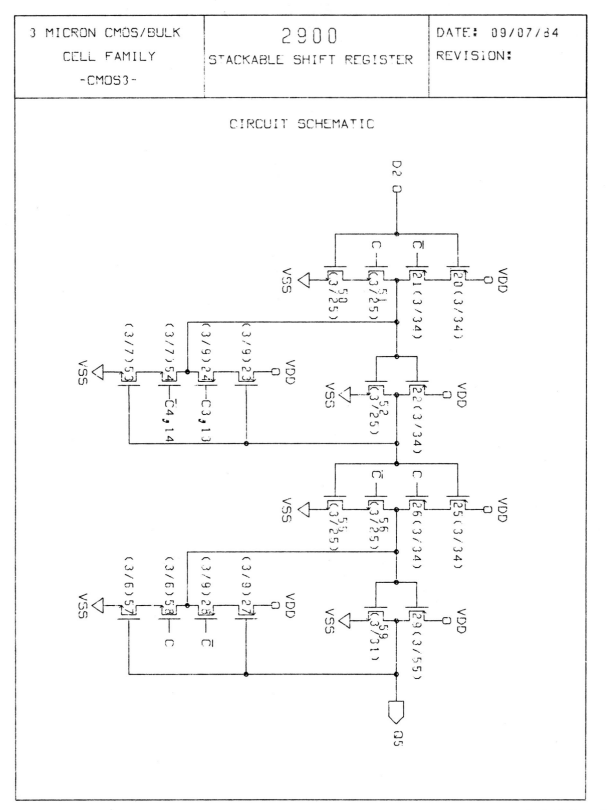

3 MICRON CMOS/BULK CELL FAMILY -CMOS3-	2900 STACKABLE SHIFT REGISTER CLOCK TO Q	DATE: 09/07/84 REVISION:

OUTPUT CHARACTERISTIC EQUATIONS

$$P_D(0-1) = P_{DC}(0-1) + .02 (T_{R/F} - 10) + .61 R_S C_L$$

$$P_D(1-0) = P_{DC}(1-0) + .06 (T_{R/F} - 10) + .57 R_S C_L$$

$$T_R = T_{RC} + .03 (T_{R/F} - 10) + 2.41 R_S C_L$$

$$T_F = T_{FC} + .04 (T_{R/F} - 10) + 2.38 R_S C_L$$

EQUATIONS

$25^{\circ}C$	$95^{\circ}C$	$125^{\circ}C$
$P_{DC}(0-1) = 1.32 C_L + 4.43$	$P_{DC}(0-1) = 2.32 C_L + 5.11$	$P_{DC}(0-1) = 2.52 C_L + 5.33$
$P_{DC}(1-0) = 1.51 C_L + 5.05$	$P_{DC}(1-0) = 1.90 C_L + 7.07$	$P_{DC}(1-0) = 2.05 C_L + 7.45$
$T_{RC} = 5.46 C_L + 2.75$	$T_{RC} = 7.01 C_L + 3.57$	$T_{RC} = 7.65 C_L + 3.93$
$T_{FC} = 3.86 C_L + 2.37$	$T_{FC} = 4.37 C_L + 3.69$	$T_{FC} = 5.29 C_L + 4.04$

$125^{\circ}C$ BC	VOLTAGE TABLE
$P_{DC}(0-1) = 1.12 C_L + 1.51$	

$125^{\circ}C$ BC

$$P_{DC}(0-1) = 1.12 C_L + 1.51$$

$$P_{DC}(1-0) = .88 C_L + 2.94$$

$$T_{RC} = 3.59 C_L + 2.05$$

$$T_{FC} = 2.42 C_L + 2.32$$

VOLTAGE TABLE

VOLTAGE	DEVIATION FACTOR			
	TRANSITION		PROP DELAY	
	TR	TF	1-0	0-1
3.0	1.54	1.52	1.88	1.78
3.5	1.35	1.41	1.53	1.52
4.0	1.17	1.20	1.23	1.26
4.5	1.09	1.10	1.14	1.13
5.0	1.00	1.00	1.00	1.00
5.5	.95	.95	.92	.92
6.0	.90	.89	.84	.84
6.5	.87	.86	.78	.79
7.0	.84	.83	.73	.73

REL 3.3   2900-3

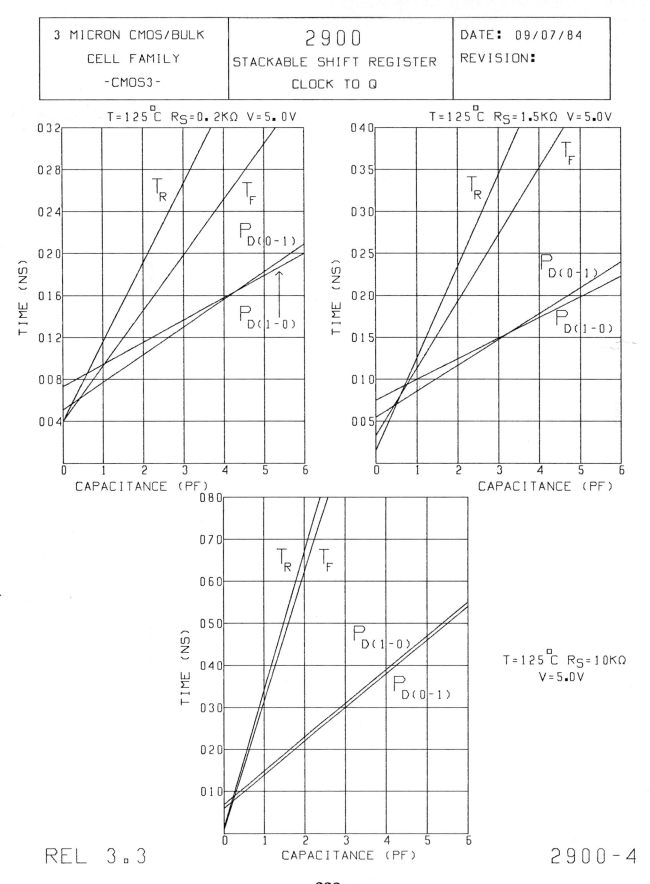

3 MICRON CMOS/BULK CELL FAMILY -CMOS3-	2900 STACKABLE SHIFT REGISTER	DATE: 09/07/8 REVISION:

SPECIAL TIMING

SPECIAL TIMING FOR KOV-1 APPLICATIONS:

SETUP TIME=11 NS (WORST) OBTAINED UNDER THE FOLLOWING CONDITIONS:

        VDD=5.0V
        WNWP 125° C, STANDARD LOAD
        0 NS CLOCK SKEW, BALANCED CLOCK AND CLOCKBAR
        RISE/FALL TIMES, 11 NS CLOCK RISE/FALL TIME
        60 NS DATA INPUT RISE/FALL TIME

HOLD TIME=2 NS (WORST) OBTAINED UNDER THE FOLLOWING CONDITIONS:

        VDD=5.0V
        BNBP 125° C, STANDARD LOAD
        0 NS CLOCK SKEW, BALANCED CLOCK AND CLOCKBAR
        RISE/FALL TIMES, 11 NS CLOCK RISE/FALL TIME
        60 NS DATA INPUT RISE/FALL TIME

REL 3.3   2900-5

SPECIAL TIMING

MINIMUM CLOCK PULSE WIDTH=15NS (W/0NS SKEW)

RIPPLE-THRU SUSCEPTABILITY

    (A)   TABLE OF RIPPLE-THRU SUSCEPTABILITY FOR MASTER-TO-SLAVE RIPPLE FOR 2900 CELL BASED ON 0NS CLOCK SKEW, BALANCED RISE AND FALL TIMES FOR CLOCK AND CLOCKBAR.

        MAXIMUM CLOCK AND CLOCKBAR RISE AND FALL TIMES W/O CAUSING RIPPLE-THRU (MASTER-TO-SLAVE)

	VDD=7.0V	5.0V	3.0V
125°C8NSP	14NS	22NS	46NS
-55°C5NSP	10NS	20NS	90NS

    (B)   THE 2900 CELL, WHEN USED IN CONJUNCTION WITH THE 2910 CLOCK DRIVER, WILL NOT RIPPLE UNDER ANY CONDITIONS OF TEMPERATURES BETWEEN -55 AND 125°C, AND VDD BETWEEN 3.0 AND 7.0 VOLTS, WITH A 100 NS RISE/FALL TIME ON THE INPUT OF THE 2910 CELL. THIS ASSUMES THAT A SINGLE 2910 CELL DRIVES A ROW OF 32 SHIFT REGISTER CELLS.

REL 3.3   2900-6

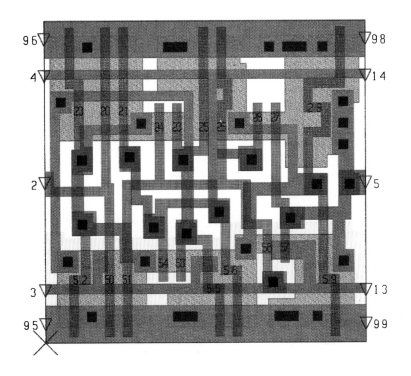

REL 3.3   2900-7

3 MICRON CMOS/BULK CELL FAMILY -CMOS3-	2910 STACKABLE TWO-PHASE CLOCK DRIVER CELL HEIGHT 105 WIDTH 180	DATE: 09/07/84 REVISION:

TERMINAL INFORMATION

TERMINAL NAME	TERMINAL NUMBER	LOGIC FIELD	CAPACITANCE (PF)
CIN	2,12	1	.281
COUT	3	6	
CBAR	4	7	

LOGIC DIAGRAM

TRUTH TABLE

CIN	COUT	CBAR
1	1	0
0	0	1
X	X	X

LOGIC SYMBOLS

WORST CASE DELAY INFORMATION

P_D = 10.59 NS $T_{R/F}$ = 7.14 NS

R_S = 0.0KΩ, C_L = 1.5PF, V=5V, T=125°C

LOGIC EQUATION(S)

COUT=CIN

CBAR=$\overline{CIN}$

NOTES

ALL SIMULATIONS WERE PERFORMED WITH A 0.0 OHM RESISTANCE ON CLOCK AND CLOCKBAR OUTPUTS EXCEPT WHERE NOTED OTHERWISE.

THE 2900-2940 CELLS ARE NON-STANDARD CMOS3 CELLS SPECIFICALLY DESIGNED FOR LONG, HIGH DENSITY SHIFT REGISTER APPLICATIONS. REFER TO THE CMOS3 CELL NOTEBOOK APPENDIX FOR GUIDELINES ON IMPLEMENTING THESE CELLS.

REL 3.3   2910-1

CIRCUIT SCHEMATIC

3 MICRON CMOS/BULK CELL FAMILY -CMOS3-	2910 STACKABLE TWO-PHASE CLOCK DRIVER CIN TO COUT	DATE: 09/07/84 REVISION:

OUTPUT CHARACTERISTIC EQUATIONS

$$P_D(0-1) = P_{DC}(0-1) + .14 (T_{R/F} - 10)$$

$$P_D(1-0) = P_{DC}(1-0) + .09 (T_{R/F} - 10)$$

$$T_R = T_{RC} + .02 (T_{R/F} - 10)$$

$$T_F = T_{FC} + .03 (T_{R/F} - 10)$$

EQUATIONS

25°C

$$P_{DC}(0-1) = .54 C_L + 6.90$$

$$P_{DC}(1-0) = .53 C_L + 7.27$$

$$T_{RC} = 1.31 C_L + 2.39$$

$$T_{FC} = 1.17 C_L + 3.02$$

95°C

$$P_{DC}(0-1) = .80 C_L + 7.99$$

$$P_{DC}(1-0) = .84 C_L + 8.70$$

$$T_{RC} = 1.53 C_L + 3.35$$

$$T_{FC} = 1.44 C_L + 4.24$$

125°C

$$P_{DC}(0-1) = .85 C_L + 8.41$$

$$P_{DC}(1-0) = .90 C_L + 9.24$$

$$T_{RC} = 1.31 C_L + 4.35$$

$$T_{FC} = 1.53 C_L + 4.85$$

125°C BC

$$P_{DC}(0-1) = .35 C_L + 3.95$$

$$P_{DC}(1-0) = .37 C_L + 4.05$$

$$T_{RC} = .71 C_L + 2.69$$

$$T_{FC} = .57 C_L + 3.15$$

VOLTAGE TABLE

VOLTAGE	DEVIATION FACTOR			
	TRANSITION		PROP DELAY	
	TR	TF	1-0	0-1
3.0	1.77	1.72	1.97	2.02
3.5	1.51	1.47	1.54	1.67
4.0	1.24	1.22	1.31	1.31
4.5	1.12	1.11	1.15	1.15
5.0	1.00	1.00	1.00	1.00
5.5	.93	.94	.91	.91
6.0	.85	.87	.82	.82
6.5	.81	.84	.75	.77
7.0	.77	.80	.71	.71

*RLOAD=0.0 OHM FOR ALL CONDITIONS.

REL 3.3   2910-3

344

3 MICRON CMOS/BULK CELL FAMILY -CMOS3-	2910 STACKABLE TWO-PHASE CLOCK DRIVER CIN TO CBAR	DATE: 09/07/84 REVISION:

OUTPUT CHARACTERISTIC EQUATIONS

$$P_D(0-1) = P_{DC}(0-1) + .11 \ (T_{R/F} - 10)$$

$$P_D(1-0) = P_{DC}(1-0) + .15 \ (T_{R/F} - 10)$$

$$T_R = T_{RC} + .01 \ (T_{R/F} - 10)$$

$$T_F = T_{FC} + .00 \ (T_{R/F} - 10)$$

EQUATIONS

25°C

$$P_{DC}(0-1) = .55 \ C_L + 5.38$$

$$P_{DC}(1-0) = .54 \ C_L + 5.71$$

$$T_{RC} = 1.33 C_L + 1.74$$

$$T_{FC} = 1.07 C_L + 1.53$$

95°C

$$P_{DC}(0-1) = .70 \ C_L + 7.48$$

$$P_{DC}(1-0) = .68 \ C_L + 7.79$$

$$T_{RC} = 1.72 C_L + 2.23$$

$$T_{FC} = 1.36 C_L + 2.09$$

125°C

$$P_{DC}(0-1) = .76 \ C_L + 7.89$$

$$P_{DC}(1-0) = .72 \ C_L + 8.21$$

$$T_{RC} = 1.88 C_L + 2.53$$

$$T_{FC} = 1.46 C_L + 2.35$$

125°C BC

$$P_{DC}(0-1) = .30 \ C_L + 3.80$$

$$P_{DC}(1-0) = .28 \ C_L + 4.12$$

$$T_{RC} = .78 C_L + 1.44$$

$$T_{FC} = .57 C_L + 1.39$$

VOLTAGE TABLE

VOLTAGE	DEVIATION FACTOR			
	TRANSITION		PROP DELAY	
	TR	TF	1-0	0-1
3.0	1.30	1.36	1.88	1.92
3.5	1.51	1.57	1.58	1.61
4.0	1.25	1.27	1.28	1.29
4.5	1.13	1.14	1.14	1.15
5.0	1.00	1.00	1.00	1.00
5.5	.93	.92	.92	.92
6.0	.85	.85	.84	.84
6.5	.81	.80	.79	.78
7.0	.75	.75	.73	.73

*RLOAD=0.0 OHM FOR ALL CONDITIONS.

REL 3.3   2910-4

3 MICRON CMOS/BULK CELL FAMILY -CMOS3-	2910 STACKABLE TWO-PHASE CLOCK DRIVER CLOCK SKEW	DATE: 09/07/84 REVISION:

OUTPUT CHARACTERISTIC EQUATIONS

$$P_D(0-1) = P_{DC}(0-1) - .01(T_{R/F} - 10)$$

$$P_D(1-0) = P_{DC}(1-0) - .02(T_{R/F} - 10)$$

*COUT DELAYED FROM CBAR.　　　$P_D(0-1)$=CLOCK RISE CKEW

EQUATIONS

$25^\circ C$	$95^\circ C$	$125^\circ C$
$P_{DC}(0-1) = .10 \ C_L + .19$	$P_{DC}(0-1) = .12 \ C_L + .20$	$P_{DC}(0-1) = .13 \ C_L + .19$
$P_{DC}(1-0) = .14 \ C_L + .90$	$P_{DC}(1-0) = .14 \ C_L + 1.22$	$P_{DC}(1-0) = .14 \ C_L + 1.35$

$125^\circ C$ BC	VOLTAGE TABLE

$P_{DC}(0-1) = .07 \ C_L - .16$

$P_{DC}(1-0) = .05 \ C_L + .27$

VOLTAGE	DEVIATION FACTOR PROP DELAY	
	1-0	0-1
3.0	2.26	5.23
3.5	1.33	3.65
4.0	1.40	2.08
4.5	1.20	1.54
5.0	1.00	1.00
5.5	.37	.74
6.0	.74	.49
6.5	.66	.35
7.0	.57	.21

*RLOAD=0.0 OHM FOR ALL CONDITIONS.

REL 3.3　　　2910-5

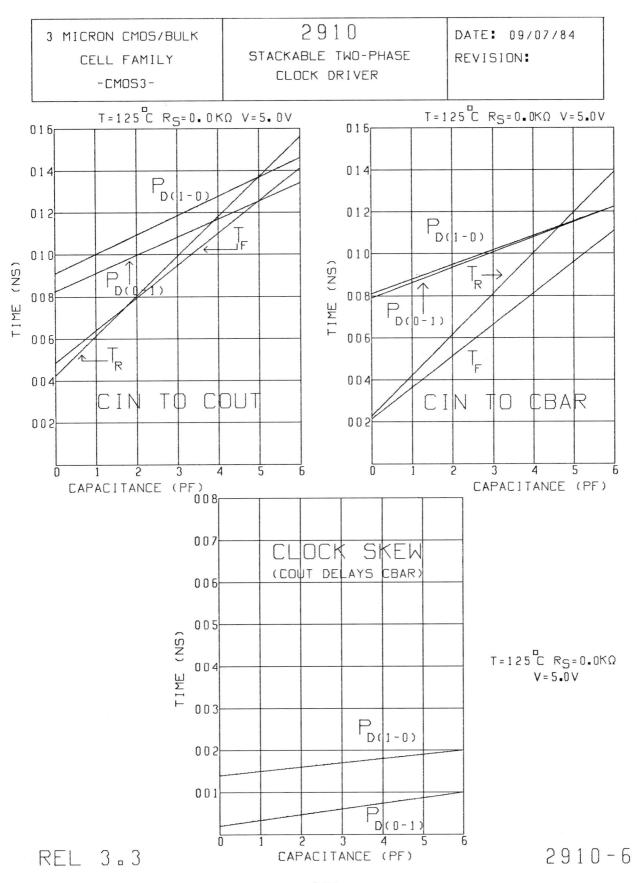

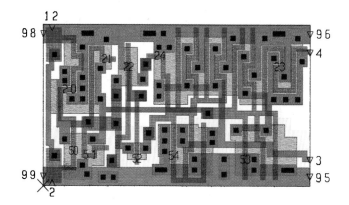

3 MICRON CMOS/BULK CELL FAMILY -CMOS3-	2920 STACKABLE DATA SELECT MUX CELL HEIGHT 105 WIDTH 72	DATE: 09/07/84 REVISION:

TERMINAL INFORMATION

TERMINAL NAME	TERMINAL NUMBER	LOGIC FIELD	CAPACITANCE (PF)
SEL	2,12	3	.297
C	3,13	4	.020
CBAR	4,14	5	.021
SD	5	2	.118
PD	6,16	1	.144
OUT	7	6	

LOGIC DIAGRAM

TRUTH TABLE

SD	PD	SEL	OUT
*	1	1	1
*	0	1	0
1	*	0	1
0	*	0	0
1	1	X	1
0	0	X	0
ALL OTHER COMBINATIONS			X

LOGIC SYMBOLS

WORST CASE DELAY INFORMATION

$P_D = 13.32\,NS$ $T_{R/F} = 20.93\,NS$

$R_S = 1.5K\Omega$, $C_L = 1.5PF$, $V = 5V$, $T = 125°C$

LOGIC EQUATION(S)

$$OUT = (\overline{SEL} * SD) + (SEL * PD)$$

NOTES

THE 2900-2940 CELLS ARE NON-STANDARD CMOS3 CELLS SPECIFICALLY DESIGNED FOR LONG, HIGH DENSITY SHIFT REGISTER APPLICATIONS. REFER TO THE CMOS3 CELL NOTEBOOK APPENDIX FOR GUIDELINES ON IMPLEMENTING THESE CELLS.
  C AND CBAR SIGNALS PLAY NO ROLE IN THE OPERATION OF THIS CELL.

REL 3.3   2920-1

CIRCUIT SCHEMATIC

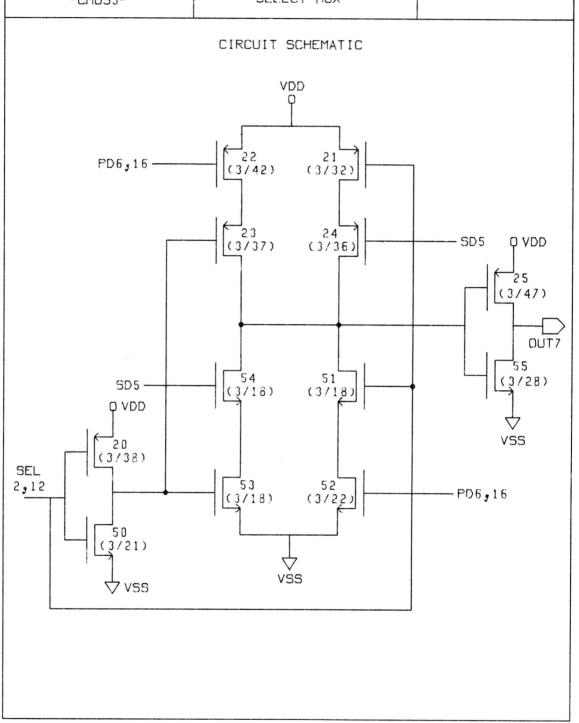

REL 3.3   2920-2

3 MICRON CMOS/BULK CELL FAMILY -CMOS3-	2920 STACKABLE DATA SELECT MUX SEL TO OUT	DATE: 09/07/84 REVISION:

OUTPUT CHARACTERISTIC EQUATIONS

$$P_D(0-1) = P_{DC}(0-1) + .13\ (T_{R/F}-10) + .60\ R_S C_L$$

$$P_D(1-0) = P_{DC}(1-0) + .14\ (T_{R/F}-10) + .55\ R_S C_L$$

$$T_R = T_{RC} + .03\ (T_{R/F}-10) + 2.38 R_S C_L$$

$$T_F = T_{FC} + .03\ (T_{R/F}-10) + 2.39 R_S C_L$$

EQUATIONS

25°C

$$P_{DC}(0-1) = 2.11 C_L + 6.55$$
$$P_{DC}(1-0) = 1.63 C_L + 7.16$$
$$T_{RC} = 6.26 C_L + 3.02$$
$$T_{FC} = 4.24 C_L + 2.54$$

95°C

$$P_{DC}(0-1) = 2.69 C_L + 7.61$$
$$P_{DC}(1-0) = 2.05 C_L + 8.49$$
$$T_{RC} = 8.06 C_L + 3.85$$
$$T_{FC} = 5.37 C_L + 3.33$$

125°C

$$P_{DC}(0-1) = 2.93 C_L + 8.02$$
$$P_{DC}(1-0) = 2.22 C_L + 9.03$$
$$T_{RC} = 8.82 C_L + 4.21$$
$$T_{FC} = 5.83 C_L + 3.70$$

125°C BC

$$P_{DC}(0-1) = 1.28 C_L + 3.30$$
$$P_{DC}(1-0) = .94\ C_L + 4.52$$
$$T_{RC} = 3.94 C_L + 3.19$$
$$T_{FC} = 2.63 C_L + 1.90$$

VOLTAGE TABLE

VOLTAGE	DEVIATION FACTOR			
	TRANSITION		PROP DELAY	
	TR	TF	1-0	0-1
3.0	1.55	1.63	1.87	1.80
3.5	1.37	1.42	1.53	1.52
4.0	1.18	1.20	1.23	1.25
4.5	1.09	1.10	1.14	1.13
5.0	1.00	1.00	1.00	1.00
5.5	.95	.94	.92	.93
6.0	.90	.89	.84	.85
6.5	.87	.86	.79	.81
7.0	.83	.82	.74	.76

REL 3.3   2920-3

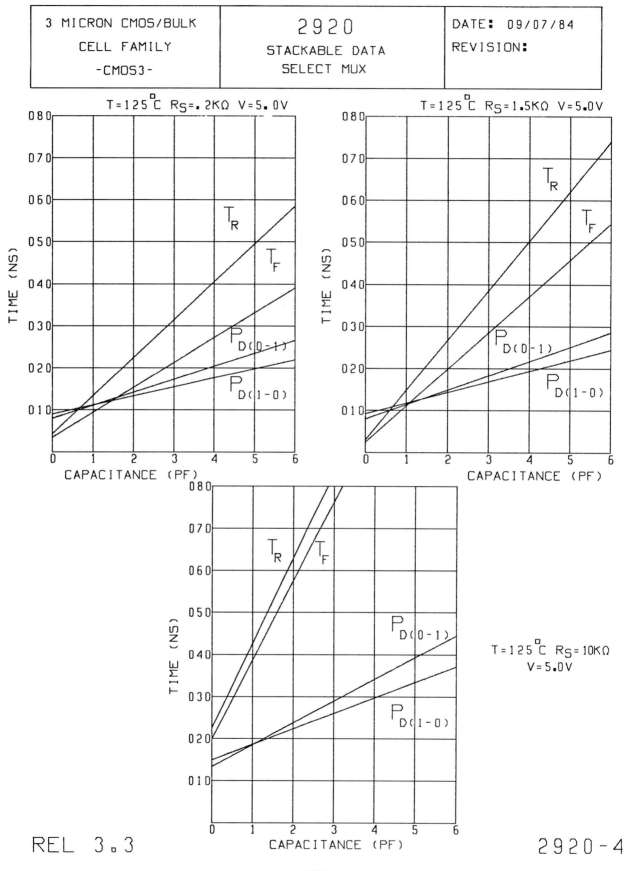

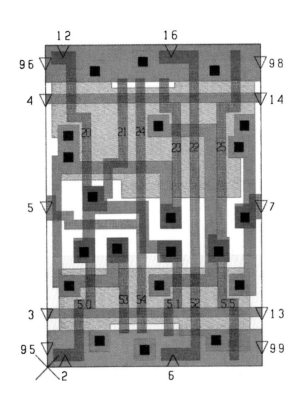

3 MICRON CMOS/BULK CELL FAMILY -CMOS3-	2930 BUS CROSSER CELL HEIGHT 105 WIDTH 12	DATE: 09/07/84 REVISION:

TERMINAL INFORMATION

TERMINAL NAME	NUMBER	LOGIC FIELD	CAPACITANCE (PF)
	2,12,5,15	N/A	.0959
C	3,13	N/A	.0036
CBAR	4,14	N/A	.0036

LOGIC DIAGRAM

N/A

TRUTH TABLE

N/A

LOGIC SYMBOLS

N/A

WORST CASE DELAY INFORMATION

$P_D =$ NS $T_{R/F} =$ NS

$R_S = 1.5 K\Omega$, $C_L = 1.5 PF$, $V = 5V$, $T = 125^{\circ}C$

LOGIC EQUATION(S)

N/A

NOTES
EQUIVALENT RESISTANCE IS 5.75 SQUARES OF POLY.

3 MICRON CMOS/BULK CELL FAMILY -CMOS3-	2930 BUS CROSSER	DATE: 09/07/84 REVISION:

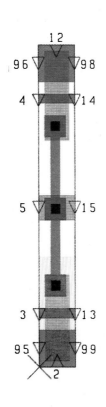

3 MICRON CMOS/BULK CELL FAMILY -CMOS3-	2940 BUS CROSSER CELL HEIGHT 105 WIDTH 12	DATE: 09/07/84 REVISION:

TERMINAL INFORMATION

NAME	TERMINAL NUMBER	LOGIC FIELD	CAPACITANCE (PF)
	2,12	N/A	.0826
C	3,13	N/A	.0036
CBAR	4,14	N/A	.0036
FEED	5,15	N/A	.0092

LOGIC DIAGRAM

N/A

TRUTH TABLE

N/A

LOGIC SYMBOLS

N/A

WORST CASE DELAY INFORMATION

$P_D =$ NS $T_{R/F} =$ NS

$R_S = 1.5K\Omega$, $C_L = 1.5PF$, $V=5V$, $T=125^\circ C$

LOGIC EQUATION(S)

N/A

NOTES

EQUIVALENT RESISTANCE IS 5.75 SQUARES OF POLY.

REL 3.3   2940-1

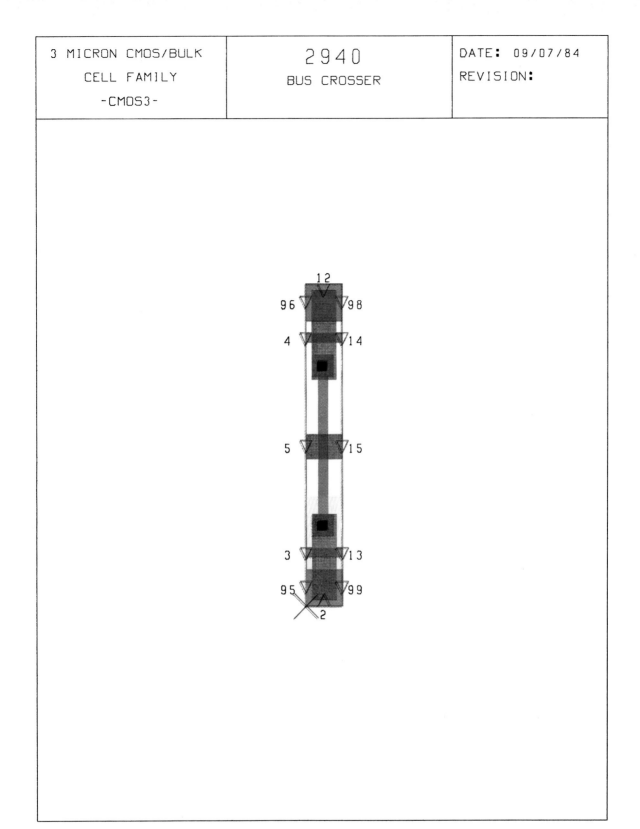

REL 3.3   2940-2

3 MICRON CMOS/BULK	8010-8140	DATE: 04/01/85
CELL FAMILY	LEVEL IDENTIFIERS	REVISION: B
-CMOS3-	CELL HEIGHT WIDTH	

TERMINAL INFORMATION

TERMINAL   LOGIC   CAPACITANCE
NAME NUMBER FIELD   (PF)

N/A

LOGIC DIAGRAM

N/A

TRUTH TABLE

N/A

LOGIC SYMBOLS

N/A

WORST CASE DELAY INFORMATION

$P_D =$ NS $T_{R/F} =$ NS

$R_S = 1.5K\Omega$, $C_L = 1.5PF$, $V=5V$, $T=125^{\circ}C$

LOGIC EQUATION(S)

N/A

NOTES

CELL NUMBER	HEIGHT	WIDTH	CELL NUMBER	HEIGHT	WIDTH
8010	13	39	8070	13	68
8030	13	41	8080	17	69
8040	13	55	8090	13	53
8050	13	42	8130	13	36
8060	13	45	8140	25	73

REL 2   8010-1

8010

8070

8030

8080

8040

8090

8050

8130

8060

8140

CIRCUIT SCHEMATIC

OUT1

OUT2

50
(3/12)

51
(3/24)

52
(3/12)

53
(12/24)

VSS

IN

OUT4

OUT3

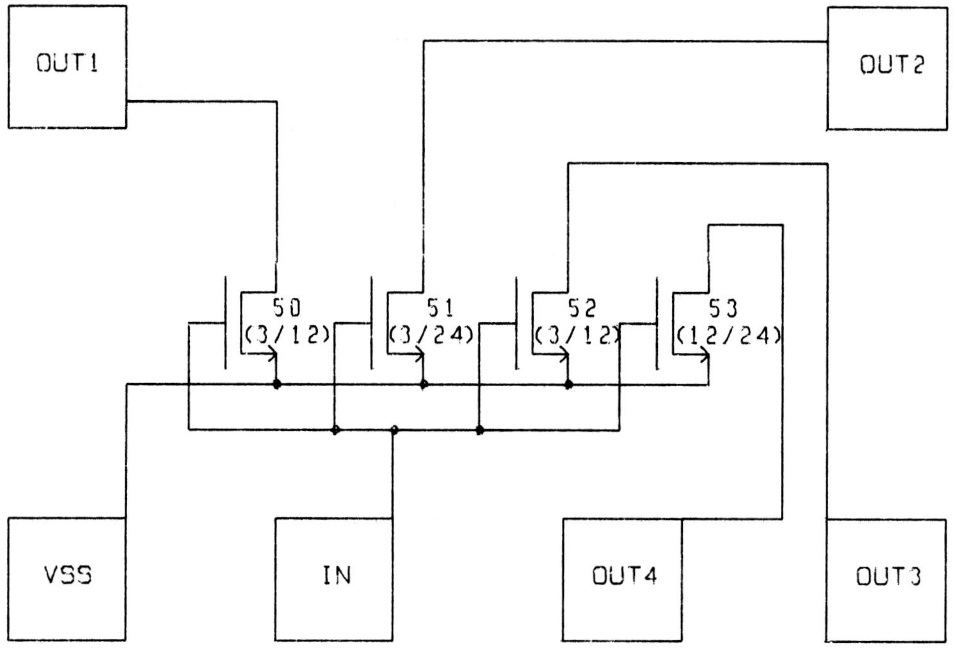

NOTES

DEVICE 50 IS A FIELD OXIDE TRANSISTOR.
DEVICE 52 IS A METAL GATE TRANSISTOR.

REL 2   8200-1

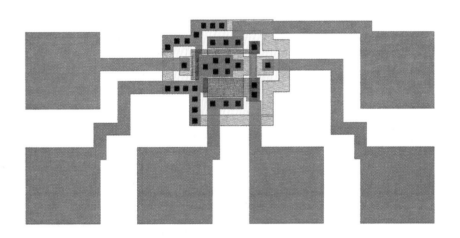

REL 2   8200-2

3˙ MICRON CMOS/BULK CELL FAMILY -CMOS3-	8210 P-CHANNEL TEST DEVICES CELL HEIGHT 137.5 WIDTH 275	DATE: 04/01/85 REVISION: C

CIRCUIT SCHEMATIC

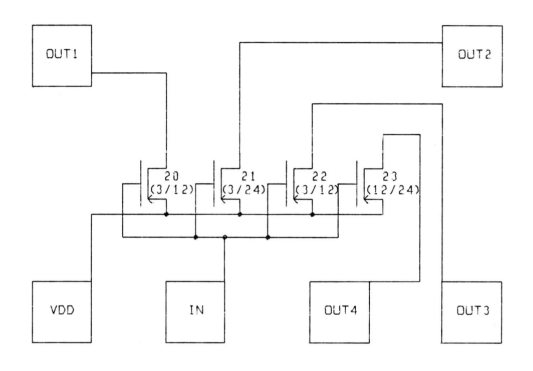

NOTES

DEVICE 20 IS A FIELD OXIDE TRANSISTOR.
DEVICE 22 IS A METAL GATE TRANSISTOR.

REL 2   8210-1

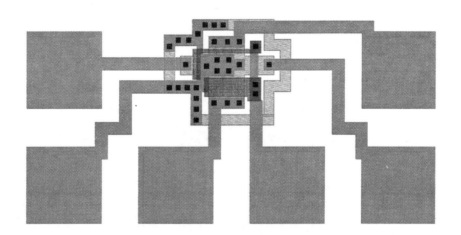

REL 2   8210-2

3 MICRON CMOS/BULK	8220	DATE: 04/01/85
CELL FAMILY	TEST RESISTORS	REVISION: C
-CMOS3-	CELL HEIGHT 137.5 WIDTH 275	

CIRCUIT SCHEMATIC

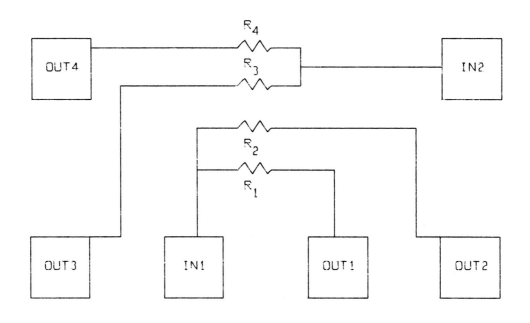

NOTES

ALL RESISTORS ARE 10 SQUARES. R_1 IS A POLY RESISTOR, R_2 IS AN N+ RESISTOR, R_3 IS A P+ RESISTOR, R_4 IS A P- RESISTOR.

REL 2   8220-1

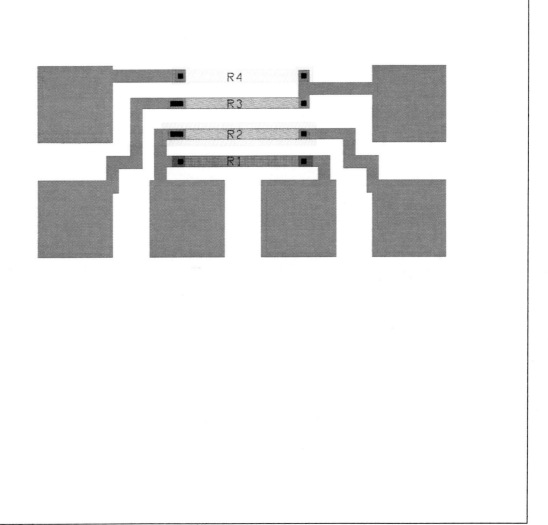

3 MICRON CMOS/BULK CELL FAMILY -CMOS3-	8630 BUS CROSSER CELL HEIGHT 150 WIDTH 12	DATE: 09/01/83 REVISION: A

TERMINAL INFORMATION

TERMINAL NAME	LOGIC NUMBER	CAPACITANCE FIELD	(PF)
1,11	N/A		.03

LOGIC DIAGRAM

N/A

TRUTH TABLE

N/A

LOGIC SYMBOLS

N/A

WORST CASE DELAY INFORMATION

$P_D =$ NS $T_{R/F} =$ NS

$R_S = 1.5K\Omega$, $C_L = 1.5PF$, $V = 5V$, $T = 125°C$

LOGIC EQUATION(S)

N/A

NOTES

EQUIVALENT RESISTANCE IS 6 SQUARES OF POLY RESISTANCE.

8630-1

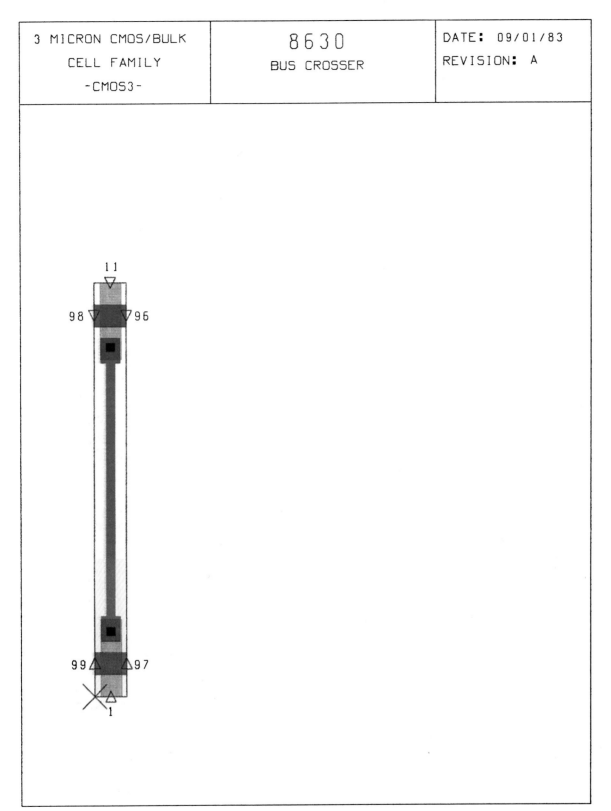

8630-2

367

3 MICRON CMOS/BULK	8640	DATE: 04/10/86
CELL FAMILY	M2 BUS CROSSER	REVISION:
-CMOS3-	CELL HEIGHT 150 WIDTH 12	

TERMINAL INFORMATION	LOGIC DIAGRAM
TERMINAL LOGIC CAPACITANCE NAME NUMBER FIELD (PF) 1,11 N/A .08	N/A

TRUTH TABLE	LOGIC SYMBOLS
N/A	N/A

WORST CASE DELAY INFORMATION

$P_D =$ NS $T_{R/F} =$ NS

$R_S = 1.5 K\Omega$, $C_L = 1.5 PF$, $V = 5V$, $T = 125 °C$

LOGIC EQUATION(S)

N/A

NOTES

EQUIVALENT RESISTANCE IS 6 SQUARES OF POLY RESISTANCE.

REL 5   8640-1

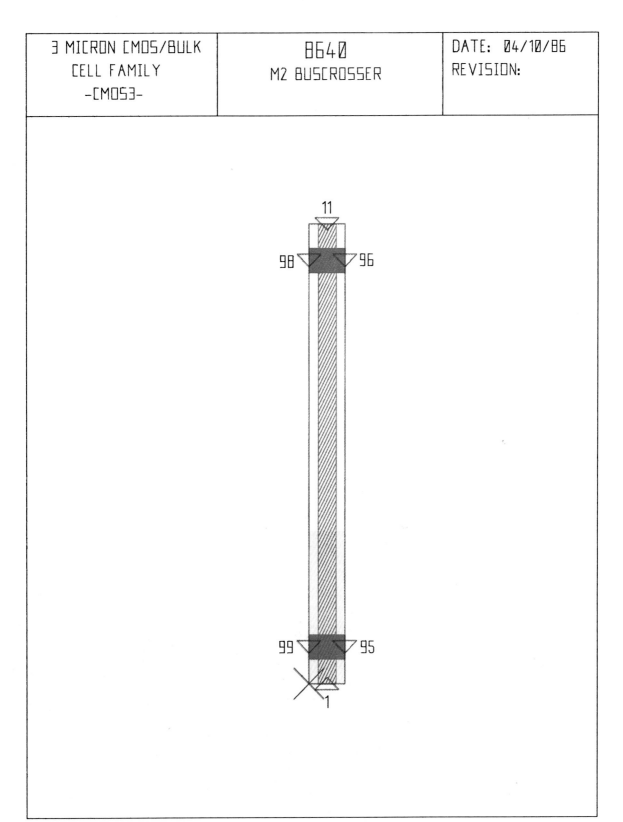

8640-2

3 MICRON CMOS/BULK CELL FAMILY -CMOS3-	8660 RC LOAD CELL CELL HEIGHT 150 WIDTH 60	DATE: 04/01/84 REVISION: 5

TERMINAL INFORMATION	LOGIC DIAGRAM

TERMINAL INFORMATION

TERMINAL NAME	LOGIC NUMBER	CAPACITANCE FIELD	(PF)
2	1		.65
3,13	5		

LOGIC DIAGRAM

N/A

TRUTH TABLE	LOGIC SYMBOLS

TRUTH TABLE

N/A

LOGIC SYMBOLS

N/A

WORST CASE DELAY INFORMATION

P_D =   NS $T_{R/F}$ =   NS

R_S =1.5KΩ, C_L =1.5PF, V=5V, T=125°C

LOGIC EQUATION(S)

N/A

NOTES

RESISTANCE- 59 SQUARES OF POLY RESISTANCE
(1.77 KΩ AT 30 Ω PER SQUARE)

IT IS RECOMMENDED THAT EITHER THE 1550 OR 1550 BE USED INSTEAD OF THE 8660.

8660-1

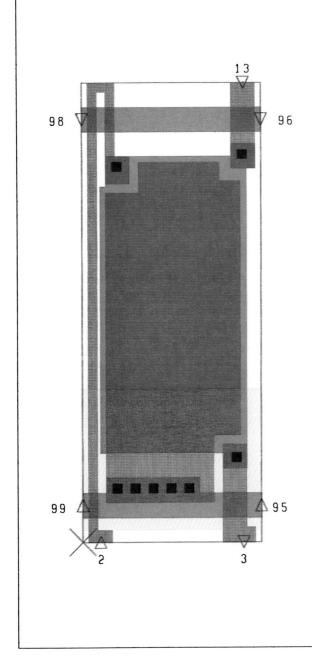

8660-2

371

3 -MICRON CMOS/BULK CELL FAMILY -CMOS3-	8670 M2 POLY VIA CELL HEIGHT 17.5 WIDTH 8	DATE: 04/10/86 REVISION:

TERMINAL INFORMATION

TERMINAL NAME	LOGIC NUMBER	CAPACITANCE FIELD	(PF)
1,2	N/A		.01

LOGIC DIAGRAM

N/A

TRUTH TABLE

N/A

LOGIC SYMBOLS

N/A

WORST CASE DELAY INFORMATION

$P_D =$ NS $T_{R/F} =$ NS

$R_S = 1.5K\Omega$, $C_L = 1.5PF$, $V = 5V$, $T = 125^{\circ}C$

LOGIC EQUATION(S)

N/A

NOTES

3 MICRON CMOS/BULK CELL FAMILY -CMOS3-	8670 M2 POLY VIA	DATE: 04/10/86 REVISION:

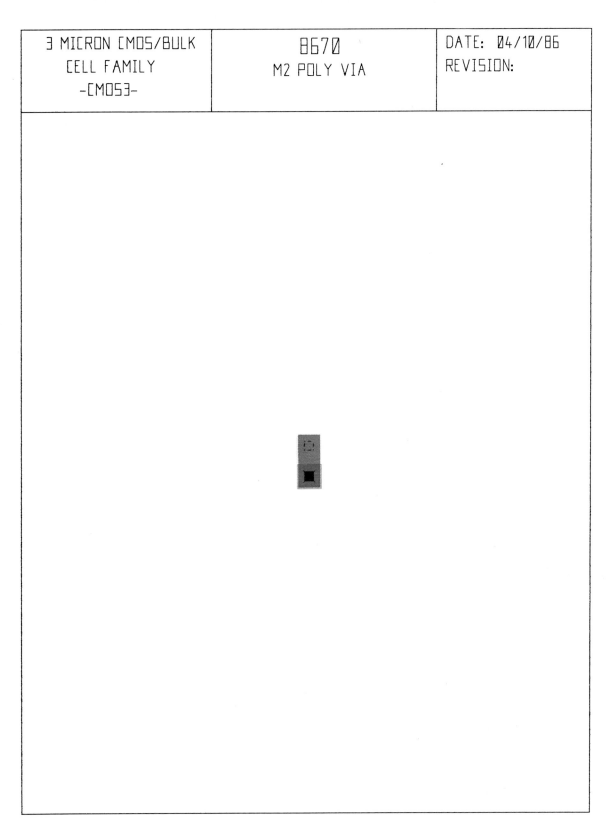

8670-2

3 MICRON CMOS/BULK CELL FAMILY -CMOS3-	8680 WIRING VIA CELL HEIGHT 8 WIDTH 8	DATE: 04/01/84 REVISION: B

TERMINAL INFORMATION

TERMINAL NAME	LOGIC NUMBER	CAPACITANCE FIELD (PF)
2	N/A	.01

LOGIC DIAGRAM

N/A

TRUTH TABLE

N/A

LOGIC SYMBOLS

N/A

WORST CASE DELAY INFORMATION

$P_D =$ NS $T_{R/F} =$ NS

$R_S = 1.5K\Omega,$ $C_L = 1.5PF,$ $V = 5V,$ $T = 125°C$

LOGIC EQUATION(S)

N/A

NOTES

8680-1

8680-2

375

3 MICRON CMOS/BULK	8690	DATE: 04/10/86
CELL FAMILY	M2 VIA	REVISION:
-CMOS3-	CELL HEIGHT 7 WIDTH 7	

TERMINAL INFORMATION	LOGIC DIAGRAM
TERMINAL LOGIC CAPACITANCE NAME NUMBER FIELD (PF) 2 N/A .005	N/A

TRUTH TABLE	LOGIC SYMBOLS
N/A	N/A

WORST CASE DELAY INFORMATION

$P_D =$ NS $T_{R/F} =$ NS

$R_S = 1.5K\Omega$, $C_L = 1.5PF$, $V = 5V$, $T = 125^{\circ}C$

LOGIC EQUATION(S)
N/A

NOTES

REL 5   8690-1

3 MICRON CMOS/BULK CELL FAMILY -CMOS3-	8690 M2 VIA	DATE: 04/10/86 REVISION:

8690-2

3 MICRON CMOS/BULK CELL FAMILY -CMOS3-	9110 VSS DIODE ONLY PAD CELL HEIGHT 313 WIDTH 204	DATE: 04/01/85 REVISION: C

TERMINAL INFORMATION

TERMINAL NAME	NUMBER	LOGIC FIELD	CAPACITANCE (PF)
OUT	2		6

LOGIC DIAGRAM

SAME AS LOGIC DIAGRAM

TRUTH TABLE

PAD	OUT
0	0
1	1
X	X

LOGICV REQUIRES THE PAD SIGNAL NAME TO BE IN LOGIC FIELD 1.

LOGIC SYMBOLS

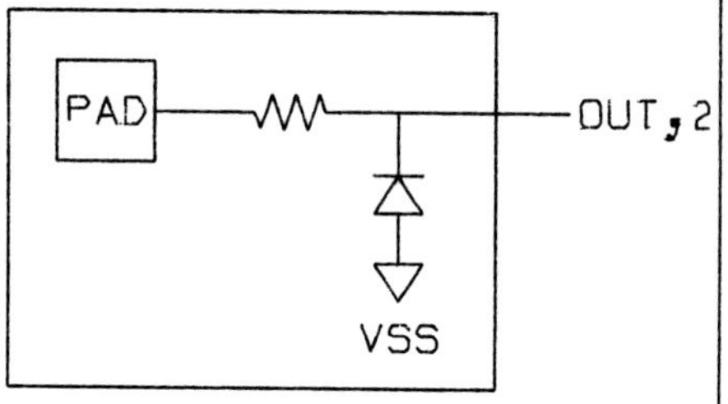

WORST CASE DELAY INFORMATION

P_D = 17.20NS $T_{R/F}$ = 4.45NS

R_S = 1.5KΩ, C_L = 1.5PF, V = 5V, T = 125°C

LOGIC EQUATION(S)

OUT = PAD

NOTES

CIRCUIT SCHEMATIC

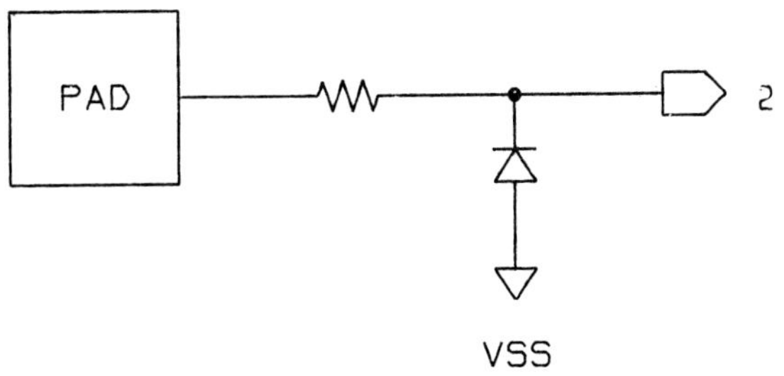

REL 3   9110-2

379

3 MICRON CMOS/BULK CELL FAMILY -CMOS3-	9110 VSS DIODE ONLY PAD	DATE: 04/01/85 REVISION: C

OUTPUT CHARACTERISTIC EQUATIONS

$$P_D(0-1) = P_{DC}(0-1) + .01 \ (T_{R/F} - 10) + .70 \ R_S C_L$$

$$P_D(1-0) = P_{DC}(1-0) + .00 \ (T_{R/F} - 10) + .63 \ R_S C_L$$

$$T_R = T_{RC} + .90 \ (T_{R/F} - 10) + 2.33 R_S C_L$$

$$T_F = T_{FC} + .87 \ (T_{R/F} - 10) + 2.41 R_S C_L$$

EQUATIONS

$25^\circ C$	$95^\circ C$	$125^\circ C$
$P_{DC}(0-1) = .92 \ C_L + 1.28$	$P_{DC}(0-1) = .94 \ C_L + 1.31$	$P_{DC}(0-1) = .96 \ C_L + 1.32$
$P_{DC}(1-0) = .92 \ C_L + 1.45$	$P_{DC}(1-0) = .94 \ C_L + 1.48$	$P_{DC}(1-0) = .96 \ C_L + 1.49$
$T_{RC} = 2.90 C_L + 9.21$	$T_{RC} = 3.01 C_L + 9.13$	$T_{RC} = 3.06 C_L + 9.12$
$T_{FC} = 2.94 C_L + 7.17$	$T_{FC} = 3.06 C_L + 7.09$	$T_{FC} = 3.12 C_L + 7.05$

$125^\circ C$ BC

$$P_{DC}(0-1) = .92 \ C_L + 1.28$$

$$P_{DC}(1-0) = .92 \ C_L + 1.45$$

$$T_{RC} = 2.90 C_L + 9.21$$

$$T_{FC} = 2.94 C_L + 7.17$$

VOLTAGE TABLE

VOLTAGE   DEVIATION FACTOR

VOLTAGE	TRANSITION		PROP DELAY	
	TR	TF	1-0	0-1
3.0	1.04	.99	1.03	1.00
3.5	1.03	.99	1.02	1.00
4.0	1.02	.99	1.01	1.00
4.5	1.01	1.00	1.01	1.00
5.0	1.00	1.00	1.00	1.00
5.5	.99	1.00	1.00	1.00
6.0	.99	1.01	1.00	1.00
6.5	.98	1.01	1.00	1.00
7.0	.97	1.01	.99	1.00

REL 3   9110-3

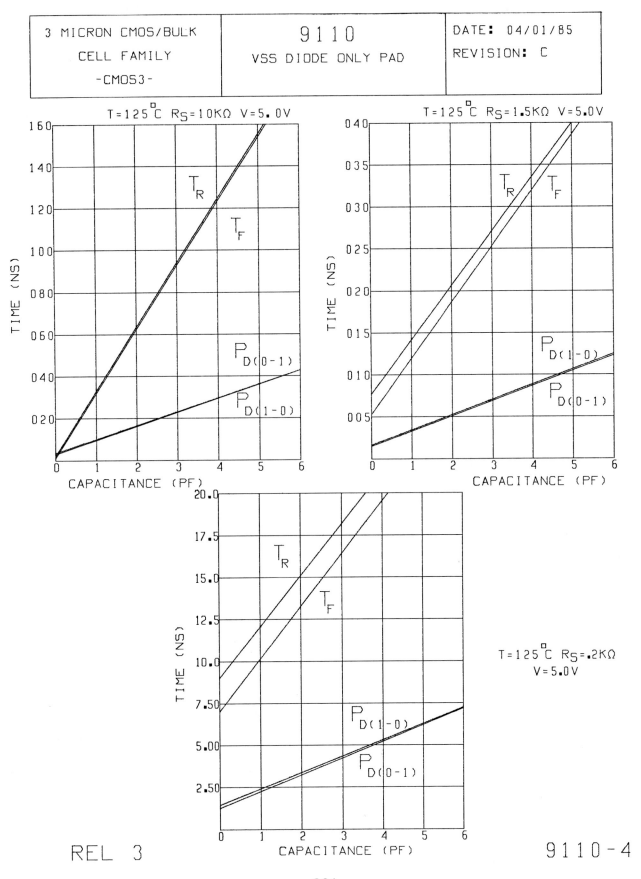

REL 3

9110-4

98

96

99

95

2

3 MICRON CMOS/BULK	9120	DATE: 04/01/85
CELL FAMILY	VSS DIODE ONLY PAD	REVISION: C
-CMOS3-	CELL HEIGHT 313 WIDTH 204	

TERMINAL INFORMATION

TERMINAL NAME	LOGIC NUMBER	CAPACITANCE FIELD	(PF)
OUT	2	6	

LOGIC DIAGRAM

SAME AS LOGIC DIAGRAM

TRUTH TABLE

PAD	OUT
0	0
1	1
X	X

LOGICV REQUIRES THE PAD SIGNAL NAME
TO BE IN LOGIC FIELD 1.

LOGIC SYMBOLS

WORST CASE DELAY INFORMATION

P_D = 4.45 NS $T_{R/F}$ = 17.19NS

R_S = 1.5KΩ, C_L = 1.5PF, V=5V, T=125°C

LOGIC EQUATION(S)

OUT=PAD

NOTES

REL 3   9120-1

383

3 MICRON CMOS/BULK CELL FAMILY -CMOS3-	9120 VSS DIODE ONLY PAD	DATE: 04/01/85 REVISION: C

CIRCUIT SCHEMATIC

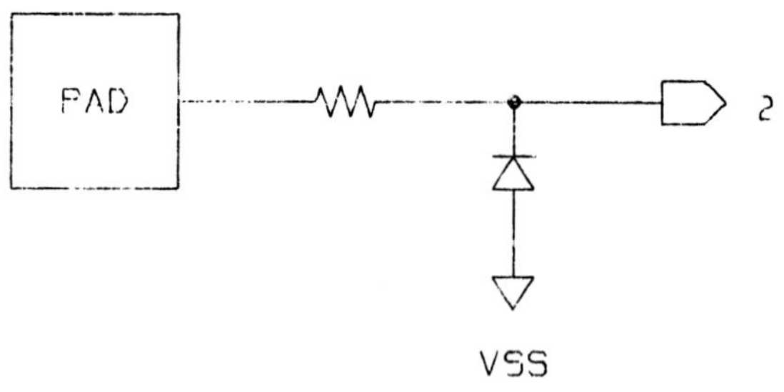

REL 3   9120-2

384

3 MICRON CMOS/BULK CELL FAMILY -CMOS3-	9 1 2 0 VSS DIODE ONLY PAD	DATE: 04/01/85 REVISION: C

OUTPUT CHARACTERISTIC EQUATIONS

$$P_D(0-1) = P_{DC}(0-1) + .01 \ (T_{R/F} - 10) + .70 \ R_S C_L$$

$$P_D(1-0) = P_{DC}(1-0) + .00 \ (T_{R/F} - 10) + .68 \ R_S C_L$$

$$T_R = T_{RC} + .90 \ (T_{R/F} - 10) + 2.33 R_S C_L$$

$$T_F = T_{FC} + .87 \ (T_{R/F} - 10) + 2.41 R_S C_L$$

EQUATIONS

$25\,^{\circ}C$

$$P_{DC}(0-1) = .92 \ C_L + 1.28$$

$$P_{DC}(1-0) = .93 \ C_L + 1.44$$

$$T_{RC} = 2.89 C_L + 9.19$$

$$T_{FC} = 2.94 C_L + 7.18$$

$95\,^{\circ}C$

$$P_{DC}(0-1) = .95 \ C_L + 1.30$$

$$P_{DC}(1-0) = .95 \ C_L + 1.47$$

$$T_{RC} = 3.01 C_L + 9.13$$

$$T_{FC} = 3.06 C_L + 7.08$$

$125\,^{\circ}C$

$$P_{DC}(0-1) = .96 \ C_L + 1.32$$

$$P_{DC}(1-0) = .96 \ C_L + 1.49$$

$$T_{RC} = 3.06 C_L + 9.13$$

$$T_{FC} = 3.12 C_L + 7.03$$

$125\,^{\circ}C$ BC

$$P_{DC}(0-1) = .92 \ C_L + 1.28$$

$$P_{DC}(1-0) = .93 \ C_L + 1.44$$

$$T_{RC} = 2.89 C_L + 9.19$$

$$T_{FC} = 2.94 C_L + 7.18$$

VOLTAGE TABLE

VOLTAGE	DEVIATION FACTOR			
	TRANSITION		PROP DELAY	
	TR	TF	1-0	0-1
3.0	1.04	.99	1.03	1.00
3.5	1.03	.99	1.02	1.00
4.0	1.02	.99	1.01	1.00
4.5	1.01	1.00	1.01	1.00
5.0	1.00	1.00	1.00	1.00
5.5	.99	1.00	1.00	1.00
6.0	.99	1.01	.99	1.00
6.5	.98	1.01	.99	1.00
7.0	.97	1.01	.99	1.00

REL 3   9120-3

385

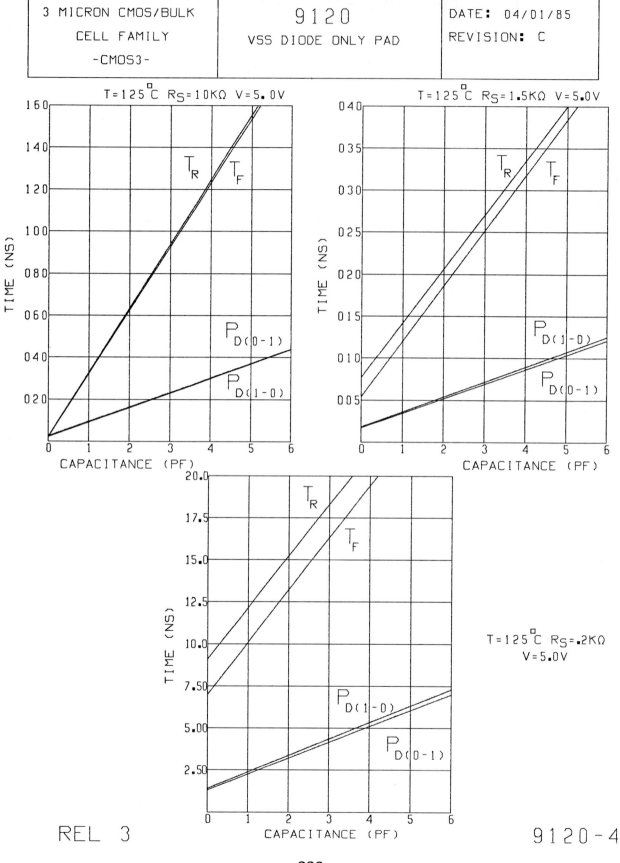

REL 3

9120-4

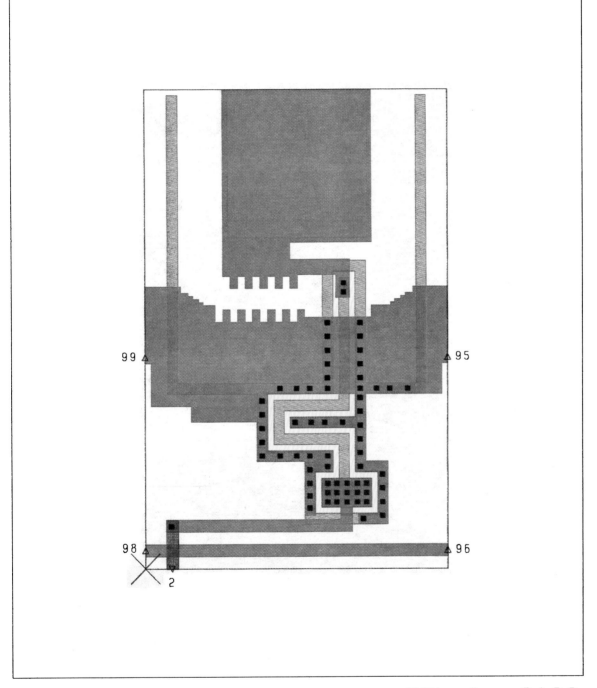

REL 3   9120-5

3 MICRON CMOS/BULK CELL FAMILY -CMOS3-	9150 INPUT PAD CELL HEIGHT 313 WIDTH 204	DATE: 04/01/85 REVISION: D

TERMINAL INFORMATION

TERMINAL NAME	LOGIC NUMBER	CAPACITANCE FIELD	(PF)
A	3	13	
OUT1	4	7	
OUT2	2	6	

LOGIC DIAGRAM

TRUTH TABLE

PAD	A	OUT1	OUT2
0	0	1	0
1	1	0	1
X	X	X	X

LOGICV REQUIRES THE PAD SIGNAL NAME
TO BE IN LOGIC FIELD 1.

LOGIC SYMBOLS

WORST CASE DELAY INFORMATION

OUT1 P_D = 8.97 NS $T_{R/F}$ = 22.06 NS

OUT2 P_D = 10.00 NS $T_{R/F}$ = 16.0 NS

R_S = 1.5KΩ, C_L = 1.5PF, V=5V, T=125°C

LOGIC EQUATION(S)

OUT1 = $\overline{A}$ = $\overline{PAD}$

OUT2 = A = PAD

NOTES
9150 AND 9160 ARE SAME FUNCTION WITH DIFFERENT BUS STRUCTURE
   0-40% OF VDD IS RECOGNIZED AS A "0"
   60-100% OF VDD IS RECOGNIZED AS A "1"
THE DELAY EQUATIONS FOR THE NON-INVERTED BUFFERED OUTPUT TAKE
INTO CONSIDERATION THE CAPACITIVE LOADING ON THE INVERTED
BUFFERED OUTPUT. RESISTIVE LOADING ON THE INVERTED OUTPUT HAS
LITTLE EFFECT ON THE NON-INVERTED BUFFERED OUTPUT. SEE DESIGN
APPLICATION NOTES FOR PROPAGATION DEVIATION OVER VOLTAGE FOR
NON-INVERTED BUFFERED DELAY WITH INVERTER OUTPUT LOADED.

REL 2   9150-1

CIRCUIT SCHEMATIC

3 MICRON CMOS/BULK CELL FAMILY -CMOS3-	9150 INPUT PAD INVERTER	DATE: 04/01/85 REVISION: D

OUTPUT CHARACTERISTIC EQUATIONS

$$P_D(0-1) = P_{DC}(0-1) + .17 (T_{R/F} - 10) + .64 R_S C_L$$

$$P_D(1-0) = P_{DC}(1-0) + .16 (T_{R/F} - 10) + .62 R_S C_L$$

$$T_R = T_{RC} + .23 (T_{R/F} - 10) + 2.28 R_S C_L$$

$$T_F = T_{FC} + .28 (T_{R/F} - 10) + 2.40 R_S C_L$$

EQUATIONS

$25^\circ C$	$95^\circ C$	$125^\circ C$
$P_{DC}(0-1) = 1.85 C_L + 3.54$	$P_{DC}(0-1) = 2.36 C_L + 3.86$	$P_{DC}(0-1) = 2.57 C_L + 3.98$
$P_{DC}(1-0) = 1.27 C_L + 3.42$	$P_{DC}(1-0) = 1.59 C_L + 3.58$	$P_{DC}(1-0) = 1.72 C_L + 3.63$
$T_{RC} = 5.48 C_L + 5.56$	$T_{RC} = 7.14 C_L + 6.70$	$T_{RC} = 7.84 C_L + 7.19$
$T_{FC} = 3.49 C_L + 3.83$	$T_{FC} = 4.48 C_L + 4.35$	$T_{FC} = 4.9 C_L + 4.59$

$125^\circ C$ BC

$$P_{DC}(0-1) = 1.15 C_L + 2.65$$

$$P_{DC}(1-0) = .85 C_L + 2.07$$

$$T_{RC} = 3.54 C_L + 5.15$$

$$T_{FC} = 2.19 C_L + 4.31$$

VOLTAGE TABLE

VOLTAGE	DEVIATION FACTOR			
	TRANSITION		PROP DELAY	
	TR	TF	1-0	0-1
3.0	1.51	1.47	1.95	1.55
3.5	1.34	1.30	1.63	1.37
4.0	1.17	1.12	1.31	1.18
4.5	1.09	1.06	1.16	1.09
5.0	1.00	1.00	1.00	1.00
5.5	.95	.96	.90	.95
6.0	.90	.92	.80	.90
6.5	.87	.90	.74	.87
7.0	.84	.87	.68	.83

REL 2   9150-3

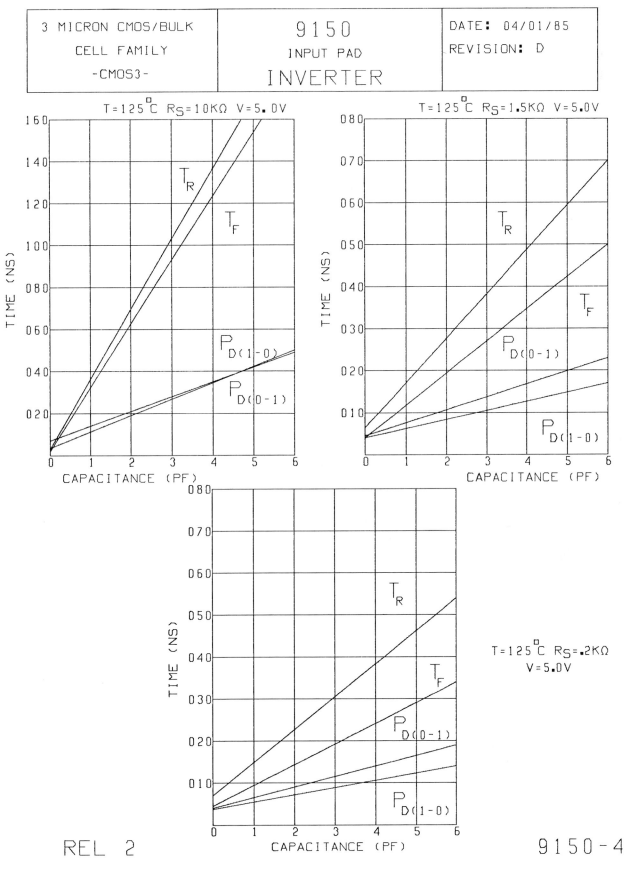

3 MICRON CMOS/BULK CELL FAMILY -CMOS3-	9150 INPUT PAD DOUBLE BUFFER	DATE: 04/01/85 REVISION: D

OUTPUT CHARACTERISTIC EQUATIONS

$$P_D(0-1) = P_{DC}(0-1) + .12 (T_{R/F} - 10) + .64 R_S C_L + 1.84 C_{LINV.}$$

$$P_D(1-0) = P_{DC}(1-0) + .14 (T_{R/F} - 10) + .61 R_S C_L + 2.77 C_{LINV.}$$

$$T_R = T_{RC} + .03 (T_{R/F} - 10) + 2.48 R_S C_L + 1.10 C_{LINV.}$$

$$T_F = T_{FC} + .04 (T_{R/F} - 10) + 2.50 R_S C_L + 1.68 C_{LINV.}$$

EQUATIONS

$25°C$
$$P_{DC}(0-1) = 1.3 C_L + 4.97$$
$$P_{DC}(1-0) = 1.0 C_L + 5.75$$
$$T_{RC} = 4.12 C_L + 2.47$$
$$T_{FC} = 2.79 C_L + 2.29$$

$95°C$
$$P_{DC}(0-1) = 1.66 C_L + 5.64$$
$$P_{DC}(1-0) = 1.26 C_L + 6.62$$
$$T_{RC} = 5.28 C_L + 3.20$$
$$T_{FC} = 3.53 C_L + 2.95$$

$125°C$
$$P_{DC}(0-1) = 1.81 C_L + 5.88$$
$$P_{DC}(1-0) = 1.34 C_L + 6.96$$
$$T_{RC} = 5.78 C_L + 3.51$$
$$T_{FC} = 3.85 C_L + 3.19$$

$125°C$ BC
$$P_{DC}(0-1) = .86 C_L + 2.81$$
$$P_{DC}(1-0) = .64 C_L + 3.62$$
$$T_{RC} = 2.9 C_L + 1.88$$
$$T_{FC} = 1.98 C_L + 1.81$$

VOLTAGE TABLE

VOLTAGE	DEVIATION FACTOR			
	TRANSITION		PROP DELAY	
	TR	TF	1-0	0-1
3.0	1.46	1.48	1.73	1.69
3.5	1.31	1.32	1.48	1.46
4.0	1.15	1.15	1.23	1.23
4.5	1.08	1.08	1.12	1.12
5.0	1.00	1.00	1.00	1.00
5.5	.96	.96	.94	.93
6.0	.92	.92	.87	.86
6.5	.89	.90	.83	.82
7.0	.86	.87	.78	.77

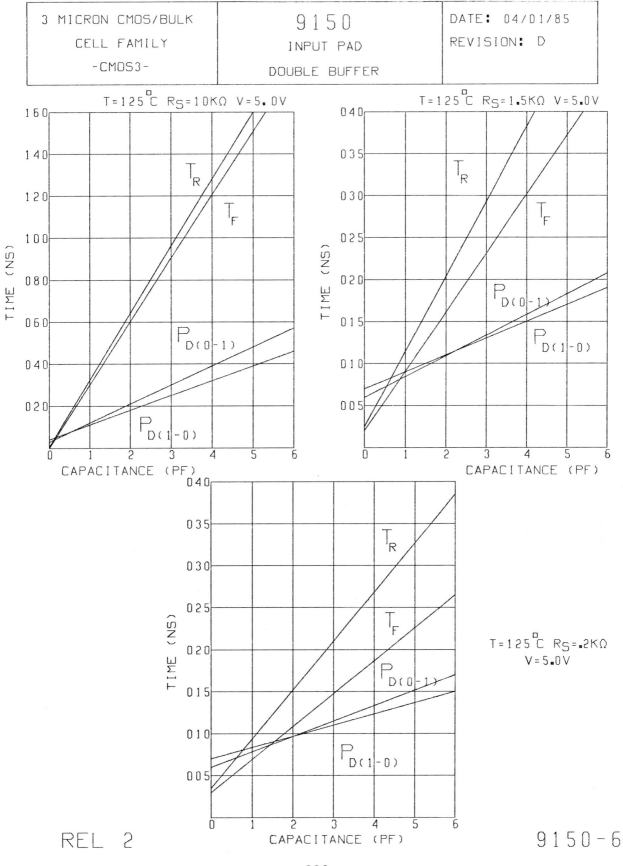

3 MICRON CMOS/BULK	9150	DATE: 04/01/85
CELL FAMILY	INPUT PAD	REVISION: D
-CMOS3-	DOUBLE BUFFER	

REL 2

9150-6

393

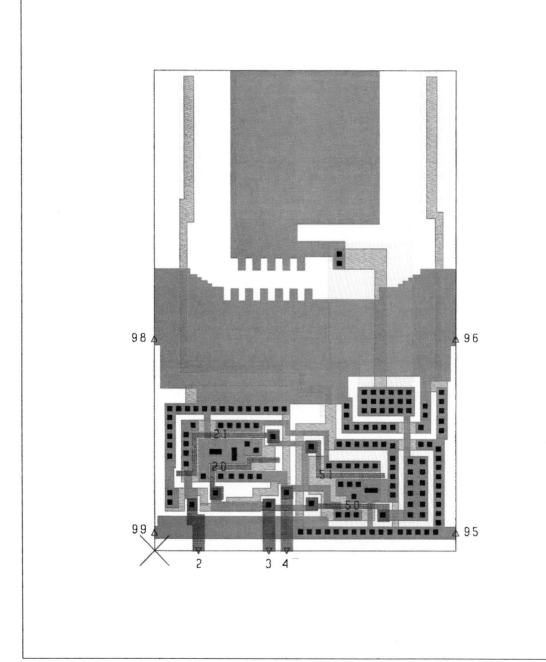

3 MICRON CMOS/BULK	9160	DATE: 04/01/85
CELL FAMILY	INPUT PAD	REVISION: D
-CMOS3-	CELL HEIGHT 313 WIDTH 204	

TERMINAL INFORMATION

TERMINAL NAME	LOGIC NUMBER	CAPACITANCE FIELD (PF)
A	3	13
OUT1	4	7
OUT2	2	5

LOGIC DIAGRAM

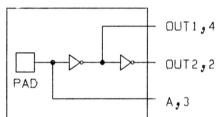

TRUTH TABLE

PAD	A	OUT1	OUT2
0	0	1	0
1	1	0	1
X	X	X	X

LOGICV REQUIRES THE PAD SIGNAL NAME
TO BE IN LOGIC FIELD 1.

LOGIC SYMBOLS

WORST CASE DELAY INFORMATION

$OUT1 \, P_D = 8.84 \, NS \qquad T_{R/F} = 22.06 \, NS$

$OUT2 \, P_D = 10.23 \, NS \qquad T_{R/F} = 16.70 \, NS$

$R_S = 1.5K\Omega, \ C_L = 1.5PF, \ V = 5V, \ T = 125°C$

LOGIC EQUATION(S)

$OUT1 = \overline{A} = \overline{PAD}$

$OUT2 = A = PAD$

NOTES
9150 AND 9160 ARE SAME FUNCTION WITH DIFFERENT BUS STRUCTURE
   0-40% OF VDD IS RECOGNIZED AS A "0"
   60-100% OF VDD IS RECOGNIZED AS A "1"
THE DELAY EQUATIONS FOR THE NON-INVERTED BUFFERED OUTPUT TAKE
INTO CONSIDERATION THE CAPACITIVE LOADING ON THE INVERTED
BUFFERED OUTPUT. RESISTIVE LOADING ON THE INVERTED OUTPUT HAS
LITTLE EFFECT ON THE NON-INVERTED BUFFERED OUTPUT. SEE DESIGN
APPLICATION NOTES FOR PROPAGATION DEVIATION OVER VOLTAGE FOR
NON-INVERTED BUFFERED DELAY WITH INVERTER OUTPUT LOADED.

REL 2   9160-1

CIRCUIT SCHEMATIC

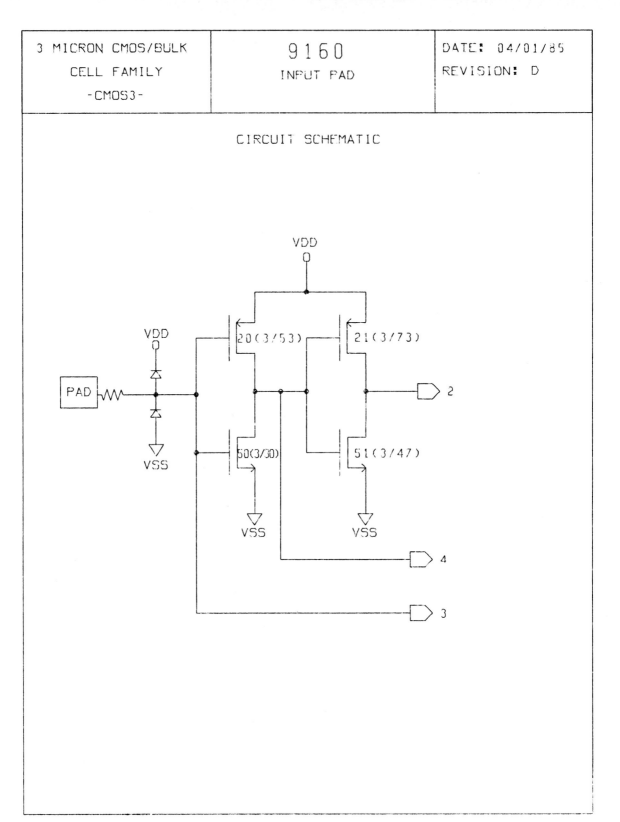

3 MICRON CMOS/BULK CELL FAMILY -CMOS3-	9160 INPUT PAD INVERTER	DATE: 04/01/85 REVISION: D

OUTPUT CHARACTERISTIC EQUATIONS

$$P_D(0-1) = P_{DC}(0-1) + .17 (T_{R/F} - 10) + .73 R_S C_L$$

$$P_D(1-0) = P_{DC}(1-0) + .18 (T_{R/F} - 10) + .70 R_S C_L$$

$$T_R = T_{RC} + .24 (T_{R/F} - 10) + 2.64 R_S C_L$$

$$T_F = T_{FC} + .26 (T_{R/F} - 10) + 2.73 R_S C_L$$

EQUATIONS

25°C

$$P_{DC}(0-1) = 1.9 C_L + 3.4$$

$$P_{DC}(1-0) = 1.50 C_L + 3.49$$

$$T_{RC} = 5.62 C_L + 5.34$$

$$T_{FC} = 4.06 C_L + 3.88$$

95°C

$$P_{DC}(0-1) = 2.43 C_L + 3.66$$

$$P_{DC}(1-0) = 1.88 C_L + 3.66$$

$$T_{RC} = 7.31 C_L + 6.40$$

$$T_{FC} = 5.22 C_L + 4.41$$

125°C

$$P_{DC}(0-1) = 2.64 C_L + 3.78$$

$$P_{DC}(1-0) = 2.04 C_L + 3.74$$

$$T_{RC} = 8.02 C_L + 6.87$$

$$T_{FC} = 5.70 C_L + 4.69$$

125°C BC

$$P_{DC}(0-1) = 1.18 C_L + 2.48$$

$$P_{DC}(1-0) = .93 C_L + 2.29$$

$$T_{RC} = 3.58 C_L + 5.11$$

$$T_{FC} = 2.46 C_L + 4.34$$

VOLTAGE TABLE

VOLTAGE	DEVIATION FACTOR			
	TRANSITION		PROP DELAY	
	TR	TF	1-0	0-1
3.0	1.51	1.54	2.00	1.55
3.5	1.34	1.35	1.66	1.37
4.0	1.16	1.16	1.32	1.18
4.5	1.08	1.08	1.16	1.09
5.0	1.00	1.00	1.00	1.00
5.5	.96	.96	.94	.95
6.0	.91	.91	.88	.89
6.5	.88	.89	.85	.86
7.0	.84	.86	.81	.83

REL 2   9160-3

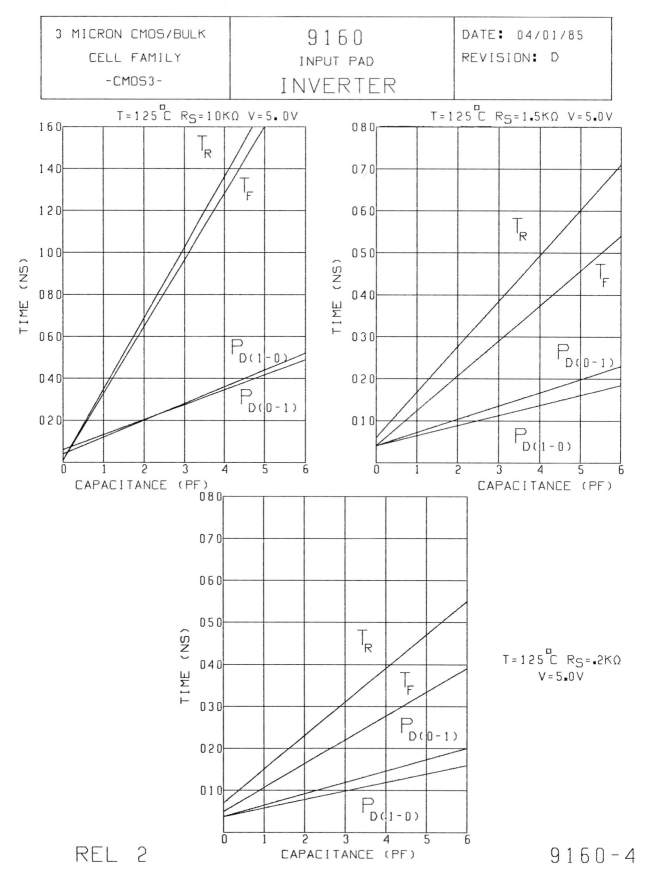

OUTPUT CHARACTERISTIC EQUATIONS

$$P_D(0-1) = P_{DC}(0-1) + .13 \ (T_{R/F} - 10) + .73 \ R_S C_L + 2.3 C_{LINV}$$

$$P_D(1-0) = P_{DC}(1-0) + .13 \ (T_{R/F} - 10) + .70 \ R_S C_L + 2.92 C_{LINV}$$

$$T_R = T_{RC} + .04 \ (T_{R/F} - 10) + 2.87 R_S C_L + 1.28 C_{LINV}$$

$$T_F = T_{FC} + .03 \ (T_{R/F} - 10) + 2.83 R_S C_L + 1.74 C_{LINV}$$

EQUATIONS

$25^{\circ}C$

$$P_{DC}(0-1) = 1.43 C_L + 5.23$$

$$P_{DC}(1-0) = 1.05 C_L + 5.59$$

$$T_{RC} = 4.46 C_L + 2.57$$

$$T_{FC} = 2.91 C_L + 2.42$$

$95^{\circ}C$

$$P_{DC}(0-1) = 1.82 C_L + 5.94$$

$$P_{DC}(1-0) = 1.33 C_L + 6.42$$

$$T_{RC} = 5.73 C_L + 3.35$$

$$T_{FC} = 3.68 C_L + 2.88$$

$125^{\circ}C$

$$P_{DC}(0-1) = 1.99 C_L + 6.21$$

$$P_{DC}(1-0) = 1.44 C_L + 6.76$$

$$T_{RC} = 6.27 C_L + 3.66$$

$$T_{FC} = 4.0 \ C_L + 3.15$$

$125^{\circ}C$ BC

$$P_{DC}(0-1) = .92 \ C_L + 3.08$$

$$P_{DC}(1-0) = .67 \ C_L + 3.41$$

$$T_{RC} = 3.08 C_L + 1.92$$

$$T_{FC} = 2.02 C_L + 1.81$$

VOLTAGE TABLE

VOLTAGE   DEVIATION FACTOR

VOLTAGE	TRANSITION		PROP DELAY	
	TR	TF	1-0	0-1
3.0	1.49	1.48	1.74	1.70
3.5	1.32	1.32	1.49	1.47
4.0	1.15	1.15	1.23	1.23
4.5	1.08	1.08	1.12	1.12
5.0	1.00	1.00	1.00	1.00
5.5	.96	.96	.94	.94
6.0	.91	.92	.87	.87
6.5	.88	.90	.83	.83
7.0	.85	.87	.78	.78

REL 2   9160-5

399

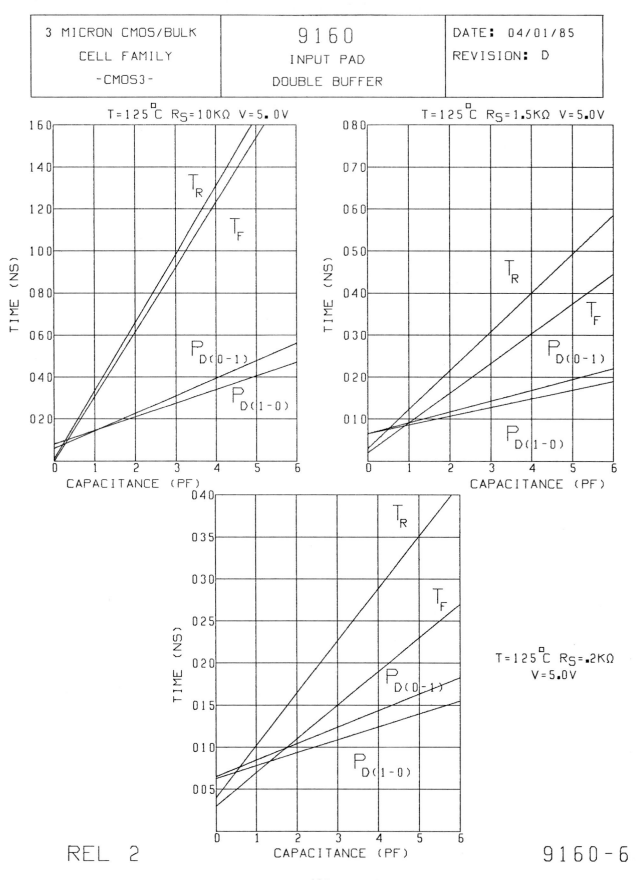

3 MICRON CMOS/BULK	9160	DATE: 04/01/85
CELL FAMILY	INPUT PAD	REVISION: D
-CMOS3-	DOUBLE BUFFER	

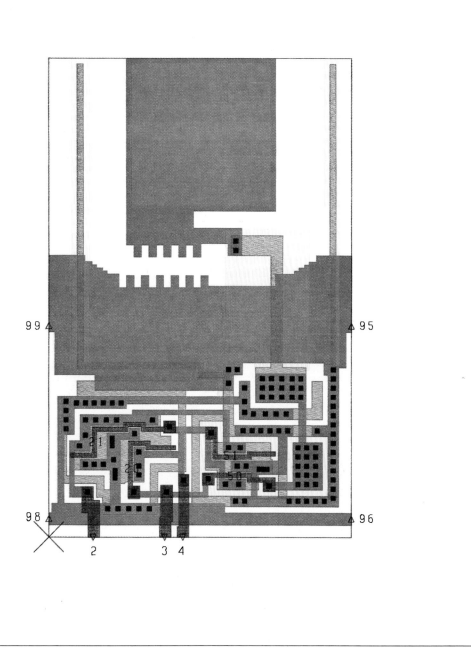

REL 2   9160-7

401

3 MICRON CMOS/BULK CELL FAMILY -CMOS3-	9250 OUTPUT BUFFER CELL HEIGHT 313 WIDTH 204	DATE: 04/01/84 REVISION: B

TERMINAL INFORMATION

TERMINAL NAME	LOGIC NUMBER	FIELD	CAPACITANCE (PF)
A	2	1	.33

LOGIC DIAGRAM

SAME AS LOGIC SYMBOL.

TRUTH TABLE

A	PAD
1	1
0	0
X	X

LOGICV REQUIRES THE PAD SIGNAL NAME TO BE IN LOGIC FIELD 6.

LOGIC SYMBOLS

WORST CASE DELAY INFORMATION

$P_D = 15.19$ NS $T_{R/F} = 34.04$ NS

$R_S = 0 K\Omega$, $C_L = 35$ PF, $V = 5V$, $T = 125^{\circ}C$

LOGIC EQUATION(S)

PAD=A

NOTES

SEE PAGE 9250-4 FOR OUTPUT DRIVE CAPABILITY.
9250 AND 9260 OUTPUT BUFFER PADS HAVE THE SAME FUNCTION EXCEPT FOR DIFFERENT BUS STRUCTURES.

REL 2   9250-1

CIRCUIT SCHEMATIC

3 MICRON CMOS/BULK CELL FAMILY -CMOS3-	9250 OUTPUT BUFFER	DATE: 04/01/84 REVISION: B

OUTPUT CHARACTERISTIC EQUATIONS

$$P_D(0-1) = P_{DC}(0-1) + .12 (T_{R/F} - 10) + .61 R_S C_L$$

$$P_D(1-0) = P_{DC}(1-0) + .14 (T_{R/F} - 10) + .46 R_S C_L$$

$$T_R = T_{RC} + .01 (T_{R/F} - 10) + 2.58 R_S C_L$$

$$T_F = T_{FC} + .02 (T_{R/F} - 10) + 2.59 R_S C_L$$

EQUATIONS

$25^\sigma C$	$95^\sigma C$	$125^\sigma C$
$P_{DC}(0-1) = .21 C_L + 4.45$	$P_{DC}(0-1) = .26 C_L + 4.93$	$P_{DC}(0-1) = 0.28 C_L + 5.13$
$P_{DC}(1-0) = .19 C_L + 5.33$	$P_{DC}(1-0) = .23 C_L + 6.10$	$P_{DC}(1-0) = 0.25 C_L + 6.41$
$T_{RC} = .71 C_L + 1.26$	$T_{RC} = .86 C_L + 1.67$	$T_{RC} = 0.92 C_L + 1.87$
$T_{FC} = .59 C_L + 1.47$	$T_{FC} = .70 C_L + 1.92$	$T_{FC} = .74 C_L + 2.13$

$125^\sigma C$ BC

$$P_{DC}(0-1) = .15 C_L + 2.47$$

$$P_{DC}(1-0) = .13 C_L + 3.40$$

$$T_{RC} = .54 C_L + 1.04$$

$$T_{FC} = .44 C_L + 1.16$$

VOLTAGE TABLE

VOLTAGE	DEVIATION FACTOR			
	TRANSITION		PROP DELAY	
	TR	TF	1-0	0-1
3.0	1.54	1.66	1.83	1.73
3.5	1.36	1.44	1.55	1.48
4.0	1.18	1.21	1.26	1.23
4.5	1.09	1.11	1.13	1.12
5.0	1.00	1.00	1.00	1.00
5.5	.95	.94	.93	.93
6.0	.90	.83	.85	.86
6.5	.37	.85	.31	.32
7.0	.33	.31	.76	.77

3 MICRON CMOS/BULK CELL FAMILY -CMOS3-	9250 OUTPUT BUFFER	DATE: 04/01/84 REVISION: B

NOTES

FOR VDD AT 5V AND VSS AT 0V THE FOLLOWING
DRIVE CAPABILITY IS ACHEIVABLE:

FOR V_{OUT} AT .5 VOLTS I_{SINK}= 2.03 MA.

FOR V_{OUT} AT 2.4 VOLTS I_{SOURCE}=7.2 MA.

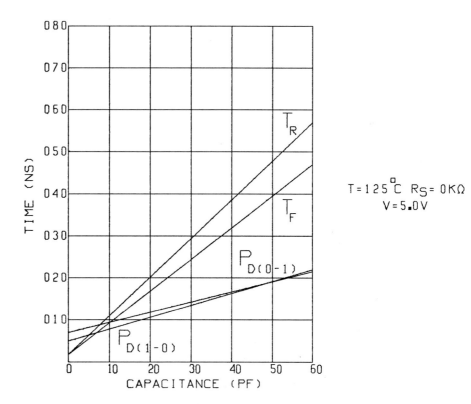

$T=125°C$ R_S= 0KΩ
$V=5.0V$

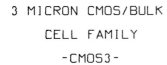

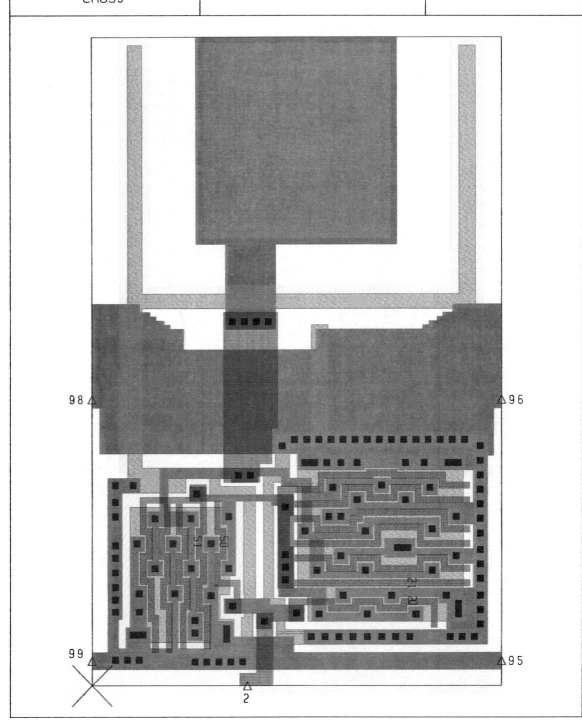

REL 2   9250-5

3 MICRON CMOS/BULK	9260	DATE: 04/01/84
CELL FAMILY	OUTPUT BUFFER	REVISION: B
-CMOS3-	CELL HEIGHT 313 WIDTH 204	

TERMINAL INFORMATION

TERMINAL NAME	LOGIC NUMBER	CAPACITANCE FIELD	(PF)
A	2	1	.32

LOGIC DIAGRAM

SAME AS LOGIC SYMBOL.

TRUTH TABLE

A	PAD
1	1
0	0
X	X

LOGICV REQUIRES THE PAD SIGNAL NAME
TO BE IN LOGIC FIELD 6.

LOGIC SYMBOLS

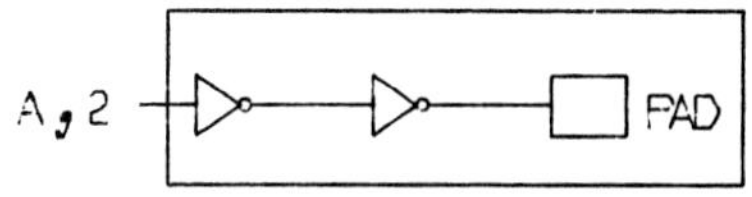

A,2 → [buffer] → [buffer] → [PAD]

WORST CASE DELAY INFORMATION

$$P_D = 15.19 \text{ NS} \qquad T_{R/F} = 35.00 \text{ NS}$$

$$R_S = 0 \text{ K}\Omega, \quad C_L = 35 \text{ PF}, \quad V=5V, \quad T=125°C$$

LOGIC EQUATION(S)

PAD=A

NOTES

SEE PAGE 4 FOR OUTPUT DRIVE CAPABILITY
9250 AND 9260 OUTPUT BUFFER PADS HAVE THE SAME FUNCTION EXCEPT FOR
DIFFERENT BUS STRUCTURES.

REL 2   9260-1

CIRCUIT SCHEMATIC

VDD

20(3/75) 21(3/540)

2

PAD

50(3/45) 51(3/266)

VSS

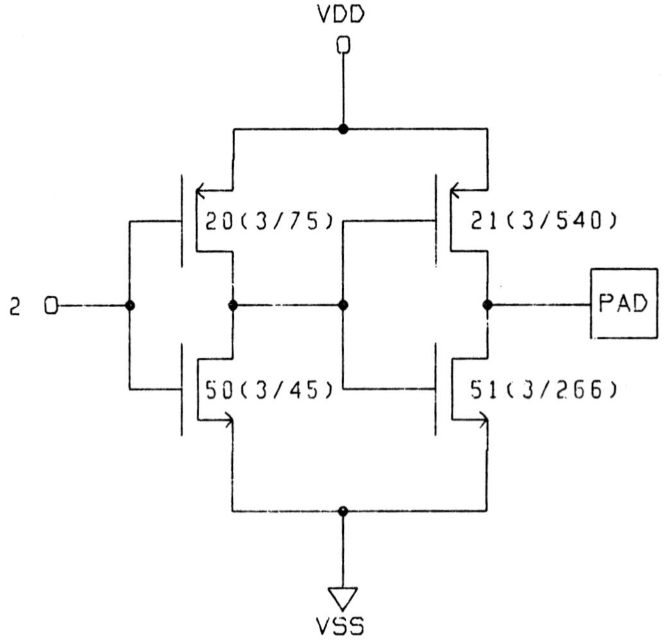

REL 2   9260-2

408

3 MICRON CMOS/BULK CELL FAMILY -CMOS3-	9260 OUTPUT BUFFER	DATE: 04/01/84 REVISION: B

OUTPUT CHARACTERISTIC EQUATIONS

$$P_D(0-1) = P_{DC}(0-1) + .12 \ (T_{R/F} - 10) + .55 \ R_S C_L$$

$$P_D(1-0) = P_{DC}(1-0) + .14 \ (T_{R/F} - 10) + .41 \ R_S C_L$$

$$T_R = T_{RC} + .01 \ (T_{R/F} - 10) + 2.33 R_S C_L$$

$$T_F = T_{FC} + .02 \ (T_{R/F} - 10) + 2.33 R_S C_L$$

EQUATIONS

25°C

$$P_{DC}(0-1) = .21 \ C_L + 4.43$$
$$P_{DC}(1-0) = .19 \ C_L + 5.43$$
$$T_{RC} = .71 \ C_L + 1.02$$
$$T_{FC} = .59 \ C_L + 1.29$$

95°C

$$P_{DC}(0-1) = .26 \ C_L + 4.98$$
$$P_{DC}(1-0) = .23 \ C_L + 6.27$$
$$T_{RC} = .86 \ C_L + 1.43$$
$$T_{FC} = .70 \ C_L + 1.74$$

125°C

$$P_{DC}(0-1) = .28 \ C_L + 5.14$$
$$P_{DC}(1-0) = .25 \ C_L + 6.56$$
$$T_{RC} = .93 \ C_L + 1.53$$
$$T_{FC} = .75 \ C_L + 1.91$$

125°C SC

$$P_{DC}(0-1) = .15 \ C_L + 2.48$$
$$P_{DC}(1-0) = .13 \ C_L + 3.43$$
$$T_{RC} = .54 \ C_L + .76$$
$$T_{FC} = .45 \ C_L + .86$$

VOLTAGE TABLE

VOLTAGE	DEVIATION FACTOR			
	TRANSITION		PROP DELAY	
	TR	TF	1-0	0-1
3.0	1.54	1.66	1.83	1.73
3.5	1.36	1.44	1.55	1.48
4.0	1.18	1.21	1.26	1.23
4.5	1.09	1.11	1.13	1.12
5.0	1.00	1.00	1.00	1.00
5.5	.95	.94	.93	.93
6.0	.90	.88	.85	.86
6.5	.87	.85	.81	.82
7.0	.83	.81	.76	.77

REL 2   9260-3

3 MICRON CMOS/BULK CELL FAMILY -CMOS3-	9260 OUTPUT BUFFER	DATE: 04/01/84 REVISION: B

NOTES

FOR VDD AT 5V AND VSS AT OV THE FOLLOWING
DRIVE CAPABILITY IS ACHIEVABLE:
FOR VOUT AT .5 VOLTS I_{SINK} IS 1.6 MA.
FOR VOUT AT 2.4 VOLTS I_{SOURCE} IS 6.5 MA.

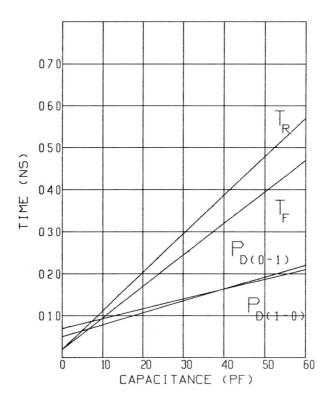

$T = 125^{\circ}C \quad R_S = 0K\Omega$
$V = 5.0V$

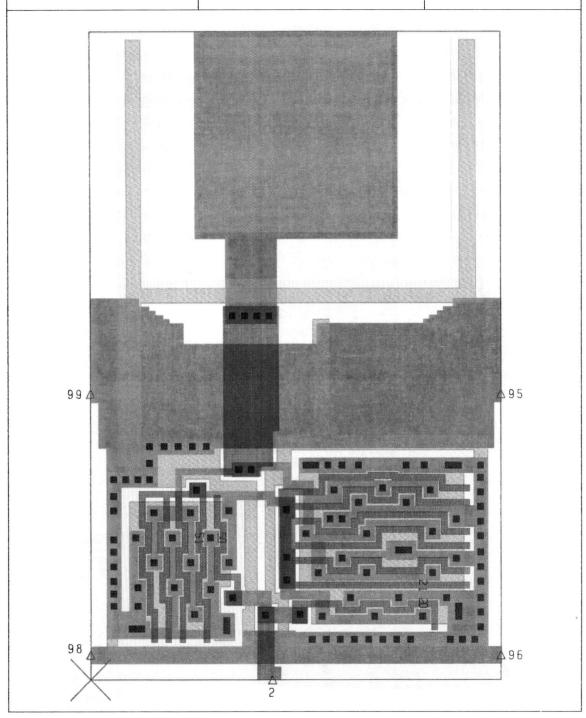

REL 2   9260-5

411

3 MICRON CMOS/BULK CELL FAMILY -CMOS3-	9320 POWER PAD CELL HEIGHT 120 WIDTH 100	DATE: 04/01/85 REVISION: B

TERMINAL INFORMATION TERMINAL LOGIC CAPACITANCE NAME NUMBER FIELD (PF) N/A	LOGIC DIAGRAM N/A
TRUTH TABLE N/A	LOGIC SYMBOLS N/A

WORST CASE DELAY INFORMATION

$P_D=$ NS $T_{R/F}=$ NS

$R_S=1.5K\Omega$, $C_L=1.5PF$, $V=5V$, $T=125^{\circ}C$

LOGIC EQUATION(S)

N/A

NOTES

THIS CELL IS TO BE USED TO BOND VDD AND VSS POWER
LINES TO THE CHIP.

REL 2   9320-1

412

3 MICRON CMOS/BULK CELL FAMILY -CMOS3-	9320 POWER PAD	DATE: 04/01/85 REVISION: B

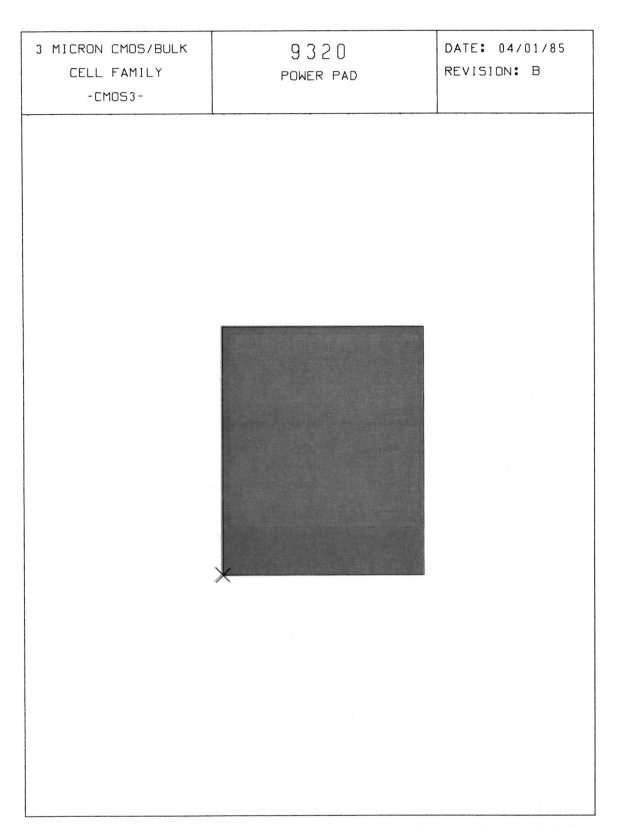

REL 2   9320-2

3 MICRON CMOS/BULK CELL FAMILY -CMOS3-	9460 SCHMITT TRIGGERED INPUT PAD CELL HEIGHT 313 WIDTH 240	DATE: 04/01/85 REVISION: D

TERMINAL INFORMATION

TERMINAL NAME	LOGIC NUMBER	CAPACITANCE FIELD (PF)
OUT	2	6

LOGIC DIAGRAM

TRUTH TABLE

PAD	OUT
1	1
0	0
X	X

LOGICV REQUIRES THE PAD SIGNAL NAME
TO BE IN LOGIC FIELD 1.

LOGIC SYMBOLS

WORST CASE DELAY INFORMATION

$P_D = 13.10$ NS $T_{R/F} = 14.0$ NS

$R_S = 1.5K\Omega$, $C_L = 1.5PF$, $V = 5V$, $T = 125°C$

LOGIC EQUATION(S)

OUT=PAD

NOTES

OUTPUT R/F TIME IS RELATIVELY INDEPENDENT OF INPUT R/F TIMES.
TRIGGER POINTS VARY AS A FUNCTION OF VOLTAGE AND OF THE RATIOS
OF K-PRIMES OF P AND N CHANNELS. TRIGGER POINTS ARE LARGELY
INDEPENDENT OF TEMPERATURE. 9460 AND 9470 ARE THE SAME
SCHMITT TRIGGER EXCEPT FOR THE BUS STRUCTURE.

REL 2   9460-1

CIRCUIT SCHEMATIC

REL 2   9460-2

415

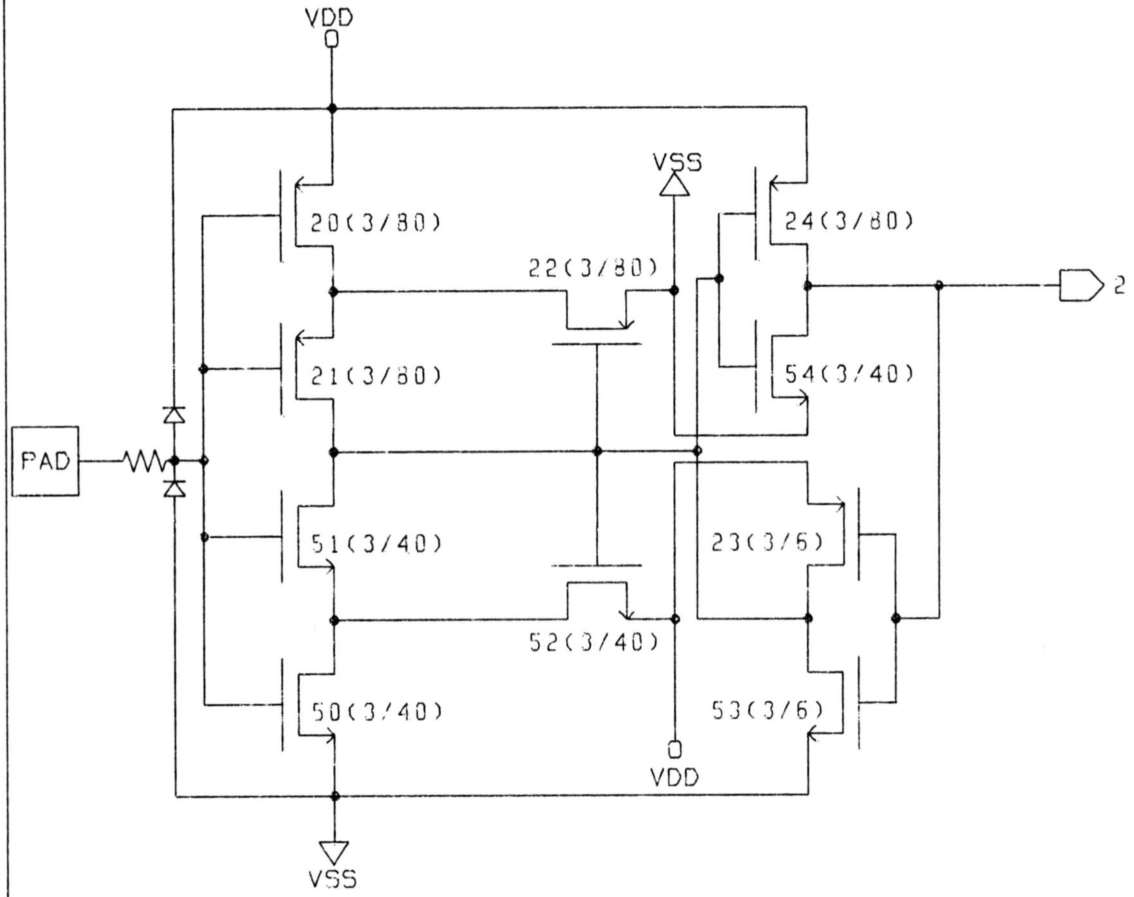

3 MICRON CMOS/BULK CELL FAMILY -CMOS3-	9460 SCHMITT TRIGGERED INPUT PAD	DATE: 04/01/85 REVISION: D

OUTPUT CHARACTERISTIC EQUATIONS

$$P_D(0-1) = P_{DC}(0-1) + 0.29(T_{R/F} - 10) + 0.61R_SC_L$$

$$P_D(1-0) = P_{DC}(1-0) + 0.32(T_{R/F} - 10) + 0.54R_SC_L$$

$$T_R = T_{RC} + 0.00(T_{R/F} - 10) + 2.49R_SC_L$$

$$T_F = T_{FC} + 0.00(T_{R/F} - 10) + 2.40R_SC_L$$

EQUATIONS

$25^\circ C$	$95^\circ C$	$125^\circ C$
$P_{DC}(0-1) = 1.30C_L + 7.15$	$P_{DC}(0-1) = 1.66C_L + 7.78$	$P_{DC}(0-1) = 1.80C_L + 8.04$
$P_{DC}(1-0) = 1.38C_L + 8.51$	$P_{DC}(1-0) = 1.74C_L + 9.48$	$P_{DC}(1-0) = 1.86C_L + 9.86$
$T_{RC} = 3.79C_L + 1.56$	$T_{RC} = 4.83C_L + 2.06$	$T_{RC} = 5.25C_L + 2.29$
$T_{FC} = 3.12C_L + 2.05$	$T_{FC} = 3.93C_L + 2.67$	$T_{FC} = 4.25C_L + 2.97$

$125^\circ C$ BC

$$P_{DC}(0-1) = .80C_L + 5.29$$

$$P_{DC}(1-0) = .77C_L + 6.28$$

$$T_{RC} = 2.53C_L + 1.03$$

$$T_{FC} = 1.95C_L + 1.53$$

VOLTAGE TABLE

VOLTAGE	DEVIATION FACTOR			
	TRANSITION		PROP DELAY	
	TR	TF	1-0	0-1
3.0	1.48	1.59	1.67	1.61
3.5	1.32	1.39	1.44	1.40
4.0	1.15	1.18	1.21	1.19
4.5	1.08	1.09	1.11	1.10
5.0	1.00	1.00	1.00	1.00
5.5	.95	.95	.94	.94
6.0	.91	.90	.89	.89
6.5	.88	.87	.84	.85
7.0	.86	.84	.80	.82

REL 2   9460-3

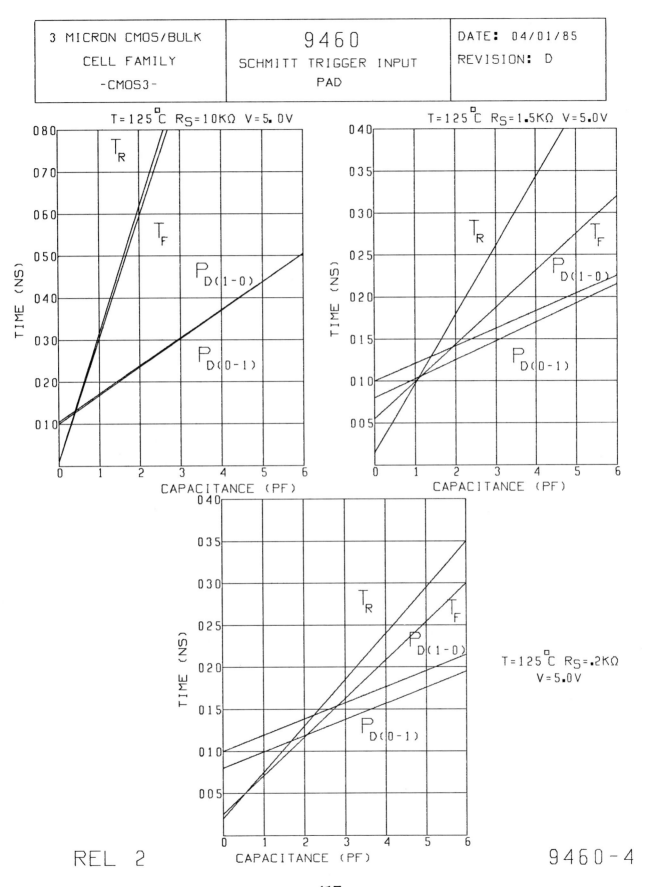

VOLTAGE TRIGGER RANGE

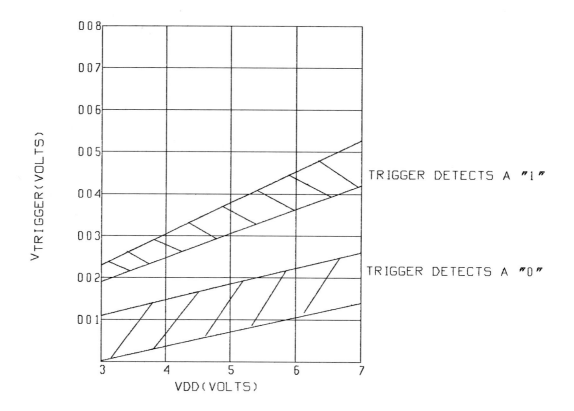

REL 2   9460-5

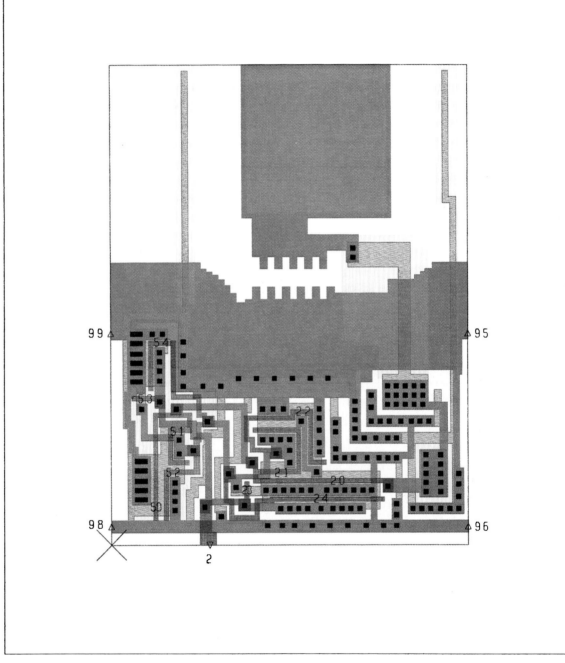

REL 2   9460-6

3 MICRON CMOS/BULK CELL FAMILY -CMOS3-	9470 SCHMITT TRIGGERED INPUT PAD CELL HEIGHT 313 WIDTH 240	DATE: 04/01/85 REVISION: C

TERMINAL INFORMATION

TERMINAL NAME	LOGIC NUMBER	CAPACITANCE FIELD	(PF)
OUT	2	6	

LOGIC DIAGRAM

TRUTH TABLE

PAD	OUT
1	1
0	0
X	X

LOGICV REQUIRES THE PAD SIGNAL NAME
TO BE IN LOGIC FIELD 1.

LOGIC SYMBOLS

WORST CASE DELAY INFORMATION

P_D = 13.10 NS $T_{R/F}$ = 14.0 NS

R_S =1.5KΩ, C_L =1.5PF, V=5V, T=125°C

LOGIC EQUATION(S)

OUT=PAD

NOTES

OUTPUT R/F TIME IS RELATIVELY INDEPENDENT OF INPUT R/F TIMES.
TRIGGER POINTS VARY AS A FUNCTION OF VOLTAGE AND OF THE RATIOS
OF K-PRIMES OF P AND N CHANNELS. TRIGGER POINTS ARE LARGELY
INDEPENDENT OF TEMPERATURE. 9470 AND 9460 ARE THE SAME
SCHMITT TRIGGER EXCEPT FOR THE BUS STRUCTURE.

REL 3   9470-1

420

CIRCUIT SCHEMATIC

3 MICRON CMOS/BULK CELL FAMILY -CMOS3-	9470 SCHMITT TRIGGERED INPUT PAD	DATE: 04/01/85 REVISION: C

OUTPUT CHARACTERISTIC EQUATIONS

$$P_D(0-1) = P_{DC}(0-1) + 0.29(T_{R/F} - 10) + 0.61 R_S C_L$$

$$P_D(1-0) = P_{DC}(1-0) + 0.32(T_{R/F} - 10) + 0.54 R_S C_L$$

$$T_R = T_{RC} + 0.00(T_{R/F} - 10) + 2.49 R_S C_L$$

$$T_F = T_{FC} + 0.00(T_{R/F} - 10) + 2.40 R_S C_L$$

EQUATIONS

$25^\circ C$	$95^\circ C$	$125^\circ C$
$P_{DC}(0-1) = 1.30 C_L + 7.15$	$P_{DC}(0-1) = 1.66 C_L + 7.78$	$P_{DC}(0-1) = 1.80 C_L + 8.04$
$P_{DC}(1-0) = 1.38 C_L + 8.51$	$P_{DC}(1-0) = 1.74 C_L + 9.48$	$P_{DC}(1-0) = 1.88 C_L + 9.86$
$T_{RC} = 3.79 C_L + 1.56$	$T_{RC} = 4.83 C_L + 2.06$	$T_{RC} = 5.25 C_L + 2.29$
$T_{FC} = 3.12 C_L + 2.05$	$T_{FC} = 3.93 C_L + 2.67$	$T_{FC} = 4.25 C_L + 2.97$

$125^\circ C$ BC

$$P_{DC}(0-1) = .80 C_L + 5.29$$

$$P_{DC}(1-0) = .77 C_L + 6.28$$

$$T_{RC} = 2.53 C_L + 1.03$$

$$T_{FC} = 1.95 C_L + 1.53$$

VOLTAGE TABLE

VOLTAGE	DEVIATION FACTOR			
	TRANSITION		PROP DELAY	
	TR	TF	1-0	0-1
3.0	1.48	1.59	1.67	1.61
3.5	1.32	1.39	1.44	1.40
4.0	1.15	1.18	1.21	1.19
4.5	1.08	1.09	1.11	1.10
5.0	1.00	1.00	1.00	1.00
5.5	.95	.95	.94	.94
6.0	.91	.90	.89	.89
6.5	.88	.87	.84	.85
7.0	.86	.84	.80	.82

REL 3   9470-3

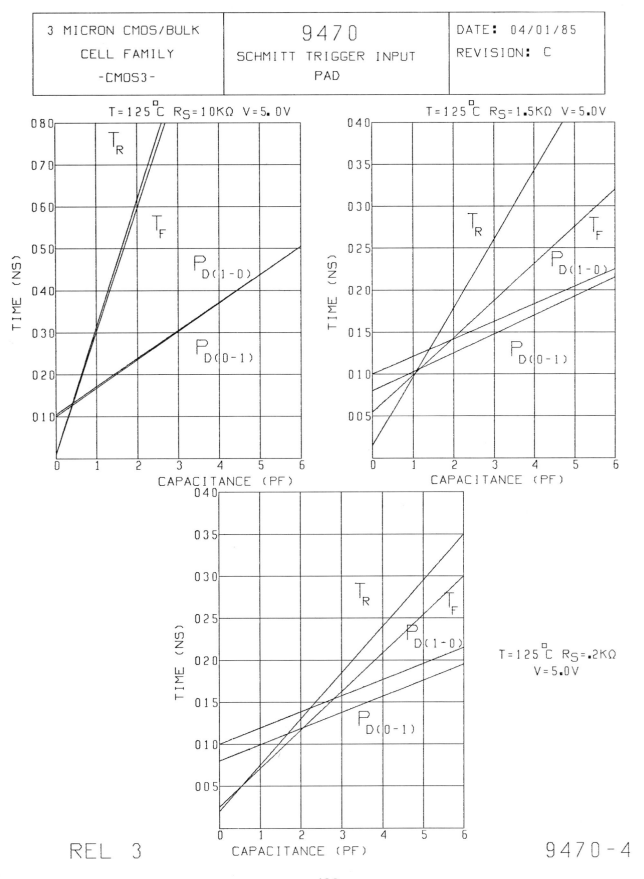

| 3 MICRON CMOS/BULK CELL FAMILY -CMOS3- | 9470 SCHMITT TRIGGER INPUT PAD | DATE: 04/01/85 REVISION: C |

REL 3

9470-4

3 MICRON CMOS/BULK CELL FAMILY -CMOS3-	9470 SCHMITT TRIGGER INPUT PAD	DATE: 04/01/85 REVISION: C

VOLTAGE TRIGGER RANGE

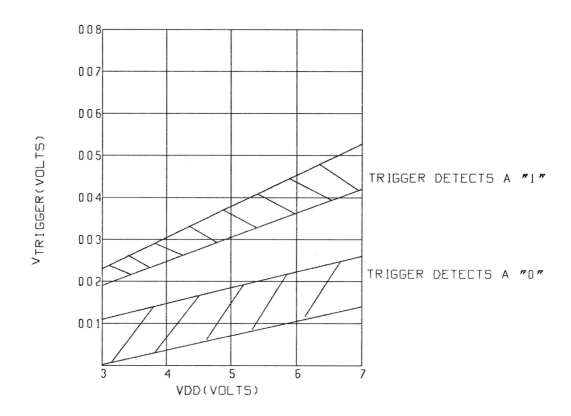

3 MICRON CMOS/BULK CELL FAMILY -CMOS3-	9470 SCHMITT TRIGGERED INPUT PAD	DATE: 04/01/85 REVISION: C

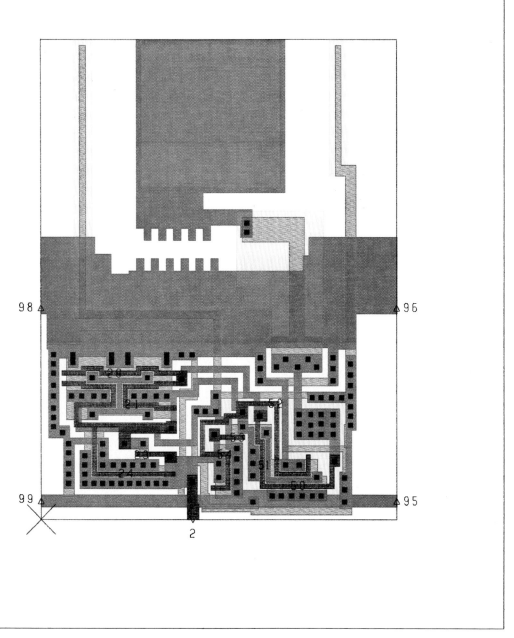

3 MICRON CMOS/BULK	9530	DATE: 04/01/85
CELL FAMILY	LEVEL SHIFTER INPUT PAD	REVISION: D
-CMOS3-	CELL HEIGHT 313 WIDTH 216	

TERMINAL INFORMATION

TERMINAL NAME	LOGIC NUMBER	CAPACITANCE FIELD	(PF)
OUT1	2	6	
OUT2	3	7	

LOGIC DIAGRAM

TRUTH TABLE

PAD	OUT1	OUT2
0	0	1
1	1	0
X	X	X

LOGICV REQUIRES THE INPUT SIGNAL NAME
TO BE IN LOGIC FIELD 1.

LOGIC SYMBOLS

WORST CASE DELAY INFORMATION

OUT1 $P_D = 11.08$ NS $T_{R/F} = 15.35$ NS

OUT2 $P_D = 12.72$ NS $T_{R/F} = 13.55$ NS

$R_S = 1.5K\Omega$, $C_L = 1.5PF$, $V=5V$, $T=125°C$

LOGIC EQUATION(S)

OUT1 = PAD

OUT2 = $\overline{PAD}$

NOTES

SUPPLY VOLTAGE OPERATING RANGE: 4.0 TO 5.5 VOLTS

INPUT SIGNAL USED FOR CHARACTERIZATION:

VIL = 0.8 V

VIH = 2.4 V

REL 3   9530-1

3 MICRON CMOS/BULK CELL FAMILY -CMOS3-	9530 LEVEL SHIFTER INPUT PAD	DATE: 04/01/85 REVISION: D

CIRCUIT SCHEMATIC

3 MICRON CMOS/BULK CELL FAMILY -CMOS3-	9530 LEVEL SHIFTER INPUT PAD NON INVERTING OUT	DATE: 04/01/85 REVISION: D

OUTPUT CHARACTERISTIC EQUATIONS

$$P_D(0-1) = P_{DC}(0-1) + .12 \ (T_{R/F} - 10) + .65 \ R_S C_L$$

$$P_D(1-0) = P_{DC}(1-0) + .12 \ (T_{R/F} - 10) + .62 \ R_S C_L$$

$$T_R = T_{RC} + .05 \ (T_{R/F} - 10) + 2.47 R_S C_L$$

$$T_F = T_{FC} + .05 \ (T_{R/F} - 10) + 2.48 R_S C_L$$

EQUATIONS

$25^{\sigma}C$	$95^{\sigma}C$	$125^{\sigma}C$
$P_{DC}(0-1) = 1.21 C_L + 6.86$	$P_{DC}(0-1) = 1.54 C_L + 6.63$	$P_{DC}(0-1) = 1.67 C_L + 6.49$
$P_{DC}(1-0) = 1.05 C_L + 5.92$	$P_{DC}(1-0) = 1.32 C_L + 7.40$	$P_{DC}(1-0) = 1.43 C_L + 8.00$
$T_{RC} = 3.80 C_L + 2.67$	$T_{RC} = 4.89 C_L + 3.34$	$T_{RC} = 5.36 C_L + 3.62$
$T_{FC} = 2.99 C_L + 2.56$	$T_{FC} = 3.78 C_L + 3.24$	$T_{FC} = 4.12 C_L + 3.53$

$125^{\sigma}C$ BC

$$P_{DC}(0-1) = .79 \ C_L + 1.73$$

$$P_{DC}(1-0) = .74 \ C_L + 6.73$$

$$T_{RC} = 2.59 C_L + 2.61$$

$$T_{FC} = 2.23 C_L + 2.31$$

VOLTAGE TABLE

VOLTAGE	DEVIATION FACTOR			
	TRANSITION		PROP DELAY	
	TR	TF	1-0	0-1
4.0	1.11	1.17	1.37	.98
4.5	1.06	1.09	1.19	.99
5.0	1.00	1.00	1.00	1.00
5.5	.97	.95	.87	1.04

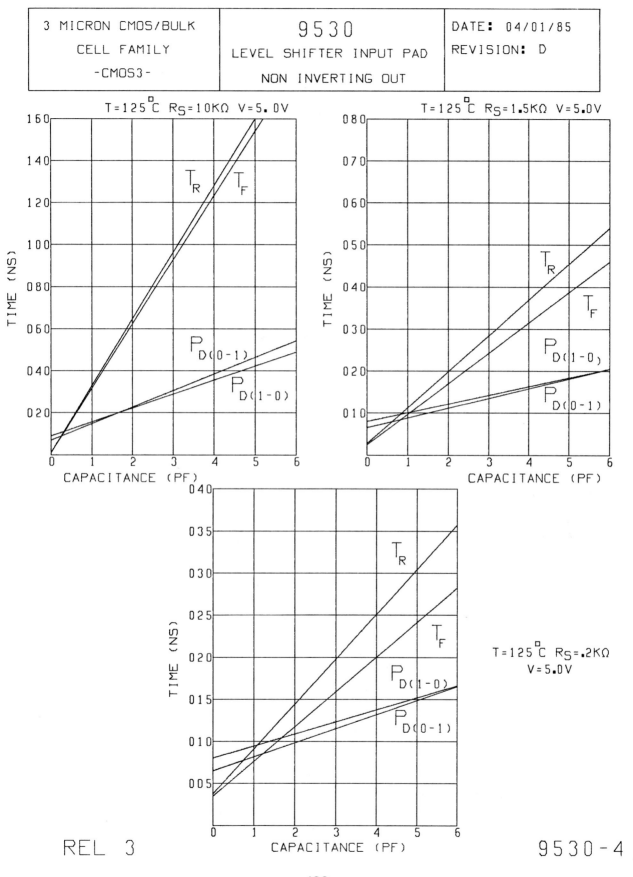

3 MICRON CMOS/BULK CELL FAMILY -CMOS3-	9530 LEVEL SHIFTER INPUT PAD INVERTING OUT	DATE: 04/01/85 REVISION: D

OUTPUT CHARACTERISTIC EQUATIONS

$$P_D(0-1) = P_{DC}(0-1) + .12 \ (T_{R/F} - 10) + .64 \ R_S C_L + 1.33 C_{LOAD}$$

$$P_D(1-0) = P_{DC}(1-0) + .12 \ (T_{R/F} - 10) + .62 \ R_S C_L + 1.76 C_{LOAD}$$

$$T_R = T_{RC} + .00 \ (T_{R/F} - 10) + 2.53 R_S C_L + .88 C_{LOAD}$$

$$T_F = T_{FC} + .01 \ (T_{R/F} - 10) + 2.54 R_S C_L + 1.17 C_{LOAD}$$

EQUATIONS

25°C

$$P_{DC}(0-1) = 1.12 C_L + 6.94$$

$$P_{DC}(1-0) = 1.00 C_L + 8.35$$

$$T_{RC} = 3.50 C_L + 1.67$$

$$T_{FC} = 2.83 C_L + 1.53$$

95°C

$$P_{DC}(0-1) = 1.42 C_L + 8.69$$

$$P_{DC}(1-0) = 1.26 C_L + 8.51$$

$$T_{RC} = 4.44 C_L + 2.22$$

$$T_{FC} = 3.56 C_L + 1.97$$

125°C

$$P_{DC}(0-1) = 1.54 C_L + 9.39$$

$$P_{DC}(1-0) = 1.36 C_L + 8.52$$

$$T_{RC} = 4.85 C_L + 2.43$$

$$T_{FC} = 3.86 C_L + 2.18$$

125°C BC

$$P_{DC}(0-1) = .73 \ C_L + 7.31$$

$$P_{DC}(1-0) = .61 \ C_L + 2.50$$

$$T_{RC} = 2.45 C_L + 1.18$$

$$T_{FC} = 1.94 C_L + 1.01$$

VOLTAGE TABLE

VOLTAGE	DEVIATION FACTOR			
	TRANSITION		PROP DELAY	
	TR	TF	1-0	0-1
4.0	1.14	1.14	1.05	1.36
4.5	1.07	1.07	1.03	1.18
5.0	1.00	1.00	1.00	1.00
5.5	.96	.96	1.01	.87

REL 3   9530-5

430

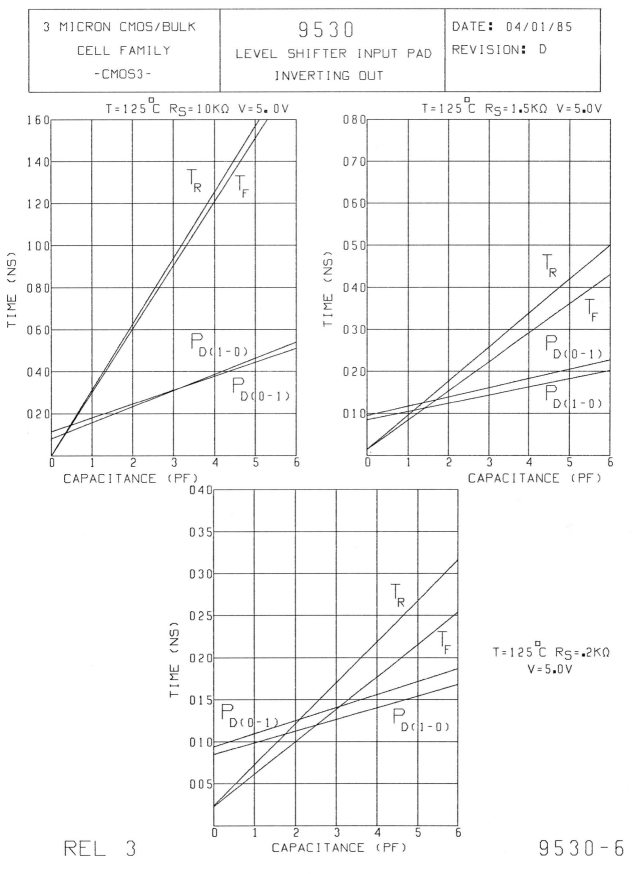

REL 3

9530-6

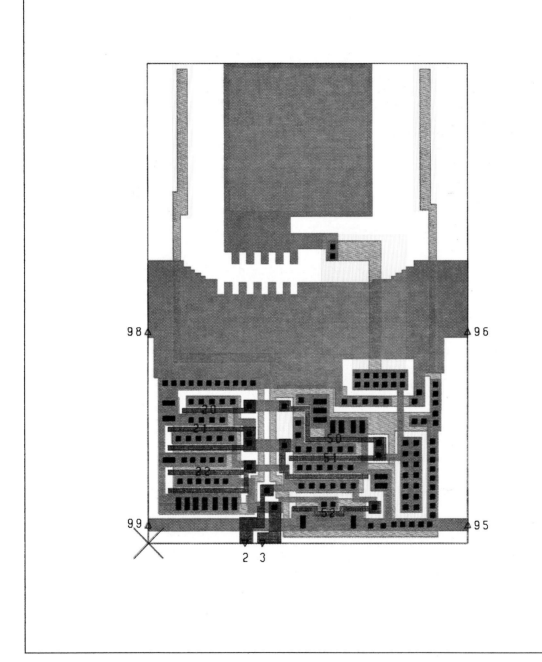

REL 3   9530-7

3 MICRON CMOS/BULK CELL FAMILY -CMOS3-	9540 LEVEL SHIFTER INPUT PAD CELL HEIGHT 313 WIDTH 216	DATE: 04/01/85 REVISION: D

TERMINAL INFORMATION

TERMINAL NAME	LOGIC NUMBER	CAPACITANCE FIELD	(PF)
OUT1	2	6	
OUT2	3	7	

LOGIC DIAGRAM

TRUTH TABLE

PAD	OUT1	OUT2
0	0	1
1	1	0
X	X	X

LOGICV REQUIRES THE INPUT SIGNAL NAME TO BE IN LOGIC FIELD 1.

LOGIC SYMBOLS

WORST CASE DELAY INFORMATION

OUT1 $P_D = 10.92$ NS $T_{R/F} = 15.20$ NS

OUT2 $P_D = 12.59$ NS $T_{R/F} = 13.55$ NS

$R_S = 1.5 K\Omega$, $C_L = 1.5 PF$, $V = 5V$, $T = 125°C$

LOGIC EQUATION(S)

OUT1 = PAD

OUT2 = $\overline{PAD}$

NOTES

SUPPLY VOLTAGE OPERATING RANGE: 4.0 TO 5.5 VOLTS

INPUT SIGNAL USED FOR CHARACTERIZATION:

VIL = 0.8 V

VIH = 2.4 V

REL 3   9540-1

433

CIRCUIT SCHEMATIC

3 MICRON CMOS/BULK CELL FAMILY -CMOS3-	9540 LEVEL SHIFTER INPUT PAD NON-INVERTING OUTPUT	DATE: 04/01/85 REVISION: D

OUTPUT CHARACTERISTIC EQUATIONS

$$P_D(0-1) = P_{DC}(0-1) + 0.12(T_{R/F} - 10) + 0.65 R_S C_L$$

$$P_D(1-0) = P_{DC}(1-0) + 0.12(T_{R/F} - 10) + 0.62 R_S C_L$$

$$T_R = T_{RC} + 0.05(T_{R/F} - 10) + 2.48 R_S C_L$$

$$T_F = T_{FC} + 0.05(T_{R/F} - 10) + 2.48 R_S C_L$$

EQUATIONS

$25^{\circ}C$

$$P_{DC}(0-1) = 1.20 C_L + 6.71$$
$$P_{DC}(1-0) = 1.04 C_L + 5.77$$
$$T_{RC} = 3.78 C_L + 2.58$$
$$T_{FC} = 2.96 C_L + 2.48$$

$95^{\circ}C$

$$P_{DC}(0-1) = 1.53 C_L + 6.49$$
$$P_{DC}(1-0) = 1.31 C_L + 7.28$$
$$T_{RC} = 4.85 C_L + 3.25$$
$$T_{FC} = 3.75 C_L + 3.12$$

$125^{\circ}C$

$$P_{DC}(0-1) = 1.66 C_L + 6.36$$
$$P_{DC}(1-0) = 1.42 C_L + 7.88$$
$$T_{RC} = 5.31 C_L + 3.53$$
$$T_{FC} = 4.08 C_L + 3.39$$

$125^{\circ}C$ SC

$$P_{DC}(0-1) = 0.78 C_L + 1.64$$
$$P_{DC}(1-0) = 0.74 C_L + 6.72$$
$$T_{RC} = 2.55 C_L + 2.58$$
$$T_{FC} = 2.20 C_L + 2.28$$

VOLTAGE TABLE

VOLTAGE	TRANSITION		PROP DELAY	
	TR	TF	1-0	0-1
4.0	1.11	1.17	1.37	.98
4.5	1.06	1.09	1.19	.99
5.0	1.00	1.00	1.00	1.00
5.5	.97	.95	.87	1.04

REL 3   9540-3

435

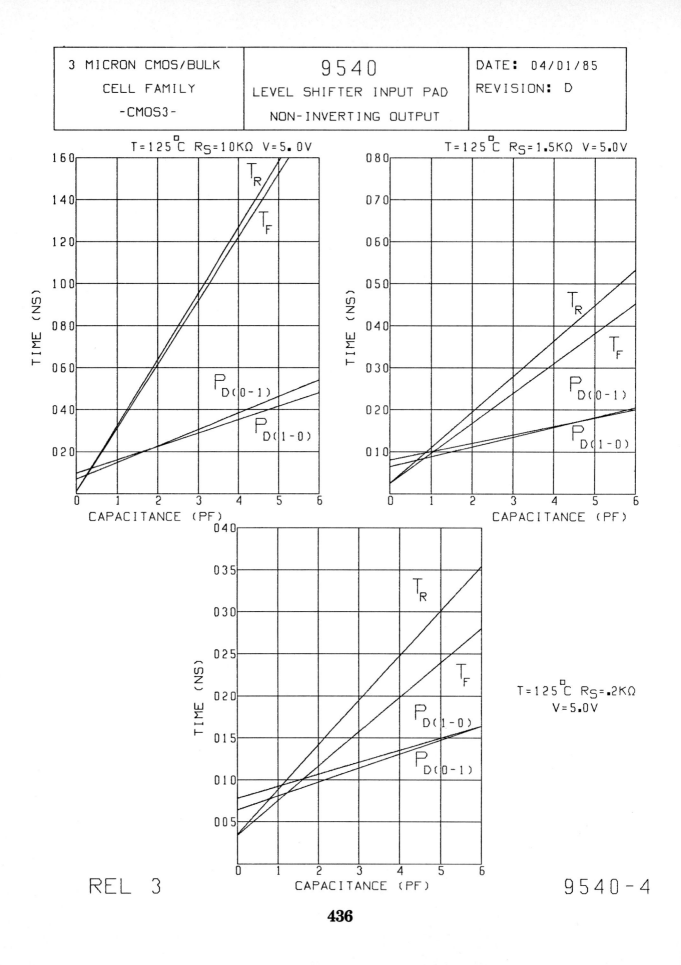

3 MICRON CMOS/BULK CELL FAMILY -CMOS3-	9540 LEVEL SHIFTER INPUT PAD INVERTING OUTPUT	DATE: 04/01/85 REVISION: D

OUTPUT CHARACTERISTIC EQUATIONS

$$P_D(0-1) = P_{DC}(0-1) + .11 \ (T_{R/F} - 10) + .64 \ R_S C_L + 1.34 C_{LOAD}$$

$$P_D(1-0) = P_{DC}(1-0) + .11 \ (T_{R/F} - 10) + .62 \ R_S C_L + 1.78 C_{LOAD}$$

$$T_R = T_{RC} + .00 \ (T_{R/F} - 10) + 2.53 R_S C_L + .88 C_{LOAD}$$

$$T_F = T_{FC} + .01 \ (T_{R/F} - 10) + 2.54 R_S C_L + 1.17 C_{LOAD}$$

EQUATIONS

25°C

$$P_{DC}(0-1) = 1.11 C_L + 6.83$$

$$P_{DC}(1-0) = 1.00 C_L + 8.24$$

$$T_{RC} = 3.50 C_L + 1.67$$

$$T_{FC} = 2.83 C_L + 1.53$$

95°C

$$P_{DC}(0-1) = 1.42 C_L + 8.56$$

$$P_{DC}(1-0) = 1.26 C_L + 8.35$$

$$T_{RC} = 4.45 C_L + 2.21$$

$$T_{FC} = 3.58 C_L + 1.87$$

125°C

$$P_{DC}(0-1) = 1.54 C_L + 9.27$$

$$P_{DC}(1-0) = 1.36 C_L + 8.37$$

$$T_{RC} = 4.85 C_L + 2.43$$

$$T_{FC} = 3.86 C_L + 2.16$$

125°C BC

$$P_{DC}(0-1) = .73 \ C_L + 7.28$$

$$P_{DC}(1-0) = .61 \ C_L + 2.41$$

$$T_{RC} = 2.46 C_L + 1.17$$

$$T_{FC} = 1.94 C_L + 1.01$$

VOLTAGE TABLE

VOLTAGE	DEVIATION FACTOR			
	TRANSITION		PROP DELAY	
	TR	TF	1-0	0-1
4.0	1.14	1.14	1.05	1.35
4.5	1.07	1.07	1.03	1.18
5.0	1.00	1.00	1.00	1.00
5.5	.96	.96	1.01	.87

REL 3   9540-5

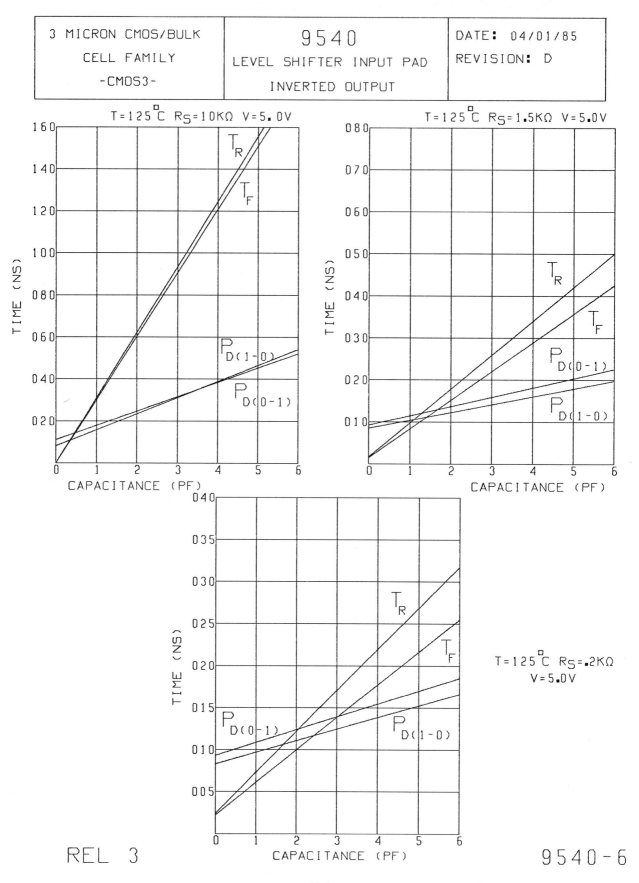

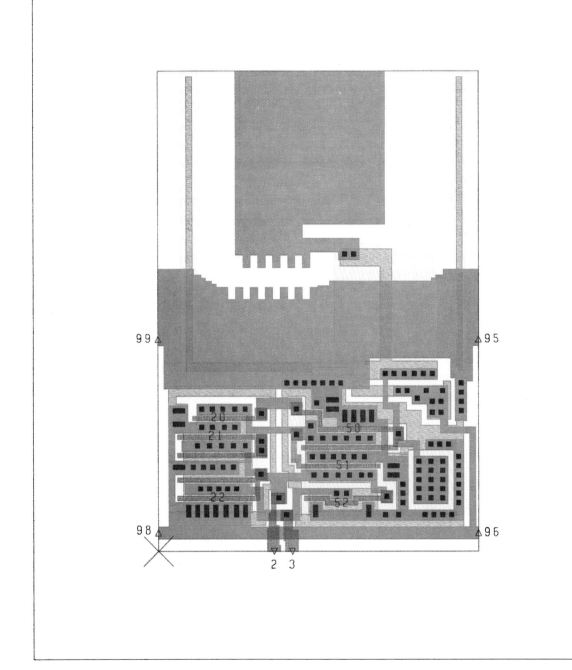

REL 3   9540-7

439

3 MICRON CMOS/BULK CELL FAMILY -CMOS3-	9620 BUTTERFLY CELL HEIGHT 100 WIDTH 100	DATE: 09/01/83 REVISION: A

TERMINAL INFORMATION	LOGIC DIAGRAM
TERMINAL LOGIC CAPACITANCE NAME NUMBER FIELD (PF) N/A	N/A

TRUTH TABLE	LOGIC SYMBOLS
N/A	N/A

WORST CASE DELAY INFORMATION	LOGIC EQUATION(S)
$P_D =$ NS $T_{R/F} =$ NS $R_S = 1.5 K\Omega$, $C_L = 1.5 PF$, $V = 5V$, $T = 125°C$	N/A

NOTES

BUTTERFLIES ARE FIDUCLE MARKS PLACED OUTSIDE OF THE SCRIBE LINES FOR ALIGNMENTS.

9620-1

3 MICRON CMOS/BULK CELL FAMILY -CMOS3-	9650 N-CHANNEL BUFFER CELL HEIGHT 313 WIDTH 204	DATE: 04/01/85 REVISION: C

TERMINAL INFORMATION

TERMINAL NAME	LOGIC NUMBER	CAPACITANCE FIELD	(PF)
A	2	1	.32

LOGIC DIAGRAM

SAME AS LOGIC SYMBOL.

TRUTH TABLE

A	PAD
0	0
1	HI-Z
X	X

LOGICV REQUIRES THE PAD SIGNAL NAME TO BE IN LOGIC FIELD 6. LOGICV SIMULATES THE HI-Z STATE AS AN X. FOR FURTHER LOGICV INFORMATION REFER TO LOGICV APPENDIX.

LOGIC SYMBOLS

WORST CASE DELAY INFORMATION

$P_D = 12.19$ NS $T_{R/F} = 27.65$ NS

$R_S = 0$ KΩ, $C_L = 35$ PF, $V = 5V$, $T = 125°C$

LOGIC EQUATION(S)

FOR A="1" PAD=HI. IMP.

FOR A="0" PAD="0"

NOTES

CIRCUIT SCHEMATIC

VDD

20(3/75)

2

50(3/45) 51(3/266)

PAD

VSS

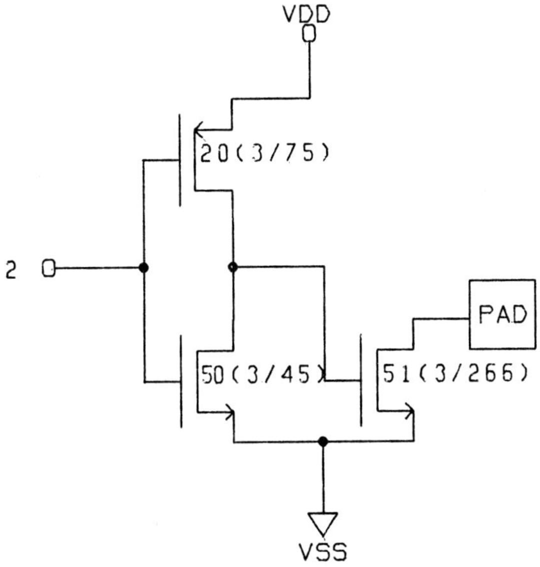

REL 2   9650-2

443

3 MICRON CMOS/BULK CELL FAMILY -CMOS3-	9650 N-CHANNEL BUFFER	DATE: 04/01/85 REVISION: C

OUTPUT CHARACTERISTIC EQUATIONS

$$P_D(1-0) = P_{DC}(1-0) + 0.09(T_{R/F} - 10) + .60\ R_S C_L$$

$$T_F = T_{FC} + 0.02(T_{R/F} - 10) + 2.59 R_S C_L$$

EQUATIONS

$25^\circ C$	$95^\circ C$	$125^\circ C$
$P_{DC}(1-0) = .19\ C_L + 3.15$	$P_{DC}(1-0) = .23\ C_L + 3.55$	$P_{DC}(1-0) = .24\ C_L + 3.69$
$T_{FC} = .59\ C_L + 1.03$	$T_{FC} = .70\ C_L + 1.34$	$T_{FC} = .75\ C_L + 1.48$

$125^\circ C$ BC

$$P_{DC}(1-0) = .13\ C_L + 1.82$$

$$T_{FC} = .45\ C_L + .95$$

VOLTAGE TABLE

VOLTAGE	DEVIATION FACTOR	
	TRANSITION	PROP DELAY
	TF	1-0
3.0	1.65	1.85
3.5	1.43	1.56
4.0	1.21	1.27
4.5	1.11	1.14
5.0	1.00	1.00
5.5	.94	.93
6.0	.88	.85
6.5	.85	.81
7.0	.81	.76

REL 2   9650-3

444

3 MICRON CMOS/BULK CELL FAMILY -CMOS3-	9650 N-CHANNEL BUFFER	DATE: 04/01/85 REVISION: C

FOR VDD AT 5V AND VSS AT 0V

THE FOLLOWING DRIVE CAPABILITY IS ACHIEVABLE:

FOR ISINK AT 1.8 MA VOUT IS .45 VOLTS.

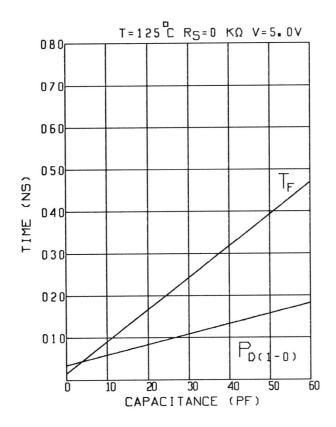

REL 2   9650-4

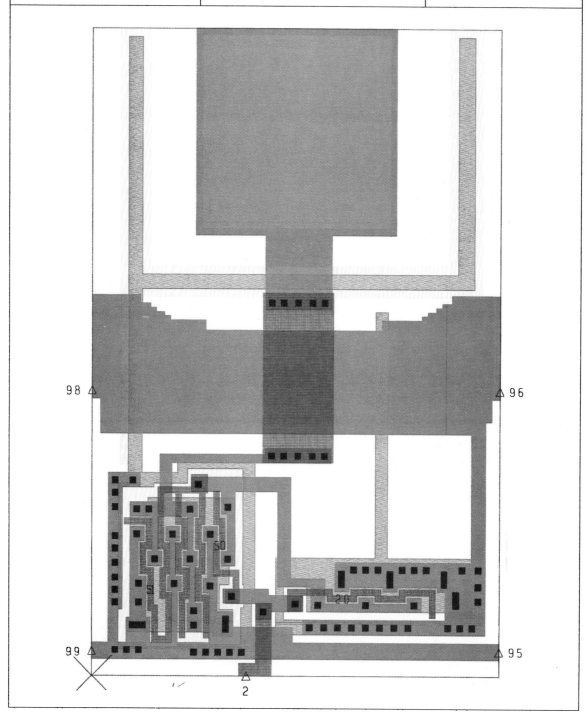

3 MICRON CMOS/BULK CELL FAMILY -CMOS3-	9660 N-CHANNEL BUFFER CELL HEIGHT 313 WIDTH 204	DATE: 04/01/85 REVISION: C

TERMINAL INFORMATION

TERMINAL NAME	LOGIC NUMBER	CAPACITANCE FIELD	(PF)
A	2	1	.32

LOGIC DIAGRAM

SAME AS LOGIC SYMBOL.

TRUTH TABLE

A	PAD
0	0
1	HI-Z
X	X

LOGICV REQUIRES THE PAD SIGNAL NAME TO BE IN LOGIC FIELD 6. LOGICV SIMULATES THE HI-Z CONDITION AS AN X. FOR FURTHER LOGICV INFORMATION REFER TO THE LOGICV APPENDIX.

LOGIC SYMBOLS

WORST CASE DELAY INFORMATION

P_D = 12.24 NS $T_{R/F}$ = 27.66 NS

R_S = 0 KΩ, C_L = 35 PF, V=5V, T=125°C

LOGIC EQUATION(S)

FOR A="1" PAD=HI.IMP,

FOR A="0" PAD="0"

NOTES

CIRCUIT SCHEMATIC

3 MICRON CMOS/BULK CELL FAMILY -CMOS3-	9660 N-CHANNEL BUFFER	DATE: 04/01/85 REVISION: C

OUTPUT CHARACTERISTIC EQUATIONS

$$P_D(1-0) = P_{DC}(1-0) + 0.09(T_{R/F} - 10) + .60 R_S C_L$$

$$T_F = T_{FC} + 0.02(T_{R/F} - 10) + 2.59 R_S C_L$$

EQUATIONS

$25^\circ C$	$95^\circ C$	$125^\circ C$
$P_{DC}(1-0) = .18 C_L + 3.19$	$P_{DC}(1-0) = .23 C_L + 3.60$	$P_{DC}(1-0) = .24 C_L + 3.74$
$T_{FC} = .59 C_L + 1.03$	$T_{FC} = .70 C_L + 1.38$	$T_{FC} = .75 C_L + 1.52$

$125^\circ C$ BC

$$P_{DC}(1-0) = .13 C_L + 1.84$$

$$T_{FC} = .45 C_L + .97$$

VOLTAGE TABLE

VOLTAGE	DEVIATION FACTOR	
	TRANSITION	PROP DELAY
	TF	1-0
3.0	1.65	1.85
3.5	1.43	1.56
4.0	1.21	1.27
4.5	1.11	1.14
5.0	1.00	1.00
5.5	.94	.93
6.0	.88	.85
6.5	.85	.81
7.0	.81	.76

REL 2   9660-3

FOR VDD AT 5V AND VSS AT 0V

THE FOLLOWING DRIVE CAPABILITY IS ACHIEVABLE:

FOR I_{SINK} AT 1.8 MA V_{OUT} IS .45 VOLTS.

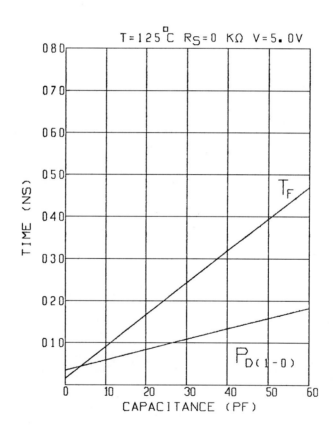

$T=125°C$ $R_S=0$ $K\Omega$ $V=5.0V$

REL 2   9660-4

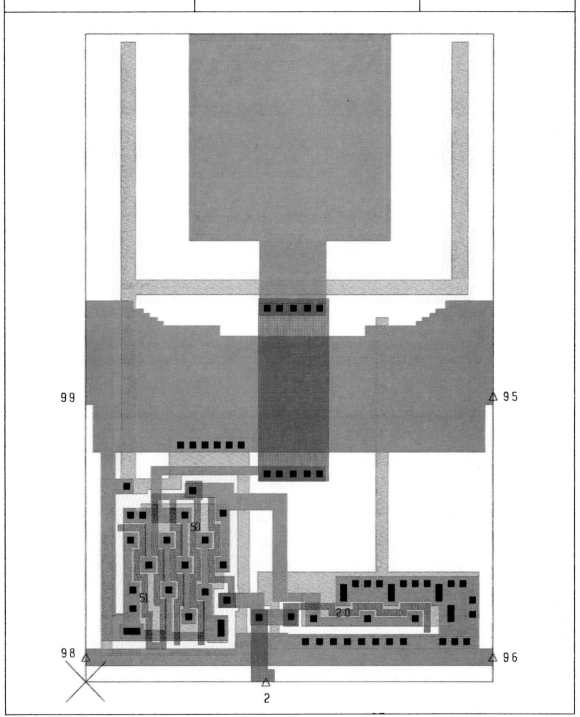

99

△ 95

98

△ 96

2

REL 2   9660-5

451

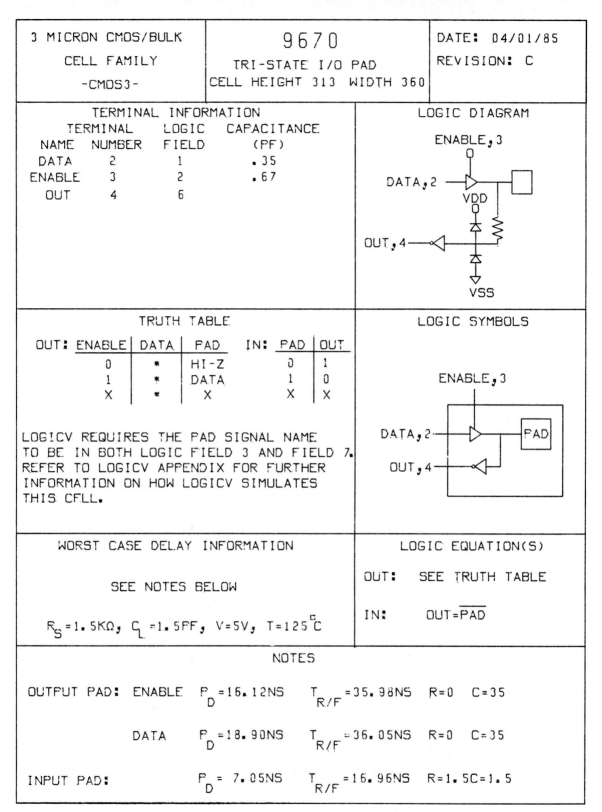

| 3 MICRON CMOS/BULK CELL FAMILY -CMOS3- | 9670 TRI-STATE I/O PAD CELL HEIGHT 313 WIDTH 360 | DATE: 04/01/85 REVISION: C |

TERMINAL INFORMATION

TERMINAL NAME	TERMINAL NUMBER	LOGIC FIELD	CAPACITANCE (PF)
DATA	2	1	.35
ENABLE	3	2	.67
OUT	4	6	

LOGIC DIAGRAM

ENABLE,3

DATA,2

VDD

OUT,4

VSS

TRUTH TABLE

OUT: ENABLE	DATA	PAD	IN: PAD	OUT
0	*	HI-Z	0	1
1	*	DATA	1	0
X	*	X	X	X

LOGICV REQUIRES THE PAD SIGNAL NAME
TO BE IN BOTH LOGIC FIELD 3 AND FIELD 7.
REFER TO LOGICV APPENDIX FOR FURTHER
INFORMATION ON HOW LOGICV SIMULATES
THIS CELL.

LOGIC SYMBOLS

ENABLE,3

DATA,2

PAD

OUT,4

WORST CASE DELAY INFORMATION

SEE NOTES BELOW

$R_S = 1.5K\Omega$, $C_L = 1.5PF$, $V = 5V$, $T = 125°C$

LOGIC EQUATION(S)

OUT: SEE TRUTH TABLE

IN: $OUT = \overline{PAD}$

NOTES

OUTPUT PAD: ENABLE $P_D = 16.12NS$ $T_{R/F} = 35.98NS$ R=0   C=35

DATA $P_D = 18.90NS$ $T_{R/F} = 36.05NS$ R=0   C=35

INPUT PAD: $P_D = 7.05NS$ $T_{R/F} = 16.96NS$ R=1.5 C=1.5

REL 3   9670-1

CIRCUIT SCHEMATIC

REL 3   9670-2

453

3 MICRON CMOS/BULK CELL FAMILY -CMOS3-	9670 TRI-STATE I/O PAD INPUT PAD	DATE: 04/01/85 REVISION: C

OUTPUT CHARACTERISTIC EQUATIONS

$$P_D(0-1) = P_{DC}(0-1) + .13 (T_{R/F} - 10) + .61 R_S C_L$$

$$P_D(1-0) = P_{DC}(1-0) + .16 (T_{R/F} - 10) + .59 R_S C_L$$

$$T_R = T_{RC} + .27 (T_{R/F} - 10) + 2.42 R_S C_L$$

$$T_F = T_{FC} + .26 (T_{R/F} - 10) + 2.44 R_S C_L$$

EQUATIONS

$25°C$	$95°C$	$125°C$
$P_{DC}(0-1) = 1.45C_L + 2.92$	$P_{DC}(0-1) = 1.84C_L + 3.05$	$P_{DC}(0-1) = 2.00C_L + 3.07$
$P_{DC}(1-0) = 1.25C_L + 3.22$	$P_{DC}(1-0) = 1.56C_L + 3.29$	$P_{DC}(1-0) = 1.59C_L + 3.32$
$T_{RC} = 4.29C_L + 3.64$	$T_{RC} = 5.58C_L + 4.08$	$T_{RC} = 6.11C_L + 4.29$
$T_{FC} = 3.32C_L + 3.12$	$T_{FC} = 4.26C_L + 3.38$	$T_{FC} = 4.66C_L + 3.51$

$125°C$ BC

$$P_{DC}(0-1) = .96 C_L + 2.04$$

$$P_{DC}(1-0) = .63 C_L + 2.09$$

$$T_{RC} = 2.76C_L + 4.13$$

$$T_{FC} = 2.04C_L + 3.86$$

VOLTAGE TABLE

VOLTAGE	DEVIATION FACTOR			
	TRANSITION		PROP DELAY	
	TR	TF	1-0	0-1
3.0	1.42	1.45	1.56	1.49
3.5	1.28	1.30	1.37	1.33
4.0	1.13	1.14	1.18	1.16
4.5	1.06	1.07	1.09	1.08
5.0	1.00	1.00	1.00	1.00
5.5	.96	.97	.95	.95
6.0	.92	.93	.89	.90
6.5	.90	.91	.86	.87
7.0	.87	.88	.82	.84

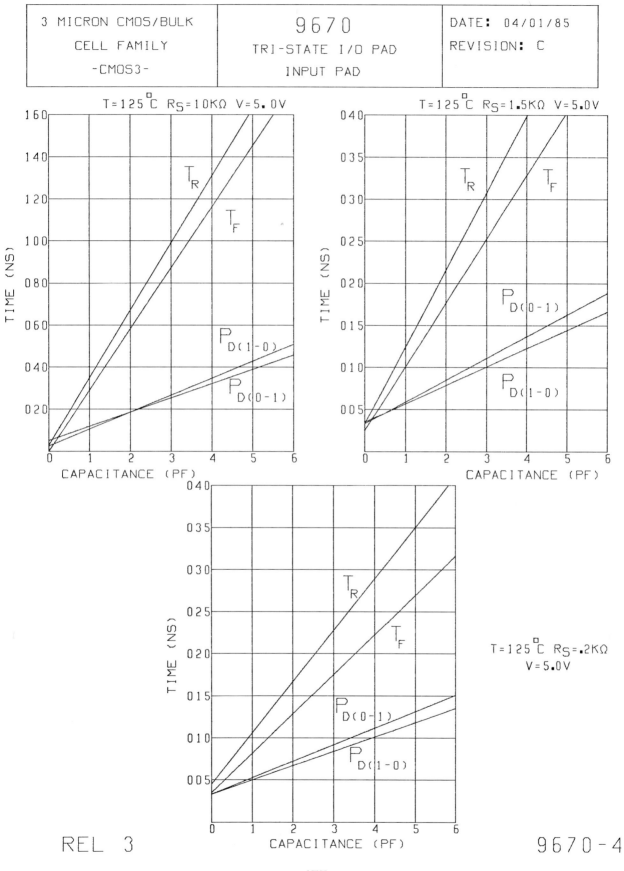

REL 3

9670-4

455

3 MICRON CMOS/BULK CELL FAMILY -CMOS3-	9670 TRI-STATE I/O PAD ENABLE OUTPUT PAD	DATE: 04/01/85 REVISION: C

OUTPUT CHARACTERISTIC EQUATIONS

$$P_D(0-1) = P_{DC}(0-1) + .11 \; (T_{R/F} - 10) + .48 \; R_S C_L$$

$$P_D(1-0) = P_{DC}(1-0) + .09 \; (T_{R/F} - 10) + .57 \; R_S C_L$$

$$T_R = T_{RC} + .01 \; (T_{R/F} - 10) + 2.82 R_S C_L$$

$$T_F = T_{FC} + 0.00 (T_{R/F} - 10) + 2.55 R_S C_L$$

EQUATIONS

$25^\circ C$

$$P_{DC}(0-1) = .22 \; C_L + 4.90$$

$$P_{DC}(1-0) = .21 \; C_L + 5.32$$

$$T_{RC} = .72 \; C_L + 2.28$$

$$T_{FC} = .63 \; C_L + 2.07$$

$95^\circ C$

$$P_{DC}(0-1) = .28 \; C_L + 5.46$$

$$P_{DC}(1-0) = .26 \; C_L + 6.08$$

$$T_{RC} = .87 \; C_L + 3.09$$

$$T_{FC} = .75 \; C_L + 2.84$$

$125^\circ C$

$$P_{DC}(0-1) = .30 \; C_L + 5.65$$

$$P_{DC}(1-0) = .28 \; C_L + 6.33$$

$$T_{RC} = .93 \; C_L + 3.44$$

$$T_{FC} = .80 \; C_L + 3.13$$

$125^\circ C$ BC

$$P_{DC}(0-1) = .16 \; C_L + 2.35$$

$$P_{DC}(1-0) = .14 \; C_L + 2.78$$

$$T_{RC} = .54 \; C_L + 1.83$$

$$T_{FC} = .48 \; C_L + 1.07$$

VOLTAGE TABLE

VOLTAGE	DEVIATION FACTOR			
	TRANSITION		PROP DELAY	
	TR	TF	1-0	0-1
3.0	1.57	1.66	2.14	1.80
3.5	1.38	1.44	1.77	1.53
4.0	1.19	1.21	1.40	1.26
4.5	1.10	1.11	1.20	1.13
5.0	1.00	1.00	1.00	1.00
5.5	.95	.94	.92	.93
6.0	.89	.87	.83	.85
6.5	.86	.83	.78	.81
7.0	.82	.79	.73	.76

REL 3   9670-5

456

3 MICRON CMOS/BULK CELL FAMILY -CMOS3-	9670 TRI-STATE I/O PAD ENABLE OUTPUT PAD	DATE: 04/01/85 REVISION: C

NOTES

FOR VDD AT 5V AND VSS AT 0V THE FOLLOWING

DRIVE CAPABILITY IS ACHIEVABLE:

FOR V_{OUT} AT .5 VOLTS I_{SINK} IS 1.93 MA.

FOR V_{OUT} AT 2.4 VOLTS I_{SOURCE} IS 7.13 MA.

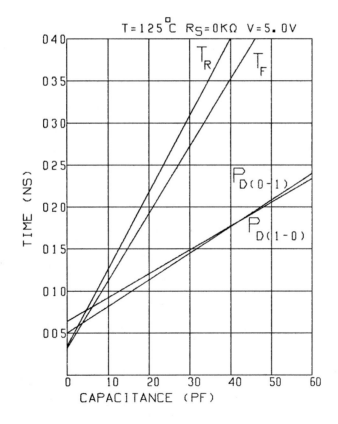

REL 3   9670-6

3 MICRON CMOS/BULK CELL FAMILY -CMOS3-	9670 TRI-STATE I/O PAD DATA CHANGING OUTPUT PAD	DATE: 04/01/85 REVISION: C

OUTPUT CHARACTERISTIC EQUATIONS

$$P_D(0-1) = P_{DC}(0-1) + .18 \ (T_{R/F} - 10) + .48 \ R_S C_L$$

$$P_D(1-0) = P_{DC}(1-0) + .14 \ (T_{R/F} - 10) + .45 \ R_S C_L$$

$$T_R = T_{RC} + .01 \ (T_{R/F} - 10) + 2.58 R_S C_L$$

$$T_F = T_{FC} + .02 \ (T_{R/F} - 10) + 2.57 R_S C_L$$

EQUATIONS

$25^{\circ}C$	$95^{\circ}C$	$125^{\circ}C$
$P_{DC}(0-1) = .22 \ C_L + 7.12$	$P_{DC}(0-1) = .23 \ C_L + 8.10$	$P_{DC}(0-1) = .30 \ C_L + 8.47$
$P_{DC}(1-0) = .21 \ C_L + 7.02$	$P_{DC}(1-0) = .26 \ C_L + 8.17$	$P_{DC}(1-0) = .28 \ C_L + 8.61$
$T_{RC} = .72 \ C_L + 2.13$	$T_{RC} = .86 \ C_L + 3.31$	$T_{RC} = .92 \ C_L + 3.68$
$T_{FC} = .62 \ C_L + 2.37$	$T_{FC} = .74 \ C_L + 3.19$	$T_{FC} = .79 \ C_L + 3.57$

$125^{\circ}C$ BC

$$P_{DC}(0-1) = .16 \ C_L + 4.14$$

$$P_{DC}(1-0) = .14 \ C_L + 4.07$$

$$T_{RC} = .54 \ C_L + 1.65$$

$$T_{FC} = .46 \ C_L + 1.71$$

VOLTAGE TABLE

VOLTAGE   DEVIATION FACTOR

VOLTAGE	TRANSITION		PROP DELAY	
	TR	TF	1-0	0-1
3.0	1.56	1.69	1.83	1.81
3.5	1.33	1.46	1.58	1.54
4.0	1.19	1.22	1.28	1.26
4.5	1.10	1.11	1.14	1.13
5.0	1.00	1.00	1.00	1.00
5.5	.95	.94	.92	.93
6.0	.89	.87	.84	.85
6.5	.86	.83	.79	.81
7.0	.82	.79	.74	.76

REL 3   9670-7

458

3 MICRON CMOS/BULK CELL FAMILY -CMOS3-	9670 TRI-STATE I/O PAD DATA CHANGING OUTPUT PAD	DATE: 04/01/85 REVISION: C

NOTES

FOR VDD AT 5V AND VSS AT 0V THE FOLLOWING

DRIVE CAPABILITY IS ACHIEVABLE:

FOR V_{OUT} AT .5 VOLTS I_{SINK} IS 1.93 MA.

FOR V_{OUT} AT 2.4 VOLTS I_{SOURCE} IS 7.13 MA.

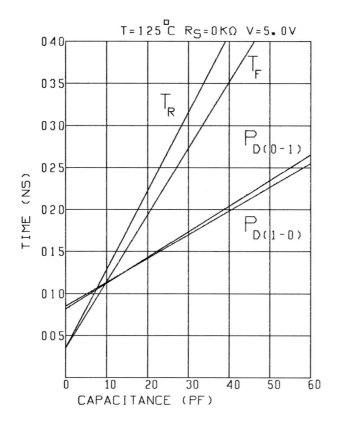

REL 3   9670-8

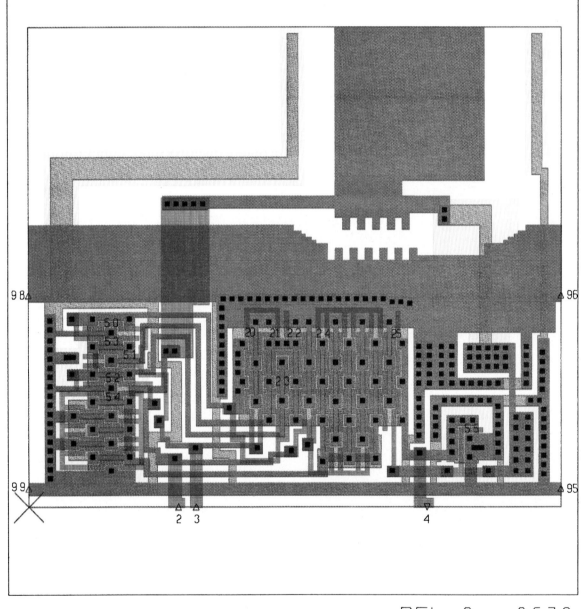

REL 3   9670-9

3 MICRON CMOS/BULK CELL FAMILY -CMOS3-	9680 TRI-STATE I/O PAD CELL HEIGHT 313 WIDTH 360	DATE: 04/01/85 REVISION: C

TERMINAL INFORMATION

TERMINAL NAME	LOGIC NUMBER	FIELD	CAPACITANCE (PF)
DATA	2	1	.39
ENABLE	3	2	.63
OUT	4	6	

LOGIC DIAGRAM

ENABLE,3

DATA,2

VDD

OUT,4

VSS

TRUTH TABLE

OUT: ENABLE	DATA	PAD	IN: PAD	OUT
0	*	HI-Z	0	1
1	*	DATA	I	0
X	*	X	X	X

LOGICV REQUIRES THE PAD SIGNAL NAME
TO BE IN BOTH LOGIC FIELD 3 AND FIELD 7.
REFER TO LOGICV APPENDIX FOR FURTHER
INFORMATION ON HOW LOGICV SIMULATES
THIS CELL.

LOGIC SYMBOLS

ENABLE,3

DATA,2 — [PAD]

OUT,4

WORST CASE DELAY INFORMATION

SEE NOTES BELOW

$R_S = 1.5K\Omega$, $C_L = 1.5PF$, $V = 5V$, $T = 125°C$

LOGIC EQUATION(S)

OUT: SEE TRUTH TABLE

IN: OUT=$\overline{PAD}$

NOTES

OUTPUT PAD: ENABLE $P_D = 16.10NS$ $T_{R/F} = 35.49NS$ R=0   C=35

DATA $P_D = 18.46NS$ $T_{R/F} = 35.56NS$ R=0   C=35

INPUT PAD: $P_D = 6.89NS$ $T_{R/F} = 16.86NS$ R=1.5 C=1.5

REL 3   9680-1

461

3 MICRON CMOS/BULK CELL FAMILY -CMOS3-	9680 TRI-STATE I/O PAD	DATE: 04/01/85 REVISION: C

CIRCUIT SCHEMATIC

VDD
2
3
21(3/77)
(3/77)22
24(3/538)
51(3/64)
(3/103)23
PAD
20
(3/68)
54(3/240)
53(3/32)
(3/32)52
50(3/32)
VSS
VDD
25
(3/69)
4
55
(3/35)
VSS
VDD
VSS

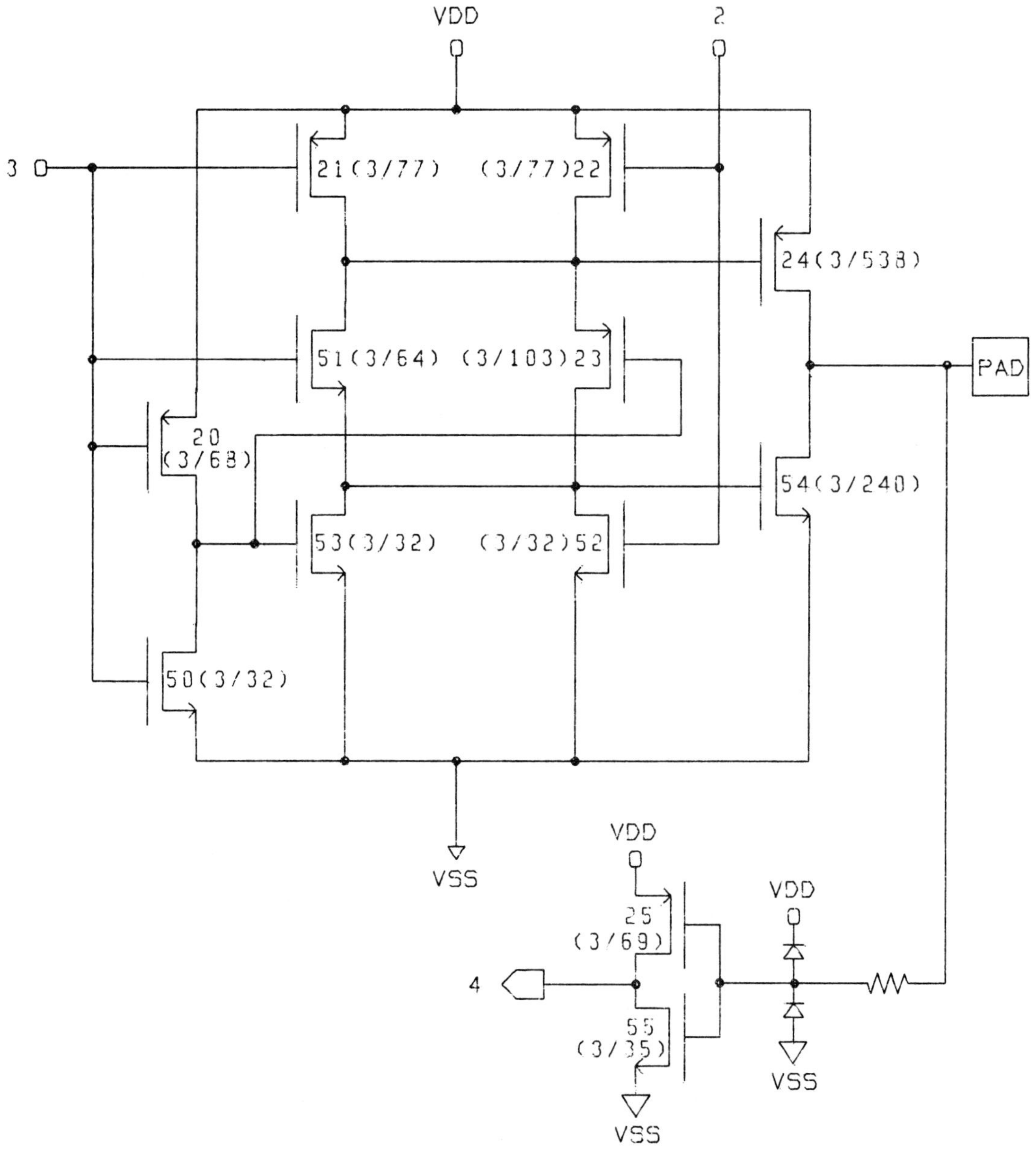

REL 3 9680-2

3 MICRON CMOS/BULK CELL FAMILY -CMOS3-	9680 TRI-STATE I/O PAD INPUT PAD	DATE: 04/01/85 REVISION: C

OUTPUT CHARACTERISTIC EQUATIONS

$$P_D(0-1)=P_{DC}(0-1)+.13\ (T_{R/F}-10)+.60\ R_S C_L$$

$$P_D(1-0)=P_{DC}(1-0)+.16\ (T_{R/F}-10)+.59\ R_S C_L$$

$$T_R=T_{RC}+.27\ (T_{R/F}-10)+2.43 R_S C_L$$

$$T_F=T_{FC}+.27\ (T_{R/F}-10)+2.46 R_S C_L$$

EQUATIONS

$25^\circ C$	$95^\circ C$	$125^\circ C$
$P_{DC}(0-1)=1.47C_L+2.61$	$P_{DC}(0-1)=1.36C_L+2.89$	$P_{DC}(0-1)=2.02C_L+2.91$
$P_{DC}(1-0)=1.29C_L+3.14$	$P_{DC}(1-0)=1.61C_L+3.20$	$P_{DC}(1-0)=1.74C_L+3.22$
$T_{RC}=4.34C_L+3.46$	$T_{RC}=5.64C_L+3.87$	$T_{RC}=6.19C_L+4.03$
$T_{FC}=3.40C_L+2.94$	$T_{FC}=4.38C_L+3.14$	$T_{FC}=4.79C_L+3.23$

$125^\circ C$ BC

$$P_{DC}(0-1)=.98\ C_L+1.95$$

$$P_{DC}(1-0)=.85\ C_L+2.06$$

$$T_{RC}=2.8\ C_L+4.08$$

$$T_{FC}=2.10C_L+3.76$$

VOLTAGE TABLE

VOLTAGE   DEVIATION FACTOR

VOLTAGE	TRANSITION		PROP DELAY	
	TR	TF	1-0	0-1
3.0	1.41	1.45	1.55	1.48
3.5	1.27	1.30	1.37	1.32
4.0	1.13	1.14	1.18	1.16
4.5	1.07	1.07	1.09	1.08
5.0	1.00	1.00	1.00	1.00
5.5	.96	.97	.95	.95
6.0	.92	.93	.89	.90
6.5	.90	.91	.86	.87
7.0	.88	.88	.82	.84

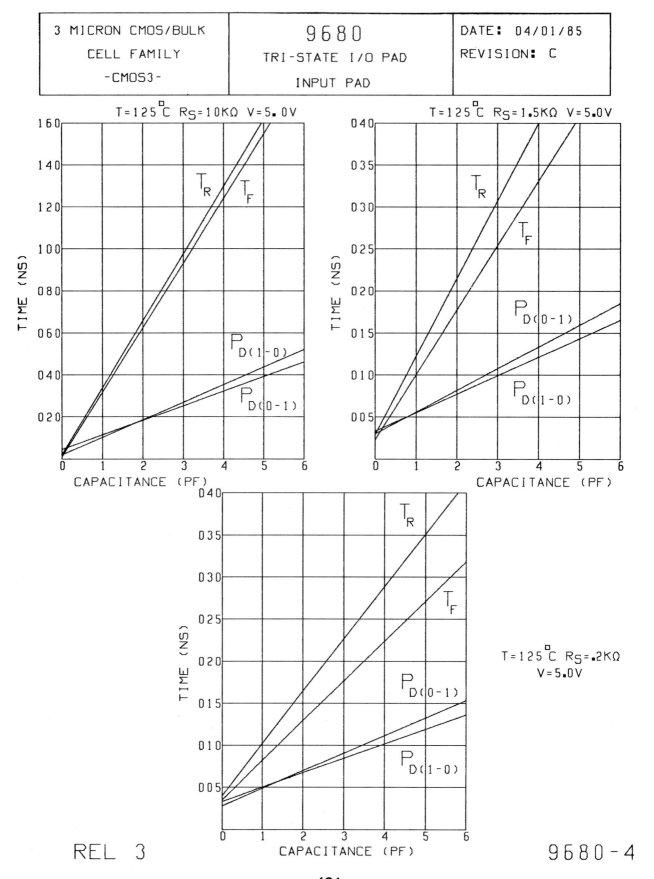

3 MICRON CMOS/BULK CELL FAMILY -CMOS3-	9680 TRI-STATE I/O PAD ENABLE OUTPUT PAD	DATE: 04/01/85 REVISION: C

OUTPUT CHARACTERISTIC EQUATIONS

$$P_D(0-1) = P_{DC}(0-1) + .10 \ (T_{R/F} - 10) + .48 \ R_S C_L$$

$$P_D(1-0) = P_{DC}(1-0) + .09 \ (T_{R/F} - 10) + .57 \ R_S C_L$$

$$T_R = T_{RC} + 0.00(T_{R/F} - 10) + 2.60 R_S C_L$$

$$T_F = T_{FC} + 0.00(T_{R/F} - 10) + 2.55 R_S C_L$$

EQUATIONS

$25^\circ C$	$95^\circ C$	$125^\circ C$
$P_{DC}(0-1) = .22 \ C_L + 4.66$	$P_{DC}(0-1) = .27 \ C_L + 5.19$	$P_{DC}(0-1) = .29 \ C_L + 5.36$
$P_{DC}(1-0) = .21 \ C_L + 5.21$	$P_{DC}(1-0) = .26 \ C_L + 5.95$	$P_{DC}(1-0) = .28 \ C_L + 6.20$
$T_{RC} = .71 \ C_L + 2.09$	$T_{RC} = .86 \ C_L + 2.84$	$T_{RC} = .92 \ C_L + 3.15$
$T_{FC} = .64 \ C_L + 2.00$	$T_{FC} = .76 \ C_L + 2.72$	$T_{FC} = .81 \ C_L + 3.01$

$125^\circ C$ BC

$$P_{DC}(0-1) = .16 \ C_L + 2.17$$

$$P_{DC}(1-0) = .14 \ C_L + 2.70$$

$$T_{RC} = .54 \ C_L + 1.75$$

$$T_{FC} = .48 \ C_L + 1.02$$

VOLTAGE TABLE

DEVIATION FACTOR

VOLTAGE	TRANSITION		PROP DELAY	
	TR	TF	1-0	0-1
3.0	1.56	1.66	2.15	1.79
3.5	1.37	1.44	1.76	1.52
4.0	1.18	1.21	1.40	1.25
4.5	1.09	1.11	1.20	1.13
5.0	1.00	1.00	1.00	1.00
5.5	.95	.94	.92	.93
6.0	.89	.87	.83	.85
6.5	.86	.83	.78	.81
7.0	.82	.79	.73	.76

REL 3   9680-5

3 MICRON CMOS/BULK CELL FAMILY -CMOS3-	9680 TRI-STATE I/O PAD ENABLE OUTPUT PAD	DATE: 04/01/85 REVISION: C

NOTES

FOR VDD AT 5V AND VSS AT 0V THE FOLLOWING
DRIVE CAPABILITY IS ACHIEVABLE:

FOR V_{OUT} AT .5 VOLTS I_{SINK} IS 1.90 MA.
FOR V_{OUT} AT 2.4 VOLTS I_{SOURCE} IS 7.20 MA.

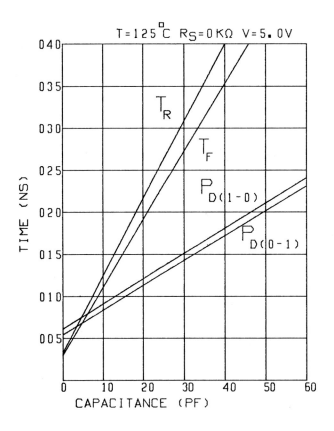

3 MICRON CMOS/BULK CELL FAMILY -CMOS3-	9680 TRI-STATE I/O PAD DATA CHANGING OUTPUT PAD	DATE: 04/01/85 REVISION: C

OUTPUT CHARACTERISTIC EQUATIONS

$$P_D(0-1) = P_{DC}(0-1) + .17\ (T_{R/F} - 10) + .48\ R_S C_L$$

$$P_D(1-0) = P_{DC}(1-0) + .14\ (T_{R/F} - 10) + .45\ R_S C_L$$

$$T_R = T_{RC} + 0.01(T_{R/F} - 10) + 2.59 R_S C_L$$

$$T_F = T_{FC} + 0.00(T_{R/F} - 10) + 2.57 R_S C_L$$

EQUATIONS

$25^\circ C$	$95^\circ C$	$125^\circ C$
$P_{DC}(0-1) = .22\ C_L + 6.38$	$P_{DC}(0-1) = .27\ C_L + 7.82$	$P_{DC}(0-1) = .29\ C_L + 8.17$
$P_{DC}(1-0) = .21\ C_L + 6.93$	$P_{DC}(1-0) = .26\ C_L + 8.05$	$P_{DC}(1-0) = .28\ C_L + 8.49$
$T_{RC} = .71\ C_L + 2.22$	$T_{RC} = .86\ C_L + 3.07$	$T_{RC} = .92\ C_L + 3.42$
$T_{FC} = .63\ C_L + 2.25$	$T_{FC} = .75\ C_L + 3.07$	$T_{FC} = .80\ C_L + 3.41$

$125^\circ C$ BC

$$P_{DC}(0-1) = .15\ C_L + 4.00$$

$$P_{DC}(1-0) = .14\ C_L + 4.04$$

$$T_{RC} = .54\ C_L + 1.57$$

$$T_{FC} = .47\ C_L + 1.65$$

VOLTAGE TABLE

VOLTAGE	DEVIATION FACTOR			
	TRANSITION		PROP DELAY	
	TR	TF	1-0	0-1
3.0	1.56	1.69	1.88	1.80
3.5	1.37	1.46	1.58	1.53
4.0	1.18	1.22	1.28	1.25
4.5	1.09	1.11	1.14	1.13
5.0	1.00	1.00	1.00	1.00
5.5	.95	.94	.92	.93
6.0	.89	.87	.84	.85
6.5	.86	.83	.79	.81
7.0	.82	.79	.74	.76

REL 3   9680-7

467

3 MICRON CMOS/BULK CELL FAMILY -CMOS3-	9680 TRI-STATE I/O PAD DATA CHANGING OUTPUT PAD	DATE: 04/01/85 REVISION: C

NOTES

FOR VDD AT 5V AND VSS AT 0V THE FOLLOWING
DRIVE CAPABILITY IS ACHIEVABLE:

FOR V_{OUT} AT .5 VOLTS I_{SINK} IS 1.90 MA.
FOR V_{OUT} AT 2.4 VOLTS I_{SOURCE} IS 7.20 MA.

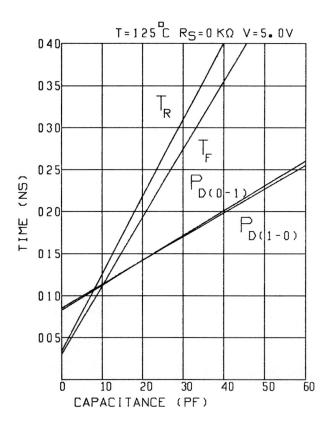

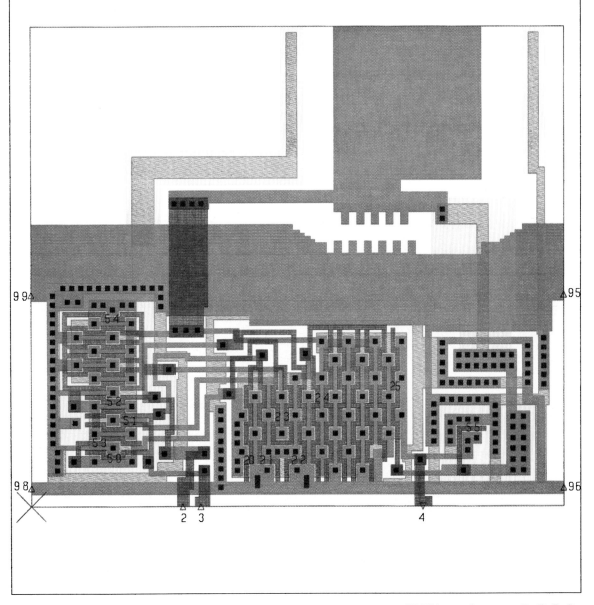

REL 3   9680-9

469

3 MICRON CMOS/BULK	9710	DATE: 04/01/85
CELL FAMILY	TRI-STATE OUTPUT PAD	REVISION: C
-CMOS3-	CELL HEIGHT 313 WIDTH 325	

TERMINAL INFORMATION

NAME	TERMINAL NUMBER	LOGIC FIELD	CAPACITANCE (PF)
DATA	2	1	.35
ENABLE	3	2	.67

LOGIC DIAGRAM

ENABLE, 3

DATA, 2 —▷—⊳

TRUTH TABLE

ENABLE	DATA	PAD
0	*	HI-Z
1	*	DATA
X	*	X

LOGICV REQUIRES THE PAD SIGNAL NAME
TO BE IN LOGIC FIELD 6. LOGICV
SIMULATES THE HI-Z STATE AS AN X.
FOR FURTHER INFORMATION REFER TO
LOGICV APPENDIX.

LOGIC SYMBOLS

ENABLE, 3

DATA, 2 —▷— PAD

WORST CASE DELAY INFORMATION

ENABLE P_D = 15.93NS $T_{R/F}$ = 35.38NS

DATA P_D = 18.25NS $T_{R/F}$ = 34.96NS

R_S = 0 KΩ, C_L = 35 PF, V=5V, T=125°C

LOGIC EQUATION(S)

SEE TRUTH TABLE

NOTES

1. DATA PRESENT WITH ENABLE CHANGING CURVES AND EQUATIONS
   ARE ON PAGES 3-4
2. ENABLE PRESENT DATA CHANGING CURVES AND EQUATIONS
   ARE ON PAGES 5-6

REL 3   9710-1

CIRCUIT SCHEMATIC

OUTPUT CHARACTERISTIC EQUATIONS

$$P_D(0-1) = P_{DC}(0-1) + .10 \ (T_{R/F} - 10) + .47 \ R_S C_L$$

$$P_D(1-0) = P_{DC}(1-0) + .09 \ (T_{R/F} - 10) + .57 \ R_S C_L$$

$$T_R = T_{RC} + .01 \ (T_{R/F} - 10) + 2.59 R_S C_L$$

$$T_F = T_{FC} + .00 \ (T_{R/F} - 10) + 2.55 R_S C_L$$

EQUATIONS

25°C

$$P_{DC}(0-1) = .22 \ C_L + 4.76$$

$$P_{DC}(1-0) = .21 \ C_L + 5.18$$

$$T_{RC} = .71 \ C_L + 2.13$$

$$T_{FC} = .62 \ C_L + 1.92$$

95°C

$$P_{DC}(0-1) = .28 \ C_L + 5.29$$

$$P_{DC}(1-0) = .26 \ C_L + 5.89$$

$$T_{RC} = .86 \ C_L + 2.87$$

$$T_{FC} = .74 \ C_L + 2.61$$

125°C

$$P_{DC}(0-1) = .30 \ C_L + 5.47$$

$$P_{DC}(1-0) = .28 \ C_L + 6.16$$

$$T_{RC} = .92 \ C_L + 3.15$$

$$T_{FC} = .79 \ C_L + 2.87$$

125°C BC

$$P_{DC}(0-1) = .16 \ C_L + 2.23$$

$$P_{DC}(1-0) = .14 \ C_L + 2.71$$

$$T_{RC} = .53 \ C_L + 1.80$$

$$T_{FC} = .47 \ C_L + 1.01$$

VOLTAGE TABLE

VOLTAGE	DEVIATION FACTOR			
	TRANSITION		PROP DELAY	
	TR	TF	1-0	0-1
3.0	1.56	1.66	2.14	1.30
3.5	1.37	1.44	1.77	1.53
4.0	1.18	1.21	1.40	1.26
4.5	1.09	1.11	1.20	1.13
5.0	1.00	1.00	1.00	1.00
5.5	.95	.94	.92	.93
6.0	.89	.87	.84	.85
6.5	.86	.83	.79	.81
7.0	.82	.79	.73	.76

REL 3   9710-3

NOTES

FOR VDD AT 5V AND VSS AT 0V THE FOLLOWING
DRIVE CAPABILITY IS ACHIEVABLE:

FOR V_{OUT} AT .5 VOLTS I_{SINK} IS 1.93 MA.
FOR V_{OUT} AT 2.4 VOLTS I_{SOURCE} IS 7.12 MA.

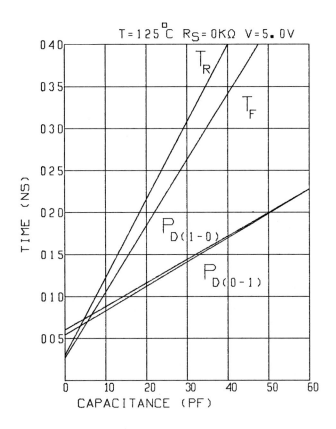

REL 3   9710-4

3 MICRON CMOS/BULK CELL FAMILY -CMOS3-	9710 TRI-STATE OUTPUT PAD DATA CHANGING	DATE: 04/01/85 REVISION: C

OUTPUT CHARACTERISTIC EQUATIONS

$$P_D(0-1) = P_{DC}(0-1) + .18 \ (T_{R/F} - 10) + .46 \ R_S C_L$$

$$P_D(1-0) = P_{DC}(1-0) + .13 \ (T_{R/F} - 10) + .45 \ R_S C_L$$

$$T_R = T_{RC} + .01 \ (T_{R/F} - 10) + 2.58 R_S C_L$$

$$T_F = T_{FC} + .02 \ (T_{R/F} - 10) + 2.57 R_S C_L$$

EQUATIONS

25°C

$$P_{DC}(0-1) = .22 \ C_L + 6.96$$

$$P_{DC}(1-0) = .21 \ C_L + 6.86$$

$$T_{RC} = .71 \ C_L + 2.25$$

$$T_{FC} = .62 \ C_L + 2.23$$

95°C

$$P_{DC}(0-1) = .28 \ C_L + 7.92$$

$$P_{DC}(1-0) = .26 \ C_L + 7.97$$

$$T_{RC} = .85 \ C_L + 3.08$$

$$T_{FC} = .74 \ C_L + 2.96$$

125°C

$$P_{DC}(0-1) = .30 \ C_L + 8.28$$

$$P_{DC}(1-0) = .28 \ C_L + 8.39$$

$$T_{RC} = .92 \ C_L + 3.40$$

$$T_{FC} = .78 \ C_L + 3.31$$

125°C BC

$$P_{DC}(0-1) = .16 \ C_L + 4.04$$

$$P_{DC}(1-0) = .14 \ C_L + 3.97$$

$$T_{RC} = .53 \ C_L + 1.60$$

$$T_{FC} = .46 \ C_L + 1.65$$

VOLTAGE TABLE

VOLTAGE	DEVIATION FACTOR			
	TRANSITION		PROP DELAY	
	TR	TF	1-0	0-1
3.0	1.56	1.69	1.88	1.81
3.5	1.38	1.46	1.58	1.54
4.0	1.19	1.22	1.28	1.26
4.5	1.10	1.11	1.14	1.13
5.0	1.00	1.00	1.00	1.00
5.5	.95	.94	.92	.93
6.0	.89	.88	.84	.85
6.5	.86	.84	.79	.81
7.0	.82	.80	.74	.76

3 MICRON CMOS/BULK CELL FAMILY -CMOS3-	9710 TRI-STATE OUTPUT PAD DATA CHANGING	DATE: 04/01/85 REVISION: C

NOTES

FOR VDD AT 5V AND VSS AT 0V THE FOLLOWING
DRIVE CAPABILITY IS ACHIEVABLE:

FOR V_{OUT} AT .5 VOLTS I_{SINK} IS 1.93 MA.
FOR V_{OUT} AT 2.4 VOLTS I_{SOURCE} IS 7.12 MA.

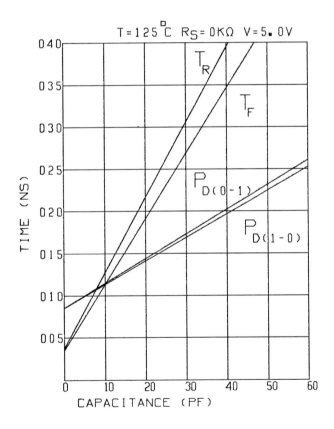

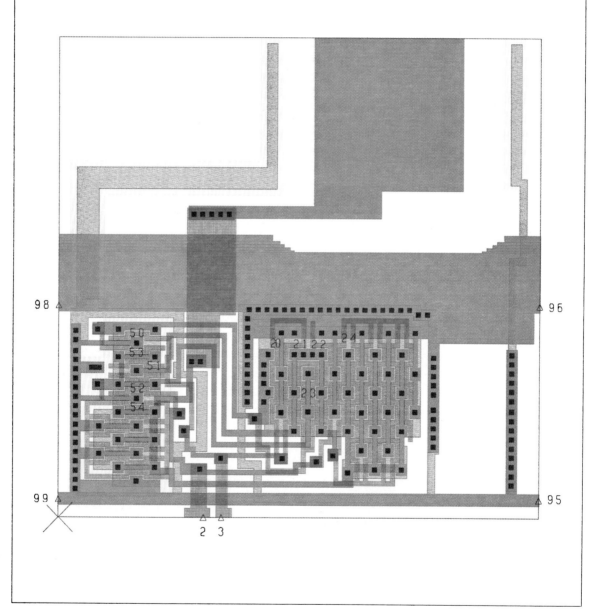

REL 3 9710-7

476

3 MICRON CMOS/BULK CELL FAMILY -CMOS3-	9720 TRI-STATE OUTPUT PAD CELL HEIGHT 313 WIDTH 325	DATE: 04/01/85 REVISION: C

TERMINAL INFORMATION

TERMINAL NAME	LOGIC NUMBER	CAPACITANCE FIELD	(PF)
DATA	2	1	.40
ENABLE	3	2	.63

LOGIC DIAGRAM

ENABLE,3

DATA,2

TRUTH TABLE

ENABLE	DATA	PAD
0	*	HI-Z
1	*	DATA
X	*	X

LOGICV REQUIRES THE PAD SIGNAL NAME
TO BE IN LOGIC FIELD 6. LOGICV
SIMULATES THE HI-Z STATE AS AN X.
FOR FURTHER LOGICV INFORMATION REFER
TO LOGICV APPENDIX.

LOGIC SYMBOLS

ENABLE,3

DATA,2 ———[> PAD

WORST CASE DELAY INFORMATION

ENABLE P_D = 15.92NS $\quad$ $T_{R/F}$ = 34.39NS

DATA P_D = 15.25NS $\quad$ $T_{R/F}$ = 34.96NS

R_S = 0 KΩ, C_L = 35 PF, V=5V, T=125°C

LOGIC EQUATION(S)

SEE TRUTH TABLE

NOTES

1. DATA PRESENT WITH ENABLE CHANGING CURVES AND EQUATIONS
   ARE ON PAGES 3-4
2. ENABLE PRESENT DATA CHANGING CURVES AND EQUATIONS
   ARE ON PAGES 5-6

REL 3   9720-1

CIRCUIT SCHEMATIC

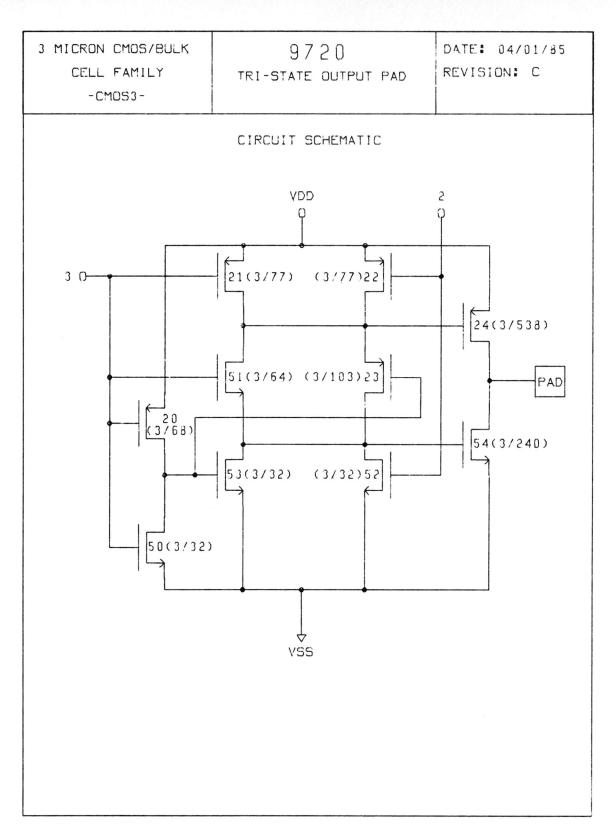

REL 3   9720-2

3 MICRON CMOS/BULK CELL FAMILY -CMOS3-	9720 TRI-STATE OUPUT PAD ENABLE CHANGING	DATE: 04/01/85 REVISION: C

OUTPUT CHARACTERISTIC EQUATIONS

$$P_D(0-1) = P_{DC}(0-1) + .10 (T_{R/F} - 10) + .48 R_S C_L$$

$$P_D(1-0) = P_{DC}(1-0) + .09 (T_{R/F} - 10) + .57 R_S C_L$$

$$T_R = T_{RC} + 0.01(T_{R/F} - 10) + 2.60 R_S C_L$$

$$T_F = T_{FC} + 0.0 (T_{R/F} - 10) + 2.55 R_S C_L$$

EQUATIONS

$25^\circ C$	$95^\circ C$	$125^\circ C$
$P_{DC}(0-1) = .22 C_L + 4.53$	$P_{DC}(0-1) = .27 C_L + 5.03$	$P_{DC}(0-1) = .29 C_L + 5.19$
$P_{DC}(1-0) = .21 C_L + 5.03$	$P_{DC}(1-0) = .26 C_L + 5.78$	$P_{DC}(1-0) = .28 C_L + 6.04$
$T_{RC} = .70 C_L + 1.98$	$T_{RC} = .85 C_L + 2.65$	$T_{RC} = .91 C_L + 2.93$
$T_{FC} = .63 C_L + 1.84$	$T_{FC} = .75 C_L + 2.52$	$T_{FC} = .80 C_L + 2.77$

$125^\circ C$ BC

$$P_{DC}(0-1) = .16 C_L + 2.07$$

$$P_{DC}(1-0) = .14 C_L + 2.61$$

$$T_{RC} = .53 C_L + 1.72$$

$$T_{FC} = .48 C_L + .97$$

VOLTAGE TABLE

VOLTAGE	TRANSITION		PROP DELAY	
	TR	TF	1-0	0-1
3.0	1.56	1.66	2.14	1.79
3.5	1.37	1.44	1.77	1.52
4.0	1.18	1.21	1.40	1.25
4.5	1.09	1.11	1.20	1.13
5.0	1.00	1.00	1.00	1.00
5.5	.95	.94	.92	.93
6.0	.89	.87	.84	.85
6.5	.86	.83	.79	.81
7.0	.82	.79	.73	.76

REL 3   9720-3

3 MICRON CMOS/BULK CELL FAMILY -CMOS3-	9720 TRI-STATE OUTPUT PAD ENABLE CHANGING	DATE: 04/01/85 REVISION: C

NOTES

FOR VDD AT 5V AND VSS AT 0V THE FOLLOWING
DRIVE CAPABILITY IS ACHIEVABLE:

FOR V_{OUT} AT .5 VOLTS I_{SINK} IS 1.90 MA.
FOR V_{OUT} AT 2.4 VOLTS I_{SOURCE} IS 7.19 MA.

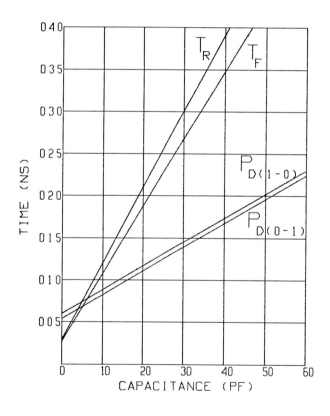

$T = 125\,^{\circ}C \quad R_S = 0K\Omega$
$V = 5.0V$

3 MICRON CMOS/BULK	9720	DATE: 04/01/85
CELL FAMILY	TRI-STATE OUTPUT PAD	REVISION: C
-CMOS3-	DATA CHANGING	

OUTPUT CHARACTERISTIC EQUATIONS

$$P_D(0-1) = P_{DC}(0-1) + .17 (T_{R/F} - 10) + .46 R_S C_L$$

$$P_D(1-0) = P_{DC}(1-0) + .13 (T_{R/F} - 10) + .46 R_S C_L$$

$$T_R = T_{RC} + .01 (T_{R/F} - 10) + 2.59 R_S C_L$$

$$T_F = T_{FC} + .01 (T_{R/F} - 10) + 2.56 R_S C_L$$

EQUATIONS

$25°C$	$95°C$	$125°C$
$P_{DC}(0-1) = .22 C_L + 6.73$	$P_{DC}(0-1) = .27 C_L + 7.64$	$P_{DC}(0-1) = .29 C_L + 7.99$
$P_{DC}(1-0) = .21 C_L + 6.77$	$P_{DC}(1-0) = .26 C_L + 7.86$	$P_{DC}(1-0) = .28 C_L + 8.29$
$T_{RC} = .70 C_L + 2.10$	$T_{RC} = .85 C_L + 2.33$	$T_{RC} = .91 C_L + 3.18$
$T_{FC} = .62 C_L + 2.10$	$T_{FC} = .75 C_L + 2.33$	$T_{FC} = .80 C_L + 3.13$

$125°C$ BC

$$P_{DC}(0-1) = .15 C_L + 3.9$$

$$P_{DC}(1-0) = .14 C_L + 3.95$$

$$T_{RC} = .53 C_L + 1.50$$

$$T_{FC} = .46 C_L + 1.57$$

VOLTAGE TABLE

VOLTAGE	DEVIATION FACTOR			
	TRANSITION		PROP DELAY	
	TR	TF	1-0	0-1
3.0	1.56	1.69	1.39	1.80
3.5	1.37	1.46	1.59	1.53
4.0	1.18	1.22	1.28	1.25
4.5	1.09	1.11	1.14	1.13
5.0	1.00	1.00	1.00	1.00
5.5	.95	.94	.92	.93
6.0	.89	.85	.84	.86
6.5	.86	.84	.79	.81
7.0	.82	.80	.74	.76

3 MICRON CMOS/BULK CELL FAMILY -CMOS3-	9720 TRI-STATE OUTPUT PAD DATA CHANGING	DATE: 04/01/85 REVISION: C

NOTES

FOR VDD AT 5V AND VSS AT 0V THE FOLLOWING
DRIVE CAPABILITY IS ACHIEVABLE:

FOR V_{OUT} AT .5 VOLTS I_{SINK} IS 1.90 MA.
FOR V_{OUT} AT 2.4 VOLTS I_{SOURCE} IS 7.19 MA.

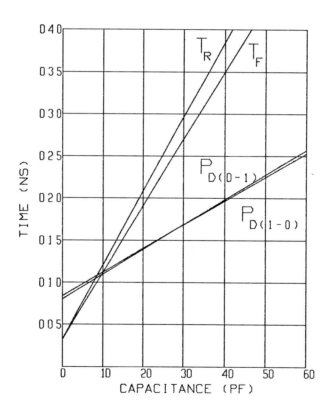

$T = 125 °C \ R_S = 0K\Omega$
$V = 5.0V$

REL 3

9720-6

482

REL 3   9720-7

12

MSI Cell
Data Pages

MSI Cell Index

CELL NUMBER	CELL NAME	CELL TYPE	NUMBER OF PAGES
4000	4–1 MUX	Function	6
4010	Custom 4–1 MUX	Custom SSI	4
4020	8–1 MUX	Function	6
4050	2–4 Decoder	Function	6
4070	Input Buffer	Custom SSI	3
4080	4-Input AND	Custom SSI	3
4090	3–8 Decoder	Function	8
4100	4-Bit R/L Shift Register	Function	7
4110	Begin	MSI Slice	4
4120	Middle	MSI Slice	4
4130	End	MSI Slice	1
4200	4-Bit Up/Down Counter	Function	7
4210	Begin	MSI Slice	5
4220	Middle	MSI Slice	5
4230	End	MSI Slice	5
4300	4-Bit Adder w/Carry	Function	6
4310	4-Bit Adder w/Carry Lookahead	Function	6
4320	C2 Generator	Custom SSI	4
4330	C3 Generator	Custom SSI	4
4340	C4 Generator	Custom SSI	5
4350	Carry Out Generator	Custom SSI	5
4360	Local Carry Lookahead Unit	Function	6
4370	Global Carry Lookahead Unit	Function	6
4400	8–Bit Parity Circuit	Function	8
4410	Begin	MSI Slice	1
4420	4-Bit Middle	MSI Slice	6
4430	8-Bit Middle	MSI Slice	12
4440	End	MSI Slice	1
4460	Begin	MSI Slice	1
4470	Middle	MSI Slice	5
4480	End	MSI Slice	6
4490	8-Bit Comparator	Function	6
4560	Begin	MSI Slice	5
4570	Middle	MSI Slice	5
4580	End	MSI Slice	5
4590	4-Bit Ripple Counter	Function	7
4610	Left Cap	Cap for MSI	2
4620	Right Cap	Cap for MSI	2

MSI Cell Index (continued)

CELL NUMBER	CELL NAME	CELL TYPE	NUMBER OF PAGES
4630	Metal1 MSI Bus Crosser	Bus Crosser	2
4640	Metal2 MSI Bus Crosser	Bus Crosser	2
4700	8-Bit Priority Encoder	Function	6
4710	Q0 Cell	Custom SSI	3
4720	Q1 Cell	Custom SSI	3
4760	Dual Half Adder	Application	6
4770	Dual Full Adder	Application	6
4780	8-Bit Population Counter	Function	6
4790	12-Bit Population Counter	Function	6

3 MICRON CMOS/BULK CELL FAMILY —CMOS3—	4000 4-to-1 Multiplexer CELL HEIGHT 363 WIDTH 240	DATE: 4/10/86 REVISION: -

RELATED CELL TYPES: 4010

The 4000 is a 4-to-1 multiplexer with enablebar (EN/). It is basically a 4010 with input decoders and an output buffer. The select inputs (S1 and S0) determine which of the data inputs (D0, D1, D2, and D3) are active. When enablebar is high, the output is always low.

While the 4000 is a 4-to-1 multiplexer, it is a CMOS multiplexer. As such when the select lines are unknown, the output is not always unknown. Please refer to the truth table on page 2 for the states of the multiplexer.

The paths chosen for characterization are: EN/ to OUT, D2 to OUT, and S1 to OUT.

TERMINAL INFORMATION

ETER NAME	PHYSICAL NAME(S)	LOGICV FIELD	FUNCTION CODE	CAPACITANCE (pfarads)	RESISTANCE(S) (Kohms)
EN/	T1, B1	1	I	0.361	0.750, 1.170
S0	T8, B8	9	I	0.378	0.750, 1.200
S1	T2, B2	2	I	0.395	0.750, 1.200
D0	T4, B4	3	I	0.357	1.170, 0.750
D1	T5, B5	4	I	0.337	1.170, 0.750
D2	T7, B7	8	I	0.370	1.170, 0.750
D3	T6, B6	5	I	0.346	1.170, 0.750
OUT	T3, B3	6	O	0.618	0.420, 0.870
P1	L1, R1	–	P	1.798	0, 0
P2	L3, R3	–	P	1.279	0, 0
G1	L2, R2	–	G	1.244	0, 0
G2	L4, R4	–	G	1.147	0, 0

RELEASE 5.0   PAGE NO.   4000 - 1

TRUTH TABLE

EN/	S0	S1	D0	D1	D2	D3	OUT
0	0	0	*	*	*	*	D0
0	0	1	*	*	*	*	D1
0	1	0	*	*	*	*	D2
0	1	1	*	*	*	*	D3
0	0	X	0	0	*	*	0
0	1	X	*	*	0	0	0
0	X	0	0	*	0	*	0
0	X	1	*	0	*	0	0
0	X	X	0	0	0	0	0
1	*	*	*	*	*	*	0
X	0	0	0	*	*	*	0
X	0	1	*	0	*	*	0
X	0	X	0	0	*	*	0
X	1	0	*	*	0	*	0
X	1	1	*	*	*	0	0
X	1	X	*	*	0	0	0
X	X	0	0	*	0	*	0
X	X	1	*	0	*	0	0
X	X	X	0	0	0	0	0
all others							X

* = Don't Care,   X = Don't Know

QUICK REFERENCE TIMING

VDD = 5 volts
C(load) = 1.5 picofarads
Input trans time = 20 nsec.
Worst case processing

D2 --> OUT (B3)   = 27.55 nsec.
S0 --> OUT (B3)   = 31.11 nsec.

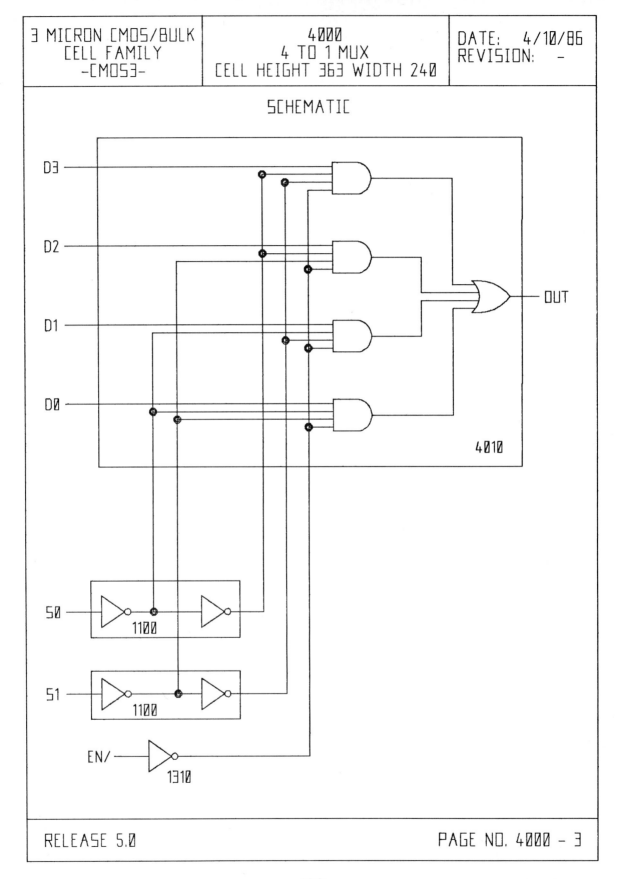

3 MICRON CMOS/BULK CELL FAMILY -CMOS3-	4000 4 TO 1 MUX CELL HEIGHT 363 WIDTH 240	DATE: 4/10/86 REVISION: -

SCHEMATIC

D3

D2

D1

D0

OUT

4010

S0

1100

S1

1100

EN/

1310

SWITCHING CHARACTERISTICS

Consult the MSI function user's guide for the conditions under which these switching characteristics were determined and for guidance on their interpretation. Cload has the units of picofarads and the results are in nanoseconds.

EN/ --> OUT (B3)   Worst Case   Best Case

```
0 --> 1  Delay =  2.51(Cload) + 23.88  OR   1.54(Cload) +  9.69
         Trans =  8.80(Cload) +  1.89  OR   5.86(Cload) +  0.53
1 --> 0  Delay =  2.13(Cload) + 13.86  OR   1.34(Cload) +  5.65
         Trans =  7.26(Cload) +  1.53  OR   5.12(Cload) +  0.34
```

D2 --> OUT (B3)   Worst Case   Best Case

```
0 --> 1  Delay =  2.51(Cload) + 23.78  OR   1.54(Cload) +  9.11
         Trans =  8.80(Cload) +  1.91  OR   5.86(Cload) +  0.53
1 --> 0  Delay =  2.13(Cload) + 22.47  OR   1.34(Cload) +  9.66
         Trans =  7.23(Cload) +  1.57  OR   5.11(Cload) +  0.34
```

S0 --> OUT (B3)   Worst Case   Best Case

```
0 --> 1  Delay =  2.51(Cload) + 27.34  OR   1.65(Cload) + 10.22
         Trans =  8.80(Cload) +  1.90  OR   5.85(Cload) +  0.54
1 --> 0  Delay =  2.13(Cload) + 24.81  OR   1.34(Cload) + 10.43
         Trans =  7.23(Cload) +  1.55  OR   5.11(Cload) +  0.34
```

OUTLINE

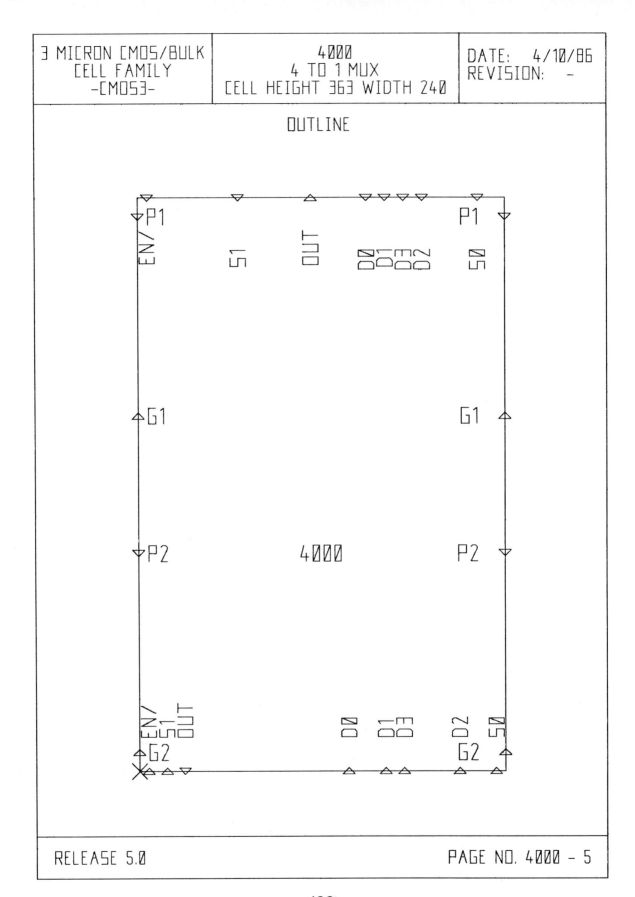

MOSTRAN RESULTS

EN/ --> OUT (B3)

		Worst Case		Best Case	
		1.5 pF	4.0 pF	1.5 pF	4.0 pF
0 --> 1	Delay	27.65	33.93	12.00	15.85
	Trans	15.10	37.11	9.31	23.95
1 --> 0	Delay	17.06	22.39	7.66	11.01
	Trans	12.41	30.55	8.01	20.80

D2 --> OUT (B3)

		Worst Case		Best Case	
		1.5 pF	4.0 pF	1.5 pF	4.0 pF
0 --> 1	Delay	27.54	33.81	11.41	15.25
	Trans	15.10	37.09	9.31	23.95
1 --> 0	Delay	25.67	31.00	11.67	15.02
	Trans	12.41	30.48	8.01	20.79

S0 --> OUT (B3)

		Worst Case		Best Case	
		1.5 pF	4.0 pF	1.5 pF	4.0 pF
0 --> 1	Delay	31.11	37.39	12.96	16.81
	Trans	15.10	37.10	9.31	23.93
1 --> 0	Delay	28.01	33.34	12.44	15.79
	Trans	12.40	30.48	8.01	20.79

All transition times have been multiplied by 1.25 to compensate for measurements taken at 80% of the signal swing.

RELATED CELL TYPES: 4000, 4020.

The 4010 is a custom CMOS SSI structure. It is a 4-to-1 multiplexer with enable. When the enable is low the output is also low. The select inputs, S1 and S0, determine which of the four data inputs are active.

TERMINAL INFORMATION

ETER NAME	PHYSICAL NAME(S)	LOGICV FIELD	FUNCTION CODE	CAPACITANCE (pfarads)	RESISTANCE(S) (Kohms)
OUT	T1, B1	6	O	0.504	.09, .09
EN	T2, B2	1	I	0.193	.750, .750
S1	T3, B3	2	I	0.245	.750, .750
S1/	T4, B4	3	I	0.225	.750, .750
S0	T7, B7	8	I	0.497	.750, .750
	T10, B10				.750, .750
S0/	T5, B5	4	I	0.508	.750, .750
	T12, B12				.750, .750
D0	T6, B6	5	I	0.236	.750, .750
D1	T8, B8	9	I	0.222	.750, .750
D2	T11, B11	11	I	0.229	.750, .750
D3	T9, B9	10	I	0.231	.750, .750
P	L1, R1	−	P	1.241	0, 0
G	L2, R2	−	G	1.109	0, 0

SCHEMATIC

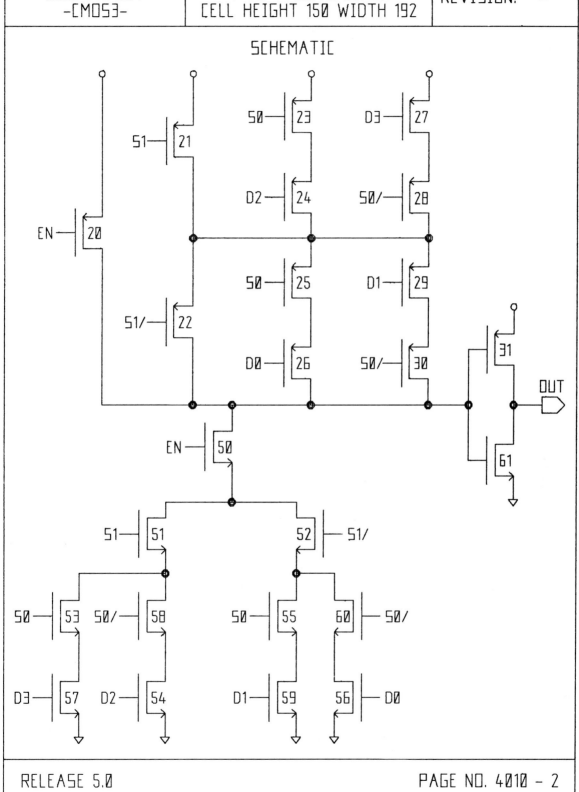

SCHEMATIC CONTINUED

DEVICE SIZES

20 3X60	50 3X40
21 3X80	51 3X40
22 3X80	52 3X40
23 3X79	53 3X40
24 3X81	54 3X40
25 3X78	55 3X40
26 3X78	56 3X41
27 3X78	57 3X40
28 3X78	58 3X41
29 3X78	59 3X40
30 3X78	60 3X40
31 3X80	61 3X30

OUTLINE

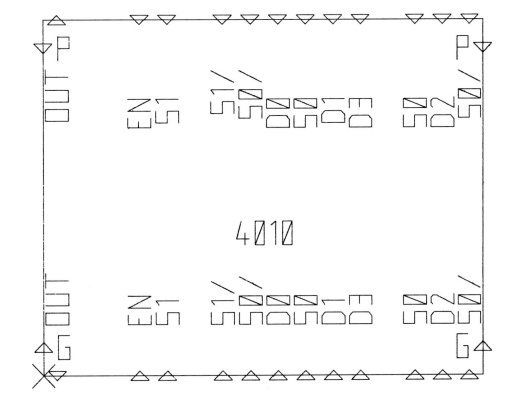

4010

3 MICRON CMOS/BULK CELL FAMILY —CMOS3—	4020 8-to-1 Multiplexer CELL HEIGHT 363 WIDTH 384	DATE 4/10/86 REVISION: –

RELATED CELL TYPES: 4010.

The 4020 is an 8-to-1 multiplexer with enablebar (EN/). To implement this function, the 4020 employs two 4010, input decoders, and an output buffer. The select line S2 determines which 4010 is selected and the other select lines, S1 and S0, choose which data which data input is active.

While the 4020 is a 8-to-1 multiplexer, the 4010 is a CMOS multiplexer. As such when the select lines are unknown, the output is not always unknown. Please refer to the truth table on page 2 for the states of the multiplexer.

The paths chosen for characterization are: EN/ to OUT, D0 to OUT, and S2 to OUT.

TERMINAL INFORMATION

ETER NAME	PHYSICAL NAME(S)	LOGICV FIELD	FUNCTION CODE	CAPACITANCE (pfarads)	RESISTANCE(S) (Kohms)
OUT	T1, B1	6	O	0.580	0.550, 0.960
EN/	T2, B2	1	I	0.346	0.750, 1.170
S0	T13, B13	16	I	0.378	1.200, 0.750
S1	T12, B12	15	I	0.381	0.750, 1.200
S2	T11, B11	12	I	0.388	0.750, 1.200
D0	T7, B7	8	I	0.380	1.200, 0.750
D1	T8, B8	9	I	0.357	1.170, 0.750
D2	T10, B10	11	I	0.382	1.230, 0.750
D3	T9, B9	10	I	0.365	1.170, 0.750
D4	T6, B6	5	I	0.384	0.750, 1.200
D5	T5, B5	4	I	0.349	0.750, 1.200
D6	T3, B3	2	I	0.355	0.750, 1.200
D7	T4, B4	3	I	0.362	0.750, 1.200
P1	L1, R1	–	P	2.560	0, 0
P2	L3, R3	–	P	2.271	0, 0
G1	L2, R2	–	G	2.318	0, 0
G2	L4, R4	–	G	1.892	0, 0

RELEASE 5.0

PAGE NO. 4020 – 1

TRUTH TABLE

EN/	S0	S1	S2	D0	D1	D2	D3	D4	D5	D6	D7	OUT
0	0	0	0	*	*	*	*	*	*	*	*	D0
0	0	0	1	*	*	*	*	*	*	*	*	D1
0	0	1	0	*	*	*	*	*	*	*	*	D2
0	0	1	1	*	*	*	*	*	*	*	*	D3
0	1	0	0	*	*	*	*	*	*	*	*	D4
0	1	0	1	*	*	*	*	*	*	*	*	D5
0	1	1	0	*	*	*	*	*	*	*	*	D6
0	1	1	1	*	*	*	*	*	*	*	*	D7
1	*	*	*	*	*	*	*	*	*	*	*	0
0/X	X	0	0	0	*	*	*	0	*	*	*	0
0/X	X	0	1	*	0	*	*	*	0	*	*	0
0/X	X	0	X	0	0	*	*	0	0	*	*	0
0/X	X	1	0	*	*	0	*	*	*	0	*	0
0/X	X	1	1	*	*	*	0	*	*	*	0	0
0/X	X	1	X	*	*	0	0	*	*	0	0	0
0/X	X	X	0	0	*	0	*	0	*	0	*	0
0/X	X	X	1	*	0	*	0	*	0	*	0	0
0/X	X	X	X	0	0	0	0	0	0	0	0	0
all others combinations												X

* = Don't Care,   0/X = The input is a 0 or an X

QUICK REFERENCE TIMING

VDD = 5 volts
C(load) = 1.5 picofarads
Input trans time = 30 nsec.
Worst case processing

D0 --> OUT (B1) =   25.20 nsec.
S2 --> OUT (B1) =   25.83 nsec.

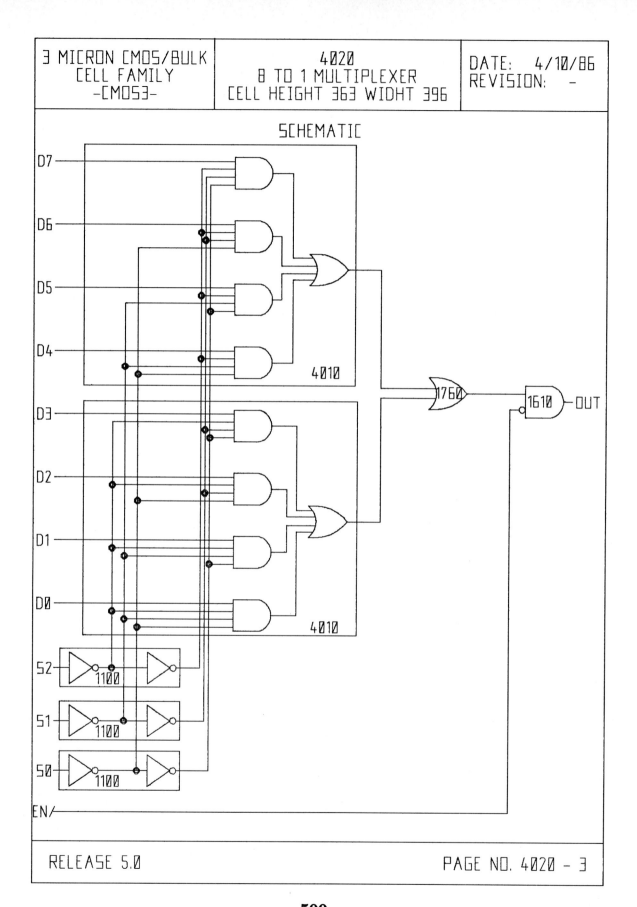

SCHEMATIC

D7

D6

D5

D4

4010

D3

D2

D1

D0

4010

S2   1100

S1   1100

S0   1100

EN/

1760

1610 — OUT

SWITCHING CHARACTERISTICS

Consult the MSI function user's guide for the conditions under which these switching characteristics were determined and for guidance on their interpretation. Cload has the units of picofarads and the results are in nanoseconds.

EN/ --> OUT (B1)   Worst Case   Best Case

0 --> 1	Delay =	3.99(Cload)	+ 6.78	OR	2.10(Cload)	+	3.45
	Trans =	12.48(Cload)	+ 8.56	OR	7.38(Cload)	+	4.15
1 --> 0	Delay =	2.16(Cload)	+ 4.44	OR	1.44(Cload)	+	1.00
	Trans =	6.08(Cload)	+ 7.58	OR	4.45(Cload)	+	4.15

D0 --> OUT (B1)   Worst Case   Best Case

0 --> 1	Delay =	3.96(Cload)	+ 18.95	OR	2.14(Cload)	+	7.40
	Trans =	13.35(Cload)	+ 3.52	OR	7.95(Cload)	+	1.17
1 --> 0	Delay =	1.90(Cload)	+ 22.37	OR	1.34(Cload)	+	9.54
	Trans =	6.75(Cload)	+ 1.44	OR	5.16(Cload)	+	0.30

S2 --> OUT (B1)   Worst Case   Best Case

0 --> 1	Delay =	3.96(Cload)	+ 19.88	OR	2.14(Cload)	+	8.22
	Trans =	13.34(Cload)	+ 3.54	OR	7.95(Cload)	+	1.17
1 --> 0	Delay =	1.87(Cload)	+ 17.80	OR	1.34(Cload)	+	6.98
	Trans =	6.76(Cload)	+ 1.42	OR	5.18(Cload)	+	0.29

OUTLINE

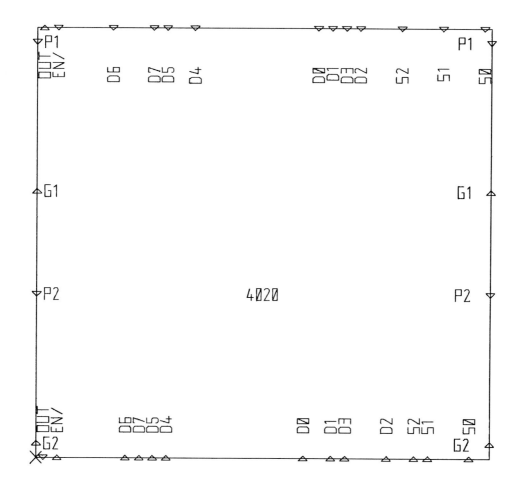

MOSTRAN RESULTS

EN/ --> OUT (B1)		Worst Case		Best Case	
		1.5 pF	4.0 pF	1.5 pF	4.0 pF
0 --> 1	Delay	12.76	22.73	6.60	11.85
	Trans	27.29	58.50	15.23	33.69
1 --> 0	Delay	7.68	13.08	3.17	6.78
	Trans	16.58	31.58	10.83	21.96

D0 --> OUT (B1)		Worst Case		Best Case	
		1.5 pF	4.0 pF	1.5 pF	4.0 pF
0 --> 1	Delay	24.88	34.77	10.61	15.96
	Trans	23.54	56.91	13.09	32.96
1 --> 0	Delay	25.21	29.95	11.54	14.88
	Trans	11.56	28.43	8.05	20.96

S2 --> OUT (B1)		Worst Case		Best Case	
		1.5 pF	4.0 pF	1.5 pF	4.0 pF
0 --> 1	Delay	25.82	35.72	11.43	16.78
	Trans	23.55	56.90	13.10	32.98
1 --> 0	Delay	20.61	25.29	8.98	12.32
	Trans	11.56	28.46	8.05	20.99

Please note that the all transition times have been multiplied by 1.25 to compensate for measurements taken at 80% of the signal swing.

RELATED CELL TYPES: 4070.

The 4050 is a 2 to 4 decoder with an enable. Once enabled only one of the outputs will be in a logic one state after a steady state condition is reached (after the control to output delay time has passed). The enable is active low.

$$D0 = (NOT(ENABLE))(C0BAR)(C1BAR)$$

$$D1 = (NOT(ENABLE))(C0)(C1BAR)$$

$$D2 = (NOT(ENABLE))(C0BAR)(C1)$$

$$D3 = (NOT(ENABLE))(C0)(C1)$$

TERMINAL INFORMATION

ETER NAME	PHYSICAL NAME(S)	LOGICV FIELD	FUNCTION CODE	CAPACITANCE (pfarads)	RESISTANCE(S) (Kohms)
ENABLE	T1, B1	1	I	0.361	1.260, 0.750
C1	T2, B2	2	I	0.297	0.750, 1.260
C0	T3, B3	3	I	0.308	1.260, 0.750
D3	T7, B7	14	O	0.607	1.260, 0.750
D2	T6, B6	13	O	0.619	0.750, 1.260
D1	T5, B5	7	O	0.619	1.260, 0.750
D0	T4, B4	6	O	0.622	0.750, 1.260
P1	L1, R1	–	P	1.471	0.0 , 0.0
G1	L2, R2	–	G	1.411	0.0 , 0.0
P2	L3, R3	–	P	1.914	0.0 , 0.0
G2	L4, R4	–	G	1.646	0.0 , 0.0

3 MICRON CMOS/BULK CELL FAMILY -CMOS3-	4050 2 TO 4 DECODER CELL HEIGHT 363 WIDTH 228	DATE: 1/01/87 REVISION: A

TRUTH TABLE

ENABLE	CONTROLS		OUTPUTS			
Enable	C1	C0	D3	D2	D1	D0
0	0	0	0	0	0	1
0	0	1	0	0	1	0
0	0	X	0	0	X	X
0	1	0	0	1	0	0
0	1	1	1	0	0	0
0	1	X	X	X	0	0
0	X	0	0	X	0	X
0	X	1	X	0	X	0
0	X	X	X	X	X	X
1	*	*	0	0	0	0
X	0	0	0	0	0	X
X	0	1	0	0	X	0
X	0	X	0	0	X	X
X	1	0	0	X	0	0
X	1	1	X	0	0	0
X	1	X	X	X	0	0
X	X	0	0	X	0	X
X	X	1	X	0	X	0
X	X	X	X	X	X	X

* = Don't Care, X = Don't Know

QUICK REFERENCE TIMING

VDD = 5 volts
C(load) = 1.5 picofarads
Input trans time = 30 nsec.
Worst case processing

C1 --> D0 (T7) = 16.69 nsec.

3 MICRON CMOS/BULK CELL FAMILY -CMOS3-	4050 2 TO 4 DECODER CELL HEIGHT 363 WIDTH 228	DATE: 1/01/87 REVISION: A

SCHEMATIC

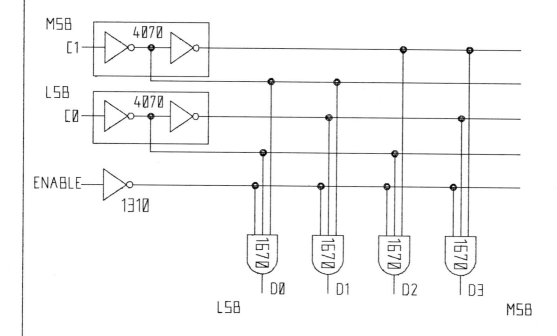

SWITCHING CHARACTERISTICS

Consult the MSI function user's guide for the conditions under which these switching characteristics were determined and for guidance on their interpretation. Cload has the units of picofarads and the results are in nanoseconds.

```
ENABLE --> D0 (T7)        Worst Case                  Best Case

0 --> 1  Delay =    2.86(Cload) + 10.92  OR   2.05(Cload) +  4.42
         Trans =   10.54(Cload) +  1.66  OR   7.97(Cload) +  0.42
1 --> 0  Delay =    2.20(Cload) + 11.88  OR   1.77(Cload) +  4.62
         Trans =    8.14(Cload) +  1.16  OR   6.90(Cload) +  0.26




C1 --> D0 (T7)            Worst Case                  Best Case

0 --> 1  Delay =    2.85(Cload) + 15.27  OR   2.05(Cload) +  5.94
         Trans =   10.53(Cload) +  1.63  OR   7.98(Cload) +  0.38
1 --> 0  Delay =    2.19(Cload) + 16.81  OR   1.78(Cload) +  6.89
         Trans =    8.19(Cload) +  1.13  OR   6.96(Cload) +  0.19
```

OUTLINE

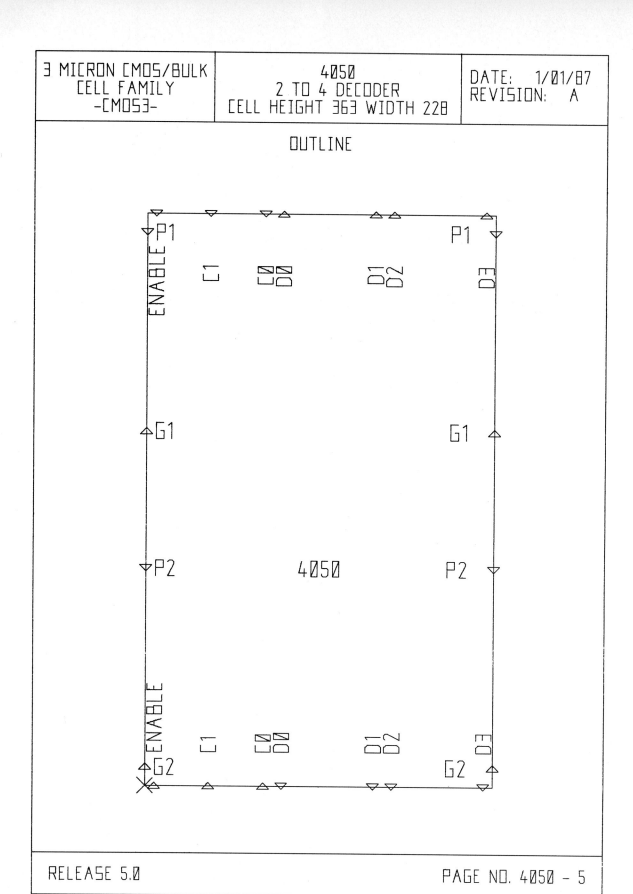

MOSTRAN RESULTS

ENABLE --> D0 (T7)	Worst Case		Best Case	
	1.5 pF	4.0 pF	1.5 pF	4.0 pF
0 --> 1 Delay	15.20	22.34	7.49	12.61
Trans	17.46	43.80	12.36	32.29
1 --> 0 Delay	15.17	20.66	7.28	11.71
Trans	13.38	33.74	10.60	27.84

C1 --> D0 (T7)	Worst Case		Best Case	
	1.5 pF	4.0 pF	1.5 pF	4.0 pF
0 --> 1 Delay	19.55	26.68	9.02	14.15
Trans	17.43	43.76	12.34	32.28
1 --> 0 Delay	20.10	25.58	9.55	13.99
Trans	13.41	33.88	10.63	28.03

Please note that transition times have been multiplied by 1.25 to compensate for measurements taken at 80% of the signal swing.

RELATED CELL TYPES: 4050, 4090.

The 4070 is an input buffer which generates both true and complemented versions of the input. This cell is useful when one needs both polarities of a signal like in decoders. This cell also contains a bus crosser.

Q = NOT(NOT(INPUT)) = INPUT

Q/ = NOT(INPUT)

TERMINAL INFORMATION

ETER NAME	PHYSICAL NAME(S)	LOGICV FIELD	FUNCTION CODE	CAPACITANCE (pfarads)	RESISTANCE(S) (Kohms)
BC1	T1, B1	–	F	0.074	0.120, 0.120
Q1	T2, B2	7	O	0.369	0.750, 0.750
Q1/	T3, B3	6	O	0.548	0.750, 0.750
I1	T4, B4	1	I	0.187	0.750, 0.750
P	L1, R1	–	P	0.271	0.0, 0.0
G	L2, R2	–	G	0.198	0.0, 0.0

3 MICRON CMOS/BULK CELL FAMILY -CMOS3-	4070 INPUT BUFFER CELL HEIGHT 150 WIDTH 36	DATE: 4/10/86 REVISION: -

SCHEMATIC

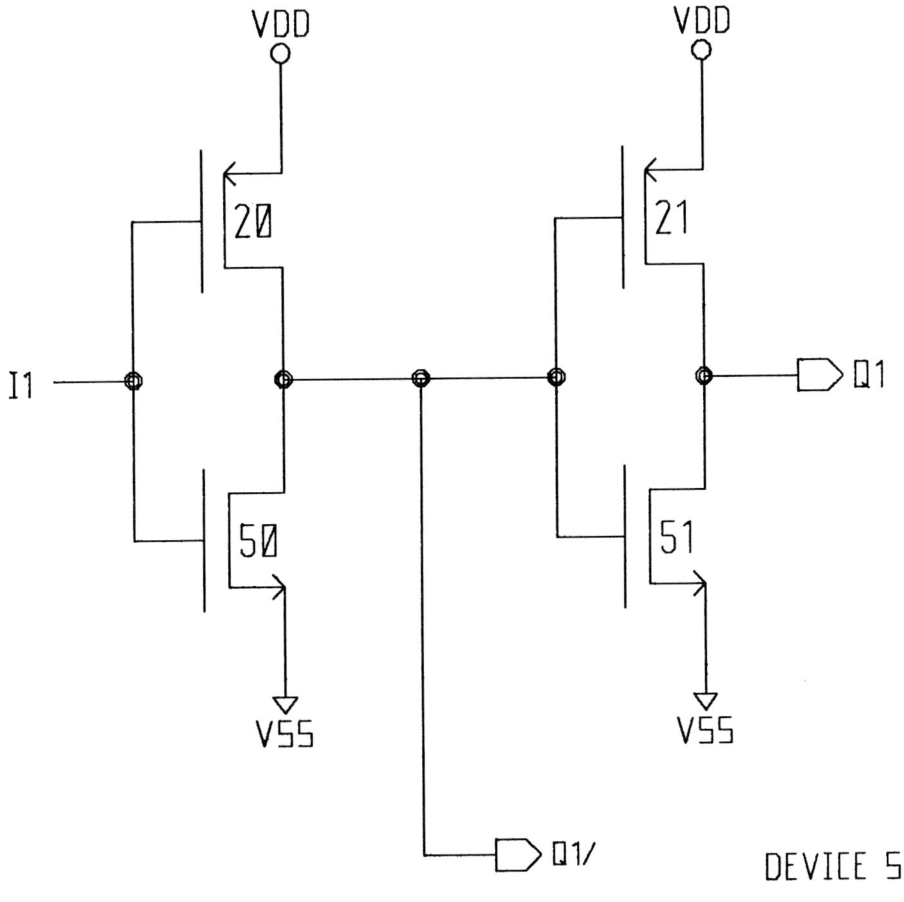

VDD
VDD
20
21
I1
Q1
50
51
VSS
VSS
Q1/

DEVICE SIZES

20 3X46
21 3X44
50 3X25.5
51 3X25

RELEASE 5.0

PAGE NO. 4070 - 2

3 MICRON CMOS/BULK CELL FAMILY -CMOS3-	4070 INPUT BUFFER CELL HEIGHT 150 WIDTH 36	DATE: 4/10/86 REVISION: -

OUTLINE

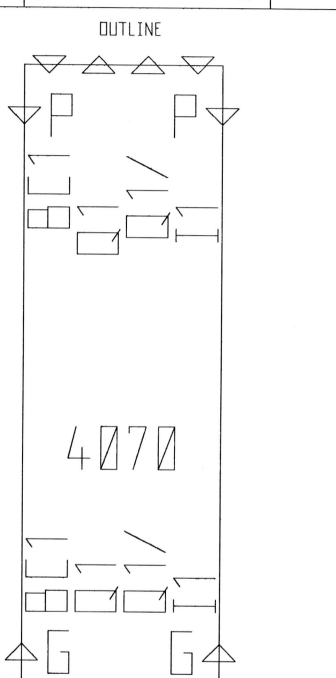

RELATED CELL TYPES: 4090.

The 4080 is a four (4) input NAND with an inverter to achieve the AND function. This cell also has a bus crosser internal to it.

$$Q1 = (I1)(I2)(I3)(I4)$$

TERMINAL INFORMATION

ETER NAME	PHYSICAL NAME(S)	LOGICV FIELD	FUNCTION CODE	CAPACITANCE (pfarads)	RESISTANCE(S) (Kohms)
BC1	T1, B1	–	F	0.076	0.135, 0.135
I1	T2, B2	1	I	0.226	0.750, 0.750
I2	T3, B3	2	I	0.213	0.750, 0.750
I3	T4, B4	3	I	0.226	0.750, 0.750
I4	T5, B5	4	I	0.232	0.750, 0.750
Q1	T6, B6	6	O	0.470	0.750, 0.750
P	L1, R1	–	P	0.604	0.0, 0.0
G	L2, R2	–	G	0.412	0.0, 0.0

3 MICRON CMOS/BULK CELL FAMILY -CMOS3-	4080 4 INPUT AND CELL HEIGHT 150 WIDTH 72	DATE: 4/10/86 REVISION: -

SCHEMATIC

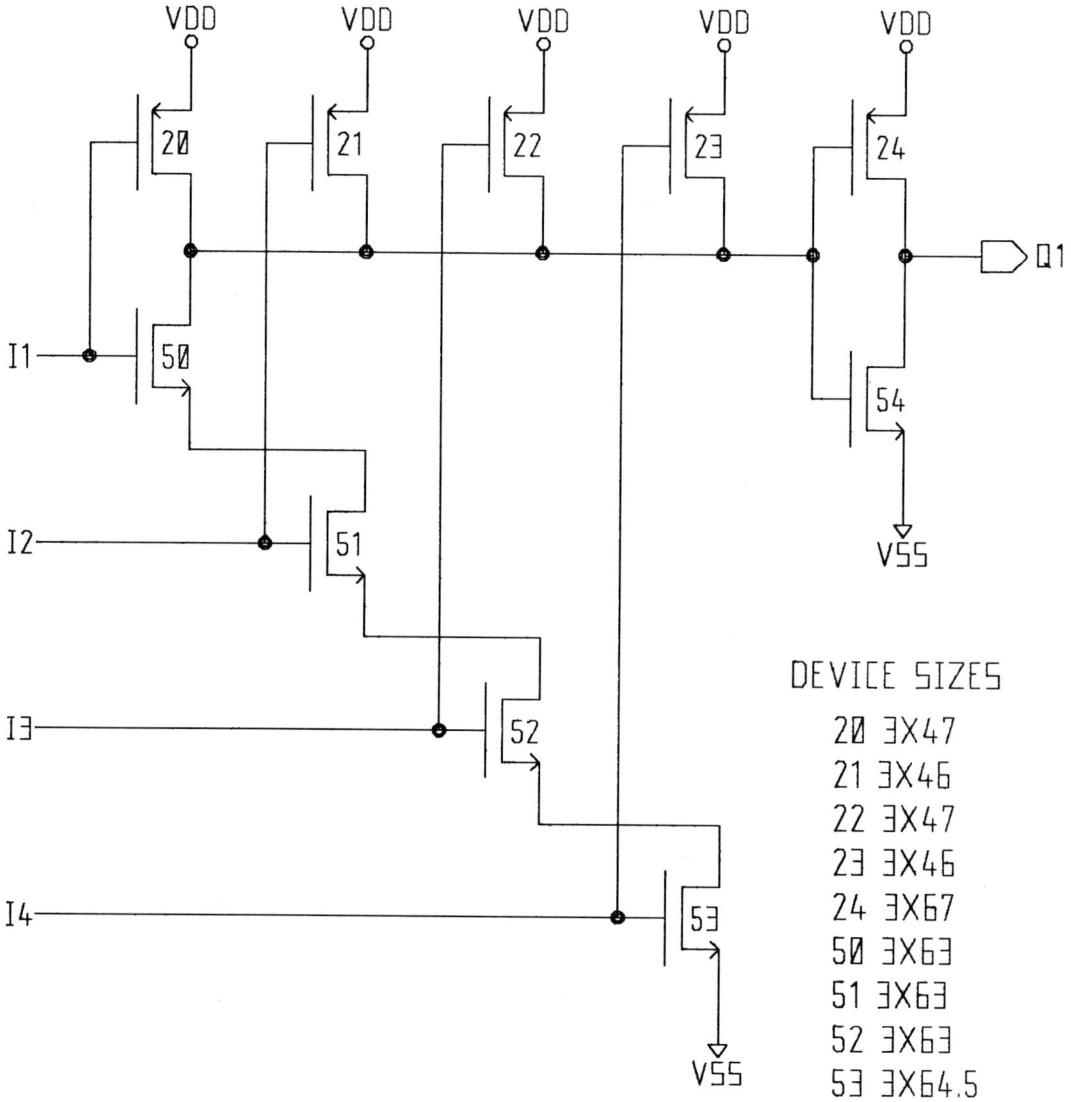

DEVICE SIZES

20	3X47
21	3X46
22	3X47
23	3X46
24	3X67
50	3X63
51	3X63
52	3X63
53	3X64.5

RELEASE 5.0

PAGE NO. 4080 - 2

OUTLINE

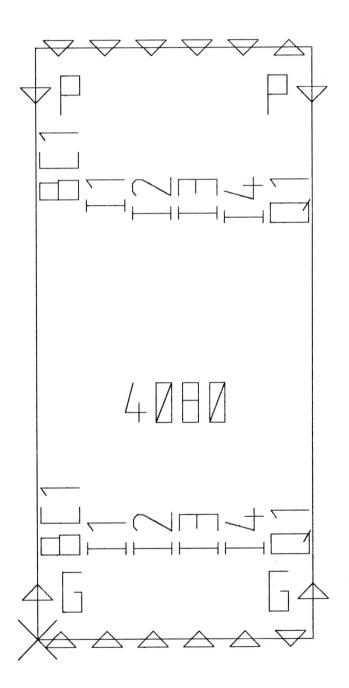

RELATED CELL TYPES: 4070 , 4080.

The 4090 is 3 to 8 decoder with a active low enable. When enabled only one of the eight outputs will be in a logic ONE state. While disabled all outputs will be a logic ZERO state.

$$Q0 = (C2BAR)(C1BAR)(C0BAR)(ENABLE)$$
$$Q1 = (C2BAR)(C1BAR)(C0)(ENABLE)$$

$$Q2 = (C2BAR)(C1)(C0BAR)(ENABLE)$$
$$Q3 = (C2BAR)(C1)(C0)(ENABLE)$$

$$Q4 = (C2)(C1BAR)(C0BAR)(ENABLE)$$
$$Q5 = (C2)(C1BAR)(C0)(ENABLE)$$

$$Q6 = (C2)(C1)(C0BAR)(ENABLE)$$
$$Q7 = (C2)(C1)(C0)(ENABLE)$$

TERMINAL INFORMATION

ETER NAME	PHYSICAL NAME(S)	LOGICV FIELD	FUNCTION CODE	CAPACITANCE (pfarads)	RESISTANCE(S) (Kohms)
ENABLE	T1, B1	1	I	0.313	0.750, 1.140
C2	T2, B2	2	I	0.313	1.140, 0.750
C1	T3, B3	3	I	0.313	0.750, 1.140
C0	T4, B4	4	I	0.313	1.140, 0.750
D7	T5, B5	28	O	0.598	0.750, 1.155
D6	T6, B6	27	O	0.598	1.155, 0.750
D5	T7, B7	21	O	0.598	0.750, 1.155
D4	T8, B8	20	O	0.598	1.155, 0.750
D3	T9, B9	14	O	0.598	0.750, 1.155
D2	T10, B10	13	O	0.598	1.155, 0.750
D1	T11, B11	7	O	0.598	0.750, 1.155
D0	T12, B12	6	O	0.598	1.155, 0.750
P1	L1, R1	−	P	2.958	0.0 , 0.0
G1	L2, R2	−	G	1.949	0.0 , 0.0
P2	L3, R3	−	P	2.958	0.0 , 0.0
G2	L4, R4	−	G	1.949	0.0 , 0.0

RELEASE 5.0

PAGE NO. 4090 − 1

TRUTH TABLE

ENABLE	C2	C1	C0	D0	D1	D2	D3	D4	D5	D6	D7
		INPUTS					OUTPUTS				
0	0	0	0	1	0	0	0	0	0	0	0
0	0	0	1	0	1	0	0	0	0	0	0
0	0	1	0	0	0	1	0	0	0	0	0
0	0	1	1	0	0	0	1	0	0	0	0
0	1	0	0	0	0	0	0	1	0	0	0
0	1	0	1	0	0	0	0	0	1	0	0
0	1	1	0	0	0	0	0	0	0	1	0
0	1	1	1	0	0	0	0	0	0	0	1
1	*	*	*	0	0	0	0	0	0	0	0

* = Don't Care

QUICK REFERENCE TIMING

VDD = 5 volts
C(load) = 1.5 picofarads
Input trans time = 30 nsec.
Worst case processing

ENABLE --> D0 (T12) = 22.78
    C0 --> D0 (T12) = 19.72

SCHEMATIC

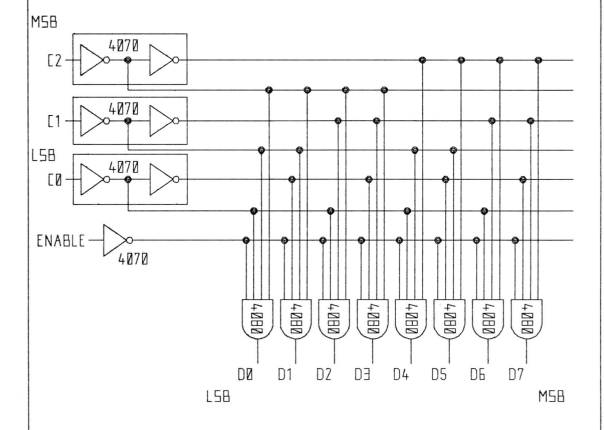

SWITCHING CHARACTERISTICS

Consult the MSI function user's guide for the conditions under which these switching characteristics were determined and for guidance on their interpretation. Cload has the units of picofarads and the results are in nanoseconds.

```
ENABLE --> D0 (T12)      Worst Case                    Best Case

0 --> 1  Delay =    2.49(Cload) + 19.04  OR   1.44(Cload) +  7.90
         Trans =    8.27(Cload) +  3.03  OR   5.28(Cload) +  1.18
1 --> 0  Delay =    2.14(Cload) + 18.57  OR   1.25(Cload) +  7.51
         Trans =    6.91(Cload) +  2.19  OR   4.64(Cload) +  0.72




C0 --> D0 (T12)          Worst Case                    Best Case

0 --> 1  Delay =    2.49(Cload) + 14.24  OR   1.44(Cload) +  5.66
         Trans =    8.26(Cload) +  3.04  OR   5.28(Cload) +  1.17
1 --> 0  Delay =    2.17(Cload) + 16.46  OR   1.25(Cload) +  6.72
         Trans =    6.88(Cload) +  2.51  OR   4.60(Cload) +  0.89
```

OUTLINE

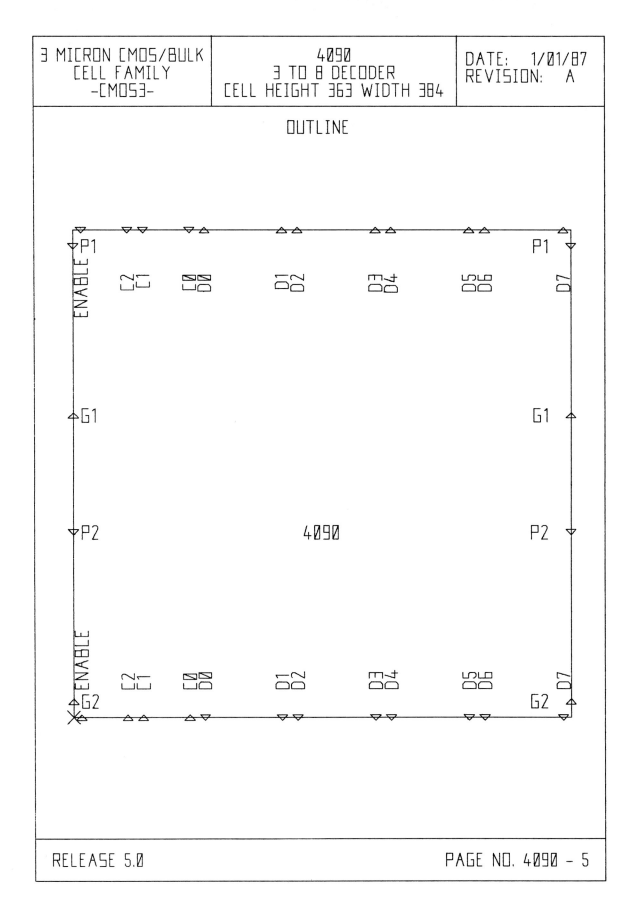

3 MICRON CMOS/BULK CELL FAMILY -CMOS3-	4090 3 TO 8 DECODER CELL HEIGHT 363 WIDTH 384	DATE: 1/01/87 REVISION: A

TRUTH TABLE

ENABLE	INPUTS				OUTPUTS							
	C2	C1	C0		D7	D6	D5	D4	D3	D2	D1	D0
0	0	0	0		0	0	0	0	0	0	0	1
0	0	0	1		0	0	0	0	0	0	1	0
0	0	0	X		0	0	0	0	0	0	X	X
0	0	1	0		0	0	0	0	0	1	0	0
0	0	1	1		0	0	0	0	1	0	0	0
0	0	1	X		0	0	0	0	X	X	0	0
0	0	X	0		0	0	0	0	0	X	0	X
0	0	X	1		0	0	0	0	X	0	X	0
0	0	X	X		0	0	0	0	X	X	X	X
0	1	0	0		0	0	0	1	0	0	0	0
0	1	0	1		0	0	1	0	0	0	0	0
0	1	0	X		0	0	X	X	0	0	0	0
0	1	1	0		0	1	0	0	0	0	0	0
0	1	1	1		1	0	0	0	0	0	0	0
0	1	1	X		X	X	0	0	0	0	0	0
0	1	X	0		0	X	0	X	0	0	0	0
0	1	X	1		X	0	X	0	0	0	0	0
0	1	X	X		X	X	X	X	0	0	0	0
0	X	0	0		0	0	0	X	0	0	0	X
0	X	0	1		0	0	X	0	0	0	X	0
0	X	0	X		0	0	X	X	0	0	X	X
0	X	1	0		0	X	0	0	0	X	0	0
0	X	1	1		X	0	0	0	X	0	0	0
0	X	1	X		X	X	0	0	X	X	0	0
0	X	X	0		0	X	0	X	0	X	0	X
0	X	X	1		X	0	X	0	X	0	X	0
0	X	X	X		X	X	X	X	X	X	X	X
1	*	*	*		0	0	0	0	0	0	0	0

* = Don't Care,   X = Don't Know,   Continued on the next page

TRUTH TABLE

ENABLE	C2	C1	C0	D7	D6	D5	D4	D3	D2	D1	D0
		INPUTS					OUTPUTS				
X	0	0	0	0	0	0	0	0	0	0	X
X	0	0	1	0	0	0	0	0	0	X	0
X	0	0	X	0	0	0	0	0	0	X	X
X	0	1	0	0	0	0	0	0	X	0	0
X	0	1	1	0	0	0	0	X	0	0	0
X	0	1	X	0	0	0	0	X	X	0	0
X	0	X	0	0	0	0	0	0	X	0	X
X	0	X	1	0	0	0	0	X	0	X	0
X	0	X	X	0	0	0	0	X	X	X	X
X	1	0	0	0	0	0	X	0	0	0	0
X	1	0	1	0	0	X	0	0	0	0	0
X	1	0	X	0	0	X	X	0	0	0	0
X	1	1	0	0	X	0	0	0	0	0	0
X	1	1	1	X	0	0	0	0	0	0	0
X	1	1	X	X	X	0	0	0	0	0	0
X	1	X	0	0	X	0	X	0	0	0	0
X	1	X	1	X	0	X	0	0	0	0	0
X	1	X	X	X	X	X	X	0	0	0	0
X	X	0	0	0	0	0	X	0	0	0	X
X	X	0	1	0	0	X	0	0	0	X	0
X	X	0	X	0	X	0	X	0	X	0	X
X	X	1	0	0	X	0	0	0	X	0	0
X	X	1	1	X	0	0	0	X	0	0	0
X	X	1	X	0	X	X	0	0	X	X	0
X	X	X	0	0	X	0	X	0	X	0	X
X	X	X	1	X	0	X	0	X	0	X	0
X	X	X	X	X	X	X	X	X	X	X	X

* = Don't Care, X = Don't Know

MOSTRAN RESULTS

ENABLE --> D0 (T12)		Worst Case		Best Case	
		1.5 pF	4.0 pF	1.5 pF	4.0 pF
0 --> 1	Delay	22.78	29.01	10.05	13.64
	Trans	15.43	36.09	9.11	22.33
1 --> 0	Delay	21.79	27.15	9.38	12.50
	Trans	12.56	29.89	7.68	19.28

C0 --> D0 (T12)		Worst Case		Best Case	
		1.5 pF	4.0 pF	1.5 pF	4.0 pF
0 --> 1	Delay	17.89	24.21	7.81	11.40
	Trans	15.44	36.10	9.10	22.31
1 --> 0	Delay	19.72	25.15	8.60	11.73
	Trans	12.83	30.02	7.80	19.31

Please note that transition times have been multiplied by 1.25 to compensate for measurements taken at 80% of the signal swing.

RELATED CELL TYPES: 4110, 4120, 4130

The 4100 MSI function is a 4-bit universal shift register with serial/parallel data in and serial/parallel data out. Control inputs S1 and S2 are decoded to determine one of four possible modes of operation of the register: stop shift, shift left, shift right, and parallel entry of data. Clock gating is not used to accomplish these functions. The flip flops change state on the negative clock edge. There are six data inputs: four for parallel entry, one for left shift serial data in, and one for right shift serial data in.

A similar bi-directional shift register of any bit size between 2 and 16, can be formed by starting with a 4110 cell, butting N 4120's next to it, and ending with a 4130 cell. The 4100 4-bit version is provided for convenience and as an example of how variable sized registers can be built. Any shift register of a user defined bit size must be formed by the user with the aid of a graphics editor, given a unique cell name, documented, and stored with every chip on which it is used.

TERMINAL INFORMATION

ETER NAME	PHYSICAL NAME(S)	LOGICV FIELD	FUNCTION CODE	CAPACITANCE (pfarads)	RESISTANCE(S) (Kohms)
CLOCK	T3, B3	1	I	0.271	0.750, 1.170
S1	T1, B1	2	I	0.368	0.990, 0.750
S2	T2, B2	3	I	0.383	0.750, 1.080
RESET	T4, B4	4	I	0.275	1.170, 0.750
DR	T5, B5	5	I	0.522	1.200, 1.230
D0	T6, B6	8	I	0.389	1.170, 0.750
D1	T8, B8	9	I	0.389	1.170, 0.750
D2	T10, B10	10	I	0.389	1.170, 0.750
D3	T12, B12	11	I	0.389	1.170, 0.750
DL	T14, B14	12	I	0.520	1.200, 1.290
Q0	T7, B7	6	O	1.443	0.260, 0.680
Q1	T9, B9	7	O	1.757	0.260, 0.680
Q2	T11, B11	13	O	1.757	0.260, 0.680
Q3	T13, B13	14	O	1.459	0.260, 0.680
P1	L1, R1	–	P	6.293	0.0, 0.0
G1	L2, R2	–	G	2.476	0.0, 0.0
P2	L3, R3	–	P	5.605	0.0, 0.0
G2	L4, R4	–	G	2.866	0.0, 0.0

RELEASE 5.0   PAGE NO.   4100 - 1

| 3 MICRON CMOS/BULK CELL FAMILY -CMOS3- | 4100 4-BIT R/L SHIFT REGISTER CELL HEIGHT 363 WIDTH 852 | DATE: 4/10/86 REVISION: - |

ABBREVIATED TRUTH TABLE

C L O C K	R E S E T	S 1	S 2	D D D D D D R 0 1 2 3 L (n)	MODE	Q 0	Q 1	Q 2	Q 3 (n+1)
*	0	*	*	*	RESET	0	0	0	0
1	1	*	*	*	SETUP	No change			
\	1	0	0	*	LOAD	D0n	D1n	D2n	D3n
\	1	0	1	*	RIGHT	DRn	Q0n	Q1n	Q2n
\	1	1	0	*	LEFT	Q1n	Q2n	Q3n	DLn
\	1	1	1	*	HOLD	No change			

"n" means signal state when the setup time was met.
"n+1" means signal state after the clock to Q time.

* = Don't Care, \ = Negative edge of clock.

QUICK REFERENCE TIMING

VDD = 5 volts
C(load) = 1.5 picofarads
Input trans time = 30 nsec.
Worst case processing

RESET --> Q3 = 29.17 nsec.

SCHEMATIC

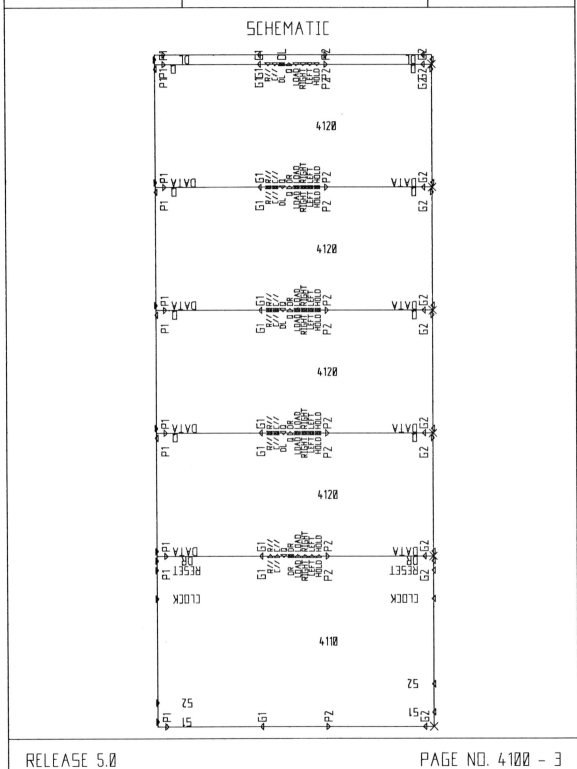

Consult the MSI function user's guide for the conditions under which these switching characteristics were determined and for guidance on their interpretation. Cload has the units of picofarads and the results are in nanoseconds.

SPECIAL TIMING

Data Setup Time . . . . = 4 nanoseconds
Data Hold Time . . . . = 12 nanoseconds
Control Setup Time . . . . . . = 37 nanoseconds
Control Hold Time . . . . = 0 nanoseconds
Minimum Clock Pulse Width . . . = 30 nanoseconds
Maximum Clock Rise Time . . . . = 200 nanoseconds
Minimum Reset Pulse Width . . . = 20 nanoseconds
Reset Hold Time . . . . = 7 nanoseconds

SWITCHING CHARACTERISTICS

CLOCK --> Q3   Worst Case   Best Case

0 --> 1	Delay =	1.96(Cload) + 22.14	OR	1.19(Cload) + 9.29
	Trans =	6.66(Cload) + 8.46	OR	4.47(Cload) + 4.10
1 --> 0	Delay =	1.73(Cload) + 29.97	OR	1.03(Cload) + 12.50
	Trans =	5.06(Cload) + 8.85	OR	3.63(Cload) + 4.48

RESET --> Q3   Worst Case   Best Case

| 1 --> 0 | Delay = | 1.59(Cload) + 26.78 | OR | 1.01(Cload) + 11.03 |
| | Trans = | 5.10(Cload) + 7.24 | OR | 3.76(Cload) + 3.42 |

OUTLINE

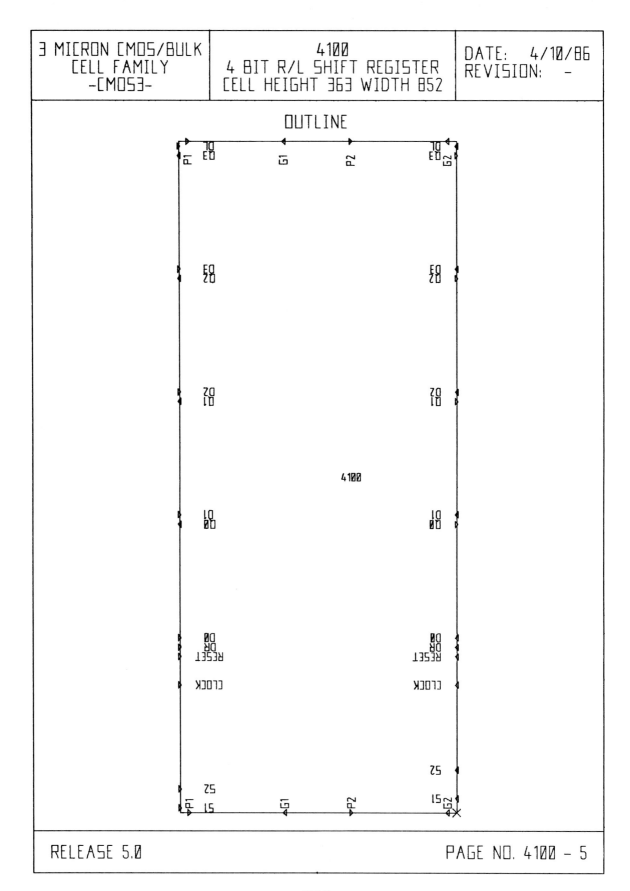

```
Time               =  Time(4110)   +    Time(4120)    +  Time(4130)
Time(N,Cload)      =  [A(N) + B]   +  [C(Cload) + D]  +      0
```

CLOCK --> Q   Worst Case

```
0 --> 1  Delay     0.71      6.36      1.96      12.94
         Trans     0.        0.        6.66       8.46
1 --> 0  Delay     0.61      6.10      1.73      21.43
         Trans     0.        0.        5.06       8.85
```

CLOCK --> Q   Best Case

```
0 --> 1  Delay     0.48      2.49      1.19       4.88
         Trans     0.        0.        4.47       4.10
1 --> 0  Delay     0.43      2.48      1.03       8.30
         Trans     0.        0.        3.63       4.48
```

RESET --> Q   Worst Case

```
1 --> 0  Delay     1.05      6.14      1.59      16.44
         Trans     0.        0.        5.10       7.24
```

RESET --> Q   Best Case

```
1 --> 0  Delay     0.81      2.38      1.01       5.41
         Trans     0.        0.        3.76       3.42
```

     In order to calculate the Delay and Transition times for
an N-bit Bi-directional shift register, use the equations at the
top of the page. The delay of the beginning 4110 depends upon the
capacitive loading presented to it by all of the 4120 cells, which
equals the input capacitance of a 4120 multiplied by N. Since the
4120 input capacitance is constant, it is contained in the coefficient A.
     Since the bi-directional shift register is synchronous, the
delay of the Mth bit of the N-bit register is dependent only on the
capacitive loading on bit M and not on M or N. Therefore, the
value of Cload in 4120 term represents the capacitive load on the
Q output in whose delay you are interested.
     Transition times do not depend upon the characteristics of
the 4110 at all.

3 MICRON CMOS/BULK CELL FAMILY -CMOS3-	4100 4 BIT R/L SHIFT REGISTER CELL HEIGHT 363 WIDTH 852	DATE: 4/10/86 REVISION: -

TRUTH TABLE

	RESET	CLOCK	DR	D0 D1 D2 D3	DL	Q0 Q1 Q2 Q3	S1	S2		Q0	Q1	Q2	Q3
			Setup time must be met.			Old outputs				After clock goes low.			
1	0	*	*	*	*	*	*	*	reset	0	0	0	0
2	1	1	*	*	*	*	*	*	setup	Q0	Q1	Q2	Q3
3	1	0	*	*	*	*	0	0	load	D0	D1	D2	D3
4	1	0	*	*	*	*	0	1	right	DR	Q0	Q1	Q2
5	1	0	*	*	*	*	1	0	left	Q1	Q2	Q3	DL
6	1	0	*	*	*	*	1	1	hold	Q0	Q1	Q2	Q3
7	1	0	0	0	0	0	*	*		0	0	0	0
8	1	0	0	0	1	0	0	X		0	0	0	0
9	1	0	1	0	0	0	X	0		0	0	0	0
10	1	0	1	*	0	0	1	X		0	0	0	0
11	1	0	*	1	0	0	1	X		0	0	0	0
12	1	0	0	1	*	0	X	1		0	0	0	0
13	1	0	0	*	1	0	X	1		0	0	0	0
14	1	0	0	0	1	1,X	0	X		0	X	X	X
15	1	0	0	0	*	1	0	X		0	X	X	X
16	1	0	1	0	0	1,X	X	0		X	X	X	0
17	1	0	*	0	0	1	X	0		X	X	X	0
18	1	0	1	0	0	0	0	X		X	0	0	0
19	1	0	1	0	1	0	0	X		X	0	0	0
20	1	0	1	0	0	0	X	1		X	0	0	0
21	1	0	1	0	1	0	X	1		X	0	0	0
22	1	0	0	0	1	0	1	X		0	0	0	X
23	1	0	1	0	1	0	1	X		0	0	0	X
24	1	0	0	0	1	0	X	0		0	0	0	X
25	1	0	1	0	1	0	X	0		0	0	0	X
26	1	0	1	0	1	0	X	X		X	0	0	X

DEFINITIONS and NOTES: * = Don't care, X = Don't know.
See the truth table for the 1570 flip flop for unknown conditions
    on the CLOCK and RESET lines.
For any other combination of inputs and previous states where
    CLOCK and RESET are known, the outputs are unknown.
Unknown conditions on S1 and/or S2 cause the D and Q lines to
    become the control lines, and the decoded states of S1 and S2
    become the the data lines.

RELEASE 5.0   PAGE NO.   4100 - 7

RELATED CELL TYPES: 4100, 4120, 4130

The 4110 cell is required for the beginning of an N-bit bi-directional shift register. It contains input terminals for all of the control signals for the register. Inside of the 4110, control signals are decoded and/or buffered. Also, there is a serial data input terminal for the right shift operation that is not buffered, but rather fed directly through to the first bit slice.

TERMINAL INFORMATION

ETER NAME	PHYSICAL NAME(S)	LOGICV FIELD	FUNCTION CODE	CAPACITANCE (pfarads)	RESISTANCE(S) (Kohms)
S1	T1, B1	2	I	0.368	0.990, 0.750
S2	T2, B2	3	I	0.383	0.750, 1.080
CLOCK	T3, B3	1	I	0.271	0.750, 1.170
RESET	T4, B4	4	I	0.275	1.170, 0.750
DR	T5, B5, R5	–	F	0.223	0.300, 0.330, 0
R//	R3	7	O	0.506	0.570
C//	R4	6	O	0.476	0.480
LOAD	R6	13	O	0.596	0.600
RIGHT	R7	14	O	0.587	0.630
LEFT	R8	20	O	0.576	0.960
HOLD	R9	21	O	0.561	0.930
P1	L1, R1	–	P	1.956	0.0, 0.0
G1	L2, R2	–	G	1.341	0.0, 0.0
P2	L3, R10	–	P	1.956	0.0, 0.0
G2	L4, R11	–	G	1.341	0.0, 0.0

RELEASE 5.0   PAGE NO.   4110 - 1

SCHEMATIC

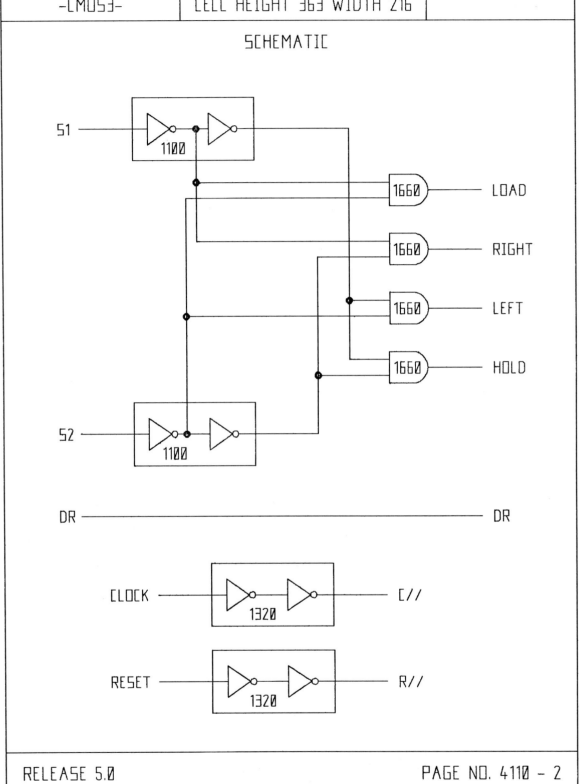

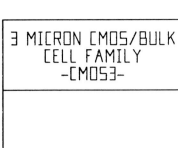

3 MICRON CMOS/BULK CELL FAMILY -CMOS3-	4100 R/L SHIFT REGISTER BEGIN CELL HEIGHT 363 WIDTH 216	DATE: 4/10/86 REVISION: -

OUTLINE

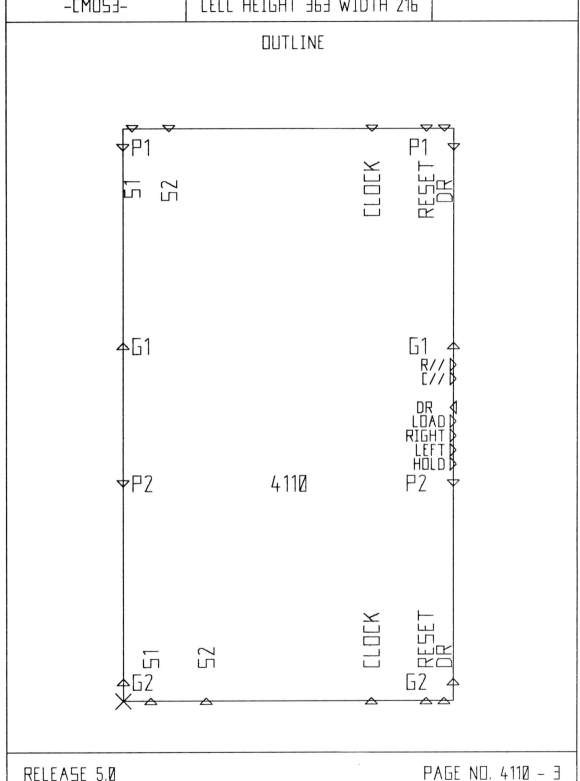

3 MICRON CMOS/BULK CELL FAMILY -CMOS3-	4110 R/L SHIFT REGISTER BEGIN CELL HEIGHT 363 WIDTH 216	DATE: 4/10/86 REVISION: -

SWITCHING CHARACTERISTICS

S2,S2 --> RIGHT   Worst Case   Best Case

		Worst Case			Best Case	
0 --> 1	Delay =	0.91(N) + 11.70	OR	0.66(N) + 4.61
	Trans =	3.38(N) + 1.25	OR	2.58(N) + 0.24
1 --> 0	Delay =	0.73(N) + 9.86	OR	0.59(N) + 3.89
	Trans =	2.78(N) + 0.77	OR	2.32(N) + 0.10

CLOCK --> C//   Worst Case   Best Case

0 --> 1	Delay =	0.71(N) + 6.36	OR	0.48(N) + 2.49
	Trans =	2.52(N) + 2.53	OR	1.84(N) + 0.98
1 --> 0	Delay =	0.61(N) + 6.10	OR	0.43(N) + 2.48
	Trans =	2.13(N) + 2.26	OR	1.66(N) + 0.80

RESET --> R//   Worst Case   Best Case

0 --> 1	Delay =	1.30(N) + 6.06	OR	0.90(N) + 2.30
	Trans =	4.79(N) + 1.52	OR	3.51(N) + 0.45
1 --> 0	Delay =	1.05(N) + 6.14	OR	0.81(N) + 2.38
	Trans =	4.08(N) + 1.35	OR	3.19(N) + 0.33

MOSTRAN RESULTS

S1,S2 --> RIGHT (R7)

		Worst Case		Best Case	
		1.22 pF	4.87 pF	1.22 pF	4.87 pF
		N = 4	N = 16	N = 4	N = 16
0 --> 1	Delay	15.32	26.18	7.26	15.20
	Trans	11.80	44.20	8.46	33.27
1 --> 0	Delay	12.78	21.53	6.25	13.33
	Trans	9.52	36.23	7.50	29.77

CLOCK --> C// (R4)

		Worst Case		Best Case	
		.985 pF	3.94 pF	.985 pF	3.94 pF
		N = 4	N = 16	N = 4	N = 16
0 --> 1	Delay	9.19	17.67	4.41	10.17
	Trans	10.10	34.33	6.66	24.30
1 --> 0	Delay	8.54	15.87	4.22	9.43
	Trans	8.63	29.10	5.95	21.87

RESET --> R// (R3)

		Worst Case		Best Case	
		1.79 pF	7.17 pF	1.79 pF	7.17 pF
		N = 4	N = 16	N = 4	N = 16
0 --> 1	Delay	11.27	26.89	5.92	16.77
	Trans	16.53	62.47	11.60	45.32
1 --> 0	Delay	10.32	22.86	5.60	15.27
	Trans	14.13	53.29	10.46	41.06

Transition times under MOSTRAN RESULTS are not multiplied by 1.25.

RELEASE 5.0	PAGE NO. 4110 - 4

RELATED CELL TYPES: 4100, 4110, 4130.

      The 4120 cell contains a 4 to 1 multiplexer and a master-slave D flip flop. N 4120 cells are required between a 4110 and a 4130 to form an N-bit bi-directional shift register. The 4120 cell contains side ports for buffered clock and reset signals, and 4 decoded control signals. There are also data ports for the shift left and shift right operations. When this cell is located in the first bit position, there is one horizontal metal wire which does not connect to anything in the 4110 cell. When this cell is located in the last bit position, there are 7 horizontal metal wires which do not connect with the 4130 cell.

TERMINAL INFORMATION

ETER NAME	PHYSICAL NAME(S)	LOGICV FIELD	FUNCTION CODE	CAPACITANCE (pfarads)	RESISTANCE(S) (Kohms)
DATA	T1,B1	3	I	0.389	1.170, 0.750
R//	L3,R3	5	I	0.448	0.780, 0.0
C//	L4,R4	1	I	0.246	0.810, 0.0
DL	R5	4	I	0.314	0.930
DR	L6	2	I	0.298	0.900
LOAD	L7,R7	8	I	0.318	0.870, 0.0
RIGHT	L8,R8	9	I	0.318	0.840, 0.0
LEFT	L9,R9	10	I	0.324	0.810, 0.0
HOLD	L10,R10	11	I	0.304	0.780, 0.0
Q	T2,B2,L5,R6	6	O	1.285	.26,.68,.38,.38
P1	L1,R1	-	P	1.179	0.0, 0.0
G1	L2,R2	-	G	0.895	0.0, 0.0
P2	L11,R11	-	P	0.910	0.0, 0.0
G2	L12,R12	-	G	1.221	0.0, 0.0

SCHEMATIC

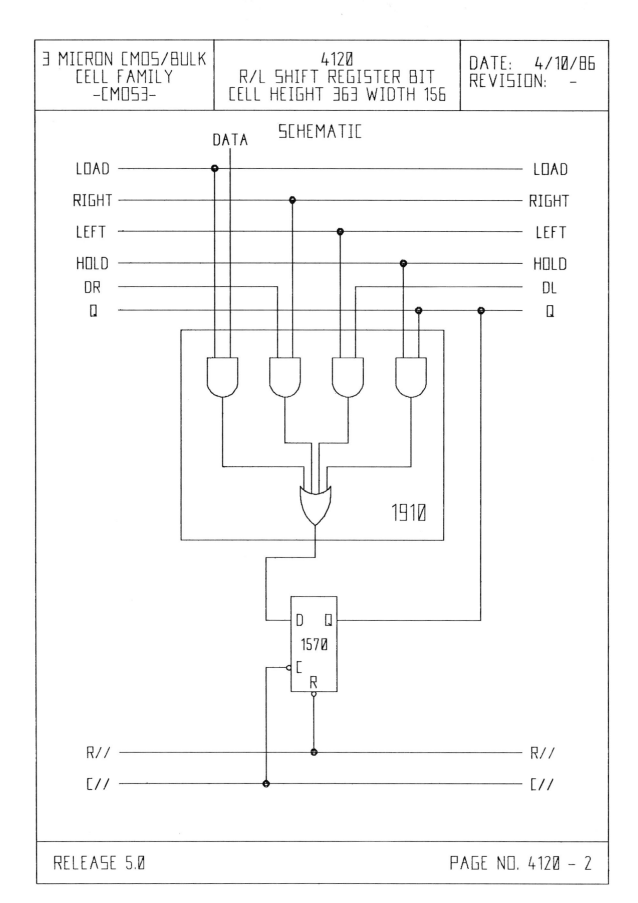

OUTLINE

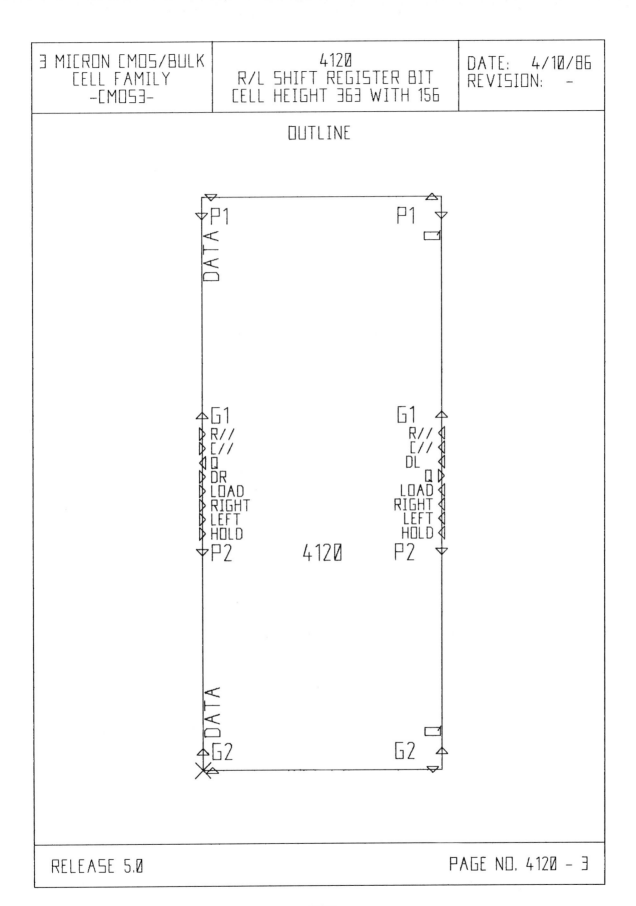

3 MICRON CMOS/BULK CELL FAMILY -CMOS3-	4120 R/L SHIFT REGISTER BIT CELL HEIGHT 363 WIDTH 216	DATE: 4/10/86 REVISION: -

SWITCHING CHARACTERISTICS

C// --> Q   Worst Case   Best Case

```
0 --> 1  Delay =  1.96(Cload) + 12.94  OR  1.19(Cload) +  4.88
         Trans =  6.66(Cload) +  8.46  OR  4.47(Cload) +  4.10
1 --> 0  Delay =  1.73(Cload) + 21.43  OR  1.03(Cload) +  8.30
         Trans =  5.06(Cload) +  8.85  OR  3.63(Cload) +  4.48
```

R// --> Q   Worst Case   Best Case

```
1 --> 0  Delay =  1.59(Cload) + 16.44  OR  1.01(Cload) +  5.41
         Trans =  5.10(Cload) +  7.24  OR  3.76(Cload) +  3.42
```

		Control --> FF,3		DATA --> FF,3	
		Worst Case	Best Case	Worst Case	Best Case
0 --> 1	Delay	14.96 (LEFT)	4.31	7.68	2.85
	Trans	6.39	3.22	4.09	2.56
1 --> 0	Delay	5.31 (RIGHT)	2.33		
	Trans	4.68	2.26		

MOSTRAN RESULTS

C// --> Q (B2)		Worst Case		Best Case	
		1.5 pF	4.0 pF	1.5 pF	4.0 pF
0 --> 1	Delay	15.89	20.80	6.67	9.65
	Trans	14.76	28.08	8.64	17.57
1 --> 0	Delay	24.03	28.36	9.85	12.43
	Trans	13.15	23.27	7.93	15.18

R// --> Q (B2)		Worst Case		Best Case	
		1.5 pF	4.0 pF	1.5 pF	4.0 pF
1 --> 0	Delay	18.83	22.81	6.92	9.44
	Trans	11.91	22.11	7.25	14.77

NOTE: The transition times under MOSTRAN RESULTS have not been multiplied by 1.25.

RELEASE 5.0	PAGE NO. 4120 - 4

3 MICRON CMOS/BULK CELL FAMILY -CMOS3-	4130 R/L SHIFT REGISTER END CELL HEIGHT 363 WIDTH 12	DATE: 4/10/86 REVISION: -

RELATED CELL TYPES: 4100, 4110, 4120.

The 4130 cell is required to complete an N-bit bi-directional shift register. It is composed of nothing more than two bus-crosser cells and some wiring. It has two purposes: to provide a data input terminal for the serial shift left operation, and to ensure that no design rule violations occur with neighboring cells.

TERMINAL INFORMATION

ETER NAME	PHYSICAL NAME(S)	LOGICV FIELD	FUNCTION CODE	CAPACITANCE (pfarads)	RESISTANCE(S) (Kohms)
DL	T1, B1, L3	–	F	0.206	0.270, 0.360, 0.0
P1	L1, R1	–	P	0.009	0.0, 0.0
G1	L2, R2	–	G	0.009	0.0, 0.0
P2	L4, R3	–	P	0.009	0.0, 0.0
G2	L5, R4	–	G	0.009	0.0, 0.0

RELEASE 5.0

PAGE NO. 4130 - 1

3 MICRON CMOS/BULK CELL FAMILY —CMOS3—	4200 4 BIT U/D COUNTER CELL HEIGHT 363 WIDTH 1128	DATE: 4/10/86 REVISION: —

RELATED CELL TYPES: 4210, 4220, 4230

The 4200 is a four bit synchronous counter that can count
up, count down, hold count, or be preset. Two control lines
SEL1 and SEL2 determine the four operational modes of the
counter.

Please note that in the preset mode, a clock pulse is needed
to load the counter. Also reset operates asynchronously.

TERMINAL INFORMATION

ETER NAME	PHYSICAL NAME(S)	LOGICV FIELD	FUNCTION CODE	CAPACITANCE (pfarads)	RESISTANCE(S) (Kohms)
SEL1	T1, B1	1	I	0.368	0.750, 0.994
SEL2	T2, B2	2	I	0.397	0.750, 1.090
RESET	T3, B3	3	I	0.267	0.750, 1.170
CLOCK	T4, B4	4	I	0.272	1.166, 0.750
DATA0	T5, B5	5	I	0.295	0.750, 1.226
DATA1	T7, B7	8	I	0.295	0.750, 1.226
DATA2	T9, B9	9	I	0.295	0.750, 1.226
DATA3	T11, B11	10	I	0.295	0.750, 1.226
QOUT0	T6, B6	6	O	1.660	1.353, 0.260
QOUT1	T8, B8	7	O	1.660	1.353, 0.260
QOUT2	T10, B10	13	O	1.660	1.353, 0.260
QOUT3	T12, B12	14	O	1.669	1.353, 0.260
COBAR	T13, B13	20	O	1.384	0.420, 0.420
P1	L1, R1		P	6.748	0.0, 0.0
G1	L2, R2		G	4.994	0.0, 0.0
P2	L3, R3		P	9.226	0.0, 0.0
G2	L4, R4		G	6.169	0.0, 0.0

RELEASE 5.0

PAGE NO.   4200 − 1

3 MICRON CMOS/BULK CELL FAMILY -CMOS3-	4200 4 BIT U/D COUNTER CELL HEIGHT 363 WIDTH 1128	DATE: 4/10/86 REVISION: -

ABBREVIATED TRUTH TABLE

CLK	RSET	SEL1	SEL2	OPERATING MODE	Q0
*	0	*	*	RESET	0
\	1	0	0	PRESET (LOAD)	LOAD WORD A
\	1	0	1	INCREMENT (COUNT UP)	COUNTING UP
\	1	1	0	DECREMENT (COUNT DOWN)	COUNTS DOWN
\	1	1	1	HOLD (STOP COUNT)	HOLDS

* = Don't Care, \ = Negative edge of clock.

QUICK REFERENCE TIMING

VDD = 5 volts
C(load) = 1.5 picofarads
Input trans time = 30 nsec.
Worst case processing

CLOCK --> Q3
  DELAY 0 --> 1 = 30.20 nsec.
  TRANS = 25.20 nsec.
RESET --> Q3
  DELAY 1 --> 0 = 40.68 nsec.
  TRANS = 38.49 nsec.

RELEASE 5.0

SCHEMATIC

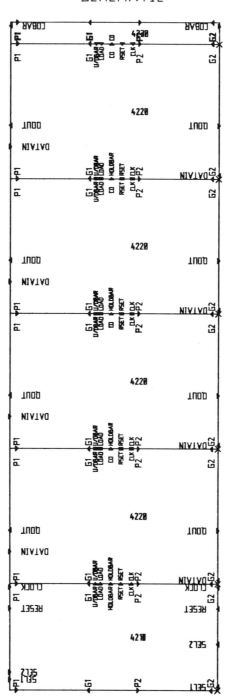

Consult the MSI function user's guide for the conditions under which these switching characteristics were determined and for guidance on their interpretation. Cload has the units of picofarads and the results are in nanoseconds.

SPECIAL TIMING

```
Data Setup Time . . . . . . . . =    9.89 nanoseconds
Data Hold Time  . . . . . . . . =    6.00 nanoseconds
Control Setup Time  . . . . . . =   16.10 nanoseconds
Control Hold Time . . . . . . . =    0.00 nanoseconds
Minimum Clock Pulse Width . . . =   30.00 nanoseconds
Maximum Clock Rise Time . . . . =  200.00 nanoseconds
Minimum Reset Pulse Width . . . =   20.00 nanoseconds
Reset Hold Time . . . . . . . . =    8.00 nanoseconds
```

SWITCHING CHARACTERISTICS

CLOCK --> Q3		Worst Case		Best Case
0 --> 1	Delay =	2.08(Cload) + 19.66	OR	2.76(Cload) + 7.87
	Trans =	2.92(Cload) + 20.82	OR	3.11(Cload) + 7.81
1 --> 0	Delay =	1.84(Cload) + 27.44	OR	2.46(Cload) + 11.00
	Trans =	5.36(Cload) + 14.11	OR	2.38(Cload) + 7.38

RESET --> Q3		Worst Case		Best Case
1 --> 0	Delay =	1.78(Cload) + 38.01	OR	1.08(Cload) + 14.33
	Trans =	5.10(Cload) + 30.84	OR	3.86(Cload) + 19.38

OUTLINE

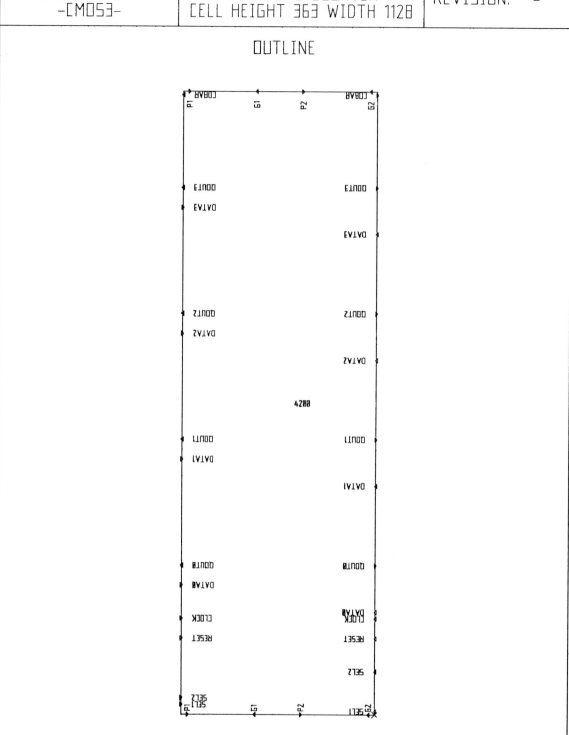

3 MICRON CMOS/BULK CELL FAMILY -CMOS3-	4200 4 BIT U/D COUNTER CELL HEIGHT 363 WIDTH 1128	DATE: 4/10/86 REVISION: -

```
Time(4200)     =   Time(4210)  +  Time(4220's)     +  Time(4230)
Time(N,Cload)  =   [A(N) + B]  +  [C(Cload) + D]   +      0
```

CLOCK --> Q

Worst Case

		A	B	C	D
0 --> 1	Delay	0.45	5.87	2.08	11.89
	Trans	1.50	2.41	2.93	12.41
1 --> 0	Delay	0.40	5.56	1.84	20.28
	Trans	1.23	2.26	5.36	6.93

Best Case

		A	B	C	D
0 --> 1	Delay	0.27	2.39	2.76	4.40
	Trans	0.96	1.29	3.11	2.38
1 --> 0	Delay	0.24	2.30	2.46	7.74
	Trans	0.83	1.18	2.38	2.80

```
Time(4200)     =   Time(4210)  +  Time(4220's)     +  Time(4230)
Time(N,Cload)  =   [A(N) + B]  +     [C]           +  [D(Cload) + E]
```

CLOCK --> COBAR

Worst Case

		A	B	C	D	E
0 --> 1	Delay	0.45	5.87	24.10	1.04	1.80
	Trans	1.50	2.41	4.90	3.55	2.26
1 --> 0	Delay	0.40	5.56	31.58	0.84	2.14
	Trans	1.23	2.26	3.60	2.67	2.18

Best Case

		A	B	C	D	E
0 --> 1	Delay	0.27	2.39	9.06	0.67	0.67
	Trans	0.96	1.27	2.60	2.52	0.69
1 --> 0	Delay	0.24	2.30	12.12	0.57	0.67
	Trans	0.83	1.18	2.14	2.14	0.53

Note: Data is assumed to be available at N-bit stage.

545

```
Time(4200)      =  Time(4210)   +   Time(4220's)    +   Time(4230)
Time(N,Cload)   =  [A(N) + B]   +   [C(Cload) + D]  +        0
```

RESET --> Q

Worst Case

		A	B	C	D
1 --> 0	Delay	1.26	7.11	1.78	25.86
	Trans	5.65	0.99	5.10	7.22

Best Case

		A	B	C	D
1 --> 0	Delay	1.03	2.57	1.08	7.64
	Trans	4.21	0.25	3.86	2.29

```
Time(4200)      =  Time(4210)   +   Time(4220's)    +   Time(4230)
Time(N,Cload)   =  [A(N) + B]   +       [C]         +   [D(Cload)+ E]
```

RESET --> COBAR

Worst Case

		A	B	C	D	E
1 --> 0	Delay	1.26	7.11	18.29	0.84	2.14
	Trans	5.65	6.99	6.44	2.67	2.18

Best Case

		A	B	C	D	E
1 --> 0	Delay	1.03	2.57	5.37	0.57	0.67
	Trans	4.21	0.25	3.43	2.14	0.53

3 MICRON CMOS/BULK CELL FAMILY —CMOS3—	4210 COUNTER FUNCTION SELECT CELL HEIGHT 363 WIDTH 180	DATE: 4/10/86 REVISION: –

RELATED CELL TYPES: 4200, 4220, 4230

The 4210, used in conjunction with the 4220 and 4230, makes an n-bit up/down counter (see the 4200 for an example). Its main purpose is to determine the operating mode of the counter. To do this it uses two control lines SEL1 and SEL2. The operating modes are as follows; preset, increment, decrement, or hold. It also buffers the clock and reset signals.

TERMINAL INFORMATION

ETER NAME	PHYSICAL NAME(S)	LOGICV FIELD	FUNCTION CODE	CAPACITANCE (pfarads)	RESISTANCE(S) (Kohms)
SEL1	T1, B1	3	I	0.368	0.750, 0.994
SEL2	T2, B2	4	I	0.397	0.750, 1.090
RESET	T3, B3	2	I	0.267	0.750, 1.170
CLOCK	T4, B4	1	I	0.272	1.166, 0.750
U/DBAR	R3	7	O	0.621	0.810
LOAD	R4	13	O	0.598	1.050
HOLDBAR	R5	6	O	0.534	1.020
RSET	R6	14	O	0.497	1.140
CLK	R7	20	O	0.469	0.810
P1	L1, R1	–	P	1.712	0.0, 0.0
G1	L2, R2	–	G	1.167	0.0, 0.0
P2	L3, R8	–	P	1.398	0.0, 0.0
G2	L4, R9	–	G	0.977	0.0, 0.0

RELEASE 5.0

SCHEMATIC

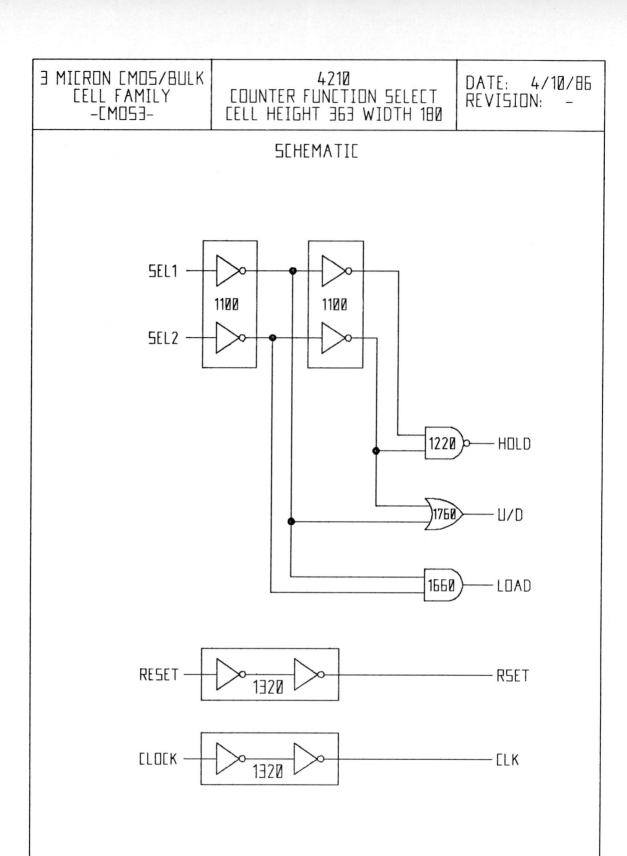

OUTLINE

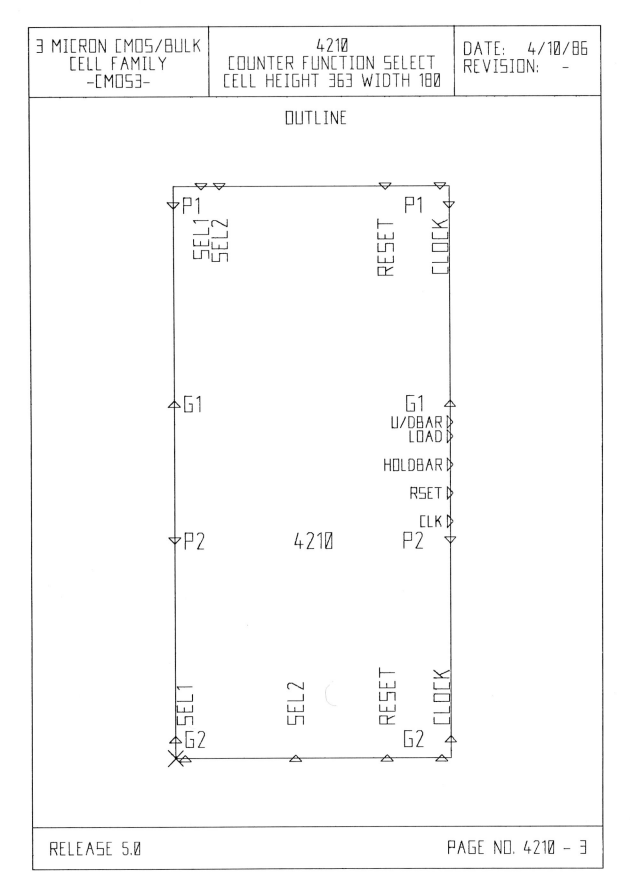

SWITCHING CHARACTERISTICS

Consult the MSI function user's guide for the conditions under which these switching characteristics were determined and for guidance on their interpretation. Cload has the units of picofarads and the results are in nanoseconds.

```
RESET --> RSET         Worst Case                  Best Case

0 --> 1  Delay =   2.72(Cload) +  6.08   OR   1.81(Cload) +  2.31
         Trans =   9.91(Cload) +  1.35   OR   6.98(Cload) +  0.39
1 --> 0  Delay =   1.88(Cload) +  7.11   OR   1.53(Cload) +  2.57
         Trans =   8.43(Cload) +  0.99   OR   6.28(Cload) +  0.25


CLOCK --> CLK          Worst Case                  Best Case

0 --> 1  Delay =   2.51(Cload) +  5.87   OR   1.49(Cload) +  2.29
         Trans =   8.31(Cload) +  2.41   OR   5.36(Cload) +  1.27
1 --> 0  Delay =   2.21(Cload) +  5.56   OR   1.31(Cload) +  2.30
         Trans =   6.81(Cload) +  2.26   OR   4.63(Cload) +  1.18


SEL1 --> LOAD          Worst Case                  Best Case

0 --> 1  Delay =   2.46(Cload) +  9.01   OR   1.65(Cload) +  3.71
         Trans =   9.01(Cload) +  1.44   OR   6.40(Cload) +  0.38
1 --> 0  Delay =   1.93(Cload) +  9.39   OR   1.42(Cload) +  3.66
         Trans =   7.08(Cload) +  0.91   OR   5.53(Cload) +  0.15
```

MOSTRAN RESULTS

RESET---> RSET	Worst Case		Best Case	
	N=4 (2.68)	N=16 (10.72)	N=4 (2.68)	N=16 (10.72)
0 --> 1 Delay	13.38	35.28	7.15	21.67
Trans	27.91	107.58	19.09	75.18
1 --> 0 Delay	12.14	27.24	6.67	18.96
Trans	23.58	91.35	17.05	67.44

CLOCK --> CLK	Worst Case		Best Case	
	N=4 (0.72)	N=16 (2.88)	N=4 (0.72)	N=16 (2.88)
0 --> 1 Delay	7.68	13.11	3.36	6.58
Trans	8.40	26.36	5.13	16.70
1 --> 0 Delay	7.15	11.93	3.25	6.09
Trans	7.16	21.86	4.51	14.51

SEL1 --> LOAD	Worst Case		Best Case	
	N=4 (1.72)	N=16 (6.88)	N=4 (1.72)	N=16 (6.88)
0 --> 1 Delay	13.23	25.95	6.55	15.07
Trans	16.93	63.40	11.35	44.35
1 --> 0 Delay	12.71	22.67	6.10	13.42
Trans	13.09	49.64	9.66	38.20

SEL1 --> U/DBAR	Worst Case		Best Case	
	N=4 (0.96)	N=16 (3.84)	N=4 (0.96)	N=16 (3.84)
0 --> 1 Delay	13.28	19.08	5.79	9.55
Trans	8.44	28.93	5.26	19.64
1 --> 0 Delay	11.85	17.73	4.99	8.40
Trans	7.59	24.93	4.85	17.64

SEL1 --> HOLDBAR	Worst Case		Best Case	
	N=4 (2.44)	N=16 (9.76)	N=4 (2.44)	N=16 (9.76)
0 --> 1 Delay	15.49	35.76	7.80	20.28
Trans	25.71	98.28	16.68	65.71
1 --> 0 Delay	16.10	35.46	7.71	19.62
Trans	23.68	90.09	15.51	61.19

NOTE: Transition times have been multiplied by 1.25 to compensate for the measurements taken at the 80% of the signal swing.

3 MICRON CMOS/BULK CELL FAMILY −CMOS3−	4220 ONE BIT COUNTER SLICE CELL HEIGHT 363 WIDTH 228	DATE: 4/10/86 REVISION: −

RELATED CELL TYPES: 4210, 4220, 4230

The 4220 is one bit of a synchronous u/d counter. To function it requires five control signals; HOLDBAR, LOAD, U/DBAR, RSET and CLK (for more information on these see the 4210). In addition to the control signals, the 4220 has a data input (used in the load mode) and provides the user with the Q output of the counter. Note that the 4220 is capable of being cascaded with other 4220s to form an n-bit counter.

TERMINAL INFORMATION

ETER NAME	PHYSICAL NAME(S)	LOGICV FIELD	FUNCTION CODE	CAPACITANCE (pfarads)	RESISTANCE(S) (Kohms)
DATAIN	T1, B1	1	I	0.378	0.750, 1.226
U/DBAR	L3, R3	2	I	0.301	0.780, 0.780
LOAD	L4, R4	3	I	0.497	0.810, 0.810
HOLDBAR	L5	4	I	0.725	0.960
RSET	L6, R6	5	I	0.776	0.0 , 0.960
CLK	L7, R7	8	I	0.237	0.780, 0.780
QOUT	T2, B2	6	O	1.743	1.353, 0.260
CO	R5	7	O	0.523	0.810
P1	L1, R1	−	P	1.930	0.0, 0.0
G1	L2, R2	−	G	1.492	0.0, 0.0
P2	L8, R8	−	P	1.851	0.0, 0.0
G2	L9, R9	−	G	1.244	0.0, 0.0

RELEASE 5.0   PAGE NO.   4220 − 1

SCHEMATIC

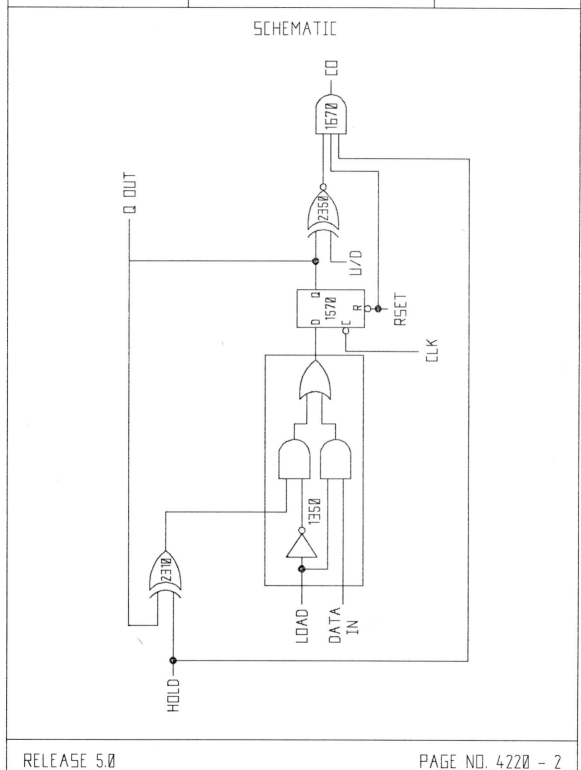

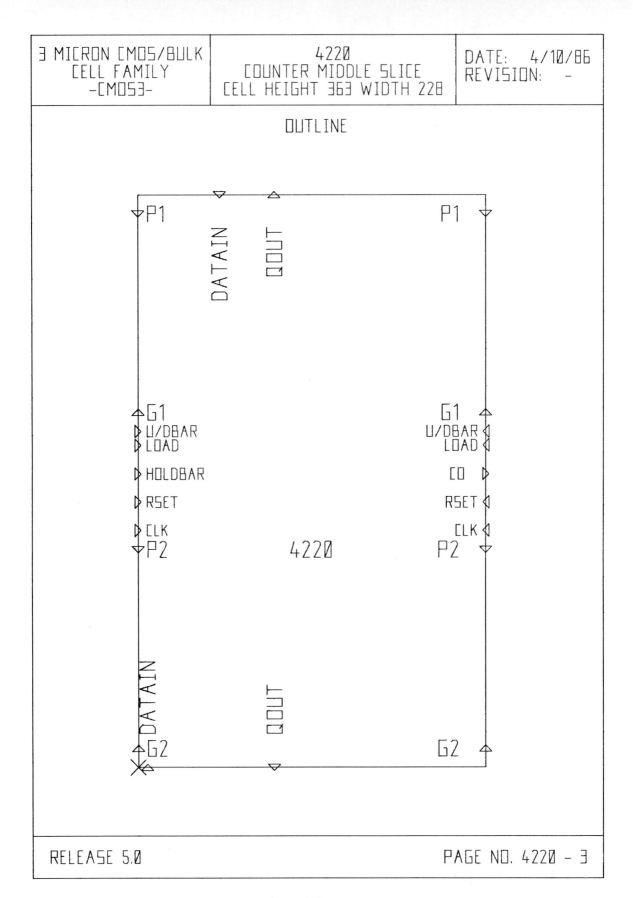

3 MICRON CMOS/BULK CELL FAMILY -CMOS3-	4220 COUNTER MIDDLE SLICE CELL HEIGHT 363 WIDTH 228	DATE: 4/10/86 REVISION: -

OUTLINE

P1   P1

DATAIN

QOUT

G1   G1
U/DBAR   U/DBAR
LOAD   LOAD

HOLDBAR   CO

RSET   RSET

CLK   CLK
P2   P2

4220

DATAIN

QOUT

G2   G2

SWITCHING CHARACTERISTICS

Consult the MSI function user's guide for the conditions under which these switching characteristics were determined and for guidance on their interpretation. Cload has the units of picofarads and the results are in nanoseconds.

```
    CLK --> QOUT        Worst Case              Best Case

0 --> 1  Delay =   2.08(Cload) + 11.99  OR   1.28(Cload) +   4.40
         Trans =   2.93(Cload) + 12.41  OR   4.61(Cload) +   2.38
1 --> 0  Delay =   1.84(Cload) + 20.28  OR   1.11(Cload) +   7.74
         Trans =   5.26(Cload) +  6.93  OR   3.82(Cload) +   2.88


    CLK --> CO          Worst Case              Best Case

0 --> 1  Delay =  11.59(Cload) + 20.62  OR   2.76(Cload) +   8.23
         Trans =   8.08(Cload) +  2.48  OR   3.11(Cload) +   1.67
1 --> 0  Delay =   8.68(Cload) + 28.98  OR   2.46(Cload) +  11.38
         Trans =   5.76(Cload) +  1.87  OR   2.38(Cload) +   1.43


   RSET --> QOUT        Worst Case              Best Case

1 --> 0  Delay =   1.78(Cload) + 25.86  OR   1.08(Cload) +   7.64
         Trans =   5.10(Cload) +  7.22  OR   3.86(Cload) +   2.29


   RSET --> CO          Worst Case              Best Case

1 --> 0  Delay =   2.76(Cload) + 17.46  OR   1.46(Cload) +   4.93
         Trans =   4.76(Cload) +  5.01  OR   3.54(Cload) +   2.37
```

3 MICRON CMOS/BULK CELL FAMILY -CMOS3-	4220 ONE BIT COUNTER SLICE CELL HEIGHT 363 WIDTH 228	DATE: 4/10/86 REVISION: -

MOSTRAN RESULTS

CLK --> QOUT		Worst Case		Best Case	
		1.5 pF	4.0 pF	1.5 pF	4.0 pF
0 --> 1	Delay	15.10	20.29	6.31	9.50
	Trans	16.81	24.14	9.29	20.81
1 --> 0	Delay	23.03	27.62	9.41	12.19
	Trans	14.81	27.95	8.60	18.14

CLK --> CO		Worst Case		Best Case	
		.30 pF	.670 pF	.30 pF	.67 pF
0 --> 1	Delay	24.31	28.39	9.06	10.08
	Trans	4.89	7.86	2.60	4.68
1 --> 0	Delay	31.58	34.79	12.12	13.03
	Trans	3.60	5.73	2.14	3.78

RSET --> QOUT		Worst Case		Best Case	
		1.5 pF	4.0 pF	1.5 pF	4.0 pF
1 --> 0	Delay	28.54	33.00	9.25	11.94
	Trans	14.88	27.64	8.08	17.73

RSET --> CO		Worst Case		Best Case	
		.30 pF	.67 pF	.30 pF	.67 pF
1 --> 0	Delay	18.29	19.31	5.37	5.91
	Trans	6.44	8.20	3.43	4.74

NOTE: Transition times have been multiplied by 1.25 to compensate for the measurements taken at 80% of the signal swing.
     Different capacitive loads were used on the COUT output. These reflect the two different slices that the 4220 drives.

RELATED CELL TYPES: 4200, 4210, 4220

The 4230 is the last stage in the synchronous counter assembly. Its only function is to invert the carry out signal to make this function compatible with its ECL equivalent.

TERMINAL INFORMATION

ETER NAME	PHYSICAL NAME(S)	LOGICV FIELD	FUNCTION CODE	CAPACITANCE (pfarads)	RESISTANCE(S) (Kohms)
CO	L3	1	I	0.529	0.780
COBAR	T1, B1	6	O	1.384	0.420, 0.420
P1	L1, R1	-	P	0.462	0.0, 0.0
G1	L2, R2	-	G	0.254	0.0, 0.0
P2	L4, R3	-	P	0.462	0.0, 0.0
G2	L5, R4	-	G	0.254	0.0, 0.0

SCHEMATIC

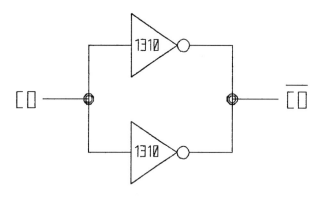

OUTLINE

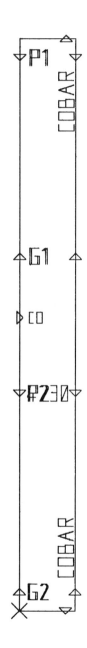

SWITCHING CHARACTERISTICS

Consult the MSI function user's guide for the conditions under which these switching characteristics were determined and for guidance on their interpretation. Cload has the units of picofarads and the results are in nanoseconds.

```
    CO --> COBAR        Worst Case              Best Case

0 --> 1  Delay =  1.04(Cload) +  1.80  OR   0.67(Cload) +  0.67
         Trans =  3.55(Cload) +  2.26  OR   2.52(Cload) +  0.69
1 --> 0  Delay =  0.84(Cload) +  2.14  OR   0.57(Cload) +  0.67
         Trans =  2.67(Cload) +  2.18  OR   2.14(Cload) +  0.53
```

MOSTRAN RESULTS

CO --> COBAR		Worst Case		Best Case	
		1.5 pF	4.0 pF	1.5 pF	4.0 pF
0 --> 1	Delay	3.36	5.96	1.68	3.36
	Trans	7.58	16.45	4.48	10.79
1 --> 0	Delay	3.40	5.50	1.52	2.94
	Trans	6.18	12.85	3.75	9.11

RELATED CELL TYPES: 4320, 4330, 4340, 4350.

   The 4300 is a 4-bit look-ahead adder. As such, it generates all internal carries at the same time, eliminating propagation delay. The carry-out is also generated this way. Essentially, there are only three gate delays from Y and Z inputs to S outputs. The 4300 can be used with the 4310, 4360, and the 4370 to create larger adders with equivalent time savings.

   The 4300 adds two 4-bit binary numbers. Y1 and Z1 are the least significant bits, incrementing to Y4 and Z4, which are the most significant bits.

   On the timing pages, timing for Y3 to S3 show the delay from an input to its sum. Y1 to S3 shows the delay through internal logic, as does the delay from A1 to COUT.

TERMINAL INFORMATION

ETER NAME	PHYSICAL NAME(S)	LOGICV FIELD	FUNCTION CODE	CAPACITANCE (pfarads)	RESISTANCE(S) (Kohms)
Y1	T1, B1	1	I	0.660	2.52, 2.52
Y2	T6, B6	4	I	0.683	2.52, 2.52
Y3	T11, B11	8	I	0.559	2.52, 2.52
Y4	T13, B13	10	I	0.573	2.61, 2.61
Z1	T2, B2	2	I	0.567	2.58, 2.58
Z2	T7, B7	5	I	0.601	2.64, 2.64
Z3	T12, B12	9	I	0.679	2.52, 2.52
Z4	T14, B14	11	I	0.660	2.52, 2.52
C1	T4, B4	3	I	0.268	1.170, .750
COUT	T10, B10	20	O	0.577	0.420, 0.840
S1	T3, B3	6	O	1.023	0.930, 1.530
S2	T5, B5	7	O	0.999	1.350, 0.930
S3	T9, B9	13	O	1.031	1.530, 0.930
S4	T8, B8	14	O	1.032	1.380, 0.930
P1	L1, R1	–	P	4.589	0.0, 0.0
P2	L3, R3	–	P	5.602	0.0, 0.0
G1	L2, R2	–	G	3.855	0.0, 0.0
G2	L4, R4	–	G	4.119	0.0, 0.0

TRUTH TABLE

The truth table for the 4300 is very lengthy. Basically it works as a binary adder. S is the sum of Y and Z and any carry bit from a previous stage. Or

$$Si = [(Yi)exor(Zi)]exor(Ci)$$

where i = 1,2,3,4
exor = Exclusive Or
Ci is either carry in, or generated by a pervious stage.

Y_i	Z_i	C_i	S_i
0	0	0	0
0	1	1	0
1	0	1	0
1	1	0	0
0	0	1	1
0	1	0	1
1	0	0	1
1	1	1	1
all others			X

To find out when C2 is unknown, refer to the 4320. Likewise, for C3, refer to the 4330, and for C4, refer to the 4340.

X = Don't know

QUICK REFERENCE TIMING

VDD = 5 volts   Y1 --> S3 (T9) = 26.31 nsec.
C(load) = 1.5 picofarads   Y1 --> COUT (B10) = 34.40 nsec.
Input trans time = 30 nsec.
Worst case processing

SCHEMATIC

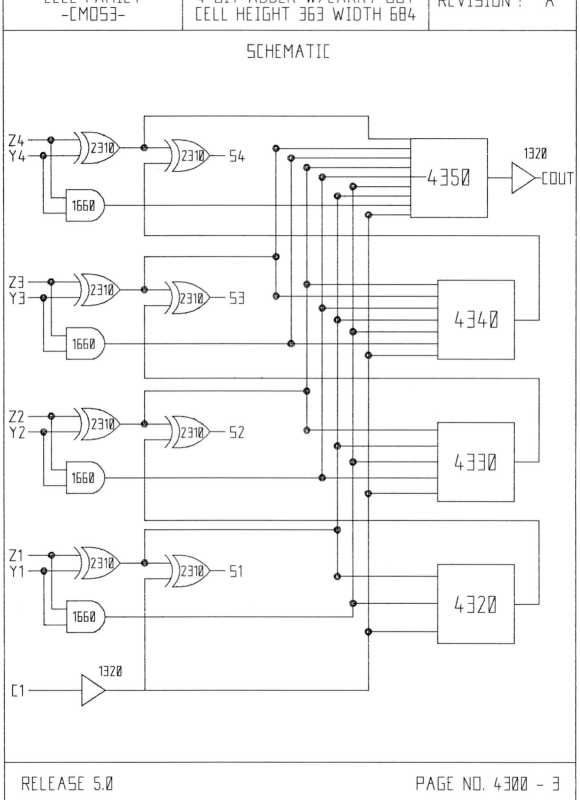

SWITCHING CHARACTERISTICS

Consult the MSI function user's guide for the conditions under which these switching characteristics were determined and for guidance on their interpretation. Cload has the units of picofarads and the results are in nanoseconds.

```
Y3 --> S3 (T9)          Worst Case              Best Case

0 --> 1  Delay =    3.28(Cload) + 15.15  OR   1.86(Cload) +  6.18
         Trans =   11.07(Cload) +  5.55  OR   6.90(Cload) +  2.00
1 --> 0  Delay =    3.18(Cload) + 14.46  OR   1.71(Cload) +  5.89
         Trans =   10.20(Cload) +  4.12  OR   6.38(Cload) +  1.24




Y1 --> S3 (T9)          Worst Case              Best Case

0 --> 1  Delay =    3.30(Cload) + 21.36  OR   1.87(Cload) +  8.75
         Trans =   11.03(Cload) +  5.91  OR   6.91(Cload) +  2.10
1 --> 0  Delay =    2.66(Cload) + 19.31  OR   1.62(Cload) +  7.78
         Trans =    9.32(Cload) +  4.30  OR   6.10(Cload) +  1.32




Y1 --> COUT (B10)       Worst Case              Best Case

0 --> 1  Delay =    2.49(Cload) + 30.66  OR   1.50(Cload) + 12.97
         Trans =    8.71(Cload) +  1.84  OR   5.74(Cload) +  0.54
1 --> 0  Delay =    2.12(Cload) + 32.07  OR   1.31(Cload) + 13.27
         Trans =    7.12(Cload) +  1.61  OR   4.97(Cload) +  0.44
```

OUTLINE

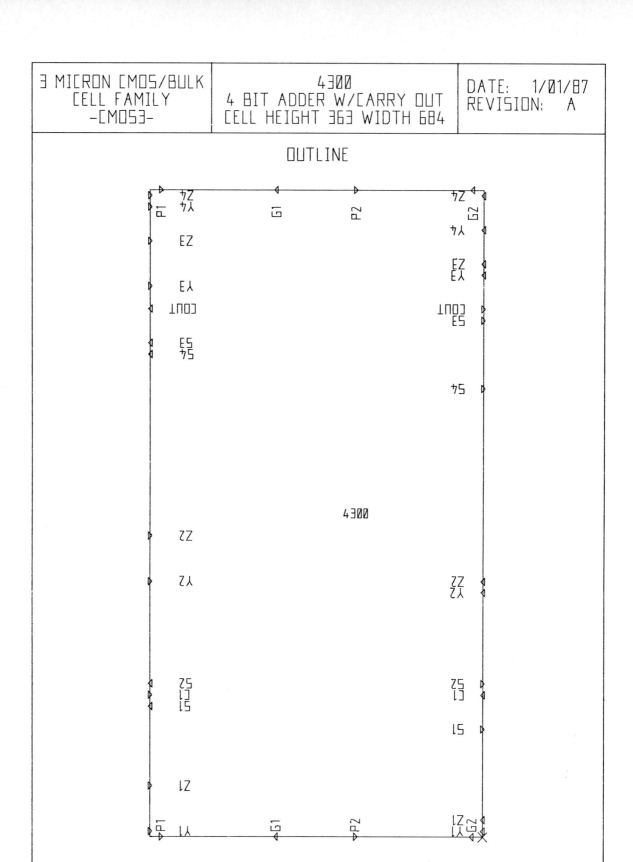

MOSTRAN RESULTS

Y3 --> S3 (B9)

		Worst Case		Best Case	
		1.5 pF	4.0 pF	1.5 pF	4.0 pF
0 --> 1	Delay	20.07	28.27	8.96	13.60
	Trans	22.16	49.84	12.35	29.60
1 --> 0	Delay	19.23	27.19	8.43	12.75
	Trans	19.41	44.90	10.81	26.76

Y1 --> S3 (B9)

		Worst Case		Best Case	
		1.5 pF	4.0 pF	1.5 pF	4.0 pF
0 --> 1	Delay	26.31	34.57	11.54	16.20
	Trans	22.46	50.04	12.46	29.73
1 --> 0	Delay	23.29	29.92	10.20	14.23
	Trans	18.28	41.58	10.48	25.74

Y1 --> COUT (B10)

		Worst Case		Best Case	
		1.5 pF	4.0 pF	1.5 pF	4.0 pF
0 --> 1	Delay	34.38	40.60	15.23	19.00
	Trans	14.91	36.69	9.14	23.48
1 --> 0	Delay	35.25	40.54	15.24	18.52
	Trans	12.30	30.11	7.89	20.31

Please note that all transition times have been multiplied by 1.25 to compensate for measurements taken at 80% of the signal swing.

RELATED CELL TYPES: 4320, 4330, 4340.

The 4310 is a 4 bit adder with look-ahead carry outputs. The 4310 can be used with the 4300, 4360, and the 4370 to make larger adders. The GEN5 and PRO5 outputs can be used with either the 4360 or the 4370, using any of the GENn or PROn inputs, where n is the number of the adder (the first adder is #1; the second, #2).

The 4310 performs binary addition on two 4-bit binary numbers. Y1 and Z1 are the least significant bits, incrementing to the most significant bits, Y4 and Z4.

For timing, Z4 to S4 delays show an input to its sum, Z1 to S4 is the longest path of internal delays to a sum, Y1 to GEN5 is the longest path to the GEN5 output, and Z1 to PRO5 also is the longest path.

TERMINAL INFORMATION

ETER NAME	PHYSICAL NAME(S)		LOGICV FIELD	FUNCTION CODE	CAPACITANCE (pfarads)	RESISTANCE(S) (Kohms)	
Y1	T1,	B1	1	I	0.660	2.520,	2.520
Z1	T2,	B2	2	I	0.567	2.580,	2.580
C1	T4,	B4	3	I	0.280	0.750,	1.230
Y2	T6,	B6	4	I	0.675	2.580,	2.580
Z2	T7,	B7	5	I	0.606	2.700,	2.700
Y3	T8,	B8	8	I	0.691	2.670,	2.670
Z3	T9,	B9	9	I	0.576	2.580,	2.580
Y4	T13,	B13	10	I	0.705	2.610,	2.610
Z4	T14,	B14	11	I	0.619	2.520,	2.520
S1	T3,	B3	6	O	1.011	0.930,	1.410
S2	T5,	B5	7	O	1.008	1.380,	0.930
S3	T10,	B10	13	O	1.032	1.410,	0.930
S4	T11,	B11	14	O	1.032	1.410,	0.930
GEN5	T12,	B12	20	O	0.619	0.870,	0.420
PRO5	T15,	B15	21	O	0.758	1.410,	1.890
P1	L1,	R1	–	P	5.377	0.0,	0.0
G1	L2,	R2	–	G	4.156	0.0,	0.0
P2	L3,	R3	–	P	5.622	0.0,	0.0
G2	L4,	R4	–	G	4.139	0.0,	0.0

ABBREVIATED TRUTH TABLE

The 4310, as an adder, works just like the 4300. Since the truth table is very lengthy, refer to the 4300 for S outputs. The PRO5 output is generated from this equation:

$$PRO5 = (PRO1)(PRO2)(PRO3)(PRO4)$$

Where $PROi = (Yi) exor (Zi)$

Y i	Z i		PRO i
0	0		0
1	1		0
0	1		1
1	0		1
*	X		X
X	*		X

PRO1	PRO2	PRO3	PRO4		PRO5
0	*	*	*		0
*	0	*	*		0
*	*	0	*		0
*	*	*	0		0
1	1	1	1		1
all others					X

where i = 1,2,3,4

For GEN5, generated by the 4340, refer to the 4340.

* = Don't Care, X = Don't know

QUICK REFERENCE TIMING

VDD = 5 volts
C(load) = 1.5 picofarads
Input trans time = 30 nsec.
Worst case processing

Z1 --> S4 (T11) = 32.66 nsec.
Y1 --> GEN5 (T12) = 29.53 nsec.
Z1 --> PRO5 (B15) = 21.71 nsec.

SCHEMATIC

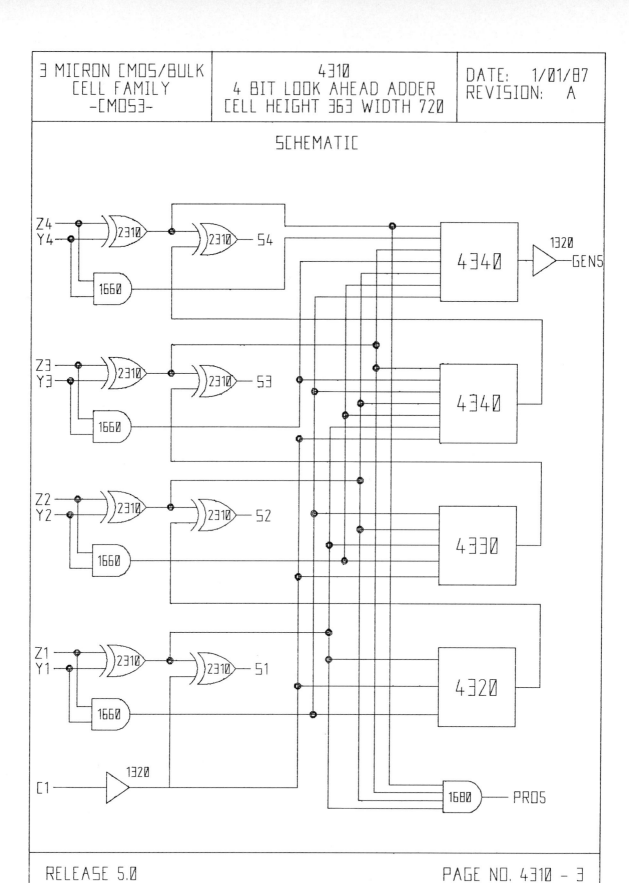

SWITCHING CHARACTERISTICS

Consult the MSI function user's guide for the conditions under which these switching characteristics were determined and for guidance on their interpretation. Cload has the units of picofarads and the results are in nanoseconds.

Z4 --> S4 (T11)   Worst Case   Best Case

```
0 --> 1  Delay =    2.79(Cload) + 17.77  OR   3.58(Cload) + 15.23
         Trans =   10.12(Cload) + 11.68  OR  12.78(Cload) +  7.67
1 --> 0  Delay =    2.97(Cload) + 14.90  OR   3.38(Cload) + 13.66
         Trans =    9.44(Cload) +  7.43  OR  11.86(Cload) +  3.80
```

Z1 --> S4 (T11)   Worst Case   Best Case

```
0 --> 1  Delay =    3.01(Cload) + 28.14  OR   3.61(Cload) + 25.90
         Trans =   10.27(Cload) +  8.92  OR  12.86(Cload) +  5.03
1 --> 0  Delay =    2.98(Cload) + 29.98  OR   3.41(Cload) + 28.58
         Trans =    9.42(Cload) +  7.31  OR  11.86(Cload) +  3.66
```

Y1 --> GEN5 (T12)   Worst Case   Best Case

```
0 --> 1  Delay =    4.27(Cload) + 23.12  OR   4.91(Cload) + 20.01
         Trans =    6.42(Cload) +  5.50  OR   8.84(Cload) +  1.89
1 --> 0  Delay =    1.68(Cload) + 24.40  OR   2.13(Cload) + 22.41
         Trans =    4.98(Cload) +  5.01  OR   7.24(Cload) +  1.62
```

Z1 --> PRO5 (B15)   Worst Case   Best Case

```
0 --> 1  Delay =    2.30(Cload) + 18.26  OR   3.01(Cload) + 15.84
         Trans =    8.36(Cload) +  6.12  OR  11.36(Cload) +  1.60
1 --> 0  Delay =    1.94(Cload) + 15.23  OR   2.64(Cload) + 13.41
         Trans =    7.16(Cload) +  5.31  OR  10.22(Cload) +  0.69
```

OUTLINE

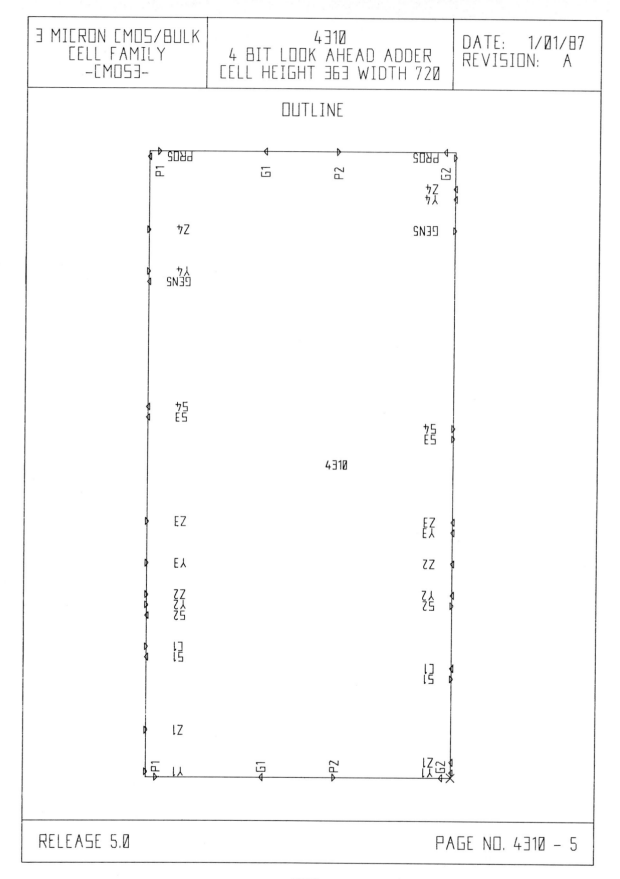

MOSTRAN RESULTS

$Z4 \rightarrow S4$ (T11)

	Worst Case		Best Case	
	1.5 pF	4.0 pF	1.5 pF	4.0 pF
0 --> 1 Delay	21.95	28.92	20.59	29.53
Trans	26.85	52.14	26.85	58.81
1 --> 0 Delay	19.51	26.93	18.73	27.17
Trans	21.59	45.19	21.59	51.24

$Z1 \rightarrow S4$ (T11)

	Worst Case		Best Case	
	1.5 pF	4.0 pF	1.5 pF	4.0 pF
0 --> 1 Delay	32.66	40.19	31.31	40.33
Trans	24.33	50.01	24.31	56.45
1 --> 0 Delay	34.46	41.93	33.69	42.20
Trans	21.45	45.01	21.44	51.08

$Y1 \rightarrow GEN5$ (T12)

	Worst Case		Best Case	
	1.5 pF	4.0 pF	1.5 pF	4.0 pF
0 --> 1 Delay	29.52	40.19	27.39	39.68
Trans	15.14	31.20	15.14	37.23
1 --> 0 Delay	27.08	31.47	25.59	30.90
Trans	12.48	24.93	12.48	30.58

$Z1 \rightarrow PRO5$ (B15)

	Worst Case		Best Case	
	1.5 pF	4.0 pF	1.5 pF	4.0 pF
0 --> 1 Delay	21.70	27.46	20.35	27.87
Trans	18.66	39.56	18.65	47.06
1 --> 0 Delay	18.13	22.96	17.36	23.95
Trans	16.04	33.93	16.03	41.59

Please note that all transition times have been multiplied by 1.25 to compensate for measurements taken at 80% of the signal swing.

RELATED CELL TYPES: 4300, 4310, 4360, 4370.

The 4320 is a multiplexer that generates the second carry bit for use in the look-ahead carry adders and the look-ahead carry units. The 4320 implements this equation:

$$C2 = [(PR1)nor(GN1)]nor[(GN1)nor(C1)]$$

where C1 is the Carry-in. PR1 and GN1 are either inputs, as for the 4360 and 4370, or are generated from Y1 and Z1 inputs, as with the 4300 and the 4310.

TERMINAL INFORMATION

ETER NAME	PHYSICAL NAME(S)	LOGICV FIELD	FUNCTION CODE	CAPACITANCE (pfarads)	RESISTANCE(S) (Kohms)
C1	T3, B3	3	I	0.237	0.750, 0.750
PR1	T4, B4	2	I	0.236	0.750, 0.750
GN1	T2, B2	1	I	0.245	0.750, 0.750
C2	T1, B1	6	O	0.515	0.750, 0.750
P	L1, R1	—	P	0.361	0.0, 0.0
G	L2, R2	—	G	0.508	0.0, 0.0

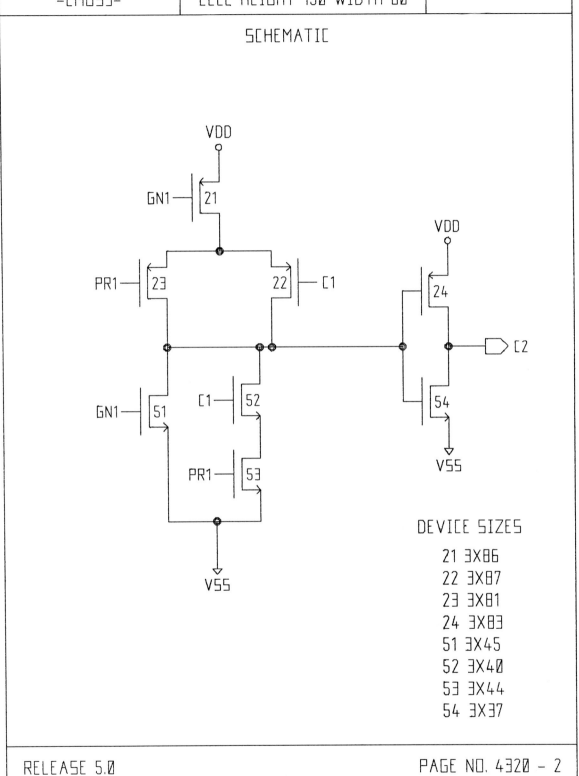

3 MICRON CMOS/BULK CELL FAMILY -CMOS3-	4320 C2 GENERATOR CELL HEIGHT 150 WIDTH 60	DATE: 1/01/87 REVISION: A

SCHEMATIC

VDD

GN1 — |21

PR1 — |23   22| — C1

VDD

|24

C2

GN1 — |51

C1 — |52

54|

PR1 — |53

VSS

VSS

DEVICE SIZES

21 3X86
22 3X87
23 3X81
24 3X83
51 3X45
52 3X40
53 3X44
54 3X37

RELEASE 5.0   PAGE NO. 4320 - 2

OUTLINE

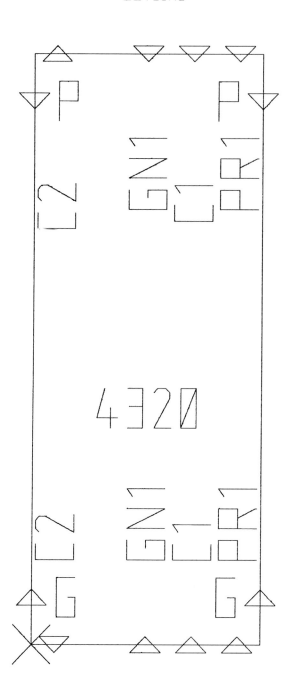

TRUTH TABLE

C 1	G N 1	P R 1		C 2
*	0	0		0
0	0	*		0
*	1	*		1
1	*	1		1
all others				X

Y 1	Z 1		G N 1
0	*		0
*	0		0
1	1		1
X	1/X		X
1	X		X

Y 1	Z 1		P R 1
0	0		0
1	1		0
0	1		1
1	0		1
X	*		X
*	X		X

* = Don't care, X = Don't know

RELATED CELL TYPES: 4300, 4310, 4360, 4370.

The 4330 is a multiplexer that generates the third carry bit for use in the look-ahead carry adders and the look-ahead carry units. The 4330 implements this equation:

$$C3 = [(C1)nor(GN2)nor(GN1)]nor[(GN2)nor(PR1)nor(GN1)]$$
$$nor[(GN2)nor(PR2)]$$

where C1 is the Carry-in. PR1, GN1, PR2, and GN2 are either inputs, as for the 4360 and 4370, or are generated from Y1, Z1, Y2, and Z2 inputs as with the 4300 and the 4310.

TERMINAL INFORMATION

ETER NAME	PHYSICAL NAME(S)	LOGICV FIELD	FUNCTION CODE	CAPACITANCE (pfarads)	RESISTANCE(S) (Kohms)
C1	T4, B4	5	I	0.206	0.750, 0.750
PR1	T5, B5	4	I	0.207	0.750, 0.750
GN1	T6, B6	3	I	0.238	0.750, 0.750
PR2	T3, B3	2	I	0.206	0.750, 0.750
GN2	T2, B2	1	I	0.214	0.750, 0.750
C3	T1, B1	6	O	0.554	0.750, 0.750
P	L1, R1	–	P	0.453	0.0, 0.0
G	L2, R2	–	G	0.678	0.0, 0.0

SCHEMATIC

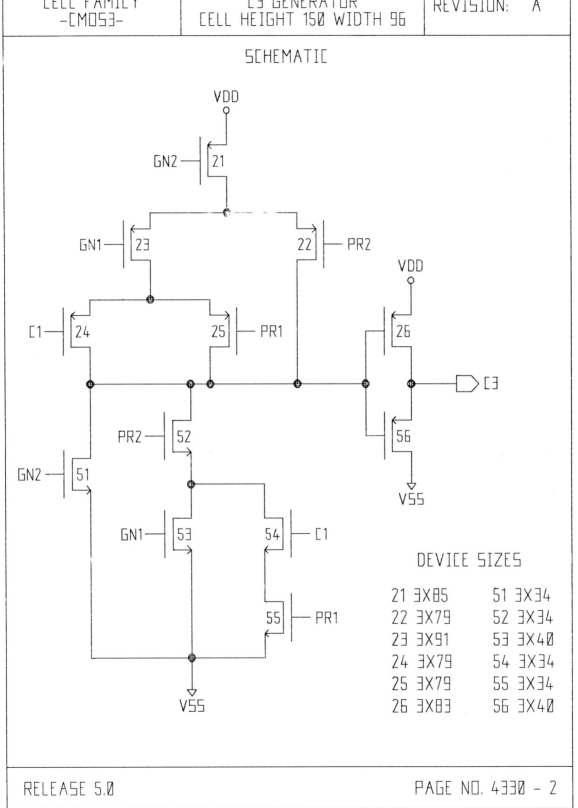

DEVICE SIZES

21 3X85	51 3X34
22 3X79	52 3X34
23 3X91	53 3X40
24 3X79	54 3X34
25 3X79	55 3X34
26 3X83	56 3X40

OUTLINE

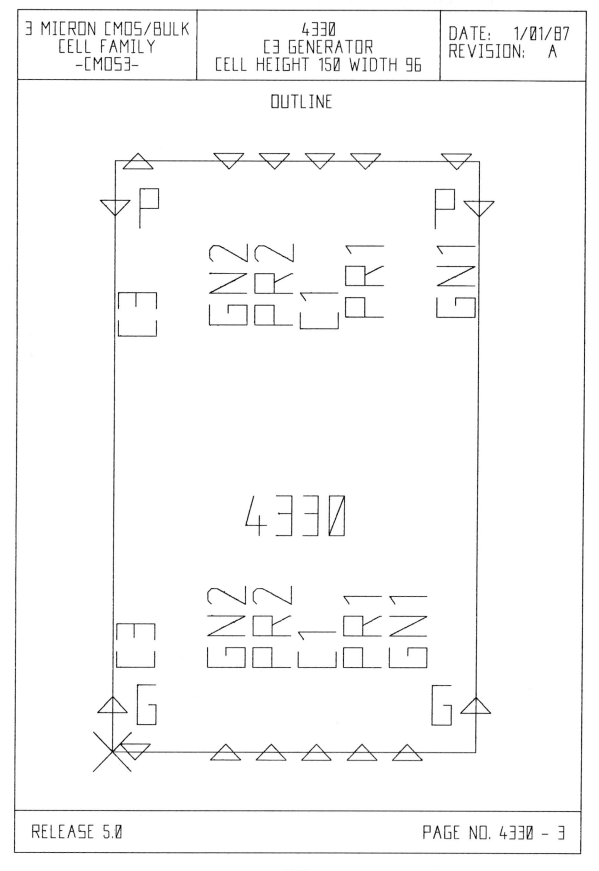

TRUTH TABLE

$GN2$	$PR2$	$GN1$	$PR1$	$C1$		$C3$
0	*	0	*	0		0
0	0	*	*	*		0
0	*	0	0	*		0
1	*	*	*	*		1
*	1	1	*	*		1
*	1	*	1	1		1
all others						X

Yi	Zi		GNi
0	*		0
*	0		0
1	1		1
X	1/X		X
1	X		X

Yi	Zi		PRi
0	0		0
1	1		0
0	1		1
1	0		1
X	*		X
X	X		X

* = Don't care,   X = Don't know,   i = 1,2

RELATED CELL TYPES: 4300, 4310, 4360, 4370.

The 4340 is a multiplexer that generates the fourth carry bit for use in the look-ahead carry adders and the look-ahead carry units. The 4330 implements this equation:

$$C4 =[(C1)nor(GN3)nor(GN2)nor(GN1)]$$
$$nor[(PR1)nor(GN3)nor(GN2)nor(GN1)]$$
$$nor[(GN2)nor(PR2)nor(GN3)]$$
$$nor[(GN3)nor(PR3)]$$

where C1 is the Carry-in. PR1, GN1, PR2, GN2, PR3, and GN3 are either inputs as for the 4360 and 4370, or are generated from Y1, Z1, Y2, Z2, Y3, and Z3 inputs as with the 4300 and the 4310.

TERMINAL INFORMATION

ETER NAME	PHYSICAL NAME(S)	LOGICV FIELD	FUNCTION CODE	CAPACITANCE (pfarads)	RESISTANCE(S) (Kohms)
C1	T7, B7	9	I	0.224	0.750, 0.750
PR1	T6, B6	8	I	0.222	0.750, 0.750
GN1	T5, B5	5	I	0.221	0.750, 0.750
PR2	T4, B4	4	I	0.219	0.750, 0.750
GN2	T8, B8	3	I	0.247	0.750, 0.750
PR3	T3, B3	2	I	0.221	0.750, 0.750
GN3	T2, B2	1	I	0.227	0.750, 0.750
C4	T1, B1	6	O	0.548	0.750, 0.750
P	L1, R1	–	P	0.532	0.0, 0.0
G	L2, R2	–	G	0.884	0.0, 0.0

SCHEMATIC

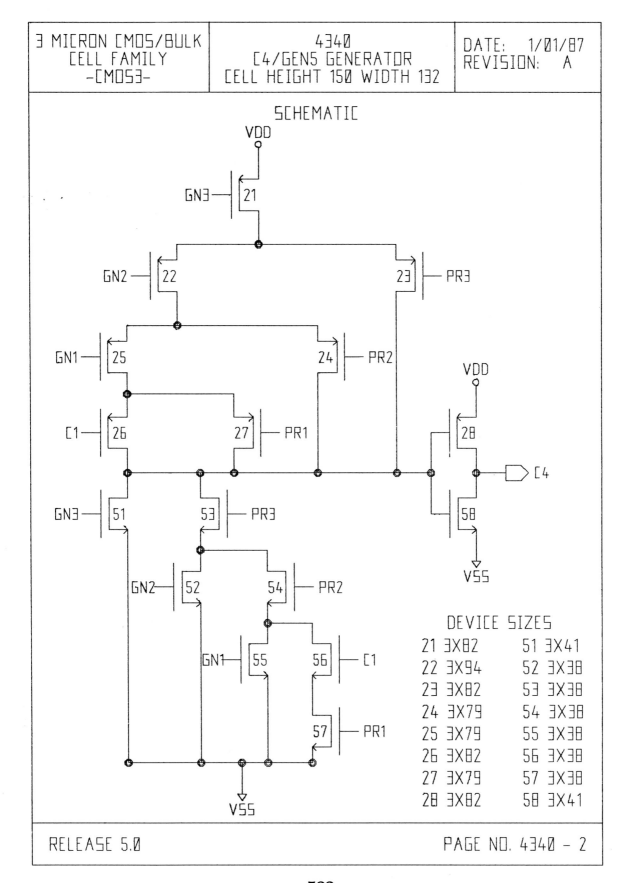

DEVICE SIZES

21 3X82	51 3X41
22 3X94	52 3X38
23 3X82	53 3X38
24 3X79	54 3X38
25 3X79	55 3X38
26 3X82	56 3X38
27 3X79	57 3X38
28 3X82	58 3X41

OUTLINE

TRUTH TABLE

GN3	PR3	GN2	PR2	GN1	PR1	C1	C4
0	0	*	*	*	*	*	0
0	*	0	0	*	*	*	0
0	*	0	*	0	0	*	0
0	*	0	*	0	*	0	0
1	*	*	*	*	*	*	1
*	1	1	*	*	*	*	1
*	1	*	1	1	*	*	1
*	1	*	1	*	1	1	1
all others							X

Yi	Zi	GNi
0	*	0
*	0	0
1	1	1
X	1/X	X
1	X	X

Yi	Zi	PRi
0	0	0
1	1	0
0	1	1
1	0	1
X	*	X
*	X	X

* = Don't Care, X = Don't know, i = 1,2,3

TRUTH TABLE

The 4340 is also used to generator GEN5 output. This truth table is for GEN5 output

GN4	PR4	GN3	PR3	GN2	PR2	GN1	GEN5
0	0	*	*	*	*	*	0
0	*	0	0	*	*	*	0
0	*	0	*	0	0	*	0
0	*	0	*	0	*	0	0
1	*	*	*	*	*	*	1
*	1	1	*	*	*	*	1
*	1	*	1	1	*	*	1
*	1	*	1	*	1	1	1
all others							X

Yi	Zi	GNi
0	*	0
*	0	0
1	1	1
X	1/X	X
1	X	X

Yi	Zi	PRi
0	0	0
1	1	0
0	1	1
1	0	1
X	*	X
*	X	X

* = Don't Care, X = Don't know, i = 1,2,3

RELATED CELL TYPES: 4300.

The 4350 is a Carry-out generator for the 4300 look-ahead adder. While carry out could be generated external to the adder by simple combinatorial logic, using the 4350 save three gate delays. The 4350 implements

$$COUT = GEN5 + (PRO5)(C1)$$

or more exactly

$$COUT = [(GN4)nor(GN3)nor(GN2)nor(GN1)nor(PR1)]$$
$$nor[(GN4)nor(GN3)nor(GN2)nor(GN1)nor(C1)]$$
$$nor[(GN4)nor(GN3)nor(GN2)nor(PR2)$$
$$nor[(GN4)nor(GN3)nor(PR3)]nor[(GN4)nor(PR4)]$$

where C1 is the Carry-in. PR1, GN1, PR2, GN2, PR3, GN3, PR4, and GN4 are either inputs as for the 4360 and 4370, or are generated from Y1, Z1, Y2, Z2, Y3, Z3, Y4, and Z4 inputs as with the 4300 and the 4310.

TERMINAL INFORMATION

ETER NAME	PHYSICAL NAME(S)	LOGICV FIELD	FUNCTION CODE	CAPACITANCE (pfarads)	RESISTANCE(S) (Kohms)
C1	T8, B8	11	I	0.230	0.750, 0.750
GN1	T6, B6	9	I	0.240	0.750, 0.750
PR1	T7, B7	10	I	0.233	0.750, 0.750
GN2	T5, B5	5	I	0.227	0.750, 0.750
PR2	T10,B10	8	I	0.222	0.750, 0.750
GN3	T9, B9	3	I	0.231	0.750, 0.750
PR3	T4, B4	4	I	0.220	0.750, 0.750
GN4	T2, B2	1	I	0.236	0.750, 0.750
PR4	T3, B3	2	I	0.219	0.750, 0.750
CO	T1, B1	6	O	0.544	0.750, 0.750
P	L1, R1	–	P	0.533	0.0, 0.0
G	L2, R2	–	G	1.169	0.0, 0.0

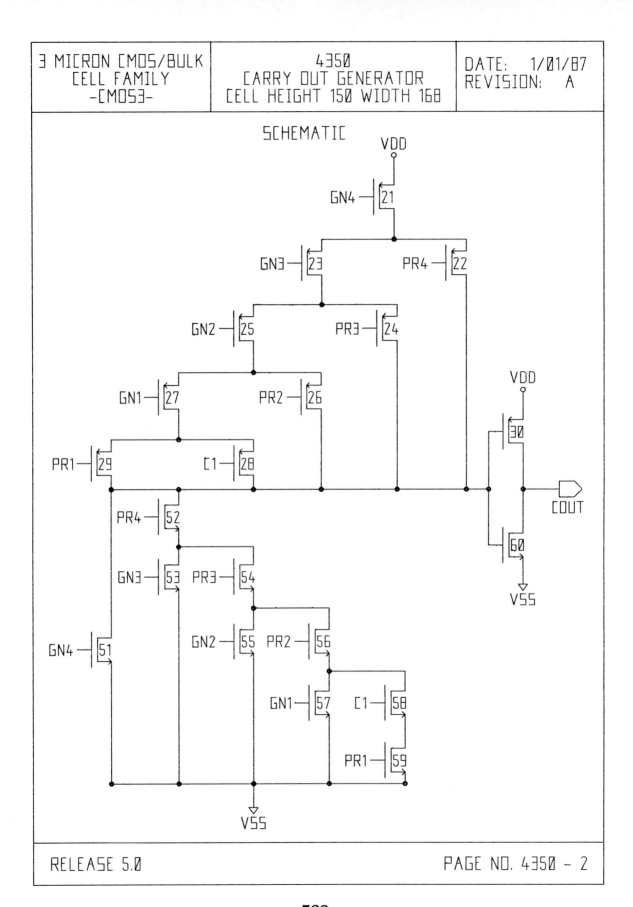

SCHEMATIC

SCHEMATIC CONTINUED

DEVICE SIZES

21 3X82	51 3X45
22 3X78	52 3X40
23 3X81	53 3X40
24 3X78	54 3X40
25 3X78	55 3X40
26 3X78	56 3X40
27 3X78	57 3X44
28 3X78	58 3X40
29 3X78	59 3X40
30 3X81	60 3X43

OUTLINE

4350

TRUTH TABLE

GN4	PR4	GN3	PR3	GN2	PR2	GN1	PR1	C1	COUT
0	0	*	*	*	*	*	*	*	0
0	*	0	0	*	*	*	*	*	0
0	*	0	*	0	0	*	*	*	0
0	*	0	*	0	*	0	0	*	0
0	*	0	*	0	*	0	*	0	0
1	*	*	*	*	*	*	*	*	1
*	1	1	*	*	*	*	*	*	1
*	1	*	1	1	*	*	*	*	1
*	1	*	1	*	1	1	*	*	1
*	1	*	1	*	1	*	1	1	1
all others									X

Y_i	Z_i	GN_i
0	*	0
*	0	0
1	1	1
X	1/X	X
1	X	X

Y_i	Z_i	PR_i
0	0	0
1	1	0
0	1	1
1	0	1
X	*	X
*	X	X

* = Don't Care,   X = Don't Know,   i = 1,2,3,4

3 MICRON CMOS/BULK CELL FAMILY -CMOS3-	4360 Look-ahead Carry w/ G5 & P5 CELL HEIGHT 363 WIDTH 564	DATE: 1/01/87 REVISION: A

RELATED CELL TYPES: 4320, 4330, 4340.

The 4360 is a look-ahead unit with look-ahead and carry outputs It can be used with the look-ahead adders, the 4300 and the 4310, and the other look-ahead unit, the 4370, to create adders larger than 4 bits.

Each output time delay is calculated for the longest input path.

If the 4360 is to be used to create larger adders, it should be remembered that input PRO1 and GEN1 come from PRO5 and GEN5 from the first adder. The C2 output is Carry-in for the second adder. The GEN5 and PRO5 are generally used as inputs for the 4370 if an adder of more than 16 bits is wanted.

TERMINAL INFORMATION

ETER NAME	PHYSICAL NAME(S)		LOGICV FIELD	FUNCTION CODE	CAPACITANCE (pfarads)	RESISTANCE(S) (Kohms)
C1	T2,	B2	3	I	0.287	0.750, 1.200
PRO1	T1,	B1	1	I	0.259	0.750, 1.170
GEN1	T3,	B3	2	I	0.301	1.230, 0.750
PRO2	T6,	B6	4	I	0.298	0.750, 1.170
GEN2	T5,	B5	5	I	0.315	0.750, 1.230
PRO3	T10,	B10	8	I	0.305	0.750, 1.200
GEN3	T9,	B9	9	I	0.283	0.750, 1.170
PRO4	T12,	B12	10	I	0.334	0.750, 1.200
GEN4	T11,	B11	11	I	0.328	0.750, 1.230
C2	T4,	B4	6	O	0.612	0.870, .420
C3	T8,	B8	7	O	0.583	0.420, 0.840
C4	T7,	B7	13	O	0.592	0.420, 0.840
GEN5	T13,	B13	14	O	0.592	1.140, 0.750
PRO5	T14,	B14	20	O	0.758	1.140, 1.820
P1	L1,	R1	-	P	4.430	0.0, 0.0
G1	L2,	R2	-	G	3.359	0.0, 0.0
P2	L3,	R3	-	P	2.477	0.0, 0.0
G2	L4,	R4	-	G	3.001	0.0, 0.0

RELEASE 5.0   PAGE NO. 4360 - 1

PRO4	GEN4	PRO3	GEN3	PRO2	GEN2	PRO1	GEN1	C1	PRO5
0	*	*	*	*	*	*	*	*	0
*	*	0	*	*	*	*	*	*	0
*	*	*	*	0	*	*	*	*	0
*	*	*	*	*	*	0	*	*	0
1	*	1	*	1	*	1	*	*	1
all others									X

The 4360 is a look-ahead carry unit. For C2 output, please refer to the 4320. Likewise, for the C3 output, refer to the 4330. And, for the C4 and GEN5, refer to the 4340.

* = Don't Care, X = Don't Know

QUICK REFERENCE TIMING

VDD = 5 volts
C(load) = 1.5 picofarads
Input trans time = 20 nsec.
Worst case processing

PRO1 --> GEN5 (T13) = 25.09 nsec.
C1 --> C4 (B7) = 25.03 nsec.
C1 --> C3 (B8) = 22.52 nsec.
PRO1 --> C2 (T4) = 19.64 nsec.

SCHEMATIC

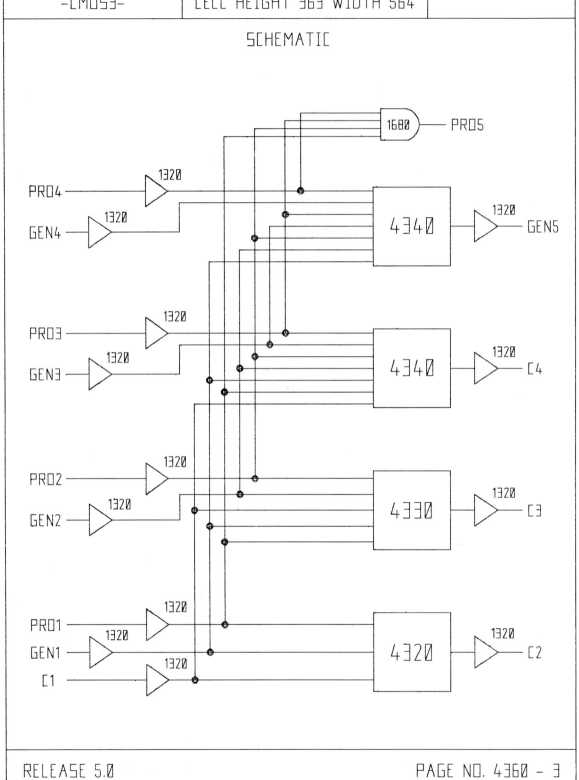

SWITCHING CHARACTERISTICS

Consult the MSI function user's guide for the conditions under which these switching characteristics were determined and for guidance on their interpretation. Cload has the units of picofarads and the results are in nanoseconds.

PRO1 --> PRO5 (B14)   Worst Case   Best Case

```
0 --> 1  Delay =   1.59(Cload) + 14.43  OR   1.11(Cload) +  5.21
         Trans =   6.24(Cload) +  2.86  OR   4.08(Cload) +  0.99
1 --> 0  Delay =   1.58(Cload) + 13.41  OR   0.95(Cload) +  5.52
         Trans =   5.03(Cload) +  2.21  OR   3.51(Cload) +  0.68
```

PRO1 --> GEN5 (T13)   Worst Case   Best Case

```
0 --> 1  Delay =   2.25(Cload) + 21.71  OR   1.17(Cload) +  8.71
         Trans =   7.42(Cload) +  2.09  OR   4.27(Cload) +  0.72
1 --> 0  Delay =   1.95(Cload) + 23.06  OR   0.98(Cload) +  9.54
         Trans =   5.92(Cload) +  1.80  OR   3.52(Cload) +  0.59
```

C1 --> C4 (B7)   Worst Case   Best Case

```
0 --> 1  Delay =   2.51(Cload) + 21.26  OR   1.54(Cload) +  8.52
         Trans =   8.84(Cload) +  1.85  OR   5.87(Cload) +  0.53
1 --> 0  Delay =   2.14(Cload) + 21.74  OR   1.34(Cload) +  8.85
         Trans =   7.26(Cload) +  1.55  OR   5.12(Cload) +  0.36
```

C1 --> C3 (B8)   Worst Case   Best Case

```
0 --> 1  Delay =   2.49(Cload) + 18.78  OR   1.50(Cload) +  7.52
         Trans =   8.72(Cload) +  1.86  OR   5.75(Cload) +  0.52
1 --> 0  Delay =   2.12(Cload) + 17.86  OR   1.31(Cload) +  7.27
         Trans =   7.15(Cload) +  1.57  OR   5.00(Cload) +  0.37
```

PRO1 --> C2 (T4)   Worst Case   Best Case

```
0 --> 1  Delay =   2.52(Cload) + 15.86  OR   1.54(Cload) +  6.38
         Trans =   8.83(Cload) +  0.92  OR   5.86(Cload) +  0.55
1 --> 0  Delay =   2.14(Cload) + 15.38  OR   1.35(Cload) +  6.26
         Trans =   7.26(Cload) +  1.60  OR   5.13(Cload) +  0.36
```

OUTLINE

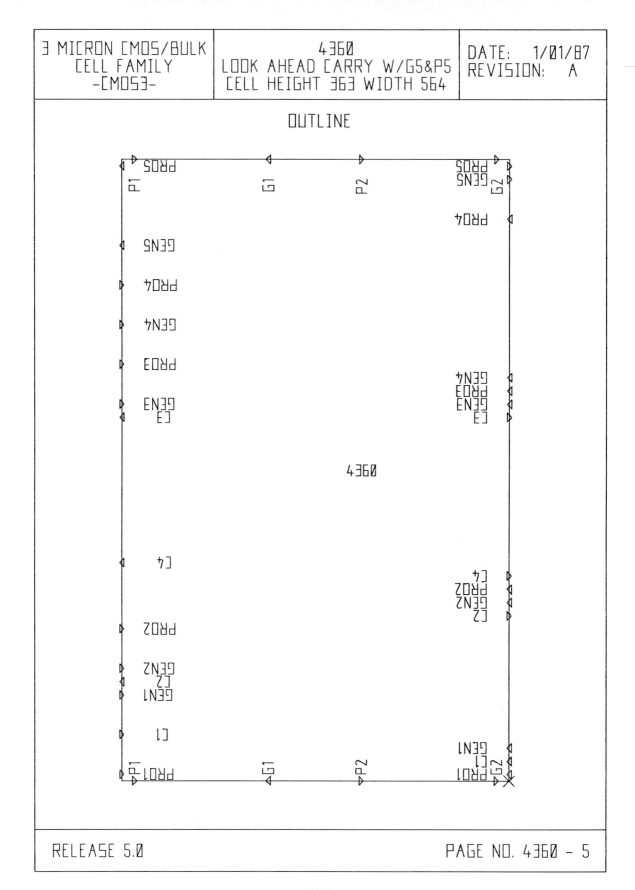

4360

MOSTRAN RESULTS

PRO1 --> PRO5 (B14)

		Worst Case		Best Case	
		1.5 pF	4.0 pF	1.5 pF	4.0 pF
0 --> 1	Delay	16.02	20.79	6.88	9.66
	Trans	12.21	27.80	7.11	17.31
1 --> 0	Delay	15.79	19.76	6.94	9.32
	Trans	9.76	22.34	5.95	14.73

PRO1 --> GEN5 (T13)

		Worst Case		Best Case	
		1.5 pF	4.0 pF	1.5 pF	4.0 pF
0 --> 1	Delay	25.09	30.71	10.46	13.38
	Trans	13.21	31.75	7.13	17.81
1 --> 0	Delay	26.00	30.89	11.01	13.45
	Trans	10.68	25.46	5.86	14.65

C1 --> C4 (B7)

		Worst Case		Best Case	
		1.5 pF	4.0 pF	1.5 pF	4.0 pF
0 --> 1	Delay	25.03	31.31	10.83	14.68
	Trans	15.11	37.21	9.33	24.00
1 --> 0	Delay	24.95	30.29	10.86	14.22
	Trans	12.45	30.61	8.05	20.86

C1 --> C3 (B8)

		Worst Case		Best Case	
		1.5 pF	4.0 pF	1.5 pF	4.0 pF
0 --> 1	Delay	22.51	28.74	9.78	13.55
	Trans	14.95	36.76	9.15	23.53
1 --> 0	Delay	21.05	26.35	9.24	12.52
	Trans	12.34	30.18	7.88	20.39

PRO1 --> C2 (T4)

		Worst Case		Best Case	
		1.5 pF	4.0 pF	1.5 pF	4.0 pF
0 --> 1	Delay	19.64	25.94	8.69	12.54
	Trans	15.16	37.23	9.35	24.01
1 --> 0	Delay	18.59	23.95	8.29	11.66
	Trans	12.49	30.64	8.06	20.89

Please note that all transition times have been multiplied by 1.25 to compensate for measurements taken at 80% of the signal swing.

RELATED CELL TYPES: 4320, 4330, 4340.

The 4370 is a look-ahead unit. It can be used with the 4300 and the 4310 to make adders larger than 4 bits. Its output are the carries that the 4300 and the 4310 use as carry-ins. Its inputs can come from the PRO5 and GEN5 output of the 4310 and the 4360.

Time delays shown for each output are longest paths.

TERMINAL INFORMATION

ETER NAME	PHYSICAL NAME(S)		LOGICV FIELD	FUNCTION CODE	CAPACITANCE (pfarads)	RESISTANCE(S) (Kohms)
C1	T1,	B1	3	I	0.259	0.750, 1.170
PRO1	T2,	B2	1	I	0.287	0.750, 1.170
GEN1	T3,	B3	2	I	0.301	1.230, 0.750
PRO2	T6,	B6	4	I	0.298	0.750, 1.170
GEN2	T5,	B5	5	I	0.311	0.750, 1.350
PRO3	T10,	B10	8	I	0.287	1.200, 0.750
GEN3	T9,	B9	9	I	0.265	0.750, 1.170
C2	T4,	B4	6	O	0.616	1.020, 0.420
C3	T8,	B8	7	O	0.571	0.420, 0.960
C4	T7,	B7	13	O	0.592	0.420, 1.020
P1	L1,	R1	–	P	2.693	0.0, 0.0
P2	L3,	R3	–	P	1.907	0.0, 0.0
G1	L2,	R2	–	G	2.153	0.0, 0.0
G2	L4,	R4	–	G	2.078	0.0, 0.0

ABBREVIATED TRUTH TABLE

The 4370 is a look-ahead carry unit. For C2 output, please refer to the 4320. Likewise, for the C3 output, refer to the 4330. And, for the C4, refer to the 4340.

QUICK REFERENCE TIMING

```
VDD = 5 volts                    C1 --> C3 (T8) =  22.79 nsec.
C(load) = 1.5 picofarads         C1 --> C2 (T4) =  18.98 nsec.
Input trans time = 20 nsec.
Worst case processing
```

SCHEMATIC

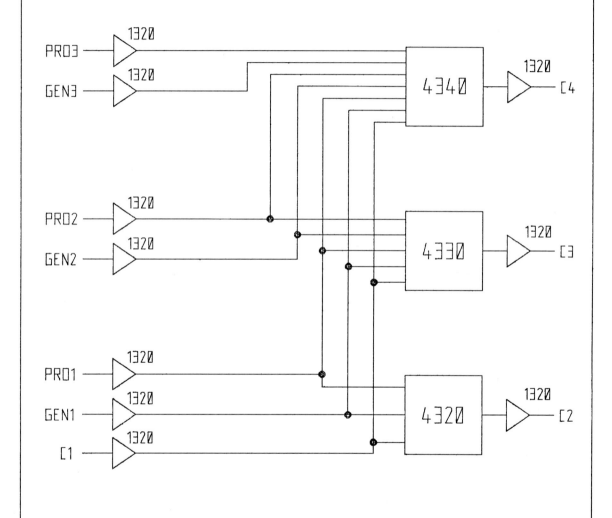

SWITCHING CHARACTERISTICS

Consult the MSI function user's guide for the conditions under which these switching characteristics were determined and for guidance on their interpretation. Cload has the units of picofarads and the results are in nanoseconds.

PRO1 --> C4 (B7)   Worst Case   Best Case

```
0 --> 1  Delay =   2.93(Cload) + 21.26  OR   1.68(Cload) +  8.51
         Trans =   9.37(Cload) +  1.79  OR   6.47(Cload) +  0.48
1 --> 0  Delay =   2.23(Cload) + 19.33  OR   1.49(Cload) +  8.83
         Trans =   7.78(Cload) +  1.46  OR   5.71(Cload) +  0.35
```

C1 --> C3 (B8)   Worst Case   Best Case

```
0 --> 1  Delay =   2.58(Cload) + 18.92  OR   1.62(Cload) +  7.43
         Trans =   9.15(Cload) +  1.77  OR   6.23(Cload) +  0.47
1 --> 0  Delay =   2.20(Cload) + 18.22  OR   1.43(Cload) +  7.41
         Trans =   7.55(Cload) +  1.53  OR   5.48(Cload) +  0.35
```

C1 --> C2 (T4)   Worst Case   Best Case

```
0 --> 1  Delay =   2.64(Cload) + 15.02  OR   1.68(Cload) +  6.03
         Trans =   9.36(Cload) +  1.88  OR   6.47(Cload) +  0.51
1 --> 0  Delay =   2.24(Cload) + 14.54  OR   1.49(Cload) +  5.90
         Trans =   7.80(Cload) +  1.52  OR   5.72(Cload) +  0.36
```

3 MICRON CMOS/BULK CELL FAMILY -CMOS3-	4370 LOOK AHEAD CARRY UNIT CELL HEIGHT 363 WIDTH 384	DATE: 4/10/86 REVISION: -

OUTLINE

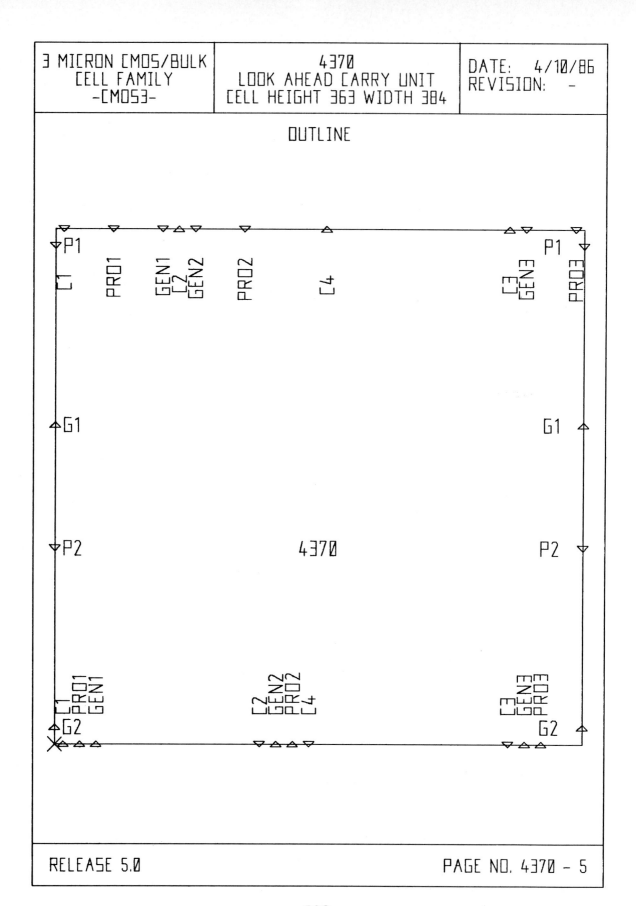

4370

MOSTRAN RESULTS

PRO1 --> C4 (B7)

		Worst Case		Best Case	
		1.5 pF	4.0 pF	1.5 pF	4.0 pF
0 --> 1	Delay	25.21	31.78	11.04	15.25
	Trans	15.84	39.26	10.18	26.35
1 --> 0	Delay	25.08	30.66	11.06	14.78
	Trans	13.14	32.60	8.91	23.18

C1 --> C3 (B8)

		Worst Case		Best Case	
		1.5 pF	4.0 pF	1.5 pF	4.0 pF
0 --> 1	Delay	22.49	28.94	9.86	13.92
	Trans	15.49	38.36	9.81	25.38
1 --> 0	Delay	21.53	27.03	9.56	13.14
	Trans	12.86	31.74	8.55	22.24

C1 --> C2 (T4)

		Worst Case		Best Case	
		1.5 pF	4.0 pF	1.5 pF	4.0 pF
0 --> 1	Delay	18.97	25.56	8.56	12.77
	Trans	15.93	39.34	10.21	26.38
1 --> 0	Delay	17.90	23.50	8.14	11.87
	Trans	13.21	32.70	8.94	23.24

Please note all the transition times have been multiplied by 1.25 to compensate for the measurement taken at 80% of the signal swing.

3 MICRON CMOS/BULK CELL FAMILY --CMOS3--	4400 8 Bit Parity Function CELL HEIGHT 363 WIDTH 360	DATE: 4/10/86 REVISION: -

RELATED CELL TYPES: 4410, 4430, 4440

The 4400 is an eight bit Parity Generator/Checker MSI function built from the 4410, 4430, and 4440 MSI slices. Its inputs are PSEL and D0 through D7. Its output is POUT.

To use it as a Parity Generator, a parity bit (PSEL) is supplied along with the data bits to generate an even (PSEL=1) or odd (PSEL=0) parity output.

To use it as a Parity Checker, the received data bit and parity are compared for a correct parity, and if an error is received it would be indicated on the output.

TERMINAL INFORMATION

ETER NAME	PHYSICAL NAME(S)	LOGICV FIELD	FUNCTION CODE	CAPACITANCE (pfarads)	RESISTANCE(S) (Kohms)
D0	T2, B2	1	I	0.497	1.17,0.75
D1	T3, B3	2	I	0.421	1.20,0.75
D2	T4, B4	3	I	0.530	0.75,1.20
D3	T5, B5	4	I	0.423	0.75,1.20
D4	T6, B6	5	I	0.503	1.17,0.75
D5	T7, B7	8	I	0.427	1.20,0.75
D6	T8, B8	9	I	0.540	0.75,1.20
D7	T9, B9	10	I	0.433	0.75,1.20
PSEL	T1, B1	11	I	0.673	1.20,1.20
POUT	T10, B10	6	O	1.101	1.23,1.23
P1	L1, R1	-	P	2.743	0.0,0.0
G1	L2, R2	-	G	1.451	0.0,0.0
P2	L3, R3	-	P	2.743	0.0,0.0
G2	L4, R4	-	G	1.451	0.0,0.0

RELEASE 5.0

PAGE NO. 4400 - 1

ABBREVIATED TRUTH TABLE

Inputs		Outputs	
D0-D7 Summation	Parity Select	Parity Even	Parity Odd
'1'=Even	1	1	0
'1'=Even	x	x	x
x	1	x	x
'1'=Odd	0	0	1
'1'=Odd	x	x	x
x	0	x	x

x = Don't Know

QUICK REFERENCE TIMING

VDD = 5 volts
C(load) = 1.5 picofarads
Input trans time = 30 nsec.
Worst case processing

PSEL --> POUT = 14.94 nsec.

SCHEMATIC

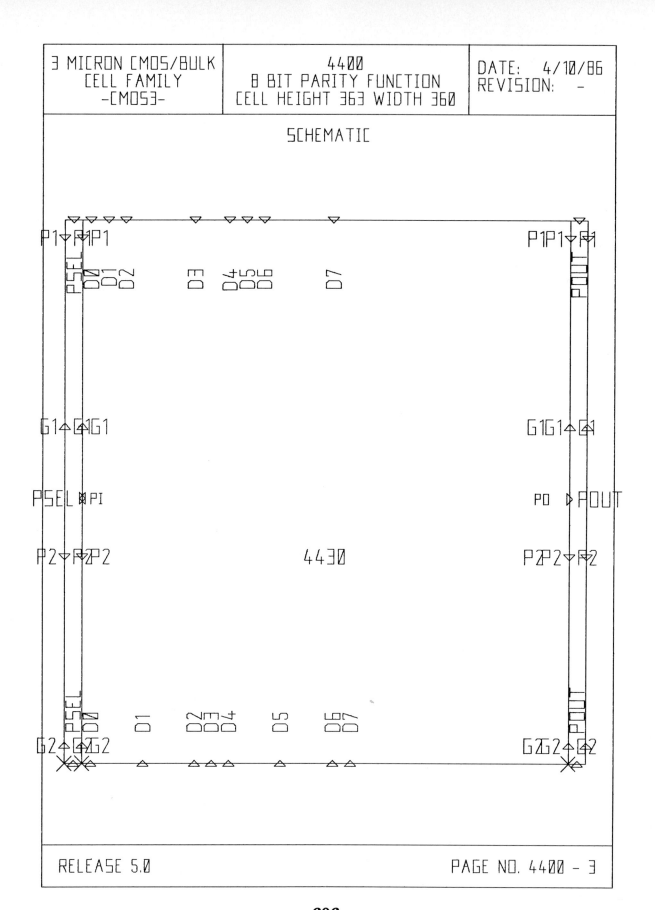

SWITCHING CHARACTERISTICS

Consult the MSI function user's guide for the conditions under which these switching characteristics were determined and for guidance on their interpretation. Cload has the units of picofarads and the results are in nanoseconds.

```
D0-D7  --> POUT          Worst Case                    Best Case

0 --> 1  Delay =    3.49(Cload) + 29.38   OR   2.16(Cload) + 12.10
         Trans =   12.28(Cload) +  4.47   OR   8.22(Cload) +  1.51
1 --> 0  Delay =    3.38(Cload) + 21.11   OR   2.04(Cload) +  7.45
         Trans =   11.35(Cload) +  3.07   OR   7.75(Cload) +   .77

PSEL   --> POUT          Worst Case                    Best Case

0 --> 1  Delay =    3.33(Cload) +  9.95   OR   2.10(Cload) +  4.55
         Trans =   11.76(Cload) +  9.20   OR   7.78(Cload) +  4.65
1 --> 0  Delay =    3.31(Cload) +  5.03   OR   2.03(Cload) +  1.25
         Trans =   11.28(Cload) +  3.57   OR   7.67(Cload) +  1.17
```

OUTLINE

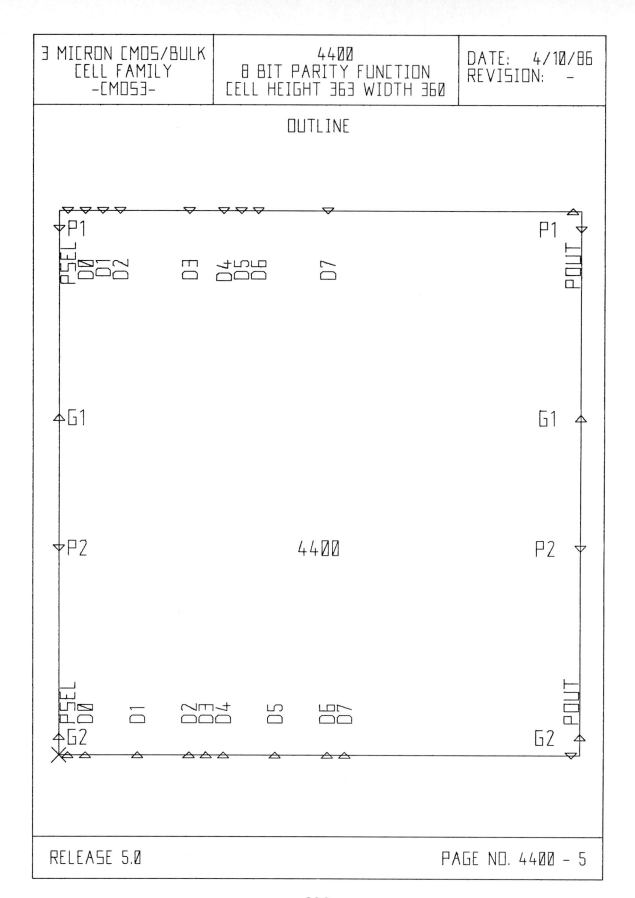

NOTE: To optimize maximum use of bits and MSI cell area, the following equation is derived from cascading as many 8 bit parity slices together as possible and ending the string with a 4 bit parity slice . n = number of 4430's.

Time(N-Bit) = Time(4410) + Time(4430) + Time(4420) + Time(4440)
Time(N,Cload) =   0   +   C(n)   + [A(Cload) + B] + 0
    N = (8n+4) = number of bits in a function.

Time(N-Bit) = Time(4410) + Time(4430) + Time(4440)
Time(N,Cload) =   0   +   C(n-1) + [D(Cload) + E] + 0
    N = 8n = number of bits in a function.

Data --> POUT		Worst Case				
		A	B	C	D	E
0 --> 1	Delay	3.96	22.80	31.09	3.94	29.52
	Trans	14.53	4.01	11.16	14.54	3.93
1 --> 0	Delay	3.78	17.42	22.73	3.78	21.18
	Trans	13.54	2.63	9.22	13.55	2.55

Data --> POUT		Best Case				
0 --> 1	Delay	2.17	8.12	13.00	2.16	12.10
	Trans	8.20	1.56	5.59	8.22	1.51
1 --> 0	Delay	2.04	5.47	8.34	2.10	7.35
	Trans	7.75	.79	4.59	7.75	.77

PSEL --> POUT		Worst Case				
0 --> 1	Delay	3.92	9.96	11.85	3.92	9.93
	Trans	14.35	7.59	17.14	14.37	7.49
1 --> 0	Delay	3.62	5.25	6.46	3.61	5.22
	Trans	13.50	3.04	9.83	13.50	2.97

PSEL --> POUT		Best Case				
0 --> 1	Delay	2.10	4.57	5.64	2.10	4.55
	Trans	7.78	4.66	10.00	7.78	4.67
1 --> 0	Delay	2.03	1.27	2.12	2.03	1.25
	Trans	7.67	1.19	5.30	7.67	1.18

TRUTH TABLE

See truth table for 4430

PSEL = PI

3 MICRON CMOS/BULK CELL FAMILY -CMOS3-	4400 8 Bit Parity Function CELL HEIGHT 363 WIDTH 360	DATE: 4/10/86 REVISION: -

MOSTRAN RESULTS

D0-D7 --> POUT		Worst Case		Best Case	
		1.5 pF	4.0 pF	1.5 pF	4.0 pF
0 --> 1	Delay	34.62	43.35	15.34	20.74
	Trans	22.89	53.59	13.84	34.39
1 --> 0	Delay	26.18	34.63	10.50	15.59
	Trans	20.09	48.46	12.39	31.76

PSEL --> POUT		Worst Case		Best Case	
		1.5 pF	4.0 pF	1.5 pF	4.0 pF
0 --> 1	Delay	14.94	23.26	7.71	12.97
	Trans	26.85	56.26	16.33	35.79
1 --> 0	Delay	9.99	18.26	4.30	9.38
	Trans	20.49	48.69	12.68	31.86

NOTE: Transition times have been multiplied by 1.25 to compensate for the measurements taken at the 80% of the signal swing.

RELEASE 5.0   PAGE NO.   4400 - 8

3 MICRON CMOS/BULK CELL FAMILY -CMOS3-	4410 Parity Stage Cap (Left) CELL HEIGHT 363 WIDTH 12	DATE: 4/10/86 REVISION: -

RELATED CELL TYPES: NA

The 4410 MSI is a parity stage cap (slice) physically consisting of a double entry data bit (PSEL) and a feed thru terminal on the right (PI) side. By adding 4420 or 4430 stages to the right of this slice and ending with a 4440 MSI slice, a N bit length Parity Generator/Checker function can be created.

TERMINAL INFORMATION

ETER NAME	PHYSICAL NAME(S)	LOGICV FIELD	FUNCTION CODE	CAPACITANCE (pfarads)	RESISTANCE(S) (Kohms)
PSEL	T1, B1, R3	NA	F	0.206	0.300,0.300,0
P1	L1, R1	-	P	0.0095	0.0,0.0
G1	L2, R2	-	G	0.0095	0.0,0.0
P2	L3, R4	-	P	0.0095	0.0,0.0
G2	L4, R5	-	G	0.0095	0.0,0.0

RELEASE 5.0

PAGE NO.   4410 - 1

3 MICRON CMOS/BULK CELL FAMILY −CMOS3−	4420 4 BIT PARITY STAGE CELL HEIGHT 363 WIDTH 168	DATE: 4/10/86 REVISION: −

RELATED CELL TYPES: NA

The 4420 MSI is a four bit Parity Generator/ Checker stage (slice), consisting of four double entry data bits D0-D3, and a terminal on the left (Parity Select) and right (Parity Output) side of MSI slice allowing other stages to be added to increase word size or to be capped and become a complete function.

To use it as a Parity Generator, a parity bit (PSEL) is supplied along with the data bits to generate an even (PSEL=1) or odd (PSEL=0) parity output.

To use it as a Parity Checker, the received data bit and parity are compared for a correct parity, and if an error is received, it would be indicated on the output.

Word length capability is expandable by cascading other 4420s' or 4430s' Parity Generator/Checker stages and capping the left and right ends with a 4410 and 4440 slice respectively.

TERMINAL INFORMATION

ETER NAME	PHYSICAL NAME(S)	LOGICV FIELD	FUNCTION CODE	CAPACITANCE (pfarads)	RESISTANCE(S) (Kohms)
D0	T1, B1	1	I	0.497	1.17, 0.75
D1	T2, B2	2	I	0.422	1.20, 0.75
D2	T3, B3	3	I	0.530	0.75, 1.20
D3	T4, B4	4	I	0.423	0.75, 1.20
PI	L3	5	I	0.435	0.90
PO	R3	6	O	0.906	0.93
P1	L1, R1	−	P	1.362	0.0, 0.0
G1	L2, R2	−	G	0.716	0.0, 0.0
P2	L4, R4	−	P	1.362	0.0, 0.0
G2	L5, R5	−	G	0.716	0.0, 0.0

TRUTH TABLE

D3	D2	D1	D0	PO PI=0	PO PI=1
0	0	0	0	0	1
0	0	0	1	1	0
0	0	1	0	1	0
0	0	1	1	0	1
0	1	0	0	1	0
0	1	0	1	0	1
0	1	1	0	0	1
0	1	1	1	1	0
1	0	0	0	1	0
1	0	0	1	0	1
1	0	1	0	0	1
1	0	1	1	1	0
1	1	0	0	0	1
1	1	0	1	1	0
1	1	1	0	1	0
1	1	1	1	0	1
0	0	0	X	X	X
1	1	1	X	X	X
0	0	X	0	X	X
1	1	X	1	X	X
0	X	0	0	X	X
1	X	1	1	X	X
X	0	0	0	X	X
X	1	1	1	X	X

X = Don't Know

QUICK REFERENCE TIMING

VDD = 5 volts   PI   --> PO   = 15.85 nsec.
C(load) = 1.5 picofarads
Input trans time = 30 nsec.
Worst case processing

SCHEMATIC

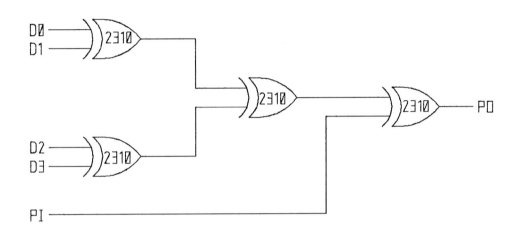

OUTLINE

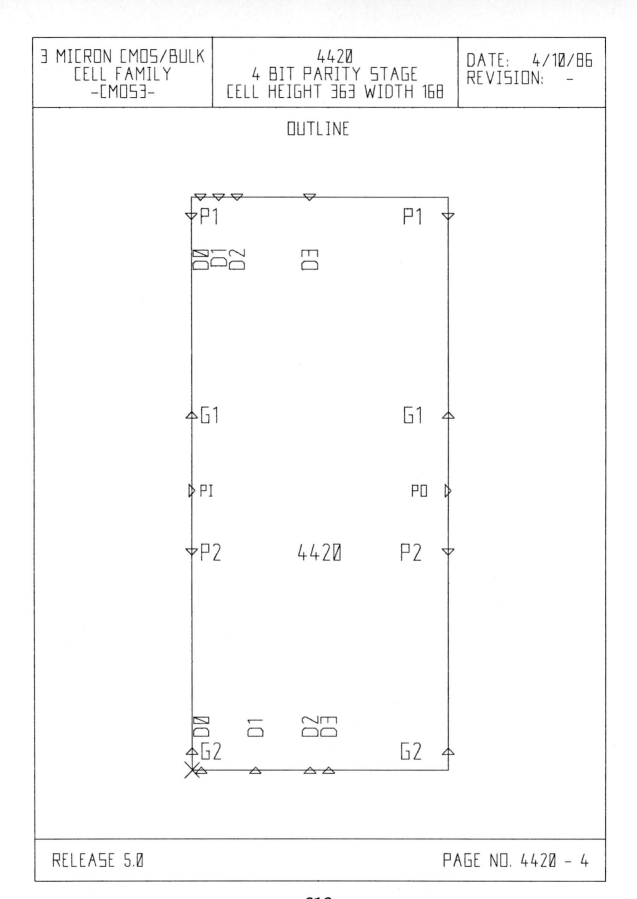

SWITCHING CHARACTERISTICS

Consult the MSI function user's guide for the conditions under which these switching characteristics were determined and for guidance on their interpretation. Cload has the units of picofarads and the results are in nanoseconds.

D0-D3 --> PO   Worst Case   Best Case

0 --> 1	Delay =	3.96(Cload) + 22.80 OR	2.17(Cload) + 8.12
	Trans =	14.53(Cload) + 4.01 OR	8.20(Cload) + 1.56
1 --> 0	Delay =	3.78(Cload) + 17.42 OR	2.04(Cload) + 5.47
	Trans =	13.54(Cload) + 2.63 OR	7.75(Cload) + .79

PI   --> PO   Worst Case   Best Case

0 --> 1	Delay =	3.92(Cload) + 9.96 OR	2.10(Cload) + 4.57
	Trans =	14.35(Cload) + 7.59 OR	7.78(Cload) + 4.66
1 --> 0	Delay =	3.62(Cload) + 5.25 OR	2.03(Cload) + 1.27
	Trans =	13.50(Cload) + 3.04 OR	7.67(Cload) + 1.19

MOSTRAN RESULTS

D0-D3 --> PO

		Worst Case			Best Case		
		.45 pF	1.5 pF	4.0 pF	.45 pF	1.5 pF	4.0 pF
0 --> 1	Delay	24.39	28.75	38.66	9.04	11.37	16.79
	Trans	11.24	25.81	62.14	5.77	13.86	34.36
1 --> 0	Delay	18.98	23.10	32.56	6.35	8.52	13.61
	Trans	9.31	22.95	56.81	4.61	12.41	31.78

PI --> PO

		Worst Case			Best Case		
		.45 pF	1.5 pF	4.0 pF	.45 pF	1.5 pF	4.0 pF
0 --> 1	Delay	11.88	15.85	25.66	5.65	7.72	12.97
	Trans	17.20	29.11	64.98	10.03	16.34	35.80
1 --> 0	Delay	6.49	10.67	19.71	2.14	4.32	9.40
	Trans	9.90	23.29	57.04	5.33	12.69	31.86

NOTE: Transition times have been multiplied by 1.25
to compensate for the measurements taken at 80% of
the signal swing.

RELATED CELL TYPES: NA

The 4430 MSI is an eight bit Parity Generator/ Checker stage (slice), consisting of eight double entry data bits D0-D7, and terminals on the left (Parity Select) side and right (Parity Output) side; allowing other stages to be added to increase word size, or to be capped and become a complete function.

To use it as a Parity Generator, a parity bit (PSEL) is supplied along with the data bits to generate an even (PSEL=1) or odd (PSEL=0) parity output.

To use it as a Parity Checker, the received data bit and parity are compared for a correct parity, and if an error is received it would be indicated on the output.

Word length capability is expandable by cascading other 4420s' or 4430s' Parity Generator/Checker stages and capping the left and right ends with a 4410 and 4440 slice respectively.

TERMINAL INFORMATION

ETER NAME	PHYSICAL NAME(S)	LOGICV FIELD	FUNCTION CODE	CAPACITANCE (pfarads)	RESISTANCE(S) (Kohms)
D0	T1, B1	1	I	0.497	1.17, 0.75
D1	T2, B2	2	I	0.422	1.20, 0.75
D2	T3, B3	3	I	0.530	0.75, 1.20
D3	T4, B4	4	I	0.423	0.75, 1.20
D4	T5, B5	5	I	0.503	1.17, 0.75
D5	T6, B6	8	I	0.427	1.20, 0.75
D6	T7, B7	9	I	0.540	0.75, 1.20
D7	T8, B8	10	I	0.433	0.75, 1.20
PI	L3	11	I	0.467	0.90
PO	R3	6	O	0.895	0.93
P1	L1, R1	–	P	2.724	0.0, 0.0
G1	L2, R2	–	G	1.432	0.0, 0.0
P2	L4, R4	–	P	2.724	0.0, 0.0
G2	L5, R5	–	G	1.432	0.0, 0.0

SCHEMATIC

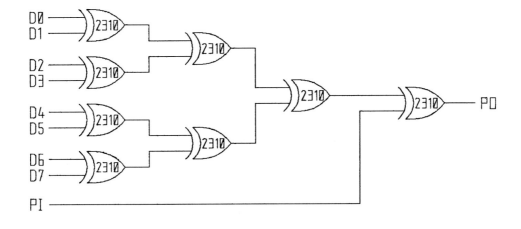

OUTLINE

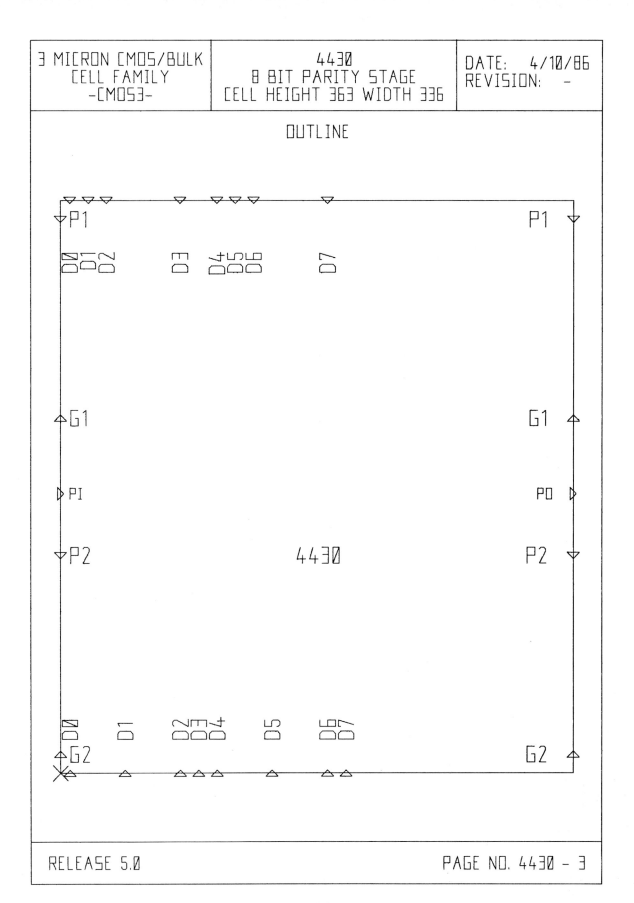

TRUTH TABLE

D7	D6	D5	D4	D3	D2	D1	D0	PO PI=0	PO PI=1
0	0	0	0	0	0	0	0	0	1
0	0	0	0	0	0	0	1	1	0
0	0	0	0	0	0	1	0	1	0
0	0	0	0	0	0	1	1	0	1
0	0	0	0	0	1	0	0	1	0
0	0	0	0	0	1	0	1	0	1
0	0	0	0	0	1	1	0	0	1
0	0	0	0	0	1	1	1	1	0
0	0	0	0	1	0	0	0	1	0
0	0	0	0	1	0	0	1	0	1
0	0	0	0	1	0	1	0	0	1
0	0	0	0	1	0	1	1	1	0
0	0	0	0	1	1	0	0	0	1
0	0	0	0	1	1	0	1	1	0
0	0	0	0	1	1	1	0	1	0
0	0	0	0	1	1	1	1	0	1
0	0	0	1	0	0	0	0	1	0
0	0	0	1	0	0	0	1	0	1
0	0	0	1	0	0	1	0	0	1
0	0	0	1	0	0	1	1	1	0
0	0	0	1	0	1	0	0	0	1
0	0	0	1	0	1	0	1	1	0
0	0	0	1	0	1	1	0	1	0
0	0	0	1	0	1	1	1	0	1
0	0	0	1	1	0	0	0	0	1
0	0	0	1	1	0	0	1	1	0
0	0	0	1	1	0	1	0	1	0
0	0	0	1	1	0	1	1	0	1
0	0	0	1	1	1	0	0	1	0
0	0	0	1	1	1	0	1	0	1
0	0	0	1	1	1	1	0	0	1
0	0	0	1	1	1	1	1	1	0
0	0	1	0	0	0	0	0	1	0
0	0	1	0	0	0	0	1	0	1
0	0	1	0	0	0	1	0	0	1
0	0	1	0	0	0	1	1	1	0
0	0	1	0	0	1	0	0	0	1
0	0	1	0	0	1	0	1	1	0
0	0	1	0	0	1	1	0	1	0
0	0	1	0	0	1	1	1	0	1
0	0	1	0	1	0	0	0	0	1
0	0	1	0	1	0	0	1	1	0
0	0	1	0	1	0	1	0	1	0

TRUTH TABLE

D7	D6	D5	D4	D3	D2	D1	D0	PO PI=0	PO PI=1
0	0	1	0	1	0	1	1	0	1
0	0	1	0	1	1	0	0	1	0
0	0	1	0	1	1	0	1	0	1
0	0	1	0	1	1	1	0	0	1
0	0	1	0	1	1	1	1	1	0
0	0	1	1	0	0	0	0	0	1
0	0	1	1	0	0	0	1	1	0
0	0	1	1	0	0	1	0	1	0
0	0	1	1	0	0	1	1	0	1
0	0	1	1	0	1	0	0	1	0
0	0	1	1	0	1	0	1	0	1
0	0	1	1	0	1	1	0	0	1
0	0	1	1	0	1	1	1	1	0
0	0	1	1	1	0	0	0	1	0
0	0	1	1	1	0	0	1	0	1
0	0	1	1	1	0	1	0	0	1
0	0	1	1	1	0	1	1	1	0
0	0	1	1	1	1	0	0	0	1
0	0	1	1	1	1	0	1	1	0
0	0	1	1	1	1	1	0	1	0
0	0	1	1	1	1	1	1	0	1
0	1	0	0	0	0	0	0	1	0
0	1	0	0	0	0	0	1	0	1
0	1	0	0	0	0	1	0	0	1
0	1	0	0	0	0	1	1	1	0
0	1	0	0	0	1	0	0	0	1
0	1	0	0	0	1	0	1	1	0
0	1	0	0	0	1	1	0	1	0
0	1	0	0	0	1	1	1	0	1
0	1	0	0	1	0	0	0	0	1
0	1	0	0	1	0	0	1	1	0
0	1	0	0	1	0	1	0	1	0
0	1	0	0	1	0	1	1	0	1
0	1	0	0	1	1	0	0	1	0
0	1	0	0	1	1	0	1	0	1
0	1	0	0	1	1	1	0	0	1
0	1	0	0	1	1	1	1	1	0
0	1	0	1	0	0	0	0	0	1
0	1	0	1	0	0	0	1	1	0
0	1	0	1	0	0	1	0	1	0
0	1	0	1	0	0	1	1	0	1
0	1	0	1	0	1	0	0	1	0
0	1	0	1	0	1	0	1	0	1

3 MICRON CMOS/BULK CELL FAMILY -CMOS3-	4430 8 Bit Parity Stage CELL HEIGHT 363 WIDTH 336	DATE: 4/10/86 REVISION: -

TRUTH TABLE

D7	D6	D5	D4	D3	D2	D1	D0	PO PI=0	PO PI=1
0	1	0	1	0	1	1	0	0	1
0	1	0	1	0	1	1	1	1	0
0	1	0	1	1	0	0	0	1	0
0	1	0	1	1	0	0	1	0	1
0	1	0	1	1	0	1	0	0	1
0	1	0	1	1	0	1	1	1	0
0	1	0	1	1	1	0	0	0	1
0	1	0	1	1	1	0	1	1	0
0	1	0	1	1	1	1	0	1	0
0	1	0	1	1	1	1	1	0	1
0	1	1	0	0	0	0	0	0	1
0	1	1	0	0	0	0	1	1	0
0	1	1	0	0	0	1	0	1	0
0	1	1	0	0	0	1	1	0	1
0	1	1	0	0	1	0	0	1	0
0	1	1	0	0	1	0	1	0	1
0	1	1	0	0	1	1	0	0	1
0	1	1	0	0	1	1	1	1	0
0	1	1	0	1	0	0	0	1	0
0	1	1	0	1	0	0	1	0	1
0	1	1	0	1	0	1	0	0	1
0	1	1	0	1	0	1	1	1	0
0	1	1	0	1	1	0	0	0	1
0	1	1	0	1	1	0	1	1	0
0	1	1	0	1	1	1	0	1	0
0	1	1	0	1	1	1	1	0	1
0	1	1	1	0	0	0	0	1	0
0	1	1	1	0	0	0	1	0	1
0	1	1	1	0	0	1	0	0	1
0	1	1	1	0	0	1	1	1	0
0	1	1	1	0	1	0	0	0	1
0	1	1	1	0	1	0	1	1	0
0	1	1	1	0	1	1	0	1	0
0	1	1	1	0	1	1	1	0	1
0	1	1	1	1	0	0	0	0	1
0	1	1	1	1	0	0	1	1	0
0	1	1	1	1	0	1	0	1	0
0	1	1	1	1	0	1	1	0	1
0	1	1	1	1	1	0	0	1	0
0	1	1	1	1	1	0	1	0	1
0	1	1	1	1	1	1	0	1	0
0	1	1	1	1	1	1	1	1	0
1	0	0	0	0	0	0	0	1	0

| 3 MICRON CMOS/BULK CELL FAMILY -CMOS3- | 4430 8 Bit Parity Stage CELL HEIGHT 363 WIDTH 336 | DATE: 4/10/86 REVISION: - |

TRUTH TABLE

D7	D6	D5	D4	D3	D2	D1	D0	PO PI=0	PO PI=1
1	0	0	0	0	0	0	1	0	1
1	0	0	0	0	0	1	0	0	1
1	0	0	0	0	0	1	1	1	0
1	0	0	0	0	1	0	0	0	1
1	0	0	0	0	1	0	1	1	0
1	0	0	0	0	1	1	0	1	0
1	0	0	0	0	1	1	1	0	1
1	0	0	0	1	0	0	0	0	1
1	0	0	0	1	0	0	1	1	0
1	0	0	0	1	0	1	0	1	0
1	0	0	0	1	0	1	1	0	1
1	0	0	0	1	1	0	0	1	0
1	0	0	0	1	1	0	1	0	1
1	0	0	0	1	1	1	0	0	1
1	0	0	0	1	1	1	1	1	0
1	0	0	1	0	0	0	0	0	1
1	0	0	1	0	0	0	1	1	0
1	0	0	1	0	0	1	0	1	0
1	0	0	1	0	0	1	1	0	1
1	0	0	1	0	1	0	0	1	0
1	0	0	1	0	1	0	1	0	1
1	0	0	1	0	1	1	0	0	1
1	0	0	1	0	1	1	1	1	0
1	0	0	1	1	0	0	0	1	0
1	0	0	1	1	0	0	1	0	1
1	0	0	1	1	0	1	0	0	1
1	0	0	1	1	0	1	1	1	0
1	0	0	1	1	1	0	0	0	1
1	0	0	1	1	1	0	1	1	0
1	0	0	1	1	1	1	0	1	0
1	0	0	1	1	1	1	1	0	1
1	0	1	0	0	0	0	0	0	1
1	0	1	0	0	0	0	1	1	0
1	0	1	0	0	0	1	0	1	0
1	0	1	0	0	0	1	1	0	1
1	0	1	0	0	1	0	0	1	0
1	0	1	0	0	1	0	1	0	1
1	0	1	0	0	1	1	0	0	1
1	0	1	0	0	1	1	1	1	0
1	0	1	0	1	0	0	0	1	0
1	0	1	0	1	0	0	1	0	1
1	0	1	0	1	0	1	0	0	1
1	0	1	0	1	0	1	1	1	0

TRUTH TABLE

D7	D6	D5	D4	D3	D2	D1	D0	PO PI=0	PO PI=1
1	0	1	0	1	1	0	0	0	1
1	0	1	0	1	1	0	1	1	0
1	0	1	0	1	1	1	0	1	0
1	0	1	0	1	1	1	1	0	1
1	0	1	1	0	0	0	0	1	0
1	0	1	1	0	0	0	1	0	1
1	0	1	1	0	0	1	0	0	1
1	0	1	1	0	0	1	1	1	0
1	0	1	1	0	1	0	0	0	1
1	0	1	1	0	1	0	1	1	0
1	0	1	1	0	1	1	0	1	0
1	0	1	1	0	1	1	1	0	1
1	0	1	1	1	0	0	0	0	1
1	0	1	1	1	0	0	1	1	0
1	0	1	1	1	0	1	0	0	1
1	0	1	1	1	0	1	1	0	1
1	0	1	1	1	1	0	0	1	0
1	0	1	1	1	1	0	1	0	1
1	0	1	1	1	1	1	0	0	1
1	0	1	1	1	1	1	1	1	0
1	1	0	0	0	0	0	0	0	1
1	1	0	0	0	0	0	1	1	0
1	1	0	0	0	0	1	0	1	0
1	1	0	0	0	0	1	1	0	1
1	1	0	0	0	1	0	0	1	0
1	1	0	0	0	1	0	1	0	1
1	1	0	0	0	1	1	0	0	1
1	1	0	0	0	1	1	1	1	0
1	1	0	0	1	0	0	0	1	0
1	1	0	0	1	0	0	1	0	1
1	1	0	0	1	0	1	0	0	1
1	1	0	0	1	0	1	1	1	0
1	1	0	0	1	1	0	0	0	1
1	1	0	0	1	1	0	1	1	0
1	1	0	0	1	1	1	0	1	0
1	1	0	0	1	1	1	1	0	1
1	1	0	1	0	0	0	0	1	0
1	1	0	1	0	0	0	1	0	1
1	1	0	1	0	0	1	0	0	1
1	1	0	1	0	0	1	1	1	0
1	1	0	1	0	1	0	0	0	1
1	1	0	1	0	1	0	1	1	0
1	1	0	1	0	1	1	0	1	0

TRUTH TABLE

D7	D6	D5	D4	D3	D2	D1	D0	PO PI=0	PO PI=1
1	1	0	1	0	1	1	1	0	1
1	1	0	1	1	0	0	0	0	1
1	1	0	1	1	0	0	1	1	0
1	1	0	1	1	0	1	0	1	0
1	1	0	1	1	0	1	1	0	1
1	1	0	1	1	1	0	0	1	0
1	1	0	1	1	1	0	1	0	1
1	1	0	1	1	1	1	0	0	1
1	1	0	1	1	1	1	1	1	0
1	1	1	0	0	0	0	0	1	0
1	1	1	0	0	0	0	1	0	1
1	1	1	0	0	0	1	0	0	1
1	1	1	0	0	0	1	1	1	0
1	1	1	0	0	1	0	0	0	1
1	1	1	0	0	1	0	1	1	0
1	1	1	0	0	1	1	0	1	0
1	1	1	0	0	1	1	1	0	1
1	1	1	0	1	0	0	0	0	1
1	1	1	0	1	0	0	1	1	0
1	1	1	0	1	0	1	0	1	0
1	1	1	0	1	0	1	1	0	1
1	1	1	0	1	1	0	0	1	0
1	1	1	0	1	1	0	1	0	1
1	1	1	0	1	1	1	0	0	1
1	1	1	0	1	1	1	1	1	0
1	1	1	1	0	0	0	0	0	1
1	1	1	1	0	0	0	1	1	0
1	1	1	1	0	0	1	0	1	0
1	1	1	1	0	0	1	1	0	1
1	1	1	1	0	1	0	0	1	0
1	1	1	1	0	1	0	1	0	1
1	1	1	1	0	1	1	0	0	1
1	1	1	1	0	1	1	1	1	0
1	1	1	1	1	0	0	0	1	0
1	1	1	1	1	0	0	1	0	1
1	1	1	1	1	0	1	0	0	1
1	1	1	1	1	0	1	1	1	0
1	1	1	1	1	1	0	0	0	1
1	1	1	1	1	1	0	1	1	0
1	1	1	1	1	1	1	0	1	0
1	1	1	1	1	1	1	1	0	1

TRUTH TABLE

D7	D6	D5	D4	D3	D2	D1	D0	PO PI=0	PO PI=1
0	1	1	1	0	1	0	X	X	X
1	0	1	0	1	0	X	1	X	X
0	1	1	0	0	X	0	0	X	X
1	0	0	0	X	1	0	0	X	X
0	0	1	X	0	0	1	1	X	X
1	0	X	1	0	0	0	0	X	X
0	X	0	0	0	1	1	1	X	X
X	1	0	0	0	0	0	0	X	X

SWITCHING CHARACTERISTICS

Consult the MSI function user's guide for the conditions under which these switching characteristics were determined and for guidance on their interpretation. Cload has the units of picofarads and the results are in nanoseconds.

```
   D0-D7 --> PO           Worst Case                   Best Case

0 --> 1  Delay =    3.94(Cload) + 29.52   OR   2.16(Cload) + 12.10
         Trans =   14.54(Cload) +  3.93   OR   8.22(Cload) +  1.51
1 --> 0  Delay =    3.78(Cload) + 21.18   OR   2.10(Cload) +  7.35
         Trans =   13.55(Cload) +  2.55   OR   7.75(Cload) +   .77

   PI    --> PO           Worst Case                   Best Case

0 --> 1  Delay =    3.92(Cload) +  9.93   OR   2.10(Cload) +  4.55
         Trans =   14.37(Cload) +  7.49   OR   7.78(Cload) +  4.67
1 --> 0  Delay =    3.61 Cload) +  5.22   OR   2.03(Cload) +  1.25
         Trans =   13.50(Cload) +  2.97   OR   7.67(Cload) +  1.18
```

MOSTRAN RESULTS

D0-D7 --> PO		Worst Case			Best Case		
		.45 pF	1.5 pF	4.0 pF	.45 pF	1.5 pF	4.0 pF
0 --> 1	Delay	31.09	35.44	45.30	13.00	15.34	20.74
	Trans	11.16	25.74	62.09	5.59	13.84	34.39
1 --> 0	Delay	22.73	26.85	36.30	8.34	10.50	15.75
	Trans	9.22	22.88	56.76	4.59	12.39	31.76

PI --> PO		Worst Case			Best Case		
		.45 pF	1.5 pF	4.0 pF	.45 pF	1.5 pF	4.0 pF
0 --> 1	Delay	11.85	15.82	25.63	5.64	7.71	12.97
	Trans	17.14	29.05	64.98	10.00	16.34	35.79
1 --> 0	Delay	6.46	10.64	19.67	2.12	4.30	9.38
	Trans	9.83	23.23	56.99	5.30	12.68	31.85

NOTE: Transition times have been multiplied by 1.25 to compensate for the measurements taken at 80% of the signal swing.

RELATED CELL TYPES: 4400

The 4440 MSI is a parity stage cap(slice) physically consisting of a feed thru terminal on the left side (PO) that becomes the double exit data bit POUT.
By adding this slice to a 4420/4430, the stages can be terminated, and there by completing an N length Parity Generator/Checker Function.

TERMINAL INFORMATION

ETER NAME	PHYSICAL NAME(S)	LOGICV FIELD	FUNCTION CODE	CAPACITANCE (pfarads)	RESISTANCE(S) (Kohms)
POUT	T1, B1, L3	NA	F	0.206	0.300,0.300,0
P1	L1, R1	–	P	0.0095	0.0,0.0
G1	L2, R2	–	G	0.0095	0.0,0.0
P2	L4, R3	–	P	0.0095	0.0,0.0
G2	L5, R4	–	G	0.0095	0.0,0.0

RELEASE 5.0

PAGE NO.   4440 - 1

RELATED CELL TYPES: 4460, 4470, 4480,

The 4450 MSI function will compare the magnitude of two 4 bit binary words. The inputs to the function are binary words Y and Z and an enable signal. Three outputs are provided : Y < Z, Y > Z, Y = Z. When the enable signal is high all of the outputs will be set to zero.

The 4450 has as its basic components a beginning slice (4460), one middle slice (4470), and an end slice (4480). The middle cells can be cascaded together to compare words of greater than 4 bits. The basic 4470 cell is a 4-bit comparator unit.

TERMINAL INFORMATION

ETER NAME	PHYSICAL NAME(S)	LOGICV FIELD	FUNCTION CODE	CAPACITANCE (pfarads)	RESISTANCE(S) (Kohms)
Y0	B1 , T1	1	I	0.490	2.50 , 2.50
Z0	B2 , T2	2	I	0.490	2.50 , 2.50
Y1	B3 , T3	3	I	0.509	2.50 , 2.50
Z1	B4 , T4	4	I	0.509	2.50 , 2.50
Y2	B5 , T5	5	I	0.493	2.46 , 2.46
Z2	B6 , T6	8	I	0.494	2.46 , 2.46
Y3	B7 , T7	9	I	0.516	2.58 , 2.58
Z3	B8 , T8	10	I	0.502	2.43 , 2.43
ENOT	B9 , T9	11	I	1.087	2.55 , 2.55
YLTZ	B10 , T10	6	O	1.171	2.10 , 0.81
YGTZ	B11 , T11	7	O	1.175	2.37 , 2.61
YEQZ	B12 , T12	13	O	1.440	0.27 , 0.27
P1	L1 , R1	N/A	P	7.411	0.00 , 0.00
G1	L2 , R2	N/A	G	5.157	0.00 , 0.00
P2	L3 , R3	N/A	P	7.699	0.00 , 0.00
G2	L4 , R4	N/A	G	5.042	0.00 , 0.00

TRUTH TABLE

INPUTS			OUTPUTS		
ENABLE	Y	Z	Y < Z	Y > Z	Y = Z
1	*	*	0	0	0
0	WORD Y =	WORD Z	0	0	1
0	WORD Y <	WORD Z	1	0	0
0	WORD Y >	WORD Z	0	1	0
0	X	X	X	X	X

* = Don't Care,   X = Don't know

QUICK REFERENCE TIMING

VDD = 5 volts	TR	WORD Y --> YGTZ =	29.23 nsec.
C(load) = 1.5 picofarads	PD0-1	WORD Y --> YEQZ =	44.05 nsec.
Input trans time = 30 nsec.	TR	WORD Y --> YEQZ =	17.97 nsec.
Worst case processing	PD0-1	ENOT --> YEQZ =	6.95 nsec.
	TR	ENOT --> YEQZ =	19.69 nsec.

SCHEMATIC

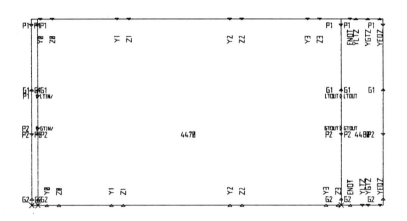

SWITCHING CHARACTERISTICS

Consult the MSI function user's guide for the conditions under which these switching characteristics were determined and for guidance on their interpretation. Cload has the units of picofarads and the results are in nanoseconds.

```
WORD Y --> YGTZ           Worst Case                Best Case

0 --> 1  Delay =    4.69(Cload) + 37.01  OR   3.52(Cload) +  9.40
         Trans =   15.16(Cload) +  6.49  OR  13.70(Cload) +  1.73
1 --> 0  Delay =    3.96(Cload) + 34.28  OR   3.26(Cload) + 15.21
         Trans =   15.30(Cload) +  4.98  OR  12.83(Cload) +  1.36

WORD Y --> YEQZ           Worst Case                Best Case

0 --> 1  Delay =    3.51(Cload) + 42.30  OR   1.20(Cload) + 11.16
         Trans =    7.64(Cload) +  6.51  OR   3.52(Cload) +  3.16
1 --> 0  Delay =    2.16(Cload) + 35.62  OR    .65(Cload) + 13.75
         Trans =    3.70(Cload) +  2.46  OR   1.64(Cload) +  2.06

 ENOT   --> YEQZ          Worst Case                Best Case

0 --> 1  Delay =    2.07(Cload) +  3.84  OR   1.00(Cload) +  1.58
         Trans =    5.34(Cload) + 11.68  OR   2.60(Cload) +  7.25
1 --> 0  Delay =    1.43(Cload) +  7.37  OR    .73(Cload) +  2.96
         Trans =    2.57(Cload) + 12.28  OR   1.38(Cload) +  7.51
```

3 MICRON CMOS/BULK CELL FAMILY -CMOS3-	4450 4 BIT COMPARATOR CELL HEIGHT 363 WIDTH 708	DATE: 1/01/87 REVISION: A

OUTLINE

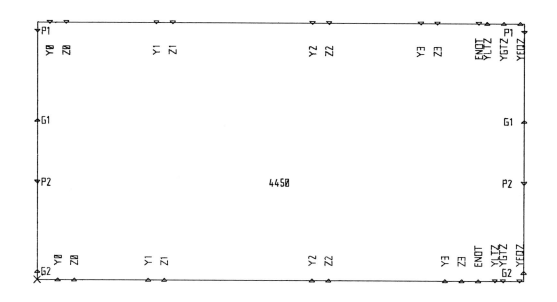

Time(4450)   = Time(4460) + Time(4470's)   + Time(4480)
                 A(N)   + B   + C(Cload)

N = # OF 4470s

WORD Y --> YGTZ		Worst Case			Best Case	
	A	B	C	A	B	C
0 --> 1 Delay	31.71	5.30	4.69	7.23	2.20	3.52
Trans	0.00	6.49	15.16	0.00	1.73	13.70
1 --> 0 Delay	27.64	6.64	3.69	12.56	2.65	3.26
Trans	0.00	4.98	15.30	0.00	1.36	12.83

WORD Y --> YEQZ		Worst Case			Best Case	
0 --> 1 Delay	31.71	10.59	3.51	7.23	3.93	1.20
Trans	0.00	6.51	7.64	0.00	3.16	3.52
1 --> 0 Delay	27.64	7.98	2.16	12.56	1.19	0.65
Trans	0.00	2.46	3.70	0.00	2.06	1.64

ENOT --> YEQZ		Worst Case			Best Case	
0 --> 1 Delay	0.00	3.84	2.07	0.00	1.58	1.00
Trans	0.00	11.68	5.34	0.00	7.25	2.60
1 --> 0 Delay	0.00	7.37	1.43	0.00	2.96	0.73
Trans	0.00	12.28	2.57	0.00	7.51	1.38

3 MICRON CMOS/BULK CELL FAMILY -CMOS3-	4460 BEGIN SLICE CELL HEIGHT 363 WIDTH 12	DATE: 4/10/86 REVISION: -

RELATED CELL TYPES: 4470, 4480, 4490,

The 4460 is the beginning cell to be used in composing an N-bit Comparator. The cell itself does not appear in the parts list for a top level structure because it is stray material that ties LTIN and GTIN to VDD for the first slice of an N-bit comparator.

This cell is part of the 4490 8 bit comparator.

TERMINAL INFORMATION

ETER NAME	PHYSICAL NAME(S)	LOGICV FIELD	FUNCTION CODE	CAPACITANCE (pfarads)	RESISTANCE(S) (Kohms)
P1	L1 , R1 , R3	N/A	P	0.065	0.00, 0.00, 0.12
G1	L2 , R2	N/A	G	0.009	0.00 , 0.00
P2	L3 , R5 , R4	N/A	P	0.007	0.00, 0.00, 0.00
G2	L4 , R6	N/A	G	0.005	0.00 , 0.00

RELEASE 5.0

PAGE NO. 4460 - 1

RELATED CELL TYPES: 4460, 4480, 4490,

The 4470 is a 4 bit cascadable slice used to form an N bit magnitude comparator, where N is a multiple of 4. An odd number of bits can be formed by tying off unused inputs. The inputs to the slice are data and greaterthan and lessthan from the previous slice. The outputs are lessthan and greaterthan to be supplied as inputs to the next stage.

A 4 bit comparator requires a 4460, one 4470, and a 4480 to provide the outputs. The 4460 ties the greaterthan and lessthan inputs of the 4470 to VDD. The 4480 takes the greater than and lessthan outputs of the 4470 to provide the outputs of the magnitude comparator.

The 4470 can be cascaded with another 4470 to form an 8 bit comparator. This has been done and is supplied to the user as the 4490 MSI function.

TERMINAL INFORMATION

ETER NAME	PHYSICAL NAME(S)	LOGICV FIELD	FUNCTION CODE	CAPACITANCE (pfarads)	RESISTANCE(S) (Kohms)
LTIN/	L3	1	I	1.378	0.87
GTIN/	L4	2	I	1.365	0.87
Y0	B1 , T1	3	I	0.490	2.50 , 2.50
Z0	B2 , T2	4	I	0.490	2.50 , 2.50
Y1	B3 , T3	5	I	0.509	2.50 , 2.50
Z1	B4 , T4	8	I	0.509	2.50 , 2.50
Y2	B5 , T5	9	I	0.493	2.46 , 2.46
Z2	B6 , T6	10	I	0.494	2.46 , 2.46
Y3	B7 , T7	11	I	0.516	2.58 , 2.58
Z3	B8 , T8	12	I	0.502	2.43 , 2.43
LTOUT	R3	6	O	0.642	0.30
GTOUT	R4	7	O	0.646	0.84
P1	L1 , R1	N/A	P	5.117	0.00 , 0.00
G1	L2 , R2	N/A	G	4.749	0.00 , 0.00
P2	L5 , R5	N/A	P	5.476	0.00 , 0.00
G2	L6 , R6	N/A	G	4.638	0.00 , 0.00

RELEASE 5.0

SCHEMATIC

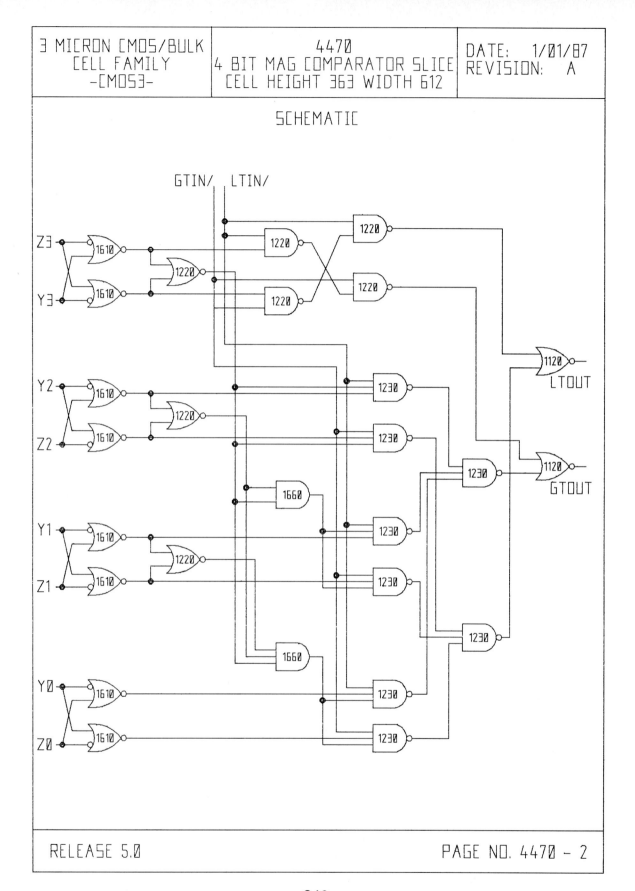

OUTLINE

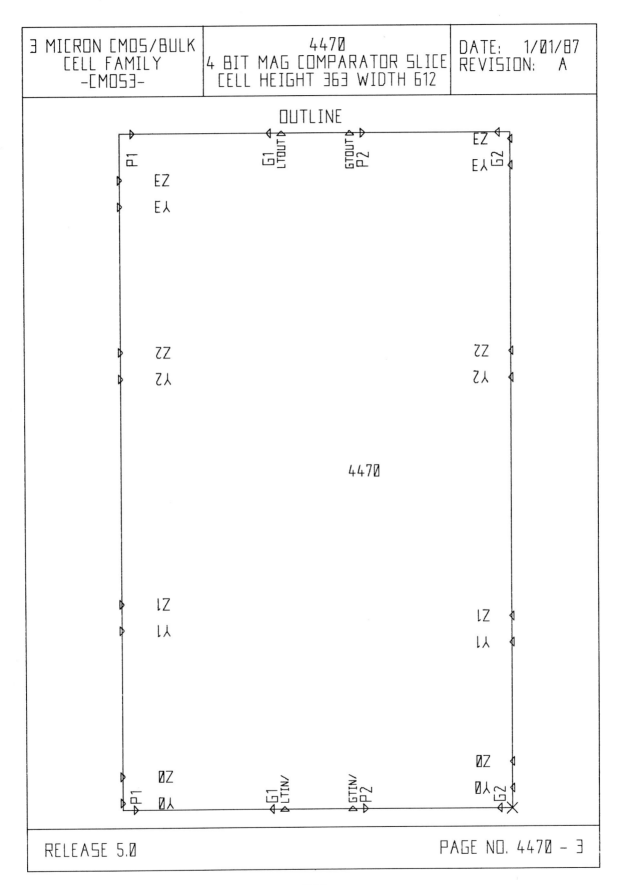

4470

TRUTH TABLE

LTIN/	GTIN/	INPUTS	LTOUT	GTOUT
0	0	Y = * Z = *	0	0
0	1	Y = * Z = *	0	1
0	X	Y = * Z = *	0	X
1	0	Y = * Z = *	1	0
X	0	Y = * Z = *	X	0
1	1	Y = Z	1	1
1	1	Y < Z	0	1
1	1	Y > Z	1	0
1	1	Y = X Z = X	X	X
1	X	Y = Z	1	X
1	X	Y < Z	X	X
1	X	Y > Z	1	0
X	1	Y = Z	X	1
X	1	Y < Z	0	1
X	1	Y > Z	X	X
X	X	Y = * Z = *	X	X

* = Don't Care , X = Don't Know

3 MICRON CMOS/BULK CELL FAMILY -CMOS3-	4470 4 BIT MAG COMPARATOR SLICE CELL HEIGHT 363 WIDTH 612	DATE: 1/01/87 REVISION: A

MOSTRAN RESULTS

Y2 --> LTOUT	Worst Case Driving a 4470	Best Case Driving a 4480
0 --> 1 Delay	18.17	7.17
Trans	20.14	12.10
1 --> 0 Delay	23.42	13.11
Trans	17.43	10.70

Y2 --> GTOUT	Worst Case Driving a 4470	Best Case Driving a 4480
0 --> 1 Delay	31.71	17.43
Trans	22.29	14.74
1 --> 0 Delay	27.64	10.96
Trans	19.39	13.33

Z0 --> GTOUT	Worst Case Driving a 4470	Best Case Driving a 4480
0 --> 1 Delay	17.49	7.23
Trans	22.29	14.75
1 --> 0 Delay	21.53	12.56
Trans	19.39	13.28

LTIN/ --> LTOUT	Worst Case Driving a 4470	Best Case Driving a 4480
0 --> 1 Delay	9.59	4.61
Trans	19.90	12.41
1 --> 0 Delay	10.69	6.27
Trans	16.14	10.44

GTIN/ --> GTOUT	Worst Case Driving a 4470	Best Case Driving a 4480
0 --> 1 Delay	10.24	5.32
Trans	22.16	15.04
1 --> 0 Delay	11.27	6.97
Trans	18.36	13.13

Note: The transition times listed on this page are from 0 - 100%.

RELEASE 5.0

PAGE NO. 4470 - 5

3 MICRON CMOS/BULK CELL FAMILY —CMOS3—	4480 COMPARATOR END CELL CELL HEIGHT 363 WIDTH 84	DATE: 1/01/87 REVISION: A

RELATED CELL TYPES: 4460, 4470, 4490,

The 4480 is the end cell used to form an N-bit comparator. The inputs are LTOUT and GTOUT from the 4470 along with an enable signal. The outputs are Y = Z, Y > Z, Y < Z. One end cell is required for an N-bit comparator function.

TERMINAL INFORMATION

ETER NAME	PHYSICAL NAME(S)	LOGICV FIELD	FUNCTION CODE	CAPACITANCE (pfarads)	RESISTANCE(S) (Kohms)
LTOUT	L3	1	I	0.244	0.93
GTOUT	L4	2	I	0.244	0.93
ENOT	B1 , T1	3	I	1.087	2.55 , 2.55
YLTZ	B2 , T2	6	O	1.171	2.10 , 0.81
YGTZ	B3 , T3	7	O	1.175	2.37 , 2.61
YEQZ	B4 , T4	13	O	1.440	0.27 , 0.27
P1	L1 , R1	N/A	P	0.850	0.00 , 0.00
G1	L2 , R2	N/A	G	0.399	0.00 , 0.00
P2	L5 , R3	N/A	P	0.850	0.00 , 0.00
G2	L6 , R4	N/A	G	0.399	0.00 , 0.00

RELEASE 5.0

SCHEMATIC

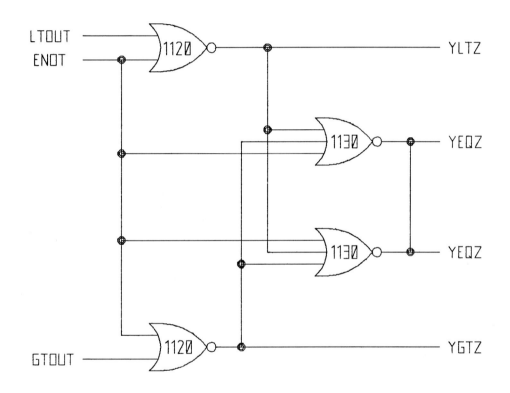

3 MICRON CMOS/BULK CELL FAMILY -CMOS3-	4480 COMPARATOR END CELL CELL HEIGHT 363 WIDTH 84	DATE: 1/01/87 REVISION: A

OUTLINE

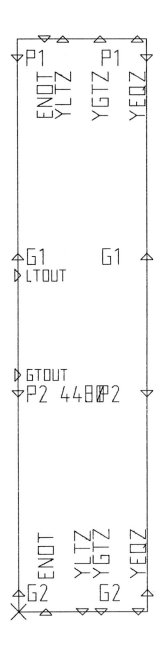

TRUTH TABLE

	INPUTS			OUTPUTS	
LTOUT	GTOUT	ENOT	YLTZ	YGTZ	YEQZ
0	0	0	1	1	0
0	1	0	1	0	0
1	0	0	0	1	0
1	1	0	0	0	1
1	X	0	0	X	X
X	1	0	X	0	X
X	X	0	X	X	X
*	*	1	0	0	0
0	0	X	X	X	X
0	1	X	X	0	X
1	0	X	0	X	X
1	1	X	0	0	X
1	X	X	0	X	X
X	1	X	X	0	X
X	X	X	X	X	X

* = Don't Care   X = Don't Know

SWITCHING CHARACTERISTICS

Consult the MSI function user's guide for the conditions under which these switching characteristics were determined and for guidance on their interpretation. Cload has the units of picofarads and the results are in nanoseconds.

```
   LTOUT --> YLTZ         Worst Case                 Best Case

0 --> 1  Delay =   4.24(Cload) +  5.49  OR   3.02(Cload) +  1.90
         Trans =  15.19(Cload) +  7.34  OR  11.62(Cload) +  1.76
1 --> 0  Delay =   3.47(Cload) +  6.91  OR   2.85(Cload) +  1.50
         Trans =  13.14(Cload) +  6.57  OR  10.72(Cload) +  1.77

   GTOUT --> YGTZ         Worst Case                 Best Case

0 --> 1  Delay =   4.69(Cload) +  5.30  OR   3.52(Cload) +  2.20
         Trans =  15.16(Cload) +  6.49  OR  13.70(Cload) +  1.73
1 --> 0  Delay =   3.96(Cload) +  6.64  OR   3.26(Cload) +  2.65
         Trans =  15.30(Cload) +  4.98  OR  12.83(Cload) +  1.36

   LTOUT --> YEQZ         Worst Case                 Best Case

0 --> 1  Delay =   3.51(Cload) + 10.52  OR   1.20(Cload) +  6.50
         Trans =   7.64(Cload) +  6.51  OR   3.52(Cload) +  3.16
1 --> 0  Delay =   2.16(Cload) +  7.90  OR    .65(Cload) +  1.19
         Trans =   3.70(Cload) +  2.46  OR   1.64(Cload) +  2.06

   GTOUT --> YEQZ         Worst Case                 Best Case

0 --> 1  Delay =   3.51(Cload) + 10.59  OR   1.20(Cload) +  3.93
         Trans =   7.64(Cload) +  6.51  OR   3.52(Cload) +  3.16
1 --> 0  Delay =   2.16(Cload) +  7.98  OR    .65(Cload) +  1.19
         Trans =   3.70(Cload) +  2.46  OR   1.64(Cload) +  2.06

   ENOT --> YEQZ          Worst Case                 Best Case

0 --> 1  Delay =   2.07(Cload) +  3.84  OR   1.00(Cload) +  1.58
         Trans =   5.34(Cload) + 11.68  OR   2.60(Cload) +  7.25
1 --> 0  Delay =   1.43(Cload) +  7.37  OR    .73(Cload) +  2.96
         Trans =   2.57(Cload) + 12.28  OR   1.38(Cload) +  7.51
```

MOSTRAN RESULTS

LTOUT --> YLTZ

		Worst Case		Best Case	
		1.5 pF	4.0 pF	1.5 pF	4.0 pF
0 --> 1	Delay	11.84	22.43	6.42	13.96
	Trans	30.00	67.76	19.20	48.26
1 --> 0	Delay	12.11	20.78	5.77	12.89
	Trans	26.29	59.15	17.85	44.65

GTOUT --> YGTZ

		Worst Case		Best Case	
		1.5 pF	4.0 pF	1.5 pF	4.0 pF
0 --> 1	Delay	12.33	24.05	7.48	16.29
	Trans	32.16	75.08	22.29	56.55
1 --> 0	Delay	12.59	22.50	7.55	15.71
	Trans	27.93	66.18	20.61	52.69

LTOUT --> YEQZ

		Worst Case		Best Case	
		1.5 pF	4.0 pF	1.5 pF	4.0 pF
0 --> 1	Delay	15.79	24.57	8.30	11.30
	Trans	17.96	37.05	8.45	17.26
1 --> 0	Delay	11.23	16.56	4.40	6.03
	Trans	8.01	17.26	4.51	8.60

GTOUT --> YEQZ

		Worst Case		Best Case	
		1.5 pF	4.0 pF	1.5 pF	4.0 pF
0 --> 1	Delay	15.86	24.64	5.73	8.73
	Trans	17.96	37.05	8.45	17.26
1 --> 0	Delay	11.23	16.64	2.17	3.80
	Trans	8.01	17.26	4.51	8.60

ENOT --> YEQZ

		Worst Case		Best Case	
		1.5 pF	4.0 pF	1.5 pF	4.0 pF
0 --> 1	Delay	6.94	12.11	3.08	5.58
	Trans	19.69	33.03	11.14	17.63
1 --> 0	Delay	9.52	13.10	4.06	5.89
	Trans	16.13	22.55	9.59	13.05

Note: The transition times recorded on this page are from 0 - 100%.

RELATED CELL TYPES: 4460, 4470, 4480,

The 4490 MSI function will compare the magnitude of two 8 bit binary words. The inputs to the function are binary words Y and Z and an enable signal. Three outputs are provided : Y < Z, Y > Z, Y = Z. When the enable signal is high all of the outputs will be set to zero.

The 4490 has as its basic components a beginning slice (4460), two middle slices (4470), and an end slice (4480). The middle cells are cascaded together to provide the 8 bits per word. The basic 4470 cell is a 4-bit comparator unit.

TERMINAL INFORMATION

ETER NAME	PHYSICAL NAME(S)	LOGICV FIELD	FUNCTION CODE	CAPACITANCE (pfarads)	RESISTANCE(S) (Kohms)
Y4	B1 , T1	1	I	0.490	2.50 , 2.50
Z4	B2 , T2	2	I	0.490	2.50 , 2.50
Y5	B3 , T3	3	I	0.509	2.50 , 2.50
Z5	B4 , T4	4	I	0.509	2.50 , 2.50
Y6	B5 , T5	5	I	0.493	2.46 , 2.46
Z6	B6 , T6	8	I	0.494	2.46 , 2.46
Y7	B7 , T7	9	I	0.516	2.58 , 2.58
Z7	B8 , T8	10	I	0.502	2.43 , 2.43
Y0	B9 , T9	11	I	0.490	2.50 , 2.50
Z0	B10 , T10	12	I	0.490	2.50 , 2.50
Y1	B11 , T11	15	I	0.509	2.50 , 2.50
Z1	B12 , T12	16	I	0.509	2.50 , 2.50
Y2	B13 , T13	17	I	0.493	2.46 , 2.46
Z2	B14 , T14	18	I	0.494	2.46 , 2.46
Y3	B15 , T15	19	I	0.516	2.58 , 2.58
Z3	B16 , T16	22	I	0.502	2.43 , 2.43
ENOT	B17 , T17	23	I	1.087	2.55 , 2.55
YLTZ	B18 , T18	6	O	1.171	2.10 , 0.81
YGTZ	B19 , T19	7	O	1.175	2.37 , 2.61
YEQZ	B20 , T20	13	O	1.440	0.27 , 0.27
P1	L1 , R1	N/A	P	12.528	0.00 , 0.00
G1	L2 , R2	N/A	G	9.906	0.00 , 0.00
P2	L3 , R3	N/A	P	13.175	0.00 , 0.00
G2	L4 , R4	N/A	G	9.681	0.00 , 0.00

RELEASE 5.0

PAGE NO.   4490 - 1

```
┌──────────────────────┬────────────────────────────┬─────────────────────┐
│ 3 MICRON CMOS/BULK   │           4490             │ DATE:    1/01/87    │
│    CELL FAMILY       │     8 BIT COMPARATOR       │ REVISION: A         │
│      -CMOS3-         │  CELL HEIGHT 363 WIDTH 1320 │                     │
├──────────────────────┴────────────────────────────┴─────────────────────┤
│                             TRUTH TABLE                                   │
│                                                                           │
│                                                                           │
│          INPUTS                              OUTPUTS                       │
│                                                                           │
│   ENABLE      Y           Z           Y < Z      Y > Z      Y = Z         │
│   ----------------------------------   ----------------------------       │
│      1        *           *      |       0          0          0          │
│      0     WORD Y  =   WORD Z    |       0          0          1          │
│      0     WORD Y  <   WORD Z    |       1          0          0          │
│      0     WORD Y  >   WORD Z    |       0          1          0          │
│      0       X           X       |       X          X          X          │
│                                                                           │
│                                                                           │
│                                                                           │
│   * = Don't Care,  X = Don't know                                         │
├───────────────────────────────────────────────────────────────────────────┤
│                      QUICK REFERENCE TIMING                               │
│                                                                           │
│  VDD = 5 volts                TR    WORD Y --> YGTZ =  29.23 nsec.        │
│  C(load) = 1.5 picofarads     PD0-1 WORD Y --> YEQZ =  79.28 nsec.        │
│  Input trans time = 30 nsec.  TR    WORD Y --> YEQZ =  17.97 nsec.        │
│  Worst case processing        PD0-1 ENOT   --> YEQZ =   6.95 nsec.        │
│                               TR    ENOT   --> YEQZ =  19.69 nsec.        │
│                                                                           │
├───────────────────────────────────────────────────────────────────────────┤
│  RELEASE 5.0                              PAGE NO.  4490 - 2              │
└───────────────────────────────────────────────────────────────────────────┘
```

SCHEMATIC

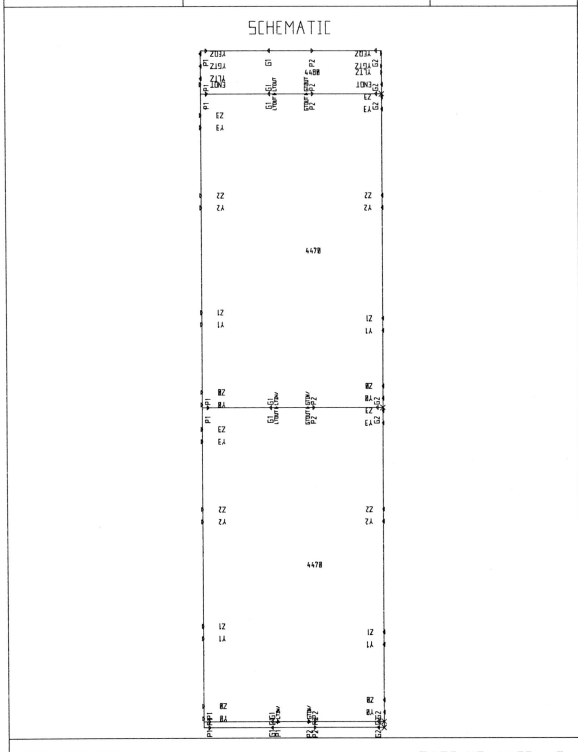

SWITCHING CHARACTERISTICS

Consult the MSI function user's guide for the conditions under which these switching characteristics were determined and for guidance on their interpretation. Cload has the units of picofarads and the results are in nanoseconds.

WORD Y --> YGTZ   Worst Case   Best Case

```
0 --> 1  Delay =    4.69(Cload) + 68.72  OR   3.52(Cload) + 16.66
         Trans =   15.16(Cload) +  6.49  OR  13.70(Cload) +  1.73
1 --> 0  Delay =    3.96(Cload) + 61.92  OR   3.26(Cload) + 27.77
         Trans =   15.30(Cload) +  4.98  OR  12.83(Cload) +  1.36
```

WORD Y --> YEQZ   Worst Case   Best Case

```
0 --> 1  Delay =    3.51(Cload) + 74.01  OR   1.20(Cload) + 18.39
         Trans =    7.64(Cload) +  6.51  OR   3.52(Cload) +  3.16
1 --> 0  Delay =    2.16(Cload) + 63.26  OR    .65(Cload) + 26.31
         Trans =    3.70(Cload) +  2.46  OR   1.64(Cload) +  2.06
```

 ENOT --> YEQZ   Worst Case   Best Case

```
0 --> 1  Delay =    2.07(Cload) +  3.84  OR   1.00(Cload) +  1.58
         Trans =    5.34(Cload) + 11.68  OR   2.60(Cload) +  7.25
1 --> 0  Delay =    1.43(Cload) +  7.37  OR    .73(Cload) +  2.96
         Trans =    2.57(Cload) + 12.28  OR   1.38(Cload) +  7.51
```

OUTLINE

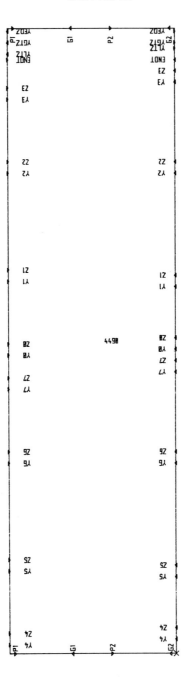

3 MICRON CMOS/BULK CELL FAMILY -CMOS3-	4490 8 BIT COMPARATOR CELL HEIGHT 363 WIDTH 1320	DATE: 1/01/87 REVISION: A

```
Time(4490)      =   Time(4460)   +   Time(4470's)      +   Time(4480)
                    A(N)         +   B                 +   C(Cload)
N = # OF 4470s
```

WORD Y --> YGTZ

		Worst Case			Best Case		
		A	B	C	A	B	C
0 --> 1	Delay	31.71	5.30	4.69	7.23	2.20	3.52
	Trans	0.00	6.49	15.16	0.00	1.73	13.70
1 --> 0	Delay	27.64	6.64	3.69	12.56	2.65	3.26
	Trans	0.00	4.98	15.30	0.00	1.36	12.83

WORD Y --> YEQZ

		Worst Case			Best Case		
0 --> 1	Delay	31.71	10.59	3.51	7.23	3.93	1.20
	Trans	0.00	6.51	7.64	0.00	3.16	3.52
1 --> 0	Delay	27.64	7.98	2.16	12.56	1.19	0.65
	Trans	0.00	2.46	3.70	0.00	2.06	1.64

ENOT --> YEQZ

		Worst Case			Best Case		
0 --> 1	Delay	0.00	3.84	2.07	0.00	1.58	1.00
	Trans	0.00	11.68	5.34	0.00	7.25	2.60
1 --> 0	Delay	0.00	7.37	1.43	0.00	2.96	0.73
	Trans	0.00	12.28	2.57	0.00	7.51	1.38

RELATED CELL TYPES: 4570, 4580, 4590

The 4560 is the first stage in an n-bit asynchronous ripple counter. Its main purpose is to determine the mode of the counter. If SELECT is low ,the counter mode is preset. If SELECT is high, the counter mode is count.

The 4560 also provides the first counter slice (THE 4570) with its data input. (DATA0)

TERMINAL INFORMATION

ETER NAME	PHYSICAL NAME(S)	LOGICV FIELD	FUNCTION CODE	CAPACITANCE (pfarads)	RESISTANCE(S) (Kohms)
SELECT	T1, B1	1	I	0.326	0.750,0.750
DATA0	T2, B2, R3	—	F	0.209	0.244,0.413,0.030
SEL	R4	6	O	0.942	0.450
P1	L1, R1	—	P	0.325	0.0,0.0
G1	L2, R2	—	G	0.216	0.0,0.0
P2	L3, R5	—	P	0.325	0.0,0.0
G2	L4, R6	—	G	0.216	0.0,0.0

RELEASE 5.0

SCHEMATIC

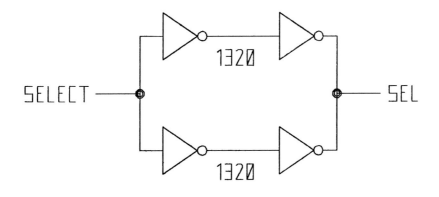

SELECT

1320

1320

SEL

DATA0 —————————————— DATA0

OUTLINE

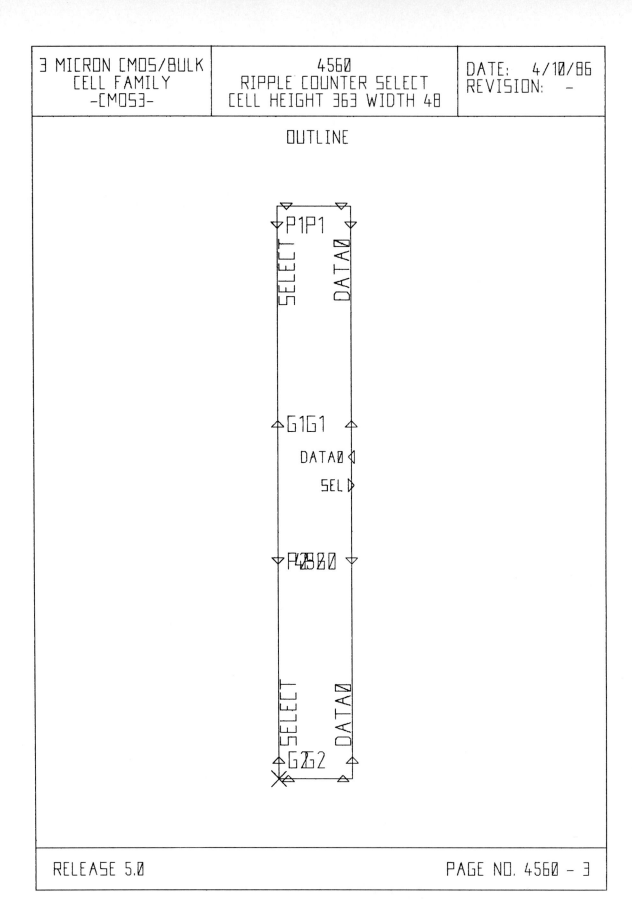

SWITCHING CHARACTERISTICS

Consult the MSI function user's guide for the conditions under which these switching characteristics were determined and for guidance on their interpretation. Cload has the units of picofarads and the results are in nanoseconds.

```
SELECT --> SEL          Worst Case              Best Case

0 --> 1  Delay =    1.19(Cload) +  5.90  OR    .98(Cload) +  2.22
         Trans =    4.60(Cload) +  1.06  OR   3.85(Cload) +   .32
1 --> 0  Delay =    1.08(Cload) +  5.49  OR    .93(Cload) +  2.18
         Trans =    4.16(Cload) +   .81  OR   3.65(Cload) +   .21
```

3 MICRON CMOS/BULK CELL FAMILY -CMOS3-	4560 RIPPLE COUNTER SELECT CELL HEIGHT 363 WIDTH 48	DATE: 4/10/86 REVISION: -

MOSTRAN RESULTS

SELECT --> SEL		Worst Case		Best Case	
		N=4 (2.28 pF)	N=20 (11.41 pF)	N=4 (2.28 pF)	N=20 (11.41 pF)
0 --> 1	Delay	10.68	29.81	6.13	21.79
	Trans	19.46	93.07	15.70	77.24
1 --> 0	Delay	9.83	27.18	5.89	20.73
	Trans	17.46	84.06	14.79	73.11

NOTE: Transition times have been multiplied by 1.25 to compensate for the measurements taken at 80% of the signal swing.

3 MICRON CMOS/BULK
CELL FAMILY
-CMOS3-

4570
RIPPLE COUNTER SLICE
CELL HEIGHT 363 WIDTH 360

DATE: 4/10/86
REVISION: -

RELATED CELL TYPES: 4560, 4580, 4590

The 4570 comprises 2-bits of an n-bit ripple counter with parallel load. To function properly it requires five input signals; DATA0 (provided by the 4560 in the first slice and by the 4570 in each subsequent slice) , LDATA0, LDATA1, SEL (4560) , and RSET (4580).

TERMINAL INFORMATION

ETER NAME	PHYSICAL NAME(S)	LOGICV FIELD	FUNCTION CODE	CAPACITANCE (pfarads)	RESISTANCE(S) (Kohms)
LDATA0	T1, B1	4	I	0.622	0.750, 1.196
LDATA1	T4, B4	5	I	0.612	1.240, 0.750
DATA0	L3	3	I	0.321	0.982
SEL	L4, R4	1	I	1.141	0.915, 0.915
RSET	L5, R5	2	I	0.626	0.915, 0.915
Q0	T2, B2	6	O	1.510	1.132, 0.086
Q1	T3, B3, R3	7	O	1.215	.086,.562,.150
P1	L1, R1	–	P	3.808	0.0, 0.0
G1	L2, R2	–	G	2.285	0.0, 0.0
P2	L6, R6	–	P	3.808	0.0, 0.0
G2	L7, R7	–	G	2.285	0.0, 0.0

SCHEMATIC

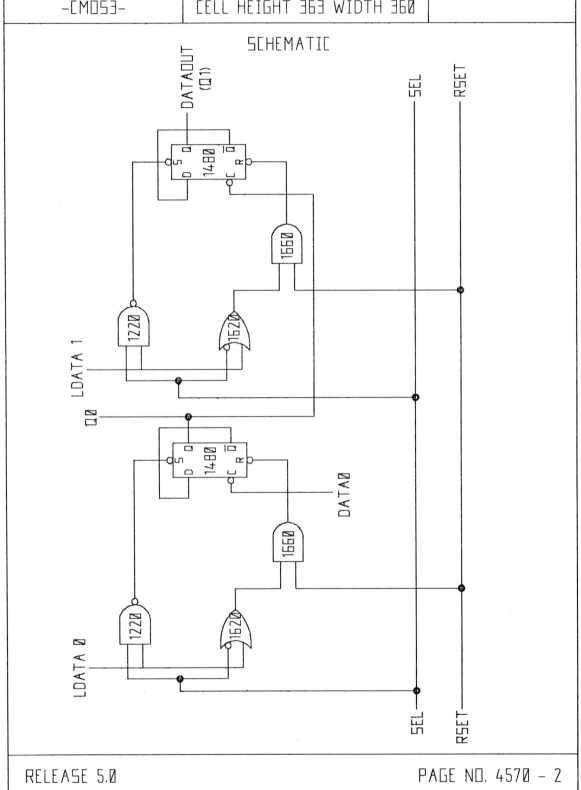

OUTLINE

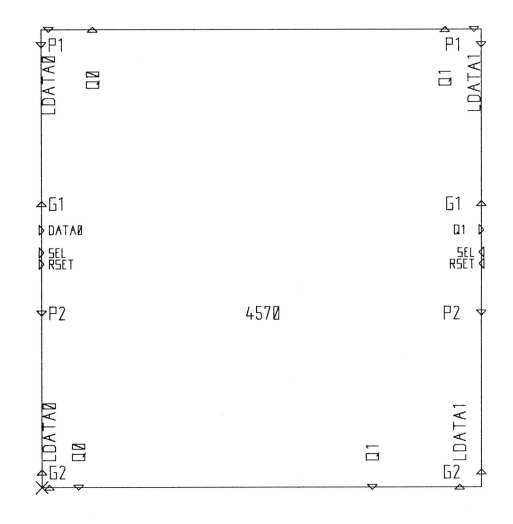

SWITCHING CHARACTERISTICS

Consult the MSI function user's guide for the conditions under which these switching characteristics were determined and for guidance on their interpretation. Cload has the units of picofarads and the results are in nanoseconds.

DATA0   --> Q1   Worst Case   Best Case

0 --> 1 Delay =   4.57(Cload) + 24.12   OR   2.25(Cload) + 9.40
         Trans =   7.15(Cload) + 4.96   OR   2.63(Cload) + 2.54
1 --> 0 Delay =   5.72(Cload) + 27.30   OR   2.70(Cload) + 10.62
         Trans =   9.78(Cload) + 6.61   OR   3.71(Cload) + 3.08

LDATA0 --> Q0   Worst Case   Best Case

0 --> 1 Delay =   1.86(Cload) + 7.83   OR   .53(Cload) + 2.79
         Trans =   6.45(Cload) + 4.39   OR   1.24(Cload) + 3.57
1 --> 0 Delay =   3.69(Cload) + 25.45   OR   1.33(Cload) + 10.15
         Trans =   11.46(Cload) + 7.95   OR   3.72(Cload) + 4.00

RSET   --> Q0   Worst Case   Best Case

1 --> 0 Delay =   3.67(Cload) + 17.06   OR   1.32(Cload) + 7.02
         Trans =   11.44(Cload) + 8.26   OR   3.68(Cload) + 4.27

RELEASE 5.0   PAGE NO.   4570 - 4

MOSTRAN RESULTS

DATA0 --> Q1

		Worst Case			Best Case		
		.32 pF	1.5 pF	4.0 pF	.32 pF	1.5 pF	4.0 pF
0 --> 1	Delay	34.24	30.97	42.39	15.64	12.78	18.41
	Trans	8.03	15.68	33.55	4.21	6.48	13.05
1 --> 0	Delay	37.63	35.89	50.20	16.94	14.67	21.42
	Trans	10.33	21.28	45.73	4.89	8.65	17.93

LDATA0 --> Q0

		Worst Case		Best Case	
		1.5 pF	4.0 pF	1.5 pF	4.0 pF
0 --> 1	Delay	10.63	15.29	3.58	4.90
	Trans	14.06	30.18	5.43	8.53
1 --> 0	Delay	30.99	40.22	12.14	15.46
	Trans	25.15	53.81	9.59	18.90

RSET --> Q0

		Worst Case		Best Case	
		1.5 pF	4.0 pF	1.5 pF	4.0 pF
1 --> 0	Delay	22.57	31.75	9.00	12.30
	Trans	25.41	54.00	9.80	19.01

NOTE: For a .32pF load, the resistance was 1132 ohms.
     Transition times have been multiplied by 1.25
to compensate for the measurements taken at 80% of
the signal swing.

RELATED CELL TYPES: 4560, 4570, 4590

The 4580 provides reset control to an n–bit ripple counter made using the 4560 and 4570 cells. It requires no other inputs than reset.

Users please note that reset is active low.

TERMINAL INFORMATION

ETER NAME	PHYSICAL NAME(S)	LOGICV FIELD	FUNCTION CODE	CAPACITANCE (pfarads)	RESISTANCE(S) (Kohms)
RESET	T1, B1	1	I	0.326	0.750, 0.750
RSET	L3	6	O	0.938	0.450
P1	L1, R1	–	P	0.316	0.0, 0.0
G1	L2, R2	–	G	0.207	0.0, 0.0
P2	L4, R3	–	P	0.316	0.0, 0.0
G2	L5, R4	–	G	0.207	0.0, 0.0

3 MICRON CMOS/BULK CELL FAMILY -CMOS3-	4580 RIPPLE COUNTER RESET CELL HEIGHT 363 WIDTH 36	DATE: 4/10/86 REVISION: -

SCHEMATIC

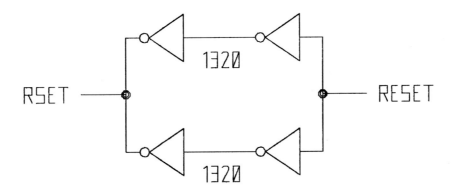

RSET

1320

1320

RESET

3 MICRON CMOS/BULK CELL FAMILY -CMOS3-	4580 RIPPLE COUNTER RESET CELL HEIGHT 363 WIDTH 36	DATE: 4/10/86 REVISION: -

OUTLINE

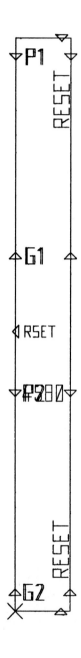

SWITCHING CHARACTERISTICS

Consult the MSI function user's guide for the conditions under which these switching characteristics were determined and for guidance on their interpretation. Cload has the units of picofarads and the results are in nanoseconds.

```
RESET  --> RSET        Worst Case                 Best Case

0 --> 1  Delay =    .66(Cload) +  5.88  OR    .54(Cload) +  2.23
         Trans =   1.86(Cload) +  4.00  OR   2.09(Cload) +   .54
1 --> 0  Delay =    .59(Cload) +  5.46  OR    .51(Cload) +  2.19
         Trans =   2.25(Cload) +  1.22  OR   1.99(Cload) +   .43
```

MOSTRAN RESULTS

RESET --> RSET		Worst Case		Best Case	
		N=4 (1.25 pF)	N=20 (6.26 pF)	N=4 (1.25 pF)	N=20 (6.26 pF)
0 --> 1	Delay	8.50	18.98	4.37	12.95
	Trans	11.42	41.10	8.92	42.46
1 --> 0	Delay	7.85	17.40	4.22	12.36
	Trans	10.24	46.31	8.37	40.14

NOTE: Transition times have been multiplied by 1.25 to compensate for the measurements taken at 80% of the signal swing.

RELATED CELL TYPES: 4560, 4570, 4580

The 4590 is a 4-bit ripple counter with parallel load.
It is comprised of one 4560 , two 4570's , and one 4580.
To function properly it requires 7 inputs; SELECT, DATA0
(see 4560), LDATA0 through LDATA3 (see 4570),and RESET
(see 4580).

Note, when loading the counter, the data must be present
on all LDATA inputs before the load command is given.

TERMINAL INFORMATION

ETER NAME	PHYSICAL NAME(S)	LOGICV FIELD	FUNCTION CODE	CAPACITANCE (pfarads)	RESISTANCE(S) (Kohms)
SELECT	T1, B1	2	I	0.326	0.750, 0.750
DATA0	T2, B2	1	I	0.530	1.230, 1.395
RESET	T11, B11	9	I	0.326	0.750, 0.750
LDATA0	T3, B3	3	I	0.622	0.750, 1.196
LDATA1	T6, B6	4	I	0.612	1.240, 0.750
LDATA2	T7, B7	5	I	0.622	0.750, 1.190
LDATA3	T10, B10	8	I	0.612	1.240, 0.750
Q0	T4, B4	6	O	1.510	1.132, 0.086
Q1	T5, B5	7	O	1.536	0.086, 1.132
Q2	T8, B8	13	O	1.510	1.132, 0.086
Q3	T9, B9	14	O	1.215	0.086, 0.562
P1	L1, R1	—	P	8.256	0.0, 0.0
G1	L2, R2	—	G	4.992	0.0, 0.0
P2	L3, R3	—	P	8.256	0.0, 0.0
G2	L4, R4	—	G	4.992	0.0, 0.0

ABBREVIATED TRUTH TABLE

DATA0 (CLK)	SELECT	RSET	OPERATING MODE	Q0,Q1,Q2,Q3
*	*	0	RESET	0 0 0 0
1	*	1	*	NO CHANGE
\	0	1	COUNT	COUNT UP (MODULUS 16)
\	1	1	LOAD	LOAD WORD A

* = Don't Care, \ = Negative edge of clock.

QUICK REFERENCE TIMING

VDD = 5 volts
C(load) = 1.5 picofarads
Input trans time = 30 nsec.
Worst case processing

DATA0 --> Q3
  DELAY 0 --> 1 = 133.69 nsec.
  TRAN   = 39.78 nsec.
RESET --> Q3
  DELAY 1 --> 0 = 28.75 nsec.

RELEASE 5.0

SCHEMATIC

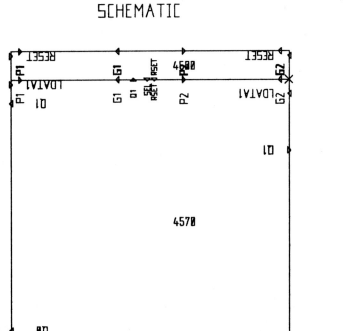

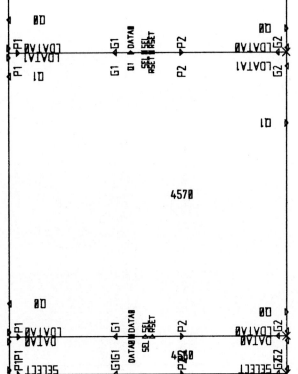

Consult the MSI function user's guide for the conditions under which these switching characteristics were determined and for guidance on their interpretation. Cload has the units of picofarads and the results are in nanoseconds.

SPECIAL TIMING

```
Data Setup Time . . . . . . . . =  26.41 nanoseconds
Data Hold Time  . . . . . . . . =   0.00 nanoseconds
Control Setup Time  . . . . . . =   7.93 nanoseconds
Control Hold Time . . . . . . . =   0.00 nanoseconds
Minimum Clock Pulse Width . . . =  28.00 nanoseconds
Maximum Clock Rise Time . . . . = 200.00 nanoseconds
Minimum Reset Pulse Width . . . =  32.00 nanoseconds
Minimum Set Pulse Width . . . . =  25.00 nanoseconds
```

SWITCHING CHARACTERISTICS

RESET --> Q0   Worst Case   Best Case

| 1 --> 0 | Delay = | 3.67(Cload) + 23.24 | OR | 1.32(Cload) + 9.85 |
| | Trans = | 11.44(Cload) + 12.28 | OR | 3.68(Cload) + 7.18 |

DATA0 --> Q3   Worst Case   Best Case

0 --> 1	Delay =	4.57(Cload) + 126.84	OR	2.25(Cload) + 56.32
	Trans =	7.15(Cload) + 29.05	OR	2.63(Cload) + 15.17
1 --> 0	Delay =	5.72(Cload) + 140.19	OR	2.70(Cload) + 61.44
	Trans =	9.78(Cload) + 37.60	OR	3.71(Cload) + 17.75

OUTLINE

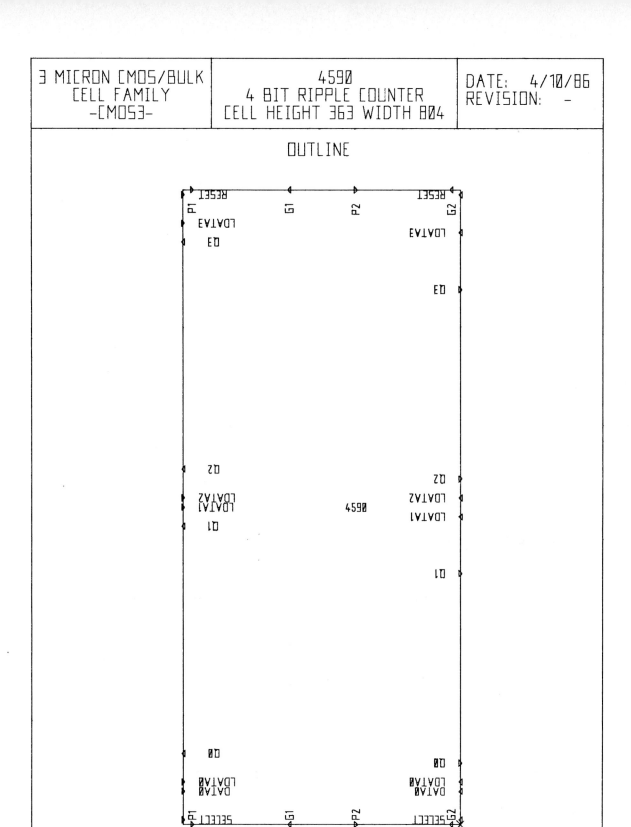

Time(4590)   = Time(4560) + Time(4570's) + Time(4580)
Time(N,Cload) =   0   + [A(Cload) + B] + [C(N) + D]

RESET --> Q   Worst Case
                      A   B   C   D

1 --> 0   Delay   3.67   17.06   0.18   5.46
          Trans   11.44   8.26   0.70   1.22

                                      Best Case

1 --> 0   Delay   1.32   7.02   0.16   2.19
          Trans   3.68   4.27   0.62   0.43

Time(4590)   = Time(4560) + Time(4570's) + Time(4580)
Time(N,Cload) = [A(N) + B] + [C(Cload) + D] +   0

LDATA --> Q   Worst Case
                      A   B   C   D

0 --> 1   Delay   0.68   5.90   1.86   7.83
          Trans   2.62   1.06   6.45   4.39
1 --> 0   Delay   0.62   5.49   3.69   25.45
          Trans   2.37   0.81   11.46   7.95

                                      Best Case

0 --> 1   Delay   0.56   2.22   0.53   2.79
          Trans   2.19   0.32   1.24   3.57
1 --> 0   Delay   0.53   2.18   1.33   10.15
          Trans   2.08   0.21   3.72   4.00

```
Time(4590)    = Time(4560)  +  Time(4570's)   +  Time(4580)
Time(N,Cload) =    0    +  A(N-1)   +  [B(Cload) + C]   +    0
```

```
LDATA  --> Q                        Worst Case
                        A               B              C

0 --> 1  Delay        34.24           4.57          24.12
         Trans         8.03           7.15           4.96
1 --> 0  Delay        37.63           5.72          27.30
         Trans        10.33           9.78           6.61

                                    Best Case
0 --> 1  Delay        15.64           2.25           9.40
         Trans         4.21           2.63           2.54
1 --> 0  Delay        16.94           2.70          10.62
         Trans         4.89           3.71           3.08
```

RELATED CELL TYPES: N/A

The 4610 is a stray cell for use on chips composed of both MSI and SSI cells. The 4610 is used to connect power and ground terminals on the left side of MSIs when rows contain both MSIs and SSIs.

TERMINAL INFORMATION

ETER NAME	PHYSICAL NAME(S)			LOGICV FIELD	FUNCTION CODE	CAPACITANCE (pfarads)	RESISTANCE(S) (Kohms)
G1	R3,	R2,	L2	N/A	G	0.099	0.00, 0.00, 0.00
P1	L1,	R1		N/A	P	0.099	0.00, 0.00,

OUTLINE

679

RELATED CELL TYPES: N/A

The 4620 is a stray cell for use on chips composed of both MSI and SSI cells. The 4620 is used to connect power and ground terminals on the right side of MSIs when rows contain both MSIs and SSIs.

TERMINAL INFORMATION

ETER NAME	PHYSICAL NAME(S)		LOGICV FIELD	FUNCTION CODE	CAPACITANCE (pfarads)	RESISTANCE(S) (Kohms)
G2	L3, R2,		N/A	G	0.010	0.00, 0.00
P2	R1, L2,	L1	N/A	P	0.102	0.00, 0.00, 0.00

OUTLINE

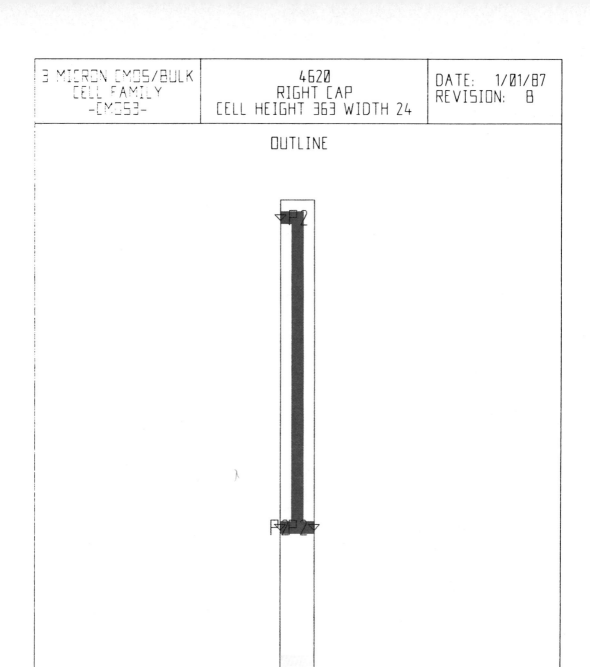

681

RELATED CELL TYPES: N/A

The 4630 is a stray cell to jump signals across an MSI cell row.

TERMINAL INFORMATION

ETER NAME	PHYSICAL NAME(S)	LOGICV FIELD	FUNCTION CODE	CAPACITANCE (pfarads)	RESISTANCE(S) (Kohms)
1	T1, B1	N/A	F	0.196	0.20, 0.20
P1	R1, L1	N/A	P	0.009	0.00, 0.00
G1	R2, L2	N/A	G	0.009	0.00, 0.00
P2	R3, L3	N/A	P	0.009	0.00, 0.00
G2	R4, L4	N/A	G	0.009	0.00, 0.00

RELEASE 5.0

PAGE NO. 4630 - 1

OUTLINE

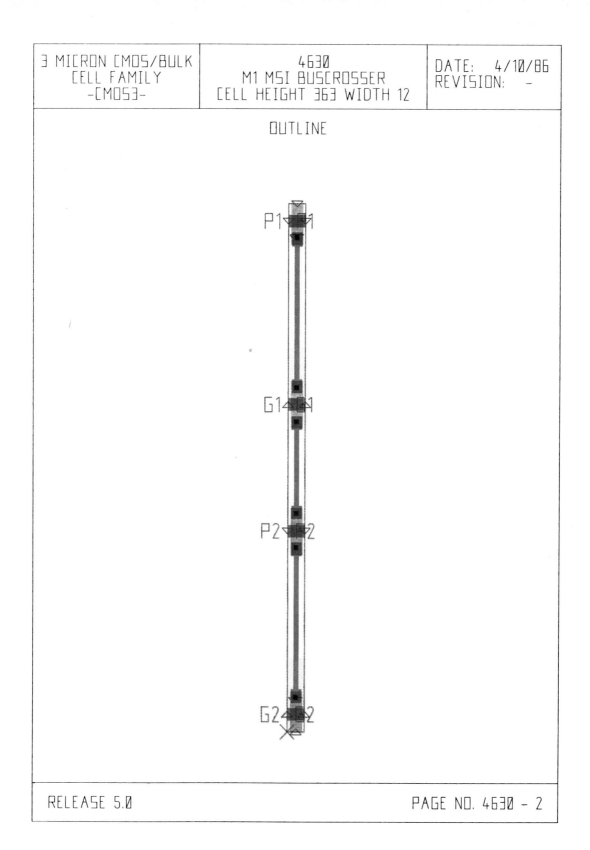

RELATED CELL TYPES: N/A

The 4640 is a stray cell to jump signals across an MSI cell row in second metal.

TERMINAL INFORMATION

ETER NAME	PHYSICAL NAME(S)	LOGICV FIELD	FUNCTION CODE	CAPACITANCE (pfarads)	RESISTANCE(S) (Kohms)
1	T1, B1	N/A	F	0.069	0.00, 0.00
P1	R1, L1	N/A	P	0.010	0.00, 0.00
G1	R2, L2	N/A	G	0.010	0.00, 0.00
P2	R3, L3	N/A	P	0.010	0.00, 0.00
G2	R4, L4	N/A	G	0.010	0.00, 0.00

OUTLINE

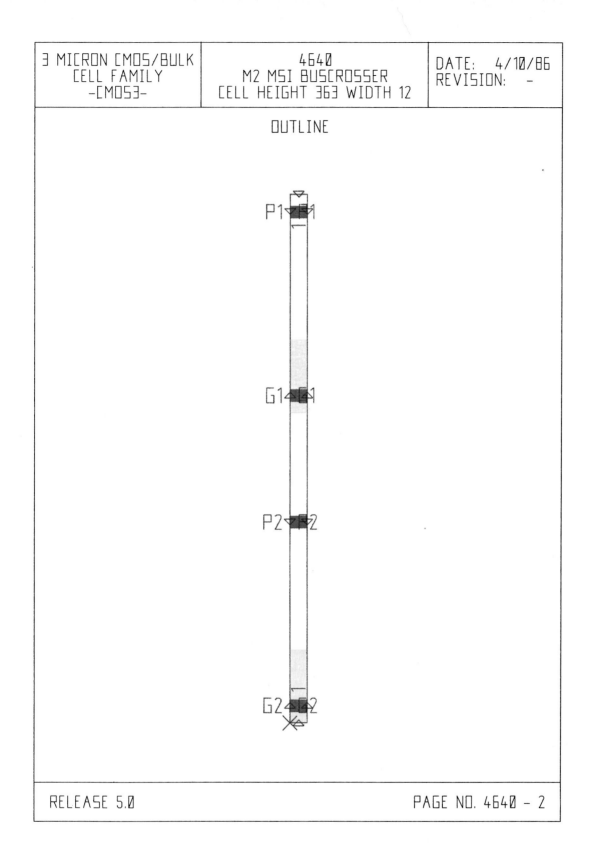

685

3 MICRON CMOS/BULK CELL FAMILY -CMOS3-	4700 8-INPUT PRIORITY ENCODER CELL HEIGHT 363 WIDTH 540	DATE: 4/10/86 REVISION: -

RELATED CELL TYPES: 4710, 4720

The 4700 is designed to encode eight inputs, D0-D7, into a binary coded output, Q0-Q3. The output code is that of the highest priority input. Any input of lower priority is ignored. D0 is the highest priority input and D7 is the lowest priority input.

The input lines are active high, (e.g., the three binary outputs are low when input D0 is high). The Q3 output is high when any input is high.

TERMINAL INFORMATION

ETER NAME	PHYSICAL NAME(S)	LOGICV FIELD	FUNCTION CODE	CAPACITANCE (pfarads)	RESISTANCE(S) (Kohms)
D0	T1, B1	1	I	0.37	0.75, 1.20
D1	T2, B2	2	I	0.38	1.20, 0.75
D2	T3, B3	3	I	0.38	1.20, 0.75
D3	T4, B4	4	I	0.29	1.20, 0.75
D4	T9, B9	5	I	0.38	0.75, 1.2
D5	T10, B10	8	I	0.42	0.75, 1.2
D6	T11, B11	9	I	0.37	0.75, 1.2
D7	T12, B12	10	I	0.26	1.20, 0.75
Q0	T5, B5	6	O	0.66	0.57, 0.12
Q1	T6, B6	7	O	0.71	0.12, 0.57
Q2	T7, B7	13	O	0.61	1.20, 0.75
Q3	T8, B8	14	O	0.74	0.75, 1.2
P1	R1, L1	–	P	5.22	0.0, 0.0
G1	R2, L2	–	G	3.67	0.0, 0.0
P2	R3, L3	–	P	4.57	0.0, 0.0
G2	R4, L4	–	G	3.40	0.0, 0.0

3 MICRON CMOS/BULK CELL FAMILY -CMOS3-	4700 8-INPUT PRIORITY ENCODER CELL HEIGHT 363 WIDTH 540	DATE: 4/10/86 REVISION: -

ABBREVIATED TRUTH TABLE

			INPUTS						OUTPUTS		
D0	D1	D2	D3	D4	D5	D6	D7	Q3	Q2	Q1	Q0
1	*	*	*	*	*	*	*	1	0	0	0
0	1	*	*	*	*	*	*	1	0	0	1
0	0	1	*	*	*	*	*	1	0	1	0
0	0	0	1	*	*	*	*	1	0	1	1
0	0	0	0	1	*	*	*	1	1	0	0
0	0	0	0	0	1	*	*	1	1	0	1
0	0	0	0	0	0	1	*	1	1	1	0
0	0	0	0	0	0	0	1	1	1	1	1
0	0	0	0	0	0	0	0	0	0	0	0
X	*	*	*	*	*	*	*	X	X	X	X
0	X	*	*	*	*	*	*	X	X	X	X
0	0	X	*	*	*	*	*	X	X	X	X
0	0	0	X	*	*	*	*	X	X	X	X
0	0	0	0	X	*	*	*	X	X	X	X
0	0	0	0	0	X	*	*	X	X	X	X
0	0	0	0	0	0	X	*	X	X	X	X
0	0	0	0	0	0	0	X	X	X	X	X

* = Don't Care   X = Don't Know

QUICK REFERENCE TIMING

VDD = 5 volts	DATA --> Q3 OUT = 21.40 nsec.
C(load) = 1.5 picofarads	DATA --> Q1 OUT = 27.62 nsec.
Input trans time = 30 nsec.	DATA --> Q0 OUT = 28.61 nsec.
Worst case processing	Tr, Tf (Q0, Q1) = 13.39 nsec.
	Tr, Tf (Q2, Q3) = 17.75 nsec.

RELEASE 5.0

SCHEMATIC

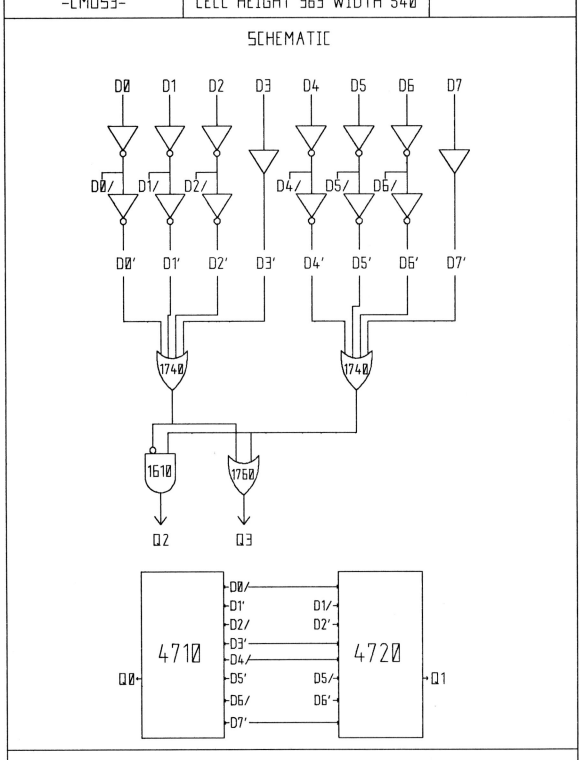

SWITCHING CHARACTERISTICS

Consult the MSI function user's guide for the conditions under which these switching characteristics were determined and for guidance on their interpretation. Cload has the units of picofarads and the results are in nanoseconds.

D7 --> Q0 OUT   Worst Case   Best Case

```
0 --> 1  Delay =   2.10(Cload) + 25.44   OR   1.15(Cload) + 11.06
         Trans =   4.99(Cload) +  9.25   OR   3.00(Cload) +  5.30
1 --> 0  Delay =   2.18(Cload) + 26.72   OR   1.10(Cload) + 11.57
         Trans =   5.16(Cload) +  7.13   OR   3.01(Cload) +  4.27
```

D1 --> Q0 OUT   Worst Case   Best Case

```
0 --> 1  Delay =   1.59(Cload) + 13.13   OR   0.94(Cload) +  5.24
         Trans =   5.18(Cload) +  2.41   OR   3.43(Cload) +  0.86
1 --> 0  Delay =   1.76(Cload) + 12.57   OR   0.95(Cload) +  5.22
         Trans =   5.29(Cload) +  2.51   OR   3.37(Cload) +  0.91
```

D7 --> Q1 OUT   Worst Case   Best Case

```
0 --> 1  Delay =   2.12(Cload) + 24.44   OR   1.10(Cload) + 10.21
         Trans =   5.33(Cload) +  8.17   OR   3.08(Cload) +  4.24
1 --> 0  Delay =   2.17(Cload) + 25.17   OR   1.09(Cload) + 10.86
         Trans =   5.14(Cload) +  7.24   OR   3.02(Cload) +  4.17
```

D2 --> Q1 OUT   Worst Case   Best Case

```
0 --> 1  Delay =   1.75(Cload) + 16.12   OR   0.94(Cload) +  6.37
         Trans =   5.52(Cload) +  3.28   OR   3.39(Cload) +  1.15
1 --> 0  Delay =   2.17(Cload) + 21.00   OR   1.09(Cload) +  9.05
         Trans =   5.13(Cload) +  7.31   OR   3.02(Cload) +  4.20
```

D7 --> Q2 OUT   Worst Case   Best Case

```
0 --> 1  Delay =   3.68(Cload) + 17.54   OR   1.78(Cload) +  7.04
         Trans =  11.95(Cload) +  3.28   OR   6.27(Cload) +  1.68
1 --> 0  Delay =   1.63(Cload) + 20.91   OR   0.92(Cload) +  8.60
         Trans =   5.22(Cload) +  2.01   OR   3.38(Cload) +  0.66
```

D7 --> Q3 OUT   Worst Case   Best Case

```
0 --> 1  Delay =   1.24(Cload) + 19.54   OR   1.04(Cload) +  7.47
         Trans =   7.02(Cload) +  1.01   OR   3.84(Cload) +  0.83
1 --> 0  Delay =   1.64(Cload) + 21.76   OR   0.92(Cload) +  8.86
         Trans =   5.12(Cload) +  2.17   OR   3.35(Cload) +  0.68
```

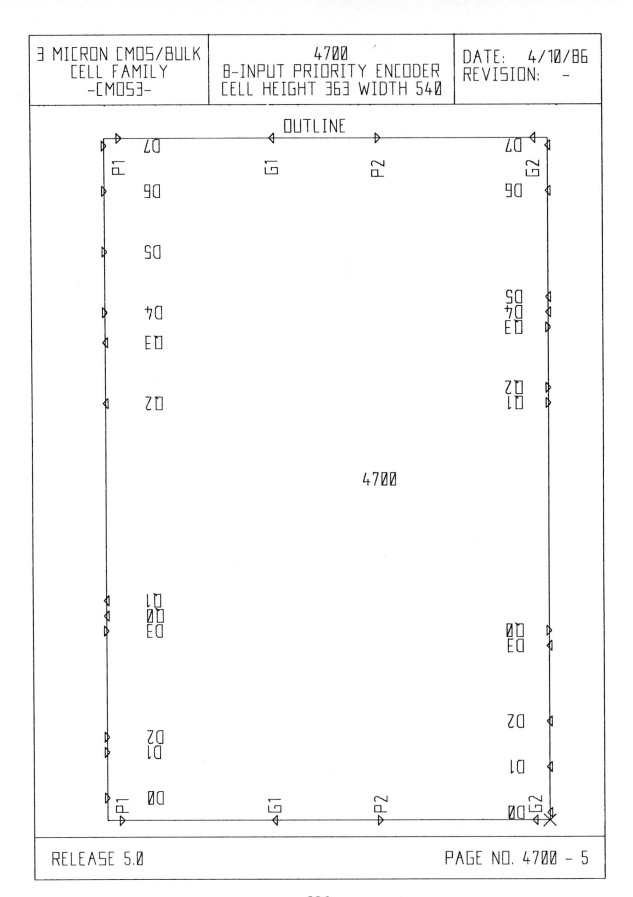

OUTLINE

4700

3 MICRON CMOS/BULK CELL FAMILY -CMOS3-	4700 8-INPUT PRIORITY ENCODER CELL HEIGHT 363 WIDTH 540	DATE: 4/10/86 REVISION: -

MOSTRAN RESULTS

D7 --> Q0 OUT	Worst Case		Best Case	
	1.5 pF	4.0 pF	1.5 pF	4.0 pF
0 --> 1 Delay	28.61	33.86	12.78	15.65
Trans	13.39	23.38	7.84	13.84
1 --> 0 Delay	30.00	35.46	13.21	15.95
Trans	11.90	22.23	7.03	13.05

D1 --> Q0 OUT	Worst Case		Best Case	
	1.5 pF	4.0 pF	1.5 pF	4.0 pF
0 --> 1 Delay	15.53	19.50	6.65	9.00
Trans	8.14	18.50	4.80	11.66
1 --> 0 Delay	15.20	19.59	6.64	9.01
Trans	8.36	18.94	4.78	11.53

D7 --> Q1 OUT	Worst Case		Best Case	
	1.5 pF	4.0 pF	1.5 pF	4.0 pF
0 --> 1 Delay	27.62	32.92	11.85	14.59
Trans	12.93	23.59	7.08	13.23
1 --> 0 Delay	28.42	33.85	12.49	15.21
Trans	11.96	22.24	6.96	13.00

D2 --> Q1 OUT	Worst Case		Best Case	
	1.5 pF	4.0 pF	1.5 pF	4.0 pF
0 --> 1 Delay	18.75	23.13	7.79	10.15
Trans	9.24	20.27	4.99	11.77
1 --> 0 Delay	24.26	29.69	10.68	13.40
Trans	12.01	22.28	6.98	13.01

D7 --> Q2 OUT	Worst Case		Best Case	
	1.5 pF	4.0 pF	1.5 pF	4.0 pF
0 --> 1 Delay	23.06	32.26	9.71	14.16
Trans	17.75	41.66	8.87	21.41
1 --> 0 Delay	23.35	27.42	9.98	12.28
Trans	7.88	18.33	4.59	11.36

D7 --> Q3 OUT	Worst Case		Best Case	
	1.5 pF	4.0 pF	1.5 pF	4.0 pF
0 --> 1 Delay	21.40	24.50	9.02	11.61
Trans	9.23	23.27	5.27	12.95
1 --> 0 Delay	24.22	28.32	10.23	12.52
Trans	7.88	16.12	4.56	11.25

NOTE: Transition times have not been multiplied by 1.25.

RELEASE 5.0

3 MICRON CMOS/BULK CELL FAMILY -CMOS3-	4710 Q_0 OF PARITY ENCODER CELL HEIGHT 150 WIDTH 180	DATE: 1/01/87 REVISION: A

RELATED CELL TYPES: 4700,4720

The 4710 is a custom SSI cell built to be a part of the 4700 MSI function. The 4700 is an 8 bit priority encoder, the 8 input bits (D0-D7) are encoded into 4 output bits, Q_0 TO Q_3. Q_0 is the least significant output bit. The 4710 cell takes the eight inputs: D0/, D1, D2/, D3, D4/, D5, D6/, and D7 to produce the Q_0 output bit.

TERMINAL INFORMATION

ETER NAME	PHYSICAL NAME(S)	LOGICV FIELD	FUNCTION CODE	CAP (pF)	RESISTANCE(S) (Kohms)
Q_0	T1, B1	6	O	0.51	0.09, 0.09
D0/	T2, B2	1	I	0.23	0.75, 0.75
D1	T3, B3	2	I	0.23	0.75, 0.75
D2/	T4, B4	3	I	0.23	0.75, 0.75
D3	T5, B5	4	I	0.23	0.75, 0.75
D4/	T6, B6	5	I	0.23	0.75, 0.75
D5	T7, B7	8	I	0.23	0.75, 0.75
D6/	T8, B8	9	I	0.23	0.75, 0.75
D7	T9, B9	10	I	0.23	0.75, 0.75
P	R1, L1	–	P	2.08	0.0, 0.0
G	R2, L2	–	G	1.22	0.0, 0.0

RELEASE 5.0

PAGE NO. 4710 - 1

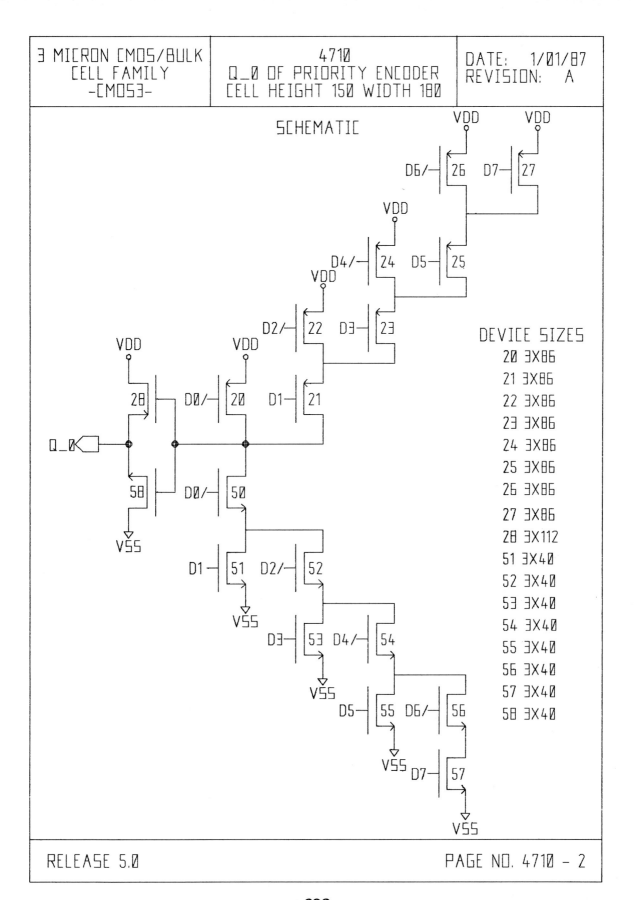

SCHEMATIC

DEVICE SIZES
20 3X86
21 3X86
22 3X86
23 3X86
24 3X86
25 3X86
26 3X86
27 3X86
28 3X112
51 3X40
52 3X40
53 3X40
54 3X40
55 3X40
56 3X40
57 3X40
58 3X40

OUTLINE

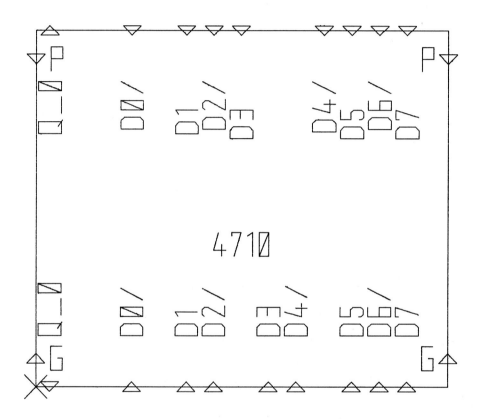

4710

RELATED CELL TYPES: 4700, 4710

The 4720 is a custom SSI cell built to be used in the 4700 MSI function. The 4700 is an 8 bit priority encoder. It takes 8 input bits (D0-D7) and encodes them into 4 output bits, Q_0 to Q_3. Q_0 is the least significant bit and Q_1 is the 2nd least significant bit of the output. The 4720 directly implements Q_1 from the eight inputs: D0/, D1/, D2, D3, D4/, D5/, D6, and D7. Note that four of these input signals are inverted.

TERMINAL INFORMATION

ETER NAME	PHYSICAL NAME(S)	LOGICV FIELD	FUNCTION CODE	CAP (pF)	RESISTANCE(S) (Kohms)
Q_1	T1, B1	6	O	0.51	0.09, 0.09
D0/	T2, B2	1	I	0.25	0.75, 0.75
D1/	T3, B3	2	I	0.23	0.75, 0.75
D2	T4, B4	3	I	0.23	0.75, 0.75
D3	T5, B5	4	I	0.23	0.75, 0.75
D4/	T6, B6	5	I	0.23	0.75, 0.75
D5/	T7, B7	8	I	0.23	0.75, 0.75
D6	T8, B8	9	I	0.23	0.75, 0.75
D7	T9, B9	10	I	0.23	0.75, 0.75
P	R1, L1	–	P	2.23	0.0, 0.0
G	R2, L2	–	G	1.26	0.0, 0.0

SCHEMATIC

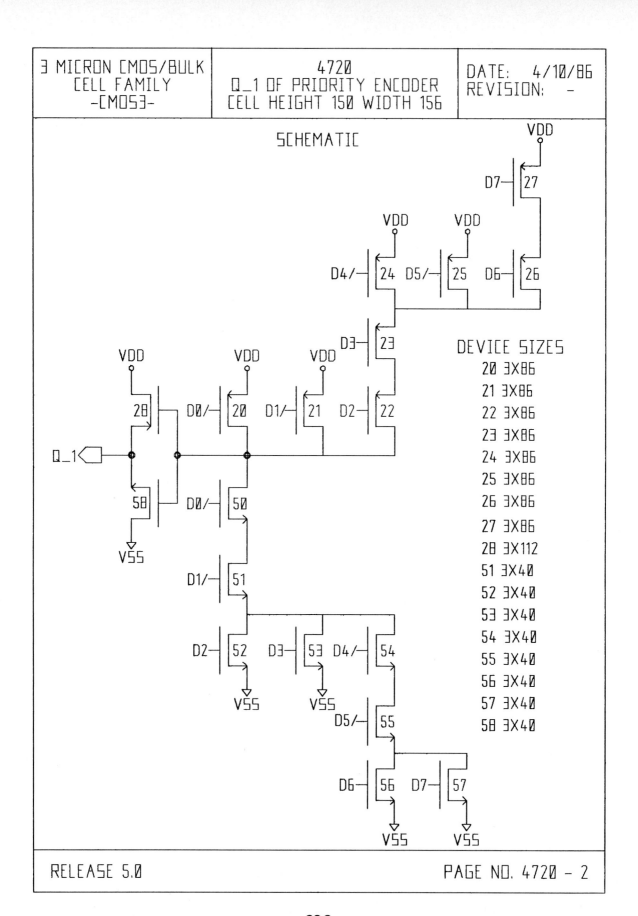

DEVICE SIZES
20 3X86
21 3X86
22 3X86
23 3X86
24 3X86
25 3X86
26 3X86
27 3X86
28 3X112
51 3X40
52 3X40
53 3X40
54 3X40
55 3X40
56 3X40
57 3X40
58 3X40

RELEASE 5.0

3 MICRON CMOS/BULK CELL FAMILY -CMOS3-	4720 Q1 OF PRIORITY ENCODER CELL HEIGHT 150 WIDTH 156	DATE: 4/10/86 REVISION: -

OUTLINE

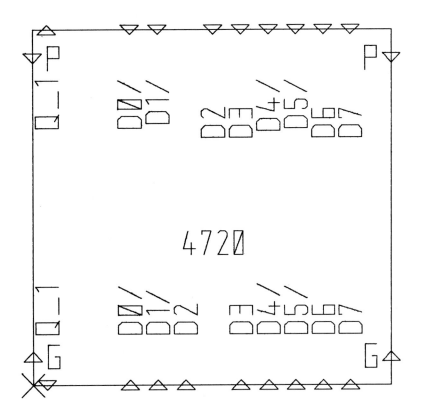

4720

RELATED CELL TYPES: NA

The 4760 is a Dual Half Adder MSI slice. Each Half Adder has two inputs (Y,Z) independent of the other adder with the results appearing at the outputs sum (S) and carry out (CO).

Its primary function is to act as a basic building block in the design of an n-word bit adder, n-bit population counter, or a n-bit multiplier.

TERMINAL INFORMATION

ETER NAME	PHYSICAL NAME(S)	LOGICV FIELD	FUNCTION CODE	CAPACITANCE (pfarads)	RESISTANCE(S) (Kohms)
Y1	T2, B2	1	I	0.663	2.28, 2.28
Z1	T3, B3	2	I	0.564	2.28, 2.28
Z2	T6, B6	4	I	0.562	2.28, 2.28
Y2	T7, B7	3	I	0.663	2.28, 2.28
S1	T4, B4	7	O	0.995	0.68, 0.47
S2	T5, B5	6	O	0.995	0.47, 0.68
CO1	T1, B1	14	O	0.648	0.75, 0.96
CO2	T8, B8	13	O	0.648	0.96, 0.75
P1	L1, R1	–	P	1.253	0.0, 0.0
G1	L2, R2	–	G	0.737	0.0, 0.0
P2	L3, R3	–	P	1.253	0.0, 0.0
G2	L4, R4	–	G	0.737	0.0, 0.0

TRUTH TABLE

Z1	Y1	CO1	S1		Z2	Y2	CO2	S2
0	0	0	0		0	0	0	0
0	1	0	1		0	1	0	1
0	X	0	X		0	X	0	X
1	0	0	1		1	0	0	1
1	1	1	0		1	1	1	0
1	X	X	X		1	X	X	X
X	0	0	X		X	0	0	X
X	1	X	X		X	1	X	X
X	X	X	X		X	X	X	X

X = Don't Know

QUICK REFERENCE TIMING

VDD = 5 volts
C(load) = 1.5 picofarads
Input trans time = 30 nsec.
Worst case processing

Y ,Z ---> CO = 12.16 nsec.
Y, Z ---> S = 14.21

3 MICRON CMOS/BULK CELL FAMILY -CMOS3-	4760 DUAL HALF ADDER CELL HEIGHT 363 WIDTH 144	DATE: 1/01/87 REVISION: A

SCHEMATIC

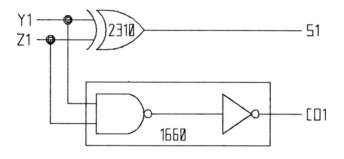

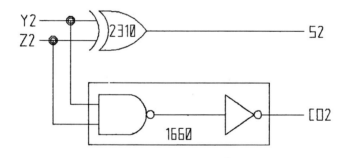

SWITCHING CHARACTERISTICS

Consult the MSI function user's guide for the conditions under which these switching characteristics were determined and for guidance on their interpretation. Cload has the units of picofarads and the results are in nanoseconds.

```
   Y ,Z   --> S            Worst Case                    Best Case

0 --> 1  Delay =    2.70(Cload) + 10.16   OR   1.14(Cload) +  3.24
         Trans =    9.29(Cload) + 11.55   OR   5.00(Cload) +  2.93
1 --> 0  Delay =    3.10(Cload) +  6.80   OR   1.38(Cload) +  1.35
         Trans =    8.08(Cload) +  9.68   OR   4.39(Cload) +  2.27

   Y ,Z   --> CO           Worst Case                    Best Case

0 --> 1  Delay =    2.42(Cload) +  8.52   OR   1.57(Cload) +  1.64
         Trans =    4.36(Cload) + 18.94   OR   5.06(Cload) +   .90
1 --> 0  Delay =    1.91(Cload) +  1.94   OR   1.02(Cload) +   .39
         Trans =    6.66(Cload) +  1.50   OR   1.15(Cload) +  5.28
```

OUTLINE

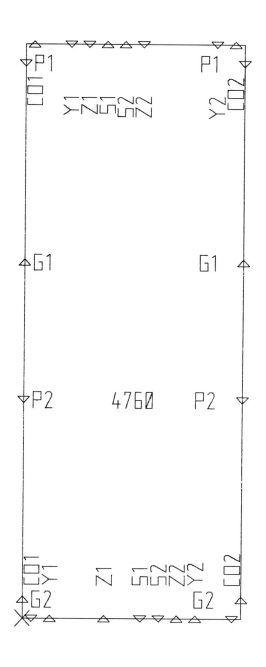

MOSTRAN RESULTS

	Worst Case		Best Case	
Y ,Z --> S	1.5 pF	4.0 pF	1.5 pF	4.0 pF
0 --> 1 Delay	14.22	20.98	4.95	7.80
Trans	25.48	48.70	10.43	22.93
1 --> 0 Delay	11.45	19.20	3.42	6.87
Trans	21.80	42.00	8.86	19.84

	Worst Case		Best Case	
Y ,Z --> CO	1.5 pF	4.0 pF	1.5 pF	4.0 pF
0 --> 1 Delay	12.16	18.22	3.99	7.91
Trans	25.48	36.38	8.50	21.16
1 --> 0 Delay	4.81	9.59	1.95	4.49
Trans	11.50	28.16	7.01	9.89

NOTE: Transition times have been multiplied by 1.25 to compensate for the measurements taken at 80% of the signal swing.

3 MICRON CMOS/BULK CELL FAMILY —CMOS3—	4770 DUAL FULL ADDER CELL HEIGHT 363 WIDTH 228	DATE: 1/01/87 REVISION: A

RELATED CELL TYPES: NA

The 4770 is a Dual Full Adder MSI slice. Each Full Adder has a set of three inputs (Y1,Z1,C1, Y2,Z2,C2) for the addition of data bits. The result of the addition appears on the sum and carry-out output terminals (S1,CO1,S2,CO2).

Its primary function is to act as a basic building block in the design of an n-bit word adder, an n-bit population counter, or an n bit multiplier.

TERMINAL INFORMATION

ETER NAME	PHYSICAL NAME(S)		LOGICV FIELD	FUNCTION CODE	CAPACITANCE (pfarads)	RESISTANCE(S) (Kohms)
C1	T2,	B2	3	I	0.880	0.96, 0.75
Y1	T3,	B3	1	I	1.182	0.96, 0.75
Z1	T4,	B4	2	I	1.159	0.96, 0.75
C2	T7,	B7	10	I	0.885	0.75, 0.96
Y2	T8,	B8	8	I	1.181	0.75, 0.96
Z2	T9,	B9	9	I	1.150	0.75, 0.96
S1	T1,	B1	6	O	0.661	0.96, 0.75
S2	T6,	B6	13	O	0.678	0.75, 0.96
CO1	T5,	B5	7	O	0.671	0.96, 0.75
CO2	T10,	B10	14	O	0.655	0.75, 0.96
P1	L1,	R1	–	P	1.875	0.0, 0.0
G1	L2,	R2	–	G	1.236	0.0, 0.0
P2	L3,	R3	–	P	1.875	0.0, 0.0
G2	L4,	R4	–	G	1.236	0.0, 0.0

TRUTH TABLE

Y1	Z1	C1	CO1	S1		Y2	Z2	C2	CO1	S1
0	0	0	0	0		0	0	0	0	0
0	0	1	0	1		0	0	1	0	1
0	0	X	0	X		0	0	X	0	X
0	1	0	0	1		0	1	0	0	1
0	1	1	1	0		0	1	1	1	0
0	X	0	0	X		0	X	0	0	X
1	0	0	0	1		1	0	0	0	1
1	0	1	1	0		1	0	1	1	0
1	1	0	1	0		1	1	0	1	0
1	1	1	1	1		1	1	1	1	1
1	1	X	1	X		1	1	X	1	X
1	X	1	X	X		1	X	1	X	X
X	0	0	0	X		X	0	0	0	X
X	1	1	X	X		X	1	1	X	X

X = Don't Know

QUICK REFERENCE TIMING

```
VDD = 5 volts                    Y ,Z --> S  = 14.73 nsec.
C(load) = 1.5 picofarads         Y ,Z --> CO = 16.50 nsec.
Input trans time = 30 nsec.
Worst case processing
```

RELEASE 5.0   PAGE NO. 4770 - 2

3 MICRON CMOS/BULK CELL FAMILY -CMOS3-	4770 DUAL FULL ADDER CELL HEIGHT 363 WIDTH 228	DATE: 1/01/87 REVISION: A

SCHEMATIC

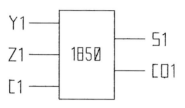

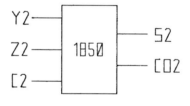

SWITCHING CHARACTERISTICS

Consult the MSI function user's guide for the conditions under which these switching characteristics were determined and for guidance on their interpretation. Cload has the units of picofarads and the results are in nanoseconds.

```
Y ,Z --> S               Worst Case               Best Case

0 --> 1  Delay =    2.17(Cload) +  8.26   OR   1.51(Cload) +  1.76
         Trans =    8.22(Cload) +  3.44   OR   5.64(Cload) +  1.20
1 --> 0  Delay =    2.00(Cload) + 11.73   OR    .60(Cload) +  5.53
         Trans =    7.04(Cload) +  3.04   OR   4.92(Cload) +  1.28


Y ,Z --> CO              Worst Case               Best Case

0 --> 1  Delay =    2.32(Cload) + 13.02   OR   1.50(Cload) +  2.70
         Trans =    7.92(Cload) +  3.05   OR   5.72(Cload) +   .78
1 --> 0  Delay =    1.91(Cload) +  5.96   OR   1.18(Cload) +   .59
         Trans =    6.55(Cload) +  1.92   OR   5.01(Cload) +   .76
```

OUTLINE

P1   P1

S1 Y1 Z1 CO1 S2   C2   Y2   Z2   CO2

G1   G1

P2   4770   P2

S1 Y1   Z1   CO1 S2 C2 Y2 Z2 CO2

G2   G2

MOSTRAN RESULTS

Y ,Z --> S		Worst Case		Best Case	
		1.5 pF	4.0 pF	1.5 pF	4.0 pF
0 --> 1	Delay	11.52	16.95	4.03	7.81
	Trans	15.78	36.34	9.65	23.74
1 --> 0	Delay	14.74	19.75	6.43	7.93
	Trans	13.59	31.18	8.66	20.96

Y ,Z --> CO		Worst Case		Best Case	
		1.5 pF	4.0 pF	1.5 pF	4.0 pF
0 --> 1	Delay	16.49	22.28	4.95	8.70
	Trans	14.93	34.73	9.36	23.66
1 --> 0	Delay	8.82	13.59	2.36	5.30
	Trans	11.74	28.11	8.28	20.81

NOTE: Transition times have been multiplied by 1.25
to compensate for the measurements taken at 80% of
the signal swing.

RELATED CELL TYPES: NA

The 4780 MSI is an 8 bit population counter, consisting of 8 double entry data bits (D0 – D7) used to
count the total number of '1's appearing in a word and
placing the result on the outputs (S0 – S3).

TERMINAL INFORMATION

ETER NAME	PHYSICAL NAME(S)	LOGICV FIELD	FUNCTION CODE	CAPACITANCE (pfarads)	RESISTANCE(S) (Kohms)
D0	T1, B1	1	I	0.920	1.20, 0.75
D1	T2, B2	2	I	1.223	1.20, 0.75
D2	T3, B3	3	I	1.196	1.20, 0.75
D3	T4, B4	4	I	0.928	0.75, 1.20
D4	T5, B5	5	I	1.220	0.75, 1.20
D5	T6, B6	8	I	1.189	0.75, 1.20
D6	T7, B7	9	I	0.669	2.49, 2.49
D7	T8, B8	10	I	0.592	2.52, 2.52
S0	T9, B9	6	O	0.648	0.72, 0.30
S1	T10, B10	7	O	0.869	0.47, 0.92
S2	T11, B11	13	O	0.859	0.92, 0.47
S3	T12, B12	14	O	0.571	0.75, 1.17
P1	L1, R1	–	P	5.935	0.0, 0.0
G1	L2, R2	–	G	2.027	0.0, 0.0
P2	L3, R3	–	P	6.025	0.0, 0.0
G2	L4, R4	–	G	2.082	0.0, 0.0

RELEASE 5.0   PAGE NO.   4780 – 1

TRUTH TABLE

INPUTS								OUTPUTS '1's			
D7	D6	D5	D4	D3	D2	D1	D0	S3	S2	S1	S0
0	0	0	0	0	0	0	0	0	0	0	0
0	0	0	0	0	0	0	1	0	0	0	1
0	0	0	0	0	0	1	1	0	0	1	0
0	0	0	0	0	1	1	1	0	0	1	1
0	0	0	0	1	1	1	1	0	1	0	0
0	0	0	1	1	1	1	1	0	1	0	1
0	0	1	1	1	1	1	1	0	1	1	0
0	1	1	1	1	1	1	1	0	1	1	1
1	1	1	1	1	1	1	1	1	0	0	0

Note: The above Truth Table lists the minimum number of
     '1' bits located in a data word to show a complete
     count at the outputs.
     The '1's can appear in any random order of a data
     word and still have the same results as shown above.
     An unknown state X in the data input would cause
     the outputs to become unknown.

QUICK REFERENCE TIMING

VDD = 5 volts   D0 --> S3 = 30.40 nsec.
C(load) = 1.5 picofarads
Input trans time = 30 nsec.
Worst case processing

SCHEMATIC

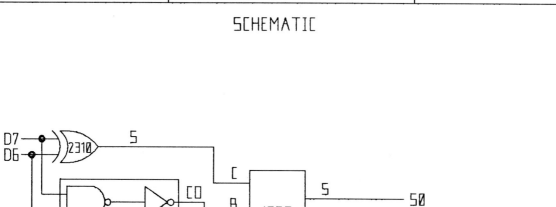
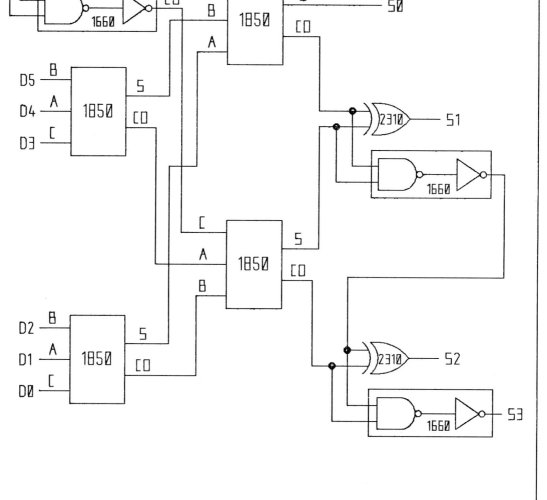

SWITCHING CHARACTERISTICS

     Consult the MSI function user's guide for the conditions under which these switching characteristics were determined and for guidance on their interpretation. Cload has the units of picofarads and the results are in nanoseconds.

```
   D0-D7 --> S0-S3          Worst Case                    Best Case

0 --> 1  Delay =    3.27(Cload) + 25.49  OR    1.48(Cload) +  2.24
         Trans =   11.28(Cload) +  6.32  OR    3.12(Cload) +  1.34
1 --> 0  Delay =    2.72(Cload) + 20.36  OR    1.12(Cload) +  4.15
         Trans =   10.14(Cload) +  4.19  OR    2.32(Cload) +  1.70
```

OUTLINE

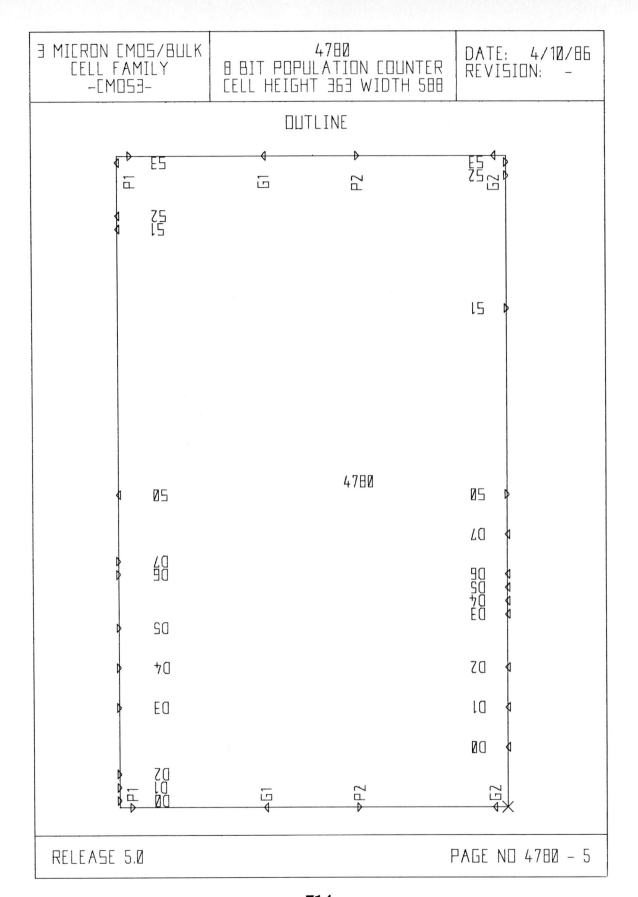

MOSTRAN RESULTS

D0-D7 --> S0-S3	Worst Case		Best Case	
	1.5 pF	4.0 pF	1.5 pF	4.0 pF
0 --> 1 Delay	30.39	38.56	4.47	8.18
Trans	23.24	51.44	6.01	13.80
1 --> 0 Delay	24.43	31.22	5.84	8.65
Trans	19.40	44.75	5.19	11.00

NOTE: Transition times have been multiplied by 1.25 to compensate for the measurements taken at 80% of the signal swing.

RELATED CELL TYPES: NA

The 4790 is a 12 bit population counter consisting of twelve double entry data bits (D0 − D11) used to count the total number of '1's appearing in a word and placing the results on the output terminals (S0 − S3).

TERMINAL INFORMATION

ETER NAME	PHYSICAL NAME(S)	LOGICV FIELD	FUNCTION CODE	CAPACITANCE (pfarads)	RESISTANCE(S) (Kohms)
D0	T1, B1	1	I	0.914	1.20, 0.75
D1	T2, B2	2	I	1.213	1.20, 0.75
D2	T3, B3	3	I	1.189	1.20, 0.75
D3	T4, B4	4	I	0.908	1.20, 0.75
D4	T5, B5	5	I	1.215	1.20, 0.75
D5	T6, B6	8	I	1.193	1.20, 0.75
D6	T7, B7	9	I	0.917	0.75, 1.20
D7	T8, B8	10	I	1.212	0.75, 1.20
D8	T9, B9	11	I	1.155	0.75, 1.17
D9	T10, B10	12	I	0.930	0.75, 1.20
D10	T11, B11	15	I	1.226	0.75, 1.20
D11	T12, B12	16	I	1.195	0.75, 1.20
S0	T13, B13	6	O	1.027	0.92, 0.47
S1	T14, B14	7	O	1.027	0.47, 0.92
S2	T15, B15	13	O	0.702	0.75, 0.30
S3	T16, B16	14	O	0.653	0.72, 0.30
P1	L1, R1	−	P	8.628	0.0, 0.0
G1	L2, R2	−	G	5.558	0.0, 0.0
P2	L3, R3	−	P	8.628	0.0, 0.0
G2	L4, R2	−	G	5.558	0.0, 0.0

RELEASE 5.0   PAGE NO.   4790 − 1

TRUTH TABLE

INPUTS												OUTPUTS '1's			
D11	D10	D9	D8	D7	D6	D5	D4	D3	D2	D1	D0	S3	S2	S1	S0
0	0	0	0	0	0	0	0	0	0	0	0	0	0	0	0
0	0	0	0	0	0	0	0	0	0	0	1	0	0	0	1
0	0	0	0	0	0	0	0	0	0	1	1	0	0	1	0
0	0	0	0	0	0	0	0	0	1	1	1	0	0	1	1
0	0	0	0	0	0	0	0	1	1	1	1	0	1	0	0
0	0	0	0	0	0	0	1	1	1	1	1	0	1	0	1
0	0	0	0	0	0	1	1	1	1	1	1	0	1	1	0
0	0	0	0	0	1	1	1	1	1	1	1	0	1	1	1
0	0	0	0	1	1	1	1	1	1	1	1	1	0	0	0
0	0	0	1	1	1	1	1	1	1	1	1	1	0	0	1
0	0	1	1	1	1	1	1	1	1	1	1	1	0	1	0
0	1	1	1	1	1	1	1	1	1	1	1	1	0	1	1
1	1	1	1	1	1	1	1	1	1	1	1	1	1	0	0

Note: The above truth table lists the minimum number of
'1' bits located in a data word to show a complete
count at the outputs.
    The '1's can appear in any random order of a data
word and still have the same results as shown above.
    An unknown state X in the data input would cause
the outputs to be unknown.

QUICK REFERENCE TIMING

VDD = 5 volts
C(load) = 1.5 picofarads
Input trans time = 30 nsec.
Worst case processing

DO --> S0 = 30.95 nsec.
DO --> S3 = 40.11 nsec.

SCHEMATIC

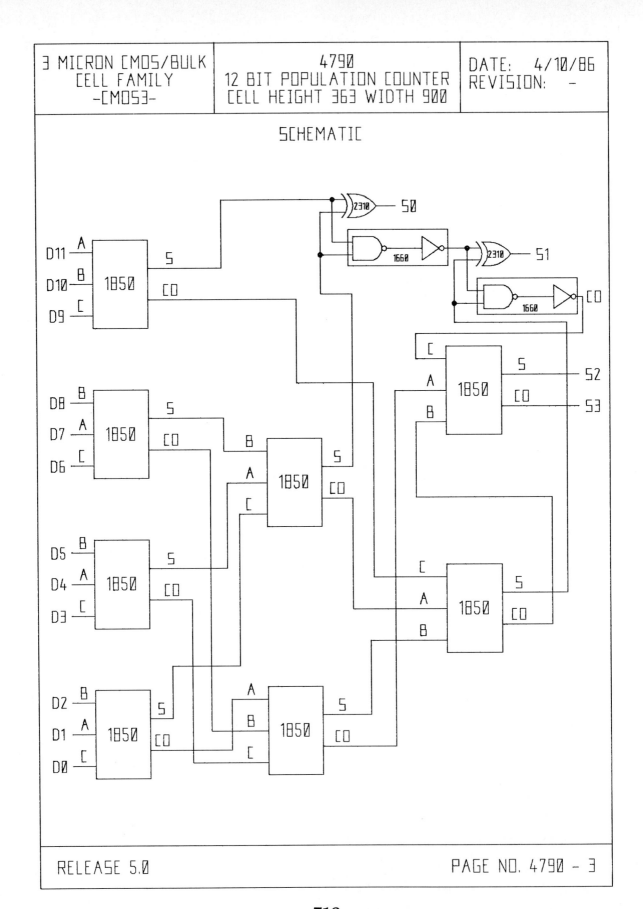

SWITCHING CHARACTERISTICS

Consult the MSI function user's guide for the conditions under which these switching characteristics were determined and for guidance on their interpretation. Cload has the units of picofarads and the results are in nanoseconds.

```
D0 --> S0                Worst Case                Best Case

0 --> 1  Delay =    3.27(Cload) + 17.36   OR    1.85(Cload) +  6.48
         Trans =   11.07(Cload) +  5.40   OR    6.86(Cload) +  1.90
1 --> 0  Delay =    3.20(Cload) + 26.15   OR    1.71(Cload) + 11.54
         Trans =   10.17(Cload) +  3.99   OR    6.34(Cload) +  1.15


D0 --> S3                Worst Case                Best Case

0 --> 1  Delay =    1.88(Cload) + 37.29   OR    0.92(Cload) + 15.67
         Trans =    5.64(Cload) +  3.28   OR    3.07(Cload) +  1.40
1 --> 0  Delay =    1.66(Cload) + 28.77   OR    0.77(Cload) + 11.21
         Trans =    4.26(Cload) +  3.29   OR    2.37(Cload) +  1.39
```

OUTLINE

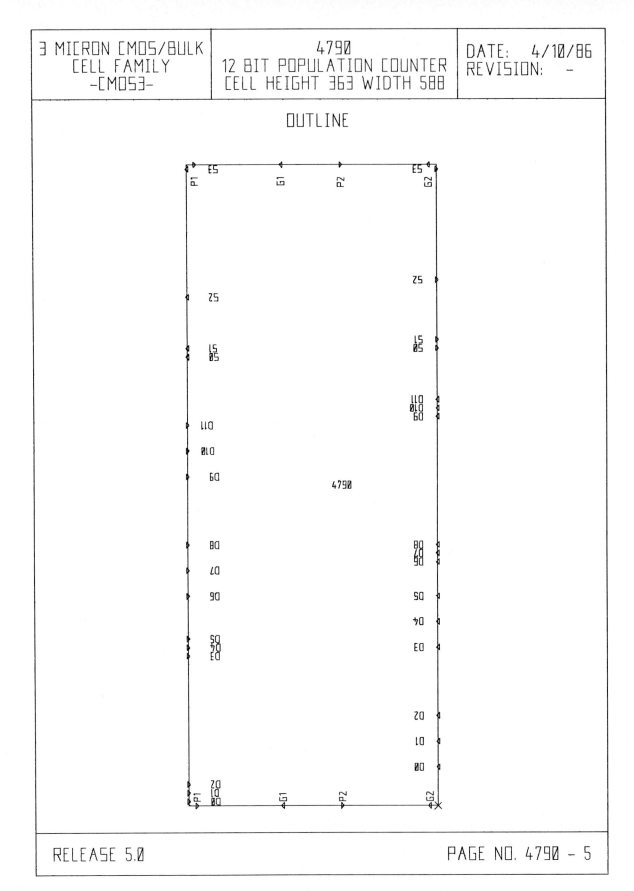

MOSTRAN RESULTS

D0 --> S0		Worst Case		Best Case	
		1.5 pF	4.0 pF	1.5 pF	4.0 pF
0 --> 1	Delay	22.27	30.45	9.25	13.87
	Trans	22.00	49.67	12.20	29.36
1 --> 0	Delay	30.94	38.93	14.11	18.39
	Trans	19.25	44.68	10.66	26.51

D0 --> S3		Worst Case		Best Case	
		1.5 pF	4.0 pF	1.5 pF	4.0 pF
0 --> 1	Delay	40.12	44.83	17.04	19.37
	Trans	11.76	25.84	6.01	13.69
1 --> 0	Delay	31.26	35.41	12.36	14.28
	Trans	9.69	20.35	4.95	10.88

NOTE: Transition times have been multiplied by 1.25 to compensate for the measurements taken at 80% of the signal swing.